Catastrophe A
The Catholic
In 'Northern Ireland'

Volume Two

Resurgence
1969-2016
by
Pat Walsh

Belfast Historical & Educational Society

Also by Dr. Pat Walsh:

Catastrophe, 1914-1968, Volume One: *The Catholic Predicament In 'Northern Ireland', Catastrophe And Resurgence*

The Rise And Fall Of Imperial Ireland. Redmondism In The Context Of Britain's War Of Conquest Of South Africa And Its Great War On Germany, 1899-1916

The Armenian Insurrection And The Great War by Pat Walsh and Garegin Pasdermadjian ("Armen Garo")

The Great Fraud Of 1914-18

Lord Hankey: **How We Planned The Great War**

Forgotten Aspects Of **Ireland's Great War On Turkey**

The Events Of 1915 In Eastern Anatolia In The Context Of Britain's Great War On The Ottoman Empire

British Geopolitics & The Balkan Wars—An Irish Perspective

Remembering Gallipoli, President McAleese's Great War Crusade

Britain's Great War, Pope Benedict's Lost Peace: How Britain Blocked The Pope's Peace Efforts Between 1915 And 1918

Introduction to: *Major C.J.C. Street*: **The Administration Of Ireland, 1920**; with a substantial extract from his *Ireland In 1921* and a review of his other writings on Britain's world role, and inter-war Europe.

Introduction to: **Lionel Curtis: Ireland**

Introduction to: **The Politics Of Pre-War Europe**: *The Catholic Bulletin* on Peace, War And Neutrality, 1937-1939

2016
Resurgence
The Catholic Predicament In 'Northern Ireland', Volume Two
ISBN 978-1-872078-26-7

This book forms Volume Five of the
Northern Ireland Contemporary Politics & History Series

Belfast Historical & Educational Society
33 Athol Street, Belfast BT12 4GX

Orders: lane.jack@gmail.com

Contents

Introduction   **5**

Chapter 1:   **The August Interregnum**   **12**
(Unheeded Warnings; Battle Begins in Belfast; Defensive Preparations; Battle of Bogside; Taoiseach's Response; Going Berserk in Belfast; Republican Let-Down; No Help from 'The Prince'; Republican Confusion; Nature of British Intervention; Westminster Takes Control; Behind the Barricades; Oliver Wright's Secret Dispatch; Arm's-Length Policy)

Chapter 2:   **The North in Flux**   **42**
(View from Derry; Thoughts of John Hume; Hunt Report; Nationalists and Security Forces; N. Catholics in 1970; Playing Stormont Charade; Oliver Wright's Second Dispatch; Seduction of North; Callaghan's Retreat from West Belfast; Why Civil Rights Led to National War)

Chapter 3:   **Dublin and the North**   **70**
(Fianna Fail and N. Nationalism; Wanted: A F F of North; What was Dublin's Policy?; Dublin's Two-Pronged Strategy; Dublin & N. Catholics; Contradictory Policy; Dublin & Northern Protestants; Dublin's Futile Policy Towards Unionism; Limitations of 'Moderation'; Fiddling While Belfast Burns)

Chapter 4:   **The New Republicanism**   **95**
(The Republican Split; New Republicanism; Character of Republicanism; Fianna Fail and the IRA; British or Irish Responsibility?; Ballymurphy Watershed?)

Chapter 5:   **Dublin's About Turn**   **115**
(A 'Republican Plot'?; Retreat from North; Arms Crisis; John Kelly on Captain Kelly; Effects of Taoiseach's volte face; Demise of Defence Committees;; Falls Curfew; The not yet Republican Catholics; Republican Strategy; Dublin on N. Republicanism)

Chapter 6:   **Moment of Truth**   **138**
(Opposition in Paralysis; Formation of SDLP; What Was SDLP?; British Labour and SDLP; Why SDLP Suited Britain; Irish Opposition to British Labour; Dublin's Attitude to SDLP; The Conceptual Blur; Fall of Chichester-Clark; Faulkner springs Surprise; Hume's Fateful Decision; Common Origins; Effects of SDLP Walk-Out)

Chapter 7:   **National War**   **169**
(Internment & Total War; SDLP & Total War; Civil Disobedience Campaign; Hume's Altered Vision; Dublin Depends on Republicans; Anti-Partition Pamphlet; Dublin's Policy of 'Stormont Must Go'; Testing Nationalist Will; After Bloody Sunday; Hume at UN; Dublin's Realpolitik; Direct Rule Imposed; Promoting 'Disengagement Policy'; Protestant Resistance; SDLP Advises Whitelaw; A Military Watershed; SDLP & Provos; IRA & Catholic Community)

Chapter 8:   **Sunningdale**   **212**
(Constitutional' Manoeuvrings; SDLP Plays Hard To Get; Heath Threat; Sunningdale; SDLP Accepts; Executive Formed; Faulkner Duped by Dublin; Election Warning; Opposition Grows; UWC Strike; SDLP in Revolt; Fall of Executive; Explaining SDLP Behaviour; British Bungling; Lost in 'N. Ireland'; S. Discomfort)

Chapter 9:   **Turning Point**   **245**
(British Bankruptcy?; SDLP after Sunningdale; SDLP acquiring an Army; SDLP Pleads With Dublin; Provo War Escalation; 1975 Truce; Rees & Ulster Nationalism; S. Armagh; Turning Point; Contracting Out the War; British Non-Target; Republicans & Ulsterisation; Sectarianising the War)

Chapter 10: **Regrouping** 275
(SDLP in Doldrums; SDLP under Fitt; Fitt Confronts Himself; SDLP under Hume; Provos Squeezed; Long War; Criminalisation Policy; Year of Hunger Strikes; Triumph of Failure; Rise of Sinn Fein; Parting of Ways; New Ireland Forum; Forum Rebuffed)

Chapter 11: **Hillsborough Ice Age** 304
(Making of Hillsborough Treaty; Lady Was For Turning; Aims of Treaty; Lancing Unionist Boil; Republicans & Hillsborough Treaty; Republican Surge; Atrocity for Atrocity; Republican Peace Moves)

Chapter 12: **War and Peace** 332
(Re-entrance of Charles Haughey; Haughey, De Valera & Lemass; Re-building Ireland; Fr. Reid's Letter to Haughey; Haughey/Adams; Bringing in Hume; Duisburg Division; Talks about Talks; Hume Changes Course; Brooke Speech; Manoeuvring for Position; Hume/Adams; Loyalist/British Reaction; Downing Street Declaration; Differences within SDLP)

Chapter 13: **Retreat from the Battlefield** 370
(IRA 1994 Ceasefire; Unionism seeks Victory; Major Problems; Clinton & Major; Major Miscalculation; Mitchell Report; End of Ceasefire; Hume's difficulty; High Noon at Drumcree; Ceasefire Resumed; Mallon Takes Control of SDLP)

Chapter 14: **The Long Good Friday** 396
(Republicans & 1998 settlement; Irredentism or Misgovernment?; Good Friday Agreement; Purpose of GFA; Manufacturing Consent; Blair's Letter; 'Pro-Agreement' Unionism?; Omagh Catastrophe; Hume opts out; Mallon's Offer to Trimble; Surrender Demands; Trimble "jumps first"; Agreement Suspended; Peace or Pacification?; Trimble & Republican Position; Crusade & Cruiser; Trimble's 'sophisticated analysis'; Trimble's 'Exotic Advisers'; Trimble & Athol Street; Neo-Conservative connection)

Chapter 15: **Whither Republicanism?** 441
(Republican Defeat View; Surrender & Re-grant?; Trouble with Treaties; War Aims; Politicians & Spooks; Secret History?; 'Revolutionaries' & Nationalist Continuum; Politics & Ideology; Missing Subject; Anti-Sinn Fein Symbiosis; Was Britain fighting itself?)

Chapter 16: **Winning the Peace** 471
(Agreement & Decommissioning; SDLP's Paradise Lost; Republicans Call Shots; A New Orbit; A Worrying Development!; North Turned Upside Down; Steak Knife Unionism; Battle of Ideas; Patton & Policing; Trimble Resigns; Arms Issue Again; Saving Dave I; SF overtakes SDLP; Saving Dave II; Bringing House Down; Saving Dave III; Whither the SDLP?; How SF Won the Peace)

Chapter 17: **The Functional Peace** 510
(Triumph of "Extremes"; Northern Bank & McCartney Killing; Republican Army bows out; Policing Obstacle; Paisley's purpose; DUP Accepts; Twisting DUP arm; The Centre Can Hold?; A Prophecy?; Illusory Opposition)

Chapter 18: **Restless in Peace** 532
(Spread of SF; British Roll-back of Agreement; Boston College Tapes; An Unfinished War?; Origins of Pursuit of Adams; Sex as a Political Weapon; Southern Discomfort; Dublin in Denial; Unionist Discomfort; Robinson's Retreat; Moving towards edge; Stormont House Crash; A Position of Stalemate; Republicanism Or Anti-Partitionism?; Consent?)

Bibliography 572
Index 575

Introduction

The problem of 'Northern Ireland' is 'Northern Ireland' itself. That is to say the problem is not the people who inhabit the entity created in the Six Counties but the political construct within which they live. That is the basic argument running through the two volumes of *'The Catholic Predicament in Northern Ireland'*. Volume One, *'Catastrophe'*, traced its origins and development; Volume Two, *'Resurgence'* traces the great attempt to overcome it.

There are many parties to the 'Northern Ireland' conflict and not just the two communities who exist within it. This book examines that conflict in relation to all the parties—including London and Dublin—that have made it what it is.

It can only be because minds are working within an established narrative which has the intention of blaming the inhabitants of the Six Counties for the trouble there, rather than those whose responsibility such things really are, that the established narrative persists regarding 'Northern Ireland'. And all the while the thing called 'Northern Ireland' continues to defy attempts to overcome it.

It will not let its people be at peace, even after so many years of Peace. It is destined to torment until the bitter end—as its architects intended.

*

In January 1965, on the orders of Taoiseach Sean Lemass, the leader of the Northern Nationalists, Eddie McAteer, reluctantly took his place as Leader of Her Majesty's Opposition at Stormont, and gave recognition to the thing called 'Northern Ireland.' The Catholics of the North, cut off from the rest of the Irish Nation in 1920 and removed from its political developments, acted as a dependent part of the Irish Nation under orders from its predominant element in the South, went along with the new policy while knowing, at the outset, that no good would come of it.

This began the sequence of events that would end in an explosion.

The new policy of Dublin with regard to Stormont, instigated by Taoiseach Lemass, was based on a number of fatal misconceptions about the nature of 'Northern Ireland,' chief of which was a fundamental misunderstanding about it being a 'state' which was reformable to something that resembled a democracy.

The First Volume, called *'Catastrophe'*, described the formation of the weird construct of 'Northern Ireland' that is fundamental to the overall story. This perverse political entity was the one surviving fragment of the 1920 *'Better Government of Ireland Act'* after the rest of it had been ditched by Britain in favour of the Anglo-Irish Treaty.

The fact 'Northern Ireland' survived, when the rest of the 1920 Act was abandoned, suggests that the 'Northern Ireland' part of the policy was the most important part for its Imperial architects who, in those days, presided over the world and did to it what they chose (or at least, what they could get away with, given the complicating emergence of the United States as a result of England's bungled Great War).

'Northern Ireland' was conceived by Whitehall as part of a Home Rule scheme for the whole of Ireland, the other part being a Parliament and Government of 'Southern Ireland'. 'Southern Ireland' had to be abandoned when the nationalist electorate stood by the independent Government it had elected in 1918 and defied the Black and Tan terror. But 'Northern Ireland' was retained, even though its southern counterpart was lost. It helped with the manipulation of the Irish delegates at the Treaty negotiations, by which Britain regained some of the ground that it had lost to the 1919 Republic. Then, having served that purpose, it was used during the following decades in an attempt to limit the growth of independence in the 26 Co. state. The argument was that the Free State might regain the North if it kept itself British in outlook and culture. It was said that the 26 Counties could gain the Six Counties by making itself similar to them. But the Whitehall masters only set up the Six Counties into the Northern Ireland system because it was certain that the one thing the Ulster Unionist majority would not do was join the Irish nation-state.

By the use of this play it hoped, like the Pharaoh with the Jews, that even though it was letting the people go, they would not go very far.

'Northern Ireland' was, first and foremost, an Imperial construction. It had never been dreamt of until it was concocted in 1920. It had no tradition behind it, no aspiration in front of it, and no hint of consensus at the time it was established by Westminster. Nobody in Ireland wanted it. The Catholic third of the population wanted to be part of an all Ireland state. The Protestant two thirds wanted to be an integral part of the British State. But Westminster decided that both should have what neither wanted and gave them a provincial statelet, subordinate to Westminster, but excluded from its politics, whose main function would be a policing of the large Catholic minority, trapped within it, by the Protestant two-thirds majority.

The British Parliament was wholly responsible for 'Northern Ireland' and the Imperial construction was a recipe for eternal communal conflict and for little else. And no rational defence was ever made of it by those who made it in Whitehall.

In its construction in the Six Counties Westminster, the sovereign body responsible for the governing of 'Northern Ireland', deliberately denied the opportunity of normal politics to the people of the area and set up an artificial body politic outside the political system of the State whose natural effect was to preserve and exacerbate the Catholic/Protestant division it established. It was a "pseudo-state" or "false front" for the remaining British State in Ireland that left Westminster free of responsibility whilst others stewed in the juice of the mess it left behind.

The Nationalist population was very unsuited to playing the part of a dominated minority within the Six Counties. It was an intensely political community, and now it was deprived of an outlet for its energies. In the years before the catastrophe that befell it in 'Northern Ireland' it had been to the forefront in the Home Rule movement under its leader, Joe Devlin, who was emerging as the most powerful man in Ireland. Then it was severed in its prime from the rest of the Nation of which it formed a part. And it was also cut off from the UK State in which it participated politically in the great Liberal/Labour reform movement which Devlin and his Northern Hibernians had been making extensive provision for participating in.

The Unionist majority was an unsuitable governing class to preside over the Catholic community. It had cheated the people it was assigned to govern of their destiny by bringing the gun into politics. It never had any experience of statecraft and it had not even wanted to rule its Catholic minority, being content to be just British.

'Northern Ireland' remained stable for a generation, probably because of the debilitating effect of the 'Treaty' and its aftermath on Northern Catholics and the fact that the Unionist leaders, who had made what they called *"the supreme sacrifice"* by agreeing to operate a Six-County system that was distanced from the political life of the state, understood that the system did not have within it the possibility of normal politics. They did not try to draw the Catholics into spurious democratic activity, as Captain O'Neill did two generations later, but just encouraged them to accept their fate passively, with the help of a system famously called 'Orange Terror' by 'Ultach'.

But then came Lemass to Belfast. The new departure in Dublin pretended that Northern Ireland was a democracy n which the minority community had refused to participate. This was an idealist fantasy of outsiders. But it did put Northern Ireland to the test. Those in the Civil Rights movement who acted within the fantasy, including the new young 'constitutionalists' and social revolutionaries alike, began to take on the same fatal assumptions.

'Northern Ireland' proved to be a façade of the remaining region of the British State in Ireland. It could not cope with the political activism that was predicated on a view of it being a 'state' that could be reformed.

A momentum developed in the new Catholic movement that sought to reform the Stormont system that was both irresistible and unstoppable. One of the slogans of the reform agitation was *"British Rights for British Citizens"*. It took the Unionist regime to be a malevolent buffer that withheld British rights from the Nationalist community in the Six Counties. The Unionists declared that Ulster was British, so the Nationalists campaigned for British Rights, only to find the Unionists, who could not function politically as British due to the political detachment they had accepted in 1921, refused them.

'Northern Ireland' was excluded from the politics of British Government

7

as an original act of the British State. It was because of that exclusion that the Unionist regime existed as the form of the British State in the Six Counties. And the Unionists themselves were, of course, no less excluded from the political life of the British democracy than were the Nationalists.

*

The naivete of the Civil Rights agitation on the issue of British Rights, combined with a degree of ambiguity about the Border, gave it the character of a nationalist "Trojan Horse" in Unionist minds. This caused elemental problems for the Unionist regime, problems that both 'constitutional' and non-constitutional varieties of Nationalism failed to anticipate, so the reform movement developed into a mass movement that eventually brought down the British subordinate government and its simulacrum parliament at Stormont.

The new departure in Catholic politics reacted with the perverse political entity that Britain had established, and the conjunction of these two elements blew everything apart in August 1969. This is where the current Volume takes up the story begun in Volume 1. A defensive Insurrection was produced within the Catholic community in response to the going berserk of the Unionist repressive apparatus which had been spoiling for a fight since the Civil Rights movement had been getting the better of the publicity war, for the preceding year.

After the August explosion something new was possible with the re-engagement of Britain with its 'Northern Ireland' region of responsibility and Dublin's reawakened activism with regard to the Six Counties.

But the new dawn was short-lived. The re-assertion of the arm's length policy of Westminster and the withdrawal of Dublin under pressure from British diplomacy facilitated the emergence of a new force in the political vacuum in the North. That force, starting from a small nucleus, went from strength to strength and there is little doubt that it became, politically, the most effective thing that was ever produced by the Northern Catholic community—much more resourceful in every way than the movement of the early 1920s.

This new internal development of the Northern Catholics, which was never inevitable, made war on the State that was exerting a purely military sovereignty over the Six Counties, and it broke free of—or was rejected by—the 26 County State. That State in the South continued to claim *de jure* sovereignty over the North, but it had lost the nerve to give purposeful guidance to Northern nationalist defence, and it therefore surrendered the political initiative and leadership of the National Aim to the new development in the Six Counties.

This new development was the defence force which had come into being to protect Catholic areas. This Republican Army had been formed under the impact of the Unionist military assault of August 1969. The organisers of it were people as diverse as Catholic ex-servicemen and republican activists who had been expelled from the Republican movement as 'reactionaries', or marginalised within it, during the 'modernisation' of the 1960s. There was a small Republican core which survived from the catastrophe of the 1920s up until 1969, which had engaged in periodic escapades that enlivened the life of the nationalist community, but this group was politically inconsequential. The bulk of the membership of the new Republican Army were people who had taken no part in Republican affairs before the Unionist assault on nationalist West Belfast and Derry in August 1969.

The ultimate objective of this new Republican Army produced by the events of August 1969 was a full British declaration of intent of withdrawal from Ireland. That ultimate objective was utopian and it proved to be militarily unachievable—although it was given its best shot between 1971 and 1972.

A War came to be fought with the nominal object of abolishing Partition. This happened because British politics was seen to be closed to the populace of the Six Counties, and because there were old Republicans who took the community in hand and ensured that life in 'Northern Ireland' would never be the same again.

It was not the effects of Partition as such that ensured the rapid growth of the new Republican Army. It was the conditions of life in the Six Counties and the effects of the devolved regime of communal Unionism, which the Westminster Government interposed between itself and the populace of the Six Counties, that gave the War its momentum and edge.

The 1969 pogrom produced an upheaval that led a great many people to believe anything was possible, and it produced the Republican War, which was an extraordinary event requiring an extravagant belief in possibilities. But wars also need realisable purposes. The War of 1969 was given a false purpose by the circumstance in which it began, a purpose which did not relate to its effective cause. But then it was given a realisable purpose, related to its cause, which enabled it to be ended through a disciplined retreat into politics rather than in military disarray, as in the past.

And so out of the War came something that was not an explicit objective but was always implicit in its cause and character—a great transformation of the Catholic community. Life in the Six Counties, after the War was concluded, was entirely different from the way things were imagined before it.

Mass support for the War the Republican Army waged was primarily based on the conditions of life that the British Government imposed upon the Catholic community as a result of the perverse system it established in 1921. As a result there was a substantial and meaningful secondary objective implicit in the character of the Provos (who were only momentarily and superficially Anti-Treatyite) which constituted a practical possibility on the way to the ultimate objective.

The new Northern Republican leadership, from around the mid-1970s, began to increasingly pursue this secondary objective, though careful to maintain their wider and ultimate demand as part of the Republican bargaining position, in maintaining the War. This was discernible to the Southern Anti-Treaty element who had associated themselves with the new Republican force that had emerged in the North in the aftermath of the events of August 1969, and they disassociated themselves as a result, in 1987.

That remarkable development of the Northern Catholics—the new Republican Army—was a product of the working out of the departure in Nationalist politics that had been originally prompted from the South. And that working out also produced the Social Democratic & Labour Party, the party of John Hume, led initially by Gerry Fitt.

On a couple of occasions (in 1971 and 1974) the SDLP was presented with the opportunity to determine the destiny of things but it funked them, and it went into decline after obtaining the substance of its heart's desire in 1998 largely through the efforts of others.

Its foremost leader, John Hume, was a very effective force in the post-1969 situation. Starting out as a most vigorous and sincere Catholic reformist within the existing parameters of 'Northern Ireland', he gradually, through his dealings with Unionism, came to understand the continuum that historically existed between 'constitutional' and non-constitutional Nationalism and exploited its potential to the full. He came to understood that the fortunes of his community counted for more than the transient political party he used as an instrument for achieving the wider objectives he pursued. After the failure of the Hillsborough Treaty of 1985 he reached outside his party in pursuance of a comprehensive political settlement and achieved this in alliance with the Republican leadership. And then he retired from the scene with his work done leaving others, not of his party but of his community, to complete his endeavours.

The rise of the Northern Catholics from the political predicament in which they had found themselves in 1921, within the communal system that had been imposed upon them, came about through a 28 Year War and the transference of the momentum built up in that War into politics which helped transform beyond recognition the conditions of life for Catholics. A profound social and political evolution occurred in the Nationalist community in conjunction with the War and through that process things were made tolerable and there developed a degree of self-confidence within the community that had not existed since the partition Catastrophe.

There was also an alteration in power relations between the Northern Catholics and the South. Despite being badly let down by the Free State, between the Collins offensive of early 1922 and the Boundary Commission of 1925, the Northern Catholics kept faith for generations in the expectation of deliverance from Dublin. And they were sorely disappointed in their waiting. The last straw came in August 1969 and in the Lynch Government's retreat from the North, under pressure from Whitehall, in early 1970.

And so the Northern Catholics had to assert themselves in independent substance for the first time or stew in the juice. Thrown back on their own resources and finally confident enough to no longer take orders from Dublin, as they had done in the past, they constructed a power centre among themselves and maintained it for nearly three decades until it was a force that had to be taken account of. And having fought a war, made a peace, proved impervious to pressure and constructed a Government, they began to direct their momentum southward, much to the alarm of the Establishment there, who went into hysteria.

That is what this Second Volume of the *Catholic Predicament in Northern Ireland* is all about and why it is called 'Resurgence'.

*

Finally, I have to agree with Robert Ramsey, Brian Faulkner's Private Secretary, when he notes that

> "… it is a myth that most government files are opened after thirty or fifty years: many are carefully filleted and many are simply reserved in their entirety in documentary limbo. An enormous amount of time and subterfuge is devoted to these precautionary measures" (*Ringside Seats*, p.152).

Ramsey had attempted, as a senior Civil Servant, to find out the origins of the Northern Ireland Office from within the system and with access to files not available to the public. He had tried to work from one file to "associated files" back to the origin but had found the task impossible. The construct of 'Northern Ireland' was truly Byzantine, for reasons of State.

There is a recent fashion among historians to write history from the files Governments have made available to them, i.e. from the official narrative. But understanding 'Northern Ireland' like that is a hopeless venture—unless the objective is to write history from the point of view of the State itself. That, of course, is a good career move in the universities but it produces history that is obscurantist for the mass of the people.

And, then again, it produces history that complements its subject and is very much an act of service to it.

What is surprising in the 'Northern Ireland' context is that some of the released files from London and Dublin do give insights into the real motivation of Government, but historians have proved unwilling or incapable of interpreting them in any way but in which the State requires them to. One has to read between the lines, so to speak, to get at the truth, but surely the finest intellects should have been capable of such!

Pat Walsh
Easter 2016

Chapter 1

The August Interregnum

August 1969 was the pivot between the catastrophe that befell the Northern Catholics between 1921 and 1925 and their resurgence. The August events were an interregnum or turning point in the life of the community. After it nothing could be the same again.

The Northern Catholics had lived quiet and law-abiding lives over generations, despite their predicament within 'Northern Ireland'. Paddy Doherty, who led resistance to the Unionist forces in Derry during the Battle of the Bogside, recalled: "I was leading a revolt and yet respect for law and order was deeply ingrained in my character" (Paddy Bogside, p.143).

The vast majority of Northern Catholics were not at all Republican in sentiment. In fact there were only a handful of active Republicans in Belfast and Derry, coming into 1969. But a year or so later the Catholics became infused with Republicanism and were actively supporting an Insurrection against the Northern Parliament that would bring it down.

It was the shock effect of the events of August 1969 that dispelled the lethargy that the Catholic community had fell into since the time of the catastrophe.

There was no form of democratic politics available to the community despite all the efforts it had made to connect up with the States to the south and on the other island. All that was available to it at the crucial moment was the Republicanism which had all but been forgotten after the great trauma of the year 1922, but which had been preserved by a few in the hope that there would be another day for it.

And there was another day. Prompted by the events of August 1969 the community moved from Civil Rights to Insurrection, taking up the Republican spirit, in a resurgence that changed their position for good within the political entity within which they were/are confined.

Unheeded Warnings

Self-defence against an assault by the 'state', to all intents and purposes, constitutes an Insurrection.

The Unionist assault of August 1969 was a response to the Catholic reform agitation in support of the Civil Rights demands—demands that were very modest and which in any functional state would have been implemented as a matter of course. The reason these modest demands were resisted by the 'Northern Ireland' sub-government, set up by Britain in 1921, was that the Nationalist community had been mobilised in support of them. In the communal conflict inherent within the 'Northern Ireland' system the issue is never really the issue. The issue is whether the other side want something, and if it does, that, therefore, is very good reason for resisting it.

By the end of July 1969 it was becoming very apparent in Belfast that discontent elements within the Unionist mass base, seeing its political leaders out-manoeuvred by the Civil Rights agitation, and failing to keep the Catholics where they were supposed to be, were threatening a counter-offensive in which the traditional position of the Protestant community was re-asserted by force.

There was much skirmishing over the marching season when the Catholics did not keep their heads down as much as they usually did. It was clear that during the summer preparations were being made in Unionist areas of Belfast for forays into Catholic areas of the city at an appropriate opportunity. The isolated Unity Flats and Ardoyne areas were particular targets for Loyalist assertiveness.

Catholic Belfast had not given its energies to Civil Rights marching. The Civil Rights movement was seen to be very much a country or student thing from the vantage point of Belfast Catholics. Perhaps the futility of it all was foreseen by a community that had been at the sharp end of things in the past and instinctively knew what was coming its way if things were pushed. It knew in its bones how Unionism would react and where it would assert its power against the uppity Fenians to maximum effect.

The Apprentice Boys march in Derry became the initial focal point for demonstrating Unionist power and re-establishing the proper order of things in the North. Derry, unlike Belfast, had been active in Civil Rights and the annual march in August provided an opportune occasion for restoring the proper order of things.

It appears that the Wilson Government in London wanted a banning of the Derry march after trouble had broken out in Dungiven on the Twelfth. However, the Stormont Government informed James Callaghan, the British Home Secretary, that the Police had not the resources to enforce a ban on the Unionist mass-base. Callaghan was also made aware that a ban would probably bring down the new Stormont Premier, Chichester-Clark. And so Westminster, fearing having to intervene in 'Ulster', thought better of insisting on a ban and left business to Stormont.

On 1st August there was a secret discussion at the British Foreign Office between Dr. Patrick Hillery, Minister for External Affairs and Michael Stewart, acting British Secretary of State for Foreign and Commonwealth Affairs. Hillery informed Stewart of his "grave concern" about the Apprentice Boys march set for Derry. He noted that this went "far beyond" the "routine annual celebration".

According to the Note of the discussion in the Irish National Archives, Hillery warned the British Foreign Secretary that:

"The scale and importance of the demonstration this year had been deliberately stepped up. It was expected that the number of bands included in this year's parade would be somewhere in the region of the 70's, as against about 17 bands in previous years. Derry has thus become a veritable powder keg. Something might be started there that might be very difficult to contain. He thought, therefore... the parade should be banned... If, however, it was not possible to ban the parade, either because the Government of Northern Ireland feared to or otherwise, at least the sponsors of the parade should be required to limit it to the normal scale and size. Otherwise, the holding of this excessively large parade was bound to be provocative, especially as it was being deliberately routed through Catholic areas in Derry. It was sheer madness to do this in present circumstances. The parade should, at the very least, be confined to Protestant areas of the city, and should be reduced to the normal scale... The reason he was there (in the Foreign Office) is that it is the British Government which carries the ultimate responsibility for what happens in Northern Ireland. " (NAI, TSCH 2000/6/657)

After making these very reasonable requests Dr. Hillery informed Stewart that, if serious violence did occur the Republic would be forced into raising the issue at the United Nations—something that had been considered by his predecessor, earlier in the year, at a time when there were previous disturbances in Derry.

The British Foreign Secretary conceded that the parade would be "an extra big one" in August 1969 but the 'Northern Ireland' Government's judgment was that "it was better to control it than to ban it". Stewart compared the Derry situation to a spot of Colonial policing in Bermuda where the Imperial Government had come close to intervening to prop up its client administration earlier in 1969, but had thought better of it with the result that all had turned out happily.

Then the British Foreign Secretary emphasised:

"... that it was a question of judgment for the Northern Ireland Government which was primarily responsible for the area in question. He then added very deliberately 'you accept, of course, that responsibility for this area rests with the Stormont and London Governments, and not with your Government'."

The official report describes how in response Hillery—

"said to the British Foreign Secretary 'you expect the situation will not get out of hand'. The Secretary of State immediately replied very firmly 'yes'... The Minister for External Affairs then said to the Secretary of State 'you want to handle this yourselves. Is the position then that we cannot discuss it further?' The Secretary of State replied 'yes'."

Responsibility for the march and its outcome were, therefore, acknowledged by London on behalf of its local sub-government in 'Northern Ireland' and Dublin was told such things were none of its business.

Battle Begins in Belfast

The August conflict began in Belfast, rather than, as often thought, in Derry. It started on the weekend of 2nd-3rd August, after a minor fracas 300 members of John McKeague's Shankill Defence Association, supporting a Junior Orange parade, besieged the largely Catholic Unity Flats at the foot of the Shankill.

Unity flats, which was intended to be a mixed dwelling and which was proclaimed by Captain O'Neill as representing the new society of his administration, had rapidly become a mostly Catholic intrusion at the bottom of the Shankill. The flats represented something of a provocation to the Unionist mass-base as a result—symbolic of all that was despised and feared in O'Neill's new world.

The attempted invasion was repulsed by residents but later in the day a crowd of over 3000 attempted to sack the flats. The attackers were aided by police in the assault (who killed one local man) and fighting went on for nine hours before the attackers were beaten off by the residents. Another attack occurred the next morning.

The situation became so serious that British troops were requested by the Police Commissioner, but he was told that the employment of the British Army was a matter for the Secretary of State at Westminster.

The British Home Secretary, Callaghan, had been advised by his Whitehall officials earlier in 1969 that his armed forces were required by law to support the civil power if called upon by the Stormont Minister of Home Affairs. However, Callaghan decided that his army could not take instructions from the sub-government at Stormont and refused to provide it to the sub-government without Stormont agreeing to relinquish powers it had been given in 1921.

Callaghan later wrote that "we were debating whether we should intervene, but hoping and praying that we should not have to. The advice that came to me from all sides was on no account to get sucked into the Irish bog" (James Callaghan, A House Divided, p.15)

On August 6th Whitehall advised Stormont that "in view of the serious constitutional consequences of the use of troops it would be advisable for Northern Ireland to endure a quite considerable degree of disorder before involving military assistance".

When the Stormont Cabinet Secretary, Sir Harold Black asked what such consequences would be he was told that Callaghan believed that "if he decided to put troops on the streets he might be committing the UK government to take over the government of Northern Ireland". Black advised Whitehall that if Westminster took control the likely consequence would be a 1912-14 situation, including:

> "... a frightening reaction from the Protestant community which could make anything that has happened up to now seem like child's play: a provisional government might be set up with extreme elements at its head" (Eamon Phoenix, Irish Times 1.1.00).

Westminster therefore decided not to intervene lest such action would disturb the 1920 settlement.

On 10th August Eddie McAteer, Leader of the Nationalist Party, observing events in Belfast and fearful of what might transpire in his own city of Derry, called for help from the South, saying:

> "I believe and hope in this, our hour of trial, if we are to be beaten into the ground as a helpless and unarmed minority, I pray to God that our watching brethren will not stand aside any longer."

The *Irish Independent* reported that: "Asked if he meant that the Irish Government should send troops across the Border in the event of trouble he said: 'In any form...'" (*Irish News* 11.8.69). The Southern Government was also made aware of the seriousness of things in the North by the Ulster Volunteer Force bombing of the RTE offices in Dublin—although this event has been long forgotten.

Defensive Preparations

The trouble in Derry began when Orange marchers were stoned by Nationalists on the edge of the Bogside. But who started it is really beside the point as it was what happened next that really mattered. By that time the heart of the Northern Nationalist masses was no longer in the Civil Rights campaign and the Unionist community felt they needed to be taught a lesson about their position.

Earlier in the year the police had entered the Bogside after a Civil Rights march, and had run amok, destroying property. A local man had been beaten to death in front of his family by the police, who then occupied the Bogside. Samuel Devenney's massive funeral took place a couple of weeks before the Apprentice Boys' march.

The Bogsiders were determined to keep the RUC out this time and had organised themselves accordingly. From early August plans for the defence of the Bogside had been prepared by the Derry Citizens' Defence Association, a group of about 20 men, most of whom were middle-aged and represented a good cross-section of non-Unionist opinion in the town.

Professor Henry Patterson suggests that the DCDA was "dominated by local republicans" (Ireland Since 1939, p.239). It was true that the Chairman of the Association, Sean Keenan, was an old Republican, but there were ex-British servicemen, a Presbyterian and an Englishman also among the committee.

Paddy Doherty, who was its Vice-Chairman and driving force, makes it clear in his autobiography that he kept a close eye on Keenan, knowing him to be an old IRA man, so that things were not turned in a Republican direction. Local activists, who were suspicious of the Republican presence, also made sure that extra members were elected onto the Association to ensure its broad community character (*Paddy Bogside*, pp.115-7).

Doherty noted in his book an episode illustrating the lack of influence of Republicans on proceedings in the Bogside. In the month before the events of August he and Keenan journeyed to Dublin to ascertain if help would be forthcoming from the Irish Government if the Bogside was again attacked. The Taoiseach was unavailable but officials in the Department of Foreign Affairs assured the Derrymen, according to Doherty, that in the event of a serious attack: "We'll not let you down." When pressed further by Doherty the reply was: "The government will act to protect our people in Northern Ireland... and you will not be abandoned" (*Paddy Bogside*, p.124).

On leaving the Taoiseach's office Doherty was persuaded by Keenan to visit Republican HQ in Gardiner Street, to secure an insurance policy in the event of a Dublin let-down of the Bogside. The old IRA man, Keenan, was apparently bewildered at the posters of Marx, Lenin and Mao decorating the walls, leading Doherty to conclude: "It began to dawn on me how little Keenan, the man of the 1940s, knew of the IRA of the 1960s" (p.126).

When the two men met the IRA Chief of Staff and asked if any assistance would be forthcoming for Derry from the Republican movement, in the event of attack, Cathal Goulding replied, according to Doherty: "I couldn't defend the Bogside. I have neither the men nor the guns to do it."

Doherty recounted:

> "Keenan stood there, motionless, as if the message hadn't sunk in yet. 'I told you the IRA was only a myth, a fantasy army, with nothing to offer the people of Ireland,' I sneered. I sat down. The toy soldier, the Commander-in-Chief of the phantom army, was shaken by my reaction. In an effort to retrieve the situation be said 'But I will have the chief of Police or Minister for Home Affairs assassinated.'... Turning to Keenan, I said, 'Let's go back to Derry, where there is work to be done" (p.126-7).

The Republican movement, under the influence of Desmond Greaves and his Communists, had helped develop the Civil Rights movement as its new instrument of progress in the North after the 1956-62 IRA invasion had failed to get the Northern Catholics to rise. The theory of the Socialist Republicans was that a campaign for Civil Rights would splinter Unionism, releasing a more moderate, democratic and ultimately republican section of the Protestant working-class from the hard-line bigots. Then the "Northern state", deprived of its sectarian prop, would crumble into an all-Ireland Socialist Republic.

It was fantasy, of course. But it was dangerous fantasy and people like Doherty knew it would lead to trouble in the North. And that is why he had contempt for Goulding when he found out that the movement that was helping create the confrontation had made no provision for it when it inevitably came.

The Battle of the Bogside

Seamus Brady, who was in his native town as an interested observer of the Irish Government during the Unionist siege of Derry, pinpointed the significance of what happened there in August:

> "The Battle of the Bogside is probably unique in the annals of civil disturbance. For forty-eight hours a civilian population, united in what was a local revolt, successfully fought off with petrol bombs and stones a police force armed with riot equipment, CS tear gas, water cannon and armoured cars, and supported moreover by Protestant civilians. The RUC acceptance of support from Protestant civilians—at times police handed the civilians their shields and batons to use while they took a rest from the fighting—was the chief factor in welding the Catholic population together in militant resistance ... The attack failed under a hail of petrol bombs and stones. But the news that Protestant civilians were fighting alongside the hated RUC electrified the Catholic population of Bogside, the Brandywell cluster of streets behind it, and the sprawling concrete ghetto of Creggan that dominates the city. The strong individualism of Derry Catholics, which is reflected in a web of political groups normally bitterly opposed, was thus bonded into a common will to resist. Priests and people, moderates, Republicans, and socialists united under the leadership of the Citizens Defence Association..." (*Arms and the Men*, pp. 22-3. See also: 'Eye-witness report by Seamus Brady on events in Derry', NAI, 2000/6/658, which supplies material for the book.)

What was unique here was the character of the Police/Unionist mob relationship. In a normal state the police do not act as the spearhead of the mob. Film footage of the *Battle of the Bogside* shows the RUC picking up stones and hurling them at residents. Those are not the actions of a normal police force. They demonstrated the real character of the Police as a kind of mob in uniform carrying out the repression of a community on behalf of the other ones of which they were part.

As Max Weber once said the State has the monopoly of violence and acts for the society—not with the mob. But the relationship between the Police and the mob was almost complementary in 'Northern Ireland'—the Police being distinguishable from the mob only by wearing the uniforms of the state and being paid for their actions.

The Battle of the Bogside quickly assumed the character of a defensive Insurrection. There was mass participation in an improvised community uprising.

The RUC probably calculated that they could not be seen to be beaten by the Insurrectionists as this would have fatal consequences in the relationship between the subordinated and those who subordinated them. So they continued their forays in conjunction with the mob until exhaustion set in.

Brady described the result in his subsequent report to the Dublin Government:

> "This was the climactic moment in the history of Derry over the last 50 years. For never before had the ordinary citizens seen the R.U.C. retreating from anyone." (Eye-witness report by Seamus Brady. ibid).

The Taoiseach's Response

The Fianna Fail Government in the South began to respond to the events in Derry. Neil Blaney, TD for Donegal and a leading Cabinet member, who had kept himself abreast of things in the North, acted as virtual Taoiseach on the first night of the Battle of the Bogside (when Taoiseach Lynch was unavailable) and then went behind the barricades during the battle to give moral support to the defenders.

The Taoiseach, upon returning to the scene, convened a Cabinet meeting in Dublin. At this two Ministers, Kevin Boland and Blaney, said they favoured an Army intervention to assist the Bogsiders and favoured military forays across the Border at various points. They were supported by Charles Haughey and by Brian Lenihan, to a degree.

But Lynch waivered and the Cabinet were not able to reach a collective decision over what to do. In the event, the Army was ordered to the Border with the setting up of field hospitals for the wounded, as a cover. The Defence Minister, James Gibbons, was instructed to quickly bring the Army up to strength and prepare it for possible incursions in a "peace-keeping" role. It was also decided to allow supply of arms across the Border without there being any harassment of gun-runners and to follow through on the threat to involve the United Nations.

The Taoiseach made a television broadcast on the evening of 13th August, in which he made his famous and momentous "*won't stand {idly} by*" speech (the "*idly*" word was in the speech but omitted by Lynch at the last minute and it is widely known as his "*idly by*" speech):

"It is clear now that the present situation cannot be allowed to continue. It is evident also that the Stormont government is no longer in control of the situation. Indeed, the present situation is the inevitable outcome of the policies pursued for decades by successive Stormont governments. It is clear also that the Irish Government can no longer stand by and see innocent people injured and perhaps worse. It is obvious that the RUC is no longer accepted as an impartial police force. Neither would the employment of British troops be acceptable nor would they be likely to restore peaceful conditions, certainly not in the long term. The Irish Government have, therefore, requested the British Government to apply immediately to the United Nations for the urgent dispatch of a Peace-Keeping Force to the Six Counties of Northern Ireland and have instructed the Permanent Representative to the United Nations to inform the Secretary General of this request. We have also asked the British Government to see to it that police attacks on the people of Derry should cease immediately. Very many people have been injured and some of them seriously. We know that many of these do not wish to be treated in Six County hospitals. We have, therefore, directed the Irish Army authorities to have field hospitals established in County Donegal adjacent to Derry and at other points along the Border where they may be necessary. Recognising, however, that the re-unification of the national territory can provide the only permanent solution for the problem, it is our intention to request the British Government to enter into early negotiations with the Irish Government to review the present constitutional position of the Six Counties of Northern Ireland… All men and women of goodwill will hope and pray that the present deplorable and distressing situation will not further deteriorate but that it will soon be ended firstly by the granting of full equality of citizenship to every man and woman in the Six Counties area regardless of class, creed or political persuasion and, eventually, by the restoration of the historic unity of our country." (NAI, TSCH 2000/6/657)

Brady described the impact of Lynch's speech:

"The effect of this statement throughout Ireland was electrifying… In Derry behind the barricades men wept openly, women went down on their knees to give thanks to God. All over the North the minority, outnumbered and alone for fifty years, rose suddenly to a new fervour of resistance with the cry: 'The South is with us.' Throughout the rest of the country, too, as people watched the impassive face of Lynch on their television sets and heard the ponderous words, a wave of enthusiasm swept all political feeling aside. Old Ireland was reaching for its final destiny after all the centuries of travail."

But, as Brady, commented: "Unfortunately... Jack Lynch was a reluctant hero at that hour. He did not, one feels, fully comprehend the import of his words that evening; and he was regretting them by the next morning." (*Arms and the Men*, p.39)

Brady noted that the reaction from the Unionists was one of dismay, many taking Lynch's speech to mean that the Irish Army was mobilised and would cross the Border. Their response was to mobilise the B Specials, its private army of 8,000. Many of them had mobilised themselves, instinctively, already, before orders were received. They raided the rural arsenals in the doing of their duty. In their black uniforms, armed with rifles, revolvers or submachine guns, they began to fan out across the countryside to deal with the Catholic Insurrection that was breaking out in other places, in support of Derry.

The defenders of Derry sent out messages calling for diversionary demonstrations that would draw off Police reinforcements bound for the Bogside. The Northern Ireland Civil Rights Association threatened these demonstrations unless the Unionist Government called off the Specials in Derry. These took place at Strabane, Dungiven, Omagh, Lurgan, Coalisland, Dungannon, Armagh, Enniskillen, Newry and Belfast. Two hundred turned up for a meeting held by the Civil Rights Association in Divis Flats, Belfast. The diversionary demonstrations led to confrontations, but nowhere did the demonstrators use firearms—which they did not possess. The Police and B Specials, however, shot one protester dead and wounded a number of others.

The spirited and unexpected Catholic defence of Derry put the police out on their feet. Then the feared Specials began to appear through the Police lines along the city walls overlooking the Bogside. But, instead of scattering, the defenders hurried their reinforcements to the barricades.

It was at this point that the British Army was deployed. The first British units began driving trucks into Derry. Brady noted a momentary confusion among the Specials who mistook them for Irish troops. But a wild cheer went up from the Catholics as the police began to withdraw. Brady noted: "It was a humiliating defeat for the forces of law and order of Northern Ireland. They withdrew with the jeers of the Bogsiders following them" (*Arms and the Men*, p.44).

This, combined with what was happening in Belfast, was something of a turning point in the life of the Northern Catholics. The Unionists had been held at bay and had their illusions of independent existence shattered; the British had been forced to re-engage with the Six Counties and the minority itself had shown it could achieve something momentous through its united efforts.

Going Berserk in Belfast

The Bogsiders secured a significant victory against 'Northern Ireland' in the siege of Derry they had resisted successfully. However, what changed everything in the North was the Unionist assault on the Catholic Falls and Ardoyne areas in Belfast.

It must be conceded that Lynch's speech had a part in bringing this about and it therefore had a much more significant effect on Belfast than it did on Derry.

In the Derry Bogside the Catholics were a majority, rather than a minority. Even before August, they had been able to live a substantial life of their own, partly due to the Derry Gerrymander that sealed them off from the political process. They also did not suffer the routine humiliation by the forces of law and order of the Catholics elsewhere, with the result that they tended to see the Police as an occupying army when it entered the Bogside in any sizeable body. They were able to make extensive preparations for battle in their secure enclave prior to August, and they always had Donegal at their back to aid them, or to fall back upon.

However, in Belfast Catholics were in the minority and were in a much more vulnerable position to attack from the majority. Unlike in Derry, the preparations for battle had been made on the Unionist side alone.

In Belfast Nationalists demonstrating outside Springfield Road and Hastings Street Police Stations at the events in Derry hurled a few petrol bombs. In response the RUC commander ordered out Shorland armoured cars, which unbeknown to the Stormont Government had been brought up from the Border by their security apparatus. This action generated a response from Nationalists who mounted further attacks on Springfield Road Police Station. The RUC opened fire, wounding a couple of people, and it was claimed that fire was returned from the crowd. Shots were later fired at an RUC armoured vehicle in Leeson St. The RUC then decided to mount their Shorlands with browning heavy machine-guns on the morning of 13th August.

Lynch's speech took place on that evening and the B Specials appeared in Belfast on the 14th August. The Stormont Cabinet had mobilised the Specials but there had been no authorisation for them carrying arms in Belfast from the Unionist Government or the RUC.

Lynch's speech had the effect of rallying the majority to the support of their defenders as the prospect of a threat from the South appeared. So they attacked the Irish "Fifth Column" in its West Belfast stronghold as it began to get pretensions of behaving like Bogsiders.

The Loyalist population of Belfast had no means of knowing what Lynch intended on doing with his army—whether it constituted an invasion force or whether it just represented a symbolic conciliation of the upsurge in Republican sentiment in Dublin. But what the Taoiseach actually said, along with statements from the Republican Movement, combined with the Insurrection in Derry, helped to confirm the Unionist populace in its view that the conflict over Civil Rights within the North, which actually arose from the internal structure of 'Northern Ireland', was really an Anti-Partitionist offensive — as Paisley had been saying for the previous few years.

The speech by the Taoiseach was experienced as inflammatory by the Unionist populace and therefore it was, to all intents and purposes, inflammatory in effect. The Taoiseach's intervention and the expectations raised by it in the Catholic community in the North played its part in consolidating the Nationalist defence into an Insurrection.

The appearance of the Specials, armed and mingling with Protestant crowds mustering at the Shankill end of the streets connecting the Shankill with the Falls, brought the Catholic populace out in defence. Tricolours were waved and a crowd of Nationalist youths entered the mixed streets leading to the Shankill. This indicated to the Protestants that the Catholic Insurrection had spread to Belfast.

The Unionist onslaught on Nationalist areas occurred within a context which is often ignored today because of the benefit of hindsight. It is now apparent that Taoiseach Lynch was quite willing to "*stand idly by*" and keep his army South of the Border and that there were no IRA brigades in Belfast to answer to the marching orders of their Chief of Staff. Instead there was the widespread belief in Nationalist areas that the day of deliverance had arrived when all arms of Nationalism were about to act together to end their nightmare. And that feeling was conveyed across into Unionist territory by what was happening in the Insurrectionary areas and by the provocative activity and rhetoric of the 'revolutionary' elements that saw in Republicanism the means of playing out their political fantasies.

The Unionist Government dithered because of the bluff that came out of Westminster about the consequences for the Unionist Government of deploying British troops to repress the Insurrection. In this situation elements in the Police, the B Specials and the Protestant community at large took the law into their own hands and launched the punitive offensive toward the Falls to do what the State, or pseudo-state, was failing to do.

How could they know that they were the victims of a great deal of bluffing from all sides?

The Police sprayed the Catholic areas with high-calibre machine-gun fire, killing a number of people. On the evening of the 14th, the Specials ordered Catholics out of their homes and the Unionist attack burnt out families from the streets intersecting the Shankill and the Falls. When the attackers ran into small pockets of resistance from Catholic residents and a handful of lightly armed Republicans, the Police intervened with armoured cars and heavy machine guns. Conflict continued into the morning of the 15th with a Unionist attack on Clonard Monastery aimed at dislodging two IRA defenders/snipers. It was in the course of this attack that Bombay Street was gutted, at the same time as streets in Ardoyne burned.

The Unionist attack was largely improvised. It was directed towards burning out the Catholic areas close to the Shankill, to put the Catholics back in their place, rather than a general massacre. However, some Catholic areas were nearly overwhelmed and some Bishops came in to give the community a General Absolution so that Judgement Day could be faced with confidence.

On the 15th the Nationalist MP Austin Currie, met the Taoiseach in Dublin and demanded assistance for Northern Catholics. The next day three Stormont MPs (Paddy Devlin, Paddy Kennedy and Paddy O'Hanlon) arrived in the Department of External Affairs and, according to a file in the National Archives, demanded several hundred guns to prevent what they claimed to be an impending massacre of Catholics in Belfast:

> "Mr. Kennedy, who was the main spokesman, said that the B Specials were on 'the loose in Belfast, that there was continuous sniping and that people were being shot down. More and more Catholics were being forced into the Falls Road area and were being forced further and further up the Falls. Soon the whole Catholic population of Belfast would be concentrated in this area and they would be massacred. Bogside in Derry was mild compared to this. The Catholics there would have to defend themselves and their homes and they were there to see the Taoiseach. They could not return to the North until they had seen him. If Irish troops would not be sent in to the North, then they wanted guns and they would not leave without definite answers to these questions. The situation of Catholics in Belfast could not continue without protection. As regards guns, nothing need be done openly or politically—a few hundred rifles could easily be 'lost' and would not be missed." (NAI, TSCH 2000/6/658, 16.8.69)

The three demanding guns were all part of the new breed of 'Constitutional Nationalists' just elected to Stormont.

The MPs, despite returning later to see Lynch, were fobbed off by the Department of Foreign Affairs, where officials claimed the Taoiseach couldn't be found. In response they headed out and addressed a meeting in O'Connell Street where they publicly repeated their call for arms for Northern Nationalists. The Northern Nationalists were then seen by Cabinet Ministers Charles Haughey and Neil Blaney, who were left to deal with the situation.

The Republican Let-Down

The small Belfast IRA—along with a much larger assortment of defenders from the general community—helped delay the Unionist attack in Belfast with a handful of weapons so that barricades could be erected preventing a more substantial assault. But it was totally unprepared for the ferocity of the attack, and seven people died along with the destruction of hundreds of homes.

The *United Irishman*, newspaper of the Republican movement, had '*The North Began*' as its front-page headline in its August edition. It predicted, before the event that:

"The North began... The question is can the North hold on? This month will give the answer. Derry is the flashpoint. The call from Derry to station UN troops in the city should not be ignored."

On the back page was a drawing of an Irish UN soldier, which urged intervention in the North. "*Every nation's battle but his own*" was the caption beneath.

On 13th August, the second day of the Battle of the Bogside, and the day on which Lynch made his momentous speech, the Sinn Fein President Tomas Mac Giolla, issued a statement saying:

"The present events in the Six Counties are the outcome of fifty years of British rule. The civil rights demands, moderate though they are, have shown up that Unionist rule is incompatible with democracy; if the minority thought they could grant them and stay in power they would have done so after the degree of pressure put on them. The question is now no longer civil rights, but the continuation of British rule in Ireland. The Irish people cannot be expected to stand idly by and allow an Orange bigoted junta to continue in power in the Six Counties...It is necessary to re-state the demands of the Republican Movement at this juncture:

"We demand, firstly, that the Dublin government, which claims the mantle of the Republic, make immediate representations to the British government at Westminster, demanding: (1) the withdrawal of troops from the North of Ireland and the holding of an all-Ireland election (2) the immediate granting of the civil rights demands... Neither must there be any reversion to direct rule of the North by Westminster; direct rule by Westminster as during the disastrous nineteenth century is no solution to either Ireland's or the civil rights problems.

"If Westminster refuses these just and reasonable demands, we insist that the Dublin government use all resources at their disposal, including military force if need be, to defend the people who are at present being assaulted in the streets and burnt out of their homes... If the Dublin government refuses to act, we call upon the Irish people to organise during the coming period to take whatever action is necessary to provide support and solidarity to our fellow-countrymen in the North, and to go on from there to the establishment of an all-Ireland democratic republic, the only ultimate solution to the problem" (NAI, TSCH 2000/6/657).

This statement, in all its confusion between Civil and National Rights, would have confirmed in Protestant minds that the Civil Rights movement had been an Anti-Partitionist manoeuvre all along and it was now moving out of cover into the open. The other aspect of it was how little it differed from the Irish Government position in such a way that the Sinn Fein President's phrase about *"not standing idly by"* became attributed to the Taoiseach, who had omitted the word *"idly"* from his original speech on TV. Its difference lay in simply stating that if Dublin did not perform its national duty there were others who would do it for them.

On 18th August the IRA Chief of Staff announced to the Southern press that the IRA had "been in action" and had "placed all volunteers on full alert" and "sent a number of fully equipped units to the aid of their comrades in the Six Counties". British troops were warned that if they intervened on behalf of "the sectarian Orange murder gangs, you will have to take the consequences". It was stressed also that:

> "The only solution acceptable to Republicans and to the Irish people as a whole is one in which Britain gets out of our country altogether, withdraws her troops, and control over the whole of Ireland passes to a 32-County, Irish Parliament, elected from among all the people of Ireland, North and South..." (NAI, TSCH 2000/6/658)

Paddy Doherty, who had returned to Derry with Keenan and was organising the defence of the Bogside at this time, took Goulding's statement to be very unhelpful in the situation:

> "Many Protestants believed that the rioting had been directed by the IRA, and they were fearful and angry. Peter Pan did nothing to allay their fears. From the safety of his builder's yard, he announced that he was sending his paper battalions north to defend the Catholic population. His nonsensical threat destroyed any residual belief Keenan and I still had in him" (*Paddy Bogside*, p.156)

The Unionist populace in the North, listening to Goulding, had no grounds for knowing that he commanded a very small army and there was very little of a Derry or Belfast Brigade or any significant weaponry in the North.

No Help from 'The Prince'

The popular Insurrection in Derry was not Republican. It began as a defensive measure with no definite political purpose beyond keeping the RUC out of the Bogside. As Seamus Brady, an eye-witness, noted:

"It was a rebellion by unarmed civilians, led by a civilian committee. It was a rebellion in which no political group had been involved... Despite the claims made by the Six-County Government the IRA has no hand or part in the rebellion that has taken part in Derry City. Arms have not been used at any stage by the defenders" (NAI, TSCH, 2000/6/658, p.3)

In the rest of the Six Counties it was a general attempt to prevent the heavily-armed Specials coming in and massacring the unarmed and defenceless community. But Mac Giolla's and Goulding's interventions confirmed in Loyalist minds that the Insurrection in Derry and Belfast was a Republican Insurrection when it was nothing of the sort.

The turmoil that was going on in the North had nothing to do with the IRA or Sinn Fein and it had little to do with mainstream Nationalism. There were later found to be a handful of guns available to Republicans in Derry and most did not work. This information only came out when the Bogsiders started to fear that, in keeping the RUC out they would then be subject to an assault by the heavily-armed Specials. In fact, at the height of the battle with the B men's arrival impending, Doherty and Keenan were offered rifles and ammunition from an Army store across the Border but refused them to make sure there were no allegations of military assistance afterwards.

Billy McMillen, the commander of the IRA in the Falls, organised some small-scale diversionary activity on 16th August in support of Derry and then helped in defensive work with the half a dozen weapons at his disposal. The defensive work was not really Republican activity since most members of the community would have engaged in it if they had had the means themselves. The defence of Ardoyne had been largely conducted by Catholic ex-British servicemen with a couple of shotguns. (Patrick Bishop and Eamonn Mallie, *The Provisional IRA*, p.113)

McMillen got little support from his Chief of Staff in Dublin. Goulding was up in the Dublin Mountains fulfilling a contract he had made with a British TV crew to film an IRA training camp in exchange for £200. When he returned to Dublin he was confronted by Northerners at his office demanding weapons for the defence of their communities. Goulding told them that the cupboard was bare. Mick Ryan, who had been with the Chief of Staff in the mountain camp, told Sean Swan:

"Goulding... asked to be excused for a few minutes and we went upstairs to an office. He was now faced with the reality of pogroms — of what several people had been warning him was inevitable — and was an extremely worried man. When we got to the office he closed the door and stood there silently for a while. He looked close to collapse. Then he turned to me and said 'This is terrible, Jesus Christ, this is terrible. What am I going to do? Living Jesus, what are we going to do?' He seemed to realise the massive error of judgement that he had made. But 'The Prince' could not help him now. There were no gullible ears to listen" (*Official Irish Republicanism, 1962 to 1972*, p. 297).

The reference to '*The Prince*' not helping him related to Goulding having been an avid reader of Machiavelli at the time and fancying himself in that role, as a political manipulator *extraordinaire*. But nothing in Machiavelli or the Revolutionary Marxism he had been fed helped the Chief of Staff to understand what was going on in the North or guided him on how he should respond to it with his small army.

Republican Confusion

On 16th August Desmond Greaves, the theoretician of the Civil Rights strategy, phoned Jack Bennett, a Republican in Belfast, to get a report on the situation. Bennett told him that the IRA was engaging the RUC in order to bring about a breakdown in law and order and the intervention of British troops. When asked why by an astonished Greaves, Bennett explained that Goulding wanted "to prove the place was under British control". Greaves then asked: "And what then?" Bennett replied: "Oh, they hadn't thought of that." Greaves asked: "But you don't mean to say that they've risked raising this sectarian frenzy?" To which Bennett replied: "Well I suppose they had. But anyway it will break the deadlock" (from C.D. Greaves' Diary, cited in Swan, *Official Republicanism*, p.293)

Goulding then, hearing of the deployment of British troops in the North, cancelled the Republican action and ordered his units to dump arms and return home across the Border.

Despite the Republican retreat at the British intervention, September's *United Irishman* had a drawing of Jack Lynch standing at the crossroads with one road signposted to Derry and "*The Nation's Honour*" and the other to "*Humiliation and Disgrace*". The editorial then spoke in ecstatic terms of what had happened in the North:

> "The risen people of the North... who would have thought that their ultimate victory would be so great? The spirit and fire of Republicanism has lighted the way to final victory, which cannot be far off. A festival of hate they have had for 50 years. Celebrating the Protestant Ascendancy, the root and basis of Unionist rule. Keep the Fenians and papists down. But the gallant Bogsiders gave them their answer. After 1969 things will never be the same in Ulster. The rock of Unionism is split to the foundations and to have caused the split is the greatest and most historic achievement of the Civil Rights Movement. Civil Rights brought the disunited Catholics together cementing over the divisions between a dozen different parties."

There is little of the new Socialism or Civil Rights programme here. The main demands of NICRA were taken to be superfluous and miserable in comparison to the main objective—the splitting of Unionism and the re-opening of the Anti-Partitionist struggle on a new plane. But how the events of August, which were not a Republican event at all, were going to lead to a situation where the "*spirit and fire of Republicanism*" would light "*the way to final victory, which cannot be far off*" was not specified.

What had happened in the North was in the nature of a 'miracle' for the Republicans. But it had ushered in a situation where British troops had been welcomed by desperate Northern Catholics and the British Government had applied itself to instituting the Civil Rights demands and reforming the system. The question was: How was that situation, and Taoiseach Lynch's seeming abrogation of his national duty, to be turned into 'final victory' for Republicanism?

The traditionalists in the Republican movement were appalled at the behaviour of the Republican leadership. They had failed to defend Belfast after warning of the danger that the situation they themselves had helped bring about had actually came about. They were then proving incapable of acting in the Republican interest within a situation of flux that presented real opportunities of advance to those who chose to grasp them.

After the dust had settled in the North the Republican movement, having acted on its instincts during the four days in August, returned to the Greaves plan of reforming the "*Northern state*". And so, having helped unleash the dogs of war, it declined into a self-induced political irrelevance.

It was clear from all this that the existing Republican movement was inadequate to the task of dealing with the situation that was emerging in the North—defending its community, being able to advance the Republican struggle or even taking a leadership position in relation to the predicament of Northern Catholics. It, therefore, required something new to step into the breach left by its confusion.

The Nature of British Intervention

The British troops were sent into Belfast to prevent a much greater escalation of conflict, which threatened the settlement of 1921. They had the desired effect of halting the Pogrom and settling things down.

The ultimate British responsibility for what happened in August 1969 was revealed in Whitehall's reaction to Minister Hillery's initiative at the start of the month, aimed at heading off the explosion. Whitehall passed the buck to Stormont, which decided that to ban the Orange muster at Derry would result in a revolt by Stormont Unionist backbenchers which would bring down the new Unionist Premier, Major Chichester-Clark, who had just replaced Captain O'Neill, who had himself been forced out by a Unionist revolt.

The British Government was not keen to get involved in 'Northern Ireland' again in August 1969. It had successfully detached itself in 1921 and it was determined to let the Unionists continue to run the local show. But, in August 1969, it did send in troops out of sheer necessity and imagined that its intervention would be both temporary and minimal. British troops were only sent to the Six Counties after Chichester-Clark had made it clear to the British that he could no longer contain the situation—which was the whole purpose of the Unionist Government in Whitehall's eyes, ever since 1921.

Tony Benn recorded in his Diary a Cabinet meeting held on 19th August to discuss the situation. He remembers Jim Callaghan, the Home Secretary, as reporting to the Cabinet:

"'The Stormont government says it is the IRA who are the cause of the trouble, but this does not conform to British intelligence. The Catholics were defending themselves with ferocity, as Jim (Callaghan) put it, and it was really because of that fear that the situation had got out of control.

"Jim said we must remove the cause of the fear i.e., get rid of the B Specials, and he would like to see (Anthony) Peacocke, the Inspector-General of the Royal Ulster Constabulary, replaced by a British chief constable.

"...Denis (Healey) said he thought it was better to get Chichester-Clark or another Ulsterman, to carry the can... (Callaghan) said he thought Chichester Clark was anxious to help because he was a very frightened man.

"...Jim then considered the possibility of a broadly based government, although it was agreed that this should not be done unless it was acceptable. But if all else fails what do we do? Denis stressed again: let's keep Chichester Clark carrying the can. Wilson agreed: 'Yes I too want to avoid responsibility'.

"...Michael Stewart (Foreign Secretary) said. 'Britain could not walk out entirely of Ulster although we have considered it as an alternative.'

"It was an interesting thing for him to have said because that would never have been admitted publicly. He thought that awful as it would be to take over responsibility, that would be less awful than walking out. But that there must be some results tonight and the B Specials are the key" (published in The Independent, 14.12.87).

It was Westminster's intention to go to all lengths to preserve the 1920 arrangement. Callaghan advised the Cabinet:

"... it would be better to avoid direct intervention and to use the Northern Ireland Government as agents... It was important to remember that the majority of the population of NI were Protestant; in seeking to allay the apprehensions of the Catholics, they must not drive the majority beyond endurance."

It was concluded that "Direct Rule... would pose a severe administrative problem and would impose the risk of armed conflict with the Protestant community" (CAB 128/46, 19.8.69).

Much of what subsequently occurred is explained in Benn's record of this meeting.

Westminster Takes Control

The *Downing Street Communiqué and Declaration* of August 1969 basically blamed the Unionist Government for the August crisis and indicated that Whitehall would now guarantee minority rights over the head of Stormont, which had been left in charge of this aspect by Britain since 1921.

After the British made the Downing Street Declaration, promising the people of 'Northern Ireland' "in all legislative and executive decisions of Government... the same equality of treatment and freedom from discrimination as obtains in the rest of the United Kingdom irrespective of political views or religion", Chichester Clark was summoned to Downing Street to inform him of the implications of being rescued by the army of the State.

At the meeting the British took the extraordinary step of placing its local civil power under the supervision of the State's military apparatus by putting its Army General Officer Commanding in control of the RUC Inspector-General and his forces, including the Specials.

This was before the British Army faced a military opposition from the Catholic community and within a situation that Westminster regarded as only a civil disturbance. It doing this it signalled to the Nationalist community that something of much greater consequence was occurring than simply that of military aid being granted by the State to the civil power of its sub-government.

A changed political relationship was evident between Westminster and Stormont. Henceforth Stormont would operate under close Whitehall supervision and its survival would depend on good behaviour. The Unionist Government would no longer have control over its own militia and would have to implement the reforms Whitehall thought necessary, whether they liked it or not.

Chichester-Clark had to agree to commission an impartial investigation into the disorder; agree to an end to the Local Government gerrymander through a redrawing of electoral boundaries; the transference of public housing allocation away from the Councils to an independent body; the creation of a community relations commission; a review of the law on incitement to religious hatred; and an anti-discrimination clause being put in public contracts. This represented the Civil Rights programme and more.

Whitehall did little to conceal Unionist humiliation. As Ken Bloomfield, a senior Civil Servant at Stormont noted the Unionist Government would no longer be just a subordinate government:

> "The Northern Ireland government was being brought very starkly to face the reality that it could no longer assure law and order within its own resources... The first two headline objectives of its own constitution, the Government of Ireland Act 1920—'peace, order and good government—

could no longer be guaranteed. The Northern Ireland government would exist for the foreseeable future as a client regime, under constant supervision both at ministerial and official levels" (*Stormont in Crisis*, p.118)

Bloomfield notes how Jack Sayers, the Editor of the *Belfast Telegraph*, shocked at the turn of events and the humiliation of the Unionist Government, wrote to him:

> "I'm being forced to the conclusion that we are incapable of normal political development and without this we cannot sustain a Parliament and system of our own. I've come a very long way from my inborn romanticism about Ulster... Forgive me for my failure—the extreme violence in Belfast was bad enough but the communiqué and the declaration have hit me as an indictment of Unionism from which it can't recover" (p.119).

This was the realisation that, after the events of August 1969, the independent existence of the Stormont idyll was an illusion and it was incapable of acting to any effect in future.

But the British view after the August events was that Unionism was recoverable and they determined to maintain their façade at Stormont. They decided upon a reform of the system in a limited way—which the Unionists had proved unable to do, particularly as regards the security forces which the Unionists had dared not tackle—and to get out again as quickly as possible.

Or, at least, that was the cunning plan.

Behind the Barricades

In looking at this moment in time I chanced to come across some surviving copies of the news-sheet produced behind the barricades of Catholic Belfast entitled *'Citizen Press'*. This was produced by the Citizens Defence Committee and seems to have appeared every 2 or 3 days during August and early September 1969. Radio Free Belfast was the Radio arm of Citizen's Press, which read from its editions, interspersed with Irish music. It contained the views of the different elements that were thrown together in defence of the community and it gave them their say. It was Republican in a sense, but not as the term would be now understood. It was, therefore, very representative of Catholic Belfast at that moment of time – a moment that did not last.

I am not sure if these views are published elsewhere so they are well worth reproducing to rediscover the lost world of Catholic Belfast in late August 1969, so we can show that what subsequently happened need not necessarily have happened. They are reproduced directly from the surviving originals with grammar and spelling left uncorrected.

The first (from one of the later editions) reveals the feelings within the community after the attacks of the B-Men and the mob:

"HOW THE B-SPECIALS CAME INTO ARDOYNE AND WHAT THEY DID TO THE PEOPLE WHO ONLY WANTED PEACE.

"Sammy McLarnan was a member of the local Peace Keeping Committee in the Hooker Street area. He was killed at 11:55 on the Thursday of the riots, as he pulled down the blind in his house in Herbert Street. The bullets were fired by 2 B-Specials from the Crumlin Road end of Herbert Street. Earlier, Sammy McLarnan had helped other local men in a desperate fight to put out fires started by B-Men and U.V.F. extremists at the top of the road...

"50 or 60 charged in about 25 B-Men and the rest with white armbands and helmets. They were shouting 'if the men aren't in we'll rape the women'. Watching from my window I saw two B-Specials tear the wire cage off the window of one of the little shops, and then the men with the white arm bands threw the petrol bombs in.

"On Friday Herbert Street was completely abandoned 'there was no point staying behind to get shot down in cold blood, there were enough of us, but we had nothing to defend our homes with'. Today the troops maintain an uneasy peace, but the people who have nearly all move backed home feel utterly insecure. 'Can the peace last? Will the troops stay? What guarantee of safety have we got for our families if the troops leave?' these are the questions that are being asked.

"Several families in Herbert Street are already talking about emigration. They are a far cry from the extremists described in the Unionist propaganda document 'Ulster-The Facts'. They are almost absurdly 'moderate' considering what they have been through. They are prepared to contemplate almost any desperate gesture, to show that all they want is peace, they are not hard line Republicans, they still talk doubtfully about measures of militant defense which are proposed. But the truth is that after the events of Thursday, the men who were ready to build barricades, and who were always synical of Unionist intentions have proved right. The choice is, defend yourselves or emigrate.

"Events in the riots immediately prior to the present outbreak, illustrate how police indiscipline help to break back of the peace committee idea. A witness said 'a petrol bomb lit a house across Butler Street from us... in Butler street police coming up from Hooker's street hurled stones at us...'

"Whatever these people felt about the police then, they have a cold hatred for the B-Men. A man who admitted that he had a sneaking sympathy for Captain O'Neill said 'if I had had a Tommy gun I would of shot the lot of them'... It is against the background such as this that the demands of the C.D.C. are right. They are the minimum concessions which will make life tolerable and secure for the people who were moderates, before Chichester-Clarke took power and the Specials went on the rampage." (Citizen Press, No.10, 7/8/9.9.69)

It should be noted that some of the hostility within the Catholic community to the Specials was of a distinctly Imperial character. As Maurice Hayes noted the B Men were regarded as *"shirkers"* from the second German war, in which the Catholic ex-servicemen had served. And these men saw themselves as a cut-above the unprofessional rabble playing at soldiers in the Specials (Minority Verdict, p.28).

The following comes from an earlier edition as the Stormont regime attempted to bull-doze "the burnt-out houses in Conway Street, Cooper Street, Percy Street and the Bombay Street area" before James Callaghan arrived to survey the scene. It noted that —

"Citizen Press sellers were detained for questioning by the military yesterday. They suggested 'this paper is seditious'. The sellers explained that it was not particularly seditious to explain the true events on the Falls Rd. and to put forward the demands of the local Defence Committee's The Officers replied 'we are not interested in politics, we do not understand the situation in Ulsterand we do not want to'. They went on 'we just have a job to do'. Could it be that that job is to act as the unwitting stooges of a reactionary government.

"After 4 days the circulation of the Citizen News has reached 5,000 each day, we go from strength to strength, so does our partner in sedition the free radio {Radio Free Belfast. P.W.} Pick it up for News Views and music from behind the barricades. In particular our all night music programme for the men on the barricades. On 240-250 metres." (No.2 22.8.69)

Under the heading *'Get the Strength of the Security Forces around you'*, the same edition said:

"On Thursday the homes of two Catholic British Army ex-service men in Derry were raided by armed troops and members of the R.U.C. who were searching for arms and 'I.R.A. men... This raid was certainly the precursor of more to follow and it has also confirmed what many of us expected all along – that the peace-keeping role of the military is a political disguise to enable the Unionist clique to round up to terrorise its political oppents and those who bravely defended their homes and lives from the attacks of the R.U.C. and the B.Specials.

"The political settlement arranged in London between Harold Wilson and Major Clark has now been exposed as a sellout to the very forces of law and order which were supposed to come under army patrol. The military forces which received such a warm welcome in bogside and Belfast are now operating as a wing of the special branch of the unionist government and are to be held in as much contempt and distrust as the rest of the organs of state security.

"For those of us living in the liberated areas the warning must be received and must be clearly understood. We must maintain our barricades... We must impress on the Westminster Government that the unionist clique in

Stormont does not have and never has had our confidence and we demand that British troops must not aid and abet the various forms of repression that they were sent to the six counties to control. As long as the B Specials and the R.U.C. exist in this area we can never relax our vigil. These forces must be disbanded and the administration of the six counties be taken over by Westminster and governed as part of the UK thus guaranteeing the people of the six counties the same rights and justice as other United Kingdom citizens. Any other political solution arranged by Stormont and Westminster is totally unacceptable to us."

The Unionist police force was the great aggravating factor in the Six Counties. Lord Brookeborough had taken a six month holiday every year and tended to his estates for most of the week while governing 'Northern Ireland'. He knew that the governing of the statelet mainly consisted of maintaining the police and letting the British welfare state do the rest.

After August that situation could not persist. The Catholic community was clearly saying that, whilst it had tolerated the hostile policing of the RUC for half a century, it would no longer do so after the events of August. Now that areas had been liberated from the Police force of the Unionist Party, it was not going to be let back in. There was a realisation that this was the great opportunity of ridding itself of the hateful Unionist policing because the police was also the representative of the UK State as a whole. The British State, however, having ceded control of policing to its Six County sub-government in 1921, had no means of acting in the liberated areas after August 1969, aside from deploying its army. This became a very significant factor in what was to subsequently happen.

The voices from behind the barricades suggest that most of the community, even those who were organised with a political will, were reformist in instinct and quite open to a settlement within the United Kingdom. In fact, most did not even conceive of any all-Ireland solution, despite their experience of life in the Six Counties.

A couple of days later under the heading, *'The Constitution'*, a further edition of Citizen Press showed that the people behind the barricades were Constitutional in the real sense of the word:

"The Northern Ireland Constitution comes from the Government of Ireland Act 1920 & 1949. The key article is article 75 of the 1920 Act under which the British Government maintains what are called residual powers, in other words Britain has and always had the final say. Our demand that Westminster invokes article 75 to disband the specials, release the political prisoners and grant full civil rights is thoroughly constitutional.

"Until now Britain has refused to accept her responsibilities for the governing of Northern Ireland. At this moment the opportunity appears of pressure from Irish voters in Britain inducing Wily Harold Wilson to get up off his backside, and use article 75, not as it has been used up to now as final defence for a privileged junta but rather as an instrument to build a new and better Northern Ireland" (CP No.6, 24.8.69).

In 1969 the demand was for use of article 75 to end Unionist policing over the Catholic community. In 1998 the demand was for a repeal of article 75. (The Good Friday Agreement implied the repeal of Article 75 but the British Constitution is tricky. Section 5.6 of the Agreement Act is in some form a transfer of article 75, and the Welfare Reform dispute of 2015 suggests the Article is still in force.)

There was also a realisation that things could not remain as they were because nature abhors a vacuum. After an important meeting was suddenly and arbitrarily cancelled by a Priest, the *Citizen's Press* warned:

"Last week we were fighting for our lives, defence is best carried out by a closed organisation. This week we are wondering how to put over our political demands, and we are faced with simple problems like keeping the streets clean, both fields in which wider participation is necessary if we are to remain effective. There are a number of possibilities apart from mass meetings. Already informal barricade committees exist. These could elect delegates to meetings at a central point in each district, this delegate body could consider political issues as they come up..." (CP No.6, 24.8.69).

The Defence Committees did indeed expand and take on broader functions, but they needed to link up with something else to generate a political expression of substance. If they did not, politics would have to be found elsewhere.

The following piece was on the front page of No.7 under the heading, '*Barricades stay unless our demands are met by Mr. Callaghan*':

"The Labour Government have always operated on the assumption that if you talk enough with your opponents you can eventually agree with them. This is the way Wilson betrayed the people of Rhodesia, he always believed that if he talked enough with Ian Smith, they would agree and become the best of friends. Now Callaghan has arrived in Ulster to play the same game, like Chamberlain at Munich he is off to speak with Mr. Paisley to consult with all opinions and he like Mr. Wilson in Rhodesia will try to turn black into white by talking.

"Rhodesia is a long way away, the British people do not have to see the cruel consequences of the Wilson goernment's sell-out. Ulster is just across the channel, the Labour government cannot leave us in the lurch and then forget about it. Now let us spell out what is necessary to save the situation, basically it is security for our homes, women and children. Our demands are reasonable demands.

1. Disband and disarm the Specials.
2. Disarm and re-organise the R.U.C.
3. Amnesty for political prisoners and those who fought to defend their homes.
4. Use of article 75 of Government of Ireland Act to force through these changes if necessary.

"... The message is simple then Mr. Callaghan. Stop talking, start acting, give us our demands and the barricades come down, but not until." (CP No.7, 28.8.69.)

On September 7th *Citizen Press* described the taking down of the Albert Street barricades as *"The Last Concession"*. It said that agreement to do so had only been forthcoming because "firm guarantees were given about the security of the area from outside attack" and "to show... the people of the Falls are not intransigent". It noted, however, that the British military had "broke pledges given to the CDC as they moved in in a military operation against the civilian population" of the Falls and Turf Lodge prior to the agreed time and method of dismantling.

On September 18th, under the heading *"Protection? For how long?"*, a final edition noted:

"The barricades are coming down. Today Stormont, Westminster, and the army commanders will be congratulating themselves on a great step forward on the road to 'normality'. BUT it is not a normal situation when thousands of troops have to stand guard throughout a city to protect one section of the community."

The same edition noted the attacks on Catholic women going to work in the factories on the fringes of Catholic areas and the failure of the British military to protect them. Unionism evidently felt that there was unfinished business with the Catholics who had not been repressed as thoroughly as in the past, due to the Westminster intervention.

Oliver Wright's Secret Dispatch

In August 1969 the Unionist sub-government had endangered the cosy arrangement Britain had established for itself in 1921 and very nearly threw it all away when their private militia, after being repulsed in Derry, attacked West Belfast and began a popular insurrection within the UK. Unionism failed to fulfil its side of the bargain with the British—it lost control of its policing function of the Catholics (or rather its police lost control of their ability to police the Catholics, without resorting to unacceptable measures from the point of view of Britain).

The British Government concluded that the administration 'needed stiffening' to preserve it and sent Oliver Wright, whom the Prime Minister termed "rather less than a governor, rather more than an Ambassador" to maintain pressure on Stormont. Wilson had previously used Wright to negotiate with Ian Smith's regime in Rhodesia in 1965 after it had declared U.D.I. and he seems to have seen Wright as the best man for dealing with difficult colonial regimes.

Oliver Wright's role was to explain British policy in the light of August to Chichester-Clark, get Westminster input into Stormont, and put some steel into the sub-government. He reported directly to Wilson and Callaghan, avoiding both the civil services in Whitehall and Stormont.

Thirty years after these events the dispatches of Wright, the representative of the UK Government in the North, were released. The first one, however, was quickly withdrawn before the Public Record Office opened to the public. The *Daily Telegraph* made a copy of it before it was restricted again (2.7.00).

On 13th September 1969 Wright sent this important dispatch to Whitehall, the British Army GOC and the British Ambassador in Dublin, setting out *'Political Guidelines for the Pacification of the Province'*. It has the private thoughts of Britain in 'Northern Ireland' rather than its public utterances. Wright's dispatch corresponds with the account of Cabinet business published by Tony Benn, in which the basis of British policy was described as *"getting Ulstermen to carry the can"*. The same phrase is used in Wright's dispatch, when he said of the Ulster Unionist Party,

> "... with the possible exception of Mr. Brian Faulkner, none of the present Northern Ireland government is so fond of power for its own sake that they will cling to office; on the contrary, altogether too many of them would be only too pleased to return to their offices and their farms and leave it to H.M.G. to carry the can."

Wright noted that: "The Catholic barricades are manned by people who genuinely fear for their lives. The Protestant barricades are manned by people who hate Catholics."

But he then argued that it was essential that the Catholic barricades come down in order to facilitate the Unionist Government's credibility with its own constituency: "In the last resort it must suit the Catholics to get clobbered by us if that is the only way we can get justice for them."

The important thing, Wright thought, was to "maintain the authority of the Northern Ireland Government", or Britain "will be left without an instrument with which to put the reforms into effect". This was essential in allaying the fears of the "Protestant settler majority", not only for,

> "... the loss of political power within his own community, but his absorption into the larger society of Southern Ireland—alien in smell,

backward in development and inferior in politics. What was the Reformation about, if not to liberate political man from the tyranny of priests? ...so little credit is given to these fears..."

Wright drew the following conclusions in the situation that confronted Westminster after August:

"1. The best hope of achieving H.M.G.'s aims for Northern Ireland lies in the programme of reforms...

2. The best instrument for achieving these aims is the Northern Ireland Government itself since it alone, representing and elected by the majority in Ulster, has the reasonable prospect of carrying majority opinion with it.

3. The danger comes from the extremists on both sides; the main danger from the Protestant extremists, since they can exploit majority opinion and have no interest in the success of the reform programme.

4. It follows that our Central purpose should be to support the Northern Ireland government, both to keep the problem of Ulster at arm's length and because they alone can accomplish our joint aims by reasonably peaceful means... This might entail the use of force against Catholics. Obviously H.M.G. would wish to avoid having to make so repugnant a decision. But it would be the only way of ensuring that Catholic grievances were eventually addressed, H.M.G. might have to be cruel to be kind. And it would be better than the use of force against the Protestant extremists, however repulsive their attitudes and behaviour, since they are the majority community and confrontation with them would fulfil Lord Craigavon's prophecy that the eventual resolution of the Ulster problem would come when the Protestants fought the British army. And that, I should think, H.M.G. would wish to avoid at all costs" (FCO 33 769).

The Irish academic Ronan Fanning (IT, 26.2.00) recently commented that, "Wright's advice provided the blueprint for British policy in Northern Ireland in 1969-70".

In fact, Wright's dispatches were merely a reiteration of the British policy of arm's-length pacification of the North from 1921 down to the present.

Wright's argument that Catholics had ultimately to be put down for their own good, and to ensure the prospect of long-term reform, was based on an understanding of the relationship established between Westminster and its sub-government in 1921 in which London was dependent on the Unionist regime to do its dirty-work in the 'Northern Ireland' part of its State. If it could not do this, or its Protestant mass base withdrew their support for it, then the UK State would have to take up its responsibility—something it wished to avoid at all costs.

Of course, the Northern Catholics did not know this was Britain's intention and they began to hold out great hopes for Westminster and how it might at last deliver them from their long-standing predicament within 'Northern Ireland'—

hopes that were to be cruelly dashed, with tragic consequences for all.

Hope was obviously greater on this score on the 'Constitutional' wing of Nationalism than on the Republican wing, with telling effects.

The Arm's-Length Policy

The British arm's-length policy towards the North began in 1921 and has continued more or less ever since. The Stormont Parliament was imposed on the Six Counties largely against the wishes of the Unionists as a price to pay for the continued British connection. There was a trade-off made— Britain would continue to support Unionist power in Ireland politically, financially, and militarily, as long as the Protestants would take care of responsibility for the policing and general pacification of the Northern Catholics, in the Imperial interest.

And everyone would live happily ever after—except the Northern Catholics, of course.

Because it suited its interests, Britain turned a blind eye to the injustices of the system she established, as long as the Ulster Unionist Party maintained control of the fiefdom allotted to them to govern on Britain's behalf.

In late 1969 the British Government's priority was to maintain the semi-detachment it had established in 1921 and to maintain it at all costs, despite the fact that this would preserve the system that was actually generating the conflict in the first place. If it came to a choice between maintaining the arm's-length position of 'Northern Ireland' and attempting to solve the problem through Britain's deeper involvement, the primary policy over-rode the secondary aim, which was believed to be transient and better avoided.

The communal system of politics established by Britain in the North took the only form it could—the Protestant subjugation and pacification of Catholics. The operable means of politics was that originated by the Ulster Unionist Party in conjunction with the British Unionist Party and British military establishment at the time of the Home Rule crisis—the use of force or the threat of force. For forty years the Ulster Unionist Party successfully managed this system by minimising activity in the devolved parliament, as well as pacifying the Catholic masses through replicating the beneficial qualities of the British welfare state, along with maximizing the powers of their police, thereby curbing those Croppies who still wouldn't lie down.

However, the fundamental weakness of this system was exposed by the Catholic Civil Rights Movement. When what Britain, the advanced liberal democracy run by a Socialist Government, was turning a blind eye to was put on TV screens, pressure built on O'Neill to manage change in the system. But, O'Neill found that the Catholic activism generated a Protestant activism determined to resist change, within his own mass-base. And the Civil Rights agitation and the adverse publicity created in the world did not bring the British to address the situation. British policy remained that of supporting Unionist power and pacifying Catholics—albeit more effectively by re-establishing control through a series of minimal reforms, after O'Neill had fallen.

What was different in the aftermath of 1969 was the changed relationship that existed between the Downing St. and its sub-government at Stormont, and the raised expectations of Catholics.

Wright noted in a letter to the Home Office on 16th September:

> "Her Majesty's Government is not allowing the Northern Ireland Government to do what they want to do; to issue statements about a proper timetable for proper action against the Catholic barricades and the extremists who seem to call the tune behind them. The result is that the Northern Ireland Government feel that the Catholics are getting away with it and they themselves are reduced more and more to the role of puppets" (PRO, CJ 3/18, 16.9.69).

The British Government had been forced to interpose itself between its sub-government and the Catholics and to impose reforms whilst restraining its local administration from acting freely in the situation. But Wright believed that, for Whitehall to successfully return to its 1920 policy, it needed to put down the Catholics and restore the Stormont set-up with renewed support from the Protestant masses.

The detachment policy was manifest in Britain's desire to avoid Direct Rule at all costs; to pull its army out of the Six Counties as soon as possible; and to dither on legislating for the formal transfer of security to Westminster. The effect of this latter failure was to let authority seep back from Whitehall to Stormont, when the pressure slackened off from early 1970, as Catholics waited patiently on reform. It also had the effect of giving more autonomy to the British Army, which was largely beyond Stormont's authority, to indulge in colonial repression, with Westminster willing to turn a blind eye.

That was the only way to maintain what had been painfully put together in 1921 in support of British Imperial interests and its new relationship with the South, which it sought continued leverage over as it asserted a National mind of its own.

The Northern Catholics were thus going to continue to be the fall-guys for this settlement—although they did not quite know it yet.

CHAPTER 2

The North in Flux

The North went into a state of flux in the period after the August explosion, meaning that great change was a possibility after 50 years of relative stability. The primary agent that could determine the nature of that change was Britain. Change there would certainly be after what had happened; but what change was the question.

'Northern Ireland' was thrown into flux by its response to the popular demand for Civil Rights, which now seems so peculiarly modest that it hardly seems believable as the subject of a major agitation at all. The heat generated by the August explosion persisted during the autumn and winter of 1969-70. And positions taken up then largely determined the working out of subsequent events, right up to the present.

One thing should be noted about this period of flux. The new Republicanism that was the major thing that emerged from it did not produce it or play a formative part in things during it. Republicanism was really a consequence of the flux, of what others did or didn't do in London, Dublin and within Unionism and 'Constitutional Nationalism'.

The New Republicanism was produced by a community whose other options were gradually closed off as the heat of August subsided. It was not realised that the fire that had been lit was still burning and was not so easily put out as imagined.

The View from Derry

Eamonn Gallagher of the Department of External Affairs went North to see how things lay on the ground there. He first went to Belfast on the last weekend of August 1969 and then journeyed up to Derry on the 6th September to meet two contacts—"an important political person and an important financier". Unfortunately, the name of the "*important political person*" from Derry, who provides most of the information, is scored out in the Report to the Taoiseach.

We know that Gallagher's initial contacts in Derry, through his sister Anna, who lived in Letterkenny, were Sean Keenan and Paddy 'Bogside' Doherty. He also met Ivan Cooper. His main contact, however, was John Hume, who secretly provided Gallagher and the Irish Government with much sensitive information about the Civil Rights Association and then about the formation of the SDLP. We cannot with certainty say if the "*important political person*" who informed Gallagher in Derry was definitely Hume in this instance, but it is confirmed by Sean Donlon of the Department of Foreign Affairs that it was Hume whom Gallagher met in his house in Derry (John Hume, Irish Peacemaker, kindle ed). Gallagher reported to Dublin:

> "The position in Derry is quiet and confident... Virtually all of the city outside the walls on the Donegal side of the river Foyle is outside Stormont police control. The area will not accept an RUC presence until the RUC is thoroughly reformed and... disarmed. It is taken for granted that the Unionists will not again politically control Derry city... In sum, the victory in Derry is complete and there is no anticipation whatever that it will not be confirmed in local elections...
>
> "The policy of the Civil Rights Association at present is to bring about the suspension of the Stormont parliament and consequent direct rule from Westminster... When this happens it is felt that a sizeable proportion of the Unionist leadership will realise that the game is up and move in the direction of fitting themselves into the new structures. They will accept the inevitability of constitutional change deriving from demographic factors, among others, and begin to face up to the need to do a deal with Dublin—the sooner they do the greater their bargaining power... The purpose and eventual result would be to reduce the extremist element to a cold and lonely minority which could be contained even in circumstances where a rapprochement with Dublin became known to be the policy of moderate unionism. Such a progress of events could lead to an agreed solution with Dublin in a matter of 10 or 15 years... The political person said that the Civil Rights policy had succeeded where an overt nationalist policy had not but that the ultimate objective was the same" (NAI, TSCH 2000/6/657).

It is presumably the last sentence, "...*the Civil Rights policy had succeeded where an overt nationalist policy had not but that the ultimate objective was the same*" that led to the name of the "*important political person*" being "abstracted in accordance with the National Archives Act, 1986". That fact is something that just should not be uttered by a prominent and important Nationalist—since it would confirm the Unionist view of NICRA as a kind of 'Trojan Horse', a more sophisticated Anti-Partitionist manoeuvre.

However, this must have been music to the ears of the Taoiseach since the view in Dublin was that Partition, rather than the mode of 'Northern Ireland', government was the source of the problem in the North and re-unification was the only policy allowable for the Catholic minority there. It removed the worry in Dublin that Civil Rights might be actually taken in earnest with a consequent settling for something acceptable within the present state.

This draws attention to something that underlies, and is made explicit, in Dublin Government correspondence at the time—the fear that the Northern Catholics might be more interested in an improvement in their position rather than the First National Aim—the re-integration of the National territory.

The other striking thing is that the aim behind the barricades seems to have been to *"bring about the suspension of the Stormont parliament and consequent direct rule from Westminster"*, according to Gallagher. If that was the case, both Dublin and the 'Constitutional Nationalists' who would begin the long-drawn out process of forming themselves into the SDLP, set themselves against this desire in the Catholic community to attempt to preserve and reform Stormont. And that community did not harness itself to rejection until Provisional Republicanism had emerged and made it a practical possibility from the middle of 1971.

One other part of Gallagher's Report should be commented upon—the view from Derry of what was happening in Belfast:

> "They are totally opposed to anything in the nature of a repartition of the Six Counties. They are well aware that the Falls Road etc. in Belfast is a hostage and they are not prepared to encourage any policy which would separate the Six Counties into two entities and thus leave the minority in Belfast to suffer interminably. I enquired whether the creation of a new city and university of Craigavon was considered to be an element in a long range Unionist policy against the day when they might be out-voted as a whole and whether it might indicate a tendency to let the 'west of the Bann' go. This interpretation was challenged by the political person who said that the intention was simply to direct internal emigration to the area of Belfast so as to diminish the population 'west of the Bann' and continue to control the entire area."

This shows the solidarity brought about within the Northern Catholics by the Civil Rights struggle followed by the August events. Between 1922 and 1925 the Nationalists of west of the Bann had been eager to escape the construct of 'Northern Ireland' by means of the Border Commission, even if it meant leaving the Belfast and eastern Catholics behind them. They had been sorely disappointed when the Commission had been so arranged to prevent their escape, leaving them with the Catholics to the east, inside 'Northern Ireland'.

But the events of 1968-9 had solidified the Northern Catholics like nothing before and they were, from then on, determined to stand or fall together.

The Thoughts of John Hume

During the August Pogrom, and after the NI Minister for Home Affairs, John Taylor, announced the mobilisation of the Specials, the seven opposition MPs walked out of Stormont. Both Gerry Fitt and Paddy Devlin were against this withdrawal but went along with what was Hume's decision.

In September 1969 a report was prepared for Seán Ronan, Assistant

Secretary to the Department of External Affairs, by "a person unknown on meetings in Derry with leaders of nationalist community". The leaders interviewed were Sean Keenan, Paddy Doherty and Hume.

The report reveals that Hume believed "no unionist government could be trusted" and because of this he favoured,

> "… a continuance of a Stormont parliament but with a completely new form of administration which would necessarily include representatives of the Opposition e.g. an administration appointed by the Governor General. He has not worked out this idea and has nothing specific to put forward but his thinking runs along the lines of a continuance of a representative Stormont Parliament but with something in the nature of a board of management drawn from the best talent in the House rather than a Party Government…"

Hume brought the nationalist MPs up to Bunbeg in Co. Donegal for a series of meetings with a view to forming a united opposition party at Stormont. With regard to this Hume reported to Dublin:

> "As a corollary to the continuance of a Stormont Parliament conversations are proceeding between himself and other Stormont M.P.s (Ivan Cooper and Austin Currie were mentioned) with the objective of creating a United Opposition. He is quite sure that Mr. Fitt will not agree to it as Mr. Fitt prefers to continue to be a one-man band…" (NAI, DFA 2000/6/660).

A few weeks later, in early October, when Westminster was still making the running in 'Northern Ireland', Hume made his thoughts known about possible solutions to the situation to an interviewer with the *Sunday Independent*. He said:

> "… To me there is no solution of the Northern Ireland problem while the Unionists remain united. The problem has always been the right wing of unionism: these are the people who started it all in 1912, who were opposed to change and are anti-Catholic. Chichester Clark is making the same mistake as O'Neill by putting party before community… party unity in Unionism means appeasing the right wing. If the party has to appease these people in order to survive it is not going to satisfy us. There are two elements in Unionism—the decent people who simply want to retain the link with Britain and the bigots. It seems to me that in a normal society these would be incompatible and would split—but Unionism wants to keep them together… The internal solution of the problem must come by a split and a political realignment. If that doesn't happen then the only other solution I can see is for Westminster to intervene and to take over for a limited period while alternative arrangements are worked out.
>
> "Q. What would the alternatives be?
>
> "A. Apart from the original mistake of Partition itself, the big mistake is that we have two parliaments—one an exact duplicate of the other—based on the two party system and a two party system has not worked in Northern

Ireland. As I say, while the Unionist party attempts to remain united we will have one party rule which interprets democracy as the right to deprive other people of rights. Therefore the type of constitution which allows a two party system—and a one-party government forever—is a failure and has got to be looked at again. Some new form of constitution which allows government by normal representation is now required. To get into normal politics here we need a conservative party and the left wing party. The realignment should be the final one, though it may take some time.

Q. Do you think the border is still an issue?

A. In the past when people talked about uniting the country they talked about uniting a piece of earth. The real border in Ireland is the border between people and to unite the people we require a definite and careful line of policy. It first of all requires acceptance of the idea that the country can only be united when the majority in the North want it, and I'm glad Mr. Lynch has come round to this point of view..." (5.10.69)

There was a lot of common sense in what Hume said at this time and it represents something of a statement of intent. The question was though: were the new 'Constitutionalists' actually in earnest about it?

In January 1970 Hume told an audience in Birmingham that Section 5 of the Government of Ireland Act (1920) should be amended to guarantee full Civil Rights in the North. The speech, which was reported as the lead item on the front page of the Irish News under the heading, *'Amending Section 5 of the 1920 Act must be C.R. Objective'*, had some very interesting things to say about the North which showed that Hume understood the perversity of the 'Northern Ireland' construct and the 1920 Constitution very well indeed:

"Mr. Hume said that while the Constitutional question was allowed to remain the party-political issue in Northern Ireland the hopes of moving away from fixed political positions into normalised politics were dim...

"Mr. Hume said that in 1969 the North of Ireland had been through what was probably one of the worse years in its history. 'Yet now, five months after the disturbances that almost erupted in a civil war that would have destroyed the whole community we are faced with what can only amount to amazing negligence on the part of those who govern us,' he said. 'The negligence... is found in the fact that while efforts were made by the British Government to produce a package of reforms to meet immediate grievances, no attempt has been made to examine the Northern Ireland problem in depth to find and deal with the underlying causes of all our unrest. In short... it would appear that the heart of the problem is to be left untouched for another generation and another Government to solve. The symptoms are being dealt with but not the cause... Mr. Hume said the fundamental question that required close scrutiny and change was what had come to be known as 'the Constitution.' 'This,' he said, 'has been the sacred cow of Northern Ireland politics, the question that can never be touched or even discussed, although the constitution of other countries change and evolve continuously, as they must, if they are to meet the needs of an ever changing world.'

"Mr. Hume said there were weaknesses in the Acts of Parliament that made up Northern Ireland's Constitution which were fundamental to it as the link with Britain itself, weaknesses which affected the whole Northern community. In the first place… the net effect of our system of Government is that no one in Northern Ireland had any say in what type of society we have. People of the North cannot decide whether they want a Socialist or Conservative society for we are totally dependent on the type of Government in power in Britain. If Britain passes Socialist legislation so does Northern Ireland. If Britain had a Conservative Government we get Conservative legislation.'

"Mr. Hume said they in the North must be unique in Western Europe in that they had one and a quarter million people in a so-called democracy who had no power to decide what sort of society they wished to live in. 'Such a situation' said Mr. Hume, 'would be a fundamental cause of unrest in any society because the desire and right to self-determination is fundamental in any democracy. And, indeed, the unrest evident even among the Unionist population had its roots in the same problem as instanced by the U.D.I. mentality.

"'The Unionists will say,' declared Mr. Hume 'that we are represented at Westminster, but even our M.P.s there cannot play any part in determining the nature of our society, for they are not allowed to speak on the Northern problem in Westminster. The last few months have established all too clearly where the power lies.'

"Mr. Hume declared that since August 15 'we have had no Government in Northern Ireland. 'For a Government that cannot control law and order is not a government'…

"And many Unionists, said Mr. Hume, seemed to feel that those who hold the view that the Irish border needed to be removed should be outlawed and that they were automatically disloyal citizens. 'It is time,' he said, 'that loyalty was defined.' For loyalty meant loyalty to the State, loyalty to its people, and anyone who believed that the people's best interests were served by an alternative Constitution was being absolutely loyal. Mr. Hume said: 'The Government of Ireland Acts, therefore, must be brought right out of cold storage and openly discussed… and pressure should be put on the British Parliament to do so. If we fail to do so then we are only ensuring that another generation of Northern Irishmen will go through what we have gone through." (IN 24.1.70)

Despite the understanding Hume displayed about the nature of 'Northern Ireland' his view that the 'Northern Ireland' Constitution could evolve into something more inclusive and palatable was novel, but misplaced. In 'Northern Ireland' the question of how the State should be governed never arose within the politics of the region because the Government was external to what was termed the 'state'. How 'Northern Ireland' was governed was, as Hume pointed out, determined in Britain by the people of Britain and 'Northern Ireland' got the Government they, i.e. the British electorate, decided upon.

Ordinarily, in a normal state, the constitution is about how a state should be governed. But 'Northern Ireland' was not a state. In 'Northern Ireland' the Constitutional question was external to the actual Constitution. There were, in fact, two constitutions—the British Constitution that was capable of evolving and changing and which had proved to be the longest lasting and most successful constitution in the history of the world, at least in the democratic era, and another constitution—the one that pertained to 'Northern Ireland,' which was incapable of change except through warfare.

It might be said that it was ironic that the government of a state that had developed the most successful constitution in the world had established the most abominable and dysfunctional constitution for its 'Northern Ireland' region in 1920 if it hadn't been so tragic for all concerned.

This shows that Hume seems to have been in favour of first trying an internal accommodation between Unionists and Nationalists, in which 'British' Unionists were split from the Ulsterish bigoted element, facilitating a coalition constructed within the Six Counties.

If this failed he was in favour of a period of Direct Rule by Westminster and the achieving of a left/right alignment in politics.

However, this was just not possible in a Six County context and was only achievable within the party politics of the State, to which Hume professed loyalty—in which a new nationalist party would play no part. Some kind of false facsimile in which the Nationalist party represented the 'left' and the Unionist party represented the 'right' could never represent a real realignment in which both Protestants and Catholics were represented on both sides of the political divide and have a real input into electing or rejecting a government at the level of state.

The problem was that the British political parties were dead against this. And Hume himself, despite the logic of his argument in 1970, later came around to supporting them in their boycott of the province when the issue was placed on the political agenda in the late 1980s.

The other problem for Hume in seeking a reform of the 'Northern Ireland' constitution to stabilise things in the region was Westminster's intentions. The State remained committed to a restoration of Unionist rule after it had seemed to Nationalists to have fatally undermined it by depriving it of its private armies. This was what Hume concluded when he said that "since August 15 we have had no Government in Northern Ireland. 'For a Government that cannot control law and order is not a government'..."

Hume's novel plea for an evolution of the 'Northern Ireland' Constitution was undermined by the determination of Britain to maintain that which it had apparently fatally wounded.

The message "*this we will maintain*" that came from Westminster, when it became clearly understood by the Catholic community, had the effect of stimulating and energising it like nothing before. Now that Humpty-Dumpty had had his great fall it determined not to let him be put together again. As a minimum prerequisite of self-respect within the Catholic community there would be a great resistance to such a thing. And it was this energising that fuelled the Insurrection and continued the Catholic resurgence.

The Hunt Report

Callaghan's signalling of the reform of the RUC represented the most fundamental challenge to Stormont's authority. Whitehall decided that policing would be placed under non-Ulsterish leadership and the Specials would be abolished—although this decision was held back from the public until an advisory committee under Lord Hunt, a former colonial governor, had reported over 6 weeks. Hunt recommended that the new police force should be disarmed; have a much higher proportion of Catholics; be placed under an independent police authority; and have a high proportion of British officers in its command structure.

London did not necessitate the reform of the RUC purely to please the Catholics, however. It needed a new strengthened and enlarged police in order to withdraw its army. Because it wanted an unarmed RUC it then decided that a new militia, separated from the police, needed to be created for the IRA campaign on the 1956-62 model that Unionism warned it of. It was reasoned in Whitehall that such a force could also draw in any disaffected elements of the Specials and neutralise them. And it could be quietly disbanded when any threat from the IRA receded (CAB, 128/46, 7.10.69).

The other important consideration from Callaghan's point of view was satisfying the British Parliament when it reassembled in mid-October. Wilson and Callaghan realised that they would be vulnerable to criticism for not having acted earlier to prevent the August explosion. With the Cameron Commission that Terence O'Neill had commissioned due to report around the same time they were also likely to be accused of not addressing the grievances that had led to all the trouble.

Callaghan was able to announce to Parliament that he had accepted the Hunt Report that had been speedily put together and the Labour backbenchers proceeded to attack the Stormont sub-government rather than the UK Government. No criticism was made of Wilson or Callaghan and the back-bench attacks on the Unionists were used as leverage against Stormont to get it to acquiesce in the reform programme being imposed on it.

Chichester-Clark accepted the Hunt Report with extreme reluctance, believing that he was handing over the Unionist defence mechanisms to

Whitehall, and fatally undermining his own leadership of the Unionist Party (Newsletter, 27.7.71).

On 17th October, 1969 the RUC returned to Catholic areas in Belfast. Jim Sullivan, number 2 to Billy McMillen in the Belfast IRA, gave permission for the police to resume patrols in the Falls as well as for the removal of some barricades. He invited the new English Chief Constable, Arthur Young to address the CCDC in the Long Bar in Leeson Street, in the heart of the Falls—where the RUC chief received a standing ovation (Interview with Tom Conaty, from Bishop and Mallie, *The Provisional IRA*, pp. 73-4).

The Irish News' headline for that day was, *'Unarmed RUC Return to Falls and the Bogside. Cheers, And Even a Few Tears, Greet Them'*. It was reported that hundreds had turned out "to welcome them and the Chief Constable along the Falls" (IN 18.10.69).

This was all too much for traditional Republicans like Joe Cahill who remembered the pain of seeing the British Army drinking with locals in the bars of the Falls Road:

> "It brought tears to my eyes. Here was the enemy, the instigators of what had just happened... and the people were collaborating with them... people were glad to see them because the IRA had betrayed them." (*The Provisional IRA*, p.74)

After the August events and seeing the obvious hostility which the minority had for the Unionist security apparatus in the North, the British government was convinced that the most pressing concern was the reform of the police. The Hunt Report recommended just that, with the disbanding of the B Specials and the disarming of the RUC.

Nationalists and the Security Forces

While there were two nights of fierce rioting in the Shankill over the demise of the Specials and the announcement that the RUC would be reformed, the announcement was greeted with approval by Catholic politicians. And they urged Catholics, to become fully involved in any new security forces established.

John Hume said:

> "On our part we feel that the impartiality of the new force can be further increased if its membership is representative of the community as a whole, and in this context we welcome the recommendation that a police liaison committee be set up in Derry and a recruiting centre be opened here. We would hope that as many of our young men would take advantage of this" (IN 11.10.69).

Austin Currie was even more enthusiastic about the police reforms. He said he "would be prepared to recommend to those who supported him politically that they should join both of these forces [the RUC and RUC Reserve]". "In fact", said Mr. Currie, "I would be prepared to join myself. A police force organised and conducted on the lines of the British police force would be acceptable to all sections in Northern Ireland" (IN 11.10.69).

Whatever about policing, it was the lack of a clear position within 'Constitutional Nationalism' that allowed the Ulster Defence Regiment to be set up. Despite the Hunt Report insisting it would be a very different body from the B Specials it replaced, being under British Army command, it acted largely as a Unionist militia with a permeable interface to more independent Unionist military forces that later assassinated Catholics as a matter of course.

The main argument against the UDR was that the force was not really necessary as, if 'Northern Ireland' were a part of the UK, the British Army should have been able to defend its borders without any trouble. This was a logical and sensible position on which all opposition should have been based and it was a point that came up in the Stormont debate (NAI, DFA 2001/43/1392, 27.11.69).

But it was not stuck to as the basis of opposition to the UDR. And instead there was a reversion to Redmondite/Devlinite calculations by the 'Constitutionalists'.

After the setting up of the UDR was announced Austin Currie said that: "....the only way to defeat the Unionist game is by non-Unionists making application to join". Hume said "we have no intention of opting out and playing into the hands of the Unionist Party" (IN 17.11.69).

The fear of the Catholic politicians was that former B Specials would swamp the new force, and all that would change would be its name. This was an understandable fear and it turned out to be correct as half the applications came from former USC men and in Border areas, where Catholics were the majority, they made up the vast bulk of those who were enrolled. The ex-B Specials simply took over the new UDR Battalions (2001/43/1392, 3.11.70 and *Hansard* 29.10.70) Although a quarter of its membership was initially Catholic this quickly declined to an insignificant proportion and the UDR became the USC under British direction.

In late 1969 Currie told a Civil Rights meeting that:

> "A very dangerous game of bluff and double bluff is being played by both the Stormont and Westminster governments. The notorious application forms, sent to the B Specials, illustrate a deliberate attempt to keep non-Unionists from joining the new force. [But] The Unionist Government will not have any control over who will or who will not be enlisted in the new force. Only Westminster can decide whether those who believe in a United Ireland will be admitted to the new force and James Callaghan has already

stated that it is no crime to believe in this ideal to be achieved by peaceful means... What better way than joining the UDR for good Republicans to get the training, the arms and ammunition." (Free Citizen, no 10)

In his autobiography Currie reveals that he really wanted the UDR to become a cross-community force. He feared that in a doomsday situation such a force with many Catholics could not be used for general massacre. He claims Kevin Mallon, a prominent Republican led a crowd in Coalisland demanding Catholics be let into the new force and be armed and Currie interpreted this as Catholic enthusiasm. But Catholic applications in Tyrone and Fermanagh were insignificant. In the Stormont debate on the Bill it was claimed that Unionist members in the localities suggested Catholics were disloyal and, therefore, would not get through vetting screens.

The Nationalists were given little overt guidance by the Irish Government in what their position should be over the UDR. Sympathetic British Labour MPs made representations to Dublin's diplomatic services but were told not to represent a position on the Republic's behalf because it did not have a public one. (NAI, DFA 2001/43/1392, 26.11.69 and 2001/43/1392, 4.12.69)

Dublin was actually firmly opposed to the UDR because it saw "the creation of any British armed force for use in Ireland" to be "utterly repugnant" (NAI DFA 2001/42/1392, p. 2), but deemed it "best to remain silent on the subject" (NAI DFA 2001/43/1392, p. 3). At the same time its propaganda organ in the Six Counties, the 'Voice of the North', made its opposition clear to the new force and criticised Nationalists who acquiesced to it in an article called 'Copper-Fastening the Border':

"British policy towards Ireland is directed towards copper-fastening Partition. The British Army is now to defend the Border. It will be assisted in this defence by a new-type B-Special force which will be equipped and trained by the British military... Are Catholics supposed to join this force in defence of the Partition of Ireland? This is the kernel crux of the entire Callaghan reform deal. Because the minority in the 6-Counties can hardly be expected to abandon their principles and their ideals of a united Ireland merely to see justice done to them" (25.10.69).

This was actually the *"kernel crux"* of the Lynch Government's position toward Northern Nationalism at this point. Anti-Partitionism was a Dublin requirement of the Northern Nationalists which over-rode any demand for justice within the State they inhabited the Catholics of the North might have desired. How such things have been forgotten!

The more Republican-minded Nationalists, like Bernadette Devlin and Eamon McCann, condemned the UDR. They had no wish for the new force to be acceptable to the Catholic community, and if they could not prevent it from being set up, they hoped it would become a Protestant militia, like the B

Specials, so that Catholic alienation from the security forces would continue. After Republican criticism of the new force the confidence of Nationalist support for it was shaken. "The wishes of Lord Hunt are no longer being carried out" declared Paddy O'Hanlon (Nationalist MP, S. Armagh). Hume discovered that the UDR was being recruited "behind the backs of the British Government and military authorities. We will fight it every inch of the way". He also added: "But we will not allow ourselves to fall into the trap of opting out, as the Unionists want us to". However, Currie still urged Catholic participation: "There are certain members of the Government who do not wish the 'minority' to join these forces... The opposition will continue to urge the 'minority' to join" (IN 24.11.69).

Going into 1970 the *Irish News* held an ambiguous position in relation to the UDR, although it was in favour of maximizing Catholic recruitment and had a positive view of the reform of the local security forces:

> "Those who still believe that the new Ulster Defence Regiment is just what the Doctor (Callaghan) ordered, cannot feel particularly enthusiastic about the present pace of recruiting... firm applications fall far short of the regiment's need... Fidelity to the idea of such a force is fading on both sides of the political fence. The Hunt Committee, in whose report the force was proposed, went far to satisfy opposition demands for police reform in the North. The R.U.C. has already lost its paramilitary character and is now an unarmed force on the British model...
>
> "The disbanded 'B' men are not flooding into the new force in any numbers. Membership of a Government-controlled and wholly sectarian Special Constabulary is one thing; joining a British military-commanded force, and serving alongside Republicans, Nationalists, Papists and Fenians, must be a horrifying thought. Reluctance is natural...
>
> "What will the Stormont Government do if it finds that it has replaced the 'B' force with one of armed members of the minority? Equally, how can the 'B' Specials be said to have been disbanded if, in fear of a possibility of minority take-over they rush to answer the recruitment call?... Taking into account the signs of the times can there be ever be any real hope of such a force ever succeeding, whatever its name" (IN 22.1.70).

There was much speculation at the time in Nationalist circles that the UDR was simply meant to be a fig-leaf for Westminster ridding themselves of the Specials and the regiment would be wound up as soon as things settled for a period of time in the context of inevitable cut-backs.

But that did not happen as Britain returned to its traditional policy of buttressing its sub-government in the North and it later found another use for the UDR in localising (or Ulsterising) the conflict a few years later. In 1975 the British Government ditched the Hunt Report and re-instituted the RUC as an armed counter-insurgency force, restoring the 1921-69 situation.

The Northern Catholics in 1970

In its New Year's Day editorial of 1970 *The Irish News* summed up the position of the Catholic community as it saw it at that point in time:

"... as ever, a New Year brings hope of change, a wistfulness of what might be, but never is; a vague feeling that in 1970 things are bound to get better, when there is really no reason why they should... In our own little shook-up world it is impossible to forget the memory of so many revolting situations, and the minority... has given up being obedient to, and calmly accepting, a Unionist hegemony. The minority will be continually watching the outcome of Westminster's intervention now enshrined in reform legislation which, it is hoped, will open the door to justice as well as peace.

"The day of 'Unionism knows best' is over and Unionists are finding it extremely difficult to adjust to the ambience of acceptance of the changed attitudes forced upon it. There is a very real sense in which Unionism in the land has lost its bearings or, to change the metaphor, has come at last to the use of reason. Beset by pressures which, however, resented, are meant to operate to create a just community, the Unionists are working off their resentments at the whole idea by fighting among themselves. Victory for moderation must come soon in this New Year because, we have been assured, the year 1970 is to be the beginning of an age of good feeling when the minority will achieve the transition from the status of an unwanted and suspected minority to that of a natural segment of the pluralistic structure of the Northern state.

"Thus, in 1970, the emphasis will be on freedom and justice for all, the legacy of Callaghan's visit. Will Unionism and its followers come of age and grow to maturity this year? In the long run, resistance to reform will solve nothing for them, and they had better accept reality now, on the first day of New Deal Year. During this transition they are going to suffer from a particularly agonising assault on their traditional views and demeanours because for fifty years they have constantly shirked the issue of what to do with the minority's claims to justice and equality... Mr. Callaghan has forced them into breaking the habits of a lifetime and this is a year of decision for them. Only by governing in the spirit of Callaghan's reforms can they prevent Unionism degenerating into total rejection" (IN 1.1.70).

This was a view of tentative confidence. Confidence because Westminster was engaging in the North, at long last, and seemed to be intent on driving through reform that would shatter the hegemony of Unionism and create a more equal playing field in the Six Counties between the two communities. But it was tentative because there was always the feeling that Britain might lose interest in what it was now doing, with the result that Unionism would reassert itself and scupper the Callaghan project. And The Irish News knew in its bones that given recent events that would spell trouble.

Playing the Stormont Charade

The question was: what should the political representatives of the Catholic community do in such a situation?

Within weeks of the Nationalist walk-out from Stormont in August 1969 Hume was marshalling the Catholic MPs into a loose coalition to act as "an official opposition", persuading 10 of the 13 to take up "Shadow portfolios" which gave them "some of the flavour of an alternative government" (Paul Routledge, *John Hume*, p.89 and p.92).

The formation of an "*alternative government*" at Stormont was, of course, a delusionary activity.

The new 'Constitutionalists' were seeking to replace the Nationalist Party with a more radical version. An attempt was made to form a "shadow cabinet" in the illusion that the Stormont Parliament contained the government of a state, and a whip was appointed at John Hume's instigation.

This represented a *de facto* recognition of 'the state' on the part of the new breed of Nationalists and it seems they only failed to become Her Majesty's Official Opposition because the Nationalist Party had only just withdrawn from the role and the move was considered impolitic (Ian McAllister, *The Northern Ireland Social and Democratic Party*, p.30).

The fact that this thinking about a cabinet occurred even before the formation of an actual party to supply it showed that there was a disconnection between the individuals who wished to set up a platform for their election to Stormont and the community itself. That might have been all well and good in the period before August 1969 but with the Catholic community aroused where was the activism to go without a political party to engage energies? Trooping into polling booths, once in a while, to put meaningless crosses on ballot papers was yesterday's politics.

The *Irish News* reported on 5th January 1970:

> "The Opposition MPs who formed themselves into a shadow cabinet claim they are ignored by the government when appointments are made to public bodies and that there is no form of consultation between them and the cabinet when the composition of boards is being considered."

The Nationalist MPs continued to support the Stormont set-up, despite the fact that it was producing little of benefit to them. Hume said in March 1970 that "those who wanted direct rule were opening up the prospect of evils which might be worse than at present. They would be an outpost of London" (IN 2.3.70). But surely that was what the problem with 'Northern Ireland' was—it was, indeed, "an outpost of London".

Gerry Fitt, who was to become leader of this 'shadow cabinet', disagreed with the 'cabinet' policy from the outset. He was intent in continuing as the indispensable power-broker between Northern Catholics and the British Labour Party. But that left very little for anyone else to do, which seemed to be part of the reason Fitt continued to plough his lonely furrow.

In August 1969 Fitt had called for Direct Rule and was still in favour of it when the 'shadow cabinet' (and then the SDLP) was formed. Sean Redmond, General Secretary of the Connolly Association revealed to Michael Murphy that "Fitt's hatred of Unionism ensured that he wanted to tear down Stormont" (*Gerry Fitt—A Political Chameleon*, p.144).

Just prior to the British General Election of June 1970, Fitt remarked how "we can only hope that the people across the channel will be sensible enough to return the Labour Party to power". He said that "he knew from personal experience that the desire of the vast majority of the electorate in West Belfast was for peace and reconciliation among all working people in the last decisive struggle against Toryism" (IN 6.6.70).

This was although Fitt had no intention of campaigning for them to have the chance to do anything about it, like joining the Labour Party, even when Jim Callaghan was putting some effort into this.

'The Voice of the North', the newspaper funded by the Lynch Government in order to exert influence in the Six Counties, urged the Nationalists to give up the legitimising of the Stormont regime:

> "The Unionist regime of the Six Counties is on its last legs and... the British Government's attempts to impose some patch-work of just government through the machinery of Stormont on this portion of the so-called UK is doomed to failure... The Unionists'... pretence at democratic government is propped up and given credence to solely by the co-operation of Opposition MPs in lending their presence to the sham parliament at Stormont. The time has now come when the Opposition MPs should refuse to participate any longer in the mockery that is Stormont... Let our MPs set up a Provisional Parliament of the Six Counties and hold their sessions in, say, the historic town of Dungannon, or the ecclesiastical capital of Armagh... The Voice of the North believes that this abandonment of Stormont will precipitate the fall of Unionism, thus making possible the resumption of Anglo-Irish negotiations—last broken off by the infamous Agreement of 1925—about the future of this whole country" (12.4.70).

This was part of the attempt by the Lynch Government to re-orientate the Northern Nationalists from their reformist proclivities to a Fianna Fail anti-Partitionist stance—something which will be dealt with more fully in the next chapter.

In later years there was something of an 'admittance' that Catholic politicians had been 'mistaken' in their antagonism to Direct Rule in 1970. Austin Currie, for instance, said in an interview with the *Irish Times* on 20th June, 1988:

"The Civil Rights movement wanted British troops in, but it should have been accompanied by a British political presence. The crunch mistake in 1969 was to keep Stormont, with Oliver Wright as the British government's watchdog in the North. That was the crucial period in which the Provisional IRA was founded and gained momentum."

The *Irish Times* noted:

"Currie blames the political deterioration on the fact that Stormont carried on for a further three years, building up pressures and providing a front for what was actually being done behind the scenes from Westminster".

But, during those years, Currie, Hume and Fitt etc. went along with the scheme designed for them by Callaghan and overseen by Oliver Wright so that the British could maintain this 'front' which represented a false front of the British State. (A false front is a military tactic aimed at drawing the enemy into an area in which he exhausts his energies before the real front appears).

In the same interview, Currie cited the establishment of the Northern Ireland Housing Executive, which took responsibility for housing away from the Local Councils, as "the only justification I would require" for having engaged in political agitation—thus implying that the NIHE was set up in response to his demands. But, in 1970, the *Irish News* reported that—

"Massive opposition is to be mounted at Stormont to the Housing Executive Bill to set up a Central Housing Authority. Mr. John Hume who, with Mr. Austin Currie, shares the responsibility of 'shadowing' Mr. Brian Faulkner, the Minister for Development, declared last night 'We do not regard these proposals as reform and we will demand changes.' ... We will strongly oppose it in parliament' he declared" (15.10.70).

Because the Bill was introduced by Brian Faulkner the Nationalist politicians could see no progressive potential in it. The Unionists could not possibly be capable of such a reform, so the Bill was opposed on the basis that it was a Unionist trick to maintain power over housing in the Councils. And because it was not the British who were forcing the reform on the Unionists, but the Unionists themselves who were introducing it, Currie and Hume could see no political advantage in it for Nationalism, and therefore mounted "massive opposition" to it.

This is what 'opposition' amounted to within the delusion of "the Northern Ireland state".

Oliver Wright's Second Dispatch

After the August conflict a kind of lull had set in with some skirmishing taking the place of Pogrom. The British Army was initially employed in defending the Catholic areas of Belfast against further sporadic Protestant attacks through late 1969 and early 1970. Nationalists were generally hopeful and Unionists sullen after their humiliation at the hands of Westminster.

Order was restored reasonably successfully, a lull set in, and by February 1970, three of the eight British Army units sent to the province in the 'emergency' had returned home. Britain felt it had coped with the 'emergency' and further involvement was unnecessary so commitments were scaled down. There was no sign of the IRA, which the Unionists had warned of. Now all that was needed was the getting out of its Army so that things could return as they were.

A second dispatch of Oliver Wright's represents his leaving assessment of 'Ulster', job done. It was written on 6th March 1970. Below are some extracts, giving a flavour of how the situation was seen at Westminster after things had seemed to settle—and could be left be again.

In the first part of the 10 page *'Confidential'* report Wright acknowledges that Britain created the problem of 'Northern Ireland' after failing to hold the entire island through a scheme for unitary Home Rule:

> "For 700 years the English in their folly sought to govern the Irish and employed every method including, alas, the plantation of colonists to achieve their aim. When they grew weary of ill-doing and decided towards the end of the 19th century to leave the Irish to their own devices their Scots-Calvinist colonists shouted, 'Hey, what about us? The inevitable non-solution was partition, with two Irish governments, an independent native Catholic one in Dublin and a subordinate, colonial Protestant one in Belfast. The main thing at the time was to wish the problem away. It is hardly surprising that, until mid-1969, Ulster was, and felt, remote, neglected and unhappy" (NIO, CJ3/18, 6.3.70)

It is interesting to note that Wright was aware of the negative effect of Britain's detachment of the province on its citizens. The *"non-solution"* (temporary expedient?) of Partition then created 'Northern Ireland' which then produced the following:

> "A land inhabited by two minorities, each with the defensive/aggressive mentality of a minority. It is a tribal society and the two tribes, the colonists who do not want to be absorbed by the natives and the natives stranded by partition on the wrong side of the border... In fear of domination by the South, Unionists took care to dominate the North. Orange-Protestant ascendancy is what Ulster has been for the fifty years of its existence; ironically enough, it has been the existence of British-style democracy based on universal adult suffrage which has guaranteed and perpetuated a most un-British style injustice towards the Catholic minority."

Wright's idea of *"two minorities"* looks a strange observation. In fact, if

Britain had simply partitioned the island and had not created 'Northern Ireland' it would have had 'two minorities' within the UK state. But it chose not to do this. There is no disputing that the Northern Catholics represented a minority so the only sense that can be made of the idea that the Ulster Protestants were one also was in their own perception as a stranded 'minority' on the island, detached from the British body politic and left to do the needful in the territory left to them. And through this act of British policy they had developed the same fears and behaviours as the real minority.

Wright notes that British-style democracy did not produce democratic outcomes in 'Northern Ireland'. But he failed to go any further into this question. But later on in his report it becomes clear by what he means in his view that "the existence of British-style democracy based on universal adult suffrage which has guaranteed and perpetuated a most un-British style injustice towards the Catholic minority". He calls this "undiluted democracy"—presumably meaning that the imposition of what normally constitutes democracy i.e. majority rule in 'Northern Ireland' has been responsible for the character of the regime. But there seems to be only two ways out of this problem—either by designing a system that 'diluted' democracy and over-ridded the majority-rule principle of democracy or else finding a way of dissolving the communal blocs. And Britain attempted neither in the crucial times between 1970 and 1973.

In his analysis of *'The Present'*, Wright expressed satisfaction and a sense of 'mission accomplished' in his report of March 1970:

> "Although gloom tends to be the prevalent physical and moral climate of Ulster, things are immeasurably better to-day than they were six months ago. When the Army moved in Ulster was on the brink of civil war; to-day, a tolerable calm prevails on the streets, Catholics sleep without intolerable fear in the beds... Then, Ulster was a land of discrimination and injustice: to-day the symptoms of discrimination are being treated by law and the causes of discrimination—too few houses and too few jobs—are being tackled by a substantial injection of finance from Westminster. Then the Unionist Government was disorientated and the Opposition in a state of near-hysteria; to-day, the Government is slowly recovering its confidence and the Opposition is pretty relaxed.
>
> "The politics of the streets are in consequence giving way to the politics of the ballot-box and the centre of interest and concern is moving from the Catholic to the Protestant community. In 1969 the Civil Rights movement could get the Catholic masses on to the streets to demand the redressal of Catholic grievances and make the reputation of John Hume in the process. Nominated bodies—the Police Authority, the Central Housing Authority, the Community Relations Commission—representative of the whole community, are now being set up to redress the built in injustice of undiluted democracy as it works out in practice in this province. In early 1970, therefore,

the steam is going out of the Civil Rights movement and men like Hume are enhancing their reputation by cooling the situation. Civil Rights demonstrations throughout the province on the 7th of February against the Public Order Act, and on subsequent week-ends in Armagh and Enniskillen, lacked real popular backing and were virtually flops. The Opposition has returned to Stormont. But in winning its cause it now seeks a new role. In trying to form a united opposition party out of the present medley of nationalists, republicans, Labour and independents it is attempting fusion with some pretty fissionable material. But it is encouraging that the attempt is being made: a non-nationalist opposition with an economic and social programme could give a lead in breaking down the sectarian divisions of Ulster politics. It deserves support. The decision of the Northern Ireland Labour Party to seek affiliation with the British Labour Party is rather at variance with this trend."

The British programme was aimed at settling things down. It included as well as the Civil Rights programme, a new central Housing authority to build and allocate council housing; finance for an emergency rebuilding programme; a £2 million programme of job creation; an increase of 5% in the level of investment grants for industry; a series of measures to deal with discrimination in public employment. Most significantly, it was announced that the government would accept the recommendations of the Hunt Committee: the RUC would be disarmed and the B Specials disbanded.

Wright was under the impression that because the programme of the Civil Rights Movement was being implemented the province could be put back in the box and the order could be given: "Carry on: As you were!" The Catholics could be returned to the old routine and 'Northern Ireland' would not be disturbing Whitehall again.

But the Catholics refused to be satisfied in returning to the old routine. This was because the Civil Rights agitation had actually run out of perspective, disoriented by its own success. Its demands had been largely met but that had not produced any real feeling of achievement in the community.

The reason for this is that the demands had not been directed at the core of the matter. The concession of *"One Man, One Vote"* changed hardly anything. It only meant the ending of extra votes for businessmen in Local Government elections, as had been done in Britain some years earlier, and it changed hardly anything on the ground. An abstract grievance was remedied with little tangible effect and the concession of the reform only removed one of the slogans against Unionism. And what satisfaction could be gained at that?

The one real grievance was the Derry City Gerrymander. That was dealt with to the satisfaction of the Catholic majority and the Catholic part of the town was now in control of it, as Eamonn Gallagher noted. But overall the feeling was that, though the reform demands had been met, the nub of the matter had not been touched. But what was the nub of the matter?

Wright noted that the 'constitutionalists' who were in the process of forming a new party were returning, to replace the Nationalist Party, as the Opposition in Stormont—just as Callaghan had urged them: "But in winning its cause it now seeks a new role."

But that was just the problem: What would this "new role" consist of now that its objectives were being met and there was nothing to actually politic about?

Wright believed that the Nationalists, as a new "non-nationalist opposition with an economic and social programme could give a lead in breaking down the sectarian divisions of Ulster politics". That was impossible when 'Northern Ireland' was not a state and it was soon proved to be a fantasy.

In contrast, the NILP's decision "to seek affiliation with the British Labour Party" was dismissed by Wright as "rather at variance with this trend"—when it had much more substantial possibilities about it in creating something different than the old communal routine.

It was, of course, the old routine that Britain wanted to re-create with slight modifications to give a more effective mask of normality, so that Whitehall could return to its own routines without the botheration of 'Ulster'.

Wright believed that the main problem, now that the Catholics had been sorted, were the Protestant Unionists. They were bound to be put out by the concessions made to Catholics, the reform of their security apparatus and the equality agenda that would prevent discrimination in their favour. The 'Protestant backlash' was anticipated and it was fortunate that "the electorate… does not have to be consulted for another four years, and in four years massive aid from Westminster ought to have improved the quality of life and therefore the mood of the province". And so the Whitehall strategy was that Protestants would be bought off while Catholics returned to normal.

Wright also thought Chichester-Clark was the right sort of chap for the job of minimizing British involvement:

> "My own view is that Major Chichester-Clark, faced with a choice of personal preference or public duty, will opt for public duty… His Army background of service to the State, will, I think, encourage him to continue, but he will need all the stiffening we can give him… But even with our full financial and moral support it will be a close run thing; without it, we will have a constitutional crisis on our hands."

Presumably by "*a constitutional crisis*" Wright meant greater Westminster involvement and Britain upsetting the settlement of 1921 by taking up its responsibility for the 'Northern Ireland' part of its state.

Wright concluded the report to his boss, James Callaghan, with congratulations on a successful policy and a job complete:

"As I pack my bags, therefore, I am cautiously optimistic. Provided it is clear what I am being optimistic about. I am not forecasting a final solution to the Irish question, nor the two tribes of Ulster into one nation. I am setting my sights rather lower, on a containment, on the management of the Ulster problem. For things are immeasurably better here than when I unpacked six months ago... Your policy has already been right: to offer help, to insist on reform, but, to allow and insist on Stormont being the instrument of reform. Indeed there is no alternative except direct rule and no-one in their right mind wants that if it can be avoided."

And so, during the two years after Wright's departure, Whitehall bolstered the Unionist regime at Stormont in order to keep the Province at arm's length. Catholic civilians were gassed, curfewed, interned without trial, and shot on the streets in order to preserve the façade at Stormont. And it was a position held until circumstances meant it could no longer be maintained.

The Seduction of the North

Oliver Wright's dispatch of 6th March had another part in it that is worth noting. It concerns the British view of the Southern Government. Wright's perspective on Dublin and the behaviour of Taoiseach Lynch's Government is very illuminating:

"Since the partition of Ireland has produced a border not a frontier... no report from Northern Ireland would be complete without a reference to relations with the South. I agree with Sir Andrew Gilchrist that to-day the North acts: the South reacts. So long as we keep the North quiet, the South will give us no trouble, for Mr. Lynch also went to the edge of disaster last August—and stepped back in time. His courageous speech to his party conference in January marked a change from fantasy to realism about the Irish question. If he recognises, as he now does, that force cannot be used to solve the problem of Partition, he must come to realise that the only prospect of Irish unity lies in the seduction not the rape of the North. The South will, I suspect, be a long time a-wooing, if they ever start: the Irish tend to marry late, I believe."

Wright, the senior British Civil Servant drafted in to bolster Britain's 'Northern Ireland' construction, seems to have immediately grasped and understood both its purpose and why it should be maintained at all costs.

It was the object of British policy in 1920-1 to make the South seduce the North. If Britain had erected a frontier rather than a Border between the suitor and the object of his desire, it would have perhaps sapped the will and ardour of the seducer. And the ardour of the seducer had to be maintained so that he could be left hanging on. For what influence could be maintained on a seducer if he did not remain up for the seduction?

'Northern Ireland' was never the major British interest in Ireland. The main part of the island which Britain feared it was losing in 1920-1 was the political object of what it established in 'Northern Ireland'. 'Northern Ireland' was created by Whitehall as the great prize that nationalists on the island, determined on developing the fullest sovereignty and independence, had to take into account before they proceeded too far in the direction they desired. It was a hostage to good nationalist behaviour. It was a lever on the 26 County State.

At the end of the day 'Northern Ireland' was a device for securing general British hegemony over the main area of its interest in Ireland—the new Irish State.

There is a real sense in what Wright concluded that Britain felt Lynch had departed from what was expected of him and his state in August 1969. He had stepped outside of the proper ambit and thought of becoming a rapist rather than a seducer. But since then he had been made see sense and had returned to the role that was expected of him by Britain—the seducer rebuffed. His ardour had cooled and he was back carrying gifts. He had been to the edge and in learning his lesson everything was satisfactory again.

Wright's dispatches presumably had an influence on his chief, Callaghan, the British Home Secretary, who was responsible for statecraft in 'Northern Ireland' during the autumn and winter of 1969-70, after Stormont had lost control of the situation.

Callaghan later described the weeks after he took control in 'Northern Ireland' as—

> "the most meaningful experience of my political life... In August 1969, the situation required me to exercise real authority, to do it quickly or be swamped. We had to take the initiative to restore the situation and I was moving with tremendous speed all the time. It was a most enviable position for any politician to be in... there I was in charge, pulling levers here, pushing levers there, saying get this, fetch so-and-so, and the whole machine absolutely buzzed" (*A House Divided*, p.70).

Callaghan initially took his responsibility in earnest, rejecting the Unionist explanation of the breakdown that it was all the work of the IRA. He had the correct view that the IRA was not a force in the August breakdown but made the mistake of concluding that it would remain negligible to the situation.

From the feel of the situation he got in the Catholic areas he visited Callaghan understood that they would welcome incorporation into British politics and the Labour Party. So he proposed the Labour Party should extend its organisation and operation to 'Northern Ireland'.

If the British Government had acted decisively on his insights that autumn by dismantling the Stormont system and launching a new departure within British policy it is likely that events would have turned out very differently than they did.

Callaghan made a proposal to the Labour Party executive that the party should become involved in the 'Northern Ireland' region of the State but he did not push the issue enough and made little fuss when the executive rejected his proposal in January 1970. He may have believed, acting on Oliver Wright's dispatches, that the crisis had passed and things were settling down and it should be business as usual with regard to 'Northern Ireland'. And that was a fatal mistake.

British politicians did not get the chance to act as pro-consuls or dictators in the way Callaghan did in Belfast in August/September 1969. And they do not naturally fit into such a role, when they act within a representative democracy for the whole of their careers. So it is unsurprising that Callaghan failed to keep up the momentum he initially generated or was able to sustain the drive that might have moved the situation forward to the place where a difference might have been made. The gravitational pull of party politics, particularly in an election year—which did not encompass 'Northern Ireland'—took him away and the moment was lost.

Callaghan's Retreat from West Belfast

Here was the situation in West Belfast *'Behind the Barricades'* as the very 'constitutional and law-abiding *Irish News* described it, post-August 1969:

"The white painted slogan on the wall of the front of the Falls Road, just above Albert Street, defiantly proclaims: 'Falls Will Never Fall'.

"The Falls came perilously close to falling three weeks ago under military-precision onslaughts with machine-gun, small arms fire and hundreds of petrol bombs. It was then that individual heroism added up to mass gallantry as men, women and children turned out to protect their homes and to 'beat' the invaders back.

"Inside the area, behind the barricades, the maze of side streets is policed by local volunteers; Free Belfast has its own radio station, broadcasting continuously 24 hours a day; and two weekly newspapers. The Citizens Press and the Barricade Bulletin are being published to supplement the news service provided by the 'Irish News' which goes into every home in the Falls. Overlooking the Free Belfast area, from the roof of Divis Towers, 20 storeys over Divis streets, troops are keeping watch with powerful binoculars, along the full length of the road from Castle Street to Springfield Road corner...

"Life behind the barricades is more complex now than before the disturbances. It is being encouraged to go on as normally as circumstances permit but strangers are closely questioned and asked to positively identify themselves. At Divis Towers, no one is permitted in or out after 9.30 p.m. Further along the road local residents are vetted and passed through the barricades until the early a.m. And throughout the day and night every house in the neighbourhood is tuned into Radio Free Belfast which has taken the place of B.B.C. sound radio and U.T.V. television except for an occasional tuning in to the news. Young people man the station keeping up an uninterrupted flow of news, comment, patriotic songs and special requests for local families and the men at the barricades...

"In an area where tension has been building up for weeks, it is natural that rumours should start, spread and gather momentum. There have been several false alarms. Local volunteers work hard at pinning down and denying rumours which only serve in place an additional burden for already hard-worked vigilantes.

"Since the week of the heavy casualties and the task of accommodating thousands of refugees from places where they had been burned out or threatened the Falls area as such has temporarily shrunk. Streets like Conway Street, Cupar Street, Dover Street and others leading to the Shankill Road have been evacuated. Bombay Street and others in the Clonard Street-Upper Cupar Street area are devastated; houses formerly occupied by Catholics lie burned, wrecked and abandoned and in places there are two barricades—one Catholic, the other Protestant—both manned, and with a no-man's-land in between.

"Between the frontage facing the Shankill and Durham Street end of Albert Street facing Sandy Row, the Falls is in a state of siege. But there is no doubt now that forewarned there can be no new surprise attacks on the road. There are too many watchful eyes, both civilian and military, on the road. And the teenagers, who rallied to the defence of the Falls with their fathers, at a moment even graver than any during the 1921 troubles, have had a breather, and are ready to rally again if the situation demands it" (IN 11.9.69).

A week later some of the barricades came down after negotiations with the British military. But they went up again as soon as Unionist attacks resumed—which were almost a daily occurrence in the autumn and winter of 1969.

Callaghan conducted a British withdrawal from the areas behind the barricades. This was not apparent to all as the British Army kept up a visible presence in Catholic districts by extravagantly patrolling in armoured vehicles for the media. Presumably, this was to reassure Unionists who were increasingly angered that the Catholics were being failed to be policed by the authorities and kept in their place.

However, when the media was gone and the motorised patrols had flitted the Catholic areas were ceded again to the locals.

On the basis of the belief that things had settled, particularly within the Catholic community, Callaghan withdrew the apparatus of State from the Nationalist areas of Belfast and Derry while neglecting to give any political leadership to them. He left the Stormont regime in being as a façade in the hope that the Westminster intervention of August 1969 could be put in reverse. In leaving the Catholic areas of 'Northern Ireland' to their own devices immediately following the trauma of August, and with Stormont still functioning as a symbol of Unionist domination and a provocation to Catholics, Callaghan set up a situation in which something like the Provisional IRA could be generated.

In a crucial period between September 1969 and June 1970, the British Government effectively abandoned West Belfast to its own devices. And it determined to remain aloof from the festering political problem as much as possible. Thus, it left the Catholics of West Belfast to decide between what was emerging in its midst and Stormont, with no other alternative course open to it.

In these nine months the British State interposed itself as a buffer between the Catholic community and the Unionist regime. The Unionist regime was prevented from repressing the Catholic Insurrection at the root and the British Army nurtured the Republican growth—first by protecting it from Unionist interference and then by antagonising the Catholic masses through adopting repressive measures taken to stem the new Republicanism growing in the areas Callaghan abandoned in order to shore up the local façade at Stormont.

In 1969-70 in parts of 'Northern Ireland', the State abdicated what had always been regarded as a basic function of states—effective government and a monopoly of force. Naturally both of these functions began to be taken up by groups of individuals who organised themselves in order to fulfil the role that a state usually performs in protecting communities, both from external threat and internal anarchy.

That is something that would have been inconceivable to have been allowed to happen anywhere else in the UK. And it was a good indication of how much the Westminster Government took its 'Northern Ireland' region to be really part of it. It was shown to be expendable like no other region.

But the State could not suspend its activity for nine months and then take back the reins as if nothing had happened. When the British Government, which became a Tory one under Edward Heath, began to reassert its authority in these areas after nine or so months a state of War began to develop with the forces which had come into existence during the time the State's authority had been suspended.

The routine of government had been disrupted; other forces were able to establish a new legitimacy and the consequences of this period were to last decades.

Why Civil Rights Led to National War

It was the activisation of the Catholic community by the Civil Rights Movement followed by the Unionist Pogrom which led to the renewal of the Anti-Partitionist campaign, despite the lack of formal Anti-Partitionism in the Civil Rights demands, because once the movement for reform had gained momentum, it could not be stopped by the concessions made to it. It was not that the concessions made to it did not satisfy its formal demands—they largely did. The problem lay in the fact that the demands themselves could not satisfy the substance of the discontent within the Catholic community—a discontent which arose because the community was sealed into a communal vacuum within a statelet in which it would always remain a minority.

That is why the grievances of the Civil Rights Movement were described in the first volume of this book as symptoms of the problem rather than the crux of it.

The British, in an opportune moment after the events of August 1969, refused to alter the system that made the Catholic existence in the Six Counties so miserable. They tinkered with it by ceding the trivial Civil Rights programme but they left the real cause of the instability in place.

Westminster sent out increasing signals in early 1970 that what they were aiming for was not a fundamental reconstitution of the system, to make life in the Six Counties at least tolerable for the Catholics, but actually support for the continuance of Unionist sub-government with some minimal adjustments that might ward off trouble. With this more radical solutions to the problem came on the agenda. These ranged from the system's reconstitution on a more favourable basis for the Catholic community to its destruction.

Within the abandonment of West Belfast by the State the Catholic community became organised for the first time since 1922. It did so through Defence Committees where a whole conglomeration of able people including trade unionists, community activists and ex-servicemen came to the fore.

One of the major factors making for the organising of the Catholic populace was the great disparity of force that had been revealed in August and how it was deployed against the community. The Unionists were heavily armed with over 100,000 in possession of private legal weapons. There were also substantial amounts of unregistered weaponry held by Unionist privateers and the local repressive apparatus which could not be relied upon for protection from this threat. In fact, it was very likely to merge with it and support it with heavy military equipment and training in confrontations with the minority.

And the continual Unionist sallies in late 1969 and 1970 against Catholic areas of Belfast showed that this threat was very real and had not gone away.

On the other side the Catholic community was hardly armed at all and had to defend its existence by improvising with whatever came to hand and through the building of maximum community solidarity. That was the only way in which Ardoyne and Unity Flats and other areas at risk were prevented from burning in August and after.

During this period British officers, seeing the defencelessness of the Catholic community, allowed small arms training sessions in private houses and sports grounds to go on unmolested. Some soldiers even facilitated it by providing informal weapons training to young men in West Belfast (Peter Taylor, *'Provos—the IRA and Sinn Fein'*, pp.71-2).

The natural desire behind the Catholic barricades was to make contingencies for the next attack that would come from the Unionist militants (called 'Paisleyites' at the time). Arms, training and organisation were required within the community and whoever had control of this process would become the power centre in Catholic areas.

After the Unionist scaremongering the British Government saw the Republican element behind the barricades as a figment of Unionist imagination. If an IRA existed at all it was a mere reflex of Unionist discrimination and gerrymandering and when these aspects of the Six County entity were sorted, all would, it was presumed, be back to normal. And there was no sign of an IRA of any consequence in early 1970.

The British initially thought that they could use what was developing within the Catholic community as a pacifying force against the 'hot-headed' masses, and British Army officers dealt with them as the legitimate expression of order in places like Ballymurphy and the Falls (see 'Freedom Struggle,' published by the Provisional IRA which details this.) So they took it that the force behind what they saw emerging were the conditions of life that Catholics faced in the political slum.

But, of course, the IRA in embryo was never entirely a reflex of oppression—it was also, in its National expression, an army of an alternative state, which derived its right and legitimacy to take up arms from the ideology which was enshrined in the Southern Constitution.

The view of Republicanism as an organised conspiracy against 'Northern Ireland' is all very well as a characterisation of the IRA that existed prior to 1969, and which continued to exist within the larger movement that developed. But the substance of the new Republican mass was the pragmatic Catholic alienation from the exterior form of state apparatus of the Six Counties. That is what the bulk of the political movement that put people into the IRA and Sinn Fein was all about.

It originated in the catastrophic events of August 1969 and later meant that the War came to be concluded on the terms of the motivation with which it fought.

What made the Northern Catholics turn toward Republicanism was the Unionist Pogrom of August 1969. That event made it impossible for Catholics in the North to drift along quiescently in the way that they had for decades. It forced them into political action and politics by other means and gave them a determination to continue until things could not be let go back to the way they were.

The IRA's smallness in August was something that became beside the point because it was something that did not continue. The new Republicanism possessed the capability, the knowledge in the military art, and the support structure, which would enable it to grow into a significant force which could train hundreds of volunteers for action, given the right circumstances.

And it was London—and, secondarily, Dublin—that provided these circumstances within a political vacuum for the development of the embryo to become the living being.

There were three approaches that were taken to the August events and all three were inadequate to the situation. The Unionists blamed a Republicanism that hardly existed for the trouble and called for a crack-down to end it. The crack-down was denied them by the State which had put them under strict supervision.

As we shall see in the next chapter Dublin publicly attributed the explosion to the failure of Partition and called on the British to proceed toward re-unification as the only solution to the problem. This view failed to take account of the Protestant resistance to such a policy.

Lastly, the British Labour Government narrowed the problem down to something they were willing to deal with. Oliver Wright wrote to Callaghan in January 1970: "I am afraid that it is illusory to imagine that there is a short- or even medium-term solution to the problem... The problem therefore is mainly one of jobs and housing." Callaghan replied: "I agree this must be the next phase." (CJ 3/18, 20.1.70)

Britain seemed to understand that the solution to the problem of 'Northern Ireland' was not just in producing more jobs and housing and an end to discrimination etc. The problem was structural. But the same policy that had made the British establish 'Northern Ireland' now resulted in them defending the structures of the 1920 arrangement. And that meant that while Callaghan and Wright believed they could get away with a programme of minimal reform they weren't allowed off the hook so easily.

CHAPTER 3

Dublin and the North

At the height of the events of August 1969 the Taoiseach said he would not *"stand (idly) by"* and for 9 months he didn't. He gave instructions to his army to prepare for the possibility of making incursions in the Six Counties, supporting the establishment and organisation of Catholic Defence Committees and the extension of Dublin's influence among the Insurrectionists.

Dublin's policy with regard to the Six Counties has been fundamentally misrepresented in recent years. It has been written with a clear political motive, in service of the reputation of Taoiseach Lynch, and in a way that creates a clear line of demarcation between him and others who supposedly wished to plunge the Twenty-Six Counties into the abyss i.e. the Six Counties.

Of course, that is history written from hindsight and from the position of the collapse of National morale that Lynch's actions mid-way through 1970 brought about. After that, it seems, events had to be written about in a way that pretended Lynch's policy had never changed, and he had simply skilfully manoeuvred around those Fianna Fail Backwoodsmen in his Government, with the result that the Southern State was saved!

But what happened in 1970, and subsequently, is inexplicable from the vantage point of this new 'history' written in service of the Taoiseach. So we need to review what Dublin was really intending to do in 1969-70, what it actually did and how its retreat from this produced something entirely new in the Six Counties that it never bargained for.

Then we have the uncomfortable and unpalatable fact that it was not what Taoiseach Lynch did in the Autumn and Winter of 1969-70 in not *"standing (idly) by"* that produced what it did in the Six Counties but what he no longer did from the Spring of the following year, after he turned tail under pressure from an exterior force which suggested serious trouble for him if he did not put an end to his active Northern policy.

That was what actually produced what flourished from behind the barricades and became the substance of things over the following decades.

Fianna Fail and Northern Nationalism

It was Taoiseach Lynch who, more than anyone else, injected Anti-Partitionism into the situation in which the Northern Catholic community found itself in late 1969-early 1970. He declared repeatedly during this period that the Border was the cause of trouble in the Six Counties, rather than the internal workings of the 'Northern Ireland' system.

At this time there was little sign of Anti-Partitionism on the ground in the North with the Catholic Defence Committees not disputing the ultimate authority of the State—being manned by British ex-servicemen and making honest efforts to facilitate the return of the areas that had been ceded to locals behind the barricades to the authorities they saw as legitimate.

But Lynch and Fianna Fail could only understand Catholic action in the Six Counties as Anti-Partitionism, because this was the explanation for everything up North for Dublin.

In commenting on the Fianna Fail Ard Fheis in January 1970 *The Irish News* welcomed the Taoiseach's speech in which he said that "Partition is a deep throbbing weal across this land, heart and soul of Ireland" and "an imposed deformity whose indefinite perpetuation eats into the Irish consciousness like a cancer" (IN 20.1.70).

It noted that Taoiseach Lynch "added that the plain truth was that they had not the capacity to impose a solution to Partition by force; and that the Government was firm in its conviction that only peaceful means can achieve the abolition of the Border". But, whilst the Taoiseach appeared "for the most part, to have the party with him... If a change of circumstances demands a shift of policy it will no doubt be voiced".

The *Irish News* commented:

> "Mr. Lynch, in ruling out force, added that it was not enough that hearts were in the right place. The right decisions must be taken at the right time. This time may not be so far away. There have been so many developments in the Northern situation since last August that the Partition issue has been given a new perspective.
>
> "Mr. Lynch can justly claim that his decision to place troops on the Border was not only a gesture to the beleaguered Catholics of Belfast and Derry, but an act that might well force the hands of the British Government, reluctant to be involved in the North and being constantly assured by Stormont that it had the situation fully in hand.
>
> "Whether Mr. Lynch's decision was born of wisdom does not much matter now. It gave encouragement to his fellow Irishmen in the North; it certainly led to the right response from Westminster with the decision to send in troops, thus averting a holocaust and ensuring a cessation of violence. The Nationalist people were left with the feeling that the Government in Dublin had not altogether forgotten the minority in Ireland's lost Green Field.
>
> "Since last August, there have been clear indications by Mr. Lynch's Government that it is determined to make the ideal of a united Ireland more acceptable to those in the North who oppose unity; to make the country as enlivened and enticing as possible; and, meanwhile, to remind Unionists

that a serious appraisal of the North's future is now going on, the principal scrutineer being Whitehall's own man installed at Stormont.

"So, too, is consideration being given at Whitehall to the larger issue of the future of Ireland as a whole.

"In the short term, the Irish Government must give continuing attention to how closer relations can be established with the North in the economic, social, cultural and political areas. It is not too fanciful to believe that... Mr. Wilson, in his search for a solution of the intractable Irish problem, may yet turn to Jack Lynch" (IN 20.1.70).

A few days after the Fianna Fail Ard Fheis Austin Currie gave a speech to the UCD Law Society which illustrates the effect Fianna Fail's activist policy from August onwards had on Northern Nationalists in narrowing down the more complex character it had developed during the 1960s into traditional Anti-Partitionism. The *Irish News* reported under the heading, *'Currie Tells U.C.D. Law Society "Unity is Inevitable"*:

"The spirit of nationality has never been higher in the North as it has been since the eruption of last August. At the beginning of the Civil Rights campaign with its emphasis on 'British Rights for British subjects' some people had been concerned lest the desire for national unity would be diminished. They need not have worried—the fire burns brighter and stronger than ever.

"Unity can only be achieved by peaceful means. Let there be no mistake in any part of the country about that... What is needed... is a union of hearts and minds. A forced unity, in the aftermath of a bloody civil war, against the majority of present-day Unionists is not worth having. Anyway, on the practical side, as has now been admitted by the Taoiseach, sufficient force to over-run and hold the North is just not available. Even if it was, what would happen to thousands of Catholics living in isolated positions before friendly troops reached them? The use of force to achieve unity by a physical take-over of the North is clearly neither desirable nor practical...

"Some political commentators were amazed at the welcome given to the 'old enemy' when they appeared on the streets of Belfast and Derry. They should not have been. With due respect to the British Army, the legions of the Devil would have been welcome replacements for the RUC and B Specials. And, one might ask, how much more welcome than British troops would fellow Irishmen have been in the Bogside, the Falls Road, Coalisland and Dungannon etc" (IN 23.1.70).

The *Irish News* editorial and Austin Currie's speech in the South present a picture of Northern understanding of Taoiseach Lynch which is very different from that presented of him today by the coterie of Southern historians who lionise the Taoiseach for his *"moderation"* in and after August. The actions and signals Taoiseach Lynch sent out to the North certainly had the effect of invigorating the Nationalism of the Catholics of the Six Counties and guided them back toward the true path of Anti-Partitionism as the solution to their predicament.

At the end of 1967, when T.K. Whitaker, representing Taoiseach Lynch, went North to meet Unionist Ministers at Stormont, his agenda was composed of cross-border trivia. There was no issue made of things like discrimination, the conditions of Northern Catholics or Partition. The political representatives of Northern Catholics were cold-shouldered as Whitaker cozied up to Unionists, leading Eddie McAteer to conclude that Dublin's desertion of his community had left them like "fatherless children".

After the dampening down of Six County Catholic spirits by Taoisigh Lemass and early Lynch and their officials, the actions of the Lynch Government from August 1969, massively raised Northern Nationalist expectations about what was possible in the circumstances and it is hardly surprising that they then began to think the (previously) unthinkable.

To Northern Nationalists the Lynch Government had provided a valuable service to their community in doing the necessary in pressurising Whitehall into engaging in the North and instituting its reform programme. Lynch had not taken the ultimate step of military incursion but had done sufficient to make sure Britain was concentrating its mind on its 'Northern Ireland' region and was being kept at it by the presence of Irish troops at the Border.

But then the Irish Government's utterances and actions began to direct the Northern Catholics toward Anti-Partitionism and put Partition and the Government of Ireland Act back on the British political agenda. And it seemed that Jack Lynch was to be the beneficiary of all this because of his activist policy with regard to the North, after the disappointments of the Lemass years.

Wanted: A Fianna Fail of the North

Further evidence for this is contained in the Irish Government archives.

In the aftermath of the August crisis the Tánaiste, Erskine Childers, prepared 'Notes on the situation in Northern Ireland' for the Taoiseach. These began with the emphatic sentence: "We examine the unity of Ireland as an objective—in depth" (NAI, TSCH 2000/6/659, 4.9.69).

Childers' *Notes for the Taoiseach* dwelt on the political character of the Catholics of the North in conjunction with Fianna Fail framing an active policy to end Partition. These *Notes* suggested that Dublin felt the Northern part of the Nation had not always played up its part in the Patriot Game and had produced a dead loss of a party, compared with Fianna Fail:

> "Partition has had divergent effects in different periods since 1921. Thirty years ago the differences in social welfare, education and investment benefits

were less marked and the Nationalist Party was more active but still not effectual... The total Nationalist group were, as a majority, anti-Republican in attitude, while there were divisions of opinion as to—abstention from Stormont; presence in Stormont without recognition of de jure status; presence with recognition; extreme Republicanism—Since 1921 there has been no Fianna Fail type movement in Northern Ireland. On the basis of the Fianna Fail evolutionary policy of 1932 to 1947 the Nationalist parties' policies have been weak, contradictory, unrealistic."

The Tánaiste's Report noted that the UK's higher social welfare benefits, free health service and better educational facilities had produced a less Anti-Partitionist minority in the North than was desirable for Dublin. Childers told the Taoiseach that if Fianna Fail were going to be successful in its policy to end Partition it would,

"... depend to a great extent on whether the great majority of the minority population will now adopt a strong Nationalist, political organisation united on entry to Stormont and Westminster, without a sectarian approach, taking the Fianna Fail Party as an example in relation to not risking fences too quickly and willing to associate with us, privately or otherwise..."

But it was felt this was "unlikely to happen" because of "the conflicting forces" present within the minority in the North.

Far from being a reconsideration of traditional policy as some recent historians have suggested this was an indication that Fianna Fail was assuming its National duty of seeking to control and guide the Northern Nationalists on the path to freedom. The assumption underlying Childers' understanding of what needed to be done was that the Southern State knew what the National interest was and the Northerners had to be moulded into an instrument capable of achieving this—rather than producing the strange manifestations of alien politics that they were throwing up.

The Northern Catholics had tried to get into Fianna Fail on numerous occasions since 1927 (see Volume One of this series, *'Catastrophe'*) but they had always been rebuffed by De Valera. Having been rebuffed they looked for other forms of politics and began producing a great variety of things. But now it seems that they were being required to create a Northern Fianna Fail, but detached from the real thing, to further the First National Aim. Failing that what was required of them was a new approach modelled on what Fianna Fail had did in the South.

From the Fianna Fail perspective, the 'Constitutional' Nationalist Party had failed to deliver what Lemass had wanted and the 'unconstitutional' IRA was seen as counter-productive to the objective. So something that was unified and 'semi-constitutional' was desired out of the disparate elements in the Catholic community of the Six Counties.

Perhaps in the Tánaiste's mind what he saw needed doing in the North, for it to be made democratic and then independent of Britain with the rest of the Nation, chimed with what Fianna Fail had done with the Free State between 1932 and 1945. But it would have been a tall order to produce a Fianna Fail in the North. Fianna Fail was, after all, built to re-direct the path of a state and 'Northern Ireland' was only the façade of a state.

However, we will never know. Such a project was never followed through. And when an effective 'semi-constitutional' force, with many of the political attributes of Fianna Fail in the 1930s, was produced by the Northern Catholics after 28 years of warfare, it was not welcomed by Fianna Fail because its ambitions strayed outside the permitted area in which it was only supposed to be operational.

What was Dublin's Policy?

It is important to understand the policy of the Dublin Government at this point as it was to have such a great effect in the North when it was altered around April 1970.

Prof. Henry Patterson is not helpful in this respect when he suggests that:

> "For those like Lynch and Whitaker who wished to maintain Lemass's approach and for whom unity would come through North-South rapprochement assisted by some gentle prodding from London, the civil rights movement was a new, unpredictable and not entirely welcome development" (Ireland Since 1939, p. 171).

It was certainly the case that the Civil Rights movement confronted Dublin as a novel and unpredictable development. It wasn't the usual Anti-Partitionist body that had periodically emerged North of the Border that could be harnessed by Dublin and let down easily when the time came. It had formal objectives (*"British Rights for British subjects"*) that were in many respects Anti-National and could have resulted in a strengthening of Partition if they had actually been promptly met by Unionism. And it really was a purely Northern development—a product of 'Northern Ireland' itself.

But the Civil Rights movement, through setting off a chain of events that led to August 1969, had presented new possibilities for Anti-Partitionism that the Dublin Government was keen to grasp.

The idea that Taoiseach Lynch was maintaining Lemass' approach needs to be qualified by what it is thought Lemass' approach actually was. This has got muddied in recent years by the desire of certain historians to present Lemass as some kind of realist who wished to let Anti-Partitionism down gently and produce a kind of Partitionist accommodation on the island.

The Fianna Fail Government in 1969, when Lemass was still in touch with it, itself believed it was maintaining the former Taoiseach's approach in exploiting the situation for a renewed assault on Partition which had been successfully opened up by his wise policy. But that is not what Prof. Patterson means when he talks about Lynch and Whitaker wishing *"to maintain Lemass's approach... for whom unity would come through North-South rapprochement"*.

Prof. Patterson's view echoes that of Prof. Dermot Keogh of Cork that Taoiseach Lynch, advised by T.K. Whitaker, enacted a basic reorientation in the Dublin attitude to the Six Counties in the autumn of 1969.

That is wishful-thinking. What Dublin in fact did, in the aftermath of August, was to hold to its traditional view of the Six Counties and begin to formulate a policy to utilise the Northern crisis in the Anti-Partitionist interest.

A Memorandum for Government "giving the views of the Minister for External Affairs {Dr. Hillery} on the attitude and policies which might be developed in relation to Northern Ireland" makes it clear that the Fianna Fail Government had a very different policy with regard to the Six Counties than Prof. Patterson and Prof. Keogh suggest. It makes it clear that Dublin held to its traditional view that 'Northern Ireland'/Partition (which were taken to be one and the same thing) had failed and needed terminating:

> "The past year has brought into question in a fundamental way the 'solution' to the Irish question expressed in the Government of Ireland Act, 1920. This solution was a purely British one and was not sought by any element of Irish opinion. Certainly a minority of the Irish people at that time, roughly identifiable with the Presbyterian and Anglican communities in the North-East, did not share the majority view in favour of the independence of the whole country from Britain and was also opposed to Home Rule for Ireland. It was not their wish that subordinate parliaments should be created in Dublin and Belfast and, in this sense, the Stormont Parliament which Unionists have defended for 50 years was not something which they had sought for its own sake. This parliament, apart from being subordinate, found itself governing an area which was far from being homogeneous. As a political entity it had no history; it was an economic absurdity, the effects of which are felt particularly harshly in Derry, Tyrone and Fermanagh to the present day; it contained within itself, but to a degree highly accentuated in the small area of the North-East the social and religious incompatibilities which those British politicians who had conceived it had used to excuse and justify dividing the area from the rest of Ireland—territorially it included an area of about half its total size in which tho majority of the population was opposed to rule from or through Belfast... Nevertheless, Stormont has governed for almost 50 years..." (NAI, TSCH, 2000/6/662, Nov. 1969).

'Northern Ireland' had survived for 50 years, despite of itself, but Fianna

Fail was now taking credit, because of the policy of Taoiseach Lemass, for opening up the issue of Partition again:

> "Radical change has now come and it begins to be possible to distinguish the main reasons for this. The first breach of the Unionist monolith... was caused by the agreement to meet and discuss mutual problems between the former Taoiseach, Mr. Sean F. Lemass, and the former Prime Minister, Capt. Terence O'Neill. Their meetings, whatever their intrinsic importance, began a series of reactions which still continue. Two of these need to be mentioned—(i) the effect on extremist elements of the majority population of O'Neill's "treason" in allowing the former Taoiseach to visit him in Belfast and (ii) the beginning of new thinking among the minority in the North as their place in society."

This chimes with Peggy Lemass' view of her father's intention of unfreezing things in the North rather than any intention of stabilising it (Irish Times 5.1.78).

According to Minister Hillery Lemass' clever policy had succeeded in working up divisions in the seemingly monolithic Unionist Party, inspiring the Catholics into new and more effective forms of activity and this had produced the sequence of events that resulted in the events of August 1969 and the new opportunity to re-open the question of Partition:

> "A really united and self-confident Unionist Party would not have indulged—or suffered the extremist reaction to O'Neill's initiative... the first revolt, one against any change in the status quo, came from them. The second came from the minority. New leaders among them were quick to grasp the possibility of appealing over the head of a divided Unionist party to British public opinion. By demanding Civil Rights within the context of the United Kingdom they forced Stormont, already under pressure from a right wing which would yield nothing, into one impossible posture after another. In doing so, and in attracting well-publicised police repression for doing so, they revealed for all to see the unmistakable sick society that unionism had created. A series of incidents... led to a confrontation in Derry on August 12th which was seen to be a massive attempt to deny civil rights to the minority in the North; although its real circumstances were much more complex. The point was fatally made in Belfast on the night of August 14th/ August 15th when Protestant extremists, encadred by B Specials and with perhaps the tacit connivance of the RUC, set about burning out the Falls Road area. The British government found itself forced to pour further troops into the North to prevent a possible civil war."

Although it was the Catholic demand for Civil Rights and their utilisation of British pressure to push for the reform of 'Northern Ireland' that provoked Unionism into a violent reaction, it was really all about Partition, according to Dublin. Hillery continues:

> "All that has happened since then has been a massive justification of the Civil Rights movement but, as seen from London, only within the context of British justice. Although the Unionist structure of control from the North has clearly failed, there has been no overt recognition by London and neither overt nor covert by Stormont that the fundamental cause of the kind of society created in the North is the division of Ireland in the interests of a minority of the people of this country, and only a belated acceptance of the right of the minority within the area cut off to advocate by peaceful means the idea of constitutional change. Nevertheless, in the light of the history of the past 50 years even this recognition of the political right to advocate constitutional change is an immense step forward and it need not be doubted that the British government is well aware of this. Equally significant is the revived direct interest and involvement in the North of both Westminster and Whitehall."

This all presented a great opportunity for pushing on to end Partition:

> "In the new circumstances there are possibilities for adopting an attitude and a policy in relation to Northern Ireland which could ease the way to the eventual realisation of the reunification of Ireland."

But:

> "Two things should always be present to the mind in this respect. The first is that a society whose origin is dishonourable and whose legitimacy is constantly challenged is at a considerable disadvantage in dealing with its neighbours and remains fundamentally impotent. The second is that this same society contains a substantial body of people ardently committed to the preservation of their own personality and peculiarities to the point of suicidal resistance if attacked direct. Policy therefore must be found in the narrow ground between these two basic factors..."

The idea that Protestant Ulster was impotent came from seeing Stormont humiliated by their loss of sole control over security—the price it paid for Westminster assistance in August—and the Unionist masses lashing out wildly in frustration. Dublin saw the new situation as a fundamental constitutional change in relation to the position of 'Northern Ireland' in which Stormont was forced to accept Westminster Civil Rights reforms as the price for the help of its army. (See NAI, 2000/6/658 for example.)

Dublin concluded that because Protestant Ulster was now both helpless and at the same time capable of one last great futile backlash it needed to be handled with a bit of care. It should not be taken on directly, but dealt with in a more tricky and sophisticated way.

This was hardly the great change of Fianna Fail policy that has been detected in Lynch's term as Taoiseach by the new breed of Irish historian.

Dublin's Two-Pronged Strategy

Contrary to Prof. Patterson's view, the Lynch Government had decided on an activist policy to deal with the situation that was developing in the North. Dublin had been told to mind its own business by Whitehall when it tried to warn of impending disaster in the North, and it was thought that the Irish had been successfully fobbed off and were returning to their usual impotent moderacy. But the British were in for a surprise. The Lynch Government made good its threat of taking Britain to the United Nations.

Angela Clifford in *'August 1969: Ireland's Only Appeal to the United Nations—a cautionary tale of humiliation and moral collapse'*, shows how the Dublin Government, in the aftermath of the August events, moved outside the British insistence that the North was an 'internal matter' for the UK and NI governments only.

A confusion at the heart of the Irish appeal enabled Britain to block the initiative and British diplomacy was able to see off the External Affairs Minister Dr, Hillery. But what Whitehall did not anticipate at that moment was that the attempted initiative inspired the Northern Catholics and they were not going to be so easily stopped as the Irish Government.

The Republic's open, public, policy was bust by the British rebuff at the UN but there was another policy that was being pursued simultaneously and it was this, rather than the diplomatic brush-off Ireland received from Britain that was to have most implications for the North.

The appeal to the UN raised the question of international peace-keepers in the North. But the military thinking and preparations which the Irish Army was ordered to undertake laid the ground for potential Irish military intervention in the Six Counties for the first time since the days of Michael Collins' offensive in 1922. This was a radical policy aimed at circumventing British arrangements for the 'hands-off' approach to the governing of 'Northern Ireland'. And as *The Irish News* noted, this concentrated British minds on the problem of the Six Counties and kept them engaged for longer than they probably hoped they would have to bother with it.

Something like 10,000 Irish troops were deployed to the Border, artillery units were sent north and the Army reserves were called up and remained on duty for months after August. The Army was also instructed to prepare to give physical help to Northerners. It started to study the Northern military position for the first time since 1922 and sent six military Intelligence Officers, including Captain Kelly, into the Six Counties, to liaise with the Catholic defenders behind the barricades.

This was not just a momentary response to the events of August. It was felt for months afterwards in Dublin that the Six County entity might break up under pressure from the National wave of sympathy expressed for the plight of Northern Catholics and the squeeze put on the Unionist regime by the Callaghan reform programme that was instituted. Dublin evidently believed that under such pressure the Northern sub-government's authority could collapse, a right-wing Unionism would take power and everything would go into the melting pot.

In such circumstances, it was reasoned, the British Army could lose control and Dublin would not be able to stand idly by (See NAI, 2001/6/513, 30.1.70, 'Department of External Affairs on various scenarios that might arise in Northern Ireland in the short to medium term, supplied to the Department of the Taoiseach', for example). In February 1970 a formal Directive was given in verbal form to senior people in the Army, which they insisted on minuting and having the minute approved by the Government.

The Irish Army presence on the Border and the calling up of reserves grated on the British. Lord Chalfont did his utmost to secure a guarantee from Dr. Hillery that his army presented no threat to 'Northern Ireland' but the External Affairs Minister refused to give it. The issue was raised again and again by British officials (e.g. NAI, 2001/6/513, 2.3.70). But the Army was still there at the time of the Ballymurphy crisis in early April 1970 when 500 rifles and other equipment were moved to Dundalk—and these were not meant for the use of the Irish Defence Forces. And the Taoiseach kept his Army mobilised and deployed at the Border for most of 1970, despite the objections of the British and Unionist authorities.

On Lynch's orders his Ministers, organised within a special sub-committee, and members of his Army, took part in a covert operation to acquire arms outside the usual channels so that they could be distributed to the Defence Committees that had sprung up in the North. Some Northern civilians received training both covertly and as enrolled members of the Defence Forces in places like Dunree.

It was made easy for various Republican elements to set up training camps in the South and supplies of weapons were permitted to go northwards without interference from the Guards. The implication was that, if another critical situation developed, those whom the Army had armed and trained for the purposes of resistance would be supported by regular Irish military assistance. (See Capt. James Kelly, *The Thimble Riggers*, for an honest and factual account on this aspect)

A Relief Fund was established in a way which enabled the Northern Defence Committees to get the guns they felt they needed and help was also given for the rebuilding of Bombay Street and other burnt-out areas. In late February 1970 the Irish Government instructed the Army to make preparations for incursions into 'Northern Ireland' and to distribute weapons to the Northern minority.

Taoiseach Lynch was responding at this time to demands from very respectable people in the North. Paddy Devlin and Paddy Kennedy were just two of the people who drove south and requested guns from the Southern authorities for defence purposes. Gerry Fitt also demanded military assistance. And the Northern Defence Committees were given every help the Irish Government could give, short of actually making military incursions into the Six Counties.

There is evidence that the British were aware of this secret policy. A Foreign Office file reveals that Ambassador Gilchrist contacted London to alert them to the fact that there was "something more" to the Irish policy of military manoeuvres that met the eye (FCO 33/575, 16.8.69)

Dublin and the Northern Catholics

This activist policy of the Lynch Government must have had fundamental effects on the Northern minority.

Since 1921 Dublin had assumed the role of vanguard of the Irish Nation. The Southern Establishment had patronised the North as the most backward part of the Nation while excluding it from any influence within its corridors of power, even with regard to its Northern policy. And Dublin had been dutifully followed by Northern Nationalists down the years in the hope of deliverance one day by the South.

The question that arises in relation to August 1969 is: just how was it possible for the remarkable change to have taken place in the relationship between North and South.

The Northern Catholics had never really developed a political mind of their own, even in the 1960s when they produced something of their own in the Civil Rights Movement. True, prior to this, there was a lot of political activism, but this did not signify any independence of mind on the part of the Northern part of the Nation. In 1965, they looked southwards to Lemass to give the lead and, when Lemass departed, they looked to Lynch. When they felt they were being ignored by the South under Lemass and then Lynch, Eddie McAteer, Leader of the Northern Nationalists, described their feeling to be like that of "fatherless children" to the Taoiseach. (NAI, 99/1/76, 3.5.67)

Taoiseach Lemass seemed to signal to the Northerners that the Patriot Game was up and it was time for Catholics to participate in "the Northern state". The Northern Catholics had held themselves apart from this "state", which they knew was not a State, ever since it was set up in 1921. They preserved themselves apart from it and awaited deliverance from it by the main part of the Nation. And then Lemass let it be known to them that deliverance was not only on hold for the present, it was cancelled.

So what were they to do? Looking for equality within this 'state' was their only option for the future. And so the Trojan Horse, as Gerry Adams described it in November 2014, was born.

The Civil Rights Trojan Horse was not a thought-out plan of Sean Lemass. It is doubtful if he had a plan at all with regard to the North. His daughter Peggy later said that he indeed had the plan to unfreeze the North through Catholic participation and open it up for a new thrust at the Border. Lemass did not advise a Civil Rights strategy, but that is where participation naturally went to after Parliamentary Opposition in Stormont proved futile and demeaning as the Nationalist Party knew it would. So the Northern Catholics had nowhere to go but to the Civil Rights strategy after the Taoiseach had re-directed their efforts into a political cul-de-sac.

There was fortuitously a man—Desmond Greaves of the London-based Connolly Association—with a plan. Greaves, in establishing relations with the Republican movement, had given it a plan for re-opening the Border question through the Trojan Horse of Civil Rights. "Demand more than O'Neill can concede" was the advice given in the Republican Education documents and it worked a treat.

As the communal tensions built up during early 1969, the Northern Catholics increasingly looked South, 'Green Tories' and revolutionary Trotskyites alike, for some signs of hope and deliverance. And, as the impending confrontation with Unionism began to loom large, looks of desperation began to appear towards the direction of Dublin.

The Southern political Establishment had a duty in August 1969 to give first priority to the North and guidance to the Catholics there. After all, for 50 years it had viewed them as an appendage of the Nation and had determined that they continue to act in the interests of the National Aim. In the 1960s the Taoiseach had prevailed upon their political instrument to become an Official Opposition in Stormont and things began to break apart as a result.

For the first time, National and social advance to some extent was clearly possible for Northern Catholics, and was being vigorously demanded by them. In such a situation it was Dublin's responsibility to harness Northern activism, guide it in a purposeful and responsible direction, and use the considerable resources of the independent State and its people to whatever degree was necessary in support of it.

During the 1960s Dublin had reasoned itself into a position that it should have no policy on the North except the advocacy of 'moderation' to all concerned, with the pursuit of unity to be a hope, with little actual prospect of achievement. This policy was intellectualised by civil servant T.K. Whitaker and instituted by Lynch and it is found in the notes and memoranda to the Taoiseach held in the National Archive. It was the position of faint heart trying to win fair lady and it was a position that was totally inadequate to the demands of the situation that emerged after August 1969.

The events of August drew Dublin into a more activist policy with regard to the North.

The Minister for External Affairs' "*Memorandum for Government on the attitude and policies which might be developed in relation to Northern Ireland*", written in November 1969, had under the heading "Short-term Objectives of Reforms in the North", the suggestion that:

> "Nothing should be done which might impede the implementation of the necessary reforms in the North. Gentle but firm pressure should be exercised to see these reforms achieved and public approval should not be withheld when substantial measures of real reform are implemented. Further action at the United Nations and in the Council of Europe to promote reform should be taken only if insufficient progress on reform seems to warrant it. Care should be taken to avoid action leading to complete direct rule from Westminster which would make the North a closer integral part of the United Kingdom unless, of course, Stormont should completely reject genuine reform."

It called for—

> "discreet contact with Whitehall on the question both at the diplomatic level and at the Ministerial level—under cover of other activities if necessary. Bilateral talks should be sought with the British not alone on the solution of the short-term problems of reform in the North but also on possible approaches to a long-term solution..." (NAI, TSCH, 2000/6/662).

Dublin attempted to bring about increased Westminster involvement in the North but at the same time wanted to avoid the imposition of Direct Rule. When Taoiseach Lynch met the British Ambassador to Dublin in September 1969 he made it clear that Direct Rule should not be imposed by Westminster, but reform and reunification be pursued by London and Dublin in conjunction.

But here was the big problem in Dublin's position that made the Anti-Partition policy conflict with the distinct interests of Northern Catholics and made it impossible for Dublin to exploit differences between London and Belfast in its interest.

The Contradictory Policy

Northern Nationalism was clear about who its great hope for change was in the post-August situation: Westminster, in the form of James Callaghan. This can be seen in the editorials of the *Irish News* from the Fall of 1969. For instance, in one entitled *'Under Duress'* the newspaper of Northern Nationalists noted:

> "... a government now under Whitehall duress cannot afford the luxury

of disagreement on how Mr. Callaghan's wishes are to be met; nor of seeking for some form of delaying tactics in case the climate may change to their advantage. Life today in the Six Counties, and likely enough for the predictable future, dwells, and will continue to dwell, very largely in the shadow cast by Mr. Callaghan during his recent visit—the shadow of ultimate dissolution of all Stormont's powers unless there is immediate change... Mr. Callaghan is to return to the North in about six weeks time to see if his programme is bearing fruit. The influence of Whitehall is irresistible, but some members of the Unionist Party do not seem to realise it even yet... A little reflection will show them how futile it is not to" (IN 4.9.69).

The duress Unionism was under from Westminster persuaded the people on the Falls in September to agree to British requests for the coming down of the barricades in return for assurances that the Stormont Special Powers Act would be suspended. The *Irish News* commented:

"The people of the Falls Road and other areas in the city have made a courageous gesture of trust, however agonisingly difficult for them, by accepting the dismantling of the barricades... Stormont is now finding that it can no longer resist pressure and that its ability to rule is becoming increasingly exposed... If the men of Stormont have not changed, they are now being faced with the necessity of change in the area over which they have held sway for nearly fifty years. One or two have seen the writing on the wall; the others preferred to continue with their reactionary politics. But now the orders are coming from Westminster. When they have to be handed down from Stormont to the grassroots of Unionism, we shall once more discover just how much democracy exists among them" (IN 18.9.69).

The bringing in of Westminster by the events of August was the great achievement of Northern Nationalism. And it was very important that pressure was maintained on Whitehall to finish the job whilst its mind was concentrated on it and before it drifted off to its default position again.

The effective exploitation of tensions between London and Belfast could have killed off Stormont quickly in 1969. And it is agreed by all that that would have been no bad thing to have happened and tragic that it had to take what happened in the next year and three-quarters before it did happen.

But Dublin's Anti-Partitionism led it to effectively support the Unionist regime at Stormont as a tactic to prevent Direct Rule. It subsumed the Northern Catholic predicament, which could only be addressed by Westminster, to the interests of ending Partition—which it knew to be a pipe-dream—even though, as Eamon Gallagher noted from his visit to Derry that what Northern Catholics wanted was their position addressed at the level of State.

The policy of Dublin was nonsensical. If Dublin believed the cause of the trouble in the North to be Partition and that trouble was incapable of being eradicated without an end to Partition and it was ruling out the use of force to achieve it, how was it to end the trouble in the North? As the "policy suggestions" in the Government files indicate: presumably through applying "gentle but firm pressure... exercised to see... reforms achieved" and through "discreet contact with Whitehall... on the solution of the short-term problems of reform in the North but also on... a long-term solution..."

In other words discreet pressure was going to be applied at Whitehall so that the Ulster Protestants, whom the Irish Government saw as fellow-Irishmen, would not know that it was ganging up on them with Britain to put them under Dublin rule.

Meanwhile Dublin was going to collaborate with Britain to alleviate the trouble, knowing London would do nothing about Partition, even though Partition was taken to be the cause of the trouble, and therefore would cause trouble again, even if the present trouble was successfully quelled. And the Irish Government was going to depend on Britain to provide the necessary arm-twisting of the Unionists to push through the reform necessary to stabilise the situation, which would preserve the thing that caused all the trouble, and which Dublin wanted to end—Partition.

It was obvious that what the Catholics of the North wanted to get out of, and had mobilised themselves against, was 'Northern Ireland', in one way or another. Yet Dublin had no answers for them on this issue.

Dublin, in all its practical efforts in the North, was pushing for cosmetic reforms that would continue to bottle the Northern Catholics up in the Six Counties with the same mode of government that was actually agitating them. In other words, whilst denouncing Partition, and scheming against it, the Irish Government was acting tactically in a Partitionist way. That is what the much praised Whitaker policy amounted to—not very much!

The problem this time was that the Northern Catholics, who had been aroused from their lethargy of nearly half a century, were not prepared to wait for Dublin anymore. And the Dublin Government was soon to find itself following them in the National War that developed out of the situation in which any meaningful activity Dublin was engaging in within the Six Counties was first withdrawn and then policy from the South became entirely absent.

Dublin and the Northern Protestants

The Southern Government had something of an activist policy for the North under Taoiseach Lynch, which involved arming the Northern minority for defence purposes and having its Army make preparations for incursions, if necessary, in the Six Counties. That was not to the taste of Whitaker's moderation but it was the only thing that had real purpose in the situation.

Whitaker urged a policy of accommodation with the Northern Protestants but this, again, amounted to little more than 'moderation'. So the policy innovation in the military sphere was not backed up by a parallel political initiative directed at the Ulster Protestants that might have stabilised the situation and presented a different path to unity.

It might seem a contradiction to have had two such policies. But what was required after August was provision for defence of the Catholics in the North, if the British Army proved unable or unwilling to provide it; purposeful engagement with them to direct their political development; and a parallel reassurance to the Protestants to calm them in the short-term and make them amenable to unity over the longer-term.

The Whitaker/Lynch policy was found to be sadly lacking in this respect.

Taoiseach Lynch's speech during the August crisis did not only say that Dublin *"would not stand {idly} by"* while Catholics were burned out and attacked. It also said that the Stormont Government had lost control of the situation and that Britain should act by declaring that "the re-unification of the national territory" was the only basis "on which a permanent solution to the problem could be found".

The Taoiseach followed up with a number of other speeches blaming Partition for the crisis and advocating a United Ireland as the only solution to the problem. For instance, on 28th August he responded to Callaghan's reassurance that the Border was not an issue with the assertion:

> "The Government reiterates its conviction that the unnatural and unjustifiable partition of Ireland is basic to the present unrest in the Six Counties and that no long-term much less permanent, solution can be contemplated without having full regard to its existence" (IN 29.8.69).

Angela Clifford has reproduced Lynch's speeches made from August 1969 until July 1970 in her book, *'The Arms Conspiracy Trial'* (pp.555-80). There is no evidence in Lynch's public statements, or those of the colleagues closest to him, Hillery and Colley, of any change in attitude toward Partition or the Ulster Protestant. All the speeches made could have no effect but to antagonise them.

Even Lynch's so-called 'conciliatory' speech at Tralee on 17th September is full of Anti-Partitionism and ridicules the whole concept of the Border. From the press reports of the time it can be seen that Unionism, whilst welcoming Lynch's statement that he was not about to impose himself militarily on them, could only see it as evidence of an escalating Anti-Partitionist offensive from Dublin. They took it that what Lynch was saying was that he could not conquer the Six Counties by force, much as he would have, if he was able to.

The *Irish News*, speaking for Northern Catholics, did not take the Tralee speech as a sign of a Dublin retreat from Anti-Partitionism. It took it as a reassertion of One Nationism and commented as follows in an editorial:

> "Mr. Lynch has said it again for the benefit of Unionist politicians that no Irish Government can concede, and never will, Britain's right to exercise jurisdiction over any part of Irish territory. The claim of the Irish nation to control the totality of Ireland has been asserted, frequently in blood, over the centuries by successive generations of Irish men and women and it is one, as Dr. Hillery recently told the Security Council, which will never be renounced. Mr. Lynch, having made the position clear, can we take it that Mr. Chichester-Clark in his offer of a 'fruitful and friendly relationship' between his Government and Dublin, is showing an appreciation that Partition cannot last, and that with Britain's positive involvement in the Northern situation, the way is beginning to open for a new relationship?" (24.9.69).

It is clear from this that Northern Nationalism felt that Unionism was on the run, squeezed between Westminster and Dublin and saw Lynch's Tralee speech as nothing more than providing a welcoming embrace that would keep up the pressure on Unionism.

A year later, after Lynch had abandoned his military interventionist policy, *The Irish Times* reported him as saying "I have never and never will accept the right of the minority who happen to be a majority in a small part of the country to opt out of a nation" (14.11.70). And this was a view he continued to maintain well into 1972.

At the same time there are no speeches by Charles Haughey inflaming the situation, since Haughey chose not to make any. In fact, Haughey was one of the earliest believers in gaining Protestant consent to a United Ireland. In a note to Frank Aiken, in March 1967, Haughey argued that Dublin had to recognise that the only way to gain unity "was through a majority decision of the people of the North" (UCDA P104/8822, 14.3.67, Aiken papers). Lemass and Lynch never acknowledged such a "consent" position, if they held it, and it was not until Haughey became Taoiseach that it was formally accepted by Fianna Fail. Haughey also communicated his view through the journalist Constantine Fitzgibbon to British Ambassador Gilchrist that Direct Rule was both "inevitable and necessary" in sorting things out in the North in 1969 (Matt Treacy, *The IRA 1956-69, Rethinking the Republic*, p. 175).

And yet Haughey is pilloried in Dublin these days whilst Lynch is lionised.

Dublin's Futile Policy Towards Unionism

There was a serious failing in Dublin's grasp of the situation in the North that disabled its politics in the post-August situation. This was the misconception of the character of the Ulster Protestants whom Dublin took to be part of the "Historic One Irish Nation". The problem with this notion, which spanned the full gamut of Nationalist politics, was that it conflicted with the reality of the situation and led to an antagonising of the situation both between the Southern and Northern parts of the island and within the Six Counties between the two communities.

Within the two communities the understanding that the Protestant community represented a second and distinct national entity on the island had greater traction. And the Catholic community in the North cannot be blamed for failing to understand the consequences of this for their political ambitions. After all they were the sufferers of the political predicament of 'Northern Ireland' in a way that Dublin was not and were trying to physically escape them. The failure to understand the problem of the distinct national expression of the Ulster Protestants was largely a Southern failing because their detachment from the situation permitted some political action that could set the relations both between South and North and within the Six Counties on a different and less antagonising course.

With the immediate crisis of August 1969 over, it was really the moment that the Taoiseach should have acknowledged that there was nothing in the Protestant community that was responding to the appeal of Irish Nationalism. It was immune to Irish Nationalism and could not be convinced it was Irish by being constantly told by Dublin that it was mistaken about what it was. National difference was the central feature of the communal conflict in 'the North' and it was quite a separate issue from the character of 'Northern Ireland' itself, which Britain had largely determined. Whilst Ulster Unionism had derived from a British projection into Ireland, it had successfully taken root like no other colonial imposition and had developed into something of such substance that it could be only called a second Irish Nation. It was, therefore, wholly different in character from the Protestant ascendancy remnants that were dotted around the South and which it was likened to. The Ulster Protestants were a substantial people who just could not be wished away as 'good Irishmen'.

The Tánaiste put his finger on the problem in this passage from his policy document:

> "The Sinn Fein 1918-1921 policy, then later Fianna Fail Six County policy, has always made it clear that the 300 year old settlers were regarded as Irish, that Britain legalised partition but that agreement without recourse to arms would be essential to bring about unity" (NAI, TSCH 2000/6/659, 4.9.69).

This was the assertion of the One Nation view of the island without any means of bringing it about as a political reality. Getting *"agreement without recourse to arms"* was a fine sentiment but what was ever done to achieve it?

The One Nation view of John Redmond and Joe Devlin within

Nationalism was passed down from the Parliamentary Party to Sinn Fein and to every derivation of Sinn Fein in the 26 Counties. The Dublin Establishment held it in 1969 and made no effort to understand the Ulster Protestant community and therefore had no understanding of it when it was time to make important decisions in the period after August, when understanding was critical.

When the British Army was employed on the streets of the North and a semblance of order was restored to the situation, that was the time that the Southern Establishment, if it was really in earnest about winning over the Protestant community in the North for unity, to adopt a radically new approach to the Northern situation.

That would have meant recognising the Protestant community as a distinct nation—a second Irish one—and would have led to a new approach that took the heat out of the situation, lifted the perceived threat from the South to the Protestants in the North, and given solid leadership to the Northern Catholics when they were still of a mind to listen to Dublin. But in a number of speeches the Taoiseach chose to forcefully assert the One-Nation ideology and categorically rejected the "Two Nations" view, which might have persuaded the Unionists to listen to him and calm things down.

The 'One-Nationist' ideology of the Southern State asserted that the island consisted of one Irish people, without any notion of how a single National entity was actually to be brought about. It was the thing that Fr. O'Flanagan, Vice-President of Sinn Fein, way back in 1916 when Partition looked a real likelihood, had questioned the advisability of. The Devlinite *Irish News* then accused Sinn Fein of being responsible for the division in the Nation that Fr. Flanagan had described with the intention of over-coming it. In fact, the division that had already been there and had been actually worked up by the Redmondite Hibernians (see Volume One).

Recognising Protestant Ulster as a second Irish Nation would have had a number of progressive effects on the situation in 1969. It would have eased the pressure on the Protestant community that was resulting in attacks on Catholic areas; it would have focused Catholic energies on addressing their predicament initially within the UK State, and put consequent pressure on Westminster as a result for deeper reform; it would have provided the South with a realistic objective in aiming to overcome the national division on the island by building a pluralistic unitary state; and it would have undermined the purpose of the 1920 Act in securing leverage over the Southern State by separating its sovereignty from the effects of the Northern problem that could be used by Britain to make in-roads into its independence and national culture.

However, One Nationism proved die-hard and it took the contest of battle to produce its collapse. And that was not a useful process for the well-being of Nationalist Ireland. Far better that it made the appropriate calculation at the vital moment instead of ridiculing those who saw the reality of the situation and asserted it when it was evident.

The Limitations of 'Moderation'

The Minister for External Affairs' "Memorandum for Government on the attitude and policies which might be developed in relation to Northern Ireland" had a number of "policy suggestions" with regard to the courting of Ulster Protestants. "Under the heading "Basic Approach" it said:

> "Reunification of Ireland should be sought by peaceful means through cooperation, agreement and consent between Irishmen. The use of force for the purpose should be dismissed publicly as frequently as may appear necessary" (NAI, TSCH, 2000/6/662, Nov. 1969).

And that seems to be the extent of Dublin rapprochement to the Protestants—uttering frequent verbal assurances that they were not about to be invaded! How generous!

In terms of "North/South Intercourse" the document suggested the encouragement of "contact at all levels in the private as well as in the official sector..." And "In teaching Irish history in the schools emphasis should be given to the positive aspects rather than the aspects which tend to be divisive... Care should be taken to avoid appearing to condone the activities of illegal organisations such as the I.R.A..." (NAI, TSCH, 2000/6/662, Nov. 1969).

The teaching of Irish history in the South had nothing to do with the outbreak of trouble in the North in 1969. It might have had something to do with the small IRA invasion/incursion of the Six Counties between 1956 and 1962. But there were no calls for a rewriting of Irish history then to dampen down Anti-Partitionism in the 26 Counties. And the people who were in insurrection in the North had been taught mainly British history in their schools and they had to re-discover the rebel tradition in the aftermath of 1969, through self-education by a small group of Republicans.

But here is an initial indication of how the Northern explosion, which seemed initially to enhance the spirit of Nationality, might have poisonous effects on Irish National culture and independence of mind. Very soon Britain was re-educating a new breed of Irish historians who were appalled at what was happening in the North and took to self-blame to explain it.

Much of the thought in these Government documents originated with Lynch's advisor, T.K. Whitaker, who Prof. Keogh of Cork University believes to have inspired a basic reorientation in Dublin's thinking with regard to the North in 1969. It was the Lynch/Whitaker policy that Prof. Patterson referred to in the passage quoted earlier.

But this "new thinking" was nothing more than pretence. Its stated aim was to build bridges to the Unionist community and nurture it toward unity. It would be an exaggeration to call it shallow because it was very much worse than that, being fundamentally empty. And when the activist military part of Dublin's policy was dramatically abandoned by Taoiseach Lynch in mid-1970 all that remained was the empty part—meaning that Northern policy itself was then completely amorphous and lacking in purpose.

Whitaker's thinking appears in 'Notes on Anti-Partition Policy, prepared by the Tánaiste, Erskine Childers, for the Taoiseach, Jack Lynch' (NAI, TSCH 2000/6/659, 2.9.69). It was the hope of Dublin that it could detach a section of the Ulster Protestants from Unionism to create a voting majority in the North for an end to Partition:

> "About 200,000 to 300,000 have to be won over, in pure electorate terms, to gain unity, assuming the whole of the anti-unionists voted for unity. We have no opinion poll analysis whatever of their views. The PRG {group or committee consisting of Civil Servants} should ask the Belfast Telegraph for the public opinion poll referred to in earlier memo. Who are the 30-47%, or is it more, who said they believed partition would end some day?... Far more enquiry is needed as to how moderate Unionist feeling is developing, of what it consists... A suitable campaign... needs mounting to get under the skin of moderate Protestant opinion... Far more attention to Unionists coming to chartered accountancy, medical dinners, games, etc arranged tactfully by PRG; men penetrating these groups here and getting help from members to <u>soften up</u>. More journeys north. More invitations to functions here. More of our people holidaying in north... All our people in touch with Northerners to be given a brief on the theme Partition must end some day, let us see how this can be done... How do we get the hard liners in the North, such as Protestant shipyard workers to come South and meet our people? How do we penetrate this mass? ..."

Winning over the Protestants to Nationalism was a forlorn hope and one senses that the Tánaiste knew it. There is even the underlying understanding in his notes for the Taoiseach that it might not be worth it if the small innovative proposals suggested might disturb the South's own routine of existence. And it is also implicit in the document that the Southern State was even beginning to think of itself as unsuitable to be an all-Ireland state, both in terms of its Catholic character and its economic deficiencies. And very little could be done there, it was felt, except a bit of a make-over.

What was very clear from this was that the Ulster Protestants were far out of the reach of Southern understanding.

In the past, it is acknowledged, little was done to try to get to know them and now some new-fangled 'market analysis' was to be employed to attempt to understand them and then charm them into a united Ireland by being nice to them. But the lack of firm understanding and the feeling that the Ulster Protestant was simply 'wrong' in their opposition to Irish unity could only result in a lack of ability to judge the reality of things and the making of superficial gestures toward them that would have no political consequences. Dublin's 'One Nationism' was proved inadequate to the situation of flux that emerged after August because the Ulster Protestants did not react to the events as a part of the Irish Nation at all, and Dublin did not react as if it believed them to be either.

Desmond Fennell, the Dublin commentator, who was a Two-Nationist and later had an association with Provisional Sinn Fein's *Eire Nua* programme, advocated a policy through the columns of the *Irish Times* in August and September 1969, which was both rational and practical. But his thoughts were wasted on the Anti-Partitionist Dublin bourgeoisie (Fennell's hesitant and part-contradictory policy, but policy nonetheless, can be read in The Irish Times, 19.8.69 and 15.9.69.)

In the August aftermath Dublin's failure to influence the situation in the North in a positive manner had great implications for what subsequently happened. It produced a vacuum that had to be filled by something. And it was—by a new activist and independent force produced in the North amongst the Catholics there, determined to grab the opportunity to do something about the predicament they were in, having suffered it for 50 years.

It was still possible that Dublin could have guided the Northern Catholics in a direction which it desired if it had maintained its hands-on approach behind the barricades. But, as we shall see, at the first point of contact with the enemy Lynch had a change of heart and revealed Dublin to have no stomach for what it had started and what was really necessary in relation to Britain and the Six Counties.

Fiddling While Belfast Burns

The moderation which Lynch took from Whitaker, behind the Anti-Partitionism, was simply not enough as Belfast continued to smoulder and then burn in 1970.

On 7th February 1970 *The Irish News* produced an extraordinary editorial entitled *'In the Name of Humanity'*. It was an explicit sign of exasperation within the Catholic community against the 'moderation' that was being urged upon it, to lower its expectations, and a plea from the heart that something substantial ought to be done to arrest the slide into disaster, which it could foresee, from within itself.

It is an unusually emotional statement that we now know went unheeded by Westminster, 'moderate' Unionism and 'moderate' Nationalism in the

Twenty-Six Counties—which it seems to have been directed at. It deserves reproduction as a glimpse into the soul of the Northern Catholics and because it reveals what was seldom revealed. It said:

> "The image of Nero fiddling while Rome burns is one which has appealed to polemicists at all times. It so accurately symbolises the detachment from other people's troubles which is an unpleasant, but undeniable feature of any human society... there are certainly in every country and every community large numbers of people who can suffer the tragedies, the struggles, the deprivations and the hardships of others in their midst with complete equanimity; if indeed they know of them at all. It is only when an outraged people rebels, and their rebellion threatens the fastnesses of the secure, that awareness often followed by real fear, penetrates their comfortably cushioned acceptance of society as they find it.
>
> "The more humane among them, as against the 'hang them and flog them brigade,' will often express shock and dismay, will sometimes even go so far as to voice some criticisms of the regime under which they so cosily sheltered. They will, of course, accompany their statements with recommendations to patience... But their new-found sympathy remains highly unconvincing, appears, indeed, as no more than evidence of anxiety when it remains at such a nebulous level.
>
> "We have been treated in this community to more than our share of lectures on the virtues of patience, moderation and reason... What we need from these self-appointed 'moderate' voices now so earnestly raised as the very real threat of physical violence, unwanted by anyone but fanatics, emerges, is some cool common-sense and realistic appraisal of what constitutes justice, of which is meant by reform, of what precisely is the definition of the word violence, which does not necessarily mean shooting or fire-raising or batoning or throwing stones.
>
> "We have heard no 'moderate' voices raised against the selective prosecutions pursued by the Stormont Government since last summer. We have heard no 'moderate' voices raised against the differences in the distribution of punishment...
>
> "For fifty years the Nationalist Party tried to obtain justice for the artificially contrived 'minority' of this part of Ireland. Well knowing that they might be committing political suicide... they accepted Mr. O'Neill's invitation to form an official Opposition. In that role they suffered the contempt in Parliament which had been meted out in all aspects of daily life to those who, like them, did not subscribe to the idea of a 'Protestant Parliament for a Protestant people.' But no single 'moderate' voice was raised to support them though the Party, with almost heroic restraint, attempted to practice 'moderation.'
>
> "Violence, by which is usually understood physical turmoil, danger and disorder, is an appalling thing, and we hope and pray that this community, which in the past six months alone has been looking at it in the red and raw,

will be spared any further experience of it.

"But those who very rightly extol the virtues of moderation, will have to understand one thing. There is violence in people being driven to live twelve in one room. There is violence in people being kept at a permanent level of unemployment. There is violence in discrimination at judicial level. There is violence in bad housing. There is violence in forced emigration. There is violence in the prevention of democratic representation by gerrymandering. There is violence in shocking the public conscience by official lies, or distortion, or misrepresentation of facts.

"None but a fool or a knave can want the disruption of civil order. Nevertheless, if truth and justice continue to be flouted, with no action from those who publicly and officially claim to speak for 'moderation,' then the very thing they, and all sane men, fear is the more likely to occur" (IN 7.2.70).

It is noticeable in this editorial that the *Irish News* identified the source of violence with the mode of government in the Six Counties rather than with Partition, as Dublin was doing. In 1998 it was proved that the Northern newspaper knew the North and its community much better than Dublin.

The *Irish News* had a policy of never criticising Dublin. The Northern Catholics had need of every friend they potentially had and such criticism would have been politically insane. But one thing gnawed away at the paper—the treatment of the Nationalist Party by Taoiseach Lemass and his sending of them on a suicide mission into Stormont. The *Irish News* knew this could only end in tears at the very least and its fears were more than realised as things started to unravel as a result of the futility it demonstrated to the community which had prompted it to adopt the activism the pseudo-state could not contend with.

Of course, Mr. O'Neill had done the inviting. But it was the Taoiseach who had done the ordering to Eddie McAteer to "*take the soup*" as the Nationalist Leader himself described it.

From there on 'moderation' had been urged on the Northern Catholic community from Dublin, from Belfast and from London, whilst the system remained that made 'moderation' an impossibility.

As *The Irish News* inferred, it was hoped that this would ensure a quiet life for those outside the Catholic ghettoes whose more tranquil existences had been disturbed by the extraordinary events of August 1969. That was the thing that was really getting under the skin of *The Irish News*, which, lying not far from the centre of things and having a long historical memory of events, knew better of the danger that lay ahead in this irresponsible attitude that was sweetened and justified with the term 'moderation'.

Chapter 4

The New Republicanism

Why did the new Republican Army develop in the aftermath of August 1969 and what was its political character? These are the questions that this chapter attempts to answer.

The basic fact of the matter was that the Provisional IRA was a product of what *The Times* in the late 1960s called "*John Bull's Political Slum*" a.k.a. 'Northern Ireland'. It was a general manifestation of the perverse political system established by Britain in 1921 and a specific product of the events of August 1969. And it became the main political instrument of a community wishing to escape the constrictions of what had produced it.

The order of responsibility for its emergence lies primarily in London, and then secondarily in Dublin.

Whitehall misjudged the situation in early 1970, believing that it had contained the crisis of August and everything could return to normality in relations between Britain and 'Northern Ireland'—except for some minimal reforms. After engaging with 'Northern Ireland' in the first meaningful way for 50 years it gravitated back toward its traditional "*arm's length*" policy without tackling the underlying problems that had generated the conflict, which it presumed had burnt itself out.

Dublin then acted as a secondary influence on events in the context of Britain's behaviour. It began to make moves to take the Northern Catholics in hand in the situation brought about by the August Pogrom. But then Taoiseach Lynch instituted a drastic policy shift, under British pressure, that resulted in the Northern Catholics being abandoned by Dublin and thrown back on their own resources.

Forced back on their own resources by London and Dublin, the Northern Catholics produced something of their own, from themselves, and sustained it under pressure as its hope of deliverance, when everyone else had let them down.

The Republican Split

The New Republican Army or Provisionals did not exist at the time of the August Pogrom and it barely existed in the early part of 1970. One of the reasons the British underestimated the situation was because of the absence of any Republican substance—which the Unionists kept telling them was there.

The Provos or Provies came about because of the August Pogrom and the conditions that existed in 'Northern Ireland' in the months after it. There was an IRA (Officials) that existed before August 1969 but it only produced a minimal growth in conditions that seemed to favour a flourishing and it fizzled out a couple of years later. It proved inappropriate to the situation and could not avail of it.

The Republican *debacle* in Belfast in August 1969 led to a split in the IRA and Sinn Fein. In essence a new Northern Republicanism was born in response to the inadequate understanding of the Southern IRA of the significance of the events of August. But the split was not a straight North/South divide because of some other outstanding issues within the movement that came to a head at the same time. And both wings of the Republican Movement were initially led from Dublin, in acknowledgement of the historic relationship that existed within Nationalism between North and South.

There was a kind of internal coup within the Belfast IRA in late September 1969 which resulted in it disassociating itself from Dublin Command and establishing what amounted to a separate Northern Command. This enabled the Belfast Brigade to engage with people outside the movement, with the local Citizens Committees, and with a range of sympathisers outside the ambit of Republicanism willing to help the community in its defence.

In December 1969 the IRA split at the Army Convention over the issue of ending abstention from the 'Partition parliaments'. The group that left and formed the 'Provisional Army Council' was composed of traditional Sinn Fein Anti-Treatyites opposed to taking seats in Leinster House. Belfast was not involved in the split since by agreement the Belfast Brigade agreed not to attend the Convention. Many Northern Republicans who supported an end to abstentionism in the South (e.g. Kevin Mallon) still went over to the new group whose position was an abstentionist one.

The split was completed at the Sinn Fein Ard Fheis in January 1970 where, although a motion proposing an end to abstention was defeated, another motion was introduced by the leadership to trump it by calling for "allegiance to the IRA leadership". As a result there was a walk-out and formation of Provisional Sinn Fein.

The group which broke away from the Official leadership accused it of being diverted from its National duty by involvement in irrelevant social issues; of being influenced by known Communists; and of not defending the Northern Catholics in their hour of need: In short, of being inappropriate to the situation that had developed and of being incapable of responding to it in a way that would advance the position of the community afterwards.

The Provisionals rejected the Marxism of the Officials as an *"alien ideology"* unsuited to the circumstances. This formulaic ideology, which was largely British in origin, had confused its adherents as to what they were supposed to be fighting for and disabled them from seizing the greatest, and perhaps never to return, opportunity to advance the Republican struggle and the general position of Northern Catholics. It led to the detachment of the Officials from purposeful activity and later resulted in their own half-hearted war going off at half-cock, and assuming the volatile and erratic character which characterised "Republican Socialism". The 'revolution' that never was, was lost.

The Republican leadership had been led to believe that the reintegration of the Republic with Britain was afoot in some kind of 'federal relationship', and they saw nothing contradictory in supporting the Stormont set-up as an obstacle to this process—while also holding to the Anti-Partitionist view. But in the aftermath of August things were reduced to their fundamentals in the North and the Officials were too concerned with the sophisticated theories they had developed in a different situation to identify what to do.

From the Officials' grandiose theory came the view that Fianna Fail was trying to buy their way into control of the Civil Rights Movement and were attempting to split the Republican movement to ensure no opposition to federalism took place. This fantasy, along with the British Marxism that the Officials had adopted, disabled them against the Provisionals' more firm practical grasp of the situation.

The Officials continued to see Civil Rights as the way forward in 1970 (as did some elements in the new grouping). But the Civil Rights Movement had achieved all it could at this stage and was well past its sell-by date. It could only be an aggravating force on things, fuelling further conflict of a communal character in the situation that had developed.

The New Republicanism

The Provisional IRA began as quite an ambiguous movement within the community during the winter of 1969-70.

The new Republican movement that August 1969 generated was not a manifestation of Anti-Treaty Republicanism—which had little impact in the North historically—but almost entirely, in its mass expression, a product of the 'Northern Ireland' political slum. The Provisionals were 'Made in Northern Ireland', not by Dublin or by Second Dail Republicanism.

Anti-Treaty Republicanism gained a new lease of life through association with the oppressed Northerners, but the new Republicanism began to slough off the Southern Anti-Treaty remnants once it had produced its own political leadership and taken command of the necessary logistical organisation and skills to maintain a war.

Within the new Republican development in the North some old Anti-

Treaty Republicans gained a new lease of life. But they were mostly just incidental attachments that provided continuity to the past and an all-Ireland dimension to what was fundamentally a Northern development. What was more significant was the development of structures to replace that which the State had withdrawn, and an all-Ireland network for the provision of materials needed for defence, when Dublin pulled the plug on the community.

The Northern Catholics, who had since 1922 been largely 'Constitutional' (or more accurately, peaceful) in their politics, aside from the protest voting for Sinn Fein in meaningless Westminster elections, started Republicanising themselves in 1970-1, under the impact of the situation. There was a great explosion in the popularity of Republican culture and the North began to produce it itself. Numerous Ballad groups sprang up to inspire the masses toward Republicanism, 'Rebel' songs were written and Free radio stations emerged playing them to connect the new development to history. But the ground of their Republicanism remained, for most of them, the experience of life in the 'Northern Ireland' statelet which the cultural revolution sought to place in Republican context.

Seamus Twomey, who led the Belfast Brigade after the introduction of Internment, in its most vigorous phase, told Simon Winchester of *The Guardian* in 1972 what the new Republicanism was all about:

"Here our people have suffered unemployment, job discrimination, housing discrimination and so on. They have had to emigrate or generally take a second place in this country for years and years... the opposition here at Stormont have been consistently laughed at over the years. None of their suggestions were ever taken up by the unionists. I know the violence of our campaign makes it sound contradictory, but this was the only way we had of bringing pressure on the British Government to realise just what was happening here. We had to do something to keep on hitting the headlines day after day" (*Guardian*, 24.7.72).

It was the conditions of life in the North that launched and gave the Provisionals their staying power and the memory of what Catholics had been subjected to for half a century since 1920. They did not depend on a National memory or some romantic idealism—although these were significant ingredients in forming the Republican character—but were continuously reinforced in their activities by everyday experience of the system.

And from the start Republicans sought increased British involvement to advance the prospects of their community, pending achievement of the final objective.

Building up a new Republican Army and organising it to fight a war against a formidable military power was no mean feat. It was actually something quite extraordinary. The general Catholic community that went into Insurrection against the Unionist regime in 1969 was not eager to engage in war against the British Government in 1970 and it was inclined to settle down again under the authority of the existing State, given half a chance, if that State made itself more reasonable to them.

It was only the British Government's use of its army to bolster its Unionist sub-government and to repress the Catholic agitation about the system that began to reveal to them that Whitehall was going to continue their imprisonment within the routine of subjugation. And it was when this became clear that the Republican project was able to succeed, from quite an unpromising initial position.

Character of Republicanism

An extraordinary thing happened in the middle of 1970 — a small nucleus of Republicans began to take the community in hand, give it a purpose and a direction, and set in motion the chain of events which led to a resurgence.

Lord Prof. Bew's statement that: "The Provisionals themselves were primarily the creation of the sectarian explosion in Belfast itself" (*Ireland, the Politics of Enmity, 1789-2006*, p.501) has the inference that the new Republican Army was a sectarian thing in itself. But whilst it would be accurate to say that the new Republican Army was a product of the sectarian pseudo-state of 'Northern Ireland' it would not be true to describe it as sectarian in its general political character.

Prof. Bew is himself partly a product of Official Republicanism—before he became advisor to Ulster Unionism and then went to the House of Lords. And it is an article of faith in Official Republicanism that the Provisionals were a sectarian deviation from True Republicanism, who sectarianised the War and lost the revolution for Gardiner Street.

There are accounts from this time that describe the Officials as the "*socialist*" IRA and the Provisionals as the "*sectarian*" IRA. They are nonsense. If there was a difference within Republicanism, it was in the Provisionals' grasp of the reality of the situation with regard to the Protestant community. The Official IRA pontificated about the Protestants being "*brother Irishmen*" who would return to the ideals of their forefathers in the United Irishmen. The Provos, although they aspired to such ideals, knew this to be wishful thinking and not a sound basis for politics.

The Provisionals realised that the Protestant community had a will that was separate from the Irish National one. They were a separate nation in Ireland—although it was not really politic to describe them as such. But it was clear that that was understood by those who constituted the Provos and they determined to deal with this problem through force, by breaking that will, shattering it in the interests of forceful nation-building.

The Provos had a programme called *Eire Nua* that promised a separate 9 County Ulster Parliament to the Northern Protestants in the event of them finding themselves in a United Ireland. *Eire Nua* described it as follows:

"The Unionist orientated people of Ulster would have a working majority within the Province (in a federal parliament, Dail Uladh) and would therefore have considerable control over their own affairs. That power would be the surest guarantee of their civil and religious liberties within a new Ireland" (p.56).

Why concede such a thing if the people the concession was being made to were not seen as distinct and wishing to live their lives in a different way? It makes no sense if they were not seen as constituting something separate from the rest of the island.

It is clear that the Provisionals saw from the start that the Ulster Protestants stood apart from the Irish Nation and had to be forced into it by a disorganising of their separate will. But it was not politic to describe them as a separate entity/nation lest the other alternative came to the fore and it was concluded that only their expulsion would solve the problem. That would unleash a sectarianism that would go against general Republican principle — so the Provos acted in one way but sustained an ideology above their War that generally insulated the war-making from the sectarian impulse of the general society within which they existed.

The separate Protestant will would have been obvious to those who experienced it, with complicating implications. Brendan Hughes, an early volunteer of the new Republicanism, later described how in the winter of 1969-70, he was taken in hand by Republicans of the old school and given an ideological perspective on the life he experienced in the Six Counties:

"... Most of us at that time did not have a great deal of political ideology. It wasn't until later that we really began to learn what republicanism meant. We were motivated by the fact that Catholic homes and streets had been burned down, that Catholics had been forced out of their homes. People like me, who joined what was later called the Provisional IRA, were the people who had been rioting for over a year, who burned lorries, who had come under fire from the Shankill Road, who had seen people shot. They had been fighting with petrol bombs and stones and whatever else they could lay their hands on. These were the people who were defending the areas, the people who were defending the Catholic Church, who were defending against the B Specials. They were like I was, the night _____ fired his Thompson over the head of the loyalist mob from the roof of St. Comgall's school; they would have wanted to fire into the crowd instead. So most of us would have been—reactionary it might be the wrong word—but I mean, that would be close enough. The older Republicans like McKee, MacAirt and the rest, saw all this as an opportunity for another war against England. The British were now on the streets and this was an opportunity to take them on... but, at the same time, for a lot of us, it was a big adventure" (Ed Moloney, *Voices from the Grave,* pp. 47-8).

Hughes noted that the ideological perspective of Republicanism was very important in giving recruits to the new Republican Army, and the wider community within which they operated, a higher purpose that prevented them from acting out of reflex in relation to the other community. He recalls one incident just after the events of August 1969:

> "In 1969 when whole streets were burnt out, I found myself in a sort of conflict... most of my friends were Protestants. And here Protestants were burning out Catholics... So, in 1969, when the rioting started on the Grosvenor Road where I lived and homes were attacked, I was conflicted. Protestant homes were attacked around Malt Street and so forth. Now, the IRA split had not taken place at that point. The...IRA were on the ground around the Leeson Street area, trying to contain the riots. And I remember coming off the Falls road and joining a gang that was headed along Cullingtree Road toward Malt Street which was seen as the centre of Loyalism in that period. People's blood was up; they were angry and it was decided that Protestant homes should be attacked. Around 100 to 250 men were heading towards Malt Street, when we were stopped by the IRA... and stopped from going in to burn the houses out. But there was a conflict within me at the time—I was with the mob, ok, but I was sort of relieved when we were stopped... " (pp.18-9)

Sectarian warfare could have been the inevitable consequence after the Unionist sub-government had sent its shock troops in against the Falls and Bogside. At that point any practical legitimacy the statelet might have had went down the pan and everything was in the air.

Peadar O'Donnell, an idealistic socialist Republican in the 1930s, called the Northern IRA a "battalion of armed Catholics". But what else could they be?

Before Partition, Joe Devlin, the leader of Nationalism in Ulster, had moulded Belfast into a hub of Hibernianism in order to secure Imperial Home Rule. And Redmondism lasted a lot longer in the North because it was cut off from the National development that the Twenty-Six Counties underwent through Sinn Fein, the Treaty War and the De Valera era. Hibernian Nationalism of the AOH variety was very much the substance of Northern Nationalism in the half century after Partition. So, in 1969, after the security forces had went berserk against Derry and West Belfast, everything was making for the sort of thing that has later happened in Iraq under US/UK supervision.

West Belfast had developed through Devlin Hibernianism and it had many remnants of the British Imperial outlook. At one time, Joe Devlin and his Party had made the two one and the same. In the 1930s Peadar O'Donnell described it as Hibernian (which usually means Catholic-sectarian). West Belfast only became Republican as a consequence of the Unionist attack on it in August 1969 and the War that followed. Initially, it threw up an army of former Imperials for its defence—that became the Catholic Ex-Servicemen's Association (CESA)—a reminder that the traditional military expression of the Falls Road was not the Irish Republican Army, but the British Army (See Volume One for an explanation and description of the origin of this). And there was a large number of families active within the new Republicanism whose previous generations had given Imperial service or had close relations in the British Army.

The new Republican Army developed behind the barricades in West Belfast in 1969-70 out of a small Republican nucleus. The Provisional IRA became more relevant to the situation than the CESA, and thrived because the Unionist statelet took it to be the more natural phenomenon of the two.

By Republicanism giving individuals and the Catholic community at large a higher mission than the fundamental conflict that they would have engaged in, a pure sectarian war was avoided and energies were channelled into a much greater political objective with wider horizons. Combative activity was primarily directed against that which was responsible for the predicament of the Northern Catholics, namely the British State, rather than those who were charged with playing the role of instruments of its maintenance.

This Republican purpose had much to do with something that was later ridiculed—the higher political pretensions of Republicanism, of the Republic of 1919-21, which enabled it to view itself as the original and legitimate independent Irish State.

It was perfectly possible that a gang of armed Hibernians could have emerged on the Catholic side after the events of August 1969 as a mirror image to the Protestant side. However, one of the achievements of Republicanism was in marshalling to a higher political cause the material produced by the conditions of life within the breeding ground of sectarianism that might have been predisposed to the kind of thing seen in loyalism. The disciplined military structures perfected by the new Republican Army provided the means by which those with a vigorous political—or purely military—disposition could channel their efforts into a strict targeting of the British State interest and, at the same time, deter others that might emerge and consider departing from the main political disposition and principles of Republicanism.

What might have become a sectarian morass on the Catholic side, resembling the Protestant paramilitaries, was averted by the directing of energies into purposeful military activity with focused political objectives. The Provos, by and large, conducted a disciplined War in a situation where sectarian slaughter may well have been the more instinctive and natural activity.

The alternative to the Republican Army would have been a kind of armed Hibernianism. The political set-up of 'Northern Ireland' had all the potential for sectarian war—even though it was designed to encourage and facilitate sectarian conflict within the controlled medium of the Protestant community policing of the Catholics.

In the moment of crisis the Northern Catholics, left to their fate in the communal pressure-cooker of the Stormont system, abandoned by Dublin under British pressure, were taken in hand by Republicanism. Some of the Provo leadership were the people who had taken part in the fifties campaign and some were young Northerners who eventually took over. But both were informed by the idealism of what Eoghan Harris, the Official Republican who became a bitter critic of the new Republicanism, once described as "the most basic myths of modern Irish republicans" (*Sunday Independent* 17.12.06).

Some of what Harris called "the most basic myths of modern Irish republicans" were the very things that kept the Republican War on a higher plane.

Sometimes "*basic myths*" are historical imperatives of good order. That is what Robespierre realised during the height of the Revolution in France. He saw that the reckless anti-clericalism of the revolutionaries was leading to a pillar of stability being removed—namely God. So, although he had little time for God himself, he tried to make sure the masses had a 'Supreme Being' to keep their feet firmly on the ground. And Robespierre was a favourite of the Belfast United Irish paper, *The Northern Star*, if I recall correctly.

If these "*basic myths of modern Irish republicans*" had been removed, if Harris and his associates had succeeded in obliterating the Irish National culture of Republicanism, what framework did he think the Northern Catholics would operate within when they were provoked into activity by the process of communal attrition they were subject to? I would suggest that it would be a kind of armed Hibernianism that would produce a lot more sectarian events than actually occurred.

Harris later pronounced that "the truth we have to face is that every generation of the IRA—with the exception of the Dublin directed fifties campaign—engaged in sectarian slaughter" (Sunday Independent 17.12.06)

But isn't it strange that if the IRA was motivated primarily by sectarianism, produced by their own extreme Catholic-Nationalism, they should be least sectarian when they were most Catholic and Nationalist?

The Border campaigning IRA of the 1950s—people like Sean South, Daithi O'Connell and Ruari O'Bradaigh—were Republicans and Catholics of the deepest hue. They said their decades of the rosaries before and after military operations and came from a society that had reached the zenith of its Catholic and Anti-Partitionist development. And they gave up their lives, in one way or another, to its great unfinished business—recapturing the Fourth Green Field. Their like, as they say, will not be seen again.

And yet this generation—the most Catholic-Nationalist—was the only "generation of the IRA" who were not "*engaged in sectarian slaughter*".

The 1956-62 Campaign had all the character of a small invasion by the Southern IRA. It had a very minimal participation from within John Bull's Political Slum. This fact suggests that sectarianism and "*sectarian slaughter*" has another progenitor, rather than Irish Republicanism, as such. Could it be found in the political innovation called 'Northern Ireland' by any chance?

History is meaningless outside of context. The thematic and sociological approach favoured by 'post modern' Irish historians removes the historical context and makes any notion palatable, notions that would be absurd within their actual historical chain of causation.

In 1970-2 the new Republican Army trained hundreds of people who could have become purposeless sectarian killers into a disciplined and purposeful fighting force, clear in ideals and disinclined to become diverted into communal conflict.

The Provos declared War on the British State and made particular efforts to direct their War against the forces of that State. Unfortunately for the Provos the Six Counties were not held directly by the British State. In return for being a semi-detached annex of the British State the Ulster Unionists were given the state security apparatus which interposed themselves between Britain and the Northern Catholics.

Fianna Fail and the IRA

In the 'Ireland' volume of the '*Oxford History of Modern Europe*' Prof. Bew writes:

> "The Provisionals themselves were primarily the creation of the sectarian explosion in Belfast itself—but it is not in doubt that the early rapid strengthening of the movement owed much to support from leading figures in the Fianna Fail Government, some of them concerned to head off the socialist radicalism of the 'official' IRA" (*Ireland, the Politics of Enmity, 1789-2006*, p.501)

And in his book '*Ireland Since 1939*' Prof. Patterson says:

> "Both Blaney and Boland favoured sending Irish troops across the border

into Derry and Newry, but the majority of their colleagues recoiled in horror from this lunatic counsel... But if the invasion option was rejected, Lynch appears to have been powerless to prevent some of his ministers from sponsoring what became a serious attempt to subvert partition by forming an alliance with those northern republicans who were to become the nucleus of the Provisional IRA" (p.172)

The Official Republican version of history is die-hard and it has its continued hold-outs in academia as well as in the House of Lords.

There is a sleight of hand going on in these passages in an attempt to connect the 'backwoodsmen' of Fianna Fail with the growth of the Provisional IRA.

Firstly, how could the Fianna Fail 'backwoods' know that they were creating the Provisional IRA as we know it from subsequent events? How were they to envisage all the events that went into its making—that could have been so different and led to completely different scenarios if different things had been done?

Prof. Patterson uses the words "*nucleus of the Provisional IRA*" to describe the group that the Fianna Fail "*Alliance*" was made with. This nucleus already existed and had existed since the 1920s. There was always an IRA nucleus in Belfast and it was not a creation of Fianna Fail in 1969. The Fianna Fail "*Alliance*" was actually made with the Defence Committees —which might or might not have contained present or future Republicans; who was to tell?

The important question is, how was the Provisional Army Council enabled to grow from a nucleus to develop into the new Republican Army. And Haughey, Blaney and Boland had nothing to do with that process, having been cut off by Lynch well before it occurred.

Chronology needs to be looked at to get at the truth of this: Half way through 1970, after Charles Haughey had been sacked and the Arms Crisis launched by Taoiseach Lynch, there was still not much evidence of the existence of the Provisional IRA. Until the last week of June no one had been killed in the Six Counties all year and there had only been a couple of dozen minor bomb attacks—nearly all in Belfast. Most of these, judging by the targets, had been the work of loyalists, who had also attacked targets in the Republic. There was a great deal of confusion over the bombings in Belfast and 'agent-provocateurs' were often blamed. If a character is ascribed to these incidents it was that of an extension of the inter-communal street violence of the summer of 1969 through the use of crude explosives by micro-groups. No attacks were made on security forces, the main thrust of Republican operations later on.

Back in November 1969 *The United Irishman*, paper of the Officials/ Stickies, carried "*an exclusive story*" of what it called "*The Fianna Fail

Attempted Takeover of the Northern CRA" describing a situation where: "These Fianna Fail politicians are doing their best to disrupt Civil Rights and anti-Unionist forces which are politically embarrassing to them."

Why the Civil Rights campaign was embarrassing to Fianna Fail was not explained but if the Irish Government were disrupting the Civil Rights organisation in any way it was in the same way as the Republicans were meddling in it—in encouraging an Anti-Partitionist character so that reforms would not take the wind out of its sails.

A year and a half later the *United Irishman* was more specific in its accusation toward Fianna Fail: "The Provisional Alliance was created after Fianna Fail's failure to subvert the IRA and Sinn Fein, in order to develop a violent situation in which true Republicanism would be lost" (June 1972).

The Sinn Fein President, Tomas MacGiolla, said:

> "As early as February 1969 the Dublin government had begun their part of the imperialist plan by making their first contact with Republicans and Civil Rights workers in the North. Following the August pogroms they intensified their work on much more fertile ground. By concentrating on those Belfast Republicans who saw their role as Catholic defence groups and by playing on their latent sectarianism and militarist desires, they created a split amongst Republicans in Belfast and offered money and guns to those who would reject the leadership of the Republican Movement. Thus the Provisionals were born."

This is a case of fitting facts to wishful thinking. That is because there is another way of looking at the same events and coming up with a much more plausible explanation. A look at the actual sequence of events suggests that the Officials' tale was a story invented to cover up their own embarrassment and political incompetence.

Before *The United Irishman* ran its exposé and the Officials mounted a news conference at the Gresham Hotel on 30th October 1969 to publicise the *"Fianna Fail attempts to destroy the Republican Movement and buy their way into the Civil Rights movement"* a story on similar lines had appeared in the London Evening Standard on 14th October. This story was written by Tom Pocock, who had previously met Roy Johnston in Dublin.

The first contacts Fianna Fail made with the IRA after the August events were with the Goulding leadership on 17th August when the Chief of Staff was given a £1,500 advance on a promised £50,000. The only proviso was the guns should only be used in the North. That was a wholly understandable request—the guns were meant for Catholic defence in the North and the Irish Government did not want them used in labour disputes, fund-raising or 'revolutionary' activities south of the Border. That is hardly heading off *"socialist radicalism"*—which was easily handled by Fianna Fail in those days and was really about the first duty of Government, to protect its state against insurrection.

Padraic (Jock) Haughey (Charlie's brother) personally delivered a consignment of weapons from England to Cathal Goulding in September 1969, brought into Dublin on a commercial flight. Padraic collected the arms consignment of two boxes of about 40 or so short arms in a van and delivered them to the IRA in Dublin. This fact was well known in the North and questions were asked as to why they were not released for service there by Goulding. Up to 3 arms consignments were ferried through Dublin Airport by Jock Haughey to the Republicans under Goulding. In November a planned assignment had to be abandoned after it was the object of a British Intelligence sting operation.

Captain Kelly's contacts with Goulding and his men continued well after the establishment of an alternative Republican grouping in Belfast and the Irish Army Intelligence Officer was in regular contact with the IRA Chief of Staff. And money was provided to the "Officials" even as they were airing their allegations of a Fianna Fail plot to split the movement and after, up to January 1970 at least (see Matt Treacy, *The IRA 1956-69, Rethinking the Republic*, pp. 173-5, for confirmation of this.)

It seems that the Officials were actually playing a double game. After the story had been fed by the "Officials" to The London *Evening Standard*, an explanation for the dealings with the Fianna Fail Government had to be concocted that portrayed the Republican Socialists with clean hands, resisting the embrace of the *"Green Tories"* and their gifts. However, the contacts and arms were accepted all the time.

When it is suggested that Fianna Fail armed the Provisionals, the attempt to utilise the military structures of the existing IRA for Catholic defence is forgotten. But it suggests that Dublin was not interested in splitting the IRA or creating an IRA—only utilising any body of men that might be able to organise and defend the Catholic communities in the North effectively.

It was also not these initiatives that created the Provisionals in the form that emerged but Lynch's drastic *volte face* in April/May 1970.

The 'Official Republicans' (whose view still permeates Irish life through Eoghan Harris and other comrades who have withdrawn to the media and metamorphosed into strange political manifestations in academia and politics) put the idea about through their influential propaganda positions that the Fianna Fail Government created the Provisionals because it feared the revolutionary Marxism of the Official leadership. The disgraced Generals of the Official IRA grandiosely called them the *"Provisional Alliance"*, which they loved to think was being artificially constructed in the North, as the cat's paw of the *"Green Tories"* in Fianna Fail, to head off the Officials' imminent *"socialist revolution"*.

It was all fantasy, of course, and it was bound to end in tears—and then loathing of those who captured Republicanism and made it something substantial through acting purposefully on the events in the North.

The Officials represented no threat to the Irish State in 1969. They aggravated that State by their attacks on German farms and property in Ireland but in all other respects they were a force in decline. Their membership had shown no increase in numbers through 1969, their finances were in a poor state, the print run of *The United Irishman* had declined by over half in the year from 1968, and the Easter 1969 Republican commemorations had been even smaller than usual, despite the tension in the North.

Were the *"revolutionaries"* so different from the *"Green Tories"*? The Sinn Fein President saw things in the traditional way from Dublin—actually in the way Fianna Fail saw them. The Northerners were an appendage of the Nation that had established itself in the 26 Counties and they could be directed as desired. He does not allow for Northern independence of mind and refuses to accept that the Catholics in Belfast had a real need for defence that overrode all the fancy ideas that Southern Sinn Fein had developed to resurrect itself.

"Militarist desires" were a given in Belfast Republicanism. It was a small rump of a much larger community that believed only force could end the Catholic predicament in the North. The events of August made it relevant to the situation it had always perceived in a certain way and it was determined to take its chance whilst the opportunity knocked.

It was all very well talking about "latent sectarianism" from Dublin, from within a state that had managed to establish a party politics of state that overcame such things and had integrated its citizens of all religions into national political structures. Belfast's "latent sectarianism" was a given. Republicans there were a product of the sectarian pseudo-state established in 1921 on the basis of a sectarian head-count that had frozen communal politics into the very marrow of things. Republicans there could not help but be influenced by its communal structures. But they also had the desire to overcome them through Republicanism.

Around 1985 the late Danny Burke, an IRA volunteer from Galway, told the present writer that, in the August aftermath, when his unit had been moved up to the Border, he had been commanded to attack Protestant targets to create diversions, by a leading member of the Official command. Having a Republican outlook Danny resigned soon after in disgust.

British or Irish Responsibility?

The Sinn Fein President could not help but blame Britain for what happened. MacGiolla was Sinn Fein President after all! But there are the seeds of revisionism in his blame game that gradually flourished into the view that the blame lay more fully in Dublin than in London. And the development from Sinn Fein to Sinn Fein the Workers Party to the Workers Party to the Democratic Left to joining the Labour Party can be detected at its origin. The names changed but the anti-Provo fundamentals remained the same. And from there it was only a short step from taking the view that there was also something rotten in the state of independent Ireland.

Actually, the Provisionals and the War in the North arose directly out of the undemocratic mode of British government there. The Irish State had no responsibility for them. But Dublin did facilitate the rise of the new Republican force by its policy, or rather by its drastic change of policy, during the six months after August 1969.

Britain, which had actual sovereignty over 'Northern Ireland' avoided responsibility for it in 1969-70 and the Republic, which asserted sovereignty over it in Articles 2 and 3 of its Constitution, backed away from taking up responsibility for it, under British influence. And in doing this Dublin not only disrupted the North but came also to ultimately disrupt itself.

The 1969 Pogrom destabilised everything in the North, and brought all major political tendencies in the Republic into active engagement with the North for the first time in generations. The masses were also roused into a range of activity. Nearly everyone became a 'Republican' and very few, outside the North, would have disagreed with Jack Lynch's speech.

The War that followed, which lasted for 28 Years, might possibly have been averted, even in the situation where the British Government abandoned West Belfast to its own devices. The Republic could have contained and moulded the Northern Catholic response to the events of August 1969 even though it had no means of suppressing its response. But Lynch was unwilling to finish what he started when a degree of British pressure was applied to him.

What subsequently occurred might have been averted by the Southern Establishment if it had resolutely kept up the position it assumed in August 1969. But, in the period from April 1970 the Southern political establishment went into a confusion after being found out by the British to have been up to something—exercising an independent policy with regard to the North.

The first evidence for this is contained in a confidential telegram sent by the British Ambassador, Andrew Gilchrist, to London in November 1969, describing how he confronted the Taoiseach with the fact that he had knowledge of what had been going on:

> "Towards the end of the interview, after Lynch had made a remark about the need for British troops to break up the extremist arsenal in the Shankill road, I reminded him of the need for the south also to keep its nose clean. It has come to my notice that there were alleged to be activities on this side of the frontier which, if reported back to the people in Stormont, whom he had

just criticised, would strengthen them in their suspicion of the Republic and furnish them with arguments in support of their old-fashioned attitude. I had no reliable information whatever on what if anything was actually going on; my concern was with the rumours, some of them plausible enough on the surface, and with the political effects which might arise from them. Lynch at first denied all knowledge of the rumours, even when I mentioned the word 'Monaghan'; but rather gave himself away by asking if the rumours might relate to activities by a certain number of his Cabinet... I said such a name had been mentioned, and we left it at that, with the promise by Lynch to look into the whole matter." (PRO FCO 33 759)

A previous telegram of Gilchrist's outlines the information that he had obtained, some from Conor Cruise O'Brien, concerning the activities of the Minister of Finance in Monaghan on behalf of the Government. Gilchrist knew that a body had been set up by Haughey with party funds containing an Intelligence unit with Irish Army Intelligence officers and a propaganda unit attached. Plans were ready for the quick support of the Northern Defence Committees in the North by way of weapons and personnel. Numerous weapons had been supplied already across the Border for defensive purposes (PRO FCO 33 759. See Angela Clifford, *The Arms Conspiracy Trial*, pp. 556-97 for the British diplomatic record relating to this period).

The British Embassy had a very different relationship with the Irish Republic than it had with other foreign states. The Dublin Embassy had reported to the British Commonwealth Office rather than the Foreign Office up until October 1968—20 years after the Republic had come into official existence. So it would have still had a colonial attitude to the Irish Government at this time, feeling its advice should be taken and acted upon for both the good of Britain and of its client. That is the role Ambassador Gilchrist would undoubtedly have taken for himself in relation to Taoiseach Lynch. And it seems that Lynch did not disavow him and came to reciprocate.

Taoiseach Lynch did not alter course at this time but he must have been aware then that the British were on to him and his Government. He maintained his course until events in April 1970 ultimately brought things to a head. That can be seen in the Irish Government's reaction to the trouble in Ballymurphy at the start of April 1970.

The Ballymurphy Watershed?

Thirty years after the events of August 1969 two articles appeared upon release of the 1970 Southern State Papers. They were penned by David Trimble's chief advisers, Prof. Bew and Steven King. Bew, in a piece in the *Sunday Independent* and King in a column in the *Belfast Telegraph* said the same thing about the events of 1969-70.

The gist of the Bew/King argument was that the origin of the 28 Year War could be found in Nationalist conduct in early 1970 rather than in Unionist conduct in August 1969. The argument was that the Provos got organised with Dublin Government assistance in a period of calm and generous British reform of the system:

> "The army found itself most often in confrontation with loyalists... The civil rights agenda had had either been accomplished or was well on its way to being so in May, 1970. Troops were already being sent back to England as tensions subdued... Meanwhile... despite Jack Lynch attacking 'those who preach force and military action' in January, directions were given to the Irish army on February 6, 1970 to prepare for incursions into Northern Ireland... While the Provisionals were stoking resentments that went way beyond reasonable Catholic grievances, some clearly anticipating an opportunity to press the constitutional issue too..." (BT 3.1.01,*Irish Political Review*, February 2001).

The subsequent military campaign was, therefore, unjustified by the grievances suffered. August 1969 had been superseded and it was taken as an event of no consequence. It was over and reform had set in. Things were settling down again until trouble was stirred up by Dublin and the Provos.

This argument was to be repeated in Prof. Bew's *Politics Of Enmity*:

> "The Provisionals themselves were primarily the creation of the sectarian explosion in Belfast itself—but it is not in doubt that the early rapid strengthening of the movement owed much to support from leading figures in the Fianna Fail government, some of them concerned to head off the socialist radicalism of the 'official' IRA, the Provisionals' challengers for support in West Belfast. It seems likely, for example, that the Dundalk weapons were intended for Ballymurphy, where the IRA was engaging the British army in three nights of serious rioting" (Ireland, *The Politics of Enmity*, p.501)

If Dublin is to be held responsible in any way for the 28 Year War that followed, its responsibility comes only after that of the British Government and the Unionists is first taken into account. That is to say, if the British Government and Unionists had not acted in the way they did first of all, anything the Dublin Government did would have been inconsequential. Britain did everything it could to prevent Dublin intervention in the North. And it was only in the context of the conditions the British and their Stormont sub-government established and operated that Dublin could act.

While there is some truth in the view that the Dublin Government was responsible for the Provos, it was not in the way that Prof. Bew and King argue. The Provos were set on a new course after Lynch left Northern defenders in the lurch.

There is much scoffing at the unpreparedness of the Irish Army by the Unionist advisors. Dublin, they suggest, obviously was deterred from direct intervention by the fact that the British Army was a large and powerful army and would undoubtedly respond with force, as it did to Collins venture across the Border in 1922. Also, direct action might have provoked the massacre of Catholics in isolated areas. The South was saturated with Anti-Partitionist ideology but there was not an aggressive militarist state south of the Border, champing at the bit to engage in a war. Any intervention would have been prompted by a possible overwhelming of Catholic areas. Its military intention in 1969-70 was for an incursion/small invasion to lead to an internationalisation of the situation or a partnership with Britain in solving it.

In many other areas of the world where there are territorial disputes there have been frequent armed clashes between states in dispute. Ukraine/Russia, Pakistan/India and many parts of the Middle East spring to mind. But since 1922 there has been no armed conflict between the Irish and British states in Ireland. In fact, as was the case in 1956-62, the Southern State, and in particular Charles Haughey, took an active part in repressing Republicans engaged in armed actiity from an Irish base.

In 1969, unlike in 1956, a new development occurred that was wholly a product of an area outside the territory of the 26 Counties. An embryonic Northern Catholic centre of power began to emerge and develop under the auspices of the British/Ulster Unionist area of responsibility. And it was in its sharply alternating dealings with this product of the Six Counties that Dublin really messed up.

In the aftermath of 1969-70, just one area in Belfast, New Barnsley, saw its Protestant population evacuated with Catholic refugees living in Ballymurphy taking over the vacated houses. Prof. Bew and Stephen King advanced the idea that the Ballymurphy conflict with the British Army and the New Barnsley evacuation of 1970 constituted a Protestant Bombay Street in reverse, with the Catholic Ballymurphy residents deliberately driving out the Protestants of New Barnsley. But the situations were very different.

The Unionist sub-government's security forces attack on the citizens of its territory in August 1969 had a significant effect on the communal distribution of population in Belfast. At that point apart from the main areas of Protestant and Catholic occupation, there were enclaves of Protestants and Catholics in adjacent areas. But, after August 1969, people were expecting further attacks and sought shelter and security amongst their own. In that situation large numbers of displaced Catholic families found themselves being given shelter and protection in Ballymurphy, across the road. The evacuation of Protestants from New Barnsley in 1970, conducted extravagantly by Paisleyites to make a political point, occurred in the general sorting out of territory that came in the wake of fears of a second August 1969. But local factors also came into play.

The housing allocation of New Barnsley, and Lenadoon further south, was an attempt by the Unionist Government to hem in the Catholics of West Belfast to a confined area, probably for electoral purposes or in the hope they would emigrate. A more realistic division would have been along the course of the Forth River, where there was a lot of waste ground. But that would have conceded all of the area of Springmartin to Catholics and allowed for their natural growth—a thing the Unionist Party was dead against, wanting to maintain the majority that their continued existence depended on.

Looking at any map of the area one can see the problem of a Protestant New Barnsley in early 1970. The Unionists, who had control of public housing in Belfast in the 1960s, had decided the dividing line between Catholic and Protestant West Belfast. New Barnsley was constructed across the road from the large Catholic estate of Ballymurphy, and it was allocated overwhelmingly to Protestants. Its housing standard was better than Ballymurphy's and that rankled with locals.

New Barnsley was doomed as a Loyalist/Protestant outpost along the top of Catholic West Belfast after August 1969. This was despite the fact that Catholics in the Ballymurphy estate went to some lengths to try to prevent the Protestants leaving by forming and maintaining a cross-community association to ease the tension.

There were 1300 Orange parades a year across the North with no account for Catholic sensibilities. Of course, to take into account Catholic sensibilities would have defeated the point of them. That sort of ritual taunting went off fairly peacefully before August 1969 (where many streets off the Falls and Grosvenor Roads were draped with extravagant loyal bunting for the Twelfth) but in the aftermath of the Pogrom it was seen as a massive provocation and invasion threat.

In this delicate situation New Barnsley Protestants went against all advice by being the source of a provocative Orange March along the front of the Springfield Road across from Ballymurphy. The marchers were attacked on their return by angry residents from the Ballymurphy estate. Then the marchers and supporters from New Barnsley acted in a lunatic manner towards Ballymurphy by invading the estate behind a Scottish regiment of the British Army who were sent into it to sort out the Catholics. Both the Citizens Defence Committee and local Provisionals tried to calm matters but to no avail. The first significant confrontation between Catholics and the British Army took place and there were such fears in Dublin that a massacre might occur that rifles were moved up to the Border for rapid transit to Ballymurphy.

This incident made the position of New Barnsley as a Protestant enclave in a Catholic area untenable. There was a territorial sorting out along the Upper Springfield with Catholic families leaving Springmartin and Highfield on the same weekend that Protestants left New Barnsley and Moyard. There is no comparison whatever with Bombay Street where Catholic residents were subject to an unprovoked attack and burnt out. In seeking to make such a comparison, Prof. Bew is using his academic credentials to give authority to what is essentially a partisan debating point.

What these events showed was how big an effect August 1969 had had on the situation. Before it, Catholic and Protestant working-class housing estates could be built across the road from each other and the Twelfth celebrated flamboyantly by mainly-Protestant streets in a swaggering manner. Catholics kept their heads down in deference to the supremacist activity of their neighbours: But, no longer, after August 1969.

In August 1969 the old world was shattered, and O'Neill's brave new world crumbled. And afterwards it was unsafe to live in close proximity to the other side without fortifications being built for mutual protection. The communal blocs were entrenched and the War was on.

Despite what Prof. Bew and Stephen King say there was no Provisional attempt to instigate trouble in an area where arms training was proceeding and a relationship of convenience had been constructed with the British Army to facilitate non-interference.

There was something of a feud shortly after the Ballymurphy affair, when a member of the Official IRA fired a shot at a soldier and the Provisionals did not take kindly to it. Informal arrangements for the preservation of order in Ballymurphy and other Catholic areas remained in existence between British and Republican Army commanders until February 1971.

It was the sectarian conflict latent in the 'Northern Ireland' system, intensified by the events of August 1969, and the actions of the British Army, for the first time acting explicitly as the instrument of Orangeism/Stormont, that brought about the confrontation between Catholics and the British Army that facilitated the rise of the new Republican Army.

CHAPTER 5

Dublin's About Turn

In the Spring of 1970 Taoiseach Lynch lost his nerve over the activist policy he had instructed State functionaries to pursue. He had been rumbled by the British and elements within the Irish State that were prepared to act on behalf of Britain. He ordered an about turn, signalled by the arrest of those who were pursuing his previous policy, leading to the Arms Trials. This drastic alteration of policy not only had the effect of hanging out to dry those who believed they were pursuing the Taoiseach's policy but also the Northern minority to which it was directed.

The revolutionary effect of this was to negate Dublin's influence in the North and produce a vacuum behind the barricades in a situation which had already been constituted into a vacuum by Westminster's previous behaviour. The Northern Catholics were suddenly left 'all dressed up and nowhere to go'. They were abandoned as in 1922 after the death of Michael Collins, and left to the mercy of 'Northern Ireland'.

But the Northern Catholics did something different this time around. They availed of the solidarity produced within them by the events of the previous two years and they emerged in independent substance as never before. They looked within themselves to deal with their predicament and decided to run with it. And that was how Dublin was the cause of what was to spring from the ashes of Bombay Street.

A 'Republican Plot'?

Here is the version of events that has become commonplace in recent histories of the period known as the 'Arms Crisis':

> "After de Valera's retirement... Lemass had... promoted a policy of engagement with the government in Belfast, something eschewed by his predecessor. Lemass's successor, Jack Lynch, had maintained his moderation in relations with Northern Ireland and London but the onset of the crisis of the northern state in 1968 created a resurgence of a more traditional republican agenda in Fianna Fail as leading members of the party used northern events to mobilise support for a challenge to Lynch's leadership. This culminated in an attempt by Charles Haughey, Minister of Finance, and a cabal of 'republican' ministers to import arms to be given to the IRA to defend vulnerable Catholic communities in the North. Although Lynch fired the ministers who were subsequently put on trial, the 'Arms Crisis' left a bitter

legacy in the party where many members were sympathetic to the plotters and wanted a tougher line on using the crisis in Northern Ireland to 'complete the national revolution'..." (Henry Patterson, *'Deeply anti-British'? The Irish State and Cross-border Security Cooperation 1970-1974*, p.2).

It has been shown in Volume One that this version of history is seriously mistaken about Lemass. And it is wrong about virtually everything else as well—although becoming the accepted version of things in the South for purposes that apparently suit all.

Prof. Dermot Keogh of Cork subscribes to this white-wash, describing Taoiseach Lynch, advised by T.K. Whitaker, as having enacted a fundamental reorientation in the Twenty-Six County attitude to the Six Counties in the Fall of 1969. This 'reorientation' is seen as being opposed by Haughey the traditionalist, according to Keogh, who, for his treasonous actions was sent for trial, but was subsequently let off by a 'Republican' jury.

But there is little evidence of a fundamental re-orientation in Southern policy toward the North at this juncture. If there is a policy innovation at all it is in the Republican direction with the order to the Irish Army to prepare for military incursions in the North.

After the intervention of the British Ambassador in early 1970 there is then a reversion to the 'moderation' policy of giving out about Partition whilst doing very little about it.

Insider knowledge at the time was not necessary to see that Lynch's Government was doing things with guns which accorded with his speech about *"not standing (idly) by"*. And there is little doubt that Lynch's whole Cabinet was implicated in the new Irish military policy after August 1969. But in May 1970 the Taoiseach proceeded to sack and then prosecute a group of people for "conspiracy" who had, in fact, been implementing his own policy.

For 30 years it was possible to deny that it was his own policy that he prosecuted people for implementing. But with the release of secret documents after 2002 belief in Lynch's denial could no longer be made in good faith. (Those documents no longer merely lie in the National Archive, accessible only to people with an appetite for research. They have been published, along with newspaper reports of the Arms Trials—the official Court Transcript having been lost—in Angela Clifford's *The Arms Conspiracy Trial*.)

It is no longer deniable that Lynch instructed his Army to make itself ready for action in the North, and in the summer of 1970 it was his own policy that he actually prosecuted as subversive conspiracy.

The Retreat from the North

The Dublin Government probably intended to harness and lead a new political force from the Catholic Community, post-August 1969. This would have been an amalgamation of different elements from behind the barricades, including the Defence Committees, and any new political force that came out of Fianna Fail intervention would have been what could be described as 'semi-constitutional'.

However, the Arms Trials effectively aborted the possibility of such a development and instead the Provos, along with the SDLP, emerged from the ashes. The SDLP was mainly an electoral force in a situation where advancement through electoral politics was both irrelevant and impossible. The Provos were much more relevant to the raw fundamentals of the situation and went from strength to strength within it.

From mid-August 1969 until April 1970 the Dublin Government provided direct and indirect military assistance to the minority in the North. The Irish Army was instructed to make preparations for incursions across the Border and to distribute arms; public funds were allocated to purchase arms and ammunition; Captain Kelly was instructed to import weaponry to Ireland; Intelligence Officers were instructed to liaise with the defence organisations; public collections were openly allowed to finance the purchase of arms for the minority; cross-Border gun-running was permitted: some Irish Army weapons were allowed to find their way to the North and Northerners were given weapons training; a blind eye was turned to the training of men by others unconnected to the Irish State and a loan was raised in West Germany by Haughey to facilitate 'contingencies'.

On 27th September 1969 a meeting initiated by Fianna Fáil members was held in Lurgan in the North. It was attended by representatives of the Citizens Defence Committees. A provisional Central Committee was established at the meeting and on the following weekend another meeting established a controlling body for all the Northern Defence Committees. The CCDCs elected Hugh Kennedy of Bord Bainne as PRO. Captain Kelly of the Irish Army assured the meeting that the suspension of arms training in Donegal was just a temporary matter due to press stories and would be resumed shortly. He also confirmed that a military training camp would be established for weapons training for Northern nationalists. (This information is from Breasal O'Caollai, a Republican at the time, *Hibernia* December 1986)

The Irish Government also produced a booklet, '*Terror in Northern Ireland*' by Seamus Brady, for the CCDCs. Another pamphlet, '*Eye Witness in Northern Ireland*', was produced and launched in Dublin by Brady on October 5th. All were paid for out of State funds.

All evidence points to the fact that the Lynch Government pursued a particular activist policy towards the North up to the end of April 1970 and then there was a dramatic *volte-face*.

The Arms Crisis

It cannot have been the case that Lynch acted as a free agent in launching what became known as the Arms Crisis, which signalled a withdrawal from the North and an abandonment of the people there. He was undoubtedly put under pressure by the British and acted out of panic, for fear of embarrassment to the Irish State if it should be made public that the Government was implicated in providing military help to Catholic defence in the North.

What happened was that the British Ambassador, Andrew Gilchrist, supplied with briefings from his Intelligence services on Irish Government activity, required Lynch's Government to desist from the Northern policy it had embarked upon with the inflammatory speech of August 1969. (It is often forgotten how much effort Britain put into establishing listening posts and running agents in the South at this time, e.g. deploying the Littlejohns, and the penetration of the Gardai at many levels.)

Under the supervision of the Ambassador, Lynch aborted his Northern policy, broke up the apparatus developed to implement it, and produced scapegoats from his own Government and Army to explain it away.

The British Ambassador in Dublin first acted through Fine Gael, confronting it with evidence of gun running. Fine Gael then confronted Lynch and then there was a drastic failure of nerve and will on the part of the Twenty Six County political Establishment as a whole in relation to Britain and the North. This failure occurred when Britain decided to make an issue of what was in the circumstances a very reasonable and moderate policy. But the Dublin Establishment acted like naughty schoolboys caught out by their Master in an act of insolence against rightful authority. The Republic returned under British Government hegemony in mid-1970.

Lynch's Government had taken part in running guns to the Catholics in the North in the months after August 1969. That was a wholly reasonable policy in the circumstances which gave Dublin the chance of exerting leverage over the situation which had become very fluid and dangerous, particularly after the British Government had abandoned West Belfast to its own devices. But nine months later Lynch prosecuted his Government colleagues, Charlie Haughey and Neil Blaney (along with Captain James Kelly of his Army), for 'illegal' gunrunning—even though they had acted on his authority in running the guns to the North in the first place. (Also prosecuted were John Kelly of the Citizens Defence Committees and businessman Albert Luykx. It decided not to prosecute Kevin Boland for reasons which are only explicable on the view that Boland would have stuck to his guns and principles and spilt the beans about Cabinet discussions in such a way to seriously damage Taoiseach Lynch's damage limitation exercise. It can also be assumed that the prosecution against Blaney did not go beyond the District Court for similar reasons. The price paid by both Ministers was an end to their Cabinet careers)

The 'Arms Crisis' involved the treating of the failed importation of arms as a criminal act instigated by the two dismissed Ministers, Haughey and Blaney, along with Captain Kelly, in defiance of, or without the authority of, the Government. Neil Blaney, a brilliant Minister, though not a defendant in the Arms Conspiracy Trials was driven out of politics by Lynch. He had adhered to Fianna Fáil policy and paid the price with his career after the Taoiseach's change of direction.

It was clearly demonstrated in court, through cross-examination of Jim Gibbons, the Defence Minister, that what Haughey and Kelly did had been done on the authority of the Government and was not therefore illegal. And the jury who took the time to listen to all the evidence (unlike the Dublin media and even those who have written books on the subject since) found them Not Guilty.

Haughey was sacked from the Finance Ministry in May 1970 and subjected to two trials before, in the second, he was exonerated. The Arms Trial clearly demonstrated that the implementation of Government policy in the North had been delegated to Haughey and Gibbons and the Minister for Defence had in his Ministerial remit the legal power to authorise the import of arms, and had in fact authorised Captain Kelly's arms dealings.

What happened was not that Haughey, Gibbon and Kelly had gone beyond what Government policy had authorised them to do, but that Government policy had been changed by Lynch under British pressure, exerted by the British Ambassador in Dublin, and the change took the form of denying that the policy implemented by Haughey, Gibbon and Kelly had ever been Government policy.

Haughey, Blaney and Boland were the activist substance of Fianna Fail in 1969. Lynch was the PR man that they sent around the country in a caravan to win elections and who rode the National mood effectively. In 1970 the substance of Fianna Fail took their punishment in the National interest. It was a case of blame the scapegoats!

Haughey was made the chief scapegoat when Lynch backed down to Britain. But he accepted the role of scapegoat willingly. He might have taken a different course of action and this would have resulted in a very different outcome. However, he chose to play the role that was necessary to help dampen down the situation and lived to fight another day—as many others also did due to his pragmatic behaviour. And in view of his subsequent political and economic achievements for the Nation there should be no argument about the wisdom of his course.

Dublin's loss of nerve in bringing to trial Ministers for implementing their own Government's policy must have had detrimental effects in encouraging Britain to take a hand with Dublin. Britain would never have conducted its affairs in such an openly subservient and self-chastising way as Lynch proceeded to do in 1970. And this must surely have resulted in a loss of respect for Dublin as something independent in the world, a position that had been won by De Valera and his Ministers. From that moment Britain knew that the days of De Valera had gone and Ireland could be made to dance to England's tune again.

John Kelly on Captain Kelly

The reality of the situation was put in a Letter to the *Irish News* by John Kelly, who was intimately involved in the events. It was published on 25th August 2005, shortly after the death of Captain James Kelly (who Dublin Governments treated disgracefully for doing his duty), and provides a good feel for the effect of the Dublin Government's actions on the Northern Catholic community:

"The recent death in Dublin of Captain James Kelly closes another chapter in the arms crisis of 1970. That crisis, which went to the heart of the then Fianna Fail Government led by Jack Lynch, resulted in the sacking and arrest of two Government ministers (C.J. Haughey and Neil Blaney), Captain Kelly, myself and Albert Luykx. We were charged with conspiring to import arms to the north for the defence of northern nationalists. Our defence then and now was that this importation was done with Government approval. After two trials, the first being aborted by the prosecution because it wasn't going to their liking, a jury of our peers accepted the defence case that the importation had indeed had Government approval and we were acquitted.

"The then government—led by Jack Lynch—and subsequent Dublin governments refused to accept that verdict. From the end of that trial in 1970 Captain Jim Kelly fought a lonely battle to wring from the establishment a declaration that he had acted on orders from his military superiors and his political masters. It is a sad reflection on the state that Captain Kelly had to die before the state through the Taoiseach acknowledged that the captain had always acted honourably.

"Taoiseach Bertie Ahern said that at all times 'Captain Kelly acted on what he believed were the proper orders of his superiors. For my part, I have never found any reason to doubt his integrity'. Captain Kelly first came into the lives of that small group of northern nationalists who in August of 1969 were frantically trying to draw the caravans of defence around the Catholics of Belfast, Derry and the other endangered areas of the rural six counties. He did not come with a rattling sabre but with a conduit of hope, a prism of political light when northern nationalists were experiencing their darkest hour since partition. He came at a time when the forces of the state, supported by loyalist mobs, were burning Catholics from their homes, when Catholics were being fired upon by the same forces and some were being murdered. The six counties witnessed the greatest mass movement of refugees since the Second World War.

"There was no military flamboyance about Captain Kelly's mission. He was to quietly and speedily ascertain what was required in personnel and material to defend vulnerable nationalist areas in what was a potential doomsday situation for northern nationalists. Parallel to that mission he sought to bring together a consensus grouping of constitutional nationalism and physical force republicanism —the first time since partition that such a broadly based northern political consensus would be brought frequently to Dublin to meet ministers individually and collectively. These meetings sometimes included Taoiseach Jack Lynch. And all of these political engagements were under the aegis of Captain Kelly. The meetings were open and transparent—no darkened corridors.

"And there was no doubt in the minds of the northern delegations that the dark night of our political soul was ended and the Dublin government was taking possession of its constitutional imperative to be the first guarantor of our security and the safe conduct of our political future. Dublin would now use political and diplomatic pressure to ensure that the British would rein in the Orange state which acted in their name. Alas these hopes and expectations were to be dashed when that same Dublin government—which had encouraged us to entertain those expectations and hopes—sacked, arrested and put on trial two government ministers who were an essential part of the political engagements with northern nationalists together with Captain Jim Kelly, their military and political emissary to the northern nationalists.

"It seemed to us then and has been confirmed since that... political integrity was sacrificed for political expediency. It was also perhaps for northern nationalists the most singular act of betrayal since the foundation of the state, resulting as it did in the abandonment of northern nationalism to a British problem. And for 30 years we have suffered the brutal consequences of that abandonment.

"It was in this political context that Captain Jim Kelly fought for 30 years for his vindication which he also saw as a vindication of the story that might have been had the then Dublin government held its political nerve and not, as it seemed, succumbed to the political pressures and intrigues of another establishment. Captain Jim Kelly lived the last three decades with the rope of injustice of the establishment in Dublin around his neck...

"Captain Kelly was a brave man maligned by political expediency. He was an honourable soldier who served his country well in difficult and dangerous times. He deserves the applause of all the decent men and women of Ireland."

John Kelly's view that Lynch's actions, under pressure from the British Ambassador in 1970, represented *"the abandonment of northern nationalism to a British problem"* cannot be disputed. And his assertion that, as a result, *"for 30 years we have suffered the brutal consequences of that abandonment"* is the brutal truth of the matter.

This view is much nearer the truth than the attempts to canonize Jack Lynch for supposedly saving the Irish State for democracy in 1969-70. The 28 Year War in 'Northern Ireland' was, amongst other things, a product of Dublin's abandonment of West Belfast in 1969-70 and John Kelly, a traditional Republican who might have simply put it down to Ireland's long struggle for freedom, is clear about this.

Effects of the Taoiseach's *volte face*

Paddy Doherty noted from the Derry Bogside: "Lynch reversed the government's policy of involvement in the North and created a vacuum which the Provisionals were only too willing to fill" (*Paddy Bogside*, pp.226-7)

A political vacuum had already appeared in Catholic areas of the North after August 1969. The effect of Westminster's behaviour was to counterpose the Unionist system, the force that had created the political vacuum by its attack on the Catholic community, to the vacuum itself. As a consequence of this, a new centre of power emerged within the Catholic communities — within the vacuum — for the first time. It did so in response to the desperately required need for leadership and moral authority in a situation of the breakdown of the legitimacy of the apparatus of state. The events of August produced a greater coherence of purpose amongst the Catholic community in the North and threw up a political leadership which began to show itself able to negotiate with both the States with which it had to deal.

The delegations that had flowed south to Dublin contained all shades of political opinion, drawn together for mutual defence. They were the representatives of a rudimentary administration for Catholics in Derry and sizeable areas of Belfast behind the barricades. But once Dublin aborted the possible development of a semi-constitutional political force in the North there was a divergence between "Constitutional" and non-constitutional elements in Northern Nationalism.

This new development grew out of practical necessity, as Catholics finally realised, in their position of isolated desperation and vulnerability to the official and unofficial repressive forces of the Unionist statelet, that they had to look to themselves for salvation. This was the beginnings of the 28 year journey which has taken them to where they are today.

The Dublin Government's initial movement to organise and exert control over what was happening in the Northern Catholic community was understandable and its aims were feasible. Its policy was to give tangible support to Catholic defence in the North. That was quite a moderate reaction in the circumstances of the August pogrom. The objective was not to arm an emerging guerrilla force. At this point there was none, except the Official IRA, which the Dublin Government was disinclined to trust with guns, not because it was scared by 'Marxist revolution', but rather because the guns might not be used for the purposes for which they were intended—namely, Catholic defence. At this time the Provos existed only in name.

Dublin's loss of nerve had fateful implications for the situation in the North. What existed at the time behind the barricades of West Belfast were the Citizens Defence Committees.

During the Arms Trials the liaison man with the CDCs, John Kelly, gave the following description of them:

> "The Citizens' Defence Committees… contained people of all shades of minority opinion… within the Six Counties. They contained people like myself… who were Republicans, but they also contained people of no particular political point of view. They were people who were drawn together because of the circumstances, because of the situation in which we found ourselves, who were drawn together to organise the defence of the minority areas in what we felt then was a Doomsday situation. They provided first-aid posts; they engaged in fire-fighting, prevention of looting and liaison with the British army. But their primary function was to organise the defence of the minority community. They were concerned with obtaining arms, they were concerned with vigilante duties; they were concerned with the manning of the barricades and the enforcing of discipline. They were, in effect, the administration of a very large part of Derry's Bogside and of a very large part of Belfast and… there are many people still active in these organisations, people who… are of some substance and standing in the community, people with varying shades of political opinion" (*The Thimbleriggers*, p.186).

The CDCs were groups mostly depending on their effectiveness on Catholics who had gained military training through employment in the British Army. The Dublin policy, which Lynch jettisoned in the face of the British pressure, was primarily aimed at making these Defence Committees effective.

Frank Burton, an English sociologist, spent eight months in Ardoyne during late 1972 and early 1973. Even at this stage, when Republicanism had gained the ascendancy in Catholic working class areas of Belfast, the

Catholic ex-servicemen were prominent and organised in CESA:

"It was not unheard of during blanket searches for British Army soldiers to come across medals awarded to men in Arno {Ardoyne, P.W.} for their contribution to the Second World War. That is, quarry and searcher had fought for the same army. Clearly fifty and more years of living as part of the United Kingdom had its effects on staunch Republican areas and one manifestation of this was the large number of middle-aged men who had been in the British Forces, including several IRA men. The CESA was made up of such individuals who had British Army records and who though largely Republican in the sense of having some emotional commitment to a united Ireland were mainly hostile to radical Republican associations. The Association had its own club which, apart from entertainment, could be used to drill its cadets and to discuss 'security' matters concerning Arno. Many members considered CESA's primary role as that of Arno's last line of defence, a trained corps of men ready to defend the community should a concerted attack upon the district materialize. Apart from this doomsday role the organization acted as a group... stopping strange cars, questioning people and generally monitoring movement in the area. CESA's relationship with both armies in Arno, the IRA and the British, was decidedly ambiguous. The IRA regarded it as a 'bunch of cronies', some of whom were collaborators, but it would... co-operate with the Association over vigilante duty... The British Army was frequently admonished by CESA for its disgraceful troop behaviour... that... never took place in other colonial campaigns. Yet at the same time CESA aided the British domination. For example, it attempted to control and stop riots and it offered an overall condemnation of IRA activity" (*The Politics of Legitimacy: Struggles in a Belfast Community*, pp. 32-3),

Whilst being informative about how the ex-servicemen vied with the Republican Army for power and influence within the Catholic districts, Burton has the relationship between Republicanism and the British Imperial servicemen the wrong way around.

Ardoyne was not a "*staunch Republican area*" prior to August 1969. Like the rest of Catholic Belfast it had many more British ex-servicemen than IRA men. A great many families, and many with Republican backgrounds, had relatives in the British forces as well as relatives who had married British servicemen. This connection had gone back, not 50 years, when the area was actually cut off from the UK by the imposition of the Northern pseudo-state, but to 1914, when West Belfast became the most Imperial part of Nationalist Ireland, providing a high level of recruits to the British Army, encouraged by Joe Devlin and the Home Rulers, who dominated Catholic politics in the city.

The British Army, along with the Welfare State, was the major connecting point between West Belfast and the UK when the area was cut off from the political life of the State in 1921. And those who joined the British Army could still be good Nationalists and hate everything that 'Northern Ireland' stood for without any sense of discomfort—until their Army began backing up the 'Orange state' from 1970. Some of the ex-servicemen were later interned in Long Kesh and wrote of their disgust to *The Irish News* from there.

The British ex-servicemen thought of themselves as the defence force of their community, whilst not challenging the authority of the State they had served in its Imperial wars and Colonial campaigns. They resented the Republican Army who they saw as amateurs who had not been in much evidence when the crunch came in 1969.

But the CDCs and the ex-servicemen who were the major element on them were undermined by the arrest of Captain Kelly and of the liaison man of the Irish Government, John Kelly, and then by the whole business of the Arms Trial on what amounted to Treason charges.

What was West Belfast to make of this erratic behaviour from Dublin?

A strong signal was sent out to West Belfast and Northern Catholics generally that they could no longer depend upon Dublin for their deliverance. As a result they started looking to their own resources. The Defence Committees that Dublin had supported and the ex-servicemen who had put their trust in the British Government were left high-and-dry. And Republicanism, freed of reliance of Dublin and London, became the relevant milieu of development.

The Republican War thereafter absorbed every vigorous element in the Nationalist community into itself. Some of the ex-servicemen participated in that offensive as the 'constitutional' element did, to a substantial degree, during its most intense phase.

Taoiseach Lynch's May 1970 sabotage of the Defence Committees, which had developed the Catholic self-defence Insurrection aimed at eventually restoring the authority of the existing State, turned Catholic energies towards a Republican War that had quite the opposite intention.

The Demise of the Defence Committees

The Central Citizens' Defence Committee was founded on 16th August 1969, apparently on the initiative of Jim Sullivan, Adjutant of the IRA in Belfast, who became its first Chairman. It acted as the co-ordinating body for the various defence groups that sprung up after August 1969. The Defence Committees rapidly expanded until they contained about 75,000 people, sending nearly 100 delegates to the Central Committee.

The Northern Defence Committees had brought together all sorts of tendencies in the North, including former British soldiers as well as Republicans of every description, along with respectable middle-class people and elected representatives of the Catholic community. The embryonic movement carried the seeds of a new political development for the Northern minority which combined political representation with an ability to physically defend Catholics that came under attack. And in many ways this represented a success since it provided something of a disincentive to continued loyalist attacks on Catholic areas.

When the Committees began to be dispersed after their abandonment by Dublin this defensive function was provided for by the emerging Provisional IRA which gained the credit for it at St. Matthews in the Short Strand when a loyalist attack was beaten off in late June 1970, after the Provisionals made their first appearance. But the defence of the Short Strand was actually conducted by the local CDC with military assistance from the Provos. The one armed defender who was killed, Henry McIlhone, was a member of the CDC, but was later honoured with posthumous membership of the IRA on its Roll of Honour.

The formation of these Committees was not done in a moment of panic, it must be stressed, but constituted a concerted policy by an all-class alliance of the Catholics of the North which started in August 1969 and did not end until Taoiseach Lynch launched the Arms Crisis.

The Dublin Government sought to influence the major power source amongst Northern Catholics, the CDCs, and make them effective. If Lynch had stood his ground on this policy, and if he had proclaimed it openly in the face of British repression, events in the North would have developed on different lines. It would have been much better to have tried to take the Northern Catholics in hand and to have challenged the British. That would have led to an intensification of solution-finding from the British Government, and might have led to an accommodation being found before a 28 Year War developed. Such a policy could not have had worse results than what actually happened.

The barricaded areas in Catholic Belfast and Derry were fully independent of Stormont jurisdiction in this period. The reasons for the barricades in both cities were different. In Catholic Derry, which had been freed from Unionism in August 1969, they were largely a political act, with their dismantlement made dependent on reform of the security forces. In Catholic Belfast they were largely to do with protection. But behind the barricades 100,000 people had virtually opted out of 'Northern Ireland' and were organising themselves to be something else. They ran their own security force of vigilantes and maintained their own law and order. They ignored the police and negotiated directly with British commanders. Most of all they maintained close contact with Dublin and for a period considered themselves as under the jurisdiction of the Dublin Government, to do with what it wished.

But the CDCs were undermined by the arrest of Captain Kelly of the

Irish Army and of their Liaison man with Dublin, John Kelly, and by the whole business of the Arms Trials, as Government policy was reversed under British pressure. The CDCs, as they were constituted, largely led by apolitical Catholic ex-servicemen and others who were practically knowledgeable in a situation demanding particular skills, not usually required in normal peacetime, were only going to be relevant while the immediate threat of pogrom was there.

Once the community had begun to sort out its defences, the CDCs would be required for other things, and, if not given a purpose outside the immediate practical requirements for defence, were going to find themselves irrelevant to the medium term needs of the community. The CDCs had to be developed as centres of political power or else political power would go elsewhere behind the barricades. And that is just what happened when Dublin ceased to see them as part of their jurisdiction.

A number of forces in the Catholic community were vying for leadership behind the barricades. The Catholic Church, various groups of nationalists, and even revolutionary socialists fancied their chances. But the main force with moral authority, the Southern Government—the centre of power that Northern Catholics had looked to down the years for guidance and ultimate deliverance—was no longer amongst them, and those who had tried to help them within that Government were being put on trial by the State!

At the start, this conflict was fought out in the power centre that had initially emerged. The only substantial moral authority that existed in the community, apart from Dublin, was the Catholic Church and it initially saw a chance to extend its temporal power where it felt it would count.

In Ballymurphy, which became a storm-centre for the War, the Catholic Church attempted to assume command of the local CDC as Dublin disengaged. But the CDCs began to decline in influence when Dublin withdrew from them. And they fell into insignifance when the Church finally managed to take them over and gave them offices on Church property. The emerging Republican Army took over the defensive functions of the CDCs and enhanced the effectiveness of Republican ideology on the strength of them. Republicanism, of the tried and tested variety, was most relevant to the situation, in the absence of positive political leadership from Dublin. (See Ciaran de Baroid, *Ballymurphy and the Irish Wa*r, pp.91-2.)

When the Central Citizens Defence Committee took out a full-page advertisement in the *Irish News* of 16th November 1971 in an attempt to curb the escalating violence with the heading: "*Stop, Stop, Stop*", its time had passed. The 'Provies' had flown the nest and were in full-flight.

Republicans began providing the future requirements for defence, the medium-term leadership in the political vacuum behind the barricades, and the long-term hope of deliverance through its traditional objective of breaking the connection with Britain.

In the only substantial investigation into the events surrounding the Arms Crisis Angela Clifford concludes:

> "The prosecution of John Kelly undermined the Defence Committees in the North, but it did not undermine the insurrection that was brought about by the action of elements of the state apparatus and of the Loyalist populace in August 1969.
>
> "What happened was that the insurrection had been a defensive operation demanding security for the Catholic communities and more reasonable and democratic opportunities for participation in public life. Lynch, by his militant speech of 13th of August 1969, and by his actions over the following seven or eight months, had made himself an intermediary between the defensive insurrection in the North and the British Government.
>
> "The relationship between the Defence Committees and Dublin was necessary in maintaining the insurrection of the Catholic community in a defensive posture pending a basic reconstruction of political life.
>
> "If Lynch thought that the defensive insurrection would collapse when he prosecuted John Kelly, disowned the Defence Committees, and denied all that had been done since August, he miscalculated badly. He miscalculated because he, no more than Lemass, had troubled to find out what Northern Ireland actually was, before interfering with it.
>
> "The Catholic community was thrown into motion by the events of August 1969 and there was no going back. When Lynch subverted the defensive posture of the insurrection by launching the Arms Crisis, the insurrection became more active and revolutionary.
>
> "It was not a case of the IRA taking it over. A new IRA was created by it after it was disowned by Dublin and when Whitehall stood by its old Northern Ireland system, which was the cause of the problem" (pp. 25-6 of *'The Arms Crisis'*—a shorter pamphlet derived from the 700 page book, *'The Arms Conspiracy Trial'* published by A Belfast Magazine).

The emerging Republican Army filled the space the CDCs vacated, taking over the defence functions of the Citizen Defence Committees and thereby enhancing the standing of the Provisionals as a result. And with the taking over of the defence function came the inculcation of Republican ideology in the defenders that made them malleable in the future for a more assertive role in the situation of flux.

The consequence of Dublin's disengagement in mid-1970 was to give free rein to what was emerging—the new Republicanism, which was the most coherent and purposeful element that arose within the Northern flux, in the absence of responsibility by the two states concerned with the problem.

The Falls Curfew

During late June 1970, some of the new Republican Army demonstrated defence capabilities by killing five loyalists in communal confrontations on the fringes of Ardoyne and the Short Strand in Belfast. This sent out a powerful signal that there would be no more pogroms like August 1969 without resistance. To this Unionism acted in a predictable way, as it did in the 1920s, putting 500 Catholic workers out of the shipyards. But this time the community was not quelled and the Insurrection actually gathered force.

The reason for this was that unlike in 1920-2, when the British administration was intent on withdrawal from the new 'Northern Ireland' and handing over responsibility for the repressing of Catholics to the locals, in 1970 the Catholic community sheltered behind the newly arrived British force.

When the British Army then raided the Lower Falls after these killings, in an attempt to re-assert the authority which the British Government had ceded the previous September, a short gun battle broke out, and the area was placed under a weekend curfew. Three people were killed and the attitude of the locals was transformed *vis a vis* the British Army, which, having been given the benefit of the doubt, was now seen as a repressive apparatus of the Orange government at Stormont.

Much has been made of the harder line of the Tories in the Falls Curfew. But this ignores the continuity of British policy in the North. The curfew had to be launched by the British Army because the Unionists needed to be sated after the June killings. And they needed to be sated because they were needed to 'carry the can'. They were hardly going to 'carry the can' if they weren't sated. There were prominent Unionists calling for the return of the "B men" or the means to be made available to go into Catholic areas and *"liquidate the enemy"* (Bill Craig). And there were plenty willing to do so, given the go-ahead. So this attitude had to be placated.

It had been placated by allowing the heavily armed Protestant community to retain their 100,000 or so gun licences, agreement to new ones being issued, and allowing former B Specials to establish gun clubs, whilst at the same time raiding for arms in the largely unarmed Catholic areas (See NAI, DFA2003/17/30, September 1971, for more information on this aspect).

Stormont politicians were brought into the Falls to inspect the captured weapons of the IRA and a photo-call was arranged to satisfy Unionist opinion. Because the British Army became the Unionist instrument, and were seen to be its instrument, there were no more tea and buns for it on the Falls or other Catholic parts of Belfast and Derry.

The Minister for External Affairs, Hillery, was forced to make a secret visit (not having gained permission from the British) to the Falls after Paddy Devlin criticised Lynch for not doing anything "positive". Hillery described the captured Republican weapons as "out-dated" and "they now found themselves unprotected" in Catholic Belfast (IN 7.7.70). The visit and the words enraged Unionists and sent a quite different message to Nationalists in the North. The British decided not to chastise the Irish Government for its temerity, judging that Lynch was now in their pocket and more harm than good would come of a public rebuke (see PRO DEFE 25/273, 6.7.70).

The not yet Republican Catholics

The pamphlet '*Law (?) and Orders — The Story of the Belfast Curfew, 3-5 July 1970*' published by the Central Citizen's Defence Committee in mid-1970 is an interesting document. It reveals how unrepublican the force behind the barricades and the Catholic community was, in general, at the time. It has a Foreword by Micheál Ó Dathlaoich (Michael Dolley), a lecturer from England at Queens University and Member, later Vice President, of the Royal Irish Academy. It was written by Seán Óg Ó Fearghail.

The pamphlet saw the Falls Curfew as a "politically motivated" act made worse by military blundering on the part of the British Army. The event was not viewed from a Republican viewpoint but in terms of "the problem of whether deemed British citizens... possess the rights of British citizens domiciled elsewhere in the United Kingdom" (p.39).

It begins with a brief historical overview with an account of the events that led to the Falls Curfew. It describes the Curfew itself before going into the results of a CCDC survey of residents of the curfewed area, which was conducted by teams of students. It lays the blame for what happened on the British Army for its overreaction, and in particular, General Sir Ian Freeland, General Officer Commanding and Director of Operations for the British Army in 'Northern Ireland', who is accused of instituting it without authority and on a whim.

Below are some extracts. In the first, in the aftermath of the August events, the British Army is given credit for defending Catholics and for their "*invasion*" of the Shankill to restore law and order:

> "The army's principal preoccupation for the first few weeks was to contain the militant loyalists who considered that they had been cheated of their prey. Thus the position was generally that the army was welcome on the Falls but highly unpopular on the Shankill... On 11 October the loyalists tried to launch a new attack on the Catholics of the Unity Walk area... The troops moved in, and it was the turn of the Shankill to be invaded by armed

men. The invaders, however, were not a rabble, but soldiers of the Queen to whom so much hypocritical loyalty had been professed down the years, and the military did their work well. Resistance was as noisy as short-lived, and in contrast to the fusillade of undisciplined fire leashed against them the soldiers contented themselves with relatively few shots but those well-aimed. The defenders of the Shankill melted away... This show of strength had been sufficient for the loyalist mobs to lose their stomach for murderous assaults on their neighbours, and with Westminster exerting pressures Unionism dared not resist openly..." (p.6)

After the trouble between the British and Ballymurphy:

"During these difficult days the local Citizens Defence Committees worked hard to defuse the situation created by the military blundering, and this is the place to recall that all through the winter, spring and early summer, the Central Citizens Defence Committee laboured unceasingly to co-ordinate the operations of local vigilantes who enjoy such an enviable record for averting breaches of the peace and even crime. During this period it has been admitted that the crime rate in large parts of Catholic Belfast was never so low. Hooliganism... at times explicable as the result of military action, was made a whipping-boy not just by Unionist politicians but by 'Castle Catholics' who still preferred to sit up and beg thankfully for the crumbs from their masters' table instead of making a stand for full equality for the Catholic people" (p.7).

On the trouble in New Barnsley:

"As they came out of the Springfield Road the crowd of loyalist roughs who headed the Orange parade proper saw a Catholic crowd standing behind a military cordon. As if at a given signal the loyalists began to pelt the Catholic crowd who, not unnaturally, retaliated. It is very significant that throughout the confrontation the military kept their backs to the Catholic crowd. The soldiers knew only too well who had begun it all. In the melee a few shots were fired, and the troops opened up with C.S. gas, and it was poetic justice that some of the canisters fell among the marching Orangemen whose persistence with the traditional route had touched off the whole confrontation... The sympathies of the troops, already angered by the childish caperings and delays, were this time very clearly with the people of Ballymurphy, and the marchers were hustled on their way" (p.8).

On the battle of St. Matthews and Ardoyne, where loyalists were killed and which preceded the Curfew on the Falls:

"A major attack on St. Matthews Church itself was launched by an armed mob of loyalists, and the only protection offered by the military was a force of sixteen men. By the time that they arrived in the early morning fighting was general and a doughty resistance on the part of the defenders cured the mob of its taste for action... In the fighting at Ballymacarret the Ulster

Volunteer Force had taken a bloody nose. When British troops belatedly came on the scene it slunk away, and there was a desperate attempt to save face by a pretence that it had never been committed to the battle. The myth was propagated of innocent Protestant passers-by mown down by I.R.A. gunmen spoiling for a fight, and relevant here are further fatalities incurred in an irresponsible follow-up of the provocative march through Ardoyne. What Stormont needed was something to salve this wounded loyalist pride..." (p.9).

This attempt *"to salve this wounded loyalist pride"* had the effect of turning the British Army on the Catholics of the Falls, who were full of ex-servicemen:

"In both World Wars... a very high proportion of the people served in the British forces, and so are in a position to draw comparisons between the army they knew and the army of to-day. Not all are impressed by high-ranking officers affecting pullovers and open-neck shirts, and others deplore the general slovenliness of bored patrols slouching up and down streets in a make-believe army of occupation. Subsequent military brutality towards innocent members of their own families have alienated disciplined men who might, in other times, have been relied upon to exert a steadying influence" (p.2).

However,

"What must be made very clear at the outset is that this work is not intended as an indictment of the whole British army... Neither is it to be construed as an attack upon militarism... It is hoped that due significance will be attached to a parallel reluctance to cite by name the different units involved. This stems from our belief that the good name of a regiment is not lightly to be besmirched, and the author is sufficiently a man of the world to appreciate that there are few baskets of any size which will not be found to contain their proportion of bad eggs" (p.3).

But:

"Reluctantly one is drawn to the conclusion that the days are gone when a British officer and gentleman could be relied upon to possess a certain chivalry... (p.4).

On a section on *'The Irish Dead'*, the first victim of the British Army, Charles O'Neill, is described:

"His experience had been typical of the Falls area. Leaving school at fourteen, he had been unable to find regular employment and after a succession of dead-end jobs he had joined the Royal Air Force. Of exemplary character he was discharged after ten years service as medically unfit. He returned to the Falls a broken man, a martyr to asthma and bronchitis. On his body was found his Royal Air Force papers... The funeral on Tuesday 7 July was to Milltown Cemetery. There was no wreath from the R.A.F." (p.23).

How unrepublican was this view in mid-1970 is emphasised in the last few lines of it:

> "Ireland and England will learn one day to live together in friendship, and in this connection one of the more helpful signs is Irish admiration for the English common law and for the best traditions of the English armed forces for which so many Irishmen volunteered in two world wars. It was precisely this admiration, though, that explains so much of the sense of outrage felt by the Falls in July and August, 1970" (p.43).

This all tends to suggest that the Falls was a much more complex place in 1970 than is imagined today and it was far from the finished Republican article.

The Republican Strategy

By the latter part of 1970, the circumstances began to exist for the blending of the Catholic Insurrection into a Republican War. These were: mounting tension between the communities, Catholic expectations raised and Unionist Government defence mechanisms (the RUC and B Specials) disorganised by the British Government; increasing conflict between the British Army being employed as an Orange/Stormont instrument and the Catholic community; and the army of the State being kept out of the areas behind the barricades, where IRA training was underway.

The Provos realised that, once roused, the Catholics would not be content with the Stormont set-up, and would be increasingly drawn to the British State to redress their grievances. And they calculated that the only way of preventing this was by turning the Catholic insurrection into a War. It was now or never for the Anti-Partitionist cause with the community roused into insurrectionary activity by the August events.

War by its very nature is a highly risky business. It is a catastrophic sort of activity, which throws everything into the mixer, and its consequences cannot be foreseen with any degree of certainty. The only certainty is that things would never be the same again.

The basic calculation the Provisionals made was that the high risk strategy of 'Total War' was preferable, no matter where it led, to letting things settle down.

So it was now or never!

The Provisionals (unlike the Officials) had a purposeful and realistic strategy for exploiting the situation. Sean MacStiofain, the Chief of Staff of the new IRA, described the Republican strategy in his autobiography:

> "... a foolish optimism seemed to be the order of the day. It was in this context, with the summer marching season of 1970 as the most likely

flashpoint, that IRA strategy had to be determined. At the council meeting in January it was agreed that the most urgent priority would be area defence. All our energies would be devoted to providing material, financial and training assistance for the Northern units. The objective was to ensure that if any area where such a unit existed came under attack, whether from British or Loyalist extremists, that it would now be capable of adequate defensive action.

"As soon as it became feasible and practical, the IRA would move from a purely defensive position into a phase of combined defence and retaliation. Should British troops ill-treat or kill civilians, counter-operations would be undertaken when the Republican units had the capability. After a sufficient period of preparation, when the movement was considered strong enough and the circumstances right, it would go into the third phase, launching an all-out offensive action against the British occupation system." (*Memoirs of a Revolutionary*, pp. 145-6)

In the first couple of months of 1970 most of the developing violence and bombings came from Unionist groups and was directed at the Catholic community. There were also attempted bombings of targets in the Republic — in Donegal and at the GPO in Dublin. It was imagined that what was done in 1922 to the Catholic community could be repeated in 1970 with success.

But things had changed. The Unionists were under restraint from the British Government in order to settle things down and the Catholics were determined not to be put down again.

The intensifying Catholic/Protestant conflict in Belfast, and the deteriorating Catholic community's relations with the British Army, were favourable conditions for the IRA. Over the summer of 1970, a bombing campaign was launched to intensify the conflict as MacStiofain described. This was mainly aimed at Unionist businesses and was highly provocative, although there was little loss of life.

The Provo strategy was shown to be sound and practically realisable as 1970 wore on and recruits began to join their ranks, rather than those of the Officials/'Stickies'. The organisation, which initially exercised a restraining influence on the masses during the Ballymurphy riots of April 1970, was able to move up the gears.

Ruari O'Bradaigh spelt out the Provisionals' strategy in an interview with '*This Week*' on 14th August 1970:

"... The most desirable sequences would be to bring down Stormont by making the area ungovernable; this would be followed by an all-out effort to force British evacuation and disengagement... We do not regard Stormont as an Irish institution. It is just a puppet parliament and, obviously, its abolition would mean the dysfunction of the Unionist powerbase... Its abolition would bring about a direct confrontation with the Irish people, particularly the people of the North, and the British occupying power. The abolition of Stormont would be a very big step towards the achievement of the national aim."

In response to this the Officials argued that an imposition of direct rule would be "a step backwards of more than 50 years in Irish history. Less British interference and not more was the Republican demand" (*United Irishman* May 1970).

Furthermore:

"Stormont is certainly a puppet parliament in the sense that it was set up by Britain originally... Certainly too it is true that Stormont is not an Irish institution in the sense that a Republican Parliament would be, but are not all of those who are members of it Irishmen, even the right-wing Unionists, and is it not a good deal more Irish than the British Parliament which would take its place if direct rule would be imposed... Would the abolition of Stormont really destroy the Unionist power base? Is not the real Unionist power base, firstly the determination of one million Protestant Irishmen not to enter a United Ireland, and secondly, the fact that this determination is backed to the hilt by the Imperial Government in London?" (*United Irishman*, September 1970).

This was a much more sophisticated argument than that of the Provisionals and it had much that was true about it. However, the sophistication of it was inappropriate to the crudity of the situation produced by British policy in the North. And, if it were taken up in earnest, it would be positively debilitating for the sort of campaign that needed waging by Republicanism in 1970.

The Officials suffered from the attempted juggling of two ideologies that were largely incompatible—Republicanism and Socialism. And both Republicanism and Socialism were indeed *ideologies* for the Stickies, being largely disconnected from reality in each case. The Officials asked themselves what was the Republican/Socialist thing to do in each situation that confronted them and they found they got contradictory answers. A Republican would behave one way, a Socialist another and they kept coming down in the middle in an attempt to reconcile the answers. So what resulted was incoherent, confused and neither here nor there.

The Provos did not have the same theoretical dilemma. They went with their instincts, which were very much Republican.

The short-term objective of the Provos—the destruction of Stormont— was highly realisable and popular with the Catholic masses. The Officials defence of Stormont as an 'Irish' institution was ridiculous to them, in the circumstances. It was a façade in front of the real power that needed to be engaged, in one way or another. Whether the real power was destructible was another question, but it was one that was better left to another day.

It was no surprise, therefore, that the Provos went from strength to strength whereas the Officials declined to something of an irrelevance, despite, or rather because of, all the grand theories and schemes they had for their 'Revolution'. The interference of the international Communist movement in the simple republicanism of the IRA in the 1960s ultimately produced Sinn Fein the Workers Party, the Workers Party, and when Communism collapsed in the 1990s, Democratic Left. Then Democratic Left went into the Irish Labour Party and all declined together.

Dublin on Northern Republicanism

Eamon Gallagher's report of a conversation he had with Paddy Devlin in December 1970 contains an estimation of Republicanism in the North that is widely off the mark and shows Dublin's failing grasp of the situation. Gallagher, who was apparently the main influence on Irish Government policy in the North, reported to those he served in Dublin:

"I must say I have come across the track of the Kelly brothers previously in Belfast, but as a common condition of life there is to tell lies about everybody else, I have been reluctant to come to any personal conclusions or even to report the things told to me as they might simply have been gross slanders. In my contact work in the North I have moved very gradually from one source to another... For reasons of prudence I have consciously kept away from two groups i.e. the Bernadette Devlin/Eamon McCann group etc. and the Provisional Republican group... In the latter case I have had serious suspicions for a long time as to their connections in the 26 Counties.

"As I conceived it my job to make overall political assessments I also tended to keep away from information relating to what I knew to be mini-groups, no matter how loud they shouted. Nevertheless it is impossible not to hear a great deal about them and to come to some assessment of their importance... This group has control of a number of people in that area {the New Lodge, P.W.} and in other parts of Belfast including Ardoyne, an element in Ballymurphy and one in Andersonstown. I am satisfied and have been satisfied for a long time that this group created riot situations on instructions from elsewhere. I am satisfied that the purpose of these situations was two-fold—

(1) to demonstrate that the Taoiseach's policies were wrong

(2) to create a situation in which the Taoiseach would be forced in a manner contrary to his general policy.

"I am also satisfied that this group is highly unrepresentative of general opinion even among the minority in Belfast. There may be a few among them who act out of idealism but I believe most of them were paid to create trouble… It appears that in the past two or three months the funds of this group have been substantially reduced and their capacity for serious trouble-making may also, therefore, have been reduced" (NAI, TSCH 2001/8/15, 13.12.70).

It should be noted that this was written at the end of 1970, just before the Provo campaign really took off.

Gallagher dismissed the new Republicanism in the North as inconsequential *"trouble-makers"* whose strings were being pulled from South of the Border—by the sacked Ministers, Blaney and Haughey, perhaps? Cut the strings and the problem would disappear—as Gallagher was predicting it was on its way in doing.

But he was proved very wrong about the independent substance of the new Republicanism. As Taoiseach Lynch cut off the funds in his hasty retreat from the North, rather than declining, the new Republican Army began to mushroom out from its core centres into the countryside. And the view that it was some instrument directed by malevolent elements in the South, opposed to the Taoiseach's new policy, was proved to be really ludicrous.

In fact, Republicanism in the North was not affected by Lynch's *volte face* in the same way as the 'constitutional' Nationalists were. It was given a great boost by it.

Northern Republicanism had been warned by its Anti-Treaty associates that the *"traitors in the Dáil"* would sell out the National Struggle. And there was historical experience in the North, from the Collins debacle in 1922, to back up this warning. It was proved to be correct by Taoiseach Lynch's about turn and his sending for trial those who administered his policy. So the new Republicanism was ready for it.

The betrayal of the Northern Insurgency then, instead of demoralising it, shocked it into a line of independent activity, free from Dublin restraint and influence. And what became the Provos, the new independent instrument of Northern Republicanism, began to take off.

These events clearly signalled that the Northern Catholics were on their own after the withdrawal of help from the Southern State. They could no longer depend upon Dublin. They could rely on sympathy and some support from the people of the South but, after their abandonment by Lynch, their future position was now clearly a matter to be determined by their own efforts. This knowledge generated the strong Republican development that began to take hold in a large section of the community.

CHAPTER 6

Moment of Truth

Two political forces had come into existence within the Catholic community as a result of August 1969—the Provisionals and the SDLP. If Dublin had maintained its initial assertive policy of taking the Catholics of the Six Counties in hand, an alternative 'semi-constitutional' movement could have emerged and things presumably proceeded very differently.

There was a realistic possibility of the construction of an effective 'semi-constitutional' Nationalism in the North, acting in conjunction with a Dublin Government with an active Northern policy that took effective leadership of the Catholic community and exerted pressure on Britain to enact a structural reform that would make things tolerable for the Catholic community, at least for a while. But when Taoiseach Lynch forced the Arms Crisis, he aborted that possible line of development. And that gave a great spur to Provisional Republicanism and cleared the way for those who were willing to act independently of Dublin, and to see what might be done without it.

The funeral of former IRA Chief of Staff, Hugh McAteer blocked the Falls Road in June 1970. The chief mourner was his brother Eddie, Leader of the Nationalist Party, who was followed up the Falls by 300 uniformed IRA men in military formation. Fr. McAteer, son of Eddie, conducted the service. This event represented the last hurrah of the old Nationalist continuum before the parting of the ways.

It has been taken-for-granted in practically every account of this period that the Provisionals and SDLP were a natural parting in the community's politics. That assumption is mistaken. Although the Provos and SDLP had the same moment of origin in August 1969 the division which they constituted was unnecessary. The last two decades have shown how the continuum within Northern Nationalism has reasserted itself, despite attempts within sections of its 'Constitutional' wing to assert distinctiveness.

The SDLP, like the Provos, started out as an ambiguous body in 1970 and initially acted as something that was indistinguishable from the Nationalist Party it replaced, except in its more modernistic rhetoric attuned to the flavours of the time. It faced the same dilemma—participation or not?

The Opposition in Paralysis

For nearly half a century the major complaint made within Nationalist ranks in the Six Counties was that anti-Unionist political forces were fatally divided and what was most needed was unity. But it took a startlingly long time to get the 'opposition' together to form a new nationalist party. And while the 'Constitutionalists' fiddled Belfast began to burn.

There had been talk for nearly a year of the establishment of an 'opposition' party and at least four attempts had been made between March 1969 and August 1970 to forge a united nationalist grouping. Yet little had happened during such a crucial juncture in the year between August 1969 and August 1970 and there had been much disagreement over finding 'Unity' candidates for the 1970 Westminster election.

The reports made by John Hume to Mr. Gallagher of the Department of External Affairs during 1970 describe the progress, or lack of, in constructing this 'opposition' party.

On 15th February Hume told Eamonn Gallagher that "plans are going ahead for the creation of a new Opposition party in the Six Counties" that would be called the "Social Democratic and Labour Party". Hume named himself, Cooper, O'Hanlon, Fitt, Currie and Devlin as being the core of it, with more individuals to follow. He noted that the term "Labour" was only included in the name "in deference to Fitt and Devlin".

Gallagher noted:

> "Hume asked me to convey to the Taoiseach and the Minister his assurance that, notwithstanding the necessary inclusion of the word Labour in the name of the party there will be no connection between it and the British, Irish and Northern Ireland Labour parties. He is anxious that the Taoiseach and the Minister should know this in advance of any announcement of the formation of the new party but he is very anxious that no word of its creation should leak out in advance" (NAI, DFA 2001/6/513, 16.2.70).

A couple of weeks later Gallagher reported the following after another conversation with Hume:

> "Gerry Fitt appears to have changed his mind about the formation of a new party but Hume and the others intend to proceed with it anyway and will probably now drop the label "Labour" from the title. Hume feels that Fitt has been persuaded against the new party by Paddy Kennedy" (NAI, DFA 2001/6/513, 3.3.70).

What was going on? It was surely not just the strong personalities of the individuals and Hume's opposition to 'Labour' that were keeping them from forming the unified instrument that Dublin was requiring they construct in the Six Counties?

It must also have been to do with the *volte face* performed by Lynch in May 1970 which brought a degree of confusion to the main men of 'Constitutional' Nationalism and the slap in the face that the Taoiseach's arrest of those aiding their community in the North gave to the 'moderates'.

What makes interesting reading are the reports of meetings made between

Eamonn Gallagher and Paddy Devlin and Gerry Fitt (NAI, TSCH 2001/8/15, 13.12.70). These conversations were part of the examination by the Republic's Public Accounts Committee of the Northern Distress Relief Fund, prompted by Lynch's Arms Trials. In short, from being distributors of the funds from Dublin aimed at relieving the position of Northern Catholics, Fitt and Devlin were suddenly under suspicion of having armed the new Republican Army that was developing behind the barricades, because of Lynch's *volte face*.

The discomfort of Fitt and Devlin is apparent in the reports. After denying any association with, and then fingering, Neil Blaney as prime suspect in any dirty business that might have taken place, Fitt pleaded that it was nothing to do with him because "he was squeezed out of the handling of the Clones Bank account and knows nothing more about it".

The Report reveals:

"Mr. Fitt said that the misuse of the fund was both obvious and tragic in Belfast since about January of this year. Thugs and lay-abouts from the New Lodge Road area, personally known to him since his childhood, were clearly in receipt of Irish money and, in his opinion, were paid to stir up trouble at will... In the initial stages he could not understand what was happening but later it became clear to him that certain riots were connected with certain situations in Dublin. The line of command, so far as he could discover, was from Mr. Blaney to Mr. Paddy Kennedy M.P. at the political level and through the Kelly brothers at the strong-arm level. The Kelly brothers, originally from the New Lodge area and one of them moved back into it about a year ago and is now in charge of what Mr. Fitt described as {name scored out} in that area. Mr. Fitt has a low opinion of these people and believes that they have set back progress at political level to a considerable degree. It has become noticeable to him, however, that funds have been less freely available since about two months ago and he is hopeful this may stop the contrived rioting... All the events of the past year, including the cynical destruction of Paddy Kennedy as a politician and as a person, convince him that Blaney's interests lay elsewhere and he has nothing good to say of him... the important thing to his mind is to expose the posturings of Mr. Kennedy and the Kelly brothers who have led many people astray and have caused death and suffering in ghetto areas of Belfast and are still doing so."

The conversation Gallagher had with Paddy Devlin is very similar in kind.

What comes out of this is the disconcerting effect the Taoiseach's reversal of policy had on Nationalist politicians in the North. Prior to this the main men were openly asking Dublin for arms and distributing funds for defence on behalf of the Irish Government. And now they were being told they had been agents of an 'illegal' and nefarious policy for which other very senior people were being prosecuted in court. What were they to make of it all?

Certainly Fitt and Devlin's political minds with regard to the Provos seem to have become deranged by the Taoiseach's actions. What they were doing was telling tales about the Provos that Dublin wanted to hear, tales that would get them off. Those tales were entirely false and misguided and if Dublin believed them it is no wonder they were taken by surprise by the Republican growth in the North.

Is it any wonder that, with the moral ground pulled from beneath them by Taoiseach Lynch, Fitt, Devlin and others around them became politically disabled and incapable of purposeful and unified activity through most of 1970, leaving Hume on his own?

One other point: If Dublin had maintained its original policy, the 'semi-constitutional' Paddy Kennedy would have represented the mainstream of the movement Fianna Fail desired to construct in the Six Counties. But Lynch's drastic change of course had made him into a scapegoat and something of a leper to the 'Constitutionalists'.

Formation of the SDLP

In mid-August, as Republicanism began to grasp the initiative, the nationalist MPs at Stormont finally got their act together to form a new "united Opposition" to the Unionists. It seems that the formation of an Alliance Party, fishing for support from middle-class Catholics, propelled the 'Constitutional' fragments into a kind of party.

There was also another important consideration. As John Hume told *The Irish Times*, "If the British Government wants to sound out opposition, where does it turn? It is a question of practical politics..." (IT 17.8.70).

The *Irish News* welcomed the move in the following terms:

> "Unity among members of the opposition is something which this paper has tirelessly advocated... The latest move to achieve this desired move, in a united front under the leadership of Mr. Gerry Fitt, of which we learned yesterday, is the most welcome news for quite some time. All anti-Unionists will watch its development anxiously and, we are sure, in the hope of seeing it succeed and so provide us at this crucial juncture in our affairs with action which we can support and a voice with which we can speak to Westminster or any other interested party." (18.8.70).

The *Irish News* editorial saw it as a good thing that Catholic MPs should unite so that a stronger front could be presented to Unionism and, more important, that a more effective propaganda organ would be present at Westminster to further the aims of Nationalism. (And it is most probable that the reason why there was little contest for the leadership of the new Party was that Gerry Fitt was by far the most influential Nationalist MP at Westminster. The new Party might well have been more appropriately led by Currie or Hume.)

When the Social Democratic and Labour Party was formed, it was criticised from two political positions. It was alleged at the time by Paddy Kennedy and others that the British Labour Party was involved in the financing and organisation of the new Party. Kennedy had represented the Falls CDC in talks with Callaghan and formed this impression from his meetings. Kennedy, who went very Republican in opposition to his Republican Labour Party colleague, Gerry Fitt, also accused the SDLP of supporting Stormont and of being a prop of Unionist rule (IN 23.8.70).

This line of criticism was also pursued by *'The Voice of the North'*, the newspaper established by Fianna Fail to influence the Catholic community in the Six Counties and its politics after August 1969. *'The Voice Of The North'* had tried to develop a new political force in the Catholic community combining defence with Fianna Fail Republicanism but it had become a remnant of the activist policy, abandoned after pressure on Lynch from the British Ambassador (Seamus Brady submitted a bill to the Government Information Bureau for the production of the first two issues but he was told by Haughey that the Government was no longer having anything to do with the paper. Lynch made a denial of involvement with the paper in the Dáil in May 1970.)

The other critics of the new Party were the old Northern Ireland Labour Party whose primary figure, Paddy Devlin, had signalled his intention of defecting to the SDLP. In rejecting the new Party, the NILP said in a statement that:

"The record of the opposition MPs throws more than a little doubt on the statement by one spokesman that the new party will be non-sectarian in character. We find it very difficult to see some of the opposition MPs giving up their alignments or forsaking the vote catering facilities provided by the sectarian platforms. Indeed the tone has already been set by the prospective leader who has stated that it is his ideal to give real leadership to the 'minority'. We find this approach indistinguishable from the expressed views of nationalist leaders from time to time and we believe it represents the other side of the sectarian coin and the further entrenchment of sectarian politics" (IN 19.8.70).

Announcing the formation of the SDLP, Gerry Fitt, its leader, said that Party policies "would be based on radical left-of-centre principles". It would have as its aims:

"To secure a just and adequate distribution of wealth: to uphold and support the democratic rights and principles of organised labour; To promote the spread of financial, consumer, industrial and agricultural co-operatives: To work for the provision of a minimum living wage for all workers and to support the principle of equal pay for equal work: to secure equal rights for all citizens, irrespective of race, creed or political outlook; to support the re-introduction of proportional representation as the fairest and most equitable means of representation and the one most suited to the needs of the people in these Six Counties; to promote and encourage the development of all aspects of our culture; to ensure public ownership of our fishing rights of all inland waters; to formulate radical policies for the agricultural, social and economic development of rural areas; to work for the establishment of state industries, particularly in areas of high unemployment; to promote co-operation, friendship and understanding between North and South with a view to the eventual re-unification of Ireland through the consent of the majority of the people in the North and in the South" (IN 22.8.70).

The SDLP Constitution set out 6 aims in its Clause II. No. 1 aim was "To organise and maintain in Northern Ireland a socialist party". No. 6b aim was for "the public ownership and democratic control of such essential industries and services as the common good requires". No. 6c aim was for "the utilisation of its powers by the state, when and where necessary, to provide employment, by the establishment of publicly owned industries" (*SDLP Constitution*).

And yet the most basic contradiction in this was never seen—socialism is impossible without state power and 'Northern Ireland' was not a state.

The SDLP Constitution was a re-hash of the British Labour Party Constitution with Irish Unity added. Fitt placed his socialist aims at the top and his nationalist objectives near the bottom of this wish list. But the most important question went unanswered—whether the new party was aiming for a political settlement within the UK or would it refuse to make a settlement short of an all-Ireland state? Fitt, of course, refused to be pinned down on this. He preferred to maintain a conceptual blur around such a decision and simply parroted the idea he had picked up that James Connolly had been a socialist and a republican and he could be too.

Austin Currie later recalled:

"At the time of the formation of the SDLP... nationalism was being put on the back burner... There was recognition that we had to live within Northern Ireland for a considerable period of time... we had to make the best of the situation, but that we were entitled to an equal spot in the sun— that was our determination and commitment."

A founder member, Ben Caraher, told the same interviewer that it was the subject of debate between those who formed the party:

"... would the unity of Ireland be a formal aim or would that formal aim be left out? There was no question of the unity of Ireland being the primary aim of the party. Their primary preoccupations were Civil Rights in Northern Ireland, and social and economic matters... Your dream would have been to share power with liberal unionists" (Gerard Murray and Jonathan Tonge, *Sinn Fein and the SDLP*, p12)

But what if "Civil Rights and social and economic matters in Northern Ireland" were really beside the point by late 1970? Had the SDLP, as a purely electoral force, the power to influence things on their own, in the direction they desired?

What Was the SDLP?

The SDLP was, from the very beginning, a conglomeration of Catholic interests. There was the British Socialist element that formally led it and which gave it purchase amongst the British left at Westminster. This element was also the Republican Socialist wing. Its Republicanism was idealist as both Fitt and Devlin had little interest in or feeling for the independent Irish State. They were fundamentally British Socialists in a region of the state that was detached from British Socialism.

There was also a more Catholic conservative wing that was devolutionary in instinct and gravitated toward a settling down in a reformed Stormont with a chastened Unionism. This was a more vigorous version of the Nationalist Party the SDLP replaced. But it was the Nationalist Party *après* Lemass rather than Cahir Healy vintage. The new party saw itself as something distinct and superior from the Republican wing of Nationalism rather than as part of a continuum. This was the section represented by Currie and Mallon.

And then there was John Hume who, although he did not lead the party, quickly began to direct it as the instrument of his political improvisation. But, whilst Hume needed a party behind him, he ultimately realised that he required more than that to achieve his political objectives and it was that which made him re-establish the continuum that the rest of his party steered clear of, a decade or two later.

The most significant thing about the SDLP was that it was essentially a collection of individuals organised for electoral purposes. If anything, it had fewer roots in the community than the Nationalist Party it replaced (although its initial membership was much more educated and younger).

By 1972 the SDLP had only 14 branches across the Six Counties. Membership figures were confidential but, assuming the average branch contained about 30 members, since new branches were opened when 50 was exceeded, SDLP strength was probably only at about 3-400 members. That meant an SDLP branch served much more than 10,000 Catholic electors in most areas of Belfast—outside of the affluent South of the city—where about half of all Catholics voted. The Alliance Party, formed just before the SDLP, had more members and a greater number of active members that the SDLP. Branch activity was very low, being confined mainly to the selection of candidates for elections (see Ian McAllister, *The Northern Ireland Social and Democratic Labour Party*, pp. 43-5, for an analysis of SDLP Executive Reports and Census material.)

Political parties organised for electoral purposes are fine for democracy. But 'Northern Ireland' was never a democracy. It had some semblance of democracy before 1969 with its government and opposition but it lacked two crucial features of democracy that make it purposeful and successful—the ability to elect an opposition into government and for the electorate to be able to cast their vote for those who govern them. The Nationalists were never going to get into government within the contrived pseudo-state that was constructed on a sectarian headcount in 1921. And real politics was not conducted at Stormont but far away in Westminster where the people of 'Northern Ireland,' excluded from the party politics of the State, had no say.

The peculiar position in 1970 also did not make for purposeful electoral politics in 'Northern Ireland'. Stormont had come under the supervision of Westminster, the real master, and its days were believed to be numbered. Where was power to go then but back to where it really belonged? This was not a time for electoral politics. Elections were relatively meaningless in the acute situation that had developed by late 1970 and so the SDLP were ineffectual as a distinct political force from the start.

The Nationalist Party had never put down roots in West Belfast, which from the time of Joe Devlin had a different character to other minority areas. It was a Catholic growth within a powerful and substantial Protestant and industrial city. Its politics reflected that.

Gerry Fitt was the main man in 'the West', but he was an electoral force more than anything else. He had acquired a broader political influence in the 1960s by linking up with British Labour, but here his influence was limited because he was never an organic part of British Labour. He remained a one-man band in detachment from the State and its politics. Fitt was the politician best able to get the Catholic masses out every couple of years for an election and he was able to beat the Unionists in his own backyard. But what then, when the celebrations of the local triumph wore off, and the situation in the rest of 'Northern Ireland' became clear and nothing had changed, again?

West Belfast had been the least Republican area of the Six Counties and the most Redmondite/Devlinite. But now it was doing a political somersault in response to the events of August 1969. It was no longer willing to settle for a limited role in merely providing ballot box fodder for Fitt every few years. It had entered the political stage in August 1969 and it was not about to troop off it, to be brought back occasionally for elections. It was becoming activist and wanted to do something, anything, to improve its position and that of its wider community, a goal that August had brought it closer to. So it needed much more than the SDLP to absorb its energies and ambitions in 1970. It required something much more meaningful and purposeful that connected the community up with real political power and influence, which it had not had since the days of Joe Devlin.

Something more robust and substantial, with strong roots in the community and with a greater spirit of activism might have emerged within the Catholic community if Dublin had not instituted its drastic change of policy signified by the Arms Trials. It was only Dublin, in the absence of British Labour, that could have provided an alternative to what developed.

As it was, the political forces of the Catholic community were divided between a purely electoral party and the Insurgency that was developing a military *cadre*. Once the Catholic masses mobilised they could not return to their former quiet existences. Energies had to go somewhere and in late 1970 there was no chance that those kinds of energies could be diverted into mere canvassing for prominent Catholic individuals, disconnected from the real politics.

So the unsatisfied energies went into street politics, which increasingly became confrontations with the British Army, and this led the more vigorous spirits on into the military side of things.

British Labour and the SDLP

Although Callaghan had been a prime advocate of Catholic political unity in the aftermath of August 1969 he resurrected his idea of Labour organisation in the 'Northern Ireland' part of the State as things began to deteriorate during the middle of 1970 and Oliver Wright's optimistic prognosis of February 1970 proved misplaced.

In March, whilst still Secretary of State, he notified the Irish Ambassador in London of his intention of creating branches of the Labour Party in the North. It seems that Callaghan had had a Bill drawn up, along with extensive plans put in place, for instituting Direct Rule after the British General Election of June 1970. He had come to the conclusion that a substantial initiative was necessary because there could be no reconciling rising Catholic expectations with mounting Unionist reluctance to accept reform. Wilson dithered about making such a momentous change in British policy and a decision was put off until after the Election—which the Tories won.

In October, then out of government, he raised the subject with the

Ambassador again. According to a Department of External Affairs report: "he was... told that Dublin would look on the development with disfavour. This does not seem to have made much impression on Mr. Callaghan" (NAI, DT 2001/6/517, 9.11.70, p.1).

According to the Ambassador's report of October 21st, Callaghan "had been working very hard on this matter in recent months and is hoping to get approval for the idea fairly soon". He was intending to set up headquarters in Belfast and appoint agents in every constituency to fight them at the next election. But, interestingly, the Ambassador reported:

> "He stressed that he is not at all motivated by any consideration of getting more Labour seats at Westminster. His plan would, in fact, be geared essentially to the building up of a genuine Labour opposition in Stormont. I recalled that he had already mentioned this matter to me when I called on him in the Home Office in March last. My understanding then was that his plan was related to Westminster seats and he told me he has changed his mind on this in the meantime" (p.1).

This seems a strange change of mind on Callaghan's part. It was at the level of State that the Labour Party was most needed in 'Northern Ireland' through which the electorate could vote for or against the people who actually governed them. To confine Labour representation to the devolved *façade* would surely prevent representative politics from developing in connection to the state.

Perhaps someone had had a word in Callaghan's ear since his proposal in late 1969/early 1970 to connect 'Northern Ireland' up to the level of the state through Labour organisation. Callaghan was thereafter attempting to reconcile what he knew to be the right thing to do in offering Labour representation, to the existing Westminster arm's length treatment of 'Northern Ireland' from 1920.

Another interesting thing that comes out of the Ambassador's report of October 1970 is his revelation to Dublin that the British parties had agreed amongst themselves that, if Chichester Clark was to fall, Unionism was to be given one last chance to run its own show at Stormont with Brian Faulkner named as being "worth a trial".

Callaghan stressed that he was personally "strongly in favour of the unification of Ireland. The present division is unnatural..."

Dublin's policy solution with regard to the North was to end Partition. But what if it couldn't be done? Callaghan shared this aspiration but he knew that it couldn't or wouldn't be done by Britain. So what then for the people of 'Northern Ireland'?

It was probably a combination of Callaghan's Irish unification aspiration and his acquiescence to the arm's length British policy of 1920 that finally led him to abandon his policy to connect the province up to the party politics of the State through Labour organisation and support the SDLP as a substitute for this.

But the SDLP provided no alternative to what was going to happen.

Why the SDLP Suited Britain

In observing events in 'Northern Ireland' between August 1969 and the end of 1970 Seamus Brady formed the view that the SDLP was the *conscious*, product of British State strategy:

> "Callaghan returned to Northern Ireland in October, 1969, for a more chastened tour. It was on this occasion, at a private dinner with some Opposition M.P.s that he outlined his plan for dealing with the Unionist leaders, whom he spoke of as 'the hardest men I have ever met'. He saw his reforms being put into practice through the creation of a strong Opposition party at Stormont, which would have links with the Labour Party in Britain. He dismissed the Northern Ireland Labour Party as 'a branch of Unionism' and, therefore, unacceptable to British Labour. Callaghan's talk over dinner that evening marked the conception of the recently formed Social Democrat and Labour Party, which is now bidding rather uncertainly to be the Opposition at Stormont that Callaghan then asked for" (*Arms and the Men*, p.71)

Brady misses out Callaghan's efforts to establish the real Labour Party of State in its 'Northern Ireland' region, but in the medium to long term he was proved right in his analysis of what British Labour wanted in 'Northern Ireland'.

Brady's argument that the SDLP's origin lies in the British requirement for a detached labour party for the semi-detached region of the British State, in the absence of itself, has a lot going for it.

Brady's thought has credence from the purpose and usefulness for British Policy in 1969-70 of what was to become the SDLP. The organisation of the British Labour Party in the North had failed to take place. There was a determination to maintain Stormont and the 'Northern Ireland' *façade* between the State and the people of the Province. The NILP lacked the potential to become the type of opposition that could fulfil this role effectively. It had been maginalised in O'Neill's cultivation of the Nationalist Party as the new Opposition to give substance to the pseudo-state and some within it were demanding the real thing—British Labour—rather than the continuance of pseudo-parties.

Therefore, it was wholly logical that Callaghan should encourage the Catholic MPs, with some Protestant kindred spirits, at Stormont to form themselves into a pseudo party of the left organised in an area that was disconnected from the State and making believe they were its Labour Party. It would do as a make believe party of the left to go with the Unionist make believe party of the right to produce a pretend normal division of party politics for a newly created functional pseudo state that replaced the dysfunctional arrangement of the past. This would please Hume and the other opposition politicians who were saying they could make something of such a system.

Callaghan, seeing what was happening between those who would form his labour 'opposition' during 1970, as they failed to form themselves into a party and then seeing how they cobbled themselves together, must have doubted anything functional would emerge, and when it did he could see it easily breaking apart.

And, presumably that is why he resurrected his scheme for real Labour representation for the North.

That scheme disappeared without trace. Perhaps Callaghan's intention was to frighten Dublin into putting some urgency into the SDLP, so that the politicians did not take their position for granted and rose to the occasion of what was required of them from the left wing of the British State.

But it was all really just dressing up the old communal division in new clothes, just as transparent as the Emperor's.

Ian McAllister's 1977 book about the SDLP, which has a Foreword by Richard Rose, gives the party its correct title: 'The Northern Ireland Social and Democratic Party'. It was a party of a pseudo-state which would never have to bother itself with the usual business of political parties, gaining power within an actual State—a practical aim at least which its rival, Sinn Fein, had going for it.

In relation to this issue: it is strange why no one ever asked what the point of the SDLP was? Why did it content itself to be a party only of 'Northern Ireland' and not of the State it aspired to be part of, or the other State that it would spend its entire and only existence operating within?

These questions lie at the heart of the origin and purpose of the SDLP as an instrument of British strategy in 'Northern Ireland' and of Dublin's desire to keep Northern Catholics as a tool of the 'national interest' whether it was going nowhere or not.

Irish Opposition to British Labour

The Irish Ambassador outlined to Callaghan the opposition of the Government he represented in Dublin to Labour organising in the North:

> "It would mean a more positive recognition by the Labour Party of the continuing division of my country… I remarked that the development he

has in mind could do serious damage to the new opposition party in Stormont and we would regard this as unfortunate. He brushed this comment aside by saying that the new party has no future. It will disintegrate quickly because it has no genuine basis of cohesion" (pp.1-2).

The various reasons why Dublin would be opposed to the state's Labour Party organising in its 'Northern Ireland' region are then given:

"1) ... an insufficient understanding of both psychology in the area and about our attitude about the country as a whole...;

2) historically there never has been a British political party in the North. The Unionist Party... is a strictly Irish party and always has been. If the British Labour Party had taken a real interest in the Northern political situation 50 years ago one might give the some credence today. The fact is, however, that they did not do so and now deserve no acquiescence from us in setting up their own operation in the North;

3) ... Mr. Callaghan should be disabused of the notion that the minority in the North will now vote for Labour out of gratitude for what Mr. Callaghan was forced to do to maintain British prestige;

4) the minority is attempting the very difficult task of forming its own political party at the present time... The intrusion of the British Labour Party into the political scene will be resented and opposed strongly by all of those elected representatives of the minority;

5) the two major political parties here, Fianna Fáil and Fine Gael, have been careful not to organise themselves in the North although any Irish political party has a greater right to do so than any British political party. Instead their policy has been to maintain a liaison with the major opposition party in the North... the Nationalist Party, which has considerably lost in prestige and influence for reasons which I need not go into now. It appears to be in the best interests of all involved that the general policy... should be continued rather than that the major parties here should themselves enter the political arena in the North. Insofar as Fianna Fáil and Fine Gael have restrained themselves in this situation for the general good then it might be expected that Mr. Callaghan should also stay out of the situation;

6) there has been an apparent attempt by the Irish Labour Party to form a liaison with the SDLP in the North. This attempt... has so far failed and, in my opinion, will continue to fail...;

7) Mr. Callaghan admits that a British Labour Party in the North would necessarily be pro-constitution... It could conceivably... create a situation where both the majority party in the North and a minority British Labour Party were equally pro-partition and this is something we have every right to oppose;

8) ... the Conservative Government in Westminster... appears to have a greater historical sense in this matter and appears dimly to realise the need for a new arrangement. Mr. Callaghan's concept may run directly contrary

to any such supposition. It would not surprise me that he privately believes that the minority in the North would be glad to remain British if they were treated equally with their neighbours. Even if he were right in this — something with which I disagree very strongly — it is in the interest of our general policy that he should not be allowed to try for such a 'solution'..."

It is clear from this that the Dublin Government understood the difference between an imitation Labour party and the real thing. It wasn't bothered by the Northern Ireland Labour Party, but if the State Labour Party decided to organise *"we should oppose it without reserve"*.

Dublin, after calling off its activist policy in May 1970 that might have produced a formidable political force in the Six Counties among Northern Catholics, was establishing a party to serve its new interests in the North in the shape of the SDLP. The SDLP policy was unity by consent, but the policy of the Labour Party would *"necessarily be pro-constitution"* — which, of course, provided for unity by consent!

The Report's author recommended that, if Callaghan pursued his scheme, the British Labour leadership (including Wilson and Healey) should be approached to block him; leverage could be gained with the Conservative Government through opposition to Labour and "If, as suggested, our long-term national interest could be affected by competition in the North from a well-financed British Labour Party, we should oppose it without reserve" (pp.2-4).

The essential thing on Dublin's part seems to have been to maintain the political isolation of the North as a political No-man's-land between the two states — legislated for in major respects, and paid for, by Britain, but excluded from British state politics. And in doing so they kept the Northern Catholics in a Limbo, dependent upon a deliverance from Dublin that was never likely to come. And they also re-activated the lever for which 'Northern Ireland' was designed: to influence things in the South.

Sean Donlon of the Dublin Ministry of Foreign Affairs has recently revealed that Hume and Dublin conspired together in this:

> "From the beginning, the SDLP had fraternal links with both the Irish Labour Party and the British Labour Party and the latter agreed that they would not run candidates in Northern Ireland for Westminster elections. Hume also reached an informal understanding with Jack Lynch that Fianna Fail would not organise or run candidates in Northern Ireland, an important arrangement at a time when there was a minority element within the party anxious to establish an assertive Northern Ireland profile." (*John Hume, Irish Peacemaker,* kindle ed.)

It seems, therefore, that Hume and Lynch were responsible for both promoting the constitutional/unconstitutional division in Catholic politics in the 6 Counties by subverting the possibility of a "Fianna Fail of the North" and in keeping the Catholic community in a political Limbo.

But the Northern Catholics had mobilised and they were no longer going to tolerate waiting in vain—having done so for 50 years.

Dublin's Attitude to the SDLP

Lynch's courting of the SDLP constituted something of a change of policy on Fianna Fail's part with regard to Northern Nationalism. Fianna Fáil under De Valera had exercised its own arm's length policy with regard to Northern Catholics, keeping them out of the Party and barring them from influence. During the 1960s Lemass had belittled the Nationalist Party, regarding it as virtually worthless in Dublin's new engagement policy with O'Neill. He had a large part in its subsequent destruction after ordering McAteer to take up the position of Her Majesty's Loyal Opposition in the pseudo-parliament at Stormont. Lynch similarly wrote off the Nationalists and cold-shouldered McAteer when he journeyed to Dublin to ask why Lynch was rejecting the Northern part of his Nation.

In February 1970 Lynch again rejected approaches by the Nationalists to establish a formal connection between them and Fianna Fáil and told them in a letter that this was pointless, given the prospect of their imminent demise after the civil rights politics had succeeded where they had failed (DFA 305/14/360). Enda Staunton believes another reason for Lynch's rejection of the Nationalist overtures was because of the secret information he had received (from Hume) on the formation of a new Catholic party . (Enda Staunton, *The Nationalists of Northern Ireland*, p. 274)

Taoiseach Lynch's provoking of the Arms Crisis and his abandonment of attempts to develop a semi-constitutional force in the North pushed him towards making links with the new SDLP. The relationship between North and South had begun to alter in the aftermath of the August explosion and Lynch seems to have decided to go where no Fianna Fáil Leader had gone before.

Although Hume had established a working relationship with Dublin even before the formation of the SDLP, providing Lynch with intelligence about political developments within Northern Nationalism, there seems to have been some reluctance from other members of the SDLP towards formalising links with Fianna Fáil. Both Fitt and Devlin were wary of Fianna Fáil both because they had a British Socialist orientation and as a consequence of the suspicion they had come under from the Taoiseach's men after they failed to anticipate Dublin's *volte face* in spending Lynch's money in ways that were now seen as undesirable after the British Ambassador's intervention.

Some Southern businessmen ('The Dublin Fund') acted as financial go-betweens between the Dublin Government and the SDLP initially, before Lynch decided to provide the 'Constitutional' Nationalists with treasure direct from his party chest. Devlin later revealed that "we made several lucrative trips to Dublin, where a support group of sympathetic business and professional people... handed over generous sums of money" to the 'socialist' party. Devlin also revealed that, after that the Fianna Fáil Government "were running after us—whatever we wanted we got" (See Staunton, *The Nationalists of Northern Ireland*, p.276, Paddy Devlin, *Straight Left*, p.145 and Stephen Kelly, *Fianna Fáil, Partition and Northern Ireland, 1926-1971*, p.329)

Being bank-rolled from the Republic meant that the SDLP could not make interventions in 26 County political affairs and would never become a political party there. When Gerry Fitt, in Connolly-socialist mode, made a gaff by calling the Ulster Unionists and Fianna Fail "Siamese twins" of bourgeois politics it was estimated that this cost the party £10,000 from lost donations. The 'Dublin Fund' required that the SDLP clarify its attitude to have its payments maintained (IT 7.11.72) The SDLP had its place and that place was the Six Counties, only. It was the pet of Dublin in the North and could be nothing more.

The change in the Fianna Fail attitude to the Northern 'Constitutionalists' did not represent a fundamental shift in the Southern position with regard to the Northern Catholic community. A provincial SDLP suited Dublin in much the same way as it suited London. It preserved the detachment of the Six Counties and its politics from both States which had been the dominant feature of the relationships with Northern Ireland of both the British and Irish Establishments since the 1920 Act and the death of Michael Collins. It maintained the 26 Counties free from contamination by the Northerners.

However, it also signalled the end of the desire to create a Fianna Fail in the North and instead placed reliance on a political party which lacked the anchor of considerations of State. This was to prove very important because, although the alternative would have been a less constitutional force, it would have been grounded in a way that the SDLP wasn't. The Republican War took off and took the SDLP with it in a way that a force anchored to the Southern State would have been able to resist, with the legitimacy of a state behind it. The SDLP, as a detached vessel within the Northern polity, proved incapable of maintaining its position when the seas around it turned stormy.

The Conceptual Blur

The slogans and phrase mongering that served Fitt well in the O'Neill era when they were employed as mere debating points for the consumption of Westminster against the Unionist government, were imported into the

SDLP, but were now beside the point. In the transformed political situation after August 1969 when hard political decisions were going to have to be made within the developing conflict, they represented an unsustainable position that only produced confusion of purpose.

The *Irish News* commenting on Fitt's statement of aims said:

> "The aims of the new left of centre Social Democratic and Labour Party... are comprehensive and reflect the views—Republican, Socialist, Nationalist and Independent—of the six most active and vocal M.P.s who form the initial membership" (22.8.70).

Fitt's statement of policy was a masterpiece, being all things to all men while at the same time being Nationalist in the mildest of language, with the aim of Irish unity almost as an afterthought. The Party could, of course, afford its radical and idealist programme more than most political parties— it would never have the problem of reconciling idealism and practicality brought about by the gaining of political power at the level of State. Its liberal and socialist phrases were politically meaningless, apart from their use as a weapon in the Nationalist interest, giving the Party a radical froth which covered over many of its more traditional attitudes.

The new Nationalism put behind it the passive ways of the old Nationalist Party, and undertook to demonstrate that progress could be made by 'constitutional' activism rather than 'constitutional' passivity. Instead of being content with "half a loaf" like Eddie McAteer they wanted the full pan. But progress towards what end was the question—a reformed 'Northern Ireland' or a United Ireland?

It appeared that there was a new page turning in Northern Nationalism with the displacement of the Nationalist Party by the SDLP. But was there really any great policy change in the changeover, in which the past was seen as obsolete and new fashionable slogans were being proclaimed? Fitt from Republican Labour, Hume, the Derry businessman, Devlin of the NILP and Currie of the old Nationalist Party certainly had reached no agreement on how they were going to achieve a settlement within the structure of the British State.

Fitt and Devlin seemed to desire the establishment of a Socialist 'Northern Ireland' prior to a United Ireland. But how was socialism to be achieved in a façade of a State—especially as that façade was in the process of crumbling? And that would just result in the State coming into view and what then—the British Labour Party?

In February 1971 Hume rejected the idea of coalition government or of opposition ministers filling government appointments. He saw this as a mere "patching up" of Stormont (6.3.71). Hume suggested that:

> "We have reached, I think, the crunch... the Right Wing of Unionism is the Northern Ireland problem: they have created this State... and until

Westminster confronts them we will always have a problem, and I hope that confrontation is coming soon" (20.3.71).

But 'Northern Ireland' was not a state, and neither was it created by Unionism. Unionists had not wanted to operate a semi-detached pseudo-state in 1920 but found it imposed on them by Westminster who required that they make the "*supreme sacrifice*" of giving up their connection with the UK for Imperial purposes. (see Volume One)

Hume appeared to suggest that the SDLP would simply remain as the opposition at Stormont until Westminster launched a big political initiative that would face down Unionism. However, Britain had no intention of doing this.

The effect of such policy was to make the SDLP restless. The formal Leader of the SDLP, Fitt, informed the UK Representative in NI, Ronnie Burroughs, by telegram that many of his MPs wanted to walk out of Stormont in order to hasten its end. Fitt pinpointed Currie in particular and urged Burroughs to "stiffen him up". The SDLP Leader also informed the British that his party was straining at the leash to organise a passive resistance campaign including the non-payment of rent and rates (PRO PREM 15/476 22.3.71).

This was even before Faulkner took office as Prime Minister and 5 months before Internment was introduced! What was clear was that Hume was directing the party towards his own strategic objective under his Leader's nose.

From its inception until June 1971 the SDLP remained in the hinterland between a new form of politics and traditional Nationalism. As a new development in Catholic politics, it was unsure of itself, and understandably wavered between the Anti-Partitionism of the old Nationalist Party and a new purposefulness in an accommodationist direction. This situation, of course, could not persist. Nature abhors a vacuum and politics even more so.

When in the summer of 1971 the new Unionist Prime Minister, Brian Faulkner, proposed a political reform, the SDLP responded enthusiastically on the spur of the moment on the basis of its reform programme, but on further consideration decided on the basis of its Anti-Partition programme to leave Stormont.

The conceptual blur over purpose came to disable the SDLP in its moment of truth in July 1971 and left it under the direction of the only part of it that had a purposeful strategy, John Hume.

Fall of Chichester-Clark

In January 1971 a further outbreak of rioting in Ballymurphy put the local community in conflict with the British Army again. The source of the conflict was a British Army discotheque which was objected to after it was attended by local girls. The Provisionals quelled the disturbances in an arrangement with the British commanders.

However, the way conflict was ended had repercussions. The 900-strong Ulster Unionist Council met and, fed up with the British Army's lack of enthusiasm in repressing the Catholic disturbances and its acquiescing to Republican authority in parts of the Six Counties, called on Chichester-Clark to resign.

This forced the British into a show of military strength which resulted in both Republican and British fatalities. Chichester Clark made a declaration of war on the Provisionals on TV on 7th February and his cabinet issued a list of demands on the British calling for more troops, more arrests, block arrests and total curfews on Catholic areas. The most astonishing demand was for British reprisals or "punitive expeditions" to be mounted (*Sunday Insight*, Ulster, p.249)

In March 1971 Chichester-Clark came under immense pressure from the Ulster Unionist Council after the Provos killed 3 off-duty Scottish soldiers. The Unionist Prime Minister's opponents, centred around the two ministers sacked by O'Neill, Bill Craig and Harry West, indicated that a motion of no confidence would be raised within the UUC on March 29th unless the Leader of the party conceded a number of demands, including the military occupation of republican areas, increased raids and searches of Catholic districts, more curfews, the closure of cross-border roads, rearmament of the RUC, reforming of the Specials and economic sanctions against Dublin.

Chichester-Clark could not meet these demands because Westminster had taken over control of these areas formerly within the remit of Stormont. The Unionist Prime Minister pleaded with Westminster for five more battalions of troops but was only given one. When he returned to Stormont empty-handed he resigned, declaring his Government powerless to meet the demands of his party. Chichester-Clark said in his final statement: "I have decided to resign because I can see no other way of bringing home to all concerned the realities of the present constitutional, political and security situation." This indicated the anomaly between Westminster power and Stormont responsibility that could not persist.

Something of a standoff then developed between Whitehall and Stormont. The Unionist Cabinet threatened to resign *en masse* and Craig said he would organise a Provisional Government and mass resistance if London imposed Direct Rule. Westminster hinted that it could not work with Craig if he was elected Unionist Leader but if his rival, Brian Faulkner, was elected a more aggressive security policy would be adopted and the reform programme ended. Faulkner was duly elected Leader of the Unionist Party and Prime Minister.

Faulkner springs a surprise

Faulkner, although seen as a 'hard-liner' by the SDLP began his Premiership in a way no other Unionist Leader had ever contemplated. He came to the job at a desperate moment and was immediately assailed by both Nationalists and hard-line Unionists. Faulkner, however, appointed a broad-based cabinet of unionists including very moderate people and a member of the NILP, David Bleakley, who was not even an MP, in a new cabinet post of Minister for Community Relations. In his March address to Stormont Faulkner promised to make "no distinction between Protestant and Roman Catholic" and "to serve all the people of Northern Ireland" (David Bleakley, *Faulkner*, p.84).

Faulkner offered to have discussions with Fitt over matters of common concern, began to legislate against discrimination against Catholics by firms with public contracts, and organised funding for the Catholic-run Mater Hospital in North Belfast. This was a far cry from the *"Protestant Parliament for a Protestant People"* and even from the O'Neill years.

Faulkner also had published a Government White Paper, *A Record of Constructive Change*, outlining the measures taken to address the commitments made in 1969 to reform the system and the extent to which they had been implemented: Local Government boundaries had been redrawn; Derry was being administered by an independent commission; Faulkner had placed housing allocation under the Housing Executive and a points system; he had brought in fair employment measures in public contracts; a Community Relations Commission had been set up under a Catholic, Maurice Hayes; a Police Authority had been established and the office of Director of Public Prosecutions set up; the RUC had been disarmed and the Specials disbanded. All that remained of the 1968 Civil Rights Programme was the Special Powers Act, which it was argued depended for its existence solely on the continuation of violence.

Despite these unprecedented attempts at a political accommodation,

> "... the SDLP, after their initial enthusiasm, appeared to drift away from meaningful contact with the government. Faulkner found it frustrating to deal with a party leadership who would turn up late for meetings, or cancel at the last minute, or fail to deliver a promised reaction to something he had put to them" (Robert Ramsey, *Ringside Seats*, p.81)

Robert Ramsey, Faulkner's Personal Secretary, put this strange behaviour or *manque de sérieux* down to the tensions between the conflicting tendencies within the SDLP, momentarily pulled towards and away from Stormont, and a political accommodation with Unionism. But it probably also had much to do with the eye the party was keeping on the increasing Republican military campaign.

Within three months of his election Prime Minister Faulkner sprang a surprise initiative on the SDLP during a meeting of the Stormont Parliament, on 22nd June, marking the 50th Anniversary of the Northern Parliament. He offered the SDLP the Chairmanship of certain new committees within Stormont that would deal with policy formation, scrutiny of government and the consideration of legislation. These would be properly funded, resourced and have special allowances paid to SDLP chairmen. There would also be comprehensive exploratory discussions about the future of the province and its government involving all parties and a proposal for Proportional Representation for Stormont elections on the table.

This was a most remarkable and unexpected initiative from Faulkner, who was considered by the SDLP to be a hard-line Orangeman and to be only interested in repression of the minority.

Faulkner, unexpectedly, had proved a very different beast from his predecessor, Chichester Clark, who had just asked the British for tougher security measures in the situation and had little political imagination beyond that. Faulkner, on the other hand, had given up his notion that the Nationalists were just a 'Fifth Column', or at least he was prepared to put it to the test. And so he offered the SDLP something neither O'Neill or his cousin dreamt of: he offered Catholic representatives, a share in power.

It represented a radical change in Unionist policy that would, for the first time in 50 years, involve Nationalists in participation in the Stormont administration. Currie notes in his autobiography that the offer was unprecedented and "represented a major, even revolutionary, advance" that "would have been enthusiastically welcomed by the opposition at any other time over the fifty years as an indication of unionist willingness to reach out to the minority community and to take their views into account in the running of the State" (*All Hell Will Break Loose*, p.166 and p.165)

It was Faulkner's tactical flexibility, unusual in Unionism, which damned him in the eyes of the Opposition. He caught the SDLP on the hop when they had not developed a policy on participation, never expecting such an offer from him. He called their bluff and the SDLP was in a quandary about what to do.

Faulkner's offer presented the SDLP with a dilemma: work within the system or reject it. But, if it rejected the offer, the Party could hardly blame the Unionists for excluding it from power.

The SDLP initially welcomed Faulkner's offer and signalled it was minded to take it up. Fitt indicated this when he answered the Prime Minister's proposals in Stormont by saying that the SDLP "certainly hope to take him up on the challenge he has thrown out to the whole community". The *Irish News* reported Paddy Devlin as saying that he was "quite surprised" by Faulkner's proposals which "showed plenty of imagination" and that—

"... it was his (Faulkner's) best hour since I came into this house... If the promise that is contained in those proposals is implemented we will possibly get over the bad period towards which we are heading as a result of trouble on the streets. The Prime Minister has given Hon. Members, and indirectly those outside, an opportunity to share in decision making".

John Hume said: "It should be made clear to all people today who say that no change has taken place, that this is simply not true. There have been changes in this community" (IN 24.6.71). Faulkner's plea for the SDLP not to press an amendment demanding deeper reform succeeded in gaining its withdrawal and the Unionist motion was put and agreed upon. As the Northern Editor of the *Irish Times* wrote:

"If Hume, the most articulate and in many ways the shrewdest SDLP spokesman around, was willing to give the Faulkner proposals a try then it was clear that the party was committed to working within the contemporary system. Faulkner must have been happy with the first signs from the Opposition... and he must have had reasonable grounds for believing that his plans would work... In other words... there was no indication whatever that its thinking was directed along lines which would demand the end of the system... Faulkner now had the stated willingness of the entire Opposition to give him a chance to make a departure within the Stormont system work. Everybody went home that Thursday night, after three days of debate, feeling that... there seemed the basis for government/opposition co-operation." (Henry Kelly, How Stormont Fell, pp.40-3)

In the Stormont debate it seemed that the Unionists and 'Constitutional' Nationalists were about to embark on a significant internal reform of the devolved system to make it amenable to Nationalists and the SDLP were going to accept the paid Chairmanships and attempt a new departure. On July 7th the SDLP entered into negotiations with the Unionists to flesh out the proposals.

Hume's Fateful Decision

There was a moment of truth for 'Constitutional Nationalism' in June 1971 that had a great bearing on the way things subsequently turned out. In this moment the new manifestation of 'Constitutional Nationalism', the SDLP, was unexpectedly offered entry into the Stormont system by the Unionist Leader, Brian Faulkner. Their response to this innovative proposal was of great significance. It represented a fork in the road that could lead only one way or another. No middle course was possible.

During the upsurge in Republican activity that followed Faulkner's offer the British Army killed two Derry men, Cusack and Beattie. Hume demanded an inquiry and called a council of war in his home. The Provos held their first mass rally in the town, addressed by Ruari O'Bradaigh, and Hume was taunted by locals about "doing the Stormont crawl". Maire Drumm of Sinn Fein made a ferocious speech in which she told the crowd: "I would personally prefer to see all the British Army going back dead... You should not just shout 'Up the IRA', you should join the IRA." Another Republican emphasised that: "Victory is within our grasp... we are going to finish it this time. We are on the high road to freedom and what we need to do now is to rock Stormont and keep it rocking until it comes down" (Brian Faulkner, 'Memoirs of a Statesman', p.108)

On the same day Taoiseach Lynch called on the British Government to override the Protestants and declare itself for a United Ireland. It seems that Dublin was also intent on scuppering a deal between the SDLP and Faulkner.

Hume issued an ultimatum to the British Government that, if it didn't hold a public enquiry into the deaths of the Derrymen, the SDLP would withdraw from Stormont.

Fitt, the SDLP Leader, was not at the meeting at which this course was decided upon. He had lost many more constituents than Hume and had seen a much more substantial Republican growth in Belfast than Hume had in Derry, and he saw it as an over-reaction on Hume's part (Murphy, *'Gerry Fitt'*, p. 167). Along with Devlin he disagreed with the ultimatum, which had not been made after similar incidents before Faulkner's offer, and tried to circumvent it by going to London for a private meeting with the Home Secretary, Reginald Maudling.

Fitt believed that Hume had taken the decision to leave Stormont in a rush of blood and that it was an error of judgment. He felt that the likely outcome of Hume's decision was a surrendering of ground to the Provos, and so he tried to avert it. But, with the SDLP announcing on 12th July that it was going to set up an "Alternative Assembly" in Catholic Dungiven, the meeting with Maudling failed.

Hume may or may not have taken his decision without reference to Dublin, even though he was keeping them abreast of all other matters in relation to the killings and other matters. Eamon Gallagher noted that there was no "substantive exchanges" between the SDLP and Dublin after that (NAI, TSCH 2002/8/78, 14.7.71)

There is another aspect to this decision of Hume.

A few weeks prior to the SDLP walkout Hume made a widely-reported statement to the local SDLP Executive calling for the scrapping of the 1920 Government of Ireland Act, declaring that:

> "The arrival of British troops to maintain law and order, the forcing by the Westminster government of a reform programme on Stormont and the continuing presence of British watchdogs is the clearest possible public

admission that the Unionist government are and were incapable of governing Northern Ireland in peace, justice and stability. Their intervention when allied to the continuing presence of a Unionist government has created a situation of permanent instability in Northern Ireland, and we have no less than three Prime Ministers in two years to prove it" (IN 1.6.71)

Hume was much more distrustful of Faulkner than his party colleagues. The statement issued by the SDLP to justify their walk-out had the mark of Hume all over it:

"We have now been driven to the point when we have been faced with a clear choice—either to continue to give credibility to the system which in itself is basically unstable and from which derives the unrest that is destroying our community, or take a stand in order to bring home to those in authority the need for strong political action to solve our problems and to prevent any further tragic loss of life which derives from the instability of our political institutions.

"Is it any wonder that we feel that the role of the military has changed from being that of impartial keepers of the peace to that of shoring up and supporting a particular individual in the office of Prime Minister? Has the British Government even yet faced up to the logic of its presence in Northern Ireland?... What did that intervention mean other than that the Northern Ireland system itself had failed to produce the basis for peace and stability?

"Now two Years later, having refused to face that logic, the British Government, without the slightest constitutional guarantee asked us to believe that the chief-architects of our injustice-ridden society, the Unionist Party, are the people who can govern us towards a solution, with the same system!... Does the British Government seriously believe that there can be any real public confidence in a Government which is still dominated by a secret sectarian society and does it believe that its army can be used to back the decisions of such a Government?...

"...it would appear to us that the British Government has no real policy beyond that of reacting to events as they happen... Insofar as we can detect any definite policy, it would appear to be the maintenance of Stormont in its present form, carrying out minimum civil rights reforms and involving the Opposition only to the point when the Unionist right-wing would not be alienated.

"In other words, British policy is still governed, as it always has been, except for a few short months in 1969, by the threat of the right-wing backlash. There can be no solution till the right-wing is confronted. The present policy, such as it is, has never had any chance of success and has now been totally shattered by our decision to withdraw from the present parliamentary system and set up an alternative assembly.

"We hope that by doing so we will bring home to the world the reality of the Northern Ireland situation, which is that Stormont is, and always has been, the voice of Unionism. The assembly that we propose will be the voice of non-Unionists" (IN 17.7.71).

It is clear by this that Hume had seen the futility of opposition at Stormont and had started to give up on the prospect of an internal solution. His speech was interpreted as a call for Direct Rule by Westminster in order to end the Stormont system and reconstitute the government of the province.

Hume was not the Leader of the SDLP and this was not party policy. But it was the first example of Hume imposing a strategic vision on the party which over-rode the views of others and which fundamentally determined its course.

The problem, however, for the SDLP is that it was obviously not judged to be a significant political force by the British Government and it was very unlikely that it would be able to *"bring home to the world the reality of the Northern Ireland situation"* by themselves. The walk-out and establishment of a rival assembly therefore had little effect and it was dependent on the Republican Army to bring them back to political influence.

There is one other part of the statement that requires comment—the notion that the Unionists were *"the chief-architects of our injustice-ridden society"*. That might have just been propaganda to flatter the British but it was fundamentally untrue. The *"chief-architects"* of the system were in Whitehall rather than in Stormont. The Unionists were merely the operators of that system, given leeway over it as long as they were able to maintain the buffer it represented between 'Northern Ireland' and the State.

The technicalities of the SDLP withdrawal revealed much about Hume's decision. The reason for the SDLP walk-out was given as the refusal of the British Government to begin an enquiry into the British Army shooting in Derry. It withdrew from Stormont, therefore, over an issue in which the power did not actually lie in Stormont, which had no control over the activities of the British Army. The SDLP remained in Westminster where the power over security actually lay. (Presumably because, despite the absurdity of this action, it felt that it was still necessary to utilise Westminster opinion against the Unionists and Fitt would never have agreed to such a course. Noticeably, it did not withdraw from Westminster after the much larger massacres in Ballymurphy, later in the year, and in Derry in 1972 either.)

The only logical reason, therefore, of walking out of Stormont was to break it up and bring about Direct Rule—perhaps so that the local parliament could be reconstituted in a different form by Whitehall. The following account from Currie seems to confirm this:

> "The alienation of the non-unionist community embraced, not only those who had never identified with the Stormont system, but also professional and business types who had been prepared to play a full part particularly under O'Neill. The alienation was so total that even if the SDLP had wished to talk, it would have been impossible. But we had no desire to talk. We had already committed ourselves to fighting internment in every non-violent

way possible and in so doing had given a lead to public opinion. Since our withdrawal from Stormont, a month earlier, we were committed to ending the Stormont system of government. It was one of those occasions when personal inclination, public opinion and political judgement absolutely and completely coincided. By refusing to talk to Faulkner or the British, by initiating a civil disobedience campaign, and by symbolising our rejection of the system through the alternative assembly, we could end internment, end Faulkner and end the System" (SDLP News 5.10.72).

In this passage Currie runs together two separate events—the SDLP withdrawal from Stormont and the British introduction of Internment. In the following years the SDLP let it be understood that the withdrawal from Stormont took place as a result of the introduction of Internment. But the reverse was closer to the truth—Internment was a consequence of the SDLP walkout.

The fact that the walkout from Stormont was so illogical in relation to its stated cause was probably a source of guilt later for the SDLP and the myth that its cause was the much more serious event of Internment was let develop.

However, the SDLP statement issued at a conference held on 12th July shows that the party, after being invited to reform the Stormont system by Faulkner, had decided instead to destroy it and depart from its stance of "restraint and responsible leadership":

"There comes a point where to continue to do so is to appear to condone the present system. That point, in our view has been reached... The British government must face up to the clear consequences of their intervention of August 1969 and reveal their determination to produce a political solution which will be meaningful and acceptable... Without such evidence we cannot continue to give our consent to a continuation of the present system... If our demand is not met... we will withdraw immediately from parliament and will take the necessary steps to set up an alternative assembly of elected representatives to deal with the problems of the people we represent, and to become the authoritative voice to negotiate a political solution on their behalf" (IN 12.7.71).

A few days later the SDLP Leader read a party statement to a press conference in which it was stated:

"We have now been driven to the point when we have been faced with a clear choice: either to continue to give credibility to the system which in itself is basically unstable and from which derives the unrest that is destroying our community or take a stand in order to bring home to those in authority the need for strong political action to solve our problems and to prevent any further tragic loss of life which derives frm the instability of our political institutions." (IN 17.7.71).

Less than a month earlier Fitt, in welcoming Faulkner's proposals, had said that the SDLP were "prepared to co-operate with the government to prevent a further tragic loss of life and were prepared to take any steps we can in conformity with the government to prevent hundreds of innocent men, women and children, Protestant and Catholics, being maimed as they have over the last two or three years." (IN 24.6.71)

But, after two deaths in disputed circumstances, the SDLP completely reversed its position, declaring that instability and violence, instead of being a result of their non-co-operation with Unionists, was a consequence of their accommodation with Faulkner. The next couple of months were to prove which of these two incompatible positions was correct as the SDLP politically fuelled the Insurrection. The week the SDLP withdrew there was a massive increase in violence across the Six Counties

Faulkner's Personal Secretary Robert Ramsey has suggested that the SDLP walkout was given its impetus by the Department of Foreign Affairs in Dublin. He gives as evidence for this view a conversation he had with Hume in 1999 in which the SDLP leader was less than categorical in denying this and the similarities that were later revealed between DFA documents and the SDLP public statement announcing the withdrawal on 16th July.

This statement, which was more in the nature of a manifesto, justifying the SDLP withdrawal, contained such odd phrases, as *"the letter of reform is not the reality without a change of heart"* and *"Stormont... is, and always has been, the voice of Unionism"*. Ramsey believed it was written in Iveagh House in Dublin—

> "... not only because its themes exactly mirrored the southern government's policies of the day, but because the style of the document is unmistakably that of the DFA, which gives the document a markedly different 'feel' to that of the SDLP's other publications of the time" (*Ringside Seats*, p.83).

Hume undoubtedly shared a similar view of Faulkner to Dublin and there is evidence that he worked more closely—and independently—with Dublin than any of his colleagues in the SDLP. As regards Dublin's view of the Unionist Leader: Patrick Hillery, for instance, told the British Ambassador that Faulkner was not trusted by Dublin and was considered more dangerous than Bill Craig because "he was plausible enough and could convey an impression of moderation which might bamboozle Westminster" (PREM 15/476, 13.3.71)

Sean Donlon of the MFA in Dublin confirmed in 2015 that Hume took his decision in consultation with Taoiseach Lynch, behind the back of his party leader. They agreed together to destroy the Stormont government (*John Hume, Irish Peacemaker*, kindle edition). Eamon Gallagher noted that there was no "substantive exchanges" between the SDLP and Dublin after that but Hume kept up a personal dialogue with Lynch (NAI, TSCH 2002/8/78, 14.7.71 and *John Hume, Irish Peacemaker*).

Common Origins

Faulkner later made the following comment about the SDLP's "*bombshell*" in rejecting his open-ended offer and its decision to walk away from Stormont and to set up its own assembly:

> "It was a serious blow to political progress in Ulster and a sad day for democracy. Since the formation of the SDLP in 1970 the party had always taken the approach then outlined by its leader Gerry Fitt: 'We believe that Stormont is the only institution through which reform can come'... Only two weeks before they had welcomed new proposals for reform, and John Hume himself had pointed out the problems of making legislative change effective... But now... they were withdrawing with a denunciation of the whole system. They no longer sought reform, they were supporting a revolutionary change, and resorting to the old dead-end Irish tactics of boycott and abstention to achieve it. They were abdicating leadership of the Catholic community at a time when firm and moderate leadership was most needed... No doubt there were pressures which it would have taken a very great deal of courage to stand up against, but many people were to die as a result of failure to grasp this opportunity" (*Memoirs of a Statesman*, p.110)

Currie's account from 1972 suggests that the SDLP declined Faulkner's offer because it would have involved a straightforward conflict with Republicanism and 'Constitutional' Nationalist representatives in Stormont would have threatened the vigour of the developing Anti-Partitionism that would give the SDLP a more substantial role in the administration than Faulkner was offering.

Brendan O'Duffy has the following to say in relation to the SDLP decision to walk away in an article entitled '*The Price of Containment*':

> "The SDLP walk-out was an important peacemaking failure. Until that moment there was considerable competition between the SDLP and the PIRA for control... By the spring of 1971 the Provisional's offensive was destabilizing but it did not enjoy unbridled support across the nationalist community... The radical nationalist argument that Faulkner's committee system was 'too little, too late,' while accurate, misses the wider point that Faulkner could not have offered a more substantial constitutional reform package, even if he wanted to... Only Westminster could have insisted on a form of power-sharing, but this required a degree of resolve which the Heath government did not have. Once again, the level of violence had not achieved a sufficient level to discredit the policy of reacting to crises" (*The Northern Ireland Question in British Politics*, p. 106).

As Austin Currie pointed out, the Westminster adversarial majority-rule system of government and opposition set up in 1921 was very unsuitable for internal political accommodation. Perhaps that was the intention at the outset—to establish a permanent antagonism. But 50 years later it hamstrung Faulkner, who found that the system was seen as a remaining 'British' manifestation by the community it had been given to, as the 'Northern Ireland' region was detached from the political life of the State.

Robert Ramsey notes:

> "Faulkner began to set out a policy which involved major changes to the status quo in the short term and which would have a built-in evolutionary element for the future. At the heart of this policy was a new assumption, the importance of which was not clearly recognised at the time. O'Neillism had been an unstructured set of ideas, based on vague wishful thinking about how the two sides of the community might be drawn closer together... 'Faulknerism', on the other hand, took as its starting point a belief in the existence of two self-aware, distinct and equally legitimate groups who would have to be catered for in practical and specific ways which gave both a stake in, and a responsibility for, the running of Northern Ireland. It was unionist in its insistence that the fundamental constitutional position of the state must reflect the wishes of the majority, but it broke free from many of the Westminster-centre concepts of the past... My impression was that the departures from earlier widely held assumptions about British democracy did not cause Faulkner any personal pain. It was his calculation that an internal settlement which bound the political opposition into the Stormont structure would be in the true interests of unionism" (*Ringside Seats*, pp.76-7)

The SDLP had decided to treat the North as a state so their behaviour in the wake of Faulkner's offer was wholly self-defeating. If the SDLP had decided to take up Faulkner's offer, this would have precipitated a political division in the Catholic community. The SDLP politicians would have had to compete with the Republican movement, on the basis of a sharply defined difference, for the mass support of the Catholics. It would have been make or break for them. They would have either gone from strength to strength after riding out the developing Republican offensive or they would have been blown away by it.

Duffy points to another important matter. The Committee System was all the SDLP was going to achieve under its own steam. The British Government would not be prepared to embark on a substantial political initiative to deal with the conflict without a great escalation of IRA activity. But that was something the SDLP could never say.

The SDLP would thereafter have to ride on the back of the Provos like the wren rides the eagle until it exhausts itself—leaving the wren to then attempt to fly on its own wings.

But there probably was a deeper reason why the SDLP failed to have the courage of its political programme at the vital hour. It, just like the Provos, had a common source in the historical experience of the Catholic community in relation to the events of August 1969. This meant that the SDLP could not act coherently and decisively against the Republicans without in some way denying itself and its own origins. It feared that by acting against itself by accepting Faulkner's offer, it would, in essence, destroy itself.

What would have emerged from Faulkner's offer to the SDLP was set out in a Stormont Green Paper published in October 1971 which fleshed out the Committee proposals of June. One significant section stated:

> "It may be argued by some that a permanent majority/minority situation creates problems for the smooth operation of the democratic process. In many ways the British democratic system, with its virtual assurance that those who control the executive will also control the legislature, represents a much greater concentration of power than say the American system, based as it is on a deliberate diffusion and separation of powers. Between general elections the power of the British government is, in some respects, as absolute as democratic power can be, but this exercise of power is accepted by a Parliamentary minority who would know that sooner or later their turn to exercise it will come. When this expectation does not exist, there is clearly a risk of disenchantment with the democratic, parliamentary process. Because of this, it has been argued in some quarters that means must be found to give 'the minority' in Northern Ireland a share in the effective exercise of power. The Government believes that this important issue should be openly and dispassionately considered by Parliament and public" (Kenneth Bloomfield, *Stormont in Crisis*, p. 152)

The Stormont Parliament celebrated its 50th Anniversary in 1971. In 49 years of 'constitutional' politics Currie's party, the Nationalist Party, had altered the Unionist position not an inch and yet the Provisionals in just over a year of War had produced ground-breaking offers. Was it any wonder that the SDLP was dancing to the Republican tune?

Effects of the SDLP Walk-Out

Michael A. Murphy makes the following comment on the consequences of the SDLP walkout:

> "It is impossible to anticipate how events would have unfolded if the SDLP had accepted Faulkner's offer and not walked out of Stormont. Undoubtedly this would have placed the new party in direct conflict with the Provos, and there is little doubt that there would have been intense pressure on them and perhaps great short-term political damage. But it is

also the case that Faulkner would have found it difficult to proceed with the policy of internment after August 1971 if he wanted to keep the SDLP onside. Internment was made probable by the nationalist withdrawal from politics because there was no reason for restraint left in unionism, and there was no reason for Britain to veto the Unionists, since the only alternative was to take responsibility themselves. Internment greatly intensified the conflict and determined that political events would be shaped by the Provos rather than the SDLP" (*Gerry Fitt*, p.169).

Currie admits as much himself in his autobiography:

"The benefit of hindsight makes it possible to see that our withdrawal from Stormont over the Cusack-Beattie killings was a mistake. It had one consequence to which we had not given sufficient consideration: it removed from Faulkner one concern which might have prevented him from introducing internment... and which made it easier for the London government to agree to support him in its introduction. Faulkner knew we would not stomach internment, and that any hope of the 'participation' he considered necessary for the continuation of Stormont would be wrecked by our threatened withdrawal if it were introduced. Our boycott of Stormont relieved him of that disincentive" (p.173).

There is no getting away from the fact that the SDLP decision to pull out of Stormont was a major contribution to the escalation of the conflict and encouraged Westminster to seek a military solution to the conflict. If the party had decided to accept a role in the administration, Internment could not conceivably have occurred, since the price Faulkner would have had to pay for their involvement would certainly have been the shelving of Internment. And Internment greatly intensified the War which put paid to Stormont.

The important political effect of the refusal of Faulkner's offer was that it placed the SDLP fortune's in the hands of the Republicans. A better offer to the SDLP could only come about through a serious deterioration of the situation. SDLP debating power was not going to bring it about from its Alternative Assembly at Dungiven. It could only rejoin the political action as a buffer, required by the British, to the Provos.

The fact that the SDLP conceded to Republican pressure in July 1971 gave a massive boost to the Provos. It forced the SDLP into its camp and away from participation. There was now a Nationalist Front against Stormont, with Republican military activity acting as the cutting edge. The War was on!

CHAPTER 7

National War

The Republican military effort gained real momentum by mid-1971. There had been 37 major explosions in April, 47 in May, 50 in June and 92 in July. There had been 34 deaths up to July and increasing hostility was developing between the British Army and the Catholic community. The IRA virtually controlled parts of Derry and West Belfast and was seen to do so. And the training of recruits was going on largely unhindered in those areas.

The heart of the Catholic community was not really in 'Constitutional' politics within the Stormont system by then. Too much water had flowed under the bridge. The community had been roused into activity by the Civil Rights agitation and found itself with nowhere to go after Britain failed to address the fundamentals of the Catholic predicament, and defended the system they had put in place in 1921 with increasing repression. The only thing in politics which really stood between the Catholic community and War was the SDLP and the decisions it took. And now the SDLP was supporting the extra-constitutional effort of the Republicans to all intents and purposes.

So what developed from August 1971 had the character of a people's war. Almost every door in Catholic Belfast was open to the Republican Army, popular support was increasing, and there was a growing confidence that Stormont (and perhaps even the British) could be seen off.

Internment and Total War

The question of employing Internment against the Insurrection was a decision for the sub-government at Stormont. Faulkner, as Minister of Home Affairs, had used it to good effect during the 1950s IRA invasion. However, he was hesitant to use it because he was unconvinced of its effectiveness in the situation of 1971, where there was growing mass Northern Catholic participation in the Republican War. On 1st April 1971 he rejected its use, doubting that it could defeat the IRA.

His problem was that it had proved effective in both North and South in the past and the Unionist community expected him to use it in the situation of Insurrection. If he didn't use Internment he had to try another policy. But there wasn't any. More radical political policies were not open to him, due to these being the preserve of Whitehall. And the SDLP's retreat from Stormont, after his offer, ruled out any new political initiative that might be attempted.

Faulkner knew Internment would have a bad effect on British public opinion and he had to consider the impact it would have in the South. Although it was considered unlikely that Lynch would follow with a similar policy Faulkner was encouraged by the Justice Minister, Desmond O'Malley's announcement in December 1970 that the policy was under consideration and Lynch's activation of legislation to facilitate it, if necessary. Also there was a recent *Irish Times* report that said, if it was introduced in the North, it would follow, as a matter of course, in the South. (IT 15.7.71).

Faulkner went to London in early August to request the resources necessary for Internment. The British were reluctant and could have refused him, since they had control of the army that was going to carry it out. General Tuzo, the GOC in the North, advised against it, believing it to be "militarily unnecessary" (Andrew Mumford, *The Counter-Insurgency Myth: The British Experience of Irregular Warfare*, p.100).

Reginald Maudling, the Home Secretary, reported to the British Cabinet in late July:

> "... that we now had seriously to contemplate the possibility that we might be compelled to institute direct rule in Northern Ireland if Mr. Faulkner's administration was unable to retain its authority and was replaced by a regime whose policies we could not accept" (CAB 128/48, 22.7.71)

Internment, Maudling concluded, was "the last action available short of direct rule" (CAB 134/3011, 29.7.71).

The decision to introduce Internment was therefore not a military but a political one, taken in Whitehall to maintain the authority of the sub-government and to avoid the greater evil of increased British political engagement. And not too many questions were asked about how effective it was going to prove.

Internment as a policy was not an illegitimate response from Faulkner. It represented the standard practice in the face of a War and it conferred that status upon the Republican campaign. Faulkner had concluded that the Provos' adoption of 'Total War', involving the bombing of businesses and public utilities, dictated a new response—and there was no other one available.

The Provos escalated the War after the Faulkner offer to the SDLP. The shooting of three Scottish soldiers produced '*Internment Now*' slogans across Protestant areas of Belfast and rallies from the shipyard workers demanding that Faulkner implement it. The route of the 12th July march in Belfast was bombed and the new *Daily Mirror* printing plant destroyed with £2 million damage caused. This had two tactical purposes: Firstly, to make it difficult for the SDLP to embed themselves within the Stormont system and secondly, to force Faulkner's hand on Internment by producing a Unionist crescendo in favour of it.

Sean MacStiofain explained in his *'Memoirs of a Revolutionary'* why this was done:

> "We could not afford to allow them to bring in internment when they were ready. Had it have been introduced a year later the British would very much have had their intelligence act together and would have hit us badly. We knew at that time that their intelligence was bad so it was to our advantage to force internment much sooner than they would have liked" (p.185).

The British Prime Minister, Edward Heath, gave the order to Michael Carver, his General Officer Commanding, "to end it, once and for all" (Sunday Express, 28.11.93)

It was not Internment itself that caused the problem with the Catholic community, although anything Unionism did at this point would have been resented. It was the way in which it was carried out by the British Army — through massacre in Ballymurphy and much general brutality exercised by the State against those interned (e.g. the "*hooded men*").

The Internment operation was experienced as a general assault by the Catholic community in Belfast. It was second only to August 1969 in its effect on the community. It was the British Army, acting on behalf of the British State in support of the Stormont sub-government, that performed the assault and made things clear for the community. The British State was prepared to make war on the people it had promised to raise from their second class citizenship only two years previously — in support of those who were intent on keeping them there.

The botched Internment operation was a great boost for the Republican Army. Firstly, it provided a massive propaganda victory in Nationalist Ireland when the brutality and treatment of internees became public — the internees being all Catholic. Secondly, it gave formal recognition to the War by the State it was fighting. Thirdly, it swept the SDLP into being the political support for the Anti-Partitionist offensive. Fourthly, it extended the toleration of the general Catholic community for the military effort, due to the perceived injustice that was visited so partially on the community (when no loyalists were lifted). Finally, it extended Republican growth into country areas, like Tyrone, that had not been as quick as Belfast to join the Insurrection.

In addition it created a cohesion and an *esprit de corps* within the IRA as its various companies got to know each other in Long Kesh.

"*Tá ré na chainte thart* — Total War" was how the Provos referred to their offensive, after the withdrawal of the Catholic representatives from Office and the introduction of Internment ('*The Time for Talking is Over*', *An Phoblacht*, September 1971). Seamus Twomey took command of the Belfast Brigade, loosened the reins on the IRA, and a major blitz of the city began.

The SDLP and Total War

The SDLP had prepared the ground for an escalation of the campaign to bring down Stormont before the introduction of Internment. At the Roger Casement commemoration at Murlough Bay, Paddy Devlin called for a disobedience campaign to be directed against the British Army and said that this would be formulated by NICRA. He also stated that, if Faulkner introduced Internment, it would be regarded as an Act of War by NICRA and the SDLP:

"If Internment was introduced in Northern Ireland it must be recognised for what it is—an act of war and opposed as such... the barricades must go up again. If the British Government is so foolish as to commit its Army in war against any section of the Irish people, we have no alternative but to resist. If the worst comes to the worst, we need have no illusions or hold out false hopes of help from Jack Lynch's Government. We must rely on our own strength. We too are no mean people and will not be crushed" (IN, 2.8.71).

It is clear in this statement what Devlin was saying: that any repressive movement against the IRA would be regarded by the SDLP and NICRA as an act of war and would be responded to with resistance from the general Catholic community. 'Constitutional' and non-constitutional Nationalism were drawing together and Dublin, after letting down Devlin and his community a year previously, had become only secondary in things.

This was part of the development of Northern Nationalism into an independent force, brought about by Lynch's *volte face*. The 'Constitutionalists' who had first looked to Dublin for assistance, who then had been demoralised into impotence after Lynch's turning tail, had now attached themselves to the new substance that had developed within the Northern Catholic community.

On the morning of Internment, on 9th August 1971, the SDLP announced that it would begin to organise a "campaign of mass civil disobedience involving the withdrawal of all Catholics from public office; the withholding of all rent and rates, expecting 100% from all opponents of the Unionist regime"; and for the demand for the suspension of Stormont (IN 10.8.71). The SDLP flew to London to demand of Maudling certain conditions for the calling off of the disobedience campaign, due to be begun on 16th August. These included the release of all internees; a new government at Stormont with formal power-sharing structures and Nationalists guaranteed a say in decision-making across all areas; an assembly at Stormont elected by Proportional Representation.

Maudling offered the SDLP Faulkner's June proposals, underwritten this time by Westminster. The SDLP declined.

A large delegation of the SDLP—including Fitt, Hume, Devlin, Currie and Devlin—met Taoiseach Lynch and Minister for Foreign Affairs Hillery, to discuss their campaign of civil disobedience. The growing belligerence of the SDLP is revealed in this report of the event in the National Archives:

> "Messrs. Currie and Hume described the present civil disobedience campaign as having good backing from NICRA and the 'official' IRA. There was in general much more support than ever for bringing down the present system. There was a problem in involving as many people as possible in the actual campaign and the rent withholding and the rates withholding were calculated to bring about active participation by the working class and the farmer/professional class respectively. They might proceed to non-payment of TV licence fees, car-tax and income tax. Organisationally, apart from their own withdrawal from Stormont, there was a campaign for the withdrawal of councillors from the system and a start had been made of promoting resignations from the UDR. In general they wanted to harness the energy of all who were in favour of opting out of the system, to involve them and to create an active loyalty in the movement away from the system. They proposed to set up an alternative assembly to Stormont to provide a forum so that the opposition voice would be better heard.
>
> "They emphasised that the whole campaign was a last effort to obtain a political solution by peaceful means and they felt they had only one or two months within which to work—if the campaign had no success in that period the non-unionist population would go over to violence... There was some Nationalist disagreement, expressed by Mr. McGill, over the alternative assembly idea and its possible extension to an underground administration.
>
> "A number of speakers felt that the British Army were underestimating the strength of the UDF. They were well armed. On the other hand it was generally felt that the 'Protestant backlash' would better be faced now—it has been the excuse for failure to implement reforms and will continue to be used as an excuse by the Stormont Government and the British Government for not moving towards a political solution in the North" (NAI, TSCH 2002/8/481, 24.8.71).

It was suggested by the SDLP delegation

> "that the following actions be taken by the 26-county Government":-
>
> "renounce its intention to introduce internment; call for an end to internment in the North...; call for the removal of the British Army as a peace-keeping force as it was not now acceptable to the minority community..."

What the SDLP did not seem to concern themselves with was that, if the British Army was withdrawn and the "well-armed" Protestant backlash came (something that "would better be faced now"), who was going to defend the

Catholics? The Provisional IRA, who the SDLP could not bear to mention, perhaps?

There was noticeably no request for Irish Army help, after the let-down in 1970.

It is probable that the action demanded by the SDLP would have resulted in the destruction of much of the Northern Catholic community, if it had been taken up.

The idea that the SDLP's civil disobedience campaign and *"underground administration"* could act as a kind of buffer between the Catholic Community and outright war was bizarre. The SDLP campaign of civil disobedience could act only as a kind of adjunct to the Republican War effort in bringing down Stormont—an objective both shared. It was very unlikely that participation in a rent and rates boycott would deter the more active and vigorous elements in the Catholic community who were increasingly taking part in full-blooded military resistance to Stormont.

The SDLP shared their primary strategic objective with the Republicans— a United Ireland. The difference between them was purely tactical—how should it be achieved? But between Internment and Direct Rule there was a great narrowing of the tactical difference between the two sides of Nationalism—the military and electoral—until they became almost identical, except that the SDLP was not doing the real, actual fighting.

In response to the SDLP disobedience campaign the IRA widened its military campaign to *"economic targets"* of a more general nature.

In June 1971, before Internment, Hume made a speech in the British House of Commons in which he admitted that those who had advocated a United Ireland by "peaceful means" had "failed utterly to present any basic strategy, plan or programme before the people who subscribe to this ideal as to how... a peaceful unity can be achieved" (IN, 25.06.71)

Hume realised that the pursuance of such a strategy through the Stormont Parliament's communal electoral contests was futile when the Unionists could muster nearly twice the votes of Nationalists. This was shown by the experience of the Nationalist Party over decades. When the SDLP aspired to be something different, this ran the risk of going against the strategic imperative of a United Ireland if it were successful.

In late 1971-early 1972 the only potential way of achieving a United Ireland appeared to be through a full commitment by the Catholic community to the Republican momentum. The SDLP committed its energies to it and rode the Provo tiger for the best part of a year. According to Eamonn Gallagher in the Department of External Affairs in Dublin, the SDLP was now explicitly cheering on the IRA: "... even the most pacific of them have now begun to say that they have a vested interest in the continuation of violence as long as Stormont exists" (NAI, TSCH 2002/8/483, 3.11.71)

It was no wonder that the Provisionals said triumphantly of the SDLP action: "This is a move towards the policy of Sinn Fein. Indeed it is a vindication of Sinn Fein policy as consistently enunciated over the years" (*An Phoblacht*, September 1971).

The Civil Disobedience Campaign

The civil disobedience campaign began on August 16th with 130 Local Councillors withdrawing from public bodies, 200 Catholics resigning from the UDR, 20,000 households withholding rent and rates from private landlords and public authorities, and 80% of priests signing a petition condemning internment as "immoral and unjust."

As Hume told the press the objective of the campaign was

"... to demonstrate clearly that a large section of this community has withdrawn its consent from the system of government... No system of government can survive if a significant section of the population is determined that it will not be governed" (IT 16.8.71).

On the day after the publication of the *Green Paper* the first and only Catholic, G.B. Newe, joined a Stormont Cabinet, under Faulkner. G.B. Newe was a man of 1958 rather than a product of 1969. He had given a paper at the Garron Tower Conference that had prompted the Basil Clancy debate on participation (see Volume One). He was Regional Organiser of the Council of Social Services and a founder member of Protestant-Catholic Encounter (PACE), a committed participator and non-sectarian activist.

Austin Currie reserved a special hatred for Newe and issued the following statement against him, published in *The Tyrone Democrat*:

"If you are a man at all, if you wish to maintain any shred of your reputation, you should resign immediately. The administration of which you are a member is no longer recognised by your co-religionists North or South of the border as having any moral or political right to their allegiance. You are like a Jew in Hitler's cabinet. Get Out" (*All Hell Will Break Loose*, p.188).

Faulkner's *Green Paper* would have satisfied all Currie asked of Stormont when Faulkner first made his offer, but, having joined the resistance, the SDLP were now looking for Irish Quislings with the best of them.

The SDLP that withdrew from public office was a parody of what Sinn Fein was in 1919-21 and what it was seeking to be in 1971-2.

The "*Alternative Assembly*" held its inaugural meeting at the Castle Ballroom in Dungiven on 26th October 1971. It was overseen by an Executive Council composed of the abstentionist Stormont MPs and Senators with

John Hume appointed President. An elaborate constitution was formulated that set conditions excluding anybody who was not a *"Constitutional Nationalist"*. Only two plenary sessions of the *"Alternative Assembly"* were ever held. At the second one, on December 4th, the Dungiven Assembly voted to assume responsibility for the administration of law and order in Catholic areas until a *"satisfactory political settlement"* was achieved (IN 6.12.71). Having no coercive power to implement this decision, the *Alternative Assembly"* of the SDLP did nothing in this respect.

The SDLP assisted the civil resistance campaign against the Unionist Government but all the time it had no serious intent to bring about anything lasting through its activities, such as building an alternate source of power, as Sinn Fein had done with Dail Eireann between 1919 and 1921, and which it was attempting with *Eire Nua*, *Dail Uladh*, *Northern Resistance* and the *Republican Co-operatives* in 1971. A little later a Republican 'civil administration' developed which ran the Incident Centres during the 1975 Truce and which ultimately developed into Sinn Fein. But the SDLP had none of this 'underground administration' that was important in contesting power with Stormont and Westminster.

At the height of the rent and rates strike almost a quarter of Catholic households were participating. The question came up within the SDLP of setting up a fund where those who were withholding their rent and rates could lodge their unpaid money. But the party baulked at this, saying that it implied saving in order to pay up in the future.

There was another alternative, which would have involved the setting up an alternative administration at Dungiven, one that opted out of the system and counter-posed an alternative power base to Stormont. But that was beyond the imagination of the SDLP. Ultimately the party was left with only the option of returning to Stormont once Britain re-constituted it.

The Stormont Cabinet Secretary, Harold Black, and the Attorney-General, Basil Kelly, discussed taking legal action against the *"Alternative Assembly"* in mid-December 1971 on the basis of the Convention Repeal Act of 1879 which made it an offence —

> "to take part in the... proceedings of any assembly, other than Parliament as by law constituted, which shall propose to take or shall take upon itself, or willfully permit to be attributed to it the functions of either House of Parliament, or any of them, or having for its object or tendency to bring Parliament into hatred or contempt".

The Attorney-General advised the Cabinet Secretary that it was not worth taking the *"Alternative Assembly"* seriously because it was not a serious attempt to subvert the Constitution and the whole thing would be more bother than it was worth:

"...is Dungiven really proposing to take upon itself the functions of Parliament? The functions of Parliament are its legislative authority and its financial duty of providing through taxes the monetary requirements of government. The Dungiven Parliament may have some of the external trappings and procedure of Parliament, etc., its title, Chairman, preliminary prayers, debate in the form of motions, etc.—but these are not obviously functions... as I have said to you many times, the most formidable barrier in the way of a prosecution to my mind is—is it in the public interest to bring such a prosecution? Would a trial or this kind give much-needed publicity to an Assembly which already at only its second meeting is declining in attendance and generally in impact? Would such a trial make this Government look 'silly'? It must be remembered that a prosecution for either conspiracy or a breach of the 1879 Act would necessarily be an indictable one—one can see the drama and publicity or Fitt, Hume, Currie, Cooper—indeed all the old Stormont opposition—in the dock with no doubt separate legal representation at a trial which would last for weeks with all its attendant publicity and with no certainty of conviction at the end—what with difficulty of proofs and the vagary of a jury" (PRONI, CAB/9/J/37/2).

While setting up its "*Alternative Assembly*" the SDLP refused to resign its seats at Stormont and MPs continued to draw their salaries. By this fact alone it was clear they were keeping one foot in each camp and lacked the full courage of their convictions.

The SDLP found itself working, in effect, to alienate the Catholic community from the Stormont system, whilst at the same time ensuring that that system's political and social authority remained intact so that, if it had to, it could resume participation.

By late 1971 the British Government, having failed to subdue the Republican Army through Internment, was stressing its aim of guaranteeing representatives of the Catholic community "*an active, permanent and guaranteed*" role at Stormont and reducing conflict to "*an acceptable level of violence*" (IN 22.8.71, Maudling in House of Commons and 16.12.71).

This was a clear signal to the SDLP that the British were prepared to make a settlement with them, whilst marginalising Republicans—if they dropped their campaign of abstentionism and civil disobedience. Of course, if the SDLP did not accept, the only thing open to the British was increased military repression.

The SDLP decided to escalate their campaign, rather than enter into negotiations with the British. In the effort to destroy Stormont leading members of the SDLP addressed large rallies, alongside representatives of all strands of Nationalism, from the two IRAs, to Peoples Democracy and the Communist Party, over the following months. At one such rally in the Falls Park, Austin Currie predicted the following, as the Provo campaign intensified:

"Within the next six or seven months, Faulkner and his rotten Unionist system will have been smashed... The so-called British Home Secretary has once again come on T.V. and said that the SDLP ought to be prepared to talk. But I say to Maudling 'Why the hell should we talk to you? We are winning and you are not'... Even if Maudling got down on his bended knees and kissed all our backsides we would not be prepared to talk." [This sentence was censored by the *Irish News* and reported only by the *News Letter*, PW.]
... The aim of this campaign is not only to end internment but to destroy this government because all the evils of this community are symptoms of that basic disease—unionism" (BNL and IN 3.1.72).

The SDLP, despite condemning individual excesses of the Provos, really got swept away by the Republican intensifying of their campaign in the face of Faulkner's Internment policy. There was obvious pleasure taken and shown at the Unionist Premier's increasingly desperate statements reassuring the public that Internment was working when it plainly wasn't, according to Currie's autobiography. At the same rally as Currie gave his speech, Devlin called on the British Army to be driven out of Catholic areas—although by whom he did not state.

These speeches by moderate 'Constitutional' Nationalists must have had an effect on Protestant attitudes to the Catholic community. They surely encouraged the view that the Catholic community was generally supportive of the shooting and bombing. And Loyalists, unfortunately, would have seen them as justifying reprisals on the Catholic community that they were only too ready to engage in.

The substantial effect of the SDLP civil disobedience campaign was in convincing the Unionist community that the SDLP and the Provos were two sides of the same coin and in solidifying opposition to the forces of Catholic-Nationalism.

Hume's Altered Vision

Eamon Gallagher of the Department of Foreign Affairs, filed the following report of meetings he had with members of the SDLP on 15th November, 1971:

"Hume takes the view that getting rid of Stormont is the main objective of policy at present and that internment is an issue which can bring this about. On the whole, therefore, one can begin to perceive a gradual shift in the SDLP target i.e. to bring down Stormont as a preliminary to anything else. Hume disclosed to me that the SDLP had a meeting last week at which they agreed on their objective... Quite simply it is to bring about Irish unity. I asked him to consider his tactics on this—for example it might be preferable to let the conference continue for a time to talk about radical reform structures in the

North plus a connection with Dublin and when, as is reasonably certain, the Unionist conferees prove intransigent about this the ultimate question could be thrown in. There is still some disagreement about whether the Provisional IRA can be beaten by the British Army. Most opinion holds that this is not possible. Fitt and Devlin have a contrary opinion. It is obvious, however, that sizeable areas of the North around the border as well as ghettos in Belfast and Derry and some towns like Coalisland are virtually outside the control of the security forces. It is also obvious that the minority have a very determined confidence that they will not be ruled again by a Unionist Government. This feeling extends into the Catholic middle class" (NAI, TSCH 2002/8/484).

This is evidence that Dublin took the Northern Catholics to be leading the Anti-Partition campaign for the first time and the Irish Government had relegated itself to taking up a subsidiary role to the Northerners and their freedom struggle.

Towards the end of 1971 Hume wrote two articles for *The Irish Times* on 'The Way Forward for Northern Ireland' that were very different to those he penned for the same paper, seven years before, in the 1960s (see Volume One). These reveal publicly what Gallagher was told privately about the changed objectives of the SDLP.

Hume started by defending the SDLP's abstention from Stormont and retreat to Dungiven, arguing the need to demonstrate that Catholics had decided on "a complete withdrawal of consent from the system of government in Northern Ireland". Hume said the Stormont system had been "an outright failure" and its failure had been "inevitable" due to "the nature of the Northern Ireland State".

Hume said he believed that most Unionists would now "admit to the inevitability of united country" (though "it should come by agreement, for the only worthwhile unity is unity by agreement"). He wanted Westminster to actively promote the goal of Irish unity:

> "The British government should declare publicly what is the private conviction of all British parties, that Irish unity is inevitable and that it will take all steps necessary to encourage the agreement that will bring it about… the British government and parliament should not fear to set in motion the movement towards the inevitable." (IT, 6.11.71).

In a second article for the same paper Hume blamed the British guarantee of Northern Ireland's constitutional position within the UK for the intransigence of Unionists (who did not agree to change toward a united Ireland because of it):

> "Any community of one million people anywhere in the world which receives a permanent guarantee of its supremacy and privileged position from a government like the British government, backed by the necessary

finance, is not going to give any thought whatsoever to any other possible constitutional position, but that, once the guarantee is withdrawn and it is stated British policy to positively encourage and bring about Irish unity by agreement, many of the million will immediately begin to reconsider their position" (IT, 31.12.71).

Here was the policy that Hume was to pursue, using the SDLP as his instrument, for the next two and a half decades.

Gallagher's report confirms that the success of the Republican campaign had become an important driver of SDLP policy. Hume and others believed the Provos were, by late 1971, unbeatable and that made a United Ireland a possibility—although Fitt and Devlin were not so sure and this tended to veer them back towards an internal solution.

Dublin was hedging its bets between the two at this point before taking up Hume's position once Stormont had been successfully taken down.

The understanding that Nationalist success depended on Republican firepower could never be said publicly, of course, and Hume developed a very sophisticated way with words to disguise this basic calculation being made, and to maintain his distance from *"the men of violence"*. Fitt and Devlin who, unlike Hume, had had their fingers burnt in Dublin's military dealings with the Northern minority, were keen to make that separation impermeable. But that was a losing hand in 1971 and Hume knew it.

The lengths that Fitt would go to against the Provos were revealed in June 2014, when a confidential file came to light about a meeting the SDLP Leader had with British Home Secretary Reginald Maudling on 22nd December 1971. A couple of weeks earlier the bomb had exploded at McGurk's Bar killing 15 Catholic civilians. The bombing was claimed by a mysterious Loyalist group, but the British Army and media put out the idea that it had been an IRA 'own goal'—a bomb that had exploded prematurely in transit in the Catholic bar.

Fitt told the British officials that

> "every effort should be taken to pin responsibility for the explosion on the Provisionals".

If the bombing could be pinned on the Provos it would "give him an excuse to join discussions". And the British officials noted: "If this can be proved it would have a dramatic effect on Catholic public opinion even to the extent of giving him the excuse to join discussions" (IN 12.6.14).

It was clear from this that while the SDLP absenteeism policy was being led by Hume, Fitt, his party leader, was hoping for an opportunity to re-open dialogue with Unionists and the British, in order to lead the party back to Stormont.

But this became impossible after the events of early 1972.

Dublin Depends on Republicans

Dublin, which had intended the SDLP to be its instrument in the North, was now riding on the coat-tails of Northern Republicans in its policy with regard to the Six Counties.

Even though Dublin's support for the disobedience campaign to bring down Stormont was a kind of re-engagement with the Northern Catholic community, after Lynch's *volte face* in mid-1970, the relationship between the two parts of the Nation had changed fundamentally since August 1969.

What is apparent is that the Northern Catholics, for the first time, were leading the Anti-Partitionist struggle and dictating the course of it. The South was acting as a political ancillary to the struggle that was being waged in the North and it was no longer being asked to provide deliverance for the part of the Nation that needed delivering.

Taoiseach Lynch and the Dublin Government were becoming a kind of fellow-traveller of the IRA, and had shelved opposition to Direct Rule in favour of the Provos' policy to bring down Stormont.

There is not much to disagree with in what Faulkner said in a statement about Dublin:

> "Mr. Lynch now clearly commits himself and his Government to support by political means what the IRA seeks to achieve by violent means—the overthrow of the Northern Ireland Government" (*Memoirs of a Statesman*, pp.126-7).

A Department of Foreign Affairs briefing document for a meeting at Chequers held in September 1971, between Taoiseach Lynch, Prime Minister Heath, and Faulkner, was officially described as dealing with "the necessity for political changes in Northern Ireland to counter the strength of the IRA". But a reading of it shows it to have been about how the Irish Government might benefit politically from the military efforts of the Republican Army. This is what it said:

> "Internment has shown, rather the failure of internment has demonstrated the potency of the IRA. The IRA, as an active phenomenon, cannot be defeated by· the military forces at present in the field in the North. It can only be beaten by anti-unionist leaders who can separate the Catholic communities from the IRA. In order to preserve and strengthen their position there must be immediate and radical policy changes in the North. Failure to face up to this will mean a continuation indefinitely of the IRA threat and all the consequences that may flow from this" (NAI, DFA 2003/17/30, September 1971),

This was the policy adopted by Dublin of using the Republican Army in the North to gain the National Aim of the Irish Government on the island. What could not be conceded completely by the British to the Northern Republicans could be conceded mostly to the SDLP and Dublin, so that the IRA would go away.

An Anti-Partition Pamphlet

In September 1971 Dublin's Department of Foreign Affairs issued a *'Pamphlet on the current and historical situation in Northern Ireland and the need for reform'*. The nine-page publication was the first official Anti-Partitionist pamphlet issued by the Irish Government since Sean Lemass had ditched the Nationalist Party, much to the annoyance of Eddie McAteer. (Seamus Brady had issued Anti-Partitionist pamphlets with Irish Government funds but in the name of private individuals or other organisations in 1969-70.)

The conclusion of the pamphlet is interesting in its blaming of the violence in the Six Counties not on the Provos or on Unionists but on 'Northern Ireland' itself, with the understanding that it was inherent in the political structures of what had been constructed in 1920-1 by Britain. It read:

> "It had seemed to many at the outset that amelioration of the lot of the deprived would be enough to meet the problem and contain violence. But in Northern Ireland as in other situations of extreme alienation, palliatives have not been sufficient to contain the explosive forces generated by oppressive political structures. Fundamental Change alone can do so.
>
> "Today there is a better understanding than ever before of the concept of 'institutionalised violence'. We have come to see that one cannot simplistically treat those who defend an existing system as 'supporters of law and order' and call 'violent' those whom it suppresses and who are provoked to react. One must rather... look critically at the system in its operation and its origins to see whether it does not enforce a kind of 'static' violence on those whom it excludes.
>
> "This is clearly true of Northern Ireland where the minority—because they have always lived under it—feel themselves prisoners of a system which has institutional violence frozen into its structures, so that their helplessness forces them either to active violence or at least to sympathy for those who seek this resort. In the end then, the remedy is clear. The institutions are faulty. They must be changed.
>
> "A British parliament enacted the Government of Ireland Act 51 years ago with an intent made explicit in its subtitle, 'An Act to provide for the better Government of Ireland'. A clear look at the nature of the basic institutions which it established at that time and which it has allowed to operate unchanged for 50 years in Northern Ireland, shows that they are not suitably adapted to achieve good government there—and a glance at the headlines after 50 years of operation shows that they have not in fact done so.

"Reforms within the structure—though well-meaning—will never be more than palliatives…" (NAI, DFA 2002/19/500).

It is very instructive to find out that at the height of the Republican War the Southern Government was putting the violence and disorder down, not to the Provos, but to 'Northern Ireland' itself. That view, which is undoubtedly accurate, is a strange thing to think of Dublin saying subsequently.

Dublin's Policy of 'Stormont Must Go'

Dublin's understanding of the situation is revealed in a note by Eamonn Gallagher on the significance of the visit of the former Prime Minister, and Leader of the Labour Party, Harold Wilson to Ireland.

> Dublin took Wilson's disbanding of "unionism's private army" the B Specials as a crucial victory which removed the Stormont government's independent power to repress the minority. The Unionist Government were thereafter dependent on the British Army which could not be used in the same way against the independent power centres of the minority that had developed in the North under the auspices of the Republican Army. As a result the writ of Stormont could not run over large parts of the North:
>
> "The logical consequences of Mr. Wilson's decision to take away the unionist private army is to take away the unionist government as well. This issue cannot be shirked. We ourselves detect a number of reasons why Mr. Heath's government refuses to face up to the issue. The most obvious one is the alleged fear of a Protestant backlash. We do not know if the backlash is a myth or a reality. We ourselves tend to discount its size because of analyses we have made in which we have some confidence. But even if it is a serious reality it has had the effect of paralysing British policy in relation to Ireland for far too long already. It cannot be allowed to carry on doing so… It is also possible that Heath, Maudling and Carrington think, or thought, that they could take out the IRA and 'free' the minority from IRA influences. Experience to date shows that such thinking is imbecilic. Even if they do succeed in taking out the IRA they will find a 40% minority of the Northern population which will still refuse to deal with a unionist government."

The note concluded that "Stormont must be suspended" so that Westminster can impose a solution on unionism:

> "Only when unionism is reduced to being an equal partner with the minority in discussions will it become realistic about its position. The question of Irish unity cannot be evaded either. The minority have a definite aspiration in that direction and nothing has eradicated it at any time in the past 50 years. Their leadership must respond to this. Their leaders cannot enter an administration designed to maintain the division of Ireland in perpetuity…

Mr. Wilson has himself referred to the desirability of creating a Council of Ireland. This idea, of course, was contained in the Government of Ireland Act 1920... Its functions should be to harmonise economic, social, cultural, and all other aspects between North and South that may have grown apart since 1921... Its objectives, however,—whether stated or not—must be to prepare for the transfer of sovereignty in the North from London to an all-Ireland Parliament in progressive steps." (NAI, TSCH, 2002/8/484, 16.11.71)

A further file in the National Archives reveals that the Dublin Government was secretly funding what it grandiosely called *'The Assembly of the Northern Irish People', the SDLP's* "Alternative Assembly" at Dungiven. The note of a meeting held on 9th March 1972 relates to whether Dublin's "financial commitment" should be continued with the fall of Stormont. It reports Hume as being "of the opinion that the Assembly's role is ended but puts in the saver that it might be worthwhile to keep it ticking over in case the political picture should change again" (NAI, DFA 2003/17/269).

The Irish Government seemed to be worried about the fact that its secret *"financial commitment"* might be exposed by having to have it renewed openly and this would have political repercussions including "embarrassing... the most able and moderate members of the Assembly, John Hume and Austin Currie, having regard to the possibility of their being denounced by colleagues who are suspicious about co-operating with the Government". This would involve the exacerbating of what the report called "internal divisions within the SDLP".

It was obvious from this that Northern Nationalists were reluctant to deal openly with the Lynch Government after being hung out to dry in 1970. And they were getting very close indeed to the Republican position, with the successes of the IRA. Ambitions were increasing right across the spectrum of Nationalism.

It has been suggested that Taoiseach Lynch instituted a kind of withdrawal from Anti-Partitionism after the Arms Trials. This view is very far from the truth, as the files from the National Archives show.

But the decision not to maintain and develop *"The Assembly of the Northern Irish people"* after Stormont was prorogued indicated that both Dublin and the SDLP lacked the courage of their Anti-Partitionist convictions. They were uninterested in establishing an alternative source of power in the North. The answer to the question posed in the report: *"Does the Government wish to gain a political foothold within the North and influence minority politics there...?"* was obviously, no, beyond aiding the SDLP.

Testing the Nationalist Will

After failing to get the SDLP to come in from the cold, the British Government escalated the conflict in order to defend its settlement of 1920-1 — its pseudo-state in the Six Counties and its sub-government at Stormont and that produced Bloody Sunday in Derry.

The sequence of events from the summer of 1971 ran like this: Fitt and Hume led the SDLP out of Stormont into the Alternative Assembly in Dungiven; The IRA campaign received the great moral boost at having detached the reformists from accommodationist politics and went into a higher gear; Internment was introduced in an attempt to stem the rising tide of violence but led to a further intensification; Bloody Sunday was an attempt to frighten Catholics off the streets but led to a further escalation of the War that finally put paid to Stormont.

The Anti-Partitionist offensive, both military and political, was reaching its high point in early 1972. There was a general feeling in Nationalist Ireland that an ending of Partition was possible through the immense effort that was going on in the North. The 'Constitutional Nationalist' *Irish News* was selling its *"Long Kesh Calendar"* to its readers for 25p (26.1.72). Next to its Anti-Internment editorials and its *"Pro Fide et Patria"* masthead it had articles such as *"Mass in Long Kesh"* in which Fr. Noel Fitzpatrick summoned up the spirit of the Martyrs in support of the Insurrection:

> "One seldom hears the Mass prayers answered with so much vigour and meaning as one does in the camp... Mass usually ends with the singing of 'Faith of Our Fathers', sung with great gusto, especially that part about 'in spite of dungeon, fire and sword" (7.2.72).

All shades of Nationalist opinion, with religious backing, were gathering behind the great effort of the community against Stormont.

The objective of the Derry march was described by its organiser, Kevin McCorry of NICRA, a few days before the Sunday, as the culmination of the disobedience campaign to destroy Stormont:

> "We are on the streets to demonstrate rejection of the Unionist regime by a large section of the community here... 30,000 people withholding rents, 10,000 people throughout the North refusing to pay rates, and other payments. Opposition representatives have been out of Stormont for six months, non-Unionist Councils have collapsed. Over this last month, thousands have demonstrated defiance of Stormont's laws in the streets."

The march, which the Stormont Government declared illegal, was intended to be a decisive confrontation with the "Orange State" by the organisers:

"It was no easy decision... for a struggling people to leave the relative safety of their homes to brave batons, rubber bullets and C.S. gas, but this was the people's way of pressing the issue to a decision" (IN 26.1.72).

NICRA demanded the unconditional release of all internees; abolition of the Special Powers Act; the withdrawal of the British Army from Republican areas; further Civil Rights legislation from Westminster and an end to the Unionist administration at Stormont.

On 30th January, at the Derry march, the British Army shot dead 13 unarmed men. In the aftermath of the massacre Hume famously said on a BBC programme that the feeling was that it was now "a United Ireland or nothing" (IN 1.2 72), and the SDLP called on all Catholics in public life to withdraw their services.

The mass killing had all the characteristics of an Imperial "*administrative massacre*" on Britain's part, in which the shooting of demonstrators/rioters was meant to deter others from bad behaviour, as had been done at Amritsar, India. 'Al Carthill', a senior Justice in the Bombay High Court said in a 1924 book that the "*administrative massacre*" was a useful device when applied to natives but was seldom used in Britain:

> "There are, however, precedents in British history which tend to show that, when the occasion arises, the British will display a surprising energy and thoroughness in this branch of administration. The 'administrative massacre', as this kind may be called, is, of course, familiar enough to the Oriental" (The Lost Dominion, pp.93-4).

A few days before the massacre at Derry it was revealed in *The Guardian* by Simon Hoggart that British Army units in Belfast had requested and obtained the withdrawal of the Paratrooper Regiment from their areas of operation because "the Army now believes that the absolute minimum of force must be used in these areas to prevent the local community from becoming more disaffected with the Army". The Paratroopers, described by one British Captain as "little better than thugs in uniform", obviously felt that the British Army was being too softly-softly in its approach and the Catholic insurgents needed to be taught a tougher lesson. (IN 26.1.72)

It later emerged that Major-General Ford, who was impatient with the developing street disorder in Derry, and who deployed the Paratroopers, had written a paper to the GOC Tuzo saying that it was time to stop the hard-core rioters that had arisen in Derry since Internment and said he was "coming to the conclusion that the minimum force necessary to achieve a restoration of law and order is to shoot selected ring leaders amongst the DYH [Derry Young Hooligans, P.W.], after clear warnings had been issued" (Peter Taylor, *'Brits: The War Against the IRA'*, p.88).

The same regiment that carried out the massacre, the Paratrooper shock troops of the British Army, had earlier carried out another massacre in August 1971 in Ballymurphy with much the same purpose—teaching the more troublesome Catholics a lesson. But the effect of such shootings was precisely the opposite to that intended and led to many demonstrators and rioters becoming IRA volunteers instead. The tactic, unlike in Amritsar, did not work.

The probability is that Bloody Sunday was an event—like the earlier massacre in Ballymurphy, which was unseen by the TV cameras—to test the will of the Nationalist community. Despite two Inquiries, it will probably never be known if there was political connivance at British Cabinet level, perhaps through *"nods and winks"*, in the decision to embark on it, or whether it was a decision taken at some level of the British Army, on the day or in advance.

After Bloody Sunday

Ian McAllister, in his book on *'The Northern Ireland Social, Democratic and Labour Party'*, saw Bloody Sunday as the inevitable outcome of the adoption of a military solution after the failure of the British Government to lure the SDLP back into Stormont. However, in its effects it ultimately spelt the end of Stormont and put a new political initiative on the table:

> "The action in shooting the marchers was in fact the logical extension of a military policy designed to extirpate the IRA, but when faced with this, and an adverse press abroad, Westminster backed away" (p.110).

When the massacre did not sap the Nationalist will, but strengthened it, Stormont had to be sacrificed to save the situation for Britain. As William Beattie Smith commented: "The Derry killings effectively terminated the strategy of using military force to uphold the Unionist administration" *('The British State and the Northern Ireland Crisis 1969-73'*, p.182).

Robert Ramsey rang Faulkner on the night of the shootings. Faulkner, who did not believe the British Army version of events that they had killed *'terrorists'*, said: "This is London's disaster, but they will use it against us" (*Ringside Seats*, p. 98). As Faulkner said, the total responsibility for Bloody Sunday lay directly with Whitehall. Stormont did not control the Army that carried it out. But it was Stormont that paid the price for it.

The events of Bloody Sunday in Derry threatened to produce a great escalation of the conflict. Catholic politicians intensified their withdrawal campaign and the IRA's military offensive surged. The last remaining Catholic legal functionaries and bureaucrats, such as Maurice Hayes, who had remained at their posts during the anti-Internment campaign withdrew from the system.

But, in fact, what was occurring was a general backing away from taking the conflict to a higher level.

A march was organised in Newry for the Sunday following Bloody Sunday. Nationalist politicians initially urged all Catholic Ireland, North and South, to be there and a mass convergence on the town from all parts of the country was predicted. Train and bus timetables were altered to take the Nation to Newry and dire predictions were made of a possible further massacre.

The situation had all the makings of a 'High Noon' in the National War. It prompted Heath to make an unprecedented appeal to Cardinal Conway, Cardinal Heenan and the Taoiseach to use their influence to have the march cancelled. It was reported that Lynch had set up "field hospitals", South of Newry, for the impending conflict (IN 4.2.72).

So the Dublin Government and the Southern Establishment, having worked things up after Bloody Sunday, thought again and spent the second half of the week calming things down and urging restraint. And the burning of the British Embassy in Dublin acted as a safety valve in the situation.

In the event, Catholic Ireland and Protestant Ulster did not come to a final reckoning. There was a strong all-class Nationalist turnout from the North but numbers did not materialise from the rest of the country as predicted earlier in the week. The march passed off peacefully.

In the moment of truth a final reckoning did not take place. Perhaps if all Ireland had converged on Newry the framework of the conflict would have been altered qualitatively with the result that anything was possible—even a Republican victory. But it didn't and the moment passed, just as at Clontarf in 1843 when Daniel O'Connell declined the challenge.

It was probably a turning point. From that moment Southern public opinion began to disengage from 'Northern Ireland' and the Northern Catholics were on their own in the situation that had developed, and had to make the best of things for themselves.

Hume at the United Nations

After the massacre in Derry, Fr. Daly, a curate in the Bogside who was present at the killings was asked on the RTE News: "What do you think should be done?" He replied:

> "... These people here have suffered for too long. I think it is about time that something was done on an international level. Obviously Britain is not either willing or interested in doing anything. I think that the Government of the South bear tremendous responsibility to do something. I think that they are the only people who have international influence and a word in an international forum. I think they must do something" (NAI, DFA 2003/17/335).

But in February 1972, after considering taking those who administered the Derry massacre to the UN, the Dublin Government gave up the notion, leaving it as an internal matter to be sorted out by those who carried it out.

So John Hume attempted an intervention at the UN, where the Irish Government had failed a year and a half before. Dublin attempted to put him off going, advising him that it was unlikely he would be received by the Secretary-General since he was not a member of a national parliament. But Kurt Waldheim had just replaced U Thant and Hume used the fact that the new man had not yet been house-trained in the conventions of his office to secure an audience—much to Dublin's surprise. The audience, however, had to take place under the auspices of the Irish Representative of the UN.

It is clear from the report that at this meeting it was Hume who represented the Northern Catholics and not the Irish Government.

In his audience with Dr. Waldheim Hume took a different approach to that taken by Dublin in September 1969. He concentrated on the peculiar conditions of 'Northern Ireland' and gave a factual presentation of the intolerable position of Catholics within it. After this:

> "As regards what action the British Government should take, Mr. Hume maintained that Westminster should take over direct responsibility for security in the North, withdraw the troops to barracks, put an end to internment without trial, and suspend or abolish Stormont. The Secretary-General enquired what would replace Stormont. Mr. Hume explained that, until a satisfactory solution has been worked out, authority should be vested in a Commission, comprising representatives of London, Dublin and the different elements in the North. It was pointed out to the Secretary-General that Stormont is a complete anomaly within the United Kingdom having no parallel in Scotland or Wales or in any of the English geographical units (like say Lancashire) with populations greater than the North and that indeed strictly speaking it is in no sense a Parliament in the normal meaning of the term. Mr. Hume added that there was much talk of London putting forward certain proposals soon but that he feared they might not be sufficiently radical to meet the situation."

In reply to this Dr. Waldheim said that

> "... he was extremely interested in what Mr. Hume had told him and that he, personally, is quite concerned about the matter. Mr. Hume would, he went on, be aware of what he (the Secretary-General) tried to do, and in particular of his offer of good offices but he could not act without the agreement of both parties, and Britain, invoking Article 2.7 of the Charter, had not so far shown any inclination to have recourse to him. Mr. Hume replied that he was indeed aware of the limitations to which the Secretary-General is subject but that he would hope he might in his talks with the British make known his anxiety and recommend that in place of their present

policy of trying to uproot violence, which is only a symptom of the disease, they might tackle the disease itself by adopting policies calculated to achieve a basic solution."

At the end of the report to the Department of Foreign Affairs, the Irish official, Mr. Cremin, reveals that he promised the Secretary-General to say nothing of the meeting to the press or about Hume's presence and to describe it as a mere routine visit if caught out (by the British?) stating: "we would not wish to do or say anything that might embarrass the Secretary-General and that it was not my intention to make any statement unless questioned" (NAI, DFA 2003/17/358, 24.3.72).

There are a number of things of interest here, quite apart from Hume's position. First of all there is the initiative that Hume was showing in taking the leadership of his people to the highest political offices in the world. Second, there is the obviously chastened attitude of Dublin, licking its wounds after its last encounter at the UN, and fearful of any exposure to Britain for any further assertion of national independence. And thirdly there is the fact that Britain had the UN stitched up as one final barrier to the Northern Catholics.

The lesson Hume must have taken from all his was that it was up to him now, in the political sphere, to arrange something for his people to escape the predicament they found themselves in.

Dublin's *Realpolitik*

After Bloody Sunday the Lynch Government announced it would "provide out of public money, finance through suitable channels for political ... action by the minority in Northern Ireland, designed to obtain their freedom from Unionist misgovernment" (IT 1.2.72).

The Lynch Government was not only going to aid *"passive resistance"* but openly finance the civil disobedience campaign in the North, aimed at destroying Stormont.

In 1971-2 there was a big fashion for *realpolitik* in Southern Establishment politics. The *realpolitik* involved a feeling of belonging to an offensive on all fronts—military, propaganda, and political—that was disorientating and demoralising the Protestant community in the Six Counties into an acceptance of a United Ireland.

This was something that was not just confined to Fianna Fail but was shared right across the political spectrum in the 26 Counties, among Fine Gael frontbenchers and Labour socialists alike. And in the period of the high point of the National War it was widely believed that one last push would shatter Ulster Unionism, and the North would fall into Dublin's lap (courtesy of some pushing from Whitehall, of course).

It was accepted in very respectable Dublin circles—and forecast in *Irish Press* editorials by Tim Pat Coogan, who authored a very popular book on the IRA at this time—that the Protestant will to stay out of a United Ireland would be sapped when it was made clear to them that the Westminster guarantees were not to be relied on.

For instance, just after Bloody Sunday, *The Irish Press* editor wrote:

> "The balloon is up and nothing will bring it down except a United Ireland... the Taoiseach's reiteration of this point on TV last night was all the more forceful for being delivered with such restrained dignity" (1.2.72).

The next day another editorial predicted:

> "There is an understandable temptation to rub the Unionists' nose in their imminent defeat... There is not a long way and probably a lot of blood before the political inevitabilities become reality. But the resolve in the direction of that 'victory' is now unstoppable." (2.2.72)

At the time that Internment was introduced in the North Coogan gave a gentle reminder to the Provos to confine their activities to the other side of the Border, where, as far as Dublin was concerned, their only unfinished business lay:

> "Whoever is responsible for the shootings across the border at Belcoo and Clady will not help the embattled Northern minority, but will only create a situation in which internment becomes necessary here" (10.8.71).

After Direct Rule was introduced *The Irish Press* congratulated the political coalition that had helped destroy Stormont thus:

> "Apart from the IRA, there was the all important and overriding diplomatic pressure from the Dublin government, with a sensible degree of political restraint; there was the staunch action of the SDLP in walking off the Stormont stage and throwing their weight behind the Civil Rights demonstrations and the people who paid no rent or rates; there were the ordinary folk who risked all in sheltering IRA men" (27.3.72)

And *The Irish Press* also described how the Provos were helping Taoiseach Lynch's policy:

> "The activities of the Provisional IRA also add strength to Mr. Lynch's increasingly urgent call for political talks by all those with a legitimate interest to seek a political solution" (24.7.72)

These editorials were gathered up in a pamphlet published by the Workers' Association, '*War Mongering! The Irish Press and the Troubles in Northern Ireland*'. The *Irish Press*, which was founded in 1931 and gave expression to the movement against the Treaty imposed by Britain in 1921, was considered expendable by Fianna Fail by 1995 when it was allowed to go out of business.

Dublin's *realpolitik* went something like this: While the Provos encouraged the British to withdraw, and attempted to soften up the Protestant will to resist with the bombing of Unionist businesses and town centres, Dublin concentrated on getting the British to 'stand up' to the Unionists, whilst the SDLP refused negotiations or entry into a new administration, and pointed the way clearly in the one direction of a United Ireland.

But it was Dublin which miscalculated in its *realpolitik*.

Direct Rule Imposed

A few days after the imposition of Internment, Faulkner met the British Prime Minister and his Ministers at Chequers in England. Faulkner later recalled that Heath and his Government made it clear to him that they were—

> "... fully behind the Stormont government in its policies. No constitutional changes were contemplated, and any political initiatives must come within the framework of existing democratic structures. Nothing could be contemplated which could even be interpreted as the first step towards direct rule. Later in the meeting I raised the subject of direct rule again; might it not come to that if things got worse? Sir Alec [Douglas Home, Foreign Secretary and former Prime Minister, P.W.] threw his hands in the air: 'Not direct rule, he exclaimed, 'anything but direct rule'. It was a point of view assented to by all present" (*Memoirs of a Statesma*n, p.128).

However, at the beginning of October 1971 Heath put together a small group called GEN 47 composed of the Ministers in his Government concerned with NI to develop a concerted policy with clear priorities of object.

Faulkner did not believe that the British would suspend Stormont. He understood the role of the 'Northern Ireland' government, ever since the 1920 settlement, as "providing a useful buffer between the problems of the region and the British government". His policy aims were given the full support of Whitehall and no criticism had been made of his actions. He was also providing the invaluable service of keeping in check the growing belligerence of the majority that might otherwise present itself in more dangerous form to all concerned (Ramsey, p.100).

In the days after Bloody Sunday, Faulkner was assured by Heath that there were no plans in his mind for Direct Rule, despite the fact that by this stage the British Prime Minister had, according to his memoirs, concluded "that we should now devote all our energies towards working for a lasting cross-community settlement—and only direct rule could offer us the breathing space necessary for building it" (Edward Heath, *'The Course of My Life'*, p.436).

At the February 4th meeting Heath assured Faulkner that he was not contemplating Direct Rule, saying, according to Ramsey who witnessed it: "I've told you Brian, we are in this together and we'll support you all the way, however long it takes". Ramsey noted that "With that, he put his arm around Faulkner's shoulder in friendly, man to man fashion… Faulkner, a man of his word, took Heath at *his* word" (*Ringside Seats*, p.101).

This led Faulkner to believe that he was still in control of things and he came up with an imaginative proposal for a political accommodation which was presented to Heath on March 1st.

This envisaged his June 1971 offer plus a review of the Special Powers Act; a scaling down of Internment; a bill of rights; a reconstruction programme for Catholic areas; and the creation of a North/South inter-governmental Council in return for the Republic dropping Articles 2 and 3 of its Constitution that claimed jurisdiction over the North. However, on the same day GEN 47 discussed two draft Bills that would legislate for Direct Rule and the transfer of security powers. Heath made it clear at this meeting, a couple of days later, that he would impose Direct Rule whether or not Faulkner agreed to a transfer of security powers—which he knew he wouldn't (CAB 130/560, 3.3.72).

However, speculation about a constitutional change began to mount in the British press, which Heath was forced to deny in a telegram to Faulkner, enabling the Unionist Leader to assure the Ulster Unionist Council that there would be no Direct Rule. This speculation led to the formation of Bill Craig's Vanguard, with its Fascist character and large Nazi-style rallies.

With the EEC vote concluded and won, Prime Minister Heath held a series of Cabinet meetings in early March to convince his Ministers of the necessity of a period of Direct Rule to launch the new political initiative it was thought essential to secure stability in the North and defeat the IRA. However, the Prime Minister failed to achieve agreement and a number of the Cabinet, particularly Lord Hailsham, left unconvinced and determined to defend the 1920 arrangements.

Direct Rule from Westminster was introduced on 24th March 1972 after Faulkner was summoned to a meeting in Downing Street, held on 22nd, where he was presented with a seeming *fait accompli*. Faulkner refused to accept a list of British conditions presented to him, including the transfer of all law and order powers to London; the phasing out of Internment; a plebiscite on Northern Ireland's position; and power-sharing with Nationalists.

Faulkner realised that these terms would reduce his administration to the role of puppets and that the Unionist Cabinet would be unwilling to take up such a role, mere fall-guys for Whitehall. Robert Ramsey later procured the information from Whitehall officials privy to it that Heath was simply using the security issue as a means of provoking Direct Rule. He had a longer list of unacceptable demands up his sleeve in case Faulkner accepted the initial ones (*Ringside Seats*, p. 102)

Heath led Faulkner to believe that he had secured Cabinet approval for his ultimatum—which he hadn't. When Faulkner refused to operate Stormont, the British Prime Minister was able on 23rd March to grind down the opposition in his own Cabinet to the striking down of Stormont by means of the stroke of a Whitehall pen on the following day. (See Smith, '*The British State*', pp. 186-9)

Heath called the bluff of the hard-line Unionists. Bill Craig set out the case for UDI (Unilateral Declaration of Independence) on the Rhodesian model and told the Monday Club that he had 80,000 men who would "shoot to kill", if necessary (*Faulkner*, p.83). His Vanguard movement called massive protests against the loss of the "Protestant Parliament" but Craig did not act. He presumably calculated, at the moment of truth, that the Protestant fear was Dublin rule rather than Direct Rule from Westminster.

Heath had decided that the Stormont system was no longer workable in the light of the escalating Republican War effort, and after Internment and Bloody Sunday had failed. A contradiction had existed at the heart of British policy since August 1969 between the desire to sustain the sub-government at Stormont and to institute sufficient reforms to preserve the 1920 arrangement. Direct Rule involved suspending the sub-government in order to resurrect it after more thorough reform had been imposed by the real Government of the state.

Robert Ramsey believes that Heath ultimately sacrificed Stormont to save his European project. At that point the UK and Ireland were seeking admission to the European Economic Community. Heath had managed to persuade President Pompidou to support Britain's entry after years of Gaullist opposition. But Bloody Sunday had given the French second thoughts and there was a fear of admitting a country on the verge of 'civil war' into the Community. Heath decided he had to take full control of the situation and put an end to Stormont. (Ramsay, pp.102-5)

Stormont was suspended for a year and the intention of Whitehall was to resurrect it as soon as was practically possible. According to Kenneth Bloomfield, the civil servant intimately involved in the process, the British—

> "... began to speak openly of the need for—and I recall the phrase vividly—'a discontinuity'... Heath by this time was convinced that the best outcome would be a limited and creative period of direct rule. The Northern Ireland politicians, under this concept, would be moved into sheltered housing while the political structures were reshaped, and would then move in again under a different tenancy agreement providing for co-ownership... If, indeed,

the British government could meet its objective of a relatively quick in and out intervention, leaving behind it more widely acceptable political structures restored to local control, this would be a great achievement..." (*A Tragedy of Errors, The Government and Misgovernment of Northern Ireland*, p.29)

Some people believed that they had destroyed a 'state' in 1972—the 'state' that was established in 1921, that is. But when a state, in the modern sense, is destroyed, it should be noticeable to everybody who lived in it. When Stormont was abolished in 1972 it was quite possible that people who were completely uninterested in politics might have lived through the experience and never suspected that a 'state' had been destroyed.

All that really happened when Stormont was prorogued was that a façade of the State was removed, and the welfare system, and every other function of the modern state, carried on operating as if nothing had happened. In fact all that really happened in 1972 was that the State came into view as the simulacrum of it dissolved. A phase of 'discontinuity' ensued until Humpty-Dumpty could be put back together again.

The British Home Secretary, Reginald Maudling, said in the House of Commons:

"I look forward, as I'm sure we all do, to the time when the political battles of Northern Ireland are fought between Conservative and Labour and not between Catholic and Protestant; there will not be a lasting solution in Northern Ireland until that is so." (Hansard, vol. 823, col. 15, 22.9.71)

He later wrote in his *Memoirs*:

"Northern Ireland will never be at peace until... the political struggles of the Province are based, as they are in the rest of the United Kingdom, not on communal issues, but on the fundamental political issues which divide the Right wing from the Left over the whole range of our public life" (Reginald Maudling, *'Memoirs'*, p.188).

But for that to happen 'Northern Ireland' needed State politics within the UK or the Republic of Ireland. And the political Establishment of which Maudling formed part was determined not to let that happen, either way. So, is it any wonder that 'Northern Ireland' could never be at peace?

Promoting 'the Disengagement Policy'

A Department of Foreign Affairs document, *'Towards a general settlement?'*, prepared for Minister Hillery's meeting with British Foreign Minister Sir Alec Douglas-Home and Secretary of State for NI William Whitelaw, reveals the policy of the Dublin Government in the period after the fall of Stormont.

It begins with the observation:

> "Mr. Brian Faulkner has remarked that Northern Ireland is in a constitutional limbo. Possibly he was thinking of this as a complaint; but the remark reveals, whether Faulkner fully appreciates it or not, what a remarkable change has taken place with the decline and final fall of Unionist Government" (NAI, DFA 2003/13/16, 21.4.72).

It ends by outlining the policy Irish Government policy in relation to the *"constitutional limbo"* after the fall of Unionism:

> "Britain should prepare to put pressure on unionism to accede to an Irish Parliament and Government. Mr. Faulkner cannot remain in his constitutional limbo... Irish policy should rightly assert that the way out of the constitutional limbo is to change the constitutional status of Northern Ireland altogether. This is not conquest, not assimilation, not victory. It is a constitutional reform which history imposes on the country as a whole."

One force in this very revolutionary and violent process which is termed a mere *"constitutional reform"* by Eamon Gallagher could not be mentioned, however, although the policy objectives was really dependent on it—the Provisional IRA.

The other main force in the situation, Britain, is mentioned—but its role is relegated to facilitating what is characterised as a kind of natural and simple evolution of things.

The Irish Government policy for a general settlement after the fall of Stormont noted that, despite the Unionist belief that their constitutional position based on the 1920 Act "virtually amounted to a treaty status on a par at least with the 1922 Treaty", it was "swept away unilaterally" by Whitehall. And now "no one really believes that a Stormont Parliament and Government is likely to be re-created at the end of 12 months—if ever".

It then suggests that the British policy of Direct Rule could not, itself, be sustained. This was because "the trouble-making potential of Northern Ireland is much too great to be contained indefinitely by Mr. Whitelaw". And sooner or later "Westminster cannot justify to the British voter, over any lengthy period of time, the idea of draining off his wealth to subsidise endemic anarchy in part of Ireland".

The document described the "Prime Factors" in "Britain's dilemma" after Direct Rule as:

> "(i) the Provisional IRA which, after the first shock, has again shown a sizeable capacity for physical destruction. So long as the ghettos are left alone the people in them have no sufficiently strong objection to bombing outside the ghettos to do anything much about it; if, in order to stop this, the British Army should again begin to harass the ghettos there seems to be a greater likelihood that the population will support the Provisional IRA than

turn against it...

"(ii) Mr. Faulkner has now taken over what was the right-wing ploy... i.e. persistent demands on the authorities to 'take out' the ghettos... if Mr. Whitelaw should succumb to it the same reaction is likely to recur i.e. total alienation of the minority."

The briefing document for the Irish Government then posed the question:

"'Given the thesis that Unionist Government will not be restored and that Whitelaw Government cannot last for very long in its present form what other alternatives are open?'... The buffer of a local parliament and government is gone; it cannot be successfully re-constituted; it seems reasonable to suppose, therefore that the British can be nudged towards considering a more general settlement. There seems to be two directions in which Britain can go — integrating the North fully with Britain or helping to bring about Irish unity... 'the integration policy' and 'the disengagement policy'...".

Dublin believed that, whilst "*the integration policy*" would be "*superficially attractive*", it was the case that —

"political, economic and military considerations should eventually tend to favour the departure of Britain from Ireland altogether on agreed conditions... However, the British may attempt to 'muddle' along with a policy of that sort unless the Government make it clear that they will resist in every way open to them. The best manner of resistance might be to promote 'the disengagement policy'."

Here are some details of "*the disengagement policy*", which are worth reproducing to give the reader a flavour of what the Irish Government's agenda for the North *actually was* in mid-1972, and to dispel the myths that have been developed by historians about Taoiseach Lynch's Government since:

"The first requirement of a successful beginning of the disengagement of Britain from Ireland is that Britain should decide, in her own interest, that she should encourage Irish unity. The Government have taken a firm stand on this. While it is comforting, indeed comfortable, to think in terms of attracting the Northern majority towards Irish unity by behaving impeccably in relation to them and in relation to the kind of unity that is sought, nothing in the history of Unionism suggests that this would have any great effect on it. From a traditional Unionist point of view, if the minority could only agree to be quiet, the Unionist position is a satisfactory one... In the circumstances Mr. Faulkner's present policy of pushing Mr. Whitelaw towards a military victory over the minority is entirely logical...

"Given the benefits of the British connection Unionism has no need to change its mind on where the future of the North should lie except for three potent reasons:

> "(i) the refusal of the minority to behave themselves;
>
> (ii) a potential demographic change at some time in the future; and
>
> (iii) the possibility that Britain will get fed up carrying the Northern Ireland state on its back.
>
> "Point No. (iii) would seem to be the one on which the Government's general policy should pivot. It can, of course, be heavily influenced by point No. (i)..."

The logic of this is not drawn out of course—it made the Irish Government's policy highly dependent on the military fortunes of the Provisional IRA.

The briefing document then emphasized that unity was not just an aspiration or a long-term ambition:

> "... the objective of Government policy is Irish unity—not unity <u>eventually</u> nor unity <u>ultimately</u>... If unity were to become available immediately the Government would be bound to take it with whatever stresses might result."

It was also indicated that Dublin's *"reconciliation"* policies towards Northern Protestants—which were really much ado about nothing—should be discarded as unnecessary in the moment of victory as Britain's was delivering them up for absorption into a United Ireland. And a new re-orientation should take place around the emerging power, the Northern Catholics:

> "It is taken for granted that some slice of the unionist population must be made favourable to Irish unity in order to make it possible to obtain a majority for Irish unity in the North i.e. as a matter of tactics—indeed good common sense—it is hoped to win over a sufficient number of unionists by persuasion. Generally speaking the matter ends there and the idea of persuasion, besides intellectual argument, without running close to 'persuasion' by bomb and bullet... Other persuasions—between the intellectual and the physical—could include political, economic, social etc. pressures from London. There is no reason why an attempt should not be made to obtain such pressures in the interests both of Britain and Ireland... a potentially powerful, yet quite legitimate persuasion. It has also become part of general thinking that an interim period might be available... while significant sections of the unionist population are won over to acquiescence in Irish unity. It seems doubtful that time is available. The gun has been out for several years in the North and the genie of Irish nationalism is also out of the battle. Neither can readily be suppressed. It is not in the long-term interest to be seen to temporise here about Irish unity—particularly if it is already too late to do so. Too careful rationalisation about the fears of the unionist population cannot be allowed safely to separate the South from the Northern minority.
>
> "Essentially the Northern minority—hold the key to Irish unity; it could be much more dangerous in the long run to under-estimate the importance

of this than to underestimate the difficulties on the unionist side... The thrust of the above argument is that an early opportunity should be taken to ask the British Government to negotiate the conditions of Irish unity in independence ... Britain should prepare to put pressure on unionism to accede to an Irish Parliament and Government."

The message in this seemed to be that the Provos were winning, the Protestants did not matter and Britain should not be let off the hook in making a final solution of its Ireland problem at the moment of an Irish victory.

Protestant Resistance

The analysis from Dublin was fantasy because it continued to misunderstand the substance of the Protestant will to resist a United Ireland and the capacity of the Unionist community to resist what the British State might want to do with it.

Whilst the Civil Rights campaign was brilliantly successful in disorientating and fragmenting Unionist politics, the Irish Government did not see that the Anti-Partitionist military and political campaign had the effect of politically uniting the whole Protestant community in defence. The 'humanitarian' appeals against Internment had little effect on the Protestants when they were on the sharp end of the Republican bombing and shooting campaign.

By December 1972 the Ulster Defence Association had grown to a membership of around 26,000 (10 times the size of the IRA) and could put large numbers on the streets in a moment. UDA members were also handily placed in industry, public utilities and transport meaning that power cuts and disruption to goods, services and movement was well within their capacity.

The Shankill was a much more powerful proletarian manifestation than the Falls. The engineering and ship-building industry had given rise to a self-reliant and coherently organised working-class. The proletariat of the Falls, where it existed, was a creation of the linen mills and was much less organised and more socially fragmented. And the Shankill was also a much better armed and drilled body of men, saturated in Imperial militarism for generations, with the power of the State apparatus behind it.

So it was something of an affront to the Shankill, between 1969 and 1971, that the Falls was getting the better of it for the first time.

That was largely to do with two factors: The organisation and coherence that Catholic Belfast had achieved as a result of the defensive insurrection it had mounted in August 1969 and the imposition of the British State as a kind of semi-protective barrier between it and Unionism since these events. (The phrase *"semi-protective"* is used because Britain employed its army in sufficient force to prevent unionist invasions from occurring but not enough to ensure complete existential security for the community—and the Army itself came to pose dangers to the community in various ways, including collusion with Loyalist elements.)

As a result of this the British presence became problematic for Unionist Belfast. It seemed to be a buffer behind which the Fenians could organise and train their forces that launched attacks against the Protestant city. And the Shankill could only stand idly by and watch. So something had to give: There had to be British total repression of the Fenians to satisfy the Unionist desire for counter-action or elements within that community would take the law into its own hands to make the *"Croppies Lie Down"* again. And so began the assassination campaign.

The *"Protestant backlash"*, when it actually came, gave little encouragement to the Nationalist politicians, who were speculating on it, since rather than manifesting itself in the form of another Pogrom, it took the form of individual assassinations and random bombings which the Catholic community was powerless to prevent.

In the intensity of emotions engendered by the success of the Republican offensive it was simply not understood, particularly in Dublin, that the reason why Anti-Partitionist *realpolitik* would ultimately lose out was because its basic assumptions were wrong.

The Protestants looked like an disorganised mob, with wild, incoherent and often brutal responses to the Anti-Partitionist offensive on all fronts— military, political and diplomatic. But this was because the Unionists were such a profoundly apolitical community and, viewed from the standpoint of the political representatives of such an intensely political community as Catholic Ireland, it was easy to mistake this incoherence and disorganisation for the lack of substance and will.

Even prior to Partition, the apolitical character of Ulster Unionism had been apparent—certainly since the days of the Revival of 1859, which seems to have set off a long process of de-politicisation in the Ulster Protestants. But the arrangement made by the British Government in 1920-1 had the deepest impact on Ulster Unionism in the democratic era. It was not an arrangement that the Unionist Party would have agreed to during the conflict over Home Rule, up to 1914. Carson understood that, by cutting Ulster off from the body politic of the UK, it would have greatly detrimental political effects on the Unionists left in Ireland.

James Craig, who had been a Junior Minister in Whitehall, presided over a sensible minimising of politics in 'Northern Ireland' in order to dampen down Catholic resentment, and a kind of apolitical idyll developed in the Six Counties in which all that needed doing was reproduction of Westminster legislation and a keeping of the Catholics in their place. But gradually this

Unionist Garden of Eden disabled Ulster Unionism politically, so that when Terence O'Neill decided to take the pretensions of the 'state' at face value, it led to an unravelling of it all. The Unionists were comprehensively outmanoeuvred by the Nationalists from the Civil Rights agitation onward when a more flexible approach was taken to 'Northern Ireland' by the Catholic community which wrong-footed Ulster Unionism in relation to Britain.

But the fact that the bulk of the Protestant community lived lives of profound respectability, apart from the vulgarity of active politics, was inconceivable to Nationalist society which was deeply political in its character and which had become intensely activist from the late 1960s.

Unionism was, however, able to respond more instinctively and coherently to the more straightforward assault it was subjected to from 1970 onwards, and the critical threat to its existence which it presented, than it was to the more subtle forms of politics that had opened up the situation for the Provos.

As a result, the Nationalist offensive tended to continue on, always looking for signs of the collapse in the will of Unionist politicians when in fact such signs were illusory, since the substance of the will of the community to resist incorporation within an all-Ireland state was largely unaffected by the inadequacies of its political representatives.

Britain could only maintain its rule in the Six Counties if there was a Protestant will to support it. But, whilst the Republican War was capable of destroying the Stormont façade, it proved incapable of breaking the Protestant will to resist incorporation into the Republic. So Dublin's *realpolitik* was left impotent.

The SDLP Advises Whitelaw

The day after Direct Rule was introduced, and Whitelaw said that he would personally review the case of each internee, the SDLP issued a statement in which it said:

> "we therefore ask those engaged in the campaign of violence to cease immediately in order to enable us to bring internment to a speedy end and in order to make a positive response to the British government's proposals" (IN 27.3.72).

But having helped turned on the tap of civil disorder the SDLP found it less easy to turn it off.

A few weeks after the start of Direct Rule, Fitt, Devlin and Hume met British Government officials, Howard Smith and Frank Steele. According to the record made by Steele "their main theme was that the SDLP was engaged in a struggle with the IRA and that we should help them in that struggle". The SDLP advised the British that the help they needed involved the release of internees and the avoiding of confrontation by the British Army with the Provos. The SDLP led the British to believe that "the IRA could be finally defeated within the next three weeks" if this approach was taken. This was because, the SDLP maintained, the Republican Army was badly split and war-weary (CJ 3/98, 11.4.72).

It is unclear whether the SDLP really believed their prediction or whether this was just an attempt to secure political advantage in relation to the situation when the SDLP felt it held a strong hand.

The IRA Chief of Staff, MacStiofain, called a press conference in Derry in which he announced the Provos' peace demands including Irish self-determination, withdrawal of British troops, and a general amnesty for political offences. He invited Whitelaw to negotiate.

The SDLP availed of the absence of any mention of the internees in MacStiofain's statement to abandon their pledge not to negotiate without their prior release. Hume and Devlin met Whitelaw on 15th June to act as go-betweens between the IRA and Britain.

William Whitelaw, the Secretary of State for NI, acted on SDLP advice, releasing over 500 internees over the next two months. He also gave formal Political Status to the Republican prisoners.

The British began to replace Internment with Detention Without Trial, a more sophisticated method of internment, to enable the SDLP to re-engage with Stormont. Along with this, Whitelaw restricted the British Army's operations in Republican areas, enhancing their *"No Go"* status. Faulkner called this a *"policy of appeasement"* and *"Killing the IRA by Kindness"*. (*'Memoirs of a Statesman'*, p.163)

In view of the SDLP Intelligence that the IRA was internally divided, the British took the opportunity of an IRA Ceasefire to meet with Provisional leaders, to ascertain if there were any 'doves' they could work with among the Republican 'hawks'. The British officials met with Daithi O'Connell and Gerry Adams, who was released from Internment, especially for the discussions. Whitelaw then met Republican leaders himself, with Sean McStiofain, Gerry Adams and Martin McGuinness being flown to London for the meeting. The IRA called a short Ceasefire to mark the occasion.

The meeting proved a non-event for Whitelaw, with the SDLP advice proving unproductive for the British.

However, the event was of immense significance to the IRA. It showed them that, if they were able to keep up the military campaign, they could ultimately force the British Establishment to the negotiating table. And, whilst complete victory might remain only a hope, some lesser, evolutionary settlement could possibly be won.

The IRA had declared 1972 as *"The Year of Victory"*, demanded a British commitment to withdraw from Ireland by 1st January 1975 with an all-

Ireland election, and they intensified their campaign, sensing that they had the British on the run. The summer saw a massive escalation of shooting and bombing, including the destruction of the huge Co-op building in Belfast, with the loss of 700 jobs, and a great increase in the number of deaths. The removal of the Stormont façade put the Republicans into the position of confronting the substance—Britain. From then on the objective was to break the British will to remain in the Six Counties and thereby demoralise the Protestant will through a British withdrawal of support.

The other thing that came out of the SDLP advice on which Whitelaw acted was a growing solidity within Unionism and, finally, the much predicted *'Protestant Backlash'*. This had begun around March, but during the summer, after Whitelaw took up the SDLP advice, it really mushroomed. Thousands of Unionist militants took to the streets and established their own *'No Go'* areas, mounted bomb and shooting assaults on Catholic areas like Ballymurphy, and began the assassination campaign against innocent Catholics, many of whom found themselves in the wrong place at the wrong time.

The SDLP portrayed itself as a buffer between the Provos and large numbers who would otherwise join or support them. In a sense this could have been the case—if the SDLP had had the courage of the convictions in their original programme—but in the practical reality, where the SDLP functioned as the less vigorous wing of Anti-Partitionism, it was a hollow claim. The SDLP, in this respect, could not guarantee an end to the Republican campaign, simply because the Provos were not fighting to install the SDLP in Stormont to assist in governing something which they wished to destroy.

The SDLP also enjoyed the advantage of being very useful to Britain. Whitelaw remarked to Donal O'Sullivan, the Irish Ambassador in London, that Hume "is behaving magnificently" after he had helped facilitate the meetings with the Provos (NA 2003/16/465, 8.6.72). In the absence of an accommodationist Republican political expression, they were all that existed that could be bargained with to stabilise the situation in the North in relation to the Catholic community. And that is why they were also useful to Dublin to prop up, and for moderate Unionism to do a deal with. This was what provided the SDLP's main political capital.

The case put by the SDLP to the Provos for suspending hostilities was that the Nationalist cause would be better received in such circumstances, and the British Government made more amenable to Anti-Partitionist argument. The IRA, however, was of the opinion that its campaign was the major, if not the only, plank sustaining the Anti-Partitionist struggle amongst the Catholic community and putting pressure on the British Government, and were determined that it should only call ceasefires for temporary tactical reasons.

The Republican concern was that there was a long-term movement within Nationalist Ireland which was manifested in a decline in Republican sentiment

South of the Border and some willingness to participate in politics North of it. In such circumstances, the Anti-Partitionism that had swelled in Dublin might only be a passing sentiment, buoyed up by the seeming success of the War in the North; and with a ceasefire the SDLP itself would soon slip back into a passive acceptance of the existence of 'Northern Ireland' again.

A Military Watershed

The Bloody Friday bombings ended what Faulkner had termed "the policy of appeasement" adopted by Whitelaw, on SDLP advice. The events of 21st July 1972 prompted the SDLP into a clear denunciation of the Provos, in which it accused the Republicans of:

> "Having no concern whatsoever for human life; no concern for democracy; not placing the same importance as did the people on internment; seeming to be intent on provoking both a Protestant backlash and military action against the Catholic areas; and showing no ability to take advantage of political opportunities" (IN 27.7.72),

Bloody Friday was distinguishable from the rest of the Provo bombing campaign only in one respect—the miscalculation they made about the effect of letting off large numbers of bombs in a smallish area in a confined period of time. Placing bombs in crowded city centres is bound to produce "*atrocities*" from time to time, no matter how conscientious the giving of warnings actually is.

Bloody Friday represented an attempted 'spectacular' against Belfast, and the security forces ability to defend it, that went badly wrong. The injuries and loss of life to civilians, on the scale produced, were probably unintended by the Republican command, as the consequence would be a large propaganda defeat for Republicanism.

Propaganda was an important element in the Republican War. The IRA, even at the height of its power, was unlikely to defeat the British Army. Its campaign was waged within a Republican morality and with a strong propaganda objective in mind. The butchering of large numbers of civilians with no connection to the security forces was not a Republican intention and deliberate steps were usually taken to avoid it.

It turned out to be a reckless and anti-working class act—but the Provos were no better or worse before than after they had committed it.

Bloody Friday had an important military consequence for the IRA. It provided the opportunity for London to launch Operation Motorman, which was a British Army surge using 27,000 troops to clear the Republican *No-Go* base areas of republican control and to occupy West Belfast and Derry. It was the biggest British military operation since Suez in 1956.

Andrew Mumford has noted that Motorman emerged from

> "… a high strategic priority to end these 'no-go' areas and send a statement to the IRA that the British still maintained the strategic upper hand in the conflict… Motorman removed the IRA's strongholds and significantly undermined the groups bargaining capacity, retarded their operational capabilities and diminished the psychological edge they thought they had over the security forces" (*'The Counter-Insurgency Myth: The British Experience of Irregular Warfare'*, p. 105).

Heath informed his military commanders that up to 100 fatalities were politically acceptable in Motorman. But the SDLP was informed of the operation beforehand in the knowledge that it would convey advance notice to the Republican Army, so that no resistance would be shown against the coming demonstration of power from the forces of the State.

The British saw the real test of the operation to be the recapturing of Derry from the Republican Army. They expected popular resistance as well as resistance from the IRA. But there was little to speak of from either. An Irish Language periodical from the time provides a knowledgeable explanation for the lack of military opposition by the Provos to Motorman in Derry. It has, of course, no knowledge of any signal given by John Hume to the Provos. However, it is very interesting with regard to the changing relationship between the Catholic masses and the Republican Army since the bombing campaign had been escalated after Stormont fell, and is worth consideration:

> "For some time lately, the Provos have been losing support in Derry. There were plenty of reasons for this, but some of the most important were:
>
> a) The bomb they planted in the Essex factory in April that was so huge that it would have destroyed half the Bogside had it exploded. The army indulged in intrigue in this matter and put everyone in the district out of their homes—impressing on them how dangerous the bomb was. Eventually they succeeded in safely dismantling the bomb and they went claiming that it was they who had saved the area. Many locals thought that this was a silly action by the Provos.
>
> b) Money was stolen from a factory in Rosemount—the wages of the girls working there (300, mostly from the Creggan). The story was put out that the Provos had done it although evidence exists that it wasn't them. But the mud was thrown and there were people who believed them to be guilty anyway.
>
> c) The Bombing Campaign. The most of the centre of this City is destroyed and it's impossible to say that the Derry which now is, is the Derry that was. In this campaign, many more Catholics were put out of work than any other crowd. There is no social life. There is no working life. To be truthful, there is no life at all worth talking about. At night everyone stays inside listening to bullets going past unsure whether or not they or one of their family will stop one today or tomorrow.

"With all these reasons, the people of the Bogside and Creggan were sick and tired of the campaign being waged by the Provos. When the big day of bombings took place in Belfast, and when they heard that more soldiers were coming to attack their own areas, that finished the issue for them. They would not fight with them but would leave the fighting to those who had brought in those forces—The Provos.

"At this point, the Provos made a major mistake. An announcement came from them saying they were going to fight to the end. If there was a chance before that the people of Bogside and Creggan would have come out, that chance was lost. None of them were prepared to throw stones and a hail of bullets whizzing around them. There is certain evidence that the Provos thought the people would do just that for the Provos were sitting in their cars and their guns with them. When the English weren't obstructed they set light to their cars and the guns as well. The game was over.

"As far as the people of Bogside and Creggan are concerned, is it true that they are now reconciled to English oppression? This is by no means true, but they are willing to wait for a while to see what's going to come out of it. One thing is certain: if the English army should be oppressive against everyone from these localities, there will be more trouble then there was before..." (*Pobal* no.18, Autumn 1972. Translated from the Irish)

It is likely that the men in the cars who threw away their guns were from the Official IRA, which the Provos had neglected to inform of the cancellation of resistance after Hume's information from the British.

But this event must have impressed on the Republican Leadership the limitations on their War. It would have placed in the mind of the Republican command what actually fuelled the Insurrection and how far it would go. It was fundamentally about misgovernment and the second-class standing of the community and the attainment of objectives beyond this were going to be a bonus.

The SDLP, which had conveyed the knowledge of Motorman to the IRA and facilitated its success, then issued a condemnation of the IRA and proceeded to re-enter talks with the British Government, without the prior release of the internees. The major political effect of Motorman was to present the SDLP with the political initiative again within the Catholic community.

Dublin seems to have exerted pressure on the SDLP. The Irish Government had the SDLP leaders flown in a helicopter from Donegal to Dublin, after which a statement was issued that "no opportunity must now be let pass to achieve political progress" (IT 2.8.72). The SDLP met Whitelaw on 7-8th August, with the party calling for a "systematic de-escalation" of the conflict until political negotiations could be entered into (IT 11.8.72). However, it refused to attend the Darlington Conference organised by Heath for September.

In *abstentia* the SDLP released its own programme '*Towards a New Ireland*', hoping to deliver their policy to the Darlington Conference without attending.

'*Towards A New Ireland*' was a vision of a semi-united, semi-independent Ireland. The main suggestions in it were, firstly, that Britain should make—

"an immediate declaration that she believes that it would be in the best interests of all sections of the Community in both islands, if Ireland were to become united on terms which would be acceptable to all the people of Ireland and that she will positively encourage the prosecution of this viewpoint".

Secondly, there should be:

"A treaty between Britain and the Republic of Ireland:- (a) Accepting joint interim responsibility for the administration of Northern Ireland through certain institutions including two commissioners, an assembly and an executive, and reserving to themselves all powers of security, defence, policing, foreign affairs and financial subventions. (b) Setting up of a National Senate drawn equally from the Northern Assembly and the Dublin Parliament to plan the integration of the whole island and the harmonisation of structures, laws and services in both parts of the island".

The latter two proposals became known as "*condominium*", in SDLP statements.

The SDLP and the Provos

'Constitutional' Nationalism, whether it was in Dublin or in the Six Counties, moved to place clear blue water between itself and the actual force which had increasingly determined its political fortunes with regard to the achievement of a United Ireland. The SDLP, which rode the Provo campaign during 1971 and early 1972, now decided to draw itself away from what it saw as its contaminating effects.

At the annual conference held in Dungiven—former site of the former 'Assembly of the Northern Irish people'—a large majority passed a motion, seconded by Hume, that "the parliamentary party enter into immediate discussions with the British Secretary of State and all interested parties" (IN 27.11.72).

The *Irish News* reported "the keynote speech" of the SDLP Leader to the Party Conference:

"Mr. Fitt said that to the question, what had been achieved by the SDLP since its last conference, he could reply: 'The SDLP has achieved the downfall of the Unionist Party. Never again in Northern Ireland will people, either Protestant or Catholic, be inflicted with such an oppressive regime. Unionism as we have known it in our lifetime has gone for ever'..." (IN 27.11.72).

Ian McAllister, has a very different view of this, saying that both the IRA and SDLP "shared a common aim" which meant:

"... they acted in a parallel yet complimentary manner. Moreover, in the virtual war situation that prevailed, the group least likely to distinguish between the two means was the Catholic community. The introduction of direct rule brought a practical end to this harmony of aims. In hastening the fall of Stormont, IRA violence rather than SDLP civil disobedience had the greater impact. While civil disobedience proved ineffective in making the governmental machinery unworkable, violence severely disrupted the province's economic life, although not to the extent where it threatened its very existence... In... the final outcome it was the sovereign power and not the IRA that precipitated Stormont's demise. Westminster's attempts to find a solution were undoubtedly retarded by the SDLP's refusal to talk until internment ended... Another consequence was the continuation of a military policy (which) led to tragedies like Bloody Sunday...

"The IRA had created the need for a political group representative of the Catholic community to negotiate with Westminster on their behalf, and the SDLP, without having fought a general election, emerged to fulfil this role.

"The *de facto* position of the IRA as the community's military force and the SDLP as its political mouthpiece underlines... conditions necessary for a successful abstentionist policy... without control of the IRA the SDLP were unable to exercise coercive powers that would have their alternative system into an embryonic state.

"The SDLP's experience in abstention made it the sole political representative of the Catholic community. After March 1972, efforts became directed at developing this role by detaching itself from the more militant groups with which it had been in formal alliance, and on releasing itself from the pledge not to negotiate while internment continued" ('*The Northern Ireland Social and Democratic Labour Party*', p.113).

The IRA was the military wing of Anti-Partitionism to the SDLP's political wing. However, neither the Republican Army could control the SDLP nor the 'Constitutional Nationalists' control the IRA.

For all the opportunistic declarations against the effects of physical force Anti-Partitionism, the SDLP was largely dependent for its political power on the Republican Army's campaign. Having walked away from Stormont, it became the electoral wing of the combined movement against the Unionist Parliament. It was hardly a 'constitutional' alternative to the Provisionals anymore, having withdrawn to its own "*Alternative Assembly*". It fitted into the ambiguous relationship between 'Constitutional' and physical force Nationalism, which had existed ever since the time of Parnell and the Fenians and which was the defining characteristic of Northern Nationalism for half a century.

Parnell, said Connolly—

"always believed in a physical force party but would never join it. This gave him the power to say to the English government that if it did not grant his moderate demands then the physical force party would take control of

Irish affairs out of his hands."

Parnell, thus,

"... had the power of an organisation of armed men behind him whilst he had no responsibility for their actions" (*Irish Worker*, 8.8.14).

The rise of the Republican Army gave the British State an incentive to make concessions to the SDLP in the absence of a Republican party to make concessions to. But the SDLP, made uncertain by its contradictory aims, was unable to seize the concessions and build on them as Parnell was able to do. It seemed to fear that, if it got too much drawn into the constitutional business of the system, it would lose support within its radicalised constituency. This concern helped maintain the de facto continuum between 'constitutional' Nationalism and physical force Republicanism.

The dynamic of the situation that developed did not present the Nationalist community with a choice between either 'Constitutional' or physical force Nationalism. It became clear that it required both to advance. It was clear that 'constitutional' Nationalism would be taken little heed of by British statesmen, if it was not seen as being in some degree an alternative to the physical force movement. And, since the physical force movement was showing that it could not win an outright military victory, it was necessary that it should have some kind of constitutional engagement to advance the struggle through the obtaining of concession.

The difference between Parnell and Fitt/Hume etc. was that Parnell actively used the Fenians as a physical force arm of his movement without being subordinate to them. He controlled a powerful political movement which was largely independent of Fenianism, and which was using Fenianism. But Fitt and Hume led no such movement. If Fenianism was the unconstitutional arm of Parnellism, the SDLP was the 'constitutional' arm of the Republican Army—until it developed one of its own.

Parnell conceived an ambitious political strategy, and showed plenty of backbone in implementing it. The most striking thing about the SDLP, however, was the lack of what Parnell possessed in abundance. It did not act out of positive political conviction, and it drifted along in the wake of the Provisionals because, at decisive moments, it lacked the understanding of what it really was.

The IRA and the Catholic Community

After Operation Motorman it was becoming clear that the Republican campaign had been stemmed, although the Catholic community remained in Insurrection. Opposition to the bombing had begun to grow within the community, and the appearance of Loyalist assassination squads on a larger scale, along with the UDA's ability to put thousands of men on the streets, made it apparent that the Anti-Partitionist campaign, far from demoralising the Protestant will to resist, was provoking a substantial response from them.

Motorman changed the character of the War by ending the Republican holding of territory. It forced the Provos to operate from areas that had large security installations built within them and regular military foot patrols policing them. No longer did the situation of dual power exist in the North that had impressed Dublin so much.

The IRA had expanded rapidly from the time of Internment and it required a large escalation of activity to realise its objective of forcing a British withdrawal. It began entrusting its explosive training, construction and delivery to less experienced and more junior volunteers. The result was premature explosions and botched operations which caused the deaths of greater numbers of volunteers and civilians.

The changed situation was noticeable to Constitutional Nationalists, North and South and the sympathy which the Provos had got over the previous couple of years began to fall away. Taoiseach Lynch made no protest against *Motorman*.

In the South, the Fianna Fail Government moved to reactivate the *Offences against the State Act*, the first substantial measure taken by Dublin against the IRA in the campaign, making the word of a police inspector sufficient proof of Republican Army membership.

Passage of the new legislation was assisted by two mysterious bombs which went off in Dublin during the Debate on 1st December 1972. It was illogical for the Provos to bomb Dublin, and Irish Government files later acknowledged these to be the result of British agents operating in the 26 Counties. (See "revelations that the British government had faked IRA... raids and bombings to discredit the IRA" in NAI, TSCH 2004/21/254, 6.10.73.) After the explosions Fine Gael and Labour dropped their opposition to the law and abstained, allowing it to pass.

While IRA activity was of a fairly restricted kind, the Anti-Partitionist politicians in the SDLP and across all parties in the South used it as a political lever to push the Nationalist objective. But, after the advent of Direct Rule, when the Provos had to broaden and escalate their campaign to prevent the SDLP from becoming involved within a reformed administration, and town-centre bombing became the dominant aspect of that campaign, hostility began to emerge to the Republican struggle. Sixty thousand had signed a peace petition organised in West Belfast by June 1972 (IN 6.6.72). Also, the sympathy, which the community had worked up in Britain and internationally, began to decline when the Provos escalated and widened the campaign, resulting in a greater level of civilian casualties. The disastrous bombing of the small village of Claudy on the day of Motorman personified this.

However, the Catholic Insurrection was far from finished.

Frank Burton, the English sociologist, noted the complex attitude to the Republican Army that had developed within Catholic communities. Whilst he estimated about a third of the community were staunchly Republican, many more were supportive of the Provos only as a defence force against Unionist attack or British repression. They were opposed to offensive IRA actions against the British Army and the bombing campaign that brought counter-actions down upon the community from the British and Loyalists. The IRA, aware of this, had to justify its bombing campaign to the wider community as a means by which the British were tied up defending the city centre, making it unavailable for offensive operations within Ardoyne.

Burton noted:

> "The IRA, in attempting to create space in the community through the bombing campaign in the city, faces the problem of alienating the will of its supporters. In this sense the war is very much one of time: time to see if the British Army and Government will capitulate to certain IRA demands before the IRA becomes inoperable through lack of support. Or, alternatively, time to bring about the conditions in which the Protestant community will reject the Union. Community support for the IRA is a complex variable which is in danger of being portrayed as static. Outside perhaps those third or so (c.1972-3) who are staunchly and consistently Provisional there is essentially a see-saw relationship between the IRA and the community. What tilts the balance of the see-saw are the various activities of the British Army, Protestant paramilitary groups and the Provos' own military profile" ('*The Politics of Legitimacy*', p.85).

Burton found that the new Republicanism sustained itself, despite criticism, not because it terrorised people but because it had—

> "... what the Civil Rights movement lacked... a strong enough organisation to contain and channel the political enthusiasm it had activated. The IRA so successfully stepped into the politico-judicial vacuum because its heritage was alive in the consciousness of the Catholic minority... In addition, the doctrinal looseness of the Provisionals has enabled them to balance some of the contradictions which their campaign resurrected... Far from terror and fear, as the counter-insurgents would have it, the main reason for their existence and persistence is the centrality of their movement in the Northern Irish Catholics' consciousness" (pp.121-2).

What is noticeable in Burton's study is the sheer absence of the SDLP from the working class Catholic community. There are only two mentions of the party in his book, one by the British press in an article he quotes. The SDLP seems to have been largely irrelevant on the ground where the War was being fought.

With the reduction of Republican power came a consequent reducing and limiting of Dublin and SDLP ambitions that would take the 'Constitutionalists' back to Stormont.

CHAPTER 8

Sunningdale

The idea has become prevalent that the failure of the Sunningdale initiative and the Power-Sharing Executive it established was somehow the fault of Republicans and intransigent Unionists. That idea was expressed succinctly in the phrase given to the Peace of 1998 by Seamus Mallon, then Leader of the SDLP— *"Sunningdale for slow learners"*.

However, the failure of the potential peace agreement of 1974 was not the responsibility of Republicans and Unionists. It was very much a result of the political bungling of the 'Constitutional' Nationalists on both sides of the Border, with some assistance from the British Labour Government.

Unionist opposition to Sunningdale was natural and a given—what else was expected of them by those who had always portrayed the Unionists as intransigent, one might ask?

What was surprising and innovative was the support given to the scheme by the most substantial leader of Unionism, Brian Faulkner, and the willingness of a sizeable section of his party to go along with it. That was something that should have been nurtured at all costs by those who stood out against conflict and were desirous of peace and political accommodation.

One of the most important aspects of politics is knowing the limits of one's power in a situation. If one is aware of this, a tactical retreat can be made in the interests of the wider strategic picture. That was the great failing of 'Constitutional' Nationalism in 1974. It over-estimated the strength of its hand and this led to the squandering of what had been hard fought and gained over the previous years.

'Constitutional' Manoeuvrings

In the face of the Republican Insurrection, and the failure of Internment and Bloody Sunday to defeat it, the British Prime Minister decided on a different course of action. It was not an 'integration' or 'disengagement' policy, as Dublin had expected.

Heath may have been influenced by a pamphlet written by Prof. Harry Calvert for the United Nations in January 1972. It placed the blame for the 'Northern Ireland' problem on the permanent majority/minority structure of the Stormont Parliament and suggested that the Civil Rights programme was beside the point and not the root of the problem:

"The 1920 Act establishes provincial institutions of government in Northern Ireland on the British pattern. The constitutional scheme provided (not surprisingly) for the vesting of power, in these institutions, in the majority party on the English model. Because of continuing insecurity on the constitutional question... parties have continued to split on sectarian lines. The majority have always been the Unionist, Protestant, party linked with the Orange Order... and it has formed the government of Northern Ireland in which all power is vested... The Roman Catholic in Northern Ireland counts for virtually nothing. It matters not how able he is, how dedicated he is, even how loyal he is. The government does not need the support of Catholic members of parliament. Unionist members of parliament normally do not need Roman Catholic votes. The Roman Catholic community has literally nothing to bargain with politically. And, politically, he who cannot bargain gets a very poor deal. I have stated what I feel to be the basic issue because it is rather different from what has been voiced as the basic issue. The continued demand of recent years has been for civil rights... But, by and large, the disabilities of Roman Catholics were not such as to vindicate the turmoil now besetting the province. They were symptoms of the disease rather than the disease itself... Thus stated, it is obvious that the problem is not so much of legal as one of social and political status and power." (*The Northern Ireland Problem*, p.1)

After abolishing Stormont in March 1972 and breaking the No-Go areas with his army in *Operation Motorman*, Heath set about the task of drawing the 'Constitutional' Nationalists into a new form of devolved Six County government, to be backed by the Dublin Government. This represented a revolutionary departure in British policy—although its strategic objective remained the same— to retain the *'arm's length'* policy and sub-government in 'Northern Ireland'— but now it was to be constituted at a wider level of inclusiveness.

'Northern Ireland' was now governed by a Secretary of State, William Whitelaw—an able and senior grandee of the Tory Party. His appointment demonstrated the seriousness which Heath saw in the situation. Whitelaw brought much tact and intense political effort into enabling the SDLP to return to 'Constitutional' politics without losing face, out of the *cul de sac* they had taken themselves down.

The SDLP insistence that it would not negotiate with the British Government until all the internees were released had handed the political initiative to the IRA. Since it was in the Republican Army's gift, and not the SDLP's, to increase or decrease military activity, on which Internment was predicated, it was in the power of the IRA to determine whether negotiations between the SDLP and the British took place or not. Therefore, the IRA called the shots and had a strong incentive to maximise its military actions to keep the SDLP out of a revived Stormont.

This was the problem Whitelaw faced in getting the SDLP off the hook it had impaled itself on.

Power-sharing represented a second chance for the SDLP to determine the political agenda within the Nationalist community in a 'Constitutional' way. If it was squandered, there would be a long wait for another bite at the cherry.

The SDLP programme, *'Towards a New Ireland'*, was not reflected in the British Government's *Green Paper*, *'The Future of Northern Ireland'*, issued in October 1972, which took little inspiration from the SDLP policy. It also crushed the belief in Dublin that Britain wanted to get shot of 'Northern Ireland' in favour of a United Ireland, due to the trouble the Provos had caused them.

The *Green Paper* emphasised two major elements in any solution—the right of the majority to remain in the UK, and removal of all discrimination against the Catholics in 'Northern Ireland'. It said that unity would be a progressive development, but one which must take place on the basis of free and mutual consent. And it suggested, as the SDLP had in its official programme, that a Plebiscite would be a necessary step to sort out the issue in the short term.

A few years earlier John Hume had said:

> "It now appears to be agreed on all sides that no change can take place in the existing constitutional position without the consent of the majority of the people in the North, and that any individual or political group has the right to campaign for eventual change of the constitution. In the light of this it would seem to follow logically that the constitutional question should be taken out of politics by having a periodic referendum on it so that elections could be real elections based on real political issues" (IN 11.11.69).

When the British Government announced the holding of a Plebiscite on the Constitutional question, the SDLP did not seize the chance to convince the people of 'Northern Ireland' of the disadvantages of living in the UK, and of the benefits of joining the Republic. Instead the SDLP joined with Sinn Fein in a boycott of the poll.

When a majority (58% of the total electorate) voted for staying in the UK, the SDLP said the result was entirely predictable, since everybody knew that there were more Protestants than Catholics in 'Northern Ireland' anyhow. This, of course, was true. But it implied that the SDLP felt the Protestants were congenital Unionists and there was no hope in persuading them of the benefits of living in a United Ireland. What then were the chances of *"consent"* being forthcoming from the majority, one might ask?

What was apparent was that the SDLP's insistence on *"consent"* rather than force, and their *"respect for the right"* of consent was conditional. Hume, in an address to the Bow Group of the Conservative Party, after "making it clear that we had no wish to coerce the Unionist people into a united Ireland against their will" said that: "... the only argument advanced to date against… proposals {for joint sovereignty} was that they were unacceptable to the majority in Northern Ireland", and "this is not a proper yardstick to apply to any solution to the Northern Ireland problem" (IT 19.1.73).

This got to the heart of the idea of "*consent*" that Hume developed. "*Consent*" only referred to the final act of transference of the Protestants into a United Ireland. Anything that was done to them, short of that, no matter how much against their will it was, did not require their consent. This policy ultimately involved putting the Unionists in a position that was so hateful to them that their 'consent' could be obtained by Britain to move them on further down the Dublin road.

But, with the decline of the Republican offensive, the SDLP had to wait 10 years and for Mrs. Thatcher to come along.

The SDLP Plays Hard To Get

William Beattie Smith notes:

> "Like the IRA, the SDLP saw direct rule as a first step toward unification. With Stormont's suspension, they believed that they had brought the major political parties in Britain and Ireland around to their view that this was the only viable long-term solution. They thus focused on how and by when that outcome could be best engineered" ('*The British State and the Northern Crisis*', p.261)

The SDLP's "*Alternative Assembly*" at Dungiven had not amounted to much and, when Dublin ceased paying for it and the Provos' military offensive started to falter, the only future for the party lay in a return/retreat to accommodationist politics at Stormont. The SDLP allowed itself to be coaxed out of the position they had boxed themselves into slowly but there was really little alternative for them, and Whitelaw knew it.

Justice Devlin described the task that Whitelaw set himself very precisely during the second of the great *Television Trials*, which took place in 1972. It was to find a way in which the SDLP might abandon its Anti-Partitionism, while appearing all the while not to do so. It was to be done by degrees and a transitional phase was to be organised in which the '*Constitutionalists*' were to suspend their ideals for a cut of the political power, while every effort was to be made to conceal what was happening. The great diplomatic skills and some of the best years of Willie Whitelaw's life went into the accomplishment of this task.

The Westminster *Green Paper* of November 1972 was followed by a *White Paper*, '*Northern Ireland Constitutional Proposals*', in March 1973 and a *Constitution Bill* in May 1973. The latter provided for the election of an 80 member Northern Ireland Assembly, which it was hoped would form the basis of a power-sharing, devolved Government.

Elections held in late June 1973 resulted in a comfortable majority for the parties who were the potential power-sharers: the Faulknerite Unionists, the SDLP, and the Alliance Party. The SDLP received 23% of the total vote.

The SDLP returned to the sphere of 'Constitutional' politics with what it saw as a good bargaining position. It saw its strength lying in its potential vote in the Catholic community, combined with the fact that it could present itself as the only realistic alternative to the IRA within that community. In its election campaign it downgraded the significance of the Assembly, describing it as a mere *"conference table"*, and committed itself to nothing. Paddy Devlin made a number of statements against Power-Sharing, which he described, quite accurately, as *"institutional sectarianism"*.

Whitelaw encouraged the metamorphosing of the SDLP in return for recognising them as the authentic voice of the Catholic community—something that was not in any way the truth of the matter.

The British Government *White Paper* put the SDLP in a tricky position. The Paper conceded none of the Party's main demands and it presented no rigidly defined scheme which could convincingly be boycotted. There was to be no *'condominium'*, and no declaration of intent to withdraw. Instead, a parliament was to he established. But it was put squarely to the parties which would be involved in it, that any substantial powers would only be granted to it when it was made workable, and it would not be considered workable unless it had substantial consent in the Catholic community. The SDLP could make it unworkable by withholding consent, so long as the Party could be seen to be representative of the will of the Catholic community in doing so.

It was feared that the Nationalists would reject the proposals entirely because of the British guarantee on the province's constitutional position. This was got over by the SDLP through the argument that such a guarantee was *"not a secure basis for constitutional stability since an Act of Parliament can be changed at any time"* (*Fortnight* 21.5.73).

The SDLP took a cautious approach when confronted with the materialisation of the logic of its political position. The Party released a statement saying that "the new Assembly... until its detailed workings have been agreed, will be little more than a conference table... We will willingly accept the opportunity to sit at that conference table" (IN 21.3.73).

The *Irish News'* Letters Page summed up the fundamental dilemma faced by the SDLP:

> "Whitelaw is offering the minority an end to discrimination, gerrymandering, victimisation and all the other manifold sectarian injustices perpetrated on them for the last half a century—but at a price—a soul

destroying price. He is asking it, or anyway its leaders, to do something they have never yet done—publicly accept the legitimacy of the state" (IN 2.7.1973).

The Nationalist press began to put pressure on the SDLP to take part in the new Assembly. The *Irish News* of July 2nd, in an editorial which endorsed the Assembly as a means of easing the situation, uttered a mild rebuke to Hume for his Party's dilatory attitude:

> "John Hume has said that the Assembly will initially supply a conference table. Normality, therefore, will not come speedily, but at least the people's desire for normal politics has been expressed."

The *Irish News* editorial of 14th July was most clear when it said of the Assembly: "for all its shortcomings, it does contain the basis for a power-sharing which, given good will and tolerance on all sides could develop into an enterprise of real success". It was recognised that the Assembly was not "an instrument for realising the political ideals" of Nationalism but, "what alternative is there at the present time? They may not be cast iron, but there are guarantees that it will be employed for justice and that it will operate for equity."

But the editorial went on to warn that "An SDLP-Faulkner collaboration is unthinkable. Internment still remains ·a score to settle", and "collaboration with the Craig-Paisley axis is even more unthinkable".

But the *"unthinkable"* was not far away.

The SDLP meantime continued to play hard to get. At the first session of the Assembly, the Unionists made it clear that they were prepared to consider a nomination for Presiding Officer from the SDLP, but the latter declined to come forward. Stressing all the while that they were laying down no preconditions for participation, their spokesmen continued to lay down preconditions.

In July the SDLP faced a further problem when the new Taoiseach, Liam Cosgrave, told a meeting of senior Conservatives in London that any initiative that raised the issue of Partition "*would dangerously exacerbate tensions and fears*" in the Six Counties. Hume rebuked the Taoiseach publicly, warning him not to underestimate the strength of Anti-Partitionism or abandon it in favour of "the false liberalism of placating the Unionists" (*Irish News* 3.7.73). SDLP delegations then appeared in Dublin to explain to Cosgrave that he was weakening their bargaining position through his words and aiding the Provos. Fine Gael, took the point, and Garret Fitzgerald was sent to London to press Heath on giving the SDLP a Council of Ireland in the political imitative he was putting together.

The Heath Threat

The SDLP was finally jolted into reality by a statement by Heath that the British Government would consider the complete integration of the Province into the United Kingdom, if the Executive of the Assembly was not formed by the following March. Heath said:

> "I would favour the total integration of Northern Ireland with Great Britain if the proposed Executive is not set up by March, as required by the Northern Ireland Constitution Act" (News Letter 18.9.73).

This was the "*integration policy*" that Dublin had most feared. But it was being used as a warning-shot across the SDLP bows, rather than as a serious British alternative to its traditional policy. The *Irish News* recognised this when it said: "Integration is simply not on because... Britain wants less not more responsibility for Northern Ireland" (21.9.73).

It was let known that the Prime Minister, who was also said to be favourable to an organisation of the Conservative Party in the Six Counties, had commissioned Whitelaw to draw up contingency plans for implementing the policy. Heath made it clear that this was not his desired policy but his fall-back position—presumably if the SDLP were unprepared to play ball. If the Executive was not able to be constructed it would be on the agenda. That gave both Dublin and the SDLP food for thought. For the SDLP, the idea of a leisurely progress towards an Executive, with a liberal interspersion of demands about police reforms, Council of Ireland, etc. was rudely shattered. Ten days after Heath's statement, the SDLP declared its willingness to take part in an all-party conference to discuss the formation of a Northern Ireland Executive.

As the SDLP and the Unionists got down to discussions about the setting up of a Northern Ireland Executive, the leader of Sinn Fein, Ruari O'Bradaigh, had this to say: "The Provos are about to win the battle and lose the war... The SDLP are about to cream off all the Provisional successes. They are poachers turned gamekeepers" (IT 11.11.73).

There was little doubt that the SDLP were about to gain a share in power in the new Executive because of the Republican War effort. The Provos' effort had destroyed the old Stormont, assisted latterly by the SDLP "*poachers*". The SDLP rode the Provo tiger, as long as it seemed to be going somewhere, and was now jumping off it to take part in establishing a new, improved, Stormont.

As Faulkner later noted:

> "Henceforth discussions were to centre on the possibilities of co-operation between Northern Ireland and the Irish Republic. One heard no more talk of a 'united Ireland or nothing': the long road back from undiluted nationalism

to constructive policies for participation in Northern Ireland had begun" (*Memoirs of a Statesman*, pp.185-6).

Sunningdale

Faulkner believed that the Sunningdale arrangement was worthwhile. It tied the SDLP into the Stormont system and allowed for two years before being put to the electorate. Over this period, he calculated, Unionist resentment would decline. Thus a functional and stable settlement was possible. After a hard battle within his party and a walk-out by a sizeable minority, led by Bill Craig, Faulkner was authorized by the Ulster Unionist Council to open discussions with Whitelaw on the basis of the British White Paper.

However, against the Unionist Leader's advice, Whitelaw was persuaded by the SDLP to exclude Faulkner's opponents within Unionism from the Sunningdale negotiations, although the White Paper had stipulated that all parties elected to the Assembly should be included. This immediately created an opposition outside the talks, one that could grow, given the right conditions.

Faulkner took considerable risks thereafter, since Unionist policy was not to admit to government any party whose primary object was to break the Union. The Unionist Leader described the mainstream Unionist attitude to the SDLP at the time:

> "To many Unionists the SDLP were the party whose leaders had started off the violence with irresponsible demonstrations on the streets, who had criticized and undermined the security forces ever since, and who had encouraged their supporters to opt out of the system by a rent and rates strike which largely continued. There was still some doubt as to their attitude on the very right of the State to exist, These matters all had to be clarified if there was to be any prospect of reaching agreement on an Executive" (*Memoirs of a Statesman*, p.204).

The Constitution Act of 1973 laid down an oath for members of the Executive to take which pledged them to "uphold the laws of Northern Ireland" and to fulfil their duties "in the interests of Northern Ireland and its people". This oath barred Republicans from the Executive and effectively made support for the rent and rates strike impossible.

Elections to an Assembly were held, in which Faulkner's party secured 32 representatives within the 78-seat body (although 10 were later to defect to the anti-Sunningdale camp); the SDLP got 19; and the Alliance Party, 8. The Unionist opposition of Paisley and Craig had 18 seats.

Negotiations concerning the setting up of the Executive were held with Whitelaw acting as go-between. First formal inter-party talks took place on 5th October 1973, when deputations from the Pro-Assembly Unionists, the SDLP, and Alliance Party met at Stormont. Agreement was reached on the formation of an Executive on November 21st. On 6-9th December, representatives of the three Parties met delegations from the British and Irish Governments at the Sunningdale Civil Service College in England to finalise the settlement.

A lengthy 20-point Communique, outlining the tri-partite agreement on the Council of Ireland, was issued from Sunningdale. It covered a number of points concerning co-operation between the UK and the Republic on security matters, and contained an acceptance from the Southern Government that there "could be no change in the status of N. Ireland until a majority of the people of N. Ireland desired a change in that status". Point Seven of the Communique revealed that the Council—

> "would be confirmed to representatives of the two parts of Ireland, with appropriate safeguards for the British Government's financial and other interests. It would comprise a Council of Ministers with executive and harmonising functions and a consultative role, and a consultative Assembly with advisory and review functions. The Council of Ministers would act by unanimity and would comprise a core of seven members of the Irish government and an equal number of members of the Northern Ireland Executive... The Consultative Assembly would consist of 60 members, 30 members from Dail Eireann... and 30 members from the Northern Ireland Assembly."

The SDLP Accepts

As Dublin began to distance itself from the Insurrection, the SDLP agreed to abandon the civil disobedience campaign and go back to participatory politics within a reformed Stormont system. At the SDLP Conference in December 1973, 235 delegates against 22 voted in favour of participation in the Government of 'Northern Ireland'. The SDLP leaders then committed themselves to the pledge in the Constitution Act 1973.

The SDLP formally withdrew its support for the rent and rates strike. As the *Irish News* of 31st January put it: "They will be challenged on all sides on their sense of responsibility: the party therefore cannot support a rent and rates strike."

Unfortunately for the people who took up the call of the SDLP in August 1971, it was not quite so simple; for many of them, the effect of taking part in the strike was with them for years, as they struggled to pay off their arrears. Unfortunately for them, the consequences of the rent and rates strike were not considered if the Provo campaign, which was proving so effective in 1971, was not to succeed in achieving final victory.

With regard to the Insurrection: the SDLP was able to support and feed it but it was not able to call it off because it was only an adjunct to it and it did not have the presence in the important areas to make a meaningful difference. But in some ways this was a boon—since its continuation meant that more concessions had to be granted to the SDLP to attempt to weaken support for it.

At its conference of December 1973 the SDLP committed itself to setting up a working party to look at the possibility of bringing about integrated education, and a motion against Internment, and against Brian Faulkner as proposed Chief of the Executive was sidestepped by the leadership.

It seemed as if the SDLP was in the process of becoming a fully 'Constitutional' party of 'Northern Ireland' to all intents and purposes. And it looked as though the only discordant ingredient in an otherwise democratic settlement, the Council of Ireland, was largely symbolic to disguise the SDLP move into politics within the Six County statelet. John Hume said:

> "What in effect that means—and this is extremely important—is that for those who seek Irish unity it is clear that Britain is not standing in the way. It's a majority of people in Northern Ireland who do not want it, and obviously no one could think that you could coerce people into uniting with other people. It can only be done by consent, and if that consent is to be achieved it can only be through this building up of trust and working together" (IN 12.12.73).

Hume had to represent this as a new state of affairs, resulting from the Sunningdale Agreement. In fact, it was the state of affairs that had existed ever since 1921.

There was, however, a lot of ambiguity about the proposed Council of Ireland. It was certainly a very important ingredient of the solution as far as the Southern Government and SDLP were concerned. But the question was, in what respect? There were grounds for believing that the Council was more important to the South, not for what it was, but for what it could be made out to be—that it was the 'constitutional' device whereby the Southern Government might abandon Anti-Partitionism while obscuring this process from public view. Its existence would enable Catholic-Nationalism to say that its United Ireland aim was being taken care of, when, in fact, it was being quietly relegated to an aspiration.

Maurice Hayes, the Catholic civil servant- charged with finding a function for it, later wrote:

> "This, I thought was a dead duck from the start; a piece of symbolic window dressing that was never going to amount to anything, and which would distract attention from the essential task of building trust in Northern Ireland… it occupied the time of the Executive, it dominated the thinking of the SDLP Ministers, and it obsessed their backbenchers" (*Minority Verdict*, p.175).

The Council of Ireland cross-border body was originally a Unionist suggestion. Even Bill Craig had approved it at the Darlington Conference. But Faulkner stuck his neck out by being in favour of it having not just consultative and advisory functions but also some executive powers, to be exercised when unanimity was achieved.

Faulkner had a very relaxed attitude to cross-border co-operation, due to his confidence in dealing with Southerners. Faulkner had been to school in Dublin and had extensive business contacts in the South. The Unionist Leader felt at ease with the Southerners and, if he had a fault, it was in being too confident in his dealings with Dublin. He did not foresee the Council as a Constitutional threat, so long as Dublin reacted in the right way to it and he had every reason to believe that it was sensible enough to do so. However, not all Unionists were so confident in dealing with the South and the phrase *"Dublin is only a Sunningdale away"* had greater resonance than Faulkner anticipated within his community.

The Dublin Government was anxious to portray the formation of the Council as a substantial concession to its United Ireland aspirations. The Nationalist press could not resist pouring out words about the possible form and function of the new Council, which would enable the South to achieve some bit of sovereignty over 'Northern Ireland', and enforce in some small way its claim to jurisdiction over the Six Counties. Politicians could hardly conceal their joy that, even if equal representation on all-Ireland bodies were conceded, the Protestants would be outnumbered even on an inter-governmental institution. And if possible functions could be acquired for the all-Ireland bodies, then at least a little bit of the Nationalist dream would come true—the South would have a little bit of sovereignty over 'Northern Ireland'.

The Executive Formed

With the Sunningdale system seemingly complete, Heath made a blunder in whisking its architect, Willie Whitelaw, off to deal with his main pressing concern, the powerful Trade Unions in Britain. He was replaced by Francis Pym, who was thrown into a situation he had little knowledge or experience of.

The 'Northern Ireland' Executive took office on 1st January, 1974. Its eleven members were: Chief Minister, Brian Faulkner (Unionist); Deputy Chief Minister, Gerry Fitt (SDLP); Legal Minister and Head of the Office of Law Reform, Oliver Napier (Alliance); Minister for Information, John Baxter (Unionist); Minister for the Environment, Roy Bradford (Unionist); Minister of Housing, Local Government & Planning, Austin Currie (SDLP); Minister for Health and Social Services, Paddy Devlin (SDLP); Minister for Commerce, John Hume (SDLP); Minister for Finance, Herbert Kirk (Unionist); Minister for Education, Basil McIvor (Unionist); Minister for Agriculture, Leslie Morrell (Unionist).

The numerical permutation gave the Unionists a majority with 6 Ministers to the SDLP's 4 and 1 Alliance. But this was largely symbolic to reassure the wider Unionist community that its majority was being taken care of.

The Sunningdale system of 1974 was very different to the Good Friday system of 1998. There were no clear and binding rules for executive formation and operation. It was a more fluid construct with a weighted-majority system in which the operative weight was never actually specified.

It was, unlike the Good Friday system, a Cabinet system conducted by a Chief Executive and his Deputy, in separate Offices, responsible to the Parliament. The Secretary of State supervised and sat in judgment over the whole affair, having the sole authority to appoint Ministers to the Executive and to decide whether or not to delegate authority to them. The governing coalition, if formed, would be voluntary and there were no mechanisms established to prevent the majority Unionists from over-riding the minority Nationalists in the Executive and Assembly. Only the British Secretary of State could prevent this happening, through his power to suspend or bring down the whole arrangement if he thought fit.

1974 was very different from 1998 and what was conceded on Good Friday was never available at Sunningdale. Considering that Sunningdale was conceded by Britain near the height of the Republican offensive and the Good Friday Agreement was a more substantial equalizing of power, the deal 1998 was a far better one.

Faulkner, frustrated at having to be held to account by the arcane democracy of the Ulster Unionist Council, then took the significant decision of resigning from the Unionist Party, to signal that his first priority was making the political settlement work.

The more hard-line Unionists condemned the Executive and the Council of Ireland as a sell-out by Faulkner, but were unable to raise much steam in the Protestant community about it. Twenty-Seven people turned up to one of Paisley's early rallies against it in Ballyclare—a far cry from the protests that came after the disbandment of the Specials and Direct Rule. What was clear was that the bulk of the Protestant community was willing to give peace a chance, even if it meant making concessions to Nationalists. The price, they felt, was worth it, as long as the settlement did not appear to be a device for getting them into a United Ireland by the back door.

In the first days of the Executive, an entirely new image was projected by the SDLP. The party threw itself with enthusiasm and dedication into its Departmental work with a great deal of confidence. The Stormont bureaucracy reciprocated and good working relations were established. After Labour spokesman Roy Mason had seemed to suggest the withdrawal of British troops from 'Northern Ireland', Currie denounced him on television for his foolishness and Fitt flew over to London to confront Wilson about the gaffe. Faulkner even went on holiday, knowing the province to be in safe hands, and Hume went to America, to persuade businessmen to invest in Ulster.

The ambiguity which the Council of Ireland gave to SDLP participation in the Executive, and the Southern Government's support for Sunningdale, seemed the means by which their Anti-Partitionism could be traded in for a new participatory approach.

But such ambiguity could not last for ever. In January 1974, it was clear that a second moment of truth was coming closer for the SDLP. In that month the Faulkner group in the Unionist Party was defeated by one vote in the Ulster Unionist Council over the Sunningdale Agreement, and Faulkner resigned as Leader. The writing was on the wall for both the SDLP and the Southern Government, telling them that the ambiguity which surrounded the operation and function of the proposed Council of Ireland—which was the obvious source of most Protestant discontent—could no longer persist and that, if the Loyalist opposition to Faulkner was to be isolated and destroyed, political clarity was becoming a necessity.

Ken Bloomfield, the senior Stormont civil servant, later wrote: "In order to stabilise opinion within the unionist community, Faulkner badly needed to be able to demonstrate that the Irish government now accorded to Northern Ireland an effective de facto recognition and legitimacy" (*Stormont in Crisis*, p.202).

There was so much ambiguity around the 1973 Agreement that there were actually two different versions of the document, one signed by the British Government and the other by the Irish Government. The version signed by the Irish gave the name of the British State as 'The United Kingdom of Great Britain', with the words 'and Northern Ireland' from the British version omitted. Evasion was the order of the day in Dublin, and Whitehall went along with the fudge in order to secure the settlement. But what could be fudged in Britain with its unwritten or uncodified constitution could not be done in relation to a written constitution which a Government could be held accountable for breaching.

Faulkner Duped by Dublin

Faulkner had led a substantial body of Unionists into the agreement and indications were that his support was increasing among Protestants in early 1974. But then came the Constitutional challenge in the South and from that moment Faulkner's position began to substantially weaken. The Fine Gael/Labour Coalition in Dublin destroyed Faulkner when it stated publicly, in considerable detail, that it had conceded no constitutional recognition to the North at Sunningdale. In effect it admitted it had duped Faulkner and this signal to the Unionists in the North proved fatal to him.

Clearing up the ambiguity was made an absolute necessity by the decision of the former Fianna Fail Minister, Kevin Boland, to take the Agreement to Court on the grounds that it was unconstitutional with regard to Articles 2 and 3 of the Southern Constitution, which asserted that the right of sovereignty over the Six Counties lay with the 26 County state, not the UK. Cosgrave's Government pleaded in defence that it had not, in fact, recognised the legitimacy of the North as part of the UK, but had merely indicated that it was not its policy to enforce the sovereignty claim over the North asserted by the Constitution. It declared that its signing of the Sunningdale Agreement did not prejudice the right of any future Irish Government to act to enforce the sovereignty claim. The Irish Supreme Court found that this was the case.

Unionist support for the Agreement was given on the understanding that the Dublin Government had revoked the sovereignty claim. When the Dublin Government was seen to declare in court that the sovereignty claim still stood, Ulster Unionist hostility towards the Agreement was immediately strengthened and Faulkner began to be seen as having been duped.

A number of Southern politicians in the Coalition Government had made it known that they supported the position of upholding the Protestant right to remain out of a United Ireland for as long as they desired. The most prominent of these were Conor Cruise O'Brien and Garret FitzGerald. The Sunningdale Agreement presented them with a golden opportunity. Here, the Unionists, led by Faulkner, were accepting unequivocally the necessity for the Assembly and for a Power-Sharing Executive and, furthermore, were prepared to accept a Council of Ireland.

In return for this, they expected a clear declaration from the South that it would drop or alter its sovereignty claim over 'Northern Ireland'. Many people supposed that this declaration was made in substance in the diplomatic language of the Sunningdale Agreement. But, when Kevin Boland's legal action established that this was not the case, and that the Belfast Coalition was therefore in jeopardy, that was clearly the time for O'Brien and FitzGerald to act if they were in earnest about reaching out to Unionists. They could have demanded that a Referendum be held on Articles 2 and 3, on the basis that an arrangement had been made on behalf of the Northern Catholics so that they would be represented in the government of the North; that a Council of Ireland had been established whose powers could be enhanced when Unionist confidence in Southern intentions had been secured; and that it was essential to build this confidence through replacing the Articles with the declaration made at Sunningdale.

Or alternatively, they could have accepted postponement of the Council of Ireland until the Power-Sharing Executive had stabilised and confidence in it had developed within the Protestant community.

Such a Referendum could have been won in the South and, if it had been, Hume, Devlin and Fitt would have remained Ministers in the North. The Catholics in the North would probably have had little objection to such moves; their objective of a share in power had been achieved and they showed little interest in 'Free State' constitutional issues. The removal of the territorial claim would have erased Protestant suspicions and would have exposed the Loyalist opposition to Sunningdale as fundamentalist and dogmatic. It is even possible that the opposition in the South would have been minimal, since a refusal to remove the claim would have been seen as destroying Sunningdale and Power-Sharing in the North.

But the moment was lost in a welter of semantics and hair-splitting. Protestant suspicions were aroused and the subsequent to-ing and fro-ing between Dublin and Belfast by Irish Ministers, in the absence of a grand gesture, did nothing to quell them.

The SDLP Ministers also posed for a photograph with members of the Dublin Government in preparation for All-Ireland Government.

The funking by the Dublin Government of the constitutional issue was fuelling Loyalist reaction against the Agreement. Paisley took a full page advert in the *News Letter* in which he printed, without comment, part of the Dublin Government's Submission to the Court in the Boland Case against Sunningdale. No comment was needed to argue the case against Unionist participation in the Council of Ireland with the Government that made this Submission.

It could be said that the Government in the South had no intention of coercing the North. But how much weight do mere declarations of intention carry in politics, particularly in the communal conflict within 'Northern Ireland'?

The Cosgrave Government was asking Unionists to believe that its professed intentions counted for everything and the official Constitution of the state counted for nothing. But the Constitution legitimised the Anti-Partitionist objective that stimulated Protestant opposition. Governments come and go—but the Constitution remains. The Cosgrave Government could not decline responsibility for the Constitution. If it did not subscribe to it, they ought to have attempted to change it. If they made no attempt to do so, all the intentions in the world counted for nought.

The Cosgrave Government thought it could evade the basic issue. But it was not allowed to do so. It was compelled to argue in Court that, by adopting a policy of voluntary unification, it had not given up either the claim to sovereignty over the North, or the right to coerce the North under Dublin rule. It could not have argued otherwise, without challenging the Constitution itself. And it lacked the moral fibre to do that. The only useful thing now open was to help the Executive to continue without the Council of Ireland. If it persisted with the Council of Ireland, there was undoubtedly trouble ahead.

The Election Warning

The UK General Election of February 1974, in which Heath's Government suffered a dramatic fall, was widely cited as the cause of the demise of the Executive.

The platform of the Anti-Agreement Unionists campaign in the Election was that either the Power-Sharing Executive should submit itself to election or the Council of Ireland should be postponed. This won over 90% of the representation of the Province, and Gerry Fitt was the sole remaining Pro-Sunningdale MP left at Westminster.

Heath could have continued in government if he had not shut the anti-Faulkner Unionists out at Sunningdale. But Labour was returned at Westminster with a slim majority.

It has been suggested that the Election result provided Anti-Agreement Unionists with an electoral opportunity before the Executive had really got down to governing and had had the opportunity to show its worth to the electorate. But, if the Executive had been politically astute enough, it would have noted the result of the Election, and the tide of public opinion which it represented, and made provisions to satisfy it to consolidate its position. For what the result demonstrated was that, after two months of Executive functioning, the majority of Protestant voters had become highly suspicious of the Council of Ireland aspect of Sunningdale.

The idea that, if the Election had not occurred, opposition to Sunningdale would have been of a lot less consequence, belongs to the realm of political fantasy. The Election result was a good indicator of public opinion, and it should have convinced the Executive that proceeding with the Council at that time was politically suicidal. It should have convinced the SDLP that statements made by it about the Council being a half-way house to a United Ireland were dangerous. And it should have shown Faulkner that his position of stating that the public should not pay too much heed to what Nationalist politicians were saying, but instead recognise that they had accepted the validity of the statelet, was not one which was sustainable in the circumstances.

But unfortunately no steps were taken to deal with causes of electoral support for those opposed to the Agreement.

The only respect in which it can be said that the Election proved disadvantageous was in the replacement of the Tories and Whitelaw in power by Labour and Merlyn Rees.

Opposition Grows

An important change took place in the Protestant opposition to Sunningdale in the first few months of 1974. In January, it was composed of a handful of cantankerous individuals. By May, it grown into a substantial and representative political force. This was an important change which the Executive chose to ignore. It would have been astonishing if there had been no political opposition to Sunningdale. Even those who saw the Protestant community as the mere dupes of British Imperialism could not have expected such. Conflict was to be expected over such an innovatory scheme as Sunningdale. But the business of responsible and far-sighted politicians is to minimise such conflict, not to help maximise it.

The Sunningdale politicians began with very great tactical advantages over their opponents, and with the consent of the majority of both Catholic and Protestant communities. If the opposition to Sunningdale was a religious one, simply stirred up by the sectarian catch cries of bigoted politicians, one would have expected it to be most intense in the weeks immediately following the signing of the Agreement and the setting up of the Executive. But in that period the anti-Sunningdale rallies were miserable affairs. Opposition contained all the paranoid and sectarian elements, and the backwoodsmen. The mainstream was quiescent.

The rallies were the limit of what could have been achieved by way of opposition on the basis of sectarian sentiment and groundless fears. But a gradual turnabout took place early in 1974, and by May, when the Ulster Workers' Council called its Strike, this had become a massive turnabout.

If the Executive Parties had profited by the warning of the February Election and suspended the Council of Ireland until Dublin could see its way to deleting Articles 2 and 3 of its Constitution, it would not have been in such a declining position in May. If the SDLP had advanced arguments on the basis of what it was achieving, the Executive would have gone from strength to strength. But, if this was too much to expect, a suspension of the Council would certainly have kept the Power-sharing structures in being. Survival meant the passing of time and the consequent consolidation of the Executive.

On 8th March an SDLP delegation including Hume, Currie and Devlin met the Taoiseach and members of the Irish Cabinet in Dublin. At this meeting it was acknowledged by the SDLP that the Westminster elections had produced "shell-shock" in the Faulkner Unionists and "there were a number... who had been disposed to panic". However, "Faulkner was ready not to panic", according to the SDLP and Devlin assured the Taoiseach that "the SDLP had succeeded in steadying up the Unionists".

There was a discussion about what could be offered to the Unionists to encourage them to proceed with the ratification of Sunningdale. Devlin suggested "some effective confrontation with the IRA... which would appeal to the mentality of the Unionists". The Irish Minister of Justice, Paddy Cooney, suggested a "shooting war" with Republicans to which Devlin replied: "it might have to come to this". The SDLP delegation then argued that "vigorous action" by Dublin against Republicans would be tolerated by Northern Catholics due to "the destruction of the centres of Omagh, Strabane and Dungannon and other largely Nationalist towns by IRA bombing".

The Republicans were to be sacrificed to retain Power-Sharing, it seems.

It was emphasised to the Irish Government by the SDLP that "if there was failure to proceed with the establishment of the Council of Ireland they would withdraw from the Executive" and "it was desirable to push ahead as fast as possible with the ratification of Sunningdale". This had been made clear to the British. And it was also stated that a large release of Republican internees to their homes was not worth any postponement of establishing the Council of Ireland.

Hume argued that:

> "It was well to recall that there had been a considerable degree of opposition to power-sharing when it was first mooted whereas it now seemed to be generally accepted. It was quite possible the same could hold true for the Council of Ireland" (NAI, TSCH 2005/7/627, 11.3.74).

But that was a fatal miscalculation—the substance of the Unionist opposition was to the Council of Ireland rather than to Power-Sharing and it was essential to separate the two in order to prolong the Executive.

In mid-March Faulkner attempted to get the SDLP to agree to a two-stage implementation of the Council of Ireland, with the transfer of executive functions only proceeding after the next Assembly election endorsed the Executive. This was in line with the unanimity originally agreed and was aimed to assuage Unionist concerns. However, the SDLP was reluctant to agree to what it saw as an amendment to the Agreement. Because of the principle of cabinet responsibility these discussions, which dragged on for 6 crucial weeks, were kept from the public, only increasing Unionist concern and opposition to the whole deal.

Further meetings and conversations held between Sean Donlon of the Department of Foreign Affairs and members of the SDLP, over the next month, made it clear that there was a division within the party as to whether Faulkner would actually ratify Sunningdale without an amendment to the implementation of the Council of Ireland:

> "Hume doubts that Faulkner will pass the test but thinks it is of vital importance that this should be found out sooner rather than later. Hume still seems to be alone in the SDLP leadership in doubting Faulkner's intentions… Devlin, Currie, O'Hanlon and a number of backbenchers… take the view that Faulkner will continue to struggle and kick right up to the ratification table but that he is the political survivor par excellence and realises that if the current package disintegrates, he has no political future… he has now

been given a guaranteed four-year period in which to sell the package and that this should be child's play in comparison to some of the changes he has had to sell in recent years" (NAI, TSCH 2005/7/629, 4.4.74).

All the SDLP agreed that: "Wilson and Rees are exerting considerable pressure on Faulkner... to keep him on the Sunningdale tracks... and he should be confronted with a date for the ratification of Sunningdale before he gets his next attack of the jitters."

It was concluded that Dublin pressure would be counter-productive in the situation.

Devlin also revealed to Irish Foreign Affairs Secretary Donlon that he had been contacted by the Provos to help arrange talks between them, the UVF, DUP and the SDLP. Donlon reported that Devlin had "thought such talks would do no harm but he said Hume was totally opposed to talking even to Sinn Fein and I gathered that Hume's view was the one most likely to prevail".

There was a fatal over-confidence present in the SDLP.

The Ulster Workers Strike

In March a new body called the Ulster Workers' Council issued a statement that they would call a General Strike if the Agreement, with the Council of Ireland, was ratified. The UWC placed a notice in the *News Letter* warning that a strike would begin that evening if Faulkner voted to support Sunningdale. The Assembly voted 44 to 28 in favour of ratification on May 14th and the strike began.

There was one last chance to avert a confrontation. David Bleakley, the sole NILP Assemblyman, proposed a compromise motion to the Assembly when it sat to decide whether or not to accept the Sunningdale Agreement. He proposed that the success to date of Power-Sharing should be welcomed and it was in the interests of everyone that it should continue, but that, owing to the decision of the Dublin High Court, that it was not possible under the present Irish Constitution to give full recognition to Northern Ireland, that Sunningdale should therefore be left in abeyance, and the Governments of North and South should engage in practical co-operation on security matters.

After Bleakley suggested that the opinions of the Strikers should be taken into account in any solution to the crisis, the following exchange took place in the Assembly, between the NILP Assemblyman and Seamus Mallon of the SDLP:

"Mr. Mallon: Mr. Bleakley's suggestion that they should be included now is as ridiculous as his remarks concerning re-negotiation of the Sunningdale Agreement. His ambiguity is matched only by his hypocrisy in referring to the need for a referendum on the Council of Ireland. As one who supported the Sunningdale Agreement from the beginning, I assure Mr. Bleakley that a referendum is a figment of his imagination: of course, that applies to other people as well. The election in June 1973, amounted to a referendum.

"Mr. Bleakley: You are not speaking for your Party.

"Mr. Mallon: I can assure you that I am speaking for my party.

"Mr. Assistant Speaker: Order, I must ask the Hon. Member to address the Chair.

"Mr. Mallon: I hope that applies also to Mr. Bleakley. I can assure him that I am speaking for my party when I say that the Agreement will be implemented in total. Mr. Bleakley can rest assured that the ideas which he filched from the bullyboys on the streets are not going to become part of my policy or the policy of my party. In his platitudinous-holier-than-thou way he talked about adjustments. Again I can assure him that there will be no adjustments.

"Mr. Bleakley: You are a not-an-inch man.

"Mr. Mallon: He has said that there should be an initiative within this House. We have all the initiatives we need. Unlike some other people, the members of my party do not have a foot in each camp. We made our initiative known on 9 December, 1973: I make that point only because Mr. Bleakley brought the matter up. Despite the platitudinous pleadings of people like him our initiative stands.

"Mr. Bleakley: The man who stood on the burning deck"(Stormont Hansard, 21.5.74, col. l069-71).

Mallon's statement that the election of June 1973 had amounted to a referendum on Sunningdale was untrue. The SDLP themselves had declared it, at the time, to be an election merely to "a conference table". But in the circumstances the hypocrisy and arrogance of Mallon's attack on Bleakley was only matched by its sheer political stupidity. For, only a couple of days later, Bleakley was proved right, and Mallon was going to have to eat his words.

If the Executive coalition had supported this amendment, the confrontation with the Loyalists would have been averted. But Faulkner and Fitt pushed ahead into a confrontation in an apparent fit of blind optimism.

The SDLP in Revolt

Sunningdale was a revolutionary achievement for the SDLP. It believed it had "smashed Stormont" and achieved something that would have taken years to get under the Faulkner offer of June 1971. This led, of course, to over-confidence and a feeling that, having won so much, more was possible, and its leaders developed a false sense of their own power and the power of their community in the situation.

When Sean Donlon met members of the SDLP on the opening day of the Strike they were actually threatening to take down the Executive themselves and planning their exit, even before the Loyalists could bring it down. Donlon's report reveals:

> "Hume and Devlin are generally pessimistic about the prospects of reaching agreement with Faulkner on phased implementation but they are determined not to take any hasty decisions since they see their survival as a political force very much influenced by the manner in which the Executive is seen to collapse, if that is what is to happen. They say they are committed to consulting both with their Assembly Party and Party Executive and in addition will consult the Government here before taking any decision which might lead to collapse. Two factors which may have a bearing on the SDLP decision should be noted. Firstly, there are considerable internal strains now becoming evident. Paddy Duffy, the Party treasurer and important backroom figure before and since the party's formal establishment, told me that he is on the verge of resigning from the party... because of the failure to implement the provisions of the Sunningdale Agreement... Seamus Mallon, the Chairman of the Assembly Party, showed me a letter signed this week by a large number of local branch officers, district councillors and prominent party supporters who wish the SDLP to pull out of the Executive before July unless Sunningdale is fully implemented. The signatories are mainly from south Down, Armagh, Tyrone and Mallon made it clear that he shares their views... and the effect of all this is to reduce considerably the room for manoeuvre which the party leadership might have in the negotiations with Faulkner" (NAI, TSCH 2005/7/630, 15 and 16.5.74).

The second reason why the SDLP might collapse the Executive involved "Gerry Fitt's position as leader".

At the Assembly Party meeting of 8th May motions had been passed "expressing concern at his lack of leadership" and at Fitt's issuing of "press statements contrary to party policy". After a letter of censure was sent to Fitt his reaction was "stuff it. I don't need a party. I've survived in politics without one for nineteen elections and I'll survive without one for another nineteen."

The revolt within the rank and file of the SDLP, which very unwisely wanted to push Faulkner when pushing him would result in a breaking-point, must have had an impact on the extravagant hostility with which the leadership reacted to the Workers' Strike. When the Strike got under way, the behaviour of the SDLP confirmed the worst suspicions of it entertained by Protestants. Fitt denounced the strikers as fascists. Devlin asked on Radio Eireann why they were not arrested. Hume demanded that the British Army take over trade and industry, although this clearly was an impossibility.

For years the constant refrain of the SDLP had been that there would be no military solution to the bombing campaign. But now the Party, in the spirit of the most reactionary Tory, was demanding a military solution to an industrial stoppage.

It was also ironic that on May 17th Austin Currie reopened the question of collection charges on those who had taken part in the Rent and Rates Strike. On the one hand, he was asking the Executive to treat one form of civil disobedience—the UWC strike—as a rebellion, while on the other asking it to condone it in another form.

Fall of the Executive

By 21st May, some in the Executive were realising that the Strike enjoyed substantial support that should be taken account of. Faulkner described the manoeuvrings within the Executive in his autobiography:

"Discussions continued on the handling of the Council of Ireland re-negotiations. Some SDLP Ministers thought it would be a mistake to announce anything until the strike was over lest it be represented as a concession and a sign of weakness. But most of us believed that the time was long overdue for putting the record straight, so that people would at least have the opportunity of knowing what they were actually supposed to be striking against. Eventually we all agreed that the best prospect of defeating the strike now lay in a combined security and political initiative and that the issue of the statement, designed to reassure those concerned about the Council of Ireland, must therefore be dependent on a palliative by the security forces designed to break the street gangs. I stressed to the Executive that time was running out and that if any benefit was to accrue from the new agreement it would have to be announced soon.

"The next day, Wednesday 22 May, it became clear that we could expect no effective initiative to restore order, although some barricades were removed in the early hours of the morning on main roads, and we decided to go ahead with our announcement. The SDLP Executive members had a meeting of their backbenchers to secure final approval, but when they came back they were more disappointed than I had ever seen them. 'I'm sorry', said Gerry Fitt. We can't get them to agree.' It seemed as if the Executive was about to break up on this issue, as neither Alliance nor ourselves were prepared to go back on what had been agreed. I got up from the Executive table and said, 'Well, if that's the case I am afraid it means the end of the Executive. I am going in to the Assembly to announce the resignation of the Executive because of the failure to agree on the re-negotiation of the Council of Ireland.' I was at the door when Gerry Fitt stopped me. 'Give us another half an hour and we will try again, Brian,' he said.

"It was about an hour later that Fitt and his colleagues returned looking more cheerful. 'We had another vote and a majority have agreed', he said. I went straight in to the Assembly and announced the new proposals. It later transpired that Orme had been rushed up from Stormont Castle to address the SDLP backbenchers, and had played a major part in changing their attitude." (*Memoirs of A Statesman*, p. 271-2).

On 22nd May, the Executive, through Faulkner, issued a statement on the Sunningdale Agreement. Faulkner remembered:

"The proposal now agreed was for a phased implementation of Sunningdale, and marked a major change in approach which, announced at any time before the strike, could have done much to take the heat out of the Council of Ireland issue. Phase One, to be implemented immediately, involved the establishment of the Council of Ministers as a body for consultation and co-operation. Phase Two, bringing the transfer of some executive functions in the areas agreed at Hillsborough, the establishment of a permanent headquarters and the election of the second tier Consultative Assembly from the Northern Ireland Assembly and the Dail would be implemented only after a test of opinion of the electorate at the next Assembly elections in 1977/8, and then only if the Assembly approved. In effect all the most controversial aspects were being postponed until people had had a chance to see a more modest form of cross-border co_operation working. In the event the announcement had little effect on the situation. The UWC and the UUUC politicians rejected it and the media, having seen the successive victories of the strikers, regarded it as a desperate attempt to turn back the strike. Our insistence that it was the product of long negotiations which were virtually complete before the strike began were treated with cynicism and the papers the next morning covered it as 'capitulation' to the demands of the UWC, and 'too little too late'. It was clearly too late, but if the junta at Hawthornden Road had not already scented victory and seen the desperate straits of the Government I do not believe it would have been too little" (p272).

Faulkner's assessment of the situation was essentially correct. The opposition to the Council of Ireland had gathered irresistible momentum and, rather than having isolated the strikers the Executive had by this stage isolated itself. And the SDLP, who had only a day previously, through Austin Currie, said that the Agreement would be instituted in full, had made a dramatic climb-down in the face of reality.

Gerry Fitt was full of hope for the attempt by Len Murray (General Secretary of the British TUC) to lead a mass march of strikers back to work. This proved to be a total fiasco and only demonstrated the gulf between the workers and the unrepresentative union officials, fostered by the Communist Party. When the *'Back To Work March'* failed on Friday 24th May, Faulkner, Fitt and Oliver Napier set off for London to persuade Harold Wilson to approve the Executive's scheme for the British Army to commandeer oil distribution. There was much reluctance from the Army to take on this plan — thinking of the likely consequences. But, after an ultimatum from the SDLP, the Government decided to approve it. On Monday 27th, the British Army took over the oil refinery at Sydenham with predictable results. Electricity supply worsened drastically.

The Strike succeeded, not through lack of action by the British Government, but because it enjoyed widespread support within the Protestant community. The British Army, of course, could have dispersed the Strike with grapeshot but who would have run the province for them then? No preparations had been made for this and Westminster was not about to attempt to do in 'Northern Ireland' what it would not do in England in relation to industrial action. This was Britain in the 1970s not Thatcher's England.

At the final meeting of the Executive, on Tuesday 28th May, the SDLP fantasy of the British Army putting down the strikers continued. Faulkner suggested negotiations would be in order. Hume still held that the Strike must be broken and the loyalists taught a lesson. He refused to resign. Gerry Fitt was in two minds. He still believed that vast numbers wanted to support the Executive, and hoped for deliverance in that quarter. But, by then, the writing was on the wall for the Executive.

Paddy Devlin was quite explicit about what the SDLP sacrificed the Power-Sharing Executive for in his book, *The Fall of The Executive*:

> "The general approach to the talks was to get All-Ireland institutions established which, with adequate safeguards, would produce the dynamic which could lead ultimately to an agreed single state for Ireland. That meant, of course, that SDLP representatives would concentrate their entire efforts on building up a set of tangible executive powers for the Council which in the fullness of time would create and sustain an evolutionary process" (p.32).

So, the Council of Ireland was seen, as the Protestant opposition to it believed, no more and no less than a stepping stone to a United Ireland.

During the negotiations over Sunningdale, Devlin had warned his colleagues and Dublin; "Look, we've got to catch ourselves on here. Brian Faulkner is being nailed to a cross" (Barry White, *John Hume; Statesman of the Troubles*, p.152). But Faulkner was hung up to die and there was to be no resurrection of devolved government for 25 years.

Explaining the SDLP Behaviour

Having been coaxed into Power-Sharing, the taste of power that it got clearly went to the SDLP's head, and it over-played its hand. By its conduct in Office from January-May 1974, it undermined the position of its Unionist ally, leading to the fall of the Executive.

Why did the SDLP behave in such a suicidal manner? A number of general observations can be made. Firstly, the divided mind of the SDLP was subjected to the pulls of both Anti-Partitionism and participationist politics within Stormont. The SDLP was disabled by having two incompatible aims. This ambiguity was its inheritance from the Civil Rights campaign and the events of August 1969 and after.

This represented a conflict between idealism and practicality, which pulled the Party in opposite directions, and which could not be resolved within the context of 'Northern Ireland'. Idealism and practicality need not be antagonistic elements in politics. For normal political parties within representative politics and government, practicality tends to involve a partial implementation of ideals—a modification or alteration of ideals insofar as they are found not to correspond with what is possible, but a movement in the general direction of the ideals subscribed to is maintained.

But the Stormont system was not a representative democracy and it produced suicidal tendencies in the SDLP when its attempt to contrive a harmony between practicality and ideals failed because none was possible.

The Provos looked at the Ulster Workers' Strike and saw substance in it. Like Padraig Pearse looking at the Ulster Volunteers, they had tried to describe it away by seeing it as a variant of Irish Nationalism—as Irishmen defying the British Government. But they saw in it substance, nonetheless, and they took account of the substance by negotiating with the Ulster Workers' Council for the provision of food and fuel supplies to Catholic areas of Belfast. And they scaled the military campaign down during the Strike.

The SDLP could not reconcile itself to negotiating with the strikers, and pretended that they represented no one. Consequently, when the Party refused to take into account the substance, it was defeated by it.

John Hume, commenting on Southern Justice Minister P. Cooney's call for the removal of Articles 2 & 3 of the Republic's Constitution said that:

> "to negotiate literally publicly with the constitution of the Republic, and to literally offer to throw it away in advance of knowing where it's going to lead, particularly when we know that one of the deepest attitudes of the majority in the North is that of ascendancy, rather than simply the link with Britain—this makes them particularly difficult to deal with and makes them not amenable to any gestures, even such a major one as this" (IN 24.9.74).

The SDLP fundamentally misconceived the nature of Protestant society. The Party misconstrued the compromising attitude of the Faulkner Unionists to be a sign of weakness, rather than being a natural characteristic within Protestant society. The response of the majority of the Protestant community to the Sunningdale Agreement was very conciliationist. There was widespread consent to the admission of the SDLP to the Executive, even though its attitude to the state remained ambiguous. It was completely in accordance with precedent that the SDLP, holding the traditional Catholic-Nationalist view that Unionist conciliation was a contradiction in terms, should interpret its response as a sign of indecisiveness or weakness, and see in it an opportunity for pushing harder on the Anti-Partitionist front. The belief was that, since the Protestants had swallowed Sunningdale so easily, they could be got to swallow a bit more.

The SDLP adopted the pretence that it differed from the Provos in the way it looked at the National division in Ireland—it recognised the *'two traditions'*. But a 'tradition' is something that is much less than a nation. It was something that for the SDLP could be disregarded in relation to one of the 'traditions' but not the other—its own, which it believed was eternal and constant. It did not see the Protestants as a separate nationality and saw Ireland as a historic territorial-political entity which should have been maintained, regardless of the opinions of the people in one quarter of the island about their nationality. That view was held despite all the reconciliation rhetoric.

The SDLP was saying that, while there were 'two traditions' on the island, there was an underlying sense of national affinity between Catholics and Protestants. But, if there was a sense of national affinity, it was surely its business to tap into it and bring it to the surface. However, the SDLP seemed to know very well, in its heart of hearts, that there was no such underlying sense of national affinity between Catholics and Protestants, so it never really attempted to develop it as a result. It knew the reality of the social situation: that there was a profound sense of national antagonism between the communities, such that whatever one of them stood for aggravated the other—even if the thing it stood for was of benefit to the other.

The SDLP did not achieve its seats at the Sunningdale Conference through its own efforts—its power was conferred upon it. And this proved a debilitating factor when the party had to govern under its own steam within the Executive. In a tricky political situation it proved to be incompetent in the exercise of power—as it was to be again 25 years later when it had another go.

Not having resolved its relationship with Republicanism in a way that would have made sense of its participation in the Executive, the SDLP in Office was naturally drawn towards attempting to ward off Republican criticism, by representing Sunningdale and the Council of Ireland as a Machiavellian manoeuvre. It presented itself as having outwitted the Unionists where the more direct approach of the IRA had failed. The Council of Ireland, in the immortal words of Hugh Logue, SDLP Assemblyman for Derry, was to be the vehicle which would *"trundle through to deliver a United Country"*. Or, as Ivan Cooper put it: *"The Council of Ireland is an all Ireland Parliament with an executive and harmonising role"*.

It seemed to be only through this trickery that the SDLP could reconcile its ideals to the practicality of its participation in a Government at Stormont. The gist of its argument being that the Provos had achieved all they could for Catholics through their campaign, and now that this campaign was in decline and was achieving no more for Nationalists, they should give way to the SDLP to do the rest.

It was these delusions, the product of the divided mind of the SDLP, which resulted in the lunatic behaviour of the Executive and which culminated in the absurdity of the last Prime Minister of 'Northern Ireland', Gerry Fitt, the Connolly Socialist (who was to be premier for sixteen hours after Faulkner resigned), declaring that he would run the society against the Protestant workers with the help of the British Army.

The Assembly majority — that is the supporters of Sunningdale in the Assembly — by that time had become grossly unrepresentative of the electorate. And, once it had detached itself from the great majority of Protestants, and tried to sustain itself by military might against the community, it was doomed.

The Assembly had little representative legitimacy after that. The Ulster Workers' Council called the Strike in support of a demand for fresh elections (in the absence of a deferral by the Executive of the Council of Ireland) and thus gained the high moral ground. The case for fresh elections was unanswerable in terms of representative practice. The elections held the previous year had been elections to a *"conference table"* (to quote John Hume). From the conference table had come a structure of government. New elections were required to give popular sanction to the structures established by the conference table. When Faulkner took office he acknowledged this to be the case, but said he would like to give the electorate six months experience of Power-sharing before he called an election. When it was clear that dissatisfaction at the situation was increasing and that the demand for fresh elections was growing, the Executive declared that no elections would be held until 1977 or 1978. By this declaration the Executive broke completely with electoral practice.

The election of a Constituent Assembly is not the election of a governing parliament (even if it is limited in its powers to 'govern' as the Executive was). The business of a Constituent Assembly is to work out a Parliamentary structure for the governing of a society. Having done that, it has exhausted its mandate and is required to hold fresh elections to see if the people want it or an alternative to govern through the structures it has set up. What the Executive did was to declare the election of the Constituent Assembly to be the election of the Government.

If the Executive had set a date for new elections and suspended (or put to a referendum) the Council of Ireland for the time being, it might have retained its governing majority in the Assembly. And, even if it had lost their governing majority, it would at least have preserved the Power-Sharing structures, and seen to it that the Assembly was the focal point of politics in Northern Ireland. But, because it was thought that fresh elections would not return the same majority to the Assembly, it was decided that elections should not be held. It was decided to maintain the Coalition majority, even if it meant detaching the Executive from the society. And, when the Executive became thoroughly detached from society, it was decided to rest its authority on the British Army. When that Army found it could not function in this role against the society, the Executive fell.

None of this was at all necessary. It only required some basic political understanding to prevent the chain of events that led to the fall of the Executive. But the understanding was just not there in the SDLP, and it came too late to Faulkner and Rees.

British Bungling

After the event some members of the SDLP began saying that the bungling of the Government was to a large degree the responsibility of Rees and his Labour colleagues, and would not have happened under the Tories. In September 1989 Hume said about the Hillsborough Agreement of 1985 that

> "it has taken Thatcher to stand up to the Unionists at present and call their bluff, like a Nixon going to China, or a De Gaulle going to Algeria. There are horses for courses. Wilson had no sympathy for the Unionists whom he described as 'spongers', but though his speeches were good his actions were non-existent" (IN 12.9.1989).

There is some truth in this. But in the opposite sense to that implied. Hume believed that the Labour Ministers, hampered by some kind of socialist conscience, just could not bring themselves to turn their army on the workers—something the Tories would have had no qualms about. But the truth of the matter is that Labour bungled the Executive because it acted upon British conceptions which, when applied to 'Northern Ireland'. proved useless, because local politics had not been developed by the functioning of British democracy. Whitelaw had worked out the Agreement, and set up the structures which formed the Executive. But the understanding and diplomacy of Whitelaw was replaced by the misunderstanding and misconceptions of Rees. And there were not the usual structures of representative government, by which Government gets feedback from civil society, to put him right.

The political ineptitude of the Labour Ministers was vividly shown when they staked so much on the success of the *"Trade Union return to work"*.

This attempt to break the Strike was led by Len Murray, the TUC General Secretary, supported by Rees and Orme. (In all fairness, it must be pointed out that Murray knew little of Northern Ireland, whose Trade Union affairs are the official responsibility of the Irish Congress of Trade Unions, Northern Ireland Committee.) About 150 men, escorted by the British Army, tried to lead a return to the shipyard, and failed—the mass of workers seeing it as a blackleg attempt. That Rees and company staked so much on this futile effort demonstrated that they held some fatal preconceptions and those preconceptions were not challenged until it was too late.

It was generally known that Rees and, in particular, Orme, held the left-wing Anti-Partitionist view of the Protestant working class—that its expressed views consisted largely of bluff and that it was essentially fascist in character. And the official Trade Union movement reinforced these preconceptions, with local leaders tending to have a different ideology to the workers they represented.

It was not a mistake by Rees to consult the Trade Union movement, and act in unison with it. This was quite usual for Labour Ministers in those days when there was beer and sandwiches waiting for Trade Union leaders at Number 10. But in 'Northern Ireland', the official Trade Union movement was grossly unrepresentative of society—dominated by a clique of Communist Party members, whose Anti-Partitionist views bore little resemblance to the views of most of their own members.

So when Rees consulted the Trade Union movement, he found his preconceptions confirmed. And, in the absence of a grass-roots Labour organisation to put him right, he acted on his preconceptions and saw the Executive go down with them. Rees's problem was that, as Secretary of State for 'Northern Ireland', he was a dictator. Or rather, his problem was that he was a bad dictator. Dictators, more than representative politicians, have a duty to understand political realities. They cannot rely on civil society or the institutions of representative government, as the normal Minister can. So they must be quick-witted and practical. The problem with Rees was that he was neither.

The conduct of the SDLP within the Power-Sharing Executive undermined the deal. But the bungling of the British Government was more than that. It represented bungling of criminal proportions.

For two weeks, Wilson, Rees and Orme stubbornly resisted the Strikers, refusing to make the slightest concession to them, which might have ended the dispute, and preserved the Power-Sharing structures. And then they capitulated in the most extravagant fashion, making a massive concession which, in destroying the Executive, along with the Council of Ireland, exceeded the hopes of the most extreme opponents of Sunningdale.

A reading of the official papers reveals that Rees seems to have thought of the Executive as expendable.

It is inconceivable that the Government could have behaved in such a ridiculous manner anywhere other than in 'Northern Ireland'.

Lost in 'Northern Ireland'

The representative politicians of the British democracy were lost when it came to operating in the unrepresentative semi-detached annex of their State.

Representative government does not produce politicians with the potential to be good dictators. Willie Whitelaw was an exception. He was an extremely· gifted dictator who operated quite skilfully outside the sphere of representative politics. A rare bird, indeed, in British politics, that came from his grandee background.

A consequence of the boycott of the province by the parties of state is that bi-partisanship reigns supreme. It is unusual that any criticism of substance is directed from one party to another over the government of the State's 'Northern Ireland' region. While argument rages over every other issue in the House of Commons, there is an abnormal consensus about political decisions relating to Northern Ireland that defies democratic practice. But at the time of Sunningdale there was the closest thing to a criticism made by one party of another's handling of matters in the province. David Howell, a former Tory Minister of State in Northern Ireland, wrote in *The Times* on 10th February 1975:

> "The Sunningdale Agreement... has been much reviled as inflexible and failing to take full account of the weight of loyalist opinion and of loyalist fears about the Council of Ireland. If one regards the Sunningdale Agreement as the last, final and formal work on an Irish settlement, this view is probably correct, though lamentable because the fears are in fact groundless. But they existed. do exist and have to be taken into account. There was, of course, nothing new about this—as Willie Whitelaw... and· Francis Pym well knew. The whole management of the Northern Ireland situation required constant temperature taking and constant attention to loyalist sensibilities and suspicions. Perhaps Sunningdale was a shade too grand on occasion, too intergovernmental, too polished to fit into this pattern of constant shift and change as one struggled to maintain an equilibrium... There was, and always must be, room for manoeuvre."

The fall of the Executive and the twenty years of War that resulted from it, before another settlement emerged, came about because of British Labour bungling, SDLP and Dublin intransigence, and rejectionist Unionism.

Although the Provos did not support Sunningdale, they did nothing to bring it down. Republicans were excluded from the settlement the SDLP pledged themselves to by taking the Constitutional Oath. The IRA eased off its campaign during the time of the Executive to see how things panned out.

Of course, if Sinn Fein had been a political force and it had produced prospective Ministers for the Executive in 1974, there would have been no Sunningdale at all. Paddy Devlin and Austin Currie, or any *"Fenian about the house"*, were intolerable to many of the same Unionists in those days who later signed up to a deal in 1998, let alone people like Gerry Adams or Martin McGuinness.

That was the situation that confronted the Provisionals. There was no Sunningdale on offer to them. It had been designed to undermine them and not to facilitate their political transformation.

And it had been brought down, not by them but by Unionism.

The Labour Government's surrender to rejectionist Unionism in 1974 was so extravagant that the Provos could only conclude from it that it was a prelude to a Pilate-like washing of hands of the whole bloody mess and a British pull-out. In such circumstances it was quite logical to keep fighting on and try to give it one more push.

After all, what was the alternative on offer to the Catholic community, with Unionism dictating terms to the Government of the State and forcing it into such an extravagant surrender?

Southern Discomfort

The loss of Sunningdale did not just have an effect in the North.

The events surrounding the collapse of Sunningdale led to Dublin conducting a sea-change in the way it looked at Northern affairs. One of the major stimuli to this sea-change was the anti-civilian bombings that occurred in Dublin and Monaghan during the Strike—the major atrocity of the War. These were quite unconnected with the Strike and there have been strong suggestions and some evidence that forces of the British State played an instrumental role in their planning and organisation. What is certain is that, if they had a political objective in relation to Dublin, it was effective.

These bombings, which caused the greatest loss of life in a single day in the War, were the main military event during the crisis of the Sunningdale system. The Provos had eased up on their military campaign in order to let events run their course with regard to the Executive.

Although the Dublin Government was supporting the SDLP in conduct that was outraging the Ulster Protestant community, it made no arrangements to defend the Republic from attacks from the North. In *The Dublin/Monaghan Bombings*, John Morgan, a retired Lieutenant-Colonel of the Irish Army, traces the course of those bombs and argues not only that there was close collaboration between the British military and the Ulster Loyalists in their execution but possibly even collaboration with elements of the Gardai to leave an escape route open for the bombers. He finds it inexplicable that no extra defences were mounted in the Republic during the Ulster Workers' Strike, when the British Army was on Red Alert.

Taoiseach Liam Cosgrave made an emergency broadcast on the day of the Bombings, implying that they were the work of the IRA. That was only momentarily credible, while the country was in shock. But Fianna Fail leader Lynch also made a statement on 26th June 1975, saying the Provos "shared the guilt" for the bombings. Afterwards the Cosgrave Government and subsequent Dublin Governments stifled investigation into the incidents in Dublin and Monaghan. They were seemingly overawed by Britain and dared not risk finding it guilty. They preferred to close their minds to the awful thought that Britain could have done such deeds. How could they possibly handle the revelation of such a fact?

Instead they decided to wash their hands of the North and the Northern Catholics.

It was said earlier that the War in the North arose directly out of the undemocratic mode of British government there and the Irish State had no responsibility for it. But the refusal of Nationalist Ireland to acknowledge the fact of national division in the North enabled Britain to foist moral responsibility onto it for the War that was the almost inevitable outcome of the way that Britain chose to govern the region. And this irrational feeling of Nationalist guilt for something that was entirely the responsibility of the British State led to a collapsing of Irish National morale under the impact of the War in the North. British propaganda is skilled at exploiting such opportunities and did so through various methods.

The opportunity for this propaganda counter-attack from Britain, which was designed to divest responsibility for the situation in 'Northern Ireland' and to get others to feel guilty for it, would have been grasped after statements like that made by the Taoiseach in June 1974. Cosgrave said that the South did not desire "unity or close association with a people so deeply imbued with violence and its effects", and that the Northern conflict was "killing here the desire for unity which has been part of our heritage" (IT 14.6.74).

A few years earlier there had been enthusiastic support for the IRA at some of the highest levels of Southern society, as the War looked like it was going to come to a short and successful conclusion. But, after the bombs in Dublin, there was a backing off by the South.

The bombings also had a deeper impact on the South. It produced a reaction against the North that impacted on the National culture itself. This happened initially through Conor Cruise O'Brien's actions as Minister for Communications in Cosgrave's Government, but it spread outwards in

Southern society, in the Dublin media, and in academia until it filtered into mainstream life. The connection was made between Irish National culture, the independent state and the disastrous state of affairs in the North.

As a result, there developed a great fear about the history of the state's beginnings, cynicism about the achievement of independence, and a strong sense of self-loathing in certain circles connected to the fact that the Provos were seen as a malevolent product of National culture, rather than a product of John Bull's political slum. And the result was an irrational repression of National culture and its replacement with the British way of seeing things, which was presented as being more reasonable, even-handed and less dangerous. The Northern Catholics, who had not produced the State's Republican culture, because they had been largely Redmondite/Devlinite, and had been cut off from its formative events, became the scapegoats of this process.

In 1921 Britain established an arena for communal conflict in the Six Counties that it hoped would provide leverage over the greater prize, regaining hegemony over the Twenty-Six. Whitehall reckoned that this conflict would be of advantage to it in influencing Southern politics, and so it has proved. The South has all but destroyed its own political culture during the thirty years since the situation exploded in Northern Ireland because of its refusal to see what 'Northern Ireland' really is, and to think about why the most experienced State in the world shaped a region of itself into such a strange and perverse thing.

However, the pay-back for this retreat of National culture in the South is that it has re-emerged in other ways—notably the spread of Sinn Fein within its territory under Northern influence.

CHAPTER 9

Turning Point

Dublin and the SDLP had availed of the Republican War effort to gain a Power-Sharing Executive and an Irish dimension from Britain. However, in the course of operating this they over-reached themselves, bungled the situation and failed to capitalise politically. As a result Nationalism was check-mated by the Unionist community, which re-asserted the balance of power through the Ulster Workers' Council Strike. Nationalism, having succeeded in seeing off Stormont, could not advance beyond that. Dublin, at that point, ran out of ideas and began a process of withdrawal from the problem. Stalemate in the conflict began to set in.

Within the Northern Catholic community the fall of Sunningdale reinforced the Republican narrative of events: The British were not "*honest brokers*" in the situation; Westminster had allowed the Power-Sharing structures to fall rather than taking on Unionist power; the Unionists had been unwilling to share power with moderate Catholics; the British had been willing to employ curfew, Internment and massacre to preserve the system. This all suggested that the only realistic option was to continue with the Insurrection. There were no other meaningful alternatives in view.

British Bankruptcy?

Britain, frustrated in reconstructing the settlement of 1920 it had imposed on 'Northern Ireland', decided on a kind of 'withdrawal' from the province, in order to localize the War to minimise its own casualties and military involvement. This was a resumption of the Ulstermen "*should carry the can*" policy outlined in the British Cabinet in the aftermath of the events of August 1969 when the full fury of the Insurrection had abated. Unfortunately, this washing of hands on Britain's part, along with the policy of containment summed up in the phrase "*acceptable level of violence*", meant that only a continuance of the Republican War could bring the conflict to a settlement.

British Secretary of State Rees stated in the Commons, in the aftermath of the fall of the Executive that he was forced to recognise the rise of "a new form of Protestant nationalism… which … has brought together many strands of what has hitherto been regarded as unionist opinion" (874 HC Deb, 5s, c882 3.6.74). The first solution Rees came up with for this new-found Ulster Nationalism was 'cantonisation' *a la* Switzerland. Believing that Protestant Nationalism had emerged and the two communities could not live together,

Rees took it that they should live apart within 'Northern Ireland'.

In response civil servant Robert Ramsey, now attached to the Direct Rule Central Secretariat at Stormont Castle, told Rees that the mixed demography of the North would only produce cantons with minority problems. So, instead of one big minority problem, there would be many small ones. Ramsey was then told to prove his case. He was charged by Sir Frank Cooper, Rees' Under Secretary and enforcer (who had been a Battle of Britain pilot under Squadron Leader Rees in the Second German War), with coming up with a ten canton map of 'Northern Ireland', having 5 Orange and 5 Green cantons. When this appeared, it was obvious that the canton idea had to be shelved.

Rees then commissioned a review of alternatives to the Westminster model of democracy that might be instituted. His Secretariat worked enthusiastically on this project, examining examples of governance from other areas of the world, only to find the end product neutered by Rees and finally dropped without explanation. Ramsey believed that Cooper, who was unenthusiastic (and who was widely believed to have been the Squadron Leader rather than the pilot), shot it down (*Ringside Seats*, pp. 133-4).

In the end Rees' July 1974 White Paper, '*The Northern Ireland Constitution*', settled for the calling of a Constitutional Convention in which the parties would make proposals leading to the adoption of whatever arrangements would "command the most widespread acceptance throughout the community". Cooper was against this too but it was decided to go through the motions since the cupboard of ideas was bare.

The collapse of the Executive signalled that British policy in 'Northern Ireland' was bankrupt and the Government at Westminster might be persuaded to consider any solution—including withdrawal. The British Government indicated that it was indeed minded to consider such a solution, if nothing else was agreed. This may have been a ruse to concentrate Unionist minds on the effect of their intransigence but it only had the effect of seriously destabilising the situation.

Dublin began to take it that it was an unquestionable fact that Britain was about to disengage and the Southern media was full of such speculation. The headline on the *Irish Press* of 13th August 1974, for instance, was "*Britain seeks Political Disengagement—Rees talks of Pull-out*". James Downey in the *Irish Times* expressed most fully the logic of this argument:

> "Only the collapse of Sunningdale could have given the psychology of disengagement such force... Britain's ultimate withdrawal from Ireland was hastened, rather than impeded, by the dispatch of troops to Northern Ireland five years ago. It was hastened by the imposition of direct rule in March 1972. It was hastened by Sunningdale. And it may have been hastened by the collapse of Sunningdale" (13.8.74).

Sean Donlon of the MFA in Dublin has revealed that Dublin helped prevent a British withdrawal:

> "Rumours began to emerge that Wilson contemplated a complete British withdrawal from Northern Ireland. State papers now released... confirm the accuracy of these rumours. Wilson contemplated a unilateral, precipitate withdrawal regardless of the implications for political and economic stability on the island of Ireland. The steadying influence of Fitt at Westminster, of the SDLP with the Labour Party and of the Irish Government in contacts with the British Government were important elements in ensuring that Wilson's idea did not become policy" (*John Hume, Irish Peacemaker*, kindle ed).

Wilson's idea to replicate Mountbatten's hasty retreat from India did not become policy. However, in a book about Hume it is noticeable that the central character does not figure. An understanding why will be provided in the State papers reproduced below, which show that things were not as simple as Donlon now suggests.

The thought of British disengagement was something of a double-edged sword for Nationalist Ireland in 1974. On one hand there was a great deal of fear about what might happen to the Catholic minority in a situation of general national war. Some hoped that the greater numbers on the island might tell in such a situation and any attempt at Ulster UDI (Unilateral Declaration of Independence on the Rhodesian model) might be bloody, but short-lived. There was a belief that, once Britain left, the game was up for Unionism, but there was not a great deal of confidence in putting such a thing to the test.

The SDLP after Sunningdale

An SDLP delegation, including Devlin, Currie and O'Hanlon, had a meeting with Irish Government Ministers in which the SDLP spelled out its position: the Northerners thought Dublin was abandoning the Northern Catholics to their fate. A confidential official report from June 1974 describes a meeting in which the SDLP believed British withdrawal was on the cards and things were about to be reduced to their fundamentals:

> "The SDLP delegation were asked if they would accept power-sharing without the Irish dimension—in order that power-sharing should exist in Northern Ireland. They were emphatic in their rejection of this possibility. They said they would not give up their aspirations in order to take part in a power-sharing administration. They were aware of the consequences—which might be involuntary repartition in a UDI situation—which could involve massive hardship. They regarded either a federal solution or Irish unity as 'outside runners'... Mr. Devlin said that he was convinced that Ministers in

Westminster had agreed in principle to the idea of withdrawal and that the only question now was one of time... Mr. Currie said... economic disaster would follow if there were no power-sharing administration. This point should be rubbed home again and again... the alternative to power-sharing was a Protestant Parliament for a Protestant people. In this sort of situation the 'defenders of the people' would come into their own. In fact, he thought that if there were an election tomorrow the result, so far as the SDLP were concerned, could well be that the electorate would hold that the 'defenders' were right. They could well say that democracy and democratic methods had failed and that the only way of getting what they wanted was the Provisional way" (NAI, TSCH 2005/7/631, 11.6.74).

The idea that Sunningdale could be put back together again after it had just been destroyed was a fantasy. But it was clung to by the SDLP in preference to anything else that might be on the horizon—a return to majority rule Stormont, British withdrawal, Ulster UDI, repartition, civil war etc. The fear had began to develop that the Catholic community would go over to the "defenders"/Provisionals en masse if the SDLP programme was not imposed by Britain on the North. But how was Power-Sharing to be reinstituted without Unionists to share power with and how was this to be done without the removal of the Irish dimension that the SDLP were insisting upon?

Despite the SDLP's insistence to the Irish Government that it would stand by its political programme, even after its failure, Taoiseach Cosgrave made a shocking statement a few days after the ministerial meeting with the SDLP in which he said that the people of the Republic "are increasingly disinclined to seek unity with an area or close association with a people so deeply imbued with violence and its effects" and that the conflict in the North was "killing here the desire for unity which has been part of our heritage" (IT 14.6.74).

That was something of a bombshell for the SDLP, which took it that Dublin—along with Britain—was now prepared to distance itself from the North after the failure of Sunningdale and the bombs in Dublin and Monaghan. Hume, when asked about the implications of the Taoiseach's statement during an RTE interview, rejected the view that this had weakened the SDLP's position. He retreated to the position that, whilst the desire for immediate unity was not as strong in Dublin, there was a desire for "the coming together" of the two parts of the island in an "agreed Ireland". He added:

> "If we get an agreed Ireland, that is unity. What constitutional or institutional forms such an agreed Ireland takes is irrelevant because it would represent agreement by the people of this country as to how they should be governed" (IT 17.6.74).

This was what was to become known as the Humespeak form of sophistry. The notion of an "agreed Ireland" was an idea which Hume continued to articulate, *ad infinitum*, in many variations from this time. It was backed up by an SDLP statement '*SDLP offers agreed Ireland*' that said:

> "The SDLP has always made it clear that it does NOT desire a take-over of the North by the South and that any coming together must be on the basis of agreement... The institutional or constitutional form is not the most important issue. What is important is that such institutions should have the agreement of the people of the North and of the South. Agreement is the essence of any real unity and we cannot see how anyone in the North can object to working for an agreed Ireland with institutions acceptable to both parts of the country" (PRONI D/3072/4/1/1).

This public position would have been all well and good if it was taken in earnest and acted upon by the SDLP. But it was not the *actual* position of the party. The actual position was insistent on the Irish dimension in institutional form, and more if possible, being imposed on the Protestants in the North, whether they agreed to it or not. The public position, however, was very much something that would have to do for the lean times ahead.

The SDLP acquiring an Army

In this situation of NI Office-induced instability, the SDLP began calling for a "radical reappraisal" of the 1920 Act, a confrontation between the British and intransigent Unionists and a British declaration that they would only remain in Ireland until "agreed institutions of government" were established. (SDLP, *Another Step Forward*).

In private, and in anticipation of a complete British 'washing of hands', Hume pulled the SDLP together behind a novel idea—the acquiring of an army (or two) that the SDLP was currently lacking. The SDLP advocated an Irish Army invasion of the North, despite the possibility of British resistance, and a subsequent occupation of the Six Counties by the Republic's military forces. A confidential report written by Gearóid Ó Broin (the future Ambassador) of an SDLP Conference held in Bunbeg, Co. Donegal at the end of August 1974 shows how the experience of the fall of the Executive and the drastic signals Britain was sending out was infecting the 'Constitutional Nationalist' mind with dangerous delusions and extraordinary remedies. The report contains this rather startling prediction—which must have amazed Dublin when they heard of it:

> "The SDLP has... arrived at a position where their policy is to achieve a united Ireland in not less than two years. They appear to have lost faith in the possibility of co-operating with the majority within the framework of Northern Ireland alone. John Hume mentioned that it could still be a federal united Ireland and not necessarily a unitary state. The feeling was that if the SDLP had been too successful at Sunningdale, the UWC had erred in the

same way last May. A straightforward trial of strength was now approaching" (NAI, TSCH 2005/7/633, 27.8.74).

The "*straightforward trial of strength*" Hume had in mind amounted to a military suppression of Protestants (described as "expendable" in the report) by the British and Irish Armies to absorb them into a United Ireland. Below are some parts of the report describing Hume's view of the situation and what he desired of the British and Irish Governments. The other SDLP views can be seen to fall in behind Hume's assessment of the situation and strategy:

> "John Hume began the briefing by saying that the purpose of the meeting was to review the present position... Because of the loyalist and British attitude, the SDLP is in an intolerably weak negotiating position. It cannot afford to walk into a Convention election which will clearly produce a loyalist majority. The party has no intention of getting into such a situation. The party now seeks a clear statement from the British that power-sharing and the Irish dimension are not negotiable. This must be accepted by loyalists before any election takes place. If this is rejected by the loyalists (as the SDLP expects) this will mean that one of the two pillars of British policy has gone and therefore the other must go too. {The two pillars in question are firstly the guarantee of the link with Britain and secondly the acceptance in Northern Ireland of British standards.}... It must be borne in upon the British Government that the SDLP and the Irish Government have done all in their power to achieve a reasonable solution but have failed because of loyalist intransigence. This has serious consequences for Dublin's policy.
>
> "Gerry Fitt continued. The SDLP began with six members and at that time was in an intolerably weak position. It fought tenaciously for quadripartite talks to achieve the involvement of the Irish Government in discussions which eventually led to Sunningdale. It has been SDLP policy up to the present to achieve a consensus in politics in Northern Ireland. The downfall of Sunningdale was brought about by loyalist intransigence. The Convention elections will return a loyalist majority. The SDLP would be absolutely mad to go into them. Such a result would enable the British to point to the majority produced as giving a veneer of legality to any 'solution' produced by the loyalists... The SDLP cannot envisage... a future government of the province which requires the party to sit down with people like Craig, Paisley and West. Without the Irish dimension, the SDLP has no basis and no seats."

The British Government's proposal that a Constitutional Convention be established to see if there was any agreement amongst the political parties on a form of sub-government was the first sign of a 'washing of hands' of the North on Whitehall's part that began to encourage general suspicions in the North and elsewhere that Britain might actually withdraw completely from the Six Counties. And that was an understanding that increasingly coloured thinking from 1974 to 1976 and which had very negative consequences in the North.

The discussion at the Bunbeg meeting moved on to the SDLP's desire for a role for the Irish Government and its Army in future proceedings, where some military action might be involved in dealing with "*loyalist intransigence*". The SDLP Leader started with a warning to Dublin that they might have to revisit their 1969 policy and enhance its objectives considerably:

"If there is an outward show of loyalist intransigence, some say that the British could come to shooting loyalists. He (Fitt) would have extreme reservations that this would be the case. The minority in Northern Ireland are in a very weak position and look to the Irish Government. The only force on which they can rely is not the illegal organisations but the Irish Army. The SDLP will do all that is possible to prevent a major civil war in Northern Ireland. Such a war would inevitably spill over into the Republic. The Irish people will be involved whether the Government wants it or not...

"Paddy O'Hanlon said that the feeling of the meeting was essentially hardline... If the British Army will not take on the loyalists, it follows that they will not take on the Irish Army... If the Irish Government is positive enough, the loyalist community can become the expendable object... Paddy O'Hanlon commented that there seemed to be no definite Irish Government policy in relation to the North. Gerry Fitt urged that in any military exercise, we should consider Belfast and the Glens of Antrim {Fitt's second home at Ballyvoy/Murlough Bay, P.W.}. O'Hanlon mentioned that Portadown would be a stubborn centre of loyalist resistance. Fitt emphasised that there could be no question of repartition under any circumstances.

"John Hume added that the military exercise hinted at must be a joint British-Irish one. The British would never take on the Irish Army. There is no question of the SDLP doing a deal on UDI. I {Ó Broin, P.W.} asked whether in a take-over of Northern Ireland we were not risking indefinite loyalist violence. John Hume replied that it had now come to be a question of a choice among evils. There must not be a precipitate British withdrawal. The British must stay until the thing is sorted out. The big question is whether the British will have the will to do this...

"With regard to an Irish military involvement, Aidan Larkin... saw the Irish Army operating in minority areas while the British Army took on the loyalists... John Hume emphasised that the party would do all in its power to provide the British with a face-saving rationale for withdrawal with honour. It is generally assumed that the British do wish to withdraw and that a precipitate withdrawal would be disastrous. The joint military operation envisaged might be violent but it would be so mainly for the loyalists. Not much credibility is given to the loyalist para-military forces in such a confrontation. Aidan Larkin urged early Irish participation in the proposed security conference. He felt that it was important for the heads of both armies to begin contacts in view of the task envisaged for them by the SDLP.

"There appears to be no agreement as to when the crunch is likely to come... The general feeling appeared to be that it would come at the time of the election... or in any event, within two years... Aidan Larkin believes we should be examining closely the history of French disengagement from Algeria which has many parallels with the case of Northern Ireland. He would see many of the majority community leaving Ireland after the final settlement but these would be people of the kind who now support Faulkner, people whose whole mental orientation is toward Britain. Paddy Devlin is greatly concerned at the amount of emigration already taking place, mostly from the minority community."

Gearóid Ó Broin then sums up the SDLP position for Dublin:

"The view was repeatedly expressed that the Irish Government cannot isolate itself from the situation. When the crunch comes (and I understand that this means that when Britain decides to confront the loyalists after their clear rejection of British standards) it will not be a question of more bombs in the Republic alone but, more importantly, there will be a groundswell of support in the Republic for the minority in Northern Ireland which no government here can afford to ignore. The big difficulty is in forming a British resolve to confront the loyalists and here the party expects the support of the Irish Government by pointing out to the British that the loyalist minority of 18% can no longer be allowed to poison relations between sovereign states. The party also expects us to prepare unilaterally for such a confrontation and not to foreclose that option by negative public statements on a possible role for the Irish Army. Such statements only strengthen the loyalist will to dominance and confirm them in their intransigence. The party... inclines to think that a final settlement will probably have to be enforced by joint military action."

Ó Broin met Ivan Cooper separately from the rest of the SDLP. Cooper still favoured the old policy of "condominium" but Ó Broin wrote: "I understand... from John Hume... that he is not to be considered a weighty figure within the party". It seems that with the conflict reduced to its communal fundamentals in 1974 and a "final solution" imminent there was little further use for pet Protestants in the SDLP.

This startling document, freely available to the general public online, has been completely ignored by historians and political commentators. It gives a completely new meaning to the term 'Constitutional' Nationalism. It appears that "Constitutionalism' does not rule out the use of force or the forcing of a million Protestants into a United Ireland against their will. Force is acceptable as long as it is legal, State force. And the only force of that kind which was powerful enough to accomplish "*the task envisioned by the SDLP*" was the military force of the British State acting in alliance with its junior partner in Dublin and its army. This was neo-Redmondism. John Redmond denied the reality of Ulster Protestant resistance to Home Rule and relied on the British Army to overcome it. But, if Britain had not coerced the Unionists in 1914, it was hardly about to do it in 1975, after the Republican offensive had been stemmed and Protestant Ulster had demonstrated its national will. And if Britain was not going to do it, Dublin could be dismissed.

It was thought at the time that it was only elements high up in the Provo leadership, like MacStiofain and O'Conaill, who had concrete thoughts of a "*doomsday scenario*", in which the Southern masses would be forced into activism by the prospect of a national war. Such notions were probably more widely shared by Provo supporters who believed that if the bit came to the bit the Southern Army would come in to rescue them if an armed backlash against Republican actions manifested itself in substantial form. However, it seems that the same delusions of Southern military intervention in the North were shared right across the SDLP leadership and actually discussed at Governmental level in Dublin.

All of it was fantasy, of course. There was really nothing to be hoped for from the South. Its army could not offer military protection to the Northern Catholics, let alone smash the loyalists and unite Ireland. And neither had Britain any intention of using its army to smash Protestant resistance to a United Ireland, or indeed to impose any settlement unacceptable to them, any more than it had at the time of the UWC Strike.

The SDLP Pleads With Dublin

The meeting at Bunbeg represented the rawest of Hibernianism and it appears that Dublin recoiled from it and retreated to a position of having, as Paddy O'Hanlon said, "no definite policy in relation to the North". However, one has to sympathise with the SDLP in this. The context of the meeting was a Dublin withdrawal from the North and an abandonment of its people there. The SDLP had to confront the Irish Government with the implications of their actions, possibly leaving the Northern Catholic to their fate in the form of a catastrophe, in the event of a similar British "*washing of the hands*". Paddy Devlin wrote of this in his book *The Fall of the Executive*:

> "In amazement, the minority watched a segment of the Southern Government, in the aftermath of the downfall of the Northern Executive, make frantic attempts to disengage from Northern affairs. They heard their own elected representatives told repeatedly by certain members of the cabinet that the Irish dimension should be dropped as a political goal. They could not comprehend this opposition in high places to the idea of Ireland becoming united by consent at some time in the future. They failed to understand when told by these Southern politicians that they were not to talk of Irish unity otherwise they would be attacked by loyalists, when their only idea of talking about it in the first place was to avoid being attacked at all. The minority realise that identification with the Southern Irish people and loyalty

to a full Irish state is their only hope of survival. They realise, as they have always done, that the strength and numbers of the loyalists can only be cancelled out, now that the British have welched on their obligations to protect the minority, by implication of the military strength of the South. The Northern minority regard some of the statements and certain actions of these Southern politicians as having dangerous consequences for them. They realise that loyalists, could interpret the statements in a way that would encourage them to pursue a policy of unlimited violence towards them" (pp. 52-3).

Whilst most of this was accurate, any supposed threat from the South did not really deter the Loyalists. The more initiatives the Southern State pushed in relation to the North, under the guise of helping the SDLP against the Provos, the more hostile the Protestant community became to the minority.

The division between the SDLP and Dublin became very apparent in December 1974 when an SDLP delegation (minus its "indisposed" Leader) met the Irish Government, including the Taoiseach. In this meeting Hume maintained the view that a Loyalist victory in the proposed 'Constitutional Convention' election would lead them to refuse power-sharing and the 'Irish dimension'; that this would lead to a British withdrawal, a Loyalist "move to seize power" and "large-scale inter-communal violence would ensue"; the South would then, as a consequence, become inevitably embroiled in this "doomsday situation". And added to this,

"... the Provisional IRA had now taken a deliberate decision to attempt to provoke a civil war which would embroil the whole of Ireland {despite being on ceasefire, P.W.}. It was likely that they saw this as the only way of vindicating themselves, in the wake of all the suffering they had caused, apparently with little success, so far as their objectives were concerned" (NAI, TSCH 2005/7/649, 4.12.74? N.B. The file is mistakenly dated 4.6.74 but the meeting obviously occurred just after the Birmingham pub bombings in late November).

So, it was best, Hume argued, that "the Irish and British Governments jointly... be prepared to confront the loyalists" and enforce the implementation of the SDLP's programme of "power-sharing within the Government and an Irish dimension, expressed through institutions". This programme Hume suggested should have "non-negotiable conditions" for Unionists. As well as this, Hume argued that Dublin should make "contingency planning" for a situation where the British failed to impose the SDLP's "non-negotiable conditions" on the Unionists, the British withdrew, and "a doomsday situation" developed.

However, Hume's insistence on pushing the SDLP programme on the Unionists alarmed the Irish Government:

"The Minister for Foreign Affairs enquired whether insistence on preconditions by the two governments would not precipitate a situation which looked like developing in any case but which might still be possible to avoid? Mr. Hume replied by asking whether we could afford to drift into the situation without having an alternative plan ready... For this reason, the SDLP were again putting forward the proposals they made in August i.e. that the Irish and British Governments jointly should be prepared to confront the loyalists and enforce the implementation of power-sharing and the Irish dimension... The Minister for Foreign Affairs, referring to the proposals put forward by the SDLP... said that it was not possible to be sure that the British would, in fact, stay in the North... The Minister for Foreign Affairs expressed the view that if the Irish Government were to say anything to the British about contingency plans, involving the possibility of a British withdrawal, before this situation actually arose, it could be very dangerous. If the Irish Government were to indicate that it was facing up to the possibility of British withdrawal, this might give the British Government the alibi they almost certainly wanted to get them out of the North; in this way we would be letting them off the hook. Mr. Hume did not agree. In his view, the British would leave. We should try to ensure therefore, that it would be in the best possible circumstances and that they would stay until stable institutions were set up... The Taoiseach enquired what were the hopes of establishing stable institutions in this situation, if the loyalists had already baulked at power-sharing and the Irish dimension? Mr. Hume agreed that it certainly would not be easy to set up such institutions. The Minister for Foreign Affairs suggested that what would be involved would be the British remaining indefinitely, as there seems little prospect of reaching agreement on such stable institutions... The Minister for Justice indicated that the Government here was faced with a dilemma. They could certainly see that the scenario painted by the SDLP could all too easily come about, including a British withdrawal. They could see the need to plan for this situation. As against this, it had to be admitted that it was also only too possible that any overt planning or recognition of this possibility, might encourage the British to proceed with withdrawal. The difference between the views of the Government and the SDLP seemed to be that the SDLP regarded as a certainty or near certainty... despite their assurances and gratitude up to now, the British Government might in fact withdraw from the North... Mr. Hume said that the question remained whether we had a policy for the situation in which the loyalists rejected the basic conditions for a settlement?..."

And so the argument went round and round in circles.

By 1975 Dublin had a "*Brits In*" policy. It was frightened to death of the prospect of a British withdrawal from the North, after the Dublin Bombs of May 1974. Dublin's policy amounted to hoping that the British would not withdraw and a determination to do nothing that might encourage them to do so. So, Dublin was bankrupt with regard to getting Britain to do anything further, in terms of taking up its responsibility in the North, because of the fear that it might wash its hands entirely of all responsibility for it and bring on "*doomsday*".

Dublin's will was broken and it was now in London's pocket. This was the culmination of the moral and political collapse that came from the Lynch *volte face* of 1970. Hume, at least, was determined to make Britain face up to its responsibilities, before it left. He was willing to gamble whereas Dublin wasn't.

The report of the meeting ends like this:

> "The SDLP delegation said that it wished to get a response from the Government to the views that it had put forward. It was agreed that the Government delegation would withdraw for a while to consider this matter."

It must have become plain to Hume that Northern Catholics were now on their own and had to finally take on board that deliverance was unforthcoming from the South.

Provo War Escalation

After the collapse of the Executive, Rees' signals that Westminster might be persuaded to consider any solution—including withdrawal—, and the constant speculation about this in Nationalist Ireland, the Provos naturally escalated the War. What else could they do?

In 1974 the situation was as follows: A substantial political initiative, involving Power-Sharing between the two communities with an Irish dimension, aimed at undermining the Republican Army's war effort, had been defeated by the Protestant working class. Britain had failed to defend this settlement with the result that the only political outcome that was on the cards was a return to Unionist majority-rule, with perhaps some dilution of the previous model. This was unacceptable to Nationalists. So Britain might just "*wash its hands*" of it all and withdraw, as it was hinting.

One feature of the Provo escalation was a wide-ranging and unpredictable shooting and bombing campaign in England, ostensively aimed at the British Establishment but which produced a sizeable amount of civilian casualties in bombings in London, Guildford and Birmingham. It is probable that this campaign, which took place between July and November 1974, in which hints were dropped that the London Underground might become a target, was one of the factors in Britain's decision to Ulsterise the War and turn Provo military efforts inward. The bombings in Britain were something of a propaganda disaster for the Provos and, in the course of this escalation of the War, the Republican Army suffered some damaging losses. There were limitations on what Republicans could do and the drift into unrestricted terrorism was counter-productive. Finally the IRA availed of an opportunity provided by a group of Protestant clergymen, whom the Provisional leaders met at Feakle, County Clare, to gain moral cover from the pressure they attracted and called a cease-fire.

The Provos ended this short ceasefire quickly, feeling that the heat was off. However, they came under some pressure within the community to call a truce again. But they knew there were great dangers in this. They understood that it had been necessary to resume military operations because the political pressure of the SDLP alone would not achieve a United Ireland. However, at the same time, the British Government was determined to get an IRA Truce and so the Secretary of State, Merlyn Rees authorised talks between his officials and Sinn Fein. At these meetings his officials apparently accepted the substance of a 12-point Provisional peace plan, although this was publicly denied. The British agreed to a sharp reduction in British Army and RUC activity in Catholic areas, the establishment of Incident Centres manned by Sinn Fein members, and a guarantee of immunity from arrest for leading IRA members. In response the Provos declared another ceasefire on the 11th of February 1975.

Prof. Bew has the following to say about the signals the British sent to the Provos which he sees as something of a game they were playing with the Republicans:

"The game carried on… The Irish Times northern correspondent at the time was subsequently to recall a dinner party given for local newspaper editors by Merlyn Rees, Secretary of State for Northern Ireland, and Frank Cooper, a senior mandarin, at which Cooper had said that withdrawal would come in about five years. He added that in the first two months of 1975, 'officials at Stormont began to lace their dinner conversations and political tête-à-têtes with predictions of a pull-out. It now seems that this was aimed at creating an atmosphere which convinced the Provos that their main aim, a declaration of intent, was soon to become a reality'…" (Ireland, The Politics of Enmity 1798-2006. p. 519. and quote, IT 9.6.78).

Prof. Bew quotes a number of other newspaper and government sources to illustrate the notions Britain was encouraging, and he comments;

"The British… seemed determined to send out a message: 'Look no hands'. It was not so much a question of not having a selfish strategic interest in Ulster policy; rather a matter of not caring less. Emotional disengagement was the order of the day" (p.520).

Rees was purposefully letting the province drift into disorder, instability and a state of nature. Whitehall's aim was to put the fear of God into all parties to the conflict—Unionists, Nationalists and in Dublin—that if Britain walked away a '*doomsday*' situation would ensue. And, by doing this, the

British presumably wished to ensure future compliance with whatever policy was come up with—when one was thought of—as a better alternative to '*doomsday*'.

It appears that Rees was no bumbler at all—but a ruthless practitioner in *realpolitik*.

Whether Rees was so Machiavellian or not, it had the required effect in Dublin. The Assistant Cabinet Secretary, Dermot Nally told the Taoiseach on 7th July 1975 that the advantages of the continued British presence in the Six Counties were "so great that we should do everything possible to bring it about" and that Northern ambitions for unity should not be allowed to threaten the stability of the Southern State (Sunday Independent, 1.1.06 and IT 29.12.05).

The British doomsday threat had had the required effect—Dublin was terrified into a complete reversal of its National policy with regard to the Six Counties. The 1920 settlement had triumphed and the South was back in London's pocket.

The 1975 Truce

According to a classified Whitehall document of January 1975 Britain, in entering into a truce and negotiations with the Provos, had two main aims. Firstly, to "string along to the point where their military capacity went soggy" and Catholic support disappeared and secondly, "to give the doves the excuse to call it all off without {the British} making substantial concessions" (*Sunday Business Post*, 1.1.06)

What is evident about the talks between Rees and the Provisionals, and British policy as a whole during this period, is that the British were going to considerable lengths to encourage the notion that a full withdrawal was on the cards. One of the Feakle clergymen, Rev. William Arlow, claimed "the British government have given a firm commitment to the Provisional IRA that they will withdraw the army from Northern Ireland. This would be under circumstances such as if the present constitutional Convention fails to produce an agreed structure of government for the province" (BT 26.5.75). Daithi O'Connell of Sinn Fein understood that this meant "the overall feature of the truce was a statement by the British government that it was committed to disengage from Ireland but could not say so publicly" (*Sunday Times*, 18.6.78).

The Truce between the British Government and the IRA proceeded largely without incident for about 6 months. The Provos had undertaken not to bomb London and they steered clear of engaging the British Army. But the most significant feature of the Ceasefire was the escalation in overt sectarian conflict. The upsurge in communal warfare was clearly to do with the ambiguous nature of British policy. On the one hand, Republicans were being convinced that British withdrawal was imminent. The Provisionals' southern leadership thought the British media was preparing the ground for an honourable withdrawal on Britain's part. Ruari O'Bradaigh said "we want a situation to come about where political advance could take the place of guerrilla warfare ... what we see is an honourable accommodation with the British coupled with an honourable accommodation with the loyalists" (*Republican News*, 5.4.75).

This, of course, on the other hand, encouraged Loyalists to believe that they were about to be sold out by Britain and they responded to this in the only way they knew how, by killing Catholics in ever-increasing numbers, to deter Whitehall from its course or to establish control of territory in the event of a contest in a post-British Ulster. Elements of the Republican Army, with little to do but man the Incident Centres and indulge in periodic inter-republican feuding with the Sticks (Official IRA), after being subject to these Loyalist provocations, began to free-lance and retaliate in kind, as Republican discipline began to break down and aggressive Hibernianism emerged.

Rees and Ulster Nationalism

In the Autumn of 1974 the Secretary of State for 'Northern Ireland' made increasing use of his Office and the State apparatus available to him to foster a sense of Ulster Nationalism. He had 'discovered' that this had been the cause of the Strike that brought down the Executive—rather than his own activity—and decided to encourage it as a thing useful in dealing with the Ulster problem.

It had generally been a British Foreign and Commonwealth Office desire that there should be an "incremental withdrawal" from 'Northern Ireland' on the part of the British State and a "push-pull" relationship established between London and Dublin with Westminster pushing the North further away and Dublin pulling it toward the Republic. In implementing this policy, senior civil servants at the NI Office established intimate contacts with Protestant paramilitary leaders and tried to encourage the belief amongst them that the British Government was in the process of disengagement from the province and they would do well to start making preparations for the establishment of a kind of UDI as Britain pulled out. At the same time Republican leaders were given to believe that this process presented possibilities for them, representing the British withdrawal they had made their declared objective and the 'breaking of the connection' with England that Republicanism had always yearned for.

As part of this encouragement, the Leaders of Loyalism were lured into adopting an Independence programme. They were buttered up by being taken to foreign parts—including Amsterdam and Boston—where they met important people and as a result were made to feel important themselves. The UDA duly repaid all this attention and patronage in September 1975 as it "moved from a position on their first day in Holland of recognising that they were without political direction to the acceptance on the third day that negotiated independence was a viable policy" (IT 3.9.75).

"Eight academics and economic advisers", supplied by the British Government, had apparently persuaded the Loyalists of the viability of this course. At a further 'conference' arranged in Boston, the UDA was encouraged by the presence of members of the Alliance Party, the SDLP, Fine Gael, the Orange Order, the Irish Republican Socialist Party and some well-known clergymen and Queen's University academics to feel they were part of something substantial and workable (see IT 3.9.75).

The other part of this policy was a concerted media campaign promoting the 'popularity' of the idea of Ulster Nationalism, particularly by *The Times* and *Sunday Times*. Stories with the following headlines appeared prominently in the newspapers of the great: *'Ulster's Growing Belief That Britain Is Planning A Withdrawal'* (9.7.74); *'How Long Will Westminster Go On Signing A Blank Check For Ulster?'* (10.9.74); *'The Retreat From Ulster Is On—And It's Working!'* (23.6.75).

This latter article, written by *The Sunday Time*s "expert on Ulster", gives the full flavour of what the British Government was attempting to promote:

"An epic change is being accomplished in Britain's relationship with N. Ireland. British withdrawal is becoming a fact. The lightening of the Ulster murk is just perceptible... What withdrawal means... is the renunciation by the Westminster government of the attempt to wield power in Northern Ireland... It can be said to have begun in March 1972 when a Conservative administration discovered (as the army has still not quite discovered) that it did not have the power to beat the IRA militarily. The movement took a leap forward under the new Labour government in May 1974, at the time of the UWC strike, when ministers perceived that the most careful and equitable British originated solution could not be made to work... The central fact about British policy... is that the government has made the clear-eyed decision to have no policy, because it has no power to enforce one...

"The British government has triumphantly completed that part of the necessary psychiatric therapy which consists in alienating the patient's affections... The ultimate release from the problem of conflicting loyalties will be the emergence of a genuine N.Ireland identity. It is already detectable. Both Dr Paisley and Mr. Fitt... have proclaimed their loyalty as Ulstermen on the floor of the Convention. An odd fate has overtaken the Provisionals. Theologians have a phrase for it: released eschatology—that condition where the long dreamt dream of the final fulfillment turns out to have become a reality here and now. The nub of the Provisionals' dream is in Ireland without British influence. Now they have it... It has "not happened in quite the way they expected it, and it will not have the consequences they once looked for; but these things never do."

In the Summer of 1975 the noted Ulster correspondent of *The Times*, Robert Fisk, published a book, amidst great publicity, whose message was summed up by its title; *'The Point Of No Return: The Strike Which Broke The British In Ulster'*. Two passages give the message Rees wished to communicate:

> "He {Rees} secured a truce with the IRA in early 1975 and if the cost was high in prestige and political integrity—all the evidence points to a British assurance that Ulster could not forever remain part of the UK" (p.241).
>
> "At least one of Rees' civil servants was widely rumoured to have told the Provisionals that if the Loyalists won a majority in the Convention... then London would consider disengagement. The name of that civil servant is widely known and he is said to have made his comments in the light of a warning from the Provisionals that they would recommence their bombing campaign in Britain" (p.246).

It is clear that Fisk had been thoroughly duped by the NIO propaganda and reported it as news and fact. In reality, Ulster Nationalism never developed a real subjective dimension and really existed only while the Northern Ireland Office, assisted by *The Times* and *Sunday Times*, could sustain some credibility about the prospect of British withdrawal. It became clear that it was all a fantasy whereby Ulster independence would promote general harmony instead of what it was more likely to produce—general war.

Only one publication at the time exposed this catastrophic policy and helped people see through it. This was *'Against Ulster Nationalism'* by Brendan Clifford and the B&ICO, from which much of the material reproduced later in this section, was gotten.

South Armagh

What happened during late 1975-early1976 in South Armagh is always brought up to tar the Provos with sectarianism. But South Armagh is a very peculiar case and this period was a very peculiar time. Some context is needed here.

South Armagh was given the title "*Bandit Country*" by the British media. But it had engaged slowly and reluctantly in conflict when 'the Troubles' came. Of all the areas encompassed by the 'Northern Ireland' construct, it had done most to keep itself to itself and live its own life free of the degrading effects of the communal system at Stormont. When Belfast was developing and escalating the War, Crossmaglen remained a quiet backwater. A couple of policemen were killed in August 1970 after a local was killed in Belfast by the British Army but that was about it in the first two years of war.

When the South Armagh Brigade of the IRA began to engage the alien, disrupting force that intruded into its quiet life, it fought a military campaign directed against the forces that sought to occupy its territory. It did this very effectively for the best part of three decades. Around 60 British soldiers were killed in and around the village of Crossmaglen alone, and twice that in the surrounding area. And it is widely believed locally that many more dead bodies of undercover soldiers were spirited away in helicopters and became casualties of 'accidents' in Germany. The South Armagh Brigade suffered very few losses in return and it would probably be still fighting if the wider Republican movement had not decided to call a halt to the War.

In 1974 the British Ministry of Defence noticed something peculiar about South Armagh that worried it. The quality of its military expertise far exceeded that of other Provisional units elsewhere. It did not go for quantity in terms of operations but what it did do was extremely effective. And the British concern was that it might export its knowledge outside its local insularity.

The key to success in South Armagh was "meticulous planning and attention to the minutest detail" (Darach MacDonald, *'The Chosen Fews, Exploding Myths in South Armagh'*, p.38). Despite the appliance of all its elite regiments—marines, paratroopers and SAS—Britain could not stop the war of attrition that South Armagh put up to its occupation forces.

The policy of Ulsterisation was instituted in most of the Six Counties, including neighbouring Tyrone. But South Armagh, from the start, resisted it fiercely. Any attempts to introduce Police into the area were met with an immediate military response. And there were no local UDR forces that Britain could place in the firing line.

North of Newtownhamilton and Bessbrook was a killing ground for Loyalist groups and the IRA there had to choose its State targets amongst the local UDR and RUC. South Armagh was determined that, if the British were going to occupy, construct and garrison fortifications in its area, they would pay with military lives and not with those of local Protestants. If the British Government was going to encroach on the lives of local people it would be made pay for it.

There was no natural communal conflict in South Armagh, as there was in Belfast, because there were so few Protestants. The small Protestant community co-existed in a neighbourly manner with Catholics and the area existed as a place apart, with greater harmony existing between locals than with their co-religionists elsewhere. It was only the external alien intrusion— the extensive billeting of the British Army in the area—that began to change this situation. The only requirement that the South Armagh IRA had of local

Protestants—as it had of local Catholics—was that they did not aid the British occupation force. Problems occurred in the mid-1970s when British forces, incapable of operating themselves in South Armagh, enlisted Loyalists from the north of the County, from the Portadown district, to do their dirty work in Armagh (and further south in Dublin and Monaghan as well).

The Loyalist Glenanne gang, which had been responsible for dozens of sectarian killings of Catholics in neighbouring Tyrone and North Armagh, began to expand its activities into the south of the County. Loyalists became open to this expansion of operations because the British Government was putting out hints of disengagement and encouraging Ulster Nationalism. Loyalists began to take more of an interest in their frontiers and the native inhabitants of them in South Armagh. These Loyalists seemed to have immunity to law and order.

On the day before the Kingsmills shootings Loyalists (who were more than likely either members of the RUC or UDR) came to the south of the County and murdered three members of the Reavey family and three members of the O'Dowd family. How often do writers when selectively introducing Kingsmills into diatribes against South Armagh mention this context? (An earlier reprisal/false flag event at Tullyvallen Orange Hall is also removed from its context of the murder by loyalists in UDR uniforms of two GAA fans returning from a match in Dublin.)

It is possible that the massacre at Kingsmills was a local Republican response aimed at stopping this kind of activity. It was impossible for Republicans to have the Loyalist perpetrators of massacre arrested, since it was the British Army, local police and UDR that were actually doing the massacring themselves. (The Pat Finucane Centre has attributed 87 killings to the 'Glenanne gang', including the Dublin and Monaghan Bombings, the Miami Showband killings, and the massacres of the Reavey and O'Dowd families.) It might have been that the 'Republican Action Force' who claimed the Kingsmills killings were determined to show this was a single act and was not part of the mainstream IRA campaign. Or it might have been just a British pseudo-gang engaging in false flag operations in an attempt to promote an Ulsterising of the conflict and tit-for-tat killings to distract the IRA from its enemy, the British army of occupation.

Allegations of British involvement in these incidents were made in a 1993 Yorkshire Television documentary about the Dublin and Monaghan Bombings of 1974 called '*Hidden Hand*'. In the programme it was stated there was evidence which confirmed suspicions of links between the British State and the Portadown loyalist paramilitaries—groupings which were apparently run before and after the Dublin bombings by Captain Nairac. According to the documentary, support for this allegation was said to have come from various sources including "officers from RUC Special Branch,

CID and Special Patrol Group; officers from the Gardai Special Branch; and key senior loyalists who were in charge of the County Armagh paramilitaries of the day".

Darach MacDonald noted that the British Ministry of Defence concern about South Armagh led to the recommendation that a permanent Intelligence Officer be installed there along with special forces and other *sub rosa* elements. The result was a great deal of intrigue, disorder and killing. (*The Chosen Fews*, p.181)

The overall situation in South Armagh and the North generally was stabilised after the replacement of Merlyn Rees by Roy Mason. Mason offered certainty and stability and put a stop to the notions of Ulster Nationalism. During his period of Office the Loyalist assassination campaign dried up and tit for tat killings decreased drastically. From then onwards the IRA/ British war resumed in South Armagh until it was ended by the Good Friday Agreement. When Mason died in 2015 he got no praise from Nationalists. That is understandable. Mason was working-class Labour and the toughest opponent the IRA faced. However, it should be noted in his defence that he reduced the levels of violence drastically by stabilising things after Rees. That, at least, should be acknowledged in his favour.

Today, South Armagh is a quiet and tranquil place, now that the military occupation has gone. With the restrictions on its contact across the Border lifted it gets on with its business and its rich social life. Locals live together in peace, with minimal interference from 'Northern Ireland'.

The Turning Point

The British promotion of Ulster Nationalism failed for two reasons. The Ulster Unionists resisted the taking of their fate into their own hands as Ulster Nationalists in order to fight their own war. They refused to be Rhodesians. And the Republican leadership refused to be diverted by Britain from its War on the State to a war on Protestants.

By late 1975 the Truce between the British and the Provos began to fall apart. It had caused divisions within the Republican Army and it was evident that the leadership had begun to lose control of many of the rank and file to Hibernian impulses. According to Brendan Hughes, the move which led to an ousting of the old Republican leadership began in prison through a collaboration between himself, Ivor Bell and Gerry Adams. They decided that the leadership of Billy McKee (a long-standing friend of the Hughes family and critic of Adams after the Good Friday Agreement) had to be ended. The issue which brought on this decision was the response of the leadership to the British Government's efforts to bring about national war, during the 1975 Truce with the Republican Army, with which it had a 'hot-line' communication.

Here is Hughes' account:

"There were communications from the outside leadership to the prisoners... telling us that 'We have fought the British to a standstill, the British want out...' At the same time... Protestants were getting shot, Catholics were getting shot. But there were no British getting shot. I was... getting more and more frustrated... I was sharing a cubicle with Gerry Adams at the time and I packed my gear. By this time the INLA had been formed and had prisoners in Cage 13, and I was heading there. I was going to leave the Republican movement and join the INLA. They had just been formed from a split within the Workers' Party. I was talked out of it by Gerry and remained. He convinced me that the only way to defeat these people was to oppose them from within... they'd be quite happy for me to walk away. But here we were in this situation; it was very demoralising. We then got the word that we must prepare for civil war and, Jesus Christ... we had to start training for that possibility... The British were pulling out and the Loyalists were going to rebel... At one time, I actually advocated shooting the Belfast leadership, which Gerry and Ivor were opposed to... This sectarian war that the British were able to manipulate the IRA into was part of the Ulsterisation of security... We started to hear words like 'Godfathers', 'Chicago-type killings'. The British sent a guy, Peter Jay, as Ambassador to America, and he went there to convince the Americans that this was a sectarian war here and the British were caught in the middle. The IRA had facilitated this image..." (*Voices from the Grave*, pp. 193-4).

The British Government's attempt to alter the basis of the conflict from a Republican/British War to a Catholic/Protestant war seems to have represented a turning point in the conflict. It provoked a change in the Republican leadership that insisted on the maintenance of the Republican War on Britain but which could subsequently entertain the possibility of an interim settlement with Britain that involved the final stage of the War being fought politically rather than militarily. With the rise of a new Northern leadership from the 1969 generation, a political adaptation to Northern realities was gradually brought about. Retaliations in kind to Loyalist atrocities, that gave the British their impression of civil war, were phased out.

The most significant effect of the ceasefire on the Provos was the undermining of the authority of O'Bradaigh, O'Connell and the southern Anti-Treatyites. The Southern leadership had represented the Truce as an honourable accommodation with the British Government to facilitate the start of a withdrawal. So, when the Truce collapsed and a British pull-out began to look less and less likely, the Northern substance of the Provos took the opportunity to throw off the Southern Anti-Treatyites. Within a year of the end of the Truce, the military command of the movement passed to a virtually autonomous

Northern command. The Southerners were then also ousted from the control of *Republican News*, which was subsumed into *An Phoblacht*.

The British duping of the Southern Leadership of the Republican movement was the catalyst for the high command of the IRA to assume a more representative character, reflecting the fact that the Provos were essentially a new Republican movement created in August 1969. This event had fundamentally changed the substance of the Republican movement from a small Southern-based military conspiracy to a much more popularly-based Northern Insurrectionary War. The Republican movement after 1970 was the product of a politically active Northern Catholic community jolted into this development by the Unionist Pogrom and the subsequent withdrawal from the scene of the British and Irish authorities. It was no longer Southerners 'playing up their part in the Patriot Game'.

Ideological Republicanism—abstentionism, political exclusivity and the primacy of physical force—kept the movement alive in the South in the lean years after the Fianna Fail defection. But it was the Republicanism of a rump, not the mass political expression of a disaffected people. It was a nucleus of development which had to be preserved while the Northern statelet remained the political abnormality it was, because the chance for another fight was always going to come. But it was a mere nucleus all the same. In 1969, Southern Anti-Treatyites like O'Bradaigh and O'Connell provided the political leadership as the Northerners got on with their War. But, once the War developed into a long haul, the young working class Catholics, like Gerry Adams and Martin McGuinness, came to the fore. The purer Northern militarists began to be increasingly sidelined as the struggle demanded greater political understanding of the Northern predicament, but they became useful political allies against the Southern dogmatists, conferring legitimacy on the new pragmatism.

The Truce of 1975-6 represented the start of the parting of the ways between Northern pragmatists and Southern Anti-Treatyites—although it took another decade or so for it to fully work itself out. (Most of the Southerners left in 1986, after the Sinn Fein Ard Fheis voted to end abstention to the Dáil.)

At the time of the Truce it is strange that in trying to identify the 'hawks' and 'doves' in their talks with the Republicans, in order to try to 'politicise' the Republicans and draw out a compromising element in the movement, the British Government got it so wrong. O'Bradaigh and O'Connell were the ones the British believed they could do business with, and Adams and McGuinness were seen as the uncompromising hardliners. Was that because the British saw how Republicanism had developed into a series of compromises over the century and felt it could do another job on it while the products of its political slum were unknown quantities and might just be lost causes?

The Southern element could only lead the Republican movement while a quick victory could be imagined. When hopes of success began to dim around 1974-5, soul-searching was required. Ruari O'Bradaigh might have searched his soul around that time. But there was nothing there but the purity of the Second Dail. Gerry Adams, who was sitting in the Kesh at the time, searched his soul and began seeing the future. And, like all good prophets, he carved out the future he himself predicted. From then onwards the Republican Army was under the command of those who had their community upmost in their thoughts in fighting and settling the War.

Contracting Out the War

Tommy McKearney, a Tyrone Republican, later recalled how Britain "*Ulsterised*" the war under cover of a Truce which the Republican leadership had thought advantageous to their own movement:

"… it had become clear to senior IRA members that in the light of a high level of attrition, a readjustment had to be made. The IRA Army Council, therefore, accepted an opportunity in late 1974 to call a temporary ceasefire that lasted into mid-autumn 1975. They did so knowing the Belfast Brigade was in a parlous position and other units in rural parts of the Six Counties were suffering from a debilitating shortage of equipment. Both the British and the IRA used this interval to review their positions and prepare for the next round.

"There was a realisation at the time within IRA circles that granting a ceasefire was a risky option. Several older veterans of the 1956-62 campaign even mentioned the Kenya uprising when General China (Waruhiu Itote) of the Land and Freedom Army arranged a temporary cessation of hostilities between his people and the British. Negotiations at the time in Kenya came to nothing. During the three-month lull in fighting the Special Branch in Nairobi gathered extensive intelligence about the group that supplied food, money, volunteers and ammunition to the fighters in the forests. When the 'China Peace Overture' as it was called, failed the British swept in and arrested more than a thousand suspects in three days.

"In spite of such anxieties, the IRA called a ceasefire and opened covert negotiations… The IRA leadership had a relatively uncomplicated view of the state of affairs. They would use the break to rearm, retrain, recruit and prepare for a return to war if their demand for a British declaration of intent to withdraw from Ireland was not met. By early summer 1975, the IRA Army Council had recognised that nothing was coming from London that would meet their demands and ordered units to drift back into action… In a few short months, the IRA learned that its preparations for a return to war were inadequate. The ceasefire had engendered a taste for peace in many, including IRA supporters, and this desire was increased by the fall-out from a relentless sectarian war being waged by Loyalist death squads. Implementation of London's decision to transfer a major portion of responsibility for combating the insurrection to locally recruited forces... caused Loyalists to intensify their onslaught...

"It is difficult to accept that Britain was unaware of the consequences arising from placing locally recruited militias... in direct conflict with the IRA. Unless the IRA abandoned its campaign, it was inevitable that as the two sides came into conflict, the struggle would assume a sectarian dimension. As history records, this happened and many RUC and UDR members died, often while off-duty. Whatever rationale the IRA offered for the imperative of acting as it did, many Protestant people viewed this campaign as a sectarian assault on their community. This anger in turn lent a semblance of justification from a Unionist point of view to a largely indiscriminate killing campaign waged on Catholics" (*The Provisional IRA, From Insurrection to Parliament*, pp.139-40).

It now began to dawn on people, and not alone Republicans, but also on Hume, that Britain had conned them about withdrawal. Britain was not withdrawing its administration from 'Northern Ireland' but it was increasingly withdrawing from the War which 'Northern Ireland' was producing for them.

Direct Rule may have appeared to signal a change in British policy with regard to 'Northern Ireland'. However, the beginnings of the Ulsterisation policy actually occurred at the very moment Direct Rule was assumed by Westminster. The British military had demanded indemnity if the Government required it to reoccupy the No-Go areas of West Belfast and Derry. This was refused by the British Cabinet. Instead, it seems that an alternative plan was adopted which involved the encouragement of the growth of Loyalist counter-gangs and an informal alliance between them and the British Army. The idea was based on the methods used by the British against the Mau Mau in Kenya and was prepared by the General Office Commanding, Henry Tuzo and the Chief of General Staff, Michael Carver.

Dr. Huw Bennett published a paper entitled *'Studies in Conflict and Terrorism'* in 2010. Ed Moloney and Bob Mitchell made the following comments on Bennett's findings:

"Tuzo... made a proposal to Whitelaw that the growth of loyalist paramilitaries should be quietly promoted. The wording of Tuzo's idea strongly implies the creation of a second front that the Provisional IRA would be forced to fight on. 'Vigilantes, whether UDA or not', he wrote to Whitelaw, 'should be discreetly encouraged in Protestant areas to reduce the load on the Security Forces'. The phrase 'to reduce the load on the Security Forces' suggests much more than turning a blind eye to groups like the UDA and UVF. It comes close to regarding the loyalist paramilitaries as allies. There is nothing... to indicate that either Whitelaw or the Heath cabinet vetoed or even objected to this aspect of the Tuzo plan" (IT 19.1.13).

The initial manifestations of this were joint British Army/UDA patrols and British Army snipers firing side by side from Springmartin into Ballymurphy and conducting joint operations against the estate that led to the killing of Catholic civilians. Bennett wrote in his paper:

> "What seems to be the case to me is that in 1972 the military really took charge of the situation... There does not seem to be that much regular cabinet interference in what they are doing."

Moloney and Mitchell commented:

> "Bennett says he found all this reminiscent of the way the British handled the Mau Mau uprising in Kenya, in the 1950s. Under the direction of a young British military officer named Frank Kitson, the British created countergangs, recruited from rival Kenyan tribes, to fight the Mau Mau. Between 1970 and 1972, the same Frank Kitson, by then a general, headed the British army's Belfast brigade and was a key figure in the military hierarchy in Northern Ireland."

Britain Ulsterised the conflict, using the loyalists to do things that *'administrative massacre'* could no longer achieve or which the official army of the State could not get away without a Government indemnity. Members of the local Protestant militias (RUC and UDR) did the killing when off-duty, assisted others in the killing, and protected them from capture.

The Loyalists themselves seem to have viewed the Republican War in the context of a general Catholic uprising. There was no effort to specifically target Republicans (only one was killed in Monaghan out of the hundred or so victims of the Glenanne Gang) but simply to kill and terrorise Catholics to "keep them down" as Sir Frank Cooper put it in a letter to the General Officer Commanding the British Army, Sir Frank King (p.320). And the British idea seems to have been to "harness their energies" in pursuit of Whitehall's objectives.

Prof. Bew, after giving the general casualty figures in 'Northern Ireland' during the conflict says in his book, *'Ireland, The Politics of Enmity' 1789-2006'* (which being part of the 'Oxford History of Modern Ireland' is meant as the official last word on the matter):

> "These are figures which describe a grim civil war, complicated only by the British State's efforts to act as a peacemaker." (p.510)

Seeing Britain as *"a peacemaker"* makes strange reading when placed against the evidence contained in Anne Cadwallader's book, *Lethal Allies*. But in one way Lord Bew is accurate. Having set up 'Northern Ireland' in 1921 and got away from its construct, Britain was ensuring that it was now merely a *'complication'* to the action that was taking place there. And it has enough historians and media professionals on both sides of the Border to write that story up—to ensure it only has a bit part in history among the carnage its misgovernment produced within its area of responsibility.

The British Non-Target

Lord Bew's long-standing associate, Prof. Patterson, has written:

"Although the Provisionals had a less nakedly sectarian agenda than that of the loyalist groups, their campaign was also tainted by sectarianism. Until the onset of the 'Ulsterisation' of security policy in the mid 1970s the Provisionals had a large and easily identifiable non-Protestant target in the British Army" (*Ireland Since 1939, The Persistence of Conflict*, p.228)

This passage implies that the Provos were fundamentally an anti-Protestant force, keen to fight and kill Protestants and it was even an inconvenience to them that before Ulsterisation they were forced to take on the British Army before they could *"take it out on the Protestants"* (to use the phrase of another historian).

One would have expected, therefore, that the Provos would have welcomed Ulsterisation as having simplified the conflict and put them up against their 'real' enemy. But far from it—the Provos condemned the Ulsterisation policy and went to great lengths to get round it and to fight their real enemy by finding and engaging the British forces whom its Government had done everything possible to put beyond the IRA reach by putting local Protestants in the firing line between itself and the Provos.

Prof. Patterson has written a book about the IRA called *'The Politics of Illusion'*. One presumes the title is about how the IRA suffered illusions about various things—chief amongst them being the Republican attitude to Protestants. But if there is an 'illusion' in Republicanism it is not a sectarian one in any respect—it is precisely the opposite. It is an 'illusion' that treats Protestants as fellow Irishmen with a long Republican tradition and which seeks to include them without prejudice, and in many ways with favour, in a non-sectarian state. The belief that this was going to be accomplished by warfare may have been illusory but it was an illusion of the better and even, necessary, kind.

Perhaps it might be argued that this 'illusion' is the ideology of Republicanism but the reality is different—individuals within the IRA could be sectarian and on occasion engage in sectarian acts that, if not objectively sectarian were perceived as such by local Protestants who felt the full force of the Republican War on themselves, family and community. But if that argument is accepted the question then arises why does some of the behaviour depart from the ideology? And the only answer to this lies in the character of the medium within which the War was conducted as a consequence of the system constructed in 1920-1.

What are the facts? We know that some IRA anti-civilian shootings and bombings took place against bars and businesses in predominantly Protestant areas. We know that these actions were disowned by both IRAs at the time. We also know that more often than not nobody was apprehended for these activities. Several possibilities emerge from these facts. Firstly, these incidents may have been perpetrated by non-Republicans aimed at tainting the Republican reputation, leading to reprisals and 'tit-for-tat' activities that would draw IRA members away from their War against the British Army. That is the counter-insurgency strategy used by Britain in previous operations in other parts of the world and which was given expression by Sir Frank Kitson and others in various published accounts and manuals for British military training.

It is also possible that individual IRA members may have become drawn into this type of activity at the time, against the orders of the organisation and general Republican principles, when fighting the British was off-limits to them. That was another aspect of the British counter-insurgency strategy of Fred Holroyd etc., particularly in relation to loyalist and 'pseudo-gangs', and it would be entirely unrealistic to believe that it did not have its successes. And it was also the natural direction of the conflict produced by the 'Northern Ireland' construct and the British policy of Ulsterisation that Republicanism was attempting to rise above.

So to have expected Republicans to have conducted their War entirely within the ideology of non-sectarianism is perhaps, unrealistic. But it must be acknowledged that they did made a great effort to do so.

Republicans and Ulsterisation

The arm's length policy of Whitehall had the effect of initially disabling the British Army against the IRA. Intelligence was poor and the geography of Belfast and its street patterns unfamiliar. The Republican Army led the British Army a merry dance in the streets of Belfast and Derry. It took a couple of years for the British to gain a degree of mastery of the urban battlefield. The earlier advantage which the IRA had of local knowledge was whittled away with occupation of the urban Republican heartlands, the appliance of surveillance technology, and increased Intelligence. An armed cordon was erected around Belfast city centre to deprive the IRA of its primary target. Then the Catholic community in the city, which was only about 100,000, was gradually squeezed in a war of attrition to wear down the Republican Army's operational capacity.

Then the country areas began to take up the War in support of Belfast and the smaller IRA units operating over larger spaces proved harder for the British Army to curtail. In the rural areas the local Protestant militias were increasingly employed to repress the Insurgency. And this forced the Republican Army into a campaign of assassination against members of these militias, the RUC and UDR, both when they were on active service and off duty.

In 1972 the British Army constituted about 55% of the security forces in the Six Counties and it took about 70% of the casualties of the Republican War. By the late 1980s, as a result of Ulsterisation, the British Army represented only about 30% of the security forces and it took about 30% of the casualties. As David McKittrick wrote in *The Independent*: "a large part of the war against the IRA is carried on by Protestants in uniform" (19.9.89).

Tommy McKearney says this about the consequences of the British policy of *'Ulsterisation'* for Republicans:

"It is difficult to accept that Britain was unaware of the consequences arising from placing locally recruited militias (Protestant Unionists for the most part) in direct conflict with the IRA. Unless the IRA abandoned its campaign, it was inevitable that as the two sides came into conflict, the struggle would assume sectarian dimensions. As history records, this happened and many RUC and UDR members died, often while off duty. Whatever rationality the IRA offered for the imperative of acting as it did, many Protestant people viewed this campaign as a sectarian assault on their community. This anger in turn led a semblance of justification from a Unionist point of view to a largely indiscriminate killing campaign waged on Catholics" (*The IRA—From Insurrection to Parliament* p.140).

The Provos attempted to deal with the Protestant complication by ignoring it and claiming that the War was against the British State and no one else. But, as McKearney notes, this posed a problem in many areas where the war against Republicans was largely undertaken by Protestant militias in conjunction with others acting independently or semi-independently from the British State:

"The British used its locally recruited part-time Regiment, the UDR, supported by an RUC Reserve to gather intelligence and act as a lightly armed counter-insurgency militia. Strenuous efforts have been made over the years to portray the two forces as well-meaning, part-timers doing their best to protect society, insinuating that any attack on their members was motivated purely by sectarianism.

"Lost amid this tendentious propaganda is the reality. Both the UDR and the RUC Reserve were recruited locally and had, therefore, a comprehensive and detailed knowledge of the areas of operation. As local men, they were able to distinguish between various accents that are so distinctive to a Northern Irish ear, but would not resonate with regular soldiers reared in Britain. A County Derry accent would go unnoticed, for example, if questioned in South Tyrone by Londoners, but would immediately draw the suspicion of a Dungannon UDR patrol. As local men with roots for many generations in an area, some UDR members were even able to recognise young Republicans by family resemblance to older relatives. They had, too, the ability to differentiate between families sharing similar names, an invaluable asset to the authorities in parts of the pre-postcode Six Counties where locals used ancient patronymics to identify each other. In closely mixed rural areas, members of the UDR or RUC Reserve were intimately familiar with the rhythm and pattern of life in their districts and could recognise instantly if something was out of place.

"Whether on or off duty, these men acted not only as the eyes and ears of the regular army but actively supported it logistically and militarily. That they had dual military and civilian roles added to the danger they posed to the IRA. Employed as school bus drivers, postmen, refuse collectors and every other position in the workforce, they had a perfect cover for travelling covertly in the Republican districts, not only to observe but also to monitor. A dustman may appear a harmless worker until he sifts through the bins for information—a routine practice by every intelligence agency" (pp.117-8).

This passage from McKearney's book is cited in a recent book by Prof. Patterson entitled *'Ireland's Violent Frontier: The Border and Anglo-Irish Relations during the Troubles'* (p.41). However, it is used by the Prof. in completely the opposite way that it was intended by McKearney. Prof. Patterson employs it to explain why the Provos particularly targeted the local Protestant militias when McKearney is actually explaining the use these militias had for the British war effort over and above their simple value as cannon-fodder. McKearney recounts how the IRA had, during the 1956-62 campaign, attempted to avoid attacks on the RUC and Specials because they saw them as 'deluded Irishmen' who would someday come to their senses. But the post-1969 Northern rural IRA units found it impossible to ignore the role they played after Ulsterisation in repressing the Catholic community and fighting Republicans. Increasingly, therefore, they were targeted by the IRA.

Repeated attempts were made by Republicans to encourage Protestants to return to the spirit of their predecessors in the United Irishmen. Of course this was futile but that does not mean that it was not sincerely and earnestly meant. And the Provos undoubtedly acted as a restraining influence on communal passions within the Catholic community—which were the natural manifestation of life in the Northern statelet.

The Loyalist campaign against Republicans was very different. It was summed up in the Loyalist phrase *'Any Taig Will Do'* and largely consisted of random attacks against individuals or groups within vulnerable locations seen as 'Catholic' or indeed in the targeting of upwardly-mobile Catholics, as Anne Cadwallader found.

Sectarianising the War

The British Government's encouragement of 'Ulster Nationalism' and then 'Ulsterisation' had the object of sectarianising the War. What else was the likely outcome of 'Ulsterising' and making the War primarily the business of the Ulster Protestants whilst at the same time encouraging a belief in

British disengagement that would make them understand they would have to stop relying on Britain and fight the War themselves—and all this at a time when there was no Stormont to protect them?

Loyalists viewed the Nationalist predictions of a British withdrawal with alarm and the strenuous attempts made by the NIO to encourage ideas of Ulster Nationalism among the Protestant community helped sharpen the conflict. This, added to the fact that the British Government was negotiating with the IRA, with the suggestion that major concessions were being made to them, possibly even secretly giving them assurances of a British pull-out, made a concerted Loyalist escalation inevitable.

Ulster Nationalism was a Whitehall attempt to work up a Protestant/ Catholic war in place of the Republican/British War that had not been supposed to be part of *"the game"*—as Prof. Bew put it. It was a programme to work up a sectarian war in its Six County region after the British Government had reached a stalemate in its war with the Provos, by changing the structure of the conflict and bringing about generalised Protestant/ Catholic mayhem.

The promotion of Ulster Nationalism ultimately failed, but a kind of watered-down version that enabled a partial British withdrawal was instituted instead, called *'Ulsterisation'*.

The British Government had taken the opportunity of the Truce to institute this new strategy of *'Ulsterisation'*. This in one sense was a withdrawal, but a withdrawal of a kind desired by Britain rather than by the Provos. What it amounted to was the increasing use of the RUC as a 'counter-terrorist' force, and the Ulster Defence Regiment replacing the Regular Army of the State in most areas outside South Armagh, Derry and West Belfast. The basic idea was to *'normalise'* the situation to create the impression that it was not a War that was being fought by Britain, and that *'The Troubles'* were just an unusually large amount of criminal activity, which was being dealt with by the local forces of law and order (which, of course, were far from ordinary).

'Ulsterisation', however, is a misnomer. It was really *re*-Ulsterisation— because it was a return to the default position of 1920 rather than an innovation after 1972. It was a return to the Stormont era military position as much as could be achieved.

The counter-offensive of the British State against Republicanism— Ulsterisation/ Normalisation/ Criminalisation—was based on the premise that things were going to settle down. No escalation of the conflict was necessary to end it, a noose had simply to be applied and closed gradually. There were probably very few within the British State apparatus who would have believed in 1974 that the Republican Army could still be fighting two decades later.

CHAPTER 10

Regrouping

There was a regrouping within Northern Nationalism in the period after the collapse of Sunningdale and the British Ulsterising of the war. Republicans re-organised themselves for the Long War they realised they were going to have to fight after the short one they had attempted to win had stalled. There was a recommitment to the War that had been started rather than the diversion that the British State had attempted to redirect the Republican Army towards. And there was also a regrouping within 'Constitutional Nationalism' as the SDLP leadership formally changed hands from its formal leader, Fitt, to its real driving force, Hume.

Regrouping was essential because it became clear that Dublin was withdrawing its support and the Northern Catholics were on their own. They would now have to resolve their predicament on the best terms they could achieve, in their own interest, without relying on Dublin.

Re-grouping was also necessary because of the change in British policy aimed at isolating the War to 'Ulster', which had began as the enormously destabilising policy of Ulster Nationalism and which settled into the policy of Ulsterisation. This Whitehall policy to confine the conflict to the Six Counties, despite having to continue bearing the burden of Direct Rule, demanded a change in tack from Northern Nationalism. Ulsterisation, with its associated policies of Normalisation and Criminalisation, was initially successful for Britain. But in the longer term it helped to rejuvenate the Catholic Insurrection and produced a new political manifestation in Sinn Fein that frustrated Britain's policy of narrowing the conflict and enabled the opening of new battlegrounds.

The SDLP in the Doldrums

Rees' Ulster Nationalist strategy and the threat of British withdrawal disorientated the SDLP and resulted in it losing its bearings. When Bill Craig, during the Constitutional Convention talks, made a proposal for an emergency voluntary coalition on the lines of a 'War Cabinet', to restore order and stability in the North, the SDLP came close to accepting this purely internal settlement in 'Northern Ireland,' before members of the UUUC refused to share power with them. Meeting with the UUUC talks negotiators at the end of August 1975 Hume is recorded to have said:

> "They were now thinking in terms of a temporary constitution—he would himself advocate 10 years—with the whole thing subject to review at the end

of that time. They thought they could prove their point that partnership in government could work over such a period—and it was desirable to have the arrangements electorally endorsed at least twice... The SDLP expressed disappointment at the poor reception of the UUUC to their points of principle. They felt they were offering quite a lot in pledging the support of the Roman Catholic community for new institutions. This would mean the SDLP themselves taking on the IRA, often at personal risk and possibly at the risk of a civil war in the Catholic community. They would be prepared to take a very strong line with IRA and to put them down by quite rugged means. They were also prepared to ask the people of the Republic for their acquiescence to the new institutions so as to rob the IRA of legitimacy. Most of the discussion centred on the possibility of a crisis government to be formed by a voluntary coalition for a fixed period. SDLP argued that the emergency was economic as well as security and that a 10 year social and economic plan was appropriate for dealing with this. This would require a government on an equal basis for that period. Mr. Hume thought there should be at least two elections on an agreed programme. At the end of that period, the constitutional arrangements could be reviewed in the light of experience. The Chairman suggested the possibility of a report or reports by the NI Parliament or participating parties to the Speaker of the House of Commons. It appeared from the discussion that SDLP would not necessarily insist on power sharing being enshrined in the enabling statute provided they could be sure the rug could not be pulled from under them after having made a gentleman's agreement to join a voluntary coalition. Their people would require some concrete reassurance and satisfactory public guarantees." (PRONI, CONV 1/1)

Hume came up with the terminology of the "*two traditions*" to magic away the national division that was apparent and undeniable in the North (*Sunday Press* 16.3.75). The word "*tradition*" however hardly did justice to the complete absence of collective feeling between the Unionist and Nationalist communities. It was a deadly national division that had pre-existed the War and which had been exacerbated by the construction of 'Northern Ireland' and the War it had ultimately generated.

Senior Catholic Civil Servant Maurice Hayes saw the Constitutional Convention as "a cynical exercise designed to keep Northern Ireland off the boil and to transfer blame for failure to solve the problems to Northern Ireland politicians and away from the British Government". (*John Hume, Irish Peacemaker*). Hayes put the SDLP willingness to partake in an internal solution down to the situation that had developed from Rees' policy: "Both Hume and Craig looked over the parapet and saw anarchy, civil war and disaster. Craig wanted agreement on a strong government that would restore order and stability" (*Minority Verdict; Experiences of a Catholic Public Servant*, p. 227).

After the fall of the Executive the SDLP were in the doldrums. It had baulked at the chance Faulkner offered it in June 1971 and bungled the

Power-Sharing Executive of 1974. The declining Provo military offensive meant that the British could ignore them and concentrate on undermining the Republican Army. Success in that would have the by-product of reducing the SDLP to irrelevance because, without the Republican offensive the SDLP, was impotent. There would be no need to satisfy the SDLP to the detriment of Unionism, and a settlement could be imposed again on the North on broadly Unionist terms.

The SDLP had presented itself as a kind of buffer between the Provos and large numbers of young men who would join them. However, by 1977, large numbers of young men had joined the IRA, been killed, imprisoned or left the struggle. And it was clear that the SDLP was not a dam holding up a torrent—it was more of something floating upon it.

Fitt had taken his strategy of blurring 'Constitutional' and unConstitutional politics with him into the SDLP. He had regularly threatened Stormont with the IRA if it did not hurry up and deliver the reforms he was demanding. Of course, during the 1960s, with the IRA virtually non-existent, unconstitutional Nationalism was seen as a largely empty threat by everyone except the Unionists, but the Unionists were Fitt's main target.

Later, at the time of the formation of the SDLP, unconstitutional Nationalism had become a threat again and a *continuum* developed between it and constitutional Nationalism that was beneficial to both, particularly in the period between the SDLP's retreat to Dungiven and the imposition of Direct Rule. However, Fitt seems to have become alarmed when the spectre of Republican political expression began to be raised, particularly in his own backyard of West Belfast. Fitt saw the electoral role within the *continuum* as very much his own and he became concerned and protested against the British for attempting to encourage the Provos into politics with the Incident Centres etc. that would give them 'respectability.'

Once things stabilised—after Rees was replaced by Mason—Hume dropped the proposal of an internal accommodation and set his stall against such a thing and against his party leader's tendency toward it. Hume predicted that the new British idea of a Constitutional Convention in 1975, to allow local politicians to suggest their own solution to the conflict, would merely result in majority-rule and was best avoided. But Fitt faced down Hume's scepticism and a Republican call for a Nationalist boycott of the Convention elections in 1975. The SDLP vote remained solid in the absence of any Republican alternative. The Convention suggested a return to majority-rule, as Hume predicted it would, and then the SDLP rejected this as unworkable after the events of the previous six years.

The SDLP under Fitt

The SDLP under Fitt had two incompatible aims—British social reform and the ending of Partition. These two reforms could not be pursued together in practical politics for very long, but Fitt could never chose between them—until near the end. At the end it was a choice of pursuing the Nationalist agenda in the direction Hume was leading the party or pursuing the will o' the wisp of socialist politics within the pseudo state with its in-built Unionist majority. Fitt and Devlin chose the latter and this led to their detachments from the SDLP, which was now being pulled in the other direction by Hume.

When the Craig initiative foundered, some of the SDLP like Seamus Mallon, Joe Hendron and Paddy Wilson began proposing "*negotiated independence*" for 'Northern Ireland'. This proposal had the merit of turning the Six Counties into a state, but how stable such a state would be was another question. There was a substantial debate about the proposal at the 1976 SDLP Conference. Both Hume and Fitt sensibly rejected this idea, as it would leave the Catholic community in a very vulnerable position. However, the SDLP overwhelmingly voted to make a study of the prospects of negotiated independence, despite Fitt's threat to resign if the party actually adopted it as a policy.

In 1977 Paddy Devlin was expelled from the party after making public criticism of the SDLP for not being serious about its Socialism. Fitt failed to support Devlin and seems to have used the opportunity to ally with his opponents, "*the countrymen*", to get rid of Devlin, whom he still presumed to be a rival. These personality clashes seemed to play a strong part in SDLP politics because the party had inherited many of the characteristics of the old Nationalist Party it replaced—too many Chiefs and not enough Indians.

In early 1978 the SDLP were taken aback by the Shadow Secretary of State, Airey Neave's, statement in the House of Commons that "power-sharing was no longer practical". Fitt quickly responded to the suggestion of integration: "Airey Neave is electioneering and is seeking the support of the unionist MP's at Westminster. He could get their support at the cost of further bloodshed". The following day Eddie McGrady, warned that the SDLP "in the face of new expressions of intolerance, intransigence and insincerity, must immediately re-appraise its approach to constitutional problems". In reaction to Neave saying that, if the Conservatives came to power, they would carry out major government reforms in 'Northern Ireland', and restore more power to the Local Councils, Fitt stated:

> "If Maggie Thatcher is ever prime minister—and this is something I doubt very much will ever happen—she would do well to think of someone else to head the representatives of the British government here. We have had our share of trouble and sorrow here but I can't help thinking that it would be a lot worse with Mr. Neave in his naivety at the helm" (IN, 31.5.78).

Fitt's last political action was to bring down the Labour Government in Britain and open the door of No 10 for Thatcher. And his reason for doing this was that it had increased Northern Ireland representation at Westminster from 12 seats to 18, which Fitt saw as a sop to Unionists, but which actually benefitted Nationalists in the longer run. At the very end, Fitt thus played out the logic of 'Northern Ireland' by opposing that which might be of benefit to his side because it was being wanted by the other side. His behaviour was the mirror-image of the Unionists who had refused to countenance the reforms Fitt advocated in the 1960s and helped bring their own system to melt-down.

Fitt never regretted his decision to subject the UK population to an unlikely Government of Mrs. Thatcher, however, and remained unrepentant regarding his decision. Michael Murphy perceptively states the following:

"Mason... asked in his memoirs: 'Did he (Fitt) really expect his constituents to do better under the Thatcherite free market than under Labour?' It is probable that Mason believed his government could get away with making concessions to unionism because Fitt, a socialist, would not dare to inflict this new radical right-wing government on the country, and his constituents. Fitt's assertion that he was primarily a socialist hardly stands examination in relation to his actions. But Mason underestimated the personal animosity in Fitt that would not countenance him suffering a small short-term defeat to his local enemies.

"Fitt had little strategic understanding of the situation in the UK as a whole. If Labour had to make a short-term concession to butter up the Ulster Unionists in order to survive the winter and fight an election in a much more favourable time of the year, when government's always try to fight elections, and stave off a great threat to the working classes, then it was in the socialist interest that this had to be done. In truth the concession they were making was in no way an undemocratic one and neither was it detrimental to the nationalist interest in the longer term. Recent elections have witnessed an increased number of seats being won by nationalist candidates.

"Furthermore, if Fitt was particularly perturbed about greater Ulster representation at Westminster (and there is considerable evidence that he was), it thus marks a distinct reversal of the sentiment and content of his maiden speech at the House of Commons in 1966. Then he demanded the same rights and privileges for the people of Northern Ireland which were enjoyed in the rest of the United Kingdom. In 1979, however, he opposed a bill to increase the number of Northern Ireland seats at Westminster. This adds fuel to the charge that his machinations at parliament in the late 1960s were merely an attempt to disrupt the unionist regime in a way which would be advantageous to the ending of partition rather than for an democratic ideal" (*Gerry Fitt, Political Chameleon*, p.271).

Fitt Confronts Himself

The Pope's visit to Ireland in 1979 seems to have accentuated the unease Fitt was developing with any *continuum* between 'Constitutional' and unconstitutional Nationalism. At Drogheda the Pope addressed a crowd of 250,000 and asked all those engaged in violence to desist from it. The Provos rejected the Pope's plea on the basis that only force could remove the British presence from Ireland. This was just after the IRA's spectacular against the Parachute Regiment at Warrenpoint and at Sligo when they assassinated Lord Mountbatten.

Austin Currie believed that the Pope's Address had a profound impact on Fitt's thinking, strengthening his determination to confront Republicanism, and created within him such an abhorrence of it that it led him to detest even the 'Constitutional' republicanism he found in the SDLP. Fitt became paranoid and considered even Seamus Mallon as one who was too close to the Provos. Fitt's hostility towards his own party gathered pace after the SDLP Conference passed a new policy document entitled *"Towards a New Ireland"*. He was also annoyed at a motion from the mid-Ulster branches which suggested the SDLP should open contacts with the leaderships of "all political and paramilitary organisations who belong to the Irish tradition with a view to establishing a common ground for reconciliation with those of the British tradition". This motion was rejected, but it signalled what was to come under Hume's direction of the SDLP.

Following the SDLP Conference, Humphrey Atkins, the new Conservative Minister of State (who had taken over after the INLA had assassinated Airey Neave), launched a new political initiative. At the end of 1979, the British Government published a document proposing a Conference between the constitutional parties but stated that the Constitutional position of 'Northern Ireland' was not a topic for discussion; and there was no mention of any Irish dimension. It signalled that, although there was to be no integration, any movement toward what the SDLP wanted was off the agenda. Although the SDLP was not at all pleased by this, Fitt gave the document a guarded welcome and said it was "worthy of the deepest consideration and that is certainly what my party will be doing at the earliest opportunity" (BT 29.11.79).

The following evening the Party Executive and Constituency Representatives met and repudiated their Leader's public endorsement by unanimously deciding not to enter into talks unless they included discussions on the Irish dimension. Fitt was present but, after mulling it over, resigned from the SDLP on the following day, blaming the party's decision not to participate in talks as the main reason for his resigning. Fitt described the ruling as "completely misguided and disastrous" and added: "I can only say that I have a feeling of unutterable sadness to see at this time the party which I helped to create with others, turning so violently on the concepts on which it was founded" (*Gerry Fitt, Political Chameleon*, p.275).

He claimed that republicans had gained greater influence in the SDLP: "I have noticed that in the absence of a political initiative being taken, there is a strong republican element emerging in the ranks of the SDLP ...", and went on to repudiate nationalism: "Nationalism has been a political concept in Ireland over many, many years but I suggest that it has never brought peace to the people of the six counties. I for one have never been a nationalist to the total exclusion of my socialist ideals" (BT, 22.11.79).

Fitt gave a bizarre interview to Michael Murphy about the final meeting with his SDLP *nemeses* in Dungannon in which he seems to have had a "*St Paul on the road to Damascus*" moment:

> "'Soon as I walked in Seamus Mallon was glaring at me and two or three others. The rural elements were glaring at me'. Fitt claims that he told the gathering that he denied that he had relinquished the Irish dimension stressing that what he believed was important 'was to try and get something going within Northern Ireland so that we could learn to live together'... 'Then I sat back. I will never forget it. I looked around and looked at them one by one. I thought he's a Derry Taig. He's not bad and he's not mad but his idea is a united Ireland and he wants to aspire to it even though he is never going to get it and if he got it tomorrow he wouldn't want it. He just doesn't see things the way I see it. And I continued going around them. There was Seamus Mallon 'sure he is a half Provo'. And I went around them all and I thought there is none of them really bad people but they are all green nationalists and I am like a nigger in a woodpile. I shouldn't be in this party at all because I don't think I'm a bad bastard either. We are never going to see eye to eye" (*Gerry Fitt, Political Chameleon*, pp. 280-1).

It might be said that Fitt was confronted by his past at Dungannon and didn't like what he saw. Perhaps he only wanted to see himself in a mirror and not in the party he led. By condemning his party he was really condemning himself. And so he left his party and took himself off to British politics at last, in the House of Lords.

It is sometimes suggested that there was a basic contradiction in impulses within the SDLP between the nationalist "*countrymen*" and the "*socialist*" Fitt and Devlin. But the contradiction in impulses was not between two wings of the party: it was within Fitt and Devlin themselves, from the beginning. So, when Fitt saw the "*countrymen*", he was actually looking at the other side of himself, which he had come increasingly to dislike the more he experienced the men he had always threatened the Unionists with.

The SDLP under Hume

The SDLP had been falling apart under Fitt and it was much more appropriately led by Hume. Hume had not played on Republican sentiment in the 1960s in the same way that Fitt had and had advocated a much more distinct approach which seemed to reject the *continuum* between 'Constitutional' and unConstitutional Nationalism. But he seems to have resigned himself to the *continuum* in the early 1970s after events convinced him that there was no other way and he began to think of ways in which the relationship could progress in its common objective more fruitfully. The SDLP's new strategy began to evolve under Hume even before he had taken the helm from Fitt.

Hume devised a position that involved an intricate juggling of words and which was articulated in a form that became known as *'Humespeak'*. It involved not quite saying something but being heard by some people as if one thing was being said whilst others heard something else as being said. To attempt to analyse this would be a pursuit that the present writer has no wish to engage in—knowing the mental contortions this would bring. But what was much more important was what Hume did.

In 1977 Hume decided that a fundamental shift was needed to alter the situation in 'Northern Ireland' and rejuvenate 'Constitutional' Nationalism to play its part. He did this in a policy document called *'Facing Reality'*, in which he diagnosed the problem as being intransigent Unionism and the inaction of the British Government. Hume reckoned that the problem needed to be taken out of the purely British context by reintroducing the Irish Government into the political process and getting London and Dublin to work together to advance a political settlement in 'Northern Ireland', despite the Unionists. The objective was to get the British and Irish Governments to impose new political structures over the heads of Unionism to create a whole new ball-game. This was sometimes referred to as *"the totality of relationships"*.

Hume removed the focus from trying to achieve an internal settlement with Unionists who were determined to hang on to their majority in a new sub-government. Along with this, Hume went to the US and to Europe, to cultivate relationships with important people that could be employed in the future against Britain and the Unionists. Particularly important here were the links developed with Irish America. This was an important characteristic that Hume shared with the Republicans—the ability to open up new Fronts when progress on the battlefield was halted by Unionist or British resistance. It was something which the rest of the SDLP, including the previous leadership, lacked. It meant that, when Fitt was blocked, all that remained was to for the SDLP to ask for less the next time.

Hume first indicated his strategy in a speech he made in Waterville, Co. Kerry in September 1979, when Fitt was still Leader. He said that:

"London... exercises a frayed somewhat reluctant sovereignty in Northern Ireland while Dublin maintains a frayed and somewhat reluctant claim to sovereignty. Events cry out for joint decisive action and underline the Republic's essential role in helping to solve the Northern Ireland problem. There will be no progress until that need is publicly acknowledged in both capitals... The British government should acknowledge that the basis of their policy is unworkable... The basis of that policy is, in fact, an unconditional guarantee of support to one section of the community, the Unionists, at the expense of the other. This has ensured both the alienation of the minority and the unwillingness, indeed, inability, of Unionist political leaders to have any meaningful dialogue with anyone about the problem... The time has come for a positive and decisive initiative. It must be taken by both governments acting together. They should firstly make it clear that there are no longer any unconditional guarantees for any section of the Northern community. There is only a commitment to achieve a situation in which there are guarantees for all. Secondly they should make it clear that there is in fact no solution but only a process that leads to a solution. They should declare themselves committed to such a process, a process of integration of the differing traditions of the islands, a process designed to lead to an agreed Ireland with positive roles for all" (IN 24.9.79).

Hume took much criticism from Unionists for advocating this strategy. Prof. Bew and Prof. Patterson accused him of producing—

"superficially new and attractive versions of what were in fact traditional nationalist notions. This is the significance of his ponderous adumbration of a third way between the status quo and a demand for a declaration of intent— the notion of an agreed Ireland" (*The British State in Northern Ireland*, p.99).

But what else could Hume do for 'Constitutional Nationalism' in the circumstances? The Unionists would only consent to a return to majority rule. The British were only prepared to offer rolling devolution, which would only roll in one way, if it rolled at all. And all the time the British were simply determined to Ulsterise and normalise the conflict in order to manage it safely away from the British island. In any case, the success of Hume's strategy was not in his own hands. The British were not to be convinced of the brilliance of it as a solution to the conflict until unconstitutional Nationalism impressed it upon them as an alternative to more worrying developments.

Hume's strategy was successful because it took things outside the 1920 Act, employing forces that were beyond the confines of 'Northern Ireland' to which Northern Catholics were supposed to be confined, including America. Fitt's British horizons were inadequate to a breakout, due to Westminster's insistence that 'Northern Ireland' remain in political quarantine.

The other important result of this strategy was to elevate Hume into the role of *'statesman'*—the first 'statesman' without an actual state to represent.

What this did was inject a new vigour into Irish diplomacy in relation to the North, led by Hume, which the diplomats and political representatives of the actual Irish State were forced to follow. And this had an important result with regard to the relationship between the two parts of the Irish Nation in that, as Dublin lost its vigour with relation to the North, it was taken up by Hume, determined that the Northern Catholics would not be let down as they had been in the previous decades by the South.

Hume rejected the Labour orientation of the SDLP under Fitt. In October 1980, after returning from Washington, he told an audience of the Marketing Institute in Dublin that he welcomed the victory of Mrs. Thatcher:

> "I have always believed that a strong Tory Government offered the best opportunity of a solution to the Irish problem if they have the courage to grasp the nettle... We must re-examine our past attitudes and recognise that there should be no 'sacred cows' in our approach to a solution to the Northern Ireland problem... We should have the self-confidence to look at a situation without having to hide behind attitudes of past leaders" (Cork Examiner, 4.10.80).

Hume was signalling that Irish Nationalism was prepared to work with the Tories in order to settle the *"Irish problem"* after the Labour man, Fitt, had taken down a socialist Government to let in Mrs. Thatcher. Four years later Hume's faith in the Tories was rewarded with the Hillsborough Treaty.

The Provos Squeezed

There was little help from the South for Northern Nationalists. In 1976, Desmond Boal, who founded the DUP with Paisley, was involved in clandestine talks in secret locations, between Republicans and Loyalists which explored whether any common ground could be found within Sinn Fein's *Eire Nua* plan for a federal Ireland. Boal represented the Loyalist viewpoint, while Sean MacBride the Republican one. Boal apparently suggested the establishment of a Federal Irish Parliament that would assume the powers formerly reserved at Westminster, with a provincial Parliament based on the Six Counties (rather than the 9 Ulster Counties of *Eire Nua*) which would hold the powers previously exercised at Stormont. But the talks crumbled after Irish Government Minister Conor Cruise O'Brien exposed and condemned them on radio, blowing the cover of the Loyalist participants who had insisted on confidentiality in their attendance.

After the breakdown of the Truce between the British and the IRA, Dublin decided to introduce a range of emergency laws designed to curb Republican activity. That was the only solution it had to the problem of 'Northern Ireland'. The *Criminal Law Act* in September 1976 increased the sentences which the Special Criminal Court could impose for membership of an unlawful organisation. It increased penalties for other offences covered by the *Offences against the State Act* and gave the Irish Army the right to arrest and detain suspects. The *Emergency Powers Act* in October permitted the Gardai to detain suspects without charge or reference to court for seven days on the word of a Superintendent. The *Broadcasting Authority Amendment Act* allowed the Minister to prevent broadcasts that might *'undermine the state'*. Sinn Fein and IRA members were banned from speaking on RTE. The *Criminal Law Jurisdiction Act* allowed for the trial of Republicans in the South for offences committed in the North.

It was now thought expedient to completely distance the Southern political establishment from Republicanism. *Section 31* of the Broadcasting Act had the effect of censoring National culture in an attempt to prevent the contamination of the Nation and mass production of Provos—when the assembly line was actually elsewhere, in the North. These measures had much more detrimental effects on the Southern State in disorientating its independence of mind than any they had on the Provos, who scored something of a propaganda coup for years around Section 31.

In the North the Peace People emerged to oppose the Insurrection. The Peace People were an impressive development but failed because they could not affect the actual conditions which generated the Insurrection. These peace movements arose out of a general war-weariness in the community. They were bolstered by a media that made them world famous for a short time. But, by the time they had collected their Nobel Prizes, they were past their sell-by date, not being able to overcome the conflict inherent within the 'Northern Ireland' system. The Peace movement had little chance of undermining the IRA because it lacked political purpose and could not provide the Catholic community with a long-term political alternative development to Republicanism. The Catholic community would not desert the Provisionals, despite intense moral propaganda directed toward them, because this would have been a victory for Unionism and Unionism was not a feasible alternative to Republicanism for Catholics. The Peace People could be easily portrayed as simply a tool of the British Government and the Unionists to subdue Catholics, offering them simply defeat, and a pre-1969 situation.

The Catholic community was not a passive community which could simply be neutralised by feelings of emotion disconnected from political context. The favourite Republican term of the Provos for the Peace People was the *'Peace at any Price Brigade'* and they were countered with the slogan *'Peace with Justice'*. The Provos knew well that Catholics would not accept unconditional surrender as an alternative to their campaign, however much it was dressed up in goodness and light. Because the Insurrection had a popular character, it had to be persisted with until the popular requirements for a settlement were met.

The Long War

By the latter part of the decade the Republican War had reached a low ebb. Mason had brought a degree of stability to the situation after the mayhem of the Rees period. He began applying steady physical pressure on the IRA and the number of convictions doubled from that of 1975. The level of self-incrimination, with Volunteers being broken under interrogation, reached particularly high levels. This was partly because of the '*truceliers*' that had been admitted into the IRA ranks during the Ceasefire. These volunteers, having little experience of active service, and having only operated within British tolerance, were careless about security and easily broken by strong interrogation methods.

From being on the offensive and proclaiming '*The Year of Victory*' again, the Republican slogan became the more defensive, '*Stone Mason' Will Not Break Us*". A document captured by Gardai in 1978 admitted that the IRA was being gradually beaten and indicated that a thorough reorganisation on cellular lines under a new Northern Command was necessary to insulate it for a Long War of attrition.

The Long War was an expression of weakness—since why would the IRA fight a long war when a short one would do? However, the Provos realised, as Tommy McKearney noted: "that the British Government would" have to "be convinced that armed Irish Republicanism was not a passing phase, but something that would stubbornly fight until satisfied" (*The Provisional IRA, From Insurrection to Parliamen*t, p. 141).

Under pressure from Mason, the Republican Army suffered a brief political disorientation during 1977 when it carried out some operations more reminiscent of continental left-wing terrorism. The kidnapping and killing of businessmen and talk of 'class war' was not popular with the Catholic community and it was quickly abandoned. However, it was from this position of weakness that the captured part of the Republican Army rejuvenated the Republican struggle and brought a new momentum to politics in the North.

The British Labour Government had presumed that it could slowly neutralise the IRA simply through vigorous security measures, bringing back the appearance of normality to the province and Ulsterising the conflict. Within such a situation IRA activity would be gradually made negligible and ineffective. That policy seemed to be working by 1977. But in response the IRA did something which was very British in character. It successfully began a process of reorganisation, digging in for a Long War of attrition. A leaner fighting force was constructed, with a developing capacity to strike the British State in its more vulnerable areas. When British forces got on top of them in certain areas, the War was taken successfully to other fields. At the same time the former internees were advising that a highly effective and durable political machine and support base should be constructed out of the necessity for a protracted struggle. Republicans had to prove they were there for the long haul politically as well as militarily.

In 1977 Jimmy Drumm dropped a bombshell at Bodenstown when he gave formal recognition that the War was not being won by the Provos. It was acknowledged that the British Government had strung them along over withdrawal and there was no economic disengagement, only the effects of capitalist recession. Once Drumm had spoken, the end of the War was in sight, although that was not apparent initially. There was little doubt that the Army Council had countenanced the Bodenstown Address and it had fundamental consequences for the War. From then on the problem was how to end the War in a functional settlement. If the British Government did not facilitate an ending of the War on reasonable terms, it would undoubtedly have to be prolonged until it did, and it would have to be enhanced with politics to make up for the declining military position. These understandings began to gestate both in the mind of the Provos and in that of the enemy command.

The Criminalisation Policy

However, the British continued to pursue a victory over the Insurrection. Alongside the policy of Ulsterisation came parallel strategies of Normalisation and Criminalisation to achieve this.

Rees had ended Special Category Status for politically motivated prisoners in 1976. For prisoners convicted of political offences after this, there was to be no special treatment and they would be treated like normal criminals and held in cells rather than the Internment compounds, as Long Kesh gave way to the H-Blocks. Rees described the security problem during 1976 in the House of Commons as involving simply "small groups of criminals". His reasoning was that, as the IRA was involved in breaking the law, its members should be given no special treatment which provided them with legitimacy. Rees used the change of character in the conflict to justify this alteration. However, the change of emphasis towards sectarian conflict which had occurred during 1975 was a direct consequence of political manipulation by a British Government seeking to Ulsterise the violence by fostering an Ulster nationalist mentality among the Loyalists, by persuading them that they should stop relying on Britain and begin to fight for themselves as a separate ethnicity since British withdrawal was on the cards.

Republicans had a strong case against the ending of Special Category Status. The IRA was clearly not criminal or criminally-motivated. The Provos undoubtedly broke the law but the conflict which had resulted in the previous six years was certainly not the result of a spontaneous crime wave amongst the Catholic community. It was not, therefore, surprising that the Provisionals should consider the issue of Special Category Status as a point of principle and begin to protest against its removal by refusing to wear prison clothes.

With the prison issue, the British provided a new battlefield for the Provos when they were losing ground on the previous one. Another Front was opened by the Republicans within the prisons and this had the effect of rejuvenating the struggle overall. For a start it rekindled the tactic of street protest that the British Army had succeeded in neutralizing after the Derry massacre.

The Provos had great powers of improvisation. After being hard pressed by Mason to the extent that some even considered calling off the War, they began regrouping in Long Kesh. This was used as a time to think about the situation and to plan for the future. The Long War strategy was conceived, but also the understanding that the military campaign might not always be sustainable. In both these circumstances Republican political struggle needed to be enhanced as a substitute for War and as a replacement for it over the long term.

Sir John Chilcott has claimed that the criminalisation policy and "the great shift" of Ulsterisation was meant as a political device to separate Dublin from the Provos and a lever to politicise the Republican movement:

> "That was profoundly resented by Sinn Fein, but that resentment could not be shared by Irish governments, of whatever colour, so in that sense they were in the same position as we were. But did it have a catalytic effect in arousing in the minds of the republican movement a wish to confront, contradict or at any rate move out of the position where they could be accused of being pure criminals to something more principled? That was part of the engineering" (*The British and Peace in Northern Ireland*, p.95).

It is clear from this that Britain did not believe its own propaganda on criminalisation. It was a political device all along.

The Year of Hunger Strikes

The H-Block campaign began with the blanket protest and then the dirty protest with the setting up of committees and marches to support it. Initially support was confined to Republicans and their immediate community and the campaign was largely ineffective. The Republican position seems to have been that support for the Republican prison protests had to be on the basis of support for the Republican military campaign itself, and the H-

Block campaign "should not be side-tracked into seeing the prisoners as a civil rights issue" (*An Phoblacht*, 10.12.77).

At an "*Anti-Repression*" Conference held in Coalisland in January 1978, Bernadette McAliskey said that the Catholic community had become passive with regard to the Anti-Partition struggle and it could be made active again only by enlisting the support of the Church, Fianna Fail and the SDLP in the prison struggle. The Provos were highly suspicious of these calls by left-wingers for a "*Broad Front*" and rejected them as attempts to "turn the clock back" to the Civil Rights days (*Republican News*, 4.2.78).

It was clerical interventions that provided the much needed boost to the H-Block campaign and stirred the Provos out of the doctrinaire position they had adopted. The Primate of Ireland, Cardinal O'Fiaich, made a visit to the H-Blocks and compared conditions to the "sewers of Calcutta". This phrase, thereafter, became a popular slogan in the campaign. Fr. Faul of Dungannon also advised the Provos to stop the military campaign to increase sympathy for the prisoners. He then wrote '*H-Block*', the most popular and well-publicised pamphlet on "the horrific conditions" in Long Kesh, with Fr. Murray.

When O'Fiaich had been nominated to the See of Armagh in succession to Cardinal Conway, there was consternation within the British Establishment which had spent much time and effort cultivating the Irish Hierarchy. The British Foreign Office made representations to the Vatican to prevent the appointment. A *Sunday Times* article by Muriel Bowen quoted an unnamed Irish Senator as criticising the "appalling choice" of the Cullyhanna Cardinal. The new Cardinal was "steeped in nationalist sentiment and constantly goes back to Crossmaglen where violence is ever present and Gaelic culture matters" according to the *Sunday Times*. (Tim Pat Coogan, *A Memoir*, p.314 and p.163).

The problem Britain had with the Cardinal (or *Sagart Mór*, as the prisoners called him) was that he had a strong sense of history and culture when England was painstakingly eroding these among the Irish political and academic Establishment. In disposition O'Fiaich was an easy-going liberal Catholic in contrast to his conservative predecessor from Belfast.

Even though the clerical interventions gave a boost to the H Block campaign, the Provos initially resisted broadening the campaign. Then, in both the British General Election and the European Elections of 1979, a number of pro-prisoner candidates performed very well against the SDLP— with the Irish Independence Party defeating Austin Currie in Fermanagh/ South Tyrone to take the Westminster seat. Even though Sinn Fein called for a boycott, Catholic voters showed their enthusiasm to vote for an alternative to "Constitutional Nationalism".

So a decision was taken to call a conference and to broaden the campaign to enlist wider support. A committee was formed chaired by a Catholic priest and containing Bernadette McAliskey. The military campaign was then subordinated to the prison campaign. In many ways this represented the point at which the future direction of Republican strategy was settled.

After a Conference in the Green Briar in Andersonstown Sinn Fein formulated the Five Demands which they believed could be supported on humanitarian grounds by the wider population. This strategy was successful at first at highlighting the issue but it made no impression on the British Government. So the prisoners themselves decided to take things into their own hands by organising a Hunger Strike for the Five Demands.

A Hunger Strike was a high risk strategy. It could result in two negative outcomes. Firstly, the prisoners might not be able to see it through to the end which would result in a British victory and immense damage to the Republican struggle. Secondly, it might result in deaths and then end in disarray as other prisoners came off the protest before their demands were met. This would also damage the Republican movement and severely harm its morale. This is probably the calculation that the Thatcher Government made when it decided to push the issue to the limit during the year of Hunger Strikes, 1980-1.

The first Hunger Strike began in late 1980 and involved about three dozen prisoners on a fast. After about a month a half, Humphrey Atkins made a statement in the House of Commons saying that, if the Hunger Strike was called off, some things might be conceded. A note was to be delivered to the prisoners that, as a priest assured them, met the substance of their Five Demands. As one of the prisoners was on the verge of death, Brendan Hughes, the Officer Commanding the prisoners, unilaterally called off the fast, having promised to do so in that event. Republicans organised a victory march in West Belfast but soon found they could not rely on the Atkins Statement. The offer in the note did not meet the main demand for the right of prisoners to wear their own clothes.

Thatcher could have defused the Hunger Strike situation by making tangible concessions after the Atkins Statement at this point, but she chose not to. She claimed victory and said that the Provos had deceived themselves into calling off the fast. It thus became clear that, if the issue was settled without concrete action on the part of the British, it would represent a Republican defeat and help the British to criminalise the struggle.

Therefore, a new Hunger Strike was started by Bobby Sands in the New Year into which prisoners entered on a staggered basis. This would maximise pressure on the British by not having all the hunger strikers dying at one time. Sands, who immediately took the dropping of the First Hunger Strike as a defeat, had a resolute will over the issue and he was determined to see the contest with Thatcher through to the end this time. Sands calculated that the Provos had to demonstrate that they were as resolute and steadfast as the British and this was a very important understanding that stayed with Republicans into the next phase of the struggle.

Some way through the Hunger Strike the Provos were presented with a stroke of luck when Frank Maguire, the Independent Nationalist MP for Fermanagh/South Tyrone, died suddenly. Austin Currie attempted to enter the contest for the seat, as he had against Maguire in 1979, but the MP's brother, Noel, indicated that he was putting himself forward. The local community would not stand for a split Catholic vote under the circumstances. Hume supported Maguire's candidacy, but other senior SDLP figures like Currie, Joe Hendron, Sean Farren and Paddy O'Hanlon, wished to contest the seat.

Currie put himself on stand-by in case Republican pressure got to Maguire and he pulled out. But Maguire waited until less than an hour before nominations closed before resigning, to prevent the SDLP stepping in, and thus gave Bobby Sands a clear run against the Unionist. The local SDLP Council Chairman then signed Sands' Nomination Papers.

Sands won a tight victory over the Unionist candidate. This had a great propaganda effect on the campaign and it drew in wider support from the Catholic Church, Hume, and Charles Haughey for a settlement to be reached. It also dealt a great moral blow against the criminalisation policy. If 30,000 voters went to the polls for a candidate and elected him MP, he was hardly a common criminal. Sinn Fein also learnt its electoral trade in the contest. It came to Fermanagh/Tyrone without experience but learnt very quickly about marshalling a vote. However, Mrs. Thatcher remained unimpressed and Sands died along with nine other Republican prisoners before the Hunger Strike was called to a halt.

Triumph of Failure

In formal terms the Hunger Strike represented a victory for Mrs. Thatcher. She believed that, if concessions were made after the Hunger Strike was abandoned, it would give little satisfaction to the Provisionals. Only under circumstances that the British Government was seen to make concessions under duress by the IRA would Republicans be satisfied and be able to claim victory. She was determined that this would not happen and that the Provos were not to be let off the hook. It began to be clear that, if the Hunger Strikers continued, they would simply die. There were no circumstances under which the British Government was going to grant political status and, only if the Hunger Strike was ended, were some concessions to be given.

However, Mrs. Thatcher had a rather narrow conception of the world and a poor knowledge of history and underestimated the Republican powers of improvisation in adversity. The Hunger Strike ended in a fairly orderly manner, with some relatives withdrawing their sons from certain death. The Catholic Church also helped to organise the retreat from the Strike, with the result that, although the Five Demands were not achieved before the calling off of the Strike, and were only achieved partially after it had ended, the fast to the death demonstrated that the Republican struggle was not a criminal enterprise. After all, criminals do not usually engage in Hunger Strikes, become elected as MPs, bring large numbers of supporters onto the streets in their cause, and carry their protest through to the bitter end, in the way Republicans were able to do. Therefore, the Republican Hunger Strike shattered the misguided policy of the British Government of attempting to criminalise the Republican War.

The Long War was in a stalemate situation. The British Military and Intelligence agencies had deployed every trick in their book to defeat the insurgency. Limits set by Downing Street on the numbers of troops allocated to fighting the Provos were constantly raised until the republicans were confronted with around 50,000 police and military (the figure varying between 40,000 and 60,000 in 1994-7 according to circumstances), in addition to the paramilitary patsies in the Loyalist militias.

It was becoming clear that neither side could expect an outright victory. But, if the British authorities could see no prospect of a clear win, neither could the Provisional leaders—who had come to realise that the Protestant obstacle to a United Ireland was as serious as the determination of a British Government which could not countenance a military defeat and the loss of around 17% of its territory, not to speak of the lever on the South represented by the existence of 'Northern Ireland'.

The new Provo tactic of mobilising the Catholic community politically in support of the military campaign presented the way out of this impasse.

As the electoral strength of the Provos grew, it became possible for a deal to be made on the political level which could not be made on the military level.

The 1981 Hunger Strike resulted in a rejuvenation of the Republican struggle. Military activity had declined to an all-time low and there was also the problem of 'supergrasses', informants at a high level, emerging within the ranks as a consequence of the Long War that was being fought. However, the prison struggle, and particularly the use of electoral politics to further it, gave the Provisionals a taste of success and an opportunity to fight the struggle on a new Front that would not just be the temporary prison Front. This electoral Front would make up for the comparative weakness in the military campaign by engaging the Catholic population in political activity and putting pressure on the British Government in a new way. It represented the chance to transfer the momentum of the War into an alternative politics—not just to the SDLP.

Bobby Sands' seat was retained by Owen Carron, another Republican candidate, and the Republican movement began to develop Sinn Fein as a serious electoral force. This was *'war by other means'*, as Sinn Fein looked on the electoral process as an alternative to raising their military profile.

A controversy has emerged over an account of a British offer to settle the Hunger Strike, given by Richard O'Rawe, a public relations officer for the IRA prisoners at the time. O'Rawe claimed in a 2005 book that a British proposal to resolve the Hunger Strike after the first four deaths was accepted by the prisoners' leader, Brendan MacFarlane, but rejected after an intervention from Gerry Adams (IN 22.10.09). The offer was made secretly by the British to an intermediary known as 'Mountain Climber', and involved a statement from the British Secretary of State to be released in the event of the Hunger Strike ending. O'Rawe claimed that Adams kept this offer secret from the Hunger Strikers. This account was denied by Danny Morrison, Brendan MacFarlane, and Adams himself (IN 12.10.09, IN 6.11.10).

There were some in the Republican movement who wanted war to the bitter end, regardless of the probable outcome of such a policy. It was: *United Ireland or Nothing*. Because Adams averted the probable result of a purely military policy—the Republican movement being beaten into the ground—and found a way to transfer the momentum of the military into a political struggle without conceding that the War was anything but just, he was regarded as a traitor from the purely militarist standpoint.

O'Rawe's allegations that Adams sacrificed the lives of hunger-strikers in order to ensure that Owen Carron held the seat that had been won by Bobby Sands, and thus maintain the political impetus started by Sands, is a conspiracy theory inspired by obvious resentment. It was not subjected to much scrutiny before being taken up by influential elements in both the British and Irish states and being broadcast as an established fact.

The British may have been forced into making a deal with Republicans, but that has not precluded them from trying to row back from it in every way possible and to discredit those with whom they were forced to negotiate a peace.

As a conspiracy theory, Rawe's construct lacks plausibility, and plausibility is the nearest it could come to proof.

In the situation as it existed, a substantial increase in military resources was not to be looked for. The dual strategy of moral/political pressure plus military action had been launched by Bobby Sands. The *Armalite and Ballot Box* strategy had already begun. And the rumour that Mrs. Thatcher, despite her publicly intransigent stance against the prisoners' demands, had decided behind the scenes to concede them and that a definite offer meeting the demands had been transmitted to the Republican leadership but had been suppressed by them, has never been confirmed. There is every reason to suppose that all that was being done on the Government side was to attempt a repeat of its achievement of deflating morale in the first Hunger Strike.

Eamon Phoenix, reviewing released Government documents from 1981, described discussions on the issue between the Provo intermediary, 'Mountain

Climber' and the British Cabinet. These exploratory talks did not result in a firm offer from the British. Phoenix concludes:

> "These documents show that the prospects of an early 'deal' to end the hunger strike evaporated over that July weekend.
> "The British never actually formulated their final statement while concessions were strongly opposed by senior NIO Ministers, led by Humphrey Atkins.
> "This seems to contradict former H-Block prisoner, Richard O'Rawe's claims in his book of a clear British offer around 5 July..." (BBC Website, 30.12.2011).

As for the suggestion that the prisoners were not told of the offer, Dr. Phoenix reports: "The British government subsequently agreed to a request to permit a Provisional representative into the Maze".

It might be added that, if the British Government was serious about ending the Hunger Strike, they could simply have made a direct approach to the prisoners, or there were plenty of neutral intermediaries they could have chosen to transmit their offer. The clear position of the Republican movement at the time of the Hunger Strikes was that the prisoners themselves had the final say over the conduct of the Hunger Strike campaign and the way it was to be ended. It was not up to the outside leadership.

The evidence suggests that a British offer was being considered by Mac Farlane and Adams but it did not meet enough of the prisoners' demands to make it acceptable. Negotiations were ongoing to get the British to clarify their offer and increase it, but then Joe McDonnell died, earlier than expected, and the talks broke off. No definitive concessions meeting prisoners' demands were on offer at the time.

The O'Rawe allegations against Adams, serialized in the *Sunday Times*, were taken up enthusiastically by the die-hard opponents of the 1998 deal. They extrapolated the incident into a full-blown theory of the Origins of the Great Betrayal, arguing that the proposals were rejected for electoral advantage. The suggestion is that the British proposal was declined and the Hunger Strike carried on so that Owen Carron would be unopposed by the SDLP for Sands' seat, thereby ensuring electoral victory and a fundamental Republican change in strategy. The future direction of Sinn Fein's political strategy was thus laid out because, if Sinn Fein had lost Fermanagh-South Tyrone, the blow to Republican morale would have been severe and support for electoral politics fatally damaged. But Carron's victory, according to the die-hards, strengthened the hand of those in the Republican leadership who saw electoral politics as the way ahead and from there came the undermining of the armed struggle and the subsequent Peace Process.

This conspiracy theory tends to ignore the political context of the new strategic direction of Republican strategy. A major escalation of the War was not on the cards. But a substantial number of people could be got out to vote and every vote helped to boost the impact of military activity by putting an electoral mandate from the community behind it. This was the '*Armalite and Ballot Box*' strategy.

Rise of Sinn Fein

One of the strangest things the British Government did at this time was their attempt to erect a new Stormont. The Prior Assembly was always going to be a powerless institution but it was very much a Protestant institution. After the SDLP decided to stay away, it bore a passing resemblance to Stormont in its latter days, from July 1971. Of course it was a shadow of the old Stormont. But shadows have a tendency to remind people of the substance, particularly in 'Northern Ireland'.

Sinn Fein represented the Prior Assembly as an embryonic form of the old Unionist Government and used the very effective slogan of "*Smash Stormont*" in the election campaign to get 10 per cent of the vote and a launching pad for future success at the polls. There was no more effective instrument designed to work up support in the Catholic community for Sinn Fein than the threat of a new Unionist parliament. So the British provided a very generous gift in restoring Republican morale after the Hunger Strike and an opportunity that Sinn Fein was determined not to let go by.

The effects were almost immediate. In the 1982 Election to Prior's Assembly Gerry Adams topped the poll in West Belfast and Sinn Fein representatives got a credible 10% of the total vote (to the SDLP's 18%). More important, Sinn Fein's entry into electoral politics wrong-footed the SDLP and forced it into a boycott of the new Stormont. Sinn Fein, the SDLP and the Irish Independence Party therefore scuppered the Thatcher/Atkins attempt at an internal settlement. Furthermore, Haughey came back to power at just the right time (March 1982) to prevent the former Taoiseach, Garret Fitzgerald, from breaking the Nationalist consensus in the North and encouraging the SDLP into Prior's Assembly.

This was an important development because it meant that the British Government could no longer rely on the SDLP to make up the numbers in any political initiative they might launch. The SDLP would be looking over their shoulder at what the Republicans were doing—only this time it was the spectre of Republicans taking over the traditional business of 'Constitutional Nationalism' in representing the Catholic community that they were worried about rather than a military campaign.

In many ways this was of greater concern to the SDLP since the military campaign of the Provos was in the past a means of gaining concessions from the British Government. The Provo electoral manifestation raised the prospect of the SDLP being put out of business altogether.

The *Irish News* called the Sinn Fein performance

> "the most significant poll in Northern Ireland's turbulent history" and "a clear unequivocal demand from the nationalist people of the north to the government—change your Irish policy: only an all Ireland solution will work." (22.10.82)

This comment demonstrated the *continuum* that exists within Nationalist politics in which the newspaper of the 'Constitutional Nationalists' could easily utilise support for the unconstitutional Nationalists to argue for the common objective. It would not be too long before increasing numbers of the Catholic community began to see the same thing. An interview with Danny Morrison around this time revealed that this was also increasingly the understanding within the Sinn Fein leadership. Morrison told Padraig O'Malley:

> "SDLP supporters in the North support the IRA. The nationalist community are fairly sophisticated, and they are betting on two horses. The SDLP may improve their position through political talks which we call collaboration, and the IRA could end up bringing about the defeat of the people who harass and oppress them. So they support both sides. If the SDLP were to lose an election to Sinn Fein, that would be the end of them. They are there solely for the purpose of constitutionalism, of collaboration..." (Uncivil Wars, pp.276-7)

Parting of the Ways

The British General Election of 1983 was another success for the new Sinn Fein. Adams won the Westminster Gerry Fitt's seat against the SDLP candidate, Dr. Joe Hendron, and Sinn Fein increased its share of the vote to 13%. The Northern electoral successes led to the final replacement of O Bradaigh as President and O'Connell also resigned as Vice President, signalling the end of the Anti-Treaty curb on the new Sinn Fein. In 1986 the Northern Leadership pushed through an end to the historic Republican principle of Abstentionism to Dáil Éireann. This showed in the clearest possible manner that the reconstructed Republicanism of the Provisionals was a product of conditions of life in the Northern statelet rather than an extension of Second Dáil Anti-Treaty Republicanism.

The parting of the ways between the original Southern Anti-Treaty leadership of the Provisionals who had mounted a small invasion of the Six Counties in the fifties and the new generation of Northerners who were currently fighting the Republican War was evident in an encounter in February 1982 between the Sinn Fein President, Ruairi O Bradaigh and

Martin McGuinness from Derry. It came after the Sinn Fein Ard Chomhairle had made a decision to contest the Southern General Election in a limited number of constituencies and O Bradaigh had sought to block the decision by encouraging local cumann not to co-operate in the election. McGuinness confronted O Bradaigh but the Sinn Fein President still refused to implement the Ard Chomhairle decision:

> "McGuinness, upset, immediately attacked him with, 'Who do you think you are, refusing to represent the people? Do you think you are back in 1922, or what?' O'Bradaigh was shocked, as much by the comment about 1922 as by the attack. The comment was, for him, counter to the basis of Republicanism and the principled stand against the Treaty and its outcomes from 1922. He replied, 'This is Free State talk.' No one else said anything and their silence spoke volumes; they supported McGuinness and possibly the recognition of Leinster House" (Robert W. White, *'Ruairi O'Bradaigh, The Life and Politics of an Irish Revolutionary*, p. 285).

It was apparent in this encounter that the Provisionals consisted of two elements thrown together by the events of August 1969. The Anti-Treatyite element, led by O Bradaigh, was the incorruptible rump of Sinn Fein. But the Northern substance that it had allied with a decade earlier was of a very different character indeed. The bulk of the membership of the new Republican Army were people who had taken no part in Republican affairs before the Unionist assault on nationalist West Belfast and Derry in August 1969 and they were very representative of the community they sprang from.

Both Southern Anti-Treatyites and Northerners had a disparaging attitude toward 'the Free State'. But they had a fundamentally different appreciation of what 'the Free State' was. To the Northerners it was the *nearly state* that failed to encompass all of the Nation and never lived up to its pretensions. But to the Anti-Treatyites like O Bradaigh the antagonism was of a much more substantial kind. The division of 1922 was the alpha and omega and the whole point of Republican existence was to resist the embrace of the Treaty institutions which the movement, although composing fewer and fewer of the faithful, had done for 60 years.

O Bradaigh began getting the feeling by this time that the movement he led was about to go the way of all the others. In an Ard Chomhairle sub-committee discussion on electoral strategy in 1982 he lectured the Northerners with the statement:

> "A revolutionary movement either succeeds or fails badly. There is hardly an in-between position. So many things are put at risk that often failure or the possibility of failure can inveigle some participants into reformism in order to 'save something from the collapse', as it is put… A big and successful heave to topple and replace is what is needed rather than tinkering with the

existing system" (Ruairi O'Bradaigh, *'The Life and Politics of an Irish Revolutionary'*, p. 289)

But the Northerners saw the possibility of an interim settlement existing between ultimate success and failure outside of the polarised possibilities open to *"a revolutionary movement"*. This was because the new Republican Army was not fundamentally *"a revolutionary movement"*. It had developed from the conditions of life in the Six Counties and the extraordinary events of August 1969 within a community which produced a *continuum* between 'constitutional' and 'revolutionary' activity. It saw the possibility of translating the War into something else without having to salvage *"something from the collapse"*, as O Braidaigh it.

It is possible to see what was about to happen as the saving of *"something from the collapse"* in that the Republican War could not be won, due to Unionist resistance, and it was now necessary to end it for the best possible deal. But those who were plotting this course did not envisage *"the collapse"* in what they were doing. *"The collapse"* was more likely if *"a revolutionary movement"* carried on regardless of circumstance, with no regarding for the facts on the ground.

The final parting of the ways came at the 1986 Ard Fheis, an event which the present writer attended. The southern Anti-Treatyites warned that a participation in parliaments would end the armed struggle and they were to be proved correct. The Sinn Fein leadership, who said that it would not, was proved to be wrong. However, the vast bulk of the movement, most of it Northern, stayed with the leadership, which judged that the southern Anti-Treatyites were expendable for the political course ahead. This was a clear indication that the struggle would be concluded on terms that satisfied the North rather than on Republican principles.

The New Ireland Forum

The decision to establish the New Ireland Forum in 1983 was clearly related to a perceived political crisis brought about by the threat posed to the SDLP by the rise of Sinn Fein. It is noticeable that the emergence of Sinn Fein troubled Dublin much more so than it did London. Mrs. Thatcher was much more concerned by the military threat posed by the IRA. An NIO paper on Sinn Fein written in early 1984 seems to have been written to answer the Dublin's Minister of Foreign Affairs' complaints about Republican constituency work in the North and whether the British would do anything about it:

"Mr. Barry has commented at some length on Sinn Fein constituency activity. It is notable that Sinn Fein has been observing the spirit of the law... Given this background I think we would simply aggravate events if we went in with the heavy hand of the law... Essentially Sinn Fein's success depends on their positively seeking out problems as well as responding quickly to express need... Their infantry hold the ground, and do so in a way which provides a service which most of the community need. I suspect that whilst the law could fire a few 'rockets' it could not deliver the force of infantry which would be needed to take over and hold enemy territory. It is fairly easy to despair and... blame the SDLP for being insufficiently active." (CENT 1/14/18A, 3.2.84)

This refers to Sinn Fein's advance into operating the British welfare state on behalf of the community, acting as gatekeeper and lubricant in access to Benefits in many parts of the province. The abandonment of the Catholic community by Britain's sub-government over half a century, followed by the Thatcherite contentment with large scale unemployment, produced a new battlefield that was quickly occupied by Sinn Fein. With Sinn Fein's superior numbers and activism, the SDLP was incapable of competing in this new arena on behalf of HM Government. And the State itself, which was in the process of being shrunk by the Thatcherites, had no means to wrest its territory back from the invading Republican voluntary sector.

The SDLP leadership pressed the Southern Government for a helpful Constitutional initiative. The result was the *Forum Report*, which sought an alternative to Republicanism by providing a set of creative proposals on the North, from the standpoint of constitutional nationalism, by involving the mainstream nationalist parties of the South.

The New Ireland Forum was very much John Hume's project. During 1982 he projected its intention as being that of finding a way that an all-Ireland state could be realised through the consent of Unionists in the North. Its remit seemed to be an honest discussion by Nationalist Ireland about what obstacles the reality of the Southern State presented to Unionists which might be removed to make unity more amenable to them. Before the meeting of the Forum, Austin Currie had been reported by the *Irish Times* as having told the SDLP Conference, to big applause, that they would tell the South's politicians: "to put your money where your mouths have been over the years". And Currie believed the SDLP would "put it up to them" (*'All Hell will Break Loose'*, p. 332) But it was Currie who was absorbed by the South a few years later, after he went home empty handed in 1984.

If Hume's intention was something of this character, he was soon dissuaded by the Southern Establishment from pursuing a radical restructuring of the Republic to make it more attractive to Northern Protestants. And his skills of persuasion and great rhetorical powers were not employed, in the way that they had been in relation to the North, in advancing his reform project at the Forum. Even Hume was unable to gain any influence on the policy of the Southern State—like all the Northerners before him.

Haughey vetoed Hume's choice of Chairman: T.K. Whittaker, Lynch's adviser. Faced with opposition on the other side of the Border, Hume gave up on changing the South and was forced to return to his usual, more successful, activity against the Unionists in the North. The *Forum Report*, therefore, was nothing out of the ordinary within Nationalist politics. It was the usual verbal Anti-Partitionist campaign. It advanced three different possible models for a Nationalist solution to the Northern conflict, and suggested 'an Irish dimension' to the governing of 'Northern Ireland'.

Much of the argument for political change in the North by the Forum participants centred on the perceived "*alienation*" of the Catholic minority from the institutions of 'Northern Ireland'. The Nationalist argument, which was expressed widely in the press at the time, went as follows: 'the increasing votes for Sinn Fein showed that the Catholic people were losing their faith in 'Constitutional' politics. The British Government should therefore give Hume what he wanted or the Catholics would turn to Sinn Fein'. But what did Hume want? More or less, the same thing as Sinn Fein. Never mind that: if it was given to John Hume it was not a surrender to the IRA, even though it was actually being given in fear of giving it to the IRA and of Sinn Fein's electoral rise.

The Taoiseach, Garret Fitzgerald, who was a strong Anglophile, was determined to bring about something that would stem the Sinn Fein growth and transfer its supporters in the North over to the SDLP. That seems to have been his main political idea with regard to solving the 'problem' of the North. Sean Farren of the SDLP later defended Fitzgerald thus:

> "I think a democratic government had a duty to arrest the rise of Sinn Fein, given that they were very committed to the Armalite and the ballot box at the time. The danger of subversion in the South was very real... Fitzgerald claims credit for being instrumental in establishing the Forum, but the idea had come from us... Our concept of it was an exclusively Nationalist Forum and always was. We justified it by saying that Nationalist Ireland had to get its act together" (*John Hume and the SDLP*, p.134).

The Forum came about due to the threat to the electoral prospects of the SDLP and it was meant "*to arrest the rise of Sinn Fein in the North*". The idea that Republicans threatened the South militarily was nonsense.

Dublin had been in denial about 'Rome Rule' in the Republic and had camouflaged it in order to prevent giving Ulster Unionism an argument against Irish nationalism. FitzGerald decided to act upon the position of the Church in the Constitution by conceding the Unionists had a case and then attempting to do away with it—so that the objections of Ulster Unionism to a United Ireland based on the "*special*" position of the Catholic Church in the Republic's Constitution would make them more amenable to unity. That was a fruitless endeavour on FitzGerald's part. And the Unionist objection was proved a baseless debating point when Church power subsequently collapsed and the Protestants proved no more taken with the prospect of a United Ireland than they were at the height of Catholic Power. When the Republic adopted an ultra-Liberal posture by approving gay marriage in 2015, the Unionists were unimpressed at the *mea culpa*.

Unionists of all shades made this clear in 1985 at a conference in Virginia:

"When Irish politicians went on to speak of the desirability of changes toward a more pluralist society, the general unionist view was that such changes should be introduced, if at all, because they were fair, just and desirable in the existing Irish State. They would have no impact at all on the determination of the Northern majority to remain British." (PRONI CENT 3/32A, 16.1.85)

This was an eminently reasonable position but nationalism just could not believe that the unionists were so reasonable, and that the real basis of their opposition to an all-Ireland state was simply that they were a different nationality.

Many of the other presumptions about the Northern Protestants made in Dublin proved to be also illusory. It was thought that the weaker economy of the Republic deterred them from unity but, when the Celtic Tiger prosperity contrasted sharply with the collapsed industrial base of the North, they showed no more inclination to join the South. When welfare and pension payments in the Republic became much more generous than those of the UK, there was no increase in enthusiasm for Dublin rule among the Protestant working class. When agricultural subsidy became much more attractive in the South than in the North, there was no movement involving Unionist farmers for Irish unity. And when the Republic began commemorating the Great War and flagellating itself over 1641 or Scullabogue, there was still no lessening in Unionist resistance to a United Ireland.

All Fitzgerald's liberalism washed over the Ulster Protestants like waves on a shore and they remained, as always, determined to resist the Dublin embrace. If anything, they saw it all as justification for their stubborn resistance, since they had now won the war in the mind of the enemy command, which had suffered moral collapse from its former certainties of existence. What made England impressive as a nation was the way it followed its own impulses without concern for others. By contrast, Dublin's concern seemed to be with how it was viewed in England and whether it measured up to British notions of Progress. And the Unionists were greatly pleased when Thatcher gave the Republic a public slap in the face whilst rejecting the Forum's proposals with "*Out! Out! Out!*"

The Forum suggested three Nationalist solutions to the issue of 'Northern Ireland'—Irish unity; a federal Irish state, or joint authority over the Six Counties between Britain and Ireland. Its preferred option was Irish unity, which meant that, after all the palaver, 'constitutional' Nationalism agreed with Sinn Fein all along! And the only criticism Sinn Fein had of the Forum was that it was all much ado about nothing, with no action being taken on the basis of it.

The Forum Rebuffed

While the Forum went about its open work, secret talks went on in parallel between Dermot Nally, representing the Taoiseach, and the British led by Cabinet Secretary Sir Robert Armstrong. Hume was kept in the picture at all times about discussions.

However, the Forum was infamously dismissed by Mrs. Thatcher with the words "Out, Out, Out" in relation to its three proposals for a solution at a press conference on 19th November 1984. The manner of the rejection by Mrs. Thatcher represented a public humiliation for Fitzgerald and explicitly exposed the limitations of 'Constitutional Nationalism'. This humiliation of Constitutional Nationalism was described in a memorable editorial in the *Irish Press*, *'Out! Out! Out! Damn Forum'*:

"... constitutional nationalism fell flat on its face in the wake of one of the most unnecessary and unfruitful summits ever staged between the two countries. Mrs. Thatcher firmly stated that Northern Ireland was British and that was that... What is rapidly being buried... is constitutional Irish nationalism... It was too bad that Brighton occurred but Brighton grew out of the same policy that Mrs. Thatcher and Douglas Hurd enunciated yesterday—the doctrine of the 'acceptable level of violence'. Violence is acceptable so long as it is happening to someone else" (20.11.84).

At an angry meeting in December 1984 between Cardinal O Fiaich, his Bishops and the Secretary of State, Bishop Edward Daly described 'Northern Ireland' as an "artificial political entity and unless the government showed itself willing to face down the unionists, the minority would not believe there was a place for them in it". Bishop Cahal Daly told Hurd that "Constitutional nationalists had nothing to show for their efforts over many years" and the IRA was able "to cultivate a pre-revolutionary situation throughout Ireland" (IN 30.12.15).

A few days after Thatcher's *"Out, Out, Out"* speech, an angry Hume retorted:

"... no serious business can be done with this British Government. The Nationalist minority in the North has outgrown the Northern state. The British Government may still prevail over us. But they should bear this in mind: You do not have our consent. You have never had our consent. All your military might cannot force our consent" (Guardian, 26.11.84).

Hume seemed to be making the point that whilst the Ulster Protestants did not consent to a United Ireland, the Northern Catholics would now, no longer, consent to 'Northern Ireland' as it existed. He said that the *"Nationalist minority in the North has outgrown the Northern state"*. Was he, by any chance, predicting the process that would result in the Sinn Fein advance Southwards three decades on?

Thatcher's rebuff seems to have had a shattering effect on the SDLP. Ken Bloomfield attended a Conference in Virginia in January 1985 at which there was a wide ranging debate between the UUP, DUP and SDLP on 'Northern Ireland'. Bloomfield was surprised at how Peter Robinson (DUP) and Robert McCartney (UUP) got the better of Hume and noted that even the Irish Americans were shocked at this novel experience of Unionism winning *"hands down"*. Bloomfield noted:

> "John Hume is normally in his element in the United States, where he is widely regarded as occupying a position somewhere between Charles Stewart Parnell and Mother Teresa. On this occasion he gave a chilling impression of political bankruptcy, rather like a man who has lost a fortune by backing a particular number consistently at the roulette table and continues to stare at that number even though he no longer has a stake to play. The unionists put him under very skilful and sustained pressure to engage in talk about arrangements for internal government, even to the extent of throwing out the willingness to recognise some sort of relevant interest on the part of the Irish Republic. In the face of this pressure, Hume took refuge in unconvincing ambiguity. He continued to rely on texts from the Forum Report as if they had been handed down on tablets of stone. He played the familiar record about needing to widen the context. He notably side-stepped an invitation to go as far as the Taoiseach had gone at the last summit conference in acknowledging that there could not be constitutional change without unionist consent. "

Unionism was in high spirits. However, Bloomfield noted a realisation, even among the DUP,

> "... that unionism as well as nationalism would suffer from a disintegration of the SDLP. Such disintegration is not, I fear, a wholly remote possibility. The limb upon which the SDLP has placed itself by its utter reliance by the Forum process is largely sawn through. The party is disunited and disorganised and its morale is low. John Hume continues to resist any thought of an internal settlement, and said privately that he did not believe devolution was workable. Yet if the SDLP is left in lonely isolation, I would fear that those small tendencies toward generosity amongst unionist parties will be choked off, leaving us with limited and unattractive options" (PRONI CENT 3/32A, 16.1.85).

The problem for the British State in early 1985—which was to become an even bigger problem for Ulster Unionism—was how was the SDLP, its bulwark against rising Sinn Fein, to be resurrected?

CHAPTER 11

Hillsborough Ice Age

The Hillsborough Treaty of 1985 came about, not as a result of the New Ireland Forum, but because of the political crisis that saw Sinn Fein emerging as an electoral force and the military crisis brought about by the Brighton Bomb, successfully placed in the hotel at which Prime Minister Thatcher was staying during a Conservative Party Conference. This breach of security encouraged Mrs Thatcher to do something she was very reluctant to do. As a result of this crisis, the British authorities attempted to undermine the Republican political and military expressions through a deal with 'Constitutional Nationalism'. The *'Out! Out! Out!'* episode threatened to shatter the 'Constitutional' Nationalist bulwark Britain relied upon and let in the Republican deluge. Something had to be done by Britain to re-balance things and Thatcher was bereft of a policy.

The Hillsborough deal, which the Iron Lady concluded with Taoiseach Fitzgerald, had a most traumatic effect on Unionism and ushered in something of an Ice Age in politics in the North, lasting for a decade. Any political fluidity that had remained in the system froze up. As a result the War, far from being stemmed, was prolonged and even intensified. And, as we shall see, the project failed in practically all its objectives with the result that Hume, whose party it was largely designed to assist in the North, decided to put his weight behind another process that was occurring and, at the crucial moment, to jump ship in favour of bigger and better things.

The Making of the Hillsborough Treaty

After the signing of the Hillsborough Treaty, Hume told the Irish Times: "We arrived where we are without the assistance of Sinn Fein and we shall not require their assistance in the future" (23.11.85).

How wrong he was proved on both counts.

What rescued the SDLP from the doldrums of the post-Sunningdale period was the Republican entry into electoral politics and its instant success. That success was not all that surprising since the Republican Army always had substantial support within the Catholic community. It was just that Republicans had not put their energies into this aspect prior to 1980 and had formally conceded the electoral ground to the SDLP. With a large base available to Republicans, and an inability to utilise this in military affairs, electoral politics initially developed as an adjunct to the War effort, before taking on a life of its own.

The British did not want Sinn Fein to become the majority representatives of Catholics in the North. This would completely destroy the Criminalisation strategy—which had been badly damaged by the Hunger Strike—since, unless the British were prepared to treat the entire Catholic community as criminal, it could not permit Republicans to overtake 'Constitutional' Nationalists as the main representatives of Northern Catholics. And it would make an internal solution on broadly Unionist terms impossible in the future—the default position of Westminster—because of political pressure on the SDLP.

The British quickly realised the effect of Thatcher's *"Out, Out, Out"* summit rebuff to 'Constitutional' Nationalism. A paper produced from the Political Affairs Division for the Secretary of State for NI in January 1985 noted:

"... for the SDLP the summit outcome came as a body blow... Though leaders like John Hume recognised the inherent problems of the 3 Forum options, they nevertheless hoped that some formal expression of the Irish identity (joint authority with a small j/a) would be forthcoming. The manner of the rejection of the Forum models... was seen as a calculated insult to the minority community in the province as well as a rebuff to the... Irish Coalition. The effect was to drive the SDLP into a corner from which it has yet to emerge... Mr. Hume... has continued to set his party's face against any form of internal settlement which does not involve Dublin and has shown himself reluctant to engage with unionist parties. Privately he has shown interest in developing Anglo-Irish relations in the 'grey area' between consultative procedures and joint authority... The rejection of the options in the Forum Report at the summit and press conference was seen as a predictable humiliation for the SDLP and the parties in the Dail, and as a vindication of the stance taken by Sinn Fein" (CENT 1/13/33A, 8.1.85).

The British knew the central importance of Hume in any deal with Dublin but also that if an acceptable agreement was not produced there was the danger of losing the SDLP altogether:

"... throughout the party, one senses the feeling that people are awaiting the outcome of the summit process and that all will look to Hume to give them the necessary lead. It is unlikely that any Anglo-Irish agreement will be signed unless Hume has been convinced of its value. If that should be the case, then there is little doubt that the party will rally behind him, whatever the misgivings of Seamus Mallon. If, however, the bi-lateral dialogue breaks down then the SDLP will be in a very difficult position. So many hopes have been built on a successful agreement. It will call for a great deal more energy and commitment from Hume within Northern Ireland if the party is not to drift into collapse." (CENT 1/14/13A, 24.7.85).

The dilemma after Thatcher's *"Out, Out, Out"* rebuff was that Britain threatened to lose its main political defence against Sinn Fein if it did not come up with something to satisfy Hume and rescue the SDLP.

The Conservative Government's 'Northern Ireland' policy was exploded by a small bomb in the Westminster Parliament car park when, in 1979, the INLA assassinated Airey Neave, a close friend of Thatcher's. With him died the Tories Manifesto commitments, which could be described as '*integrationist*' in relation to the province: that is to say the ending of devolution and the treatment of Northern Ireland as an integral part of the UK. Neave was the only strong advocate of the policy and Thatcher, who knew or cared little about places outside the Home Counties, dropped it when her friend was killed. Humphrey Atkins, who became Secretary of State, went back to the default position and immediately embarked on an initiative designed to bring the constitutional communal parties together at Stormont. When that went up a blind alley, Thatcher, having just won a second term in Office, was devoid of a policy for the 'Northern Ireland' problem that had become very pressing with the Sinn Fein development. So, in November 1985, the British Government introduced something similar to the Joint Sovereignty suggested in the New Ireland Forum report as part of the Hillsborough Treaty.

It seems that a number of influential people within the British State conspired to produce an Irish policy for Thatcher. Sir Robert Armstrong and Sir David Goodall (of Ampleforth) were both dismissive of Ulster Unionism and favourable to the Irish. The senior NIO Civil Servant, Kenneth Bloomfield, who suspected these Foreign Office men had "dangerous ideas" was excluded from dealings. Lord Gowrie, who had been appointed to the Prime Minister's Cabinet Sub-Committee on Irish policy, suggested to Irish Ambassador Noel Dorr that, on Irish policy, Foreign Secretary Geoffrey Howe was "the key figure" Dublin should do business with. He was, according to Gowrie, "essentially a country solicitor" who would "always want to settle the case out of court". Gowrie also told Dorr that, although Thatcher was "central" to everything, she was not "all-important". She was capable, despite her reputation, of being "brought along by others, in something she did not initially want". Thatcher, who was usually obsessive over detail, was preoccupied by other responsibilities at this time, and was apparently inattentive to the finer points of the ongoing negotiations led by Sir Robert Armstrong and Dermot Nally, Secretary to the Taoiseach's Office.

FitzGerald was advised by the British to concentrate on things closer to Thatcher's heart than Ireland. The Taoiseach warned the British that Libya's Colonel Gaddafi was "deeply involved"in backing the IRA and was "trying to manipulate the Irish state in that way". This represented a potential revolutionary situation helpful to the "Evil Empire" and a strategic threat to Britain's security she should head-off (IT 30.12.15).

The Dublin Government congratulated itself on having "bounced" Thatcher into the Hillsborough Accord (with the help of friendly British officials) against her better judgement, through its skills of diplomacy. (Sir Edward Grey, a master of the art, who started a World War through it, once told the British Cabinet about the limits of the diplomatic process: "Diplomacy in war is futile without military success to back it. In time of war, military success is to diplomacy what heavy artillery, with plenty of munitions, is to an army in the field", Memo, 27.11.16, Cab 37/160/20.)

It is almost certainly true to say that the major reason for Thatcher's change of heart was the Provisional IRA's bombing of the Grand Hotel in Brighton during the Conservative Party's Conference. That was a serious attempt to destroy the British Cabinet, and especially Mrs Thatcher herself, and it nearly succeeded. The IRA calculated that, if it had, serious repression would have re-ignited the War. It was also a reply to the repeated claims made by British Ministers during 1983-4 that violence was being reduced, and to the belief within the Republican Army that Sinn Fein's entry into electoral politics was being taken advantage of by its opponents (see Mary Holland, IT 16.10.84).

Of course, it could never be said that the Brighton Bomb caused Mrs Thatcher to sign the Hillsborough Treaty, since the British never give in to *"terrorism"*. But it was plain to see that the desire for security began to override the Unionist convictions of the Iron Lady after the dust of Brighton settled and emotions receded. Thatcher then capitulated to her advisers and the genial Dr. Fitzgerald, while the Tories pretended that they were still holding the line against *"the terrorists"*.

The Lady Was For Turning

Margaret Thatcher's Cabinet Secretary, Sir Robert Armstrong, confided to the Irish Ambassador Noel Dorr that she had "very much wanted" to ignore Ireland. But by 1985, it had been brought up "on her list of priorities" (presumably by the bomb at Brighton). She lacked "much real deep feeling for the history of the issue" and had, according to Lord Gowrie, "No sense of history". (IT 30.12.15) When Thatcher was forced to think about Ireland she was by instinct drawn to a final solution to the problem: a Cromwellian policy of ethnic cleansing of Northern Catholics. Sir David Goodall, adviser to the Prime Minister, later recalled: "She said, if the northern Catholic population want to be in the south, well why don't they move over there? After all, there was a big movement of population in Ireland, wasn't there?" Goodall asked her, "Are you talking about Cromwell, Prime Minister? "She said, that's right, Cromwell" (BT, 17.4.13).

Having being advised against the adoption of this policy, which conflicted with the purposes of the 1920-1 settlement, Thatcher then proposed the redrawing of the Border and the establishment of an Israeli-style 'security zone' on either side of the Border. Having been talked out of that by those in the State who knew better, she settled for the policy instituted at Hillsborough in 1985.

She wrote in her Memoirs, *'The Downing Street Years'*:

> "There are terrorists in both the Catholic and Protestant communities, and all too many people prepared to give them support or at least to acquiesce in their activities ... The result is that it is impossible to separate entirely the security policy... from the wider political approach to the long-standing 'Northern Ireland problem'. For some people that connection implies that you should make concessions to the terrorist, in particular by weakening the Union between Ulster and Britain. But it never did so for me" (p.384).

No act of British policy, since 1921, weakened the Union more than what Thatcher did in the Treaty of 1985. Before Hillsborough London and Dublin asserted sovereignty over the North. However, British sovereignty took no account whatever of the Irish claim. Hillsborough formally constituted the Six Counties a disputed territory and an area of disputed sovereignty. And through her actions Thatcher gave a status to Dublin that it had not possessed before. Everything had changed and changed utterly in terms of sovereignty.

Thatcher considered that "the best chance of beating" the IRA was through them being "rejected by the nationalist minority on whom they depend for shelter and support. This requires that the minority should be led to support or at least acquiesce in the constitutional framework of the state in which they live." (p.384)

But on the other hand:

> "My own instincts are profoundly Unionist... Airey Neave and I felt the greatest sympathy with the Unionists while we were in Opposition. I knew that these people shared many of my own attitudes, derived from my staunchly Methodist background... any Conservative should in his bones be a Unionist too. Our Party has always, throughout its history, been committed to the defence of the Union: indeed on the eve of the First World War the Conservatives were not far short of provoking civil disorder to support it. That is why I could never understand why leading Unionists... suggested that in my dealings with the South and above all in the Anglo-Irish Agreement... I was contemplating selling them out to the Republic" (p.385).

But the actions of the Iron Lady counted for far more than what was in her mind. She explained her decision to sign the Hillsborough Treaty thus:

"I started from the need for greater security, which was imperative. If this meant making limited political concessions to the South, much as I disliked this kind of bargaining I had to contemplate it. But the results in terms of security must come through. In Northern Ireland itself my first choice would have been a system of majority rule—devolved government on the same lines as Westminster, and subject to its supremacy... That is broadly the approach which Airey and I had in mind when the 1979 manifesto was drafted. But it was not long before it became clear to me that this model was not going to work, at least for the present. The nationalist minority were not prepared to believe that majority rule would secure their rights— whether it took the form of an assembly in Belfast, or more powerful local government. They insisted on some kind of 'power-sharing'—that in some way both sides should participate in the executive function—as well as demanding a role for the Republic in Northern Ireland, both of which proposals were anathema to the Unionists. I had always had a good deal of respect for the old Stormont system..." (pp. 385-6).

From the above we can conclude that the Iron Lady was *"for turning"*. She was a firm Protestant Unionist by instinct and conviction. She was supposedly a 'conviction politician'. She believed in Stormont majority rule as the best form of government for Ulster. Her Government firmly rejected the view that Catholic alienation needed addressing. Just before Hillsborough Douglas Hurd described predictions of the consequences of such dissatisfaction as a "self-fulfilling" prophecy advanced by Dublin (IT 22.11.84). Yet security concerns did lead her to go against all her principles and convictions and appease Dublin. The only conclusion that can be drawn is that Thatcher was severely rattled by the IRA—both by the assassination of Airey Neave and the attempted assassination of herself—into going against everything she really believed in. There was a momentary and flamboyant slapping down of Nationalist Ireland in the aftermath of the Bomb and then a substantial surrender to it at Hillsborough.

In her book Thatcher misrepresents the 1979 integrationist policy of Neave that died with him in the House of Commons car-park. She instead attributes it to Enoch Powell (who also espoused it):

"Enoch's view was that the terrorists thrived on uncertainty about Ulster's constitutional position: that uncertainty would, he argued, be ended by full integration combined with a tough security policy. I disagreed with this for two reasons. First, as I have said, I did not believe that security could be disentangled from other wider political issues. Second, I never saw devolved government and an assembly for Northern Ireland as weakening, but rather strengthening the Union. Like Stormont before it, it would provide a clear alternative focus to Dublin—without undermining the sovereignty of the Westminster Parliament" (pp. 386-7).

The policy of integration is what would have been expected from a real Unionist like Thatcher. And yet she baulked at it in favour of a fundamental revision to the 1920-1 settlement. It is almost certain that it was not only the IRA threat that deterred her from it. It would surely have been made clear to her along the corridors of power in Whitehall that Integration was just not on. 'Northern Ireland' had a purpose for the British State that over-rode any convictions about what was the right thing to do, even for someone like Mrs Thatcher.

The Ulster Unionist Leader, James Molyneaux, an exponent of integration with the UK and an opponent of political initiatives, had seen Thatcher slap down the Forum Report and he was well pleased. Unionism was confident it had seen off the Insurrection and now believed that 'Northern Ireland' could drift back towards the UK with a strong Unionist at its helm. However, the exclusion of the Unionists from the Talks worried them. Thatcher knew that insisting there would be no compromising of British sovereignty would not cut it with Unionists. The files of the NIO in 1985 are full of acknowledgement that the Hillsborough Treaty would produce turmoil in Unionism because of what it would do. And so the most disastrous and tumultuous political initiative of all was foisted on Unionism and 'Northern Ireland' by their Unionist Prime Minister.

Alex Kane, UUP Director of Communications, remembered the Unionist reaction in Belfast upon hearing of the Treaty:

> "They were bewildered. They were seething with anger. People talked of armed rebellion and of Lord Carson's original UVF. Many... believed that Margaret Thatcher had betrayed them and that a civil war was a distinct possibility. It was the first time in my life... that I had seen real panic, real fear in the eyes of ordinary unionists. They knew, even in those first few hours, that things were never going to be the same again" (IT 14.11.15).

Upon the death of the Iron Lady in April 2013 she was showered with accolades by Ulster Unionists of all varieties. Hardly a word was said about her betrayal of the Union in 1985. In fact she was described as a good Unionist who had latterly seen the error of her ways and as such could be buried with praise. Perhaps it was her hard-line military policy against the Fenians, or what was inside her head, that won her the forgiveness of Unionism? But it reveals how much Ulster Unionism is a fundamentalist spiritual movement of the Revival, rather than a political development: feeling outweighs action and repentance is imperative. Some are predestined to be lost souls for eternity, beyond redemption; others, despite their sins, are the veritable righteous chosen ones. It is as simple-minded as that.

Aims of the Treaty

The Hillsborough Treaty was represented to the people of 'Northern Ireland' by the British Government as having a number of objectives. It was meant to decrease the level of violence. But violence increased steadily in the three years after the 1985 Treaty was made, even though it had been in decline beforehand. The number of Troubles-related deaths rose from a total of 195 in the three years prior to it to 247 in the three years after.

The 1985 Treaty was also meant to exert a reconciling influence on relations between Protestant and Catholic communities. However from the start it became another irritating factor within the conflict between the two communities and gave a sharper edge to it. It was also supposed to reduce "*Catholic alienation*" from 'Northern Ireland'. This aspect was vigorously promoted by clerics such as Fr. Denis Faul and Fr. Raymond Murray during the period prior to Hillsborough. A typical example of this argument went as follows:

> "The repeated British political failures: their failure to support the Executive against the Loyalist Workers Strike, the five year use of Internment with torture and ill-treatment, the five year blanket and no-wash protest with wide public support, the Hunger Strike. All these failures called forth demonstrations and expressions of concern from responsible Catholic leaders, lay and clerical. Stony faced British governments showed the maximum of disinterest and the maximum of contempt for these cries for help... Moderate Catholic politicians and anybody who tried to deal with the Northern Ireland Office and Downing Street were left politically naked because they got nothing and lacked credibility by dealing with the old oppressor in any of his new forms. Sinn Fein reaped the harvest and Gerry Adams the man single-handedly responsible for bringing the Republican element into politics, got a reward for his astonishing feat in making physical force men see usefulness in elections. The Catholic population in this sad situation, handed over by the British misgovernment and Loyalist bullying to Sinn Fein/IRA and IRSP/INLA bullying, must be given an alternative. The flock is corralled by the savage circumstances described above and has only one way to go... Such a substantial people must be shown some other way by which they can have some control of their own lives, culture, style of life and destiny" (IN 26.3.84).

But there was little evidence of a reduction of "*Catholic alienation*" from 'Northern Ireland' being achieved. The Republican military campaign, which had been in decline before Hillsborough, received a boost and the IRA engaged in some of its most spectacular actions in the Six Counties, England and on the European continent.

Prof. John A. Murphy later argued that the Hillsborough Treaty had "radically changed" Westminster's attitude and made British sovereignty in the North "conditional on the wishes of the people of Northern Ireland" (*Sunday Press*, 15.3.92).

Article 1 of the Treaty involved Dublin conceding "that any change in the status of Northern Ireland would only come about with the consent of a majority of the people of Northern Ireland" in return for the British affirming that "if in the future a majority of the people of Northern Ireland clearly wish for and formally consent to the establishment of a united Ireland" they would "introduce and support... legislation to give effect to that wish".

But it was never the case that Britain asserted sovereignty over the North, over-riding the wishes of the populace. That was the position of the Southern State, which Taoiseach Lynch had emphasised by saying that Articles 2 and 3 would remain, even if everyone in the Six Counties were a Unionist.

It is hard to see any purpose to the setting up of a sub-government in the Six Counties, when it divided the island instead of letting the region simply be part of the democratic system of the state, if it wasn't to influence Nationalist opinion in the 26 Counties with the delusion that a United Ireland was achievable if the Irish state limited its impulse towards independence and kept itself substantially British in culture and political orientation.

Long before Sunningdale, John Hume had welcomed Heath's Statement that "Northern Ireland would remain part of the United Kingdom only as long as its people wish" as an event that "shook the world" (*Voice of the North*, 18.11.70).

Britain had never asserted that Northern Ireland would remain part of the British state, even if a majority of the population in the area expressed a wish to join the Irish state. It said from the start that the two parts into which it divided Ireland might join together if both sides wanted to. It could say this in the absolute certainty that the last thing the Protestant majority in the North would agree to was a united Ireland. It was on the basis of this certainty that it set up the Six County sub-government. Westminster statements about the right of Ireland to unite by agreement are made for the purpose of influencing opinion in the 26 County state.

The final objective of the deal was to get the SDLP into an internal solution, a devolved government with the Unionists to replace Direct Rule, the long-standing aim of British policy with regard to its 'Northern Ireland' region. Hume had made it clear that his party would not consider devolution until it saw what the product of the Anglo-Irish negotiations was. It was realised, as the released files from 1985 have shown (e.g. PRONI, 1/13/38, 9.9.85), that this would take time. The Unionists would have to be given shock treatment, above all to please Hume and bolster his party, and such a trauma would take time to wear off. The hope was that this strategy would encourage Hume, who was playing hard to get with regard to an internal settlement, into talks with the chastened Unionists. As we shall see, this policy proceeded and reached its culmination at Duisburg. But by then it was not the only game in town and Hume scuppered it in favour of a greater prize.

Lancing the Unionist Boil

Even though the Dublin/Belfast Secretariat, set up by the Treaty to give Dublin a "consultative role" in 'Northern Ireland', had no actual power and the Dublin Government's intention was largely to keep the North at bay in the face of the rise of Sinn Fein, it inserted a thorn into the body of Unionism that drove it into a great frenzy. The Unionists (including senior civil servant Kenneth Bloomfield in the NIO) were excluded from the negotiations because it was anticipated they were not going to agree with the final product. It has been thought that it was because the Treaty was sprung on the Unionists it was so devastating for them. However that does not seem to have been entirely the case. NIO Briefing Notes for Ministers' meetings with Unionists exist for May and June 1985 which show them as being given an indication of ongoing negotiations. They were given to understand that, whilst Dublin was to get no executive role under forthcoming arrangements, there was to be the creation of "a framework" through which "the Irish can put their views to us", not in the way that currently existed but through "formalising and regularising" contacts (CENT 1/13/38A, 21.5.85 and 1/13/38, 17.6.85).

In an NIO document produced in July 1985, Peter Robinson of the DUP is reported as saying that "assurances had been given that the Irish Government would be given no more than a consultative role and as far as he was concerned that was wearable if progress could be made internally and on the security front" (PRONI 3/32A, 1.7.85). But, just before the Treaty was revealed, his leader, Paisley, along with James Molyneaux, had a meeting with Thatcher, who had been non-committal on this aspect, only saying that British sovereignty would not be compromised in any agreement with Dublin. In a post-meeting interview with Dennis Murray, the DUP leader made the Unionists' position clear:

> "... we are totally against part of the United Kingdom being picked out and structures brought into operation whereby the South of Ireland is going to have a consultative role in the future government of NI, that is a diminution of sovereignty and is something we cannot wear..." (PRONI 3/32A, 30.10.85).

Secretary of State Douglas Hurd warned Thatcher that the Treaty was a "one-sided affair" in favour of Dublin which contained sections which were "not consultative at all" and language "which seems to convey a more executive flavour". The "ambiguity" and "fudge" could not be sustained after it became public, Hurd warned (CENT 3/36A, no date)

The primary reason for Unionist trauma therefore lies with Thatcher herself. She built up Unionist hopes as the Iron Lady with her "*Out, Out, Out*" and then crushed them a year later with Dublin being let in by a great betrayal.

The 1985 Treaty also had its disturbing and disorientating effect on the Protestant community, because of the manner in which it was made public in November at Hillsborough. The great show of togetherness and common purpose between the British Prime Minister and the Irish Taoiseach maximised the aggravating effect on the Protestant community at the outset. Perhaps that was an objective, or perhaps the Protestants were forgotten about in the desire to make a great show on behalf of the SDLP that was thought would give it a serious edge over Sinn Fein in subsequent elections. Whatever the case, the end-result was the same—the Protestants felt betrayed by Britain and were seriously aggravated that it was Mrs Thatcher, the great Imperial warrior of Empire, who had done the betraying.

The Protestant community was unusually united and practically unanimous in its opposition to Hillsborough. It produced the most impressive electoral performance by Unionism in the 15 By-Elections held in January 1986 when MPs resigned their seats in protest. It produced the biggest demonstrations for years by the Protestant community in Belfast and elsewhere. John Hume's 1970 policy of separating the moderates of Unionism from the bigots was in ruins—the moderates and bigots were united as never before.

For that reason alone it gave great satisfaction to many in the Catholic community. Support for Hillsborough was nowhere near as strong in the Catholic community as opposition to it was in the Protestant. But the Catholic community thereafter passively supported the Treaty, largely on the basis that it was a humiliation of the Unionist community by the Iron Lady. That is the nature of things in 'Northern Ireland'. And there was no contradiction in people who voted for Sinn Fein, who it was meant to undermine, giving some support for it. The expectation of the British Government in 1985 that the Treaty would bring the two communities together, cause the erosion of Catholic support for Sinn Fein, bring increasing Catholic support for the 'security forces', and turn the tide against the IRA, were unrealistic in the extreme and were never realised.

On the 30th anniversary of the Hillsborough Treaty the Irish negotiator from the Department of Foreign Affairs, Michael Lillis, said:

"Fitzgerald and Hume agreed that the only solution which could have any chance of enduring would have to be 'unboycottable' and proofed against the 1974 (Unionist) veto... A solution could only be found strictly in an international treaty framework within which the two governments would work together." (IT 14.11.15)

Lillis also revealed that Dublin only confided in Hume ("who meticulously maintained confidentiality even with his closest supporters") during the negotiations with the British. The rest of the SDLP was not trusted, presumably so that they would not let the cat out of the bag in their desire to taunt the Unionists, until just before the Hillsborough meeting. The Unionists were to be overridden by something that would take them by surprise and which they could not touch. The negotiations that resulted in what happened at Hillsborough had to be conducted behind closed doors because the Unionists were a substantial community who could not be sold out by an "ascendancy" element—something which the community was often characterised as consisting of by Nationalism at that time.

The British presumed that Hume had been informed of the details of the proposed Treaty and had removed himself from the North to avoid his colleagues, whom he had "made no effort to keep informed". A briefing paper for Douglas Hurd before an important meeting with Hume to be held with the SDLP Leader 5 months before Hillsborough advised:

"In describing the agreement... it may be helpful to stress two points. First, what is on offer to Dublin is an altogether unique institutionalised structure for another Government to involve itself in Northern Ireland's affairs; that is a major concession by HMG. Secondly, Mr. Hume must be under no illusions—we cannot offer the Irish an executive role... The Secretary of State will also wish to make clear to Mr. Hume that he does not see an Anglo-Irish agreement as the whole answer. It could be an important part of the picture, but unless it is likely to allow Mr. Hume to be more forthcoming about internal developments in Northern Ireland much of its value will be lost" (CENT 1/13/38, 17.6.85).

The British were relying on the SDLP moving toward devolution in a situation in which the Governmental structures established by the Treaty would make Direct Rule redundant (1/14/19A, 10.10.85). But, whilst the British objective was to tie the SDLP into an internal arrangement, the main achievement of the Hillsborough Treaty in Hume's memorable phrase lay in its potential in "*lancing the Unionist boil*".

Interviewed on BBC Radio's 'File on Four' on 3rd December 1985 Hume said that the Treaty would be of little value if the Unionists did not come out in substantial opposition to it, in order for their opposition to be faced down by Britain. It was Hume's view that the Unionist mindset could only be changed after a decisive conflict with their Government at Westminster which the Unionists lost: "once that boil is lanced, then you will find the Unionist population for the first time in a position where they must talk to their neighbours".

This aspect of things was alluded to in a meeting the NIO Political Affairs Division had with Brian Feeney of the SDLP just before the Hillsborough Treaty was announced. Feeney, who was among a small group briefed by Hume ten days before the launch, told the British:

> "The agreement was itself of enormous symbolic importance, but what really mattered was implementation... he was worried that unionist pressure would persuade the British Government to take a 'softly softly' approach" (CENT 1/14/19A, 10.10.85).

The *"lancing of the Unionist boil"* would mean pain and trauma for the Unionists but it would be for the best, according to Hume. It meant that, "if the British Parliament decides by a majority that that is what it will do", the Unionists would be traumatised by the British betrayal. The sight of Dublin Ministers flying in and interfering in the affairs of their 'Northern Ireland' would make them withdraw into themselves for a while and perhaps go berserk—but in the end they would come round, faced with the sheer will and power arrayed against them, including that of the Iron Lady herself. The Unionists, no longer being sustained by the British, would be incapable of holding out against an ultimatum from the British Government that it was determined to implement and would eventually suffer internal collapse, making them ripe for being remoulded into something that was more congenial to agreement about Hume's way forward toward Irish unity.

Hume seemed to be confident through an awareness of history. If the Unionists had accepted the 'supreme sacrifice' they had made in being semi-detached from the Union in 1921, they would surely accept the lesser act being done to them in 1985. (He mentioned this on the same BBC Radio programme. See *'Northern Ireland: What is it?* p.49).

If their consent to being semi-detached from the Union was obtained by the British Government in 1920, something similar could be achieved in 1986 by directing them towards Dublin. And the value of that would be that the change was not obtained by force, which Hume realised the Provos could not muster enough of, but by forced consent, which the British Government was surely much more able to muster up against the Unionists. Hume instinctively felt that the Unionists, despite their bluster, would eventually have to negotiate with Nationalists within the desired political structures. His confidence stemmed from the belief that the Hillsborough Treaty had achieved one of his primary objectives. This concerned Britain's Constitutional guarantee to the majority in 'Northern Ireland', which Hume felt was an obstacle to political progress. In Hume's view unqualified support of the British State for the Unionist position meant that they had no incentive to negotiate with Nationalists. The British guarantee underpinned the Unionist veto on political progress. However, the Hillsborough Treaty, by involving Dublin in the governing of 'Northern Ireland' changed the nature of the guarantee to the majority to a qualified one, and this effectively ended the Unionist veto over political progress in the Six Counties.

Hume told the *Irish Times*:

"There is a lot of talk about the veto. The real veto is not what is written on a piece of paper but the real veto is the ability of the Unionist political establishment to threaten the British government and Parliament to make them back down. As long as that card is in their hands no dialogue takes place between the people of this island—none whatsoever... Since the signing of the agreement the Unionists were trying to exercise their veto against the sovereignty of the British Parliament... I believe that this is a very interesting political development. I believe the Unionist leadership have not thought out where they are leading the people in that regard. I believe that in the end if this veto is shown not to work, Irish politics, in terms of Catholic and Protestant, will be transformed. It is for that reason that there is no point in the British Government trying to placate the Unionists. What the British government must do is to stand by the agreement it has made. I believe that will create the circumstances for real dialogue and that will transform the political situation" (7.12.85).

Following the signing of the Treaty, Hume suggested to Radio Éireann'*s* '*Northview*' on 3rd December that

"... there aren't any unconditional guarantees any more. I think it has been made clear to the Unionists that they don't have a veto over British policy in Northern Ireland... I think that is what is very significant. In many ways it may turn out to be more significant than the Agreement itself. The guarantee is no longer an unconditional guarantee" (*John Hume and the SDLP*, p. 152).

According to Mary Holland, writing in the *Irish Times* on 16th July 1986, Hume's strategy vis a vis the Unionists had been accepted both in Dublin and London:

"One British Minister told me recently that he believed there was one overriding criterion by which the Anglo-Irish Agreement should now be judged: that by the end of this summer the Unionists would have been confronted once and for all. Their will would have been broken and this would, in turn, have a salutary effect on their political attitudes. When some observers suggested this was a risky strategy..., they were severely taken to task. Facing down the Loyalists was compared to the lancing of a boil, a necessary if painful step in the healing process... It was Dublin and London which made this the cornerstone of joint Anglo-Irish policy, not the Unionists, many of whom had signalled for months that they would like to talk. Well, we are all wiser now, the Loyalists included."

However, even at this time there were signs that Britain would not collaborate in forcing a showdown with the Ulster Protestants in which their will would finally crumble. Irish Foreign Minister Peter Barry was perturbed when the Orange March down the Garvaghy Road in Portadown, which had been stopped in 1985, before the Hillsborough Treaty, was allowed in 1986 when the Agreement had promised an end to "Nationalist alienation". For the next decade the Orangemen marched the Road with renewed determination and vigour, understanding that much more was at stake for them, after the Hillsborough Treaty. Also, the detested (by the Catholics) UDR, which Hume described in 1985 as "a group of Rangers supporters put in uniforms, supplied with weapons and given the job of policing the area where Celtic supporters live" (IT 31.12.15) continued in existence, despite its permeable relationship with loyalist assassination squads, until 1992.

For the Hillsborough Treaty to have been successful in *"lancing the Unionist boil"* there needed to be an intensifying process conducted by Mrs. Thatcher against the Ulster Protestants. Mrs Thatcher, of course, was interested in the Agreement for quite different reasons—for the security co-operation that the Irish Republic would supply against the IRA and in its ability to undermine the Republican struggle in the North. So there was a basic ambiguity at the heart of the Agreement that led to conflict between the interests of 'constitutional nationalism' and Mrs Thatcher in the longer term. Thatcher would need increased support from Nationalist Ireland in dealing with the IRA if she would proceed with dealing with the Unionists.

It was not enough for the British to simply 'stand firm' on the Treaty— there needed to be a lot of well-directed political activity on the part of the two Governments to produce the political transformation that Hume desired in Unionism from the 1985 Treaty. Thatcher, the Iron Lady, was the British Leader most likely to attempt such a thing. But, after 5 or 6 years of its implementation, and despite the trauma it produced, no such transformation occurred. The close Dublin-London partnership which the SDLP and the Irish Government hoped for, failed to materialise. The NI Secretary, Tom King, succeeded in minimising change, delaying reforms and diluting them until the Treaty became meaningless for Catholics—except in the aggravating effect it had on Unionism. And, by the middle of 1987, according to the *Irish Times*, Northern Nationalists were complaining of Haughey's *"benign indifference"* to the Hillsborough Treaty (21.9.87).

Mrs Thatcher herself concluded that the Hillsborough Treaty and her policy of appeasement had been a failure: "Our concessions had alienated the Unionists without gaining the level of security cooperation we had a right to expect" (*The Downing Street Years*, p.415). The Premier then directed her new Secretary of State, Peter Brooke, to attempt to find a more broadly-based settlement.

The Hillsborough Treaty was, as Harvey Cox has suggested:

> "... a recipe for stalemate, unless and until the Unionists were to climb down and accept, de facto, the hated Agreement. In 1912-14 and again in 1974, the unionist community had been prepared to fight a government taking a route they detested. On this occasion the Agreement was not sufficiently tangible a threat, and 'fight' not a sufficiently plausible or effective response. Hence the main actual response: sullen impotence" (*'From Hillsborough to Downing Street'* in *'The Northern Ireland Question in British Politics'*, p. 186).

It made Unionism ultra-defensive and ushered in something of an Ice Age in politics that was only melted by the Republican Peace initiative that first began to take shape parallel to, and then over-take, Hume's strategy.

Republicans and the Hillsborough Treaty

The 1985 Treaty was trumpeted by the SDLP and the Dublin Government as a triumph for 'Constitutional Nationalism' and, at the beginning, much was made of Sinn Fein's formal rejection of it. Those who negotiated the Hillsborough Agreement would have been horrified if Sinn Fein had come out in support of it. For the Treaty to stand a chance, it was imperative that Sinn Fein come out against it. This was the part Sinn Fein had to play in the Treaty game, to give it any traction on the Unionists. If Sinn Fein had declared it was advantageous it would have died at birth.

There were anxious people in Dublin and London when Sinn Fein delayed its response. Eventually, in statesmanlike tones, the Republicans rejected it whilst claiming credit for it. There was no reason to believe that the Sinn Fein rejection was anything other than formal, however, and it soon became clear that the IRA intended nothing other than to campaign to create conditions within which the SDLP could argue to extend the scope of the Treaty, or move on to something even more congenial. Nevertheless, left-wing supporters of Sinn Fein took its formal rejectionist rhetoric seriously and looked forward to building on it to develop an anti-Imperialist movement in opposition to the Treaty.

To that end a Conference was held in Belfast's Conway Mill, chaired by Bernadette (Devlin) McAliskey. The slogan of the Conference took up Fine

Gael Foreign Minister Peter Barry's phrase, *'The Nationalist Nightmare'*. The Conference promoted the belief that the lot of Catholics had actually got worse since the signing of the 1985 Treaty, rather than improving as had been promised. The theme of the Conference was that the Agreement was a disaster for Catholics, and that a broad Front, on the lines of the H-Block campaign, should be resurrected so that Hillsborough could be brought down by mass demonstrations. The Left was understandably enthusiastic about this, seeing the Treaty as a manifestation of the British Imperialist and Southern Bourgeois alliance against the anti-Imperialist struggle.

But the present writer, who attended the aforementioned Conference (and a smaller Republican Socialist one a little later in Conway Mill), remembers well how Sinn Fein made it clear that it would have none of it. It vetoed motions calling for substantial opposition to the Treaty, making the construction of a broad Front impossible. Adams made it clear that he found such a strategy impolitic from Sinn Fein's point of view. So, in the event, nothing at all came of the biggest conference of Nationalists since the Hunger Strike. At the same time Danny Morrison offered the SDLP an electoral pact against Unionists who were intending to resign their seats in protest at Hillsborough.

Adams said in An Phoblacht: "Unionist opposition was immaterial to Republicans but the proposed resignation of Unionists from Westminster seats presented an opportunity for pan-nationalist unity" (21.11.85).

I think this was the first use of the term that alarmed and was taken up subsequently by Unionists — *'the pan nationalist front'*. It signified something very worrying: that, whilst Dublin was trumpeting a formal division being established between 'Constitutional Nationalism' and the physical-force men, in fact Hillsborough had brought the two wings of nationalism closer together and Sinn Fein had an intuitive and non-dogmatic understanding of its distinct role in the Patriot Game.

Sinn Fein revealed that it considered Republicanism not to be an independent phenomena but more naturally part of a wider Nationalist *continuum*. This was a bit of a shock for those who believed in Republican Socialism and the Broad Front. Some of the left anti-imperialists accused Sinn Fein of standing for an alliance with the pro-Imperialist and bourgeois Catholic-Nationalist SDLP, even though it stood for a Treaty that was supposedly aimed at isolating and defeating Republicanism.

Sinn Fein instead stressed the relationship between Republicanism and 'Constitutional Nationalism' which enabled Catholics to interchange easily between them at elections. Danny Morrison argued that "SDLP bartering power flows from IRA fire power" (AP, 28.11.85), and the SDLP was described as "a party which through the last 15 years had built its fortunes on the blood, sweat and tears of the national resistance" (AP, 5.12.85).

Sinn Fein's Tom Hartley has confirmed that the 1985 Treaty led to a reassessment by Republicans of their relationship with 'Constitutional Nationalism':

> "Prior to this reassessment, republicans saw the SDLP as a six-county party with a six-county agenda that needed to be robustly opposed. As a result of the review, our attitude toward the SDLP changed fundamentally: while still seeing the SDLP as a six-county party, we recognised the need to engage with it... What followed was a private dialogue between Gerry Adams and John Hume that led to an early stage of a peace initiative" (In *'The Long Road'* from 'Towards Commemoration: Ireland in War and Revolution 1912-1923' p.86).

The use of the SDLP (or rather Hume, himself) was seen in Hume's achievement of the Treaty—an extra-Six Counties event—and Republicans evidently decided to establish the *continuum* on a more formal basis by working with the SDLP Leader. This illustrated well the relationship which always existed between the 'Constitutional' and physical force wings of the Nationalist movement: the 'Constitutionalists' condemned the activities of *'the men of violence'*, all the while insisting that only concessions to their demands would persuade them to lay down their arms. But, when the concessions were made, the 'violence' still continued, which the 'Constitutionalists' continued to condemn, all the while insisting that only concessions to a new set of demands would bring peace, and so on and so on. At the same time, the 'men of violence' condemned the apparent willingness to compromise of the 'Constitutionalists', and their dependence on republican sacrifices to obtain concessions which they claimed credit for. While this strategy was understood by Hume and a few others in the SDLP, it was much more generally appreciated in the Catholic community.

The Hillsborough Treaty produced a momentary stemming of the Sinn Fein tide at the 1986 by-elections (caused by the resignation of Unionists in protest at the Thatcher betrayal) and the 1987 local elections which was used by the Nationalist press to present the case for the success of the 1985 Treaty. However, an analysis of the results showed that Catholic voters were doing what they always did in 'Northern Ireland' elections—transferring from one party to another wherever and whenever they believed they could support the party which had greatest chance of unseating a Unionist.

The British realised, as one official put it, that policy must reflect "our interest in fostering the SDLP as the party of constitutional nationalism". The British first considered the Proscription of Sinn Fein to prevent further success at the ballot box. This was ruled out due to the difficulties in implementation for the RUC (PRONI CENT/1/14/16A, 17.10.85). Another proposal, made by Unionists, of introducing a mandatory "declaration of non-violence" for candidates was considered but ruled out as "counter-productive" (PRONI CENT/1/14/16A, 26.2.85). The second alternative was to "wean Sinn Fein away from violence" and "split the Provisionals into a mainstream non-violent party". Or Britain could "mark out Sinn Fein as a party which supports violence", relying on the IRA "to damage Sinn Fein support through terrorist outrages like Enniskillen and bolstering the SDLP" (NIO memo, 26.1. 88, IN 30.12.15).

The Republican Surge

In a memorable passage in its edition of December 1985 *The Irish Communist* noted:

> "There is a story which frequently occurs in the warfare of the Napoleonic period. Cannon-balls which missed their target rolled along the ground for a considerable distance, getting slower and slower. When they slowed to a snail's pace there were soldiers who, despite repeated warnings, could not resist putting a foot on them to stop them. The result was that a foot was destroyed and the cannon-ball continued at its snail's pace... Republicanism is like that now. It appears to have no movement left in it, and yet it remains an irresistible force... Though it is going nowhere anymore, it is unstoppable."

Prior to the Treaty of 1985, Republican activity in the Six Counties was in decline. Operations in England and the European mainland were sporadic. After Hillsborough there was a renewed vigour to Republican activities in the North and a purposefulness about their campaign in England and on the continent. The Treaty gave the IRA the clearest signal in 20 years that its efforts had not been in vain and that it was paying dividends, despite the fact that the War was at a relatively low ebb in Belfast and Derry. What the Provisionals understood by Hillsborough was that, if they could bring the War home to Mrs Thatcher, she certainly was for turning. If anything, it had the effect of strengthening the die-hard military element against those who were moving toward a political compromise.

The Ulsterisation policy was, of course, designed to ensure that the War would not be brought home to Mrs. Thatcher's England. But the IRA ensured that Ulsterisation could not succeed. It demonstrated this by striking in Mrs Thatcher's own constituency, showing that, while Ulster may not be as British as Finchley, Finchley would not remain immune from Ulster. The British Government hoped by its policy of Ulsterisation that casualties in the War would be increasingly borne by locals—mostly Protestants. This, of course, was increasingly the case, since by the late 1980s 85% of security was being undertaken by the local militias of the UDR and the RUC.

Adams revealed to *The Observer* on 19th June 1988 that he much preferred British military casualties to those amongst the Protestant militias of the RUC or UDR. He said: "Callous as it may sound, when British soldiers die it removes the worst of the agony from Ireland and the policy of Ulsterisation had made to possible for Britain to reduce the violence to Irish people killing each other."

The Provisionals realised that the killing of RUC and UDR personnel had little effect on the British Government. They were expendable in the *"acceptable level of violence"* Britain had allowed for and enabled Whitehall to portray the conflict as being a sectarian squabble in Ulster. So the Republican Army determined to increasingly try to kill members of the regular British Army. This took it overseas both to Great Britain and to the continent of Europe, to Germany and Gibraltar.

The greatest Republican military upsurge in the North occurred in Tyrone. The Republican War had begun in Belfast, in many ways the area that was least Republican in the North. The events of August 1969 had seen to that. It was remarkable that a War effort was sustained from a minor part of a city. Cities cannot be self-sufficient in the way that country areas can. But the War in the Six Counties was generated in Catholic Belfast (and to a lesser extent in Derry) and it had to be urban. After a couple of years South Armagh organised itself for War and established a most effective base for Republican activity that became largely impenetrable by British forces. It settled down to a long war of attrition from what was in many ways a liberated area. Around 1971 Tyrone, which was historically a Republican area and which had a very strong Republican heritage, began to participate in War. So War was established in the countryside. But this was not a case in which rural war would encircle the cities. After 1972 the Republican War was largely incapable of expansion and the British adopted an effective strategy of confinement.

As the Republican War in Belfast and Derry was wound down in the 1980s, it was escalated in Tyrone. Part of the reason for this was the receipt of a sizable quantity of military ordinance from Colonel Gaddafi. The bulk of Gaddafi's gift was captured by the Southern authorities and this scuppered an ambitious plan by some elements to drastically escalate the War by taking and holding territory in Fermanagh and Tyrone, which it was thought would have the effect of qualitatively changing the situation by forcing the British to retake areas and engaging them in direct military confrontation.

Ed Moloney in his book *'The Secret History of the IRA'* has it that this was an attempt to emulate the Tet Offensive during the Vietnam War. He suggests that the loss of the element of surprise disabled the impact. It is also inferred that Gerry Adams sabotaged the plan.

The Tet Offensive, however, was not a military victory for the Vietcong. While it had the element of surprise and achieved an initial success, it was effectively contained and subdued by the US enemy. Its main achievement was in its value as 'armed propaganda' and in its effect on American opinion, at a peculiar time in US history and society.

The Republican Tet plan had one thing to be said for it. The war of attrition could be kept up for years against the British, but it was unlikely to be brought to the required level of mass participation to force a British disengagement. Something new was required to qualitatively escalate it and bring about a final settlement, of whatever kind. It is unlikely the plan would have succeeded, however. The IRA did not have the personnel to utilise the new arsenal to maximum effect. It had been slimmed down, by necessity, in the late 1970s to protect it, and a rapid enlistment of volunteers was impossible without compromising its security. It was also the case that only an extreme situation would have produced such a large enlistment and an extreme situation was not something the wider community desired. It also did not have the secure base the Viet Cong had in neighbouring states that would provide the infrastructure needed to supply military ordinance. It was constrained by military circumstance into what it was actually doing.

The defeat of the British Army was never a possibility in the situation. Flying Columns hiding in the mountains or operating in open countryside might have been effective in 1919-21 but satellite technology and modern surveillance made such a strategy unlikely to result in success in the 1980s. Nor was a revolt of British public opinion against the War in response to a Republican *"Tet offensive"* a probability. The British public is fairly comfortable with continuous warfare at anything but an extreme level, as recent conflicts have shown. Military spirit has been successfully generated by the British State to garner support for its war-fighting through Remembrance etc.

After much of the military material bound for the IRA was captured on the Eksund, a decision was presumably taken about whether to proceed with the *"Tet"* plan or not. It is probable that there were two viewpoints — one that wanted to go ahead regardless and the other that was against, because it was preparing for the political initiative that would end the War. In the end it was more than likely reasoned that going ahead with an escalation in Tyrone would sort out the issue, one way or another, and would not compromise the alternative.

Tommy McKearney argues that "In the course of time, the Libyan shipments were not used to pursue military objectives but as bargaining chips in a political negotiation" (*'The Provisional IRA, From Insurrection to Parliament'*, p.146) That is certainly the main political significance of the weaponry. The IRA was supplied with enough material to both sustain the War for a long period and make it more deadly with a more limited supply of volunteers. That is something which would have encouraged the British to make peace rather than chasing a military victory.

The "military objective" of the IRA had previously been ruled out as a solution to ending the conflict. Pursuing it would have taken the war outside the limits imposed upon it with future peace negotiations in mind (both with the British and, in the longer term, with local Protestants) and it would have had unforeseen consequences in relation to the Catholic and Republican community itself. Was an orderly withdrawal from the War, which was considered someday inevitable, possible after the great upsurge of killing and dying that a change in strategy would entail?

The Tyrone IRA waged a serious guerrilla war in the late 1980s, ambushing the regular British Army, assassinating local security force members, destroying military installations, and assassinating those employed to rebuild them, something that had been privatised to local Protestants. British casualties were even concealed on occasion. When the IRA wiped out an SAS unit in Cappagh, bodies were spirited away by helicopter. The incident was reported in *The Irish News* by eye-witnesses but the British denied all knowledge.

A problem for the Republicans was that Ulsterisation had been embedded to such a degree outside of South Armagh and West Belfast that anything aimed to reverse this needed to inflict large amounts of casualties on local Protestants. When the surge occurred in County Tyrone, it began to be seen in sectarian terms by the Protestant community there as it was suffering most of the casualties from IRA activity. It began to be countered by reprisals from local Unionist militias, official and not. When that happened, Republicans were faced with a dilemma: divert resources toward dealing with this development, greatly antagonising local relations and falling into the trap of being depicted as communal "*defenders*"; or ignore it and continue to seek out British targets, which now existed largely in the form of undercover troops, who were spirited in and spirited away if killed. British efforts were thereafter concentrated on degrading the fighting ability of the Tyrone Brigades and utilising the local opposition to sap the morale of the base by targeting the water in which the fish swam.

Atrocity for Atrocity

When Mrs. Thatcher realised she was not going to get extradition from the Southern judiciary and was being made to look like she had been led a merry dance by Dublin, she decided to get her own back by reneging on the Treaty she had signed. When the decision was made by her Government not to prosecute individual policemen engaged in nefarious activities named in the *Stalker Report*, with Stalker himself being then dismissed, the Irish

Government was not informed of that fact through the Maryfield Secretariat. It was not treated as the interested party it should have been under the Treaty. And that had the effect of working up the very *"Nationalist alienation"* that Hillsborough was supposed to reduce. Sir John Hermon, the Chief Constable of the RUC, who was something of a hero to 'Constitutional' Nationalism when he was helping to suppress Protestant opposition to Hillsborough a couple of years earlier, suddenly became the villain when he was revealed as presiding over State assassination squads outside the law, back in 1982.

The negotiators of the Hillsborough Treaty said that one of its chief purposes was to isolate the IRA by making the security forces acceptable to, and supported by, the Catholic community. And the RUC was particularly singled out as the main instrument of this, increasingly replacing the British Army in a situation in which the UDR was to be phased out. However, the RUC, by its very nature, was irreformable. It was a covertly-directed counter-insurgency force rather than a real police force. It put the defeat of Republicanism on a higher plane than the reduction of crime. In fact, its Special Branch regularly utilised ordinary crime (including serious sexual offences when people were prepared to report them) to fight 'terrorism', turning a blind eye to criminal activities so as to create and run informers. And it was a force overwhelming recruited within the Protestant community and directed largely towards the policing of the Catholic community, along with some freelance terrorism by some members, on the side.

The British Government was also seen as conducting what effectively constituted State terrorism under the pretence of civil policing and the law. In doing this, it actually helped subvert the law and produce greater disorder. This process had begun with the *"Ulsterisation of the violence"* policy which involved replacement of the British Army by the RUC and UDR in the role of counter-insurgency, and which marked the end of any pretensions toward civil policing in 'Northern Ireland'. It led to the British State being responsible for the semi-autonomous local forces which desired to put down the Insurrection by fair means or foul. That was the price the Westminster Government paid for *"letting Ulstermen carry the can"* in upholding the settlement it had made in 1920-1 and which it wished to preserve at all cost.

The IRA campaign was treated *de facto* as a War by the British Government until 1974. After the ending of Internment, and of Prisoner of War status, police *'counter-terrorism'* was used as an alternative to maintain a façade of normality. This process of debasing policing and law was the only alternative to continuing the previous policy, aside from allowing the IRA complete freedom of action. Whitehall then authorised the training of a special squad of police by the SAS. Sir Jack Hermon, the Chief Constable, masterminded this policy of *"Ulsterising the violence"* and the 'shoot-to-kill' activities of his police assassins.

The Stalker Affair broke in 1988 when an honest Englishman, John Stalker (Deputy Chief Constable Greater Manchester Police), was charged with investigating the twisted way in which 'law' was operating in 'Northern Ireland'. He was frustrated in his efforts by the RUC, had his career ruined by character assassination, and finally published a book about his experiences. He had conducted a too thorough investigation, refusing to be steered away by nods and winks. All Stalker did was to apply the standards of ordinary policing to what was a counter-insurgency force engaged in very dirty deeds.

When the SAS was used to shoot down Republicans, armed or unarmed, at Dunloy, Gibraltar, Loughgall, Drumnakilly, Coagh, Strabane and various other places, it was suggested that they should accept such treatment without complaint. In fact, the Republicans did actually accept their casualties in a professional military spirit without the hypocrisy that was characteristic of the enemy. The fact that the British Government on the one hand treated the IRA as an army by shooting on sight in a situation they refused to recognise as war, while on the other hand pretending to be engaged in civil policing, provided very effective propaganda for Republicans within the Catholic community.

The Iron Lady's frustration at the failure of the Treaty of 1985 to defeat the Republican Army led her in the direction of a military policy that could only be termed '*atrocity for atrocity*'. 'Atrocity' propaganda and '*atrocity*' *for 'atrocity'* seemed to be the only answer Thatcher had for dealing with the IRA and its continued ability and persistence in waging its War, despite the Agreement. And the policy encouraged Loyalist groups out of a period of relative dormancy to add to the atrocities in their own way.

When Mrs Thatcher employed her undercover troops (rather than reverse the Ulsterisation policy by putting back more of her regular army), it was not long before it was being said that the IRA was losing the War— particularly after the reverses at Loughgall and Gibraltar. However the Republican Army proved the "*experts*" wrong and setbacks remained just that—setbacks. The Provos demonstrated their ability to 'up the ante' and strike simultaneously in 'Northern Ireland', Great Britain and on the European Continent. The British Government found it impossible to insulate the Great Britain mainland from the IRA's War effort as the Provos sought to overcome the Ulsterisation policy.

The upsurge and increase in the range of Provo activity resulted in stern and utterly meaningless condemnations of *criminality*, issued in the strongest possible terms by all and sundry, along with demands for a wider range of new security measures by Unionists. Much attention was focused on calls for '*selective internment*'. This was what Gerry Adams accurately labelled "*the politics of the last atrocity*". The media became full of 'atrocities', with the general aim of milking them for all they were worth to sap support for Sinn Fein and "to bolster the SDLP". In November 1987 the British Government imagined that it had secured a devastating propaganda victory against the Provos after the Enniskillen Bomb killed many Protestant civilians at a Poppy Day commemoration. This catastrophe produced a strong reaction against Republicans in the South. But the 'atrocity' politics had greater success outside of the Six Counties than within. The sentimentality generated by these events could grab the temporary attention of the outsider but had minimal effect on those who experienced the conditions of life and the conflict it generated in 'Northern Ireland'.

The media hyping of 'atrocities' actually tended to render the Catholic community largely immune to all State propaganda. This was because there was a historical community reserve against such onslaughts, dating back to the 1920s when Fr. Hassan had written *'Facts and Figures of the Belfast Pogrom 1920-22'* to expose early manifestations within the press. Since then, there had been continued recourse to disinformation by the media. As a result, there was almost total distrust and cynicism about anything that originated from the British State or was given credence by the histrionics of journalists.

The SDLP also felt morally obliged to indulge in this ritual condemnation of 'atrocities', to emphasize that there was clear green water between the party and Sinn Fein, and to gather up the votes produced by the barrage of emotionalism deployed to justify the 1985 Treaty. The problem for the SDLP was that, no sooner had there been a Provo 'atrocity' to condemn, than it was countered by a British 'atrocity' or a Loyalist 'atrocity'. When the IRA killed Justice Gibson and his wife in April 1987, this was followed by the Loughgall Ambush, where 9 people were killed by the SAS; after the IRA killed 3 RAF members in the Netherlands during May 1988, 3 Catholics were killed by the UVF in a Belfast bar; after the Ballygawley Bus Bombing in August, 3 IRA men were killed by the SAS at Drumnakilly in Co. Tyrone etc. etc.

The Tyrone surge confirmed the limitations of the military struggle to the Republican leadership. Any sloppiness in operations or breaches of Republican security would be ruthlessly punished by the British. The failure of the IRA to extend its hegemony out of South Armagh and west into Tyrone emphasised that military stalemate would persist and this strengthened the hand of those in the movement who had already begun the covert initiatives to end the War on favourable terms.

There were suggestions that in view of the attacks being made on the wider Republican community by the unofficial forces of the State, i.e. loyalist death squads, the conflict should be taken to the community from which they derived. These suggestions, despite the provocations, were not taken up. Such a course would have diverted the Republicans onto another path, one that the State and its proxies were only too willing to engage them on, a path which, once travelled, despite any intention of precision targeting, would have inevitably resulted in greater communal hurt and division.

Republican Peace Moves

After the death of the Iron Lady, official memos contained in the Thatcher Foundation Papers, revealed what *the Irish Times* described as the "conviction in senior British government circles up to and including the British prime minister... that 'some' in the IRA wanted its campaign to stop". The same report said: "The papers also disclose that the British government held this view for some time" (27.4.13).

In the Papers there is a memo by the Cabinet Secretary, Sir Robert Armstrong, dated 13th April 1981 (four days after Bobby Sands' election as an MP) which was conveyed to Mrs. Thatcher. It said:

> "There is reason to believe that the PIRA have been thinking seriously about an end to the campaign of violence, but feel they need a success, an avenue to pursue their aims politically, and something more on the prison regime... The Fermanagh by-election has given them the success, and a political opening, which is reason to think they hope to follow up in the local government elections."

Gerry Moriarty commenting on this information wrote in *The Irish Times*:

> "This new information is likely to lead to speculation about how the British government had this belief and whether it was gained through MI5, M16, agents, informers or some other form of communication or contact. It also raises questions about why the IRA did not end its violent campaign earlier."

The mind of *The Irish Times* is, like most of the Irish media (or British media in Ireland), locked into propaganda mode. It instinctively asks the questions it feels might be damaging to the Sinn Fein leadership. (A further diversion here is mention of the Richard O'Rawe claim as a "*long-running dispute with Republicanism*" that the Army Council of the IRA vetoed a deal acceptable to the prisoners after the deaths of the first four hunger strikers). That is its 'angle' on things—revealing what its purpose of existence really is, as '*the paper of record*' *i*n Ireland. It cannot simply ask the most obvious and pertinent political question surrounding this revelation—namely why, if the British Government were fully aware, as far back as 1981 or before, that there was an influential section of the Republican Movement aiming at bringing the IRA campaign to a close and opting for a peace strategy, more was not done to facilitate this?

For it was undoubtedly the case that, not only did the Hunger Strike, or the hard-line British position in relation to it, provide the means by which the electoral strategy of Sinn Fein got off the ground, it also provided for a rejuvenation of Republican activity in the following years, producing another generation of volunteers. The Thatcher Papers confirm that a Republican peace strategy existed long before it was imagined to exist.

Sir John Chilcot, Permanent Secretary at the NIO under Thatcher and Major, provides a clue why such an opportunity may not have been grasped, in an interview with Graham Spencer:

> "I think there was a short-term perception on the right side of British politics that the PIRA could be beaten, but there was little advantage in that perception. I think that kind of thinking may have been more prevalent in the mid to late 1980s after the hunger strikes, but that was also true on the other side of the political divide. However, as time went on the possibility and expectation of military victory certainly lost appeal." ('*The British and Peace in Northern Ireland*', pp.87-8)

In 1982-3 Gerry Adams begun to put out feelers through Fr. Alex Reid, a Redemptorist priest in Clonard monastery (Belfast), about the possible reaction to an IRA ceasefire and what type of settlement might be on offer from the British Government in that event. The Redemptorist Order in Clonard were a significant part of the fabric of West Belfast since the turn of the century and their Confraternities and Novenas were important events in the lives of many, from childhood, including Gerry Adams. Many Republicans were also members of the Boy's and Men's' Confraternities whose membership reached nearly 10,000 in the late 1950s.

Fr. Reid's efforts were backed by Cardinal O'Fiaich at Armagh, who was a solid South Armagh Nationalist, and who proved a useful counter-weight to the strongly anti-Republican Bishop of Down and Connor, Cahal Daly. Tim Pat Coogan described him as "the single most influential figure prepared to take the initiative in furthering" the objective of providing an alternative way forward for the Republican Army, and he provided Church property for the meetings facilitating this process. The Cardinal met a Republican delegation privately and had planned to go public about this when he died suddenly in Lourdes in May 1990. Just before his death he had gone secretly to meet the Chief Constable of the RUC with information regarding his officers being involved in assassination squads. Despite the secrecy of the meeting, the information found its way to the RUC rank and file and he was told that loyalists were planning to assassinate him. (Tim Pat Coogan, '*A Memoir*', pp.313-4)

Fr. Reid and other Redemptorists also had the advantage of being constitutionally independent of Daly's Down and Connor diocese, despite occupying its territory in West Belfast. Fr. Reid, who was trusted more than other clergy outside the Redemptorists, opened a line of communication between Adams and Tom King, the new Northern Ireland Secretary, in 1986. Adams sent a letter to King asking six pertinent questions about the nature of Britain's presence in Ireland and its intentions in the event of a dialogue with Republicans, as well as its attitude to the Unionist veto. The secret reply from the British Government, which was apparently not seen by the Secretary of State, stated: "... no matter what has been the position in the past the British government has no political, military, strategic, or economic interest in staying in Ireland".

But the reply also put the nature of the conflict down to the antagonism between the people on the island of Ireland, rather than admitting that Britain had any responsibility itself, and stated that there would be no negotiation until the IRA campaign was ended. It gave a promise to place any settlement that might be arrived at in British law. And it stated that a British withdrawal would not entail a complete physical withdrawal (although Britain would minimise its presence) but would involve withdrawing "politically" from 'Northern Ireland'. But the British refused to make this reply public or state a timescale for the process to take place within.

Fr. Reid was also frustrated in his initial attempts to get Dublin or the SDLP to talk to Sinn Fein. Finally, in 1986, he took the initiative in sending a 15 page letter to Hume and to the leader of the Opposition, Haughey. Adams went public with his own intentions, telling an interviewer in *Hot Press* of December 1987 that he would personally be in favour of calling a halt to the armed struggle if the political conditions allowed it:

> "I said that I would be prepared to consider an alternative, unarmed struggle, to attain Irish independence. If someone would outline such a course I would not only be prepared to listen, but I would be prepared to work in that direction. The difficulty is that no one has outlined a scenario by which an unarmed struggle would achieve Irish independence and peace... Most of my discussions, and most of my statements... are aimed at... opening up a dialogue to seek an end to the causes of violence... There is no military solution, none whatsoever. Military solutions by either of the two main protagonists only mean more tragedies. There can only be a political solution. And Dublin has failed to show any vestige of any political solution. They don't give a damn at all as far as I can see."

At this point, therefore, although the Republican surge was taking place in Tyrone, and Thatcher was engaging her special forces in a policy of *"atrocity for atrocity"*, the end of the Insurrection was potentially in sight for both sides and the only issue was how an end could come about. In 1987 Sinn Fein signalled this by issuing '*A Scenario for Peace*' in which the word '*peace*' was used repeatedly and then '*Towards a Strategy for Peace*' a year later.

CHAPTER 12

War and Peace

There was another game in town as well as the Hillsborough Treaty. What is known as the Peace Process has its origin in the late 1970s, when sections of the higher command of the Republican movement began to draw the conclusion that military victory was impossible and the conflict was going to end at the negotiating table. Of course, it was by no means inevitable that this was how the War would end. The British State was determined to wear away Republican military capacity until it was of little consequence and to confine what was left of it to 'Northern Ireland' with the hope that it could be channelled in a sectarian direction.

The objective of the Republican High Command therefore was a difficult one: to pursue a political strategy that led towards an acceptable peace whilst maintaining Republican military capacity at an effective level.

The sequence of the Peace Process as it developed during the mid-1980s should be stated at the outset. It started within the Republican command, around Gerry Adams; it availed of the unique figure of Charles J. Haughey to kick-start it; it was facilitated by the Redemptorist Priest, Fr. Alec Reid; it then took in John Hume, who blocked his party from the devolutionary course it had set itself upon. It then began to take in other elements of Fianna Fail and the SDLP, before utilising the important force of Irish-America against the British State.

The policy instituted by Thatcher and Taoiseach Fitzgerald at Hillsborough ultimately failed in its stated objectives and Hume decided to give way to the Adams/Fr. Reid Peace Initiative that Haughey was facilitating. In conjunction with the Republican leadership around Adams, another direction for political development was then carved out which aimed at a more comprehensive and enduring Peace settlement that would finally end the Ice Age.

Re-entrance of Charles Haughey

An important development occurred in the 26 Counties in December 1979 when Lynch, the allegedly *"reluctant Taoiseach"*, was replaced by Charles Haughey, whose objective was always to be Taoiseach. Haughey was the one first-rank politician in Dublin who had a sound understanding of the Northern Catholic predicament. He was not from a traditional Fianna

Fail background and his family had lived out the catastrophe suffered by the Catholics of the North between 1921 and 1925. His father, Sean/Jock was Commander of the IRA in Swatragh, Co. Derry, and his mother Sarah Mc Williams was also involved. Sean, like most other Northerners put his faith in Collins and, like many others, went South to join his Free State Army after 'the Treaty'. Collins left these men high and dry after attempting to use them in an offensive in his manoeuvring against the British, whom he signed the 'Treaty' with. When Collins got himself killed in an adventure in Cork, and his colleagues conceded to the Boundary Commission in 1925, this completed the disaster for the North.

Charlie was born in Co. Mayo but spent many holidays back in South Derry, where he saw the conditions of life for Northern Catholics during the 1930s. This gave him something that other Southerners lacked—an instinctive feel for the Northerners' position which led to an understanding of how to deal with 'Northern Ireland'.

Haughey as Minister for Justice repressed the small IRA invasion from the South that took place from 1956-62, seeing it as a futile external event. In 1969, however, he saw the internal Northern Catholic Resistance/Insurrection as a much more substantial event, deserving of Governmental assistance from Dublin. When his Taoiseach dramatically changed course, however, Haughey was put on trial, accused of Treason, and acquitted by a jury that understood he had acted on foot of Cabinet policy, which was then denied.

As Taoiseach Haughey immediately set his stall out in relation to the North in a speech at the Fianna Fail Ard Fheis of 1980 at which he said:

> "We must face the reality that Northern Ireland, as a political entity, has failed and that a new beginning is needed. The time has surely come for the two sovereign Governments to work together to find a formula and lift the situation on to a new plane, that will bring permanent peace and stability to the people of these islands" (IN 18.2.80).

Haughey stated that his Government "sees Northern Ireland as the major national issue, and its peaceful solution as our first political priority". He talked of "enlisting the support of all our friends in support of our interests", and working with the British Government to declare "their interest in encouraging the unity of Ireland". This represented a vocal departure from Dublin's policy of timidity since the fall of the Executive.

Haughey also communicated a message to the Republican leadership that he was prepared to conduct *uisce faoi thalamh* (confidential) talks with them in a Carmelite monastery in New York. But this offer was turned down by the IRA, according to Tim Pat Coogan ('*A Memoir*', p. 307). Haughey was confronted by a new Government at Westminster that would initially have no truck with outside interference. Mrs. Thatcher told the British Commons in

May 1980 that "The future of the constitutional affairs of Northern Ireland is a matter for the people of Northern Ireland, this Government and this Parliament alone, and no one else" (IN 21.5.80). Haughey had a summit meeting with Thatcher to try to persuade her otherwise, of which Mary Holland commented, "Mr. Haughey has embarked on a courtship of Mrs. Thatcher but he is by nature a man who expects some return for his courting" (New Statesman 30.5.80). In the event, Humphrey Atkins announced another attempt at an internal solution in August 1980 and Haughey's initiative was blocked off.

When Haughey was proposed as Taoiseach in the Dáil his character was blackened by a series of extraordinary innuendos by the self-righteous Fine Gaeler, Garret FitzGerald, who was later to say that the new Taoiseach had a *"flawed pedigree"*. This was the opening salvo of sneering that became the stock-in-trade of those who wished to do down Haughey in favour of progress toward British values in the Republic. The following example of this kind of thing, written by a History Professor, is typical:

> "With a self-image that seemed to blend the Renaissance prince and the Gaelic chieftain, Charles Haughey did not regard himself as bound by the conventional values that applied to ordinary mortals… The many rumours about how Haughey financed such a lavish life-style did not damage his immense popularity with a substantial section of the party and the electorate. Like the 'whiff of cordite' associated with the Arms Trial such rumours made him appealingly dangerous. As the Irish political journalist Stephen Collins has noted, Haughey's popularity revealed the continuing influence of 'deep ambivalence to politics and law, coupled with the atavistic anti-English strain in Irish nationalism' amongst many Irish people" (Henry Patterson, *'Ireland Since 1939: The Persistence of Conflict'*, pp.276-7).

Prof Patterson furthermore stated that Haughey "positioned his party on the side of traditional Catholic values and irredentism" (p.290).

Haughey's aristocratic posturing sent out a signal to those in Ireland, who fawned over the lost world of regal Britain, telling them that there was a new boss about the place and he was Irish. The new boss was no longer going to tug the forelock to those looked up to on the other island and was aiming to establish independent Ireland as the equal of Britain, or by-pass it completely. Haughey did this by embracing the European ideal and by-passing the debilitating social, political and economic influence of the island in between. He made Ireland a committed and useful member of the European Community just as the UK under Thatcher was making a nuisance of itself in a reassertion of the Balance of Power principle of British Foreign Policy. The European Irishness of Haughey combined with the Christian Democracy of the Continent to halt the creeping back to the Anglosphere. (That was before the Cold War ended and the EU lost its bearings.)

Haughey, De Valera and Lemass

Haughey proceeded to return to one aspect of De Valera's approach with regard to the North, non-interference in Northern governing arrangements, rejecting the disastrous political approach of the Lemass/Whittaker/Lynch era. In doing so he helped kick-start the Peace Process and give it the reach, out of the North, it needed to succeed.

De Valera had been convinced that the manner in which 'Northern Ireland' had been established, with its unique form of semi-detachment from the British state and the role imposed on the reluctant Unionists, was purposefully designed as a lever to establish British control over the new Irish State, and a curb on its potential sovereignty. Britain, in effect, teased the new Irish State with the 'unity' it could have with the lost 6 Counties, if only it ditched its desire for sovereignty and independence. De Valera came to the understanding that he had to ignore the North, to minimise any leverage its politics gave Britain in disrupting the establishing of full Irish State sovereignty. This included ruthlessly excluding any role for the Irish State in assisting the Northern Catholics in their predicament of imprisonment in their Six County confinement. In establishing Southern sovereignty he was undoubtedly right in this, although Northern Catholics were cut off from the Irish State as a result.

Haughey combined De Valera's realistic view of the North with a more instinctive grasp of the predicament of Northern Catholics there. He was really unique in this and a vital element in what subsequently happened.

In Volume One I described how Lemass (Haughey's father-in-law) as Taoiseach naively pursued a political *rapprochement* with Stormont in the misguided belief that joint business-dealing could melt away the political problems within the pseudo-state. He and his adviser, T.K. Whittaker, reasoned that business would be a cure-all for politics. In encouraging Captain O'Neill to start running the place as if he was the actual Prime Minister of an actual State— a fantasy-activity his Unionist predecessors had scrupulously avoided—Lemass, intentionally or otherwise, unleashed the political energies that 'Northern Ireland' could not cope with, ending in the events of August 1969. But, having helped "*unfreeze the North*" and let the Genie out of the bottle, the about-turn performed by Lynch in 1970 followed by disengagement, and culminating in the d*ebacle* of the Arms Conspiracy Trial, had the effect of thoroughly disorienting the Irish State. The Northern Catholics reacted more purposefully, being forced into dealing with their predicament themselves, for the first time since Partition.

The Lemass delusion, that politics was largely about facilitating business and market as cure-alls, was found wanting also in the South as the brief economic rise, lavishly praised by academics ever since, gave way to further stagnation and economic bust. Along with the economic crises, the State became incapacitated politically by the ongoing Northern situation which was to have the effect of a substantial renewal of British influence in Southern affairs—something the outrageously slandered *Catholic Bulletin* had warned against more than a generation before.

Re-building Ireland

Haughey's great strength was in making inspired decisions and getting things to happen. It was he who succeeded in breaking both the cycle of Irish economic dependency and the creeping return to political dependency in the 26 Counties. His Governments of the 1980s represented a turning point in the overturning of the two-decade experiment in Lemass-type non-political Government, in which economics was seen as the remedy for social ills. Haughey helped produce the Republic's greatest ever economic boom— that was later unfortunately to be squandered by those of lesser ability.

In 1984 Sean Feehan, former Irish Army Captain and founder of Mercier Press, compared Haughey's task as Taoiseach with that of Adenauer's as post-War Chancellor of Germany:

> "In one sense the task facing Haughey is almost as great as that which faced Konrad Adenauer when he began the labours of rebuilding Germany after the Second World War... The parallel with Ireland is clear. Haughey will be faced by... the ruins of hundreds of empty factories, and hundreds more of small businesses, destroyed by politicians who were really unable to run a country and by civil servants who pontificated nonsense from their armchairs. Haughey will be faced by a public debt higher per capita than that of Germany... Perhaps, worst of all, he will be faced by an active opposition party, spiritually aligned with the occupying power and more often than not ready to make obeisance to that power and do its bidding. Yet Adenauer built Germany into one of the greatest and most prosperous countries in Western Europe. Can Haughey do the same?" (*Operation Brogue,* p.112).

For Haughey, the issues of the Northern Insurrection, the Republic's sovereignty, and the chronic economic underdevelopment of the South, were all inter-related, parts of a whole, requiring national rejuvenation. Haughey centralised under his leadership at an expanded Department of the Taoiseach the strategic matters of foreign policy, Northern policy and the management of the Social Partnership strategy (based on the German model operated by Helmut Schmidt). The 1985 State Papers show that he distrusted his own Department of Foreign Affairs, presumably for its deference to England. He had something that other Dublin politicians lacked—a view of Britain as a *foreign* state for which a real Foreign Policy was required. From this understanding came his achievement in reviving the Southern State so that it was able to have a purposeful direction with regard to the North and Britain. And it was this spirit and activity that was so necessary for the Peace Process begun by Adams and Fr. Reid.

In 1984, Captain Feehan alleged, Haughey was the subject of a British Intelligence operation to split Fianna Fail and to oust him as leader. Captain Feehan says in *'Operation Brogue'* that he had information that members of Irish Special Branch had been working for MI5, politicians had been bugged, and British agents were operating on a substantial scale to influence the composition of the Dublin Government. He also said that many sections of the Dublin media had been cultivated by British operators. Britain had also attempted to break international confidence in the Irish economy, to prevent Haughey's rejuvenation of the economy (see *Business Week*, November 1982). The heavily-funded *'Operation Brogue'* may have been called after *'Operation Boot'*, "a British plot in the 1950s aimed at overthrowing the Iranian prime minister, Mossadeq, who had nationalised the British controlled oil wells". Captain Feehan was amazed at the disinterest of the Dublin media in the allegations and in the evidence supporting them (Irish Press 7.11.84).

Sir Alan Goodison, the British Ambassador to Dublin, noted in 1986:

"Mr Haughey's record reveals him a highly pragmatic and astute politician with few scruples and a keen eye for the main chance. It also displays him as the Irish statesman who did most to promote the Anglo-Irish dialogue which culminated in the present Agreement" (BT 25.8.15)..

An NIO report of 12th December 1986, written by P.N. Bell said:

"The present Anglo-Irish Agreement stems from initiatives taken on the Irish side by a Fianna Fáil administration, led by Mr Haughey. At his summit meeting with Mrs Thatcher in December 1980, a series of joint studies were started. The most important conclusion of these was that "formal institutional structures should be created between the heads of government, ministers and officials". The bodies established provided the formal framework for summit meetings of the Anglo-Irish Intergovernmental Conference. Bell added that in the period 1980-2, Mr Haughey had attached considerable importance to institutional changes and on getting the UK to commit 'to study the totality of relationships in these islands'..." (Ibid).

In October 1983 Haughey proposed to the New Island Forum the establishment of an Irish/British Conference, including Unionists and Sinn Fein, to formulate institutions for a political solution on an all-island basis. He put forward the view, taken up later by Sinn Fein, that Unionist consent to a final settlement needed to be sought but there should be no veto to all-embracing negotiations (Ed Moloney, *'A Secret History of the IRA'*, p. 267).

Haughey criticised the part of the Forum Report recommending joint authority, seeing this as a recipe for civil war. He desired full Unionist participation in any settlement through a Constitutional Conference (Irish Press 26.9.84). He recognised that Northern Catholics had been the biggest losers in 1921 and warned Taoiseach FitzGerald in late 1984 not to attempt to subdue the Insurrection:

> "It is not a legitimate role for any Irish government to attempt to push the nationalist community in the North back into some subordinate position, a disadvantaged minority in an artificial political entity" (IT 1.10.84).

Haughey opposed the Hillsborough Treaty, despite considerable pressure, even from within his own party, on the basis that it was a purely inter-Governmental arrangement that excluded the internal political forces of the North. He pointed out to the Irish negotiators of the Hillsborough Treaty that any recognition made of British sovereignty in the North would be unConstitutional. The Agreement they signed could not override the Constitution. He described the North as a *"failed entity"* that should not be meddled with. In this way he made a grand Republican gesture against the Treaty that helped him disengage from the North on the basis that to do so would be futile and simply create antagonism. This was surely evidence that Haughey had thought more deeply about the North than any politician of his generation from the South. Haughey was the only true statesman of Nationalist Ireland.

Haughey's view of the Hillsborough Treaty, and his refusal to fish in troubled waters, was proved to be fully justified by the extent of Unionist opposition to the Treaty. Later, taking it to be an established fact, he moved towards lukewarm support of it. And, when he returned as Taoiseach, he kept its apparatus in being, but operated it in the most minimal form possible in co-operation with Tom King, the new British Secretary of State, who also saw it as an antagonising influence on the North. At the same time he refused to renege on the Treaty, even after Sir Patrick Mayhew had decided not to prosecute RUC officers named in the Stalker-Sampson 'shoot to kill' investigation.

Haughey wished to transcend rather than implement the 1985 Treaty and offered to convene a committee to make possible changes in the Constitution that would establish better relations between North and South (IT 25.3.87). He also volunteered to meet with Unionists and at the 1988 Fianna Fail Ard Fheis declared his belief that the framework within which the North was being administered needed to be broadened with the establishment of more widely representative political structures (IN 22.2.88).

This was very different to the SDLP/Dublin Establishment objective of forcing the Unionists into a new phase of devolution through the Hillsborough lever. Both former Taoiseach FitzGerald and Tánaiste Spring wanted suspension or the creating of a window to allow the Unionists to submit to devolution with the SDLP under the auspices of the Hillsborough Treaty. Haughey was thoroughly opposed to devolution of this kind. He wanted a much wider settlement rather than the same-old journey down the one-way street to failure.

Fr. Reid's Letter to Haughey

Haughey persisted in his wider strategy and played the pivotal role in the development of the Peace Process. Without him the subsequent efforts of Albert Reynolds and Bertie Ahern would never have taken place. Haughey, though, has been all but written out of the Peace Process. Adams and Fr. Reid had ruled out the possibility of contacting Taoiseach FitzGerald in 1986, about their Peace initiative after previous attempts at contact were rebuffed. They instead contacted Haughey, although he was in Opposition at the time. When this historic opportunity occurred to do something about the North, Haughey saw it and seized it. Haughey had contributed something publicly in 1985-6 that was very positive by describing the North as a *"failed entity"* and disengaging from it. But Haughey did something in the private sphere that was even more positive, by engaging with the elements that were actually going to transform it. As Sir Alan Goodison had said, Haughey had *"a keen eye for the main chance"*.

The Haughey/Fr. Reid dialogue began in late 1985. Through Fr. Reid, Adams began sending messages to Haughey which explored various ideas. The first was a note written by Adams on jotter paper contained in a plain brown envelope. It was the first direct written communication between the Northern Republicans and a Taoiseach and was an endorsement of Haughey's stance on the Hillsborough Agreement. It said that FitzGerald's signing of the 1985 Treaty had involved a copper-fastening of Partition with Internment waiting in the wings. This helped convince Haughey that his political instincts on the North were correct, in the face of the huge opposition mounted in Dublin against his anti-Treaty stance.

Haughey had been impressed by the Republican Army's operation at Brighton. According to Tim Pat Coogan he had said: "Think of it… What an operation! If it had come off, they'd have got nearly the whole British cabinet. It would have been greater than 1916." (A *Memoir,* p.308).

Fr. Reid met Haughey at his base in Kinsealy:

> "The Fianna Fail leader listened to Reid outline a scenario detailing how the IRA could be persuaded to call a ceasefire… Reid argued that the Adams-led Republican leadership could be convinced to lay down their arms, but

that this could only come about through face-to-face discussion. Talks had to be aimed, in the first instance, at ending the isolation of the Republican Movement. Adams and his supporters had to be shown that a broad constitutional and nationalist family existed which they could join to pursue the objective of a united Ireland. But this would only come about when the IRA no longer felt that it was out on its own" (Kevin Rafter, *Nicholas Mansergh, A Biography*, p. 182)

In May 1987 a significant letter was communicated between Adams/Fr. Reid and Haughey, setting out Adams' terms for an IRA ceasefire, seven years before it happened. Within it were the principles and compromises that formed the basis of what became the Agreement of 1998. These were that dialogue between Republicans and the British should be "open-ended" and that the Republican Army would only end its campaign through the creation of an acceptable "alternative method" which involved "the right of the Nationalist and Unionist people of Ireland to decide their own constitutional and political future through dialogue among themselves and without dictation from the British authorities". This sentence altered the key demand of the IRA for a British declaration of intent to withdraw to something very different.

Fr. Reid revealed to Haughey in a letter dated 28th November 1986, on Clonard Monastery notepaper, the principles on which the Insurrection rested and on which a peace could be made with the British State to end it:

"These principles as I understand them may be set out as follows:

"1) The aim of 'the armed struggle' is to establish the right of all the Irish people to decide their own political future through dialogue among themselves. The establishment of a 32 county socialist republic is not therefore the aim of this struggle. From the Sinn Féin point of view this is a political ideal to be pursued and achieved by political strategies only.

"2) The British must in some formal and credible way declare their willingness to set aside the claim enshrined in the Government of Ireland Act, 1920 that they have in their own right the power of veto of the democratic decisions of the Irish people as a whole. In practice it would be sufficient for them to declare their willingness to set aside the Government of Ireland Act, 1920 in view of any agreements that the representatives of the people of Ireland in dialogue among themselves might make about their constitutional and political future.

"Such a declaration would set the scene for a ceasefire by the IRA.

"This principle relates only to the right of veto which the British authorities claim in Ireland on the basis of the 1920 Act. It should not therefore be taken to mean that Sinn Féin want the British to withdraw from Ireland at the present time. On the contrary they accept and would even insist on the need for a continuing British presence to facilitate the processes through which the constitutional and political structures of a just and lasting peace would be firmly and properly laid by the democratic decisions of the Irish people as a whole.

"Once the representatives of all the Irish people, Nationalist and Unionist, could meet together in accordance with the principle of independence outlined in (2) above, all options for a settlement of the national question, for organising the constitutional and political structures of a just and lasting peace would be open for dialogue and decision" (IT 5.7.07).

This was very much what happened in the subsequent staging of the Peace Process.

In the conclusion to his letter Fr. Reid wrote to Haughey:

"I can....say that the opportunity which now exists is the best that has presented itself since the present Troubles began in 1969 and that it is an opportunity not just for a ceasefire but for making final peace with the IRA and taking the gun out of Nationalist politics forever".

Fr. Reid's letter outlined the core of the new Republican proposal to Haughey of the creation of a Nationalist political consensus which would begin with talks between Sinn Féin and Fianna Fail aimed at agreeing a common approach to the North. Haughey was informed that Adams would consider calling on the IRA to implement a ceasefire if the Irish Government would pursue the issue of Irish reunification (BBC Panorama 30.1.95).

Haughey/Adams

Adams trusted Haughey as "a genuine nationalist" and Cardinal O'Fiaich indicated that he would give Haughey the necessary political cover if the initiative was discovered and Fine Gael or other anti-Republican elements in the South attempted to be shoot it down. The Dublin Establishment hated him, so Haughey had to proceed carefully. Irish Special Branch and the Gardai were penetrated by British agents and knew nearly everything that went on. His first choice for negotiator was Padraig O'hAnrachain, but he died in 1986. Martin Mansergh acted subsequently as go-between for Haughey with Adams. Secret meetings were held between Fianna Fail and Sinn Fein in Dundalk during 1988 but Haughey denied his Government was involved in talks with Republicans when questioned by Fine Gael in the Dáil. Mansergh remembers what Adams said at the first meeting:

"The point was made that northern nationalists were alienated from Dublin... They needed an alternative political strategy, if violence were to stop. The view was expressed that the Anglo-Irish Agreement was not worth the candle, as the cost of the provocation of unionists was not commensurate with any substantial gain" (Martin Mansergh, *'The Legacy Of History',* p.188).

Both Haughey's men and the Republicans agreed that the Hillsborough Treaty was an obstacle to the development of the Peace initiative and Fr. Reid maintained that it delayed the political process. Mansergh told Fr. Reid that Dublin, being a sovereign Government, had to respect the international obligations left to it by its predecessor (p. 191).

Haughey had to contend with an unfavourable political atmosphere for risk-taking on the North. There was the Enniskillen Bombing in late 1987 and then in 1988 the events at Gibraltar, and Milltown Cemetery with the subsequent public killing of the British undercover soldiers in Andersonstown that Fr. Reid got caught up in, administering Last Rites to the victims.

The period after the Hillsborough Treaty was one in which *"moderation"* was urged on the two communities by both London and Dublin as a solution to the conflict. That was the typical *"non-political"* stance that had reigned in the Southern Establishment since the Whittaker era—moderation up North for a quiet life down South. But, in order for *"moderation"* to have broken out within the 'Northern Ireland' cauldron, there would have had to have been political structures available to the communities to harness social energy in a manner that diverted it away from communal conflict. Political normality which makes *"moderation"* possible is political activity connected with the electing of a party to govern a state. It could not develop in the absence of such normal political activity in a situation where communal parties within communal blocs harness communal grievances against the other community in a political system disconnected from governing a state. Normal politics could only exist within the UK or an Irish Republic but not in such a concoction as 'Northern Ireland'.

In the South only Haughey seemed to recognise this fundamental fact. He kept emphasising that 'Northern Ireland' was not a *"viable entity"* and he refused to follow others in fishing in the troubled waters of the North. The implication of Haughey's view was that the Six Counties could only settle down within the political system of one or other of the states which asserted sovereignty over them and, if Britain was not going to do the necessary, it should not obstruct what could be necessarily accomplished in the other direction.

The later meetings organised by Haughey between an Irish Government delegation and Sinn Fein, during March and June 1988, encouraged Haughey in his belief that the Hillsborough Treaty should be transcended. Most significantly, they re-established relations with the Northern Catholic community that lay outside the Constitutional sphere. These are the relations that Lynch authorised and then broke off in 1970. After that, the Department of Foreign Affairs maintained a relationship with the SDLP alone, and an official policy of non-contact with Sinn Fein.

Haughey's paradigm shift in this respect gave Adams and his colleagues important leverage with the IRA, in encouraging movement toward an unarmed strategy: the power of the Irish Government was now behind him. It was Haughey's crossing of the Rubicon with regard to Dublin's relations with the Northern Republicans that provided the big breakthrough that enabled future Dublin Governments to provide what was necessary to the Peace Process to make it a going concern. Part of the reason why Haughey was able to engage with Adams was because the Leader of Fianna Fail was a substantial Republican himself who had confined the Sinn Fein vote to less than 2% in the Republic.

Albert Reynolds replaced Haughey as Taoiseach in February 1992 and continued his Northern policy. Reynolds had entered politics as a supporter of Haughey in the wake of the Arms Conspiracy Trials of 1970. He was an outsider to the Dublin Establishment, and understood Haughey's purposeful Northern policy, that had replaced the disastrous legacy of the Lemass and Lynch era which had incapacitated the Southern State. But Reynolds only continued—very effectively—what Haughey had managed to ignite.

During the period of Haughey and Reynolds the Northern Catholics had the allies in Dublin necessary to finally effectively pursue an ending of the Insurrection. On the Republican side the understanding of the necessity of allies in the wider Nationalist movement for a successful conclusion to the struggle was a product of the isolation suffered in the Truce of 1975 and the advantages seen in having allies during the H-Block campaign. The Fr. Reid letter suggested a Nationalist Front that in its effectiveness would persuade the members of the IRA to trust in a political struggle that would establish a momentum to the situation. Haughey was also told that the Sinn Fein objective was 'national self-determination' rather than 'a 32 county socialist republic'. It was up to the Irish people to determine their own future in free negotiations after that, according to Adams.

Adams wanted the British to set aside Section 75 of the *1920 Government of Ireland Act* that he claimed gave Westminster supreme authority over 'Northern Ireland'. But Adams stressed that he also wished Britain to remain, for the time being, in the province to oversee a political settlement and an orderly disengagement. Adams also signalled that Sinn Fein was prepared to accept the need for consent to a United Ireland in Northern Ireland and it was redefining self-determination away from the simple all-Ireland majority towards general agreement on the island. This was the first indication that the Consent principle was being accepted by Republicans, although they were unwilling to say so explicitly.

Adams and Haughey decided on a 'stepping stones' policy that choreographed the phased entry and participation of nationalist Ireland into a process for Peace, and this formed the basis of the Peace Process with slight modifications as events required. The Republican Army Council made the decision in 1988 to abandon the demand of the British that they should withdraw from 'Northern Ireland' within the lifetime of a single parliament. This had been a key demand of the southern Republicans who had led the Provos in the early 70s and its withdrawal signalled another retreat from their dogmatic position. It was decided to set no new deadline on a British withdrawal and rely on it taking place 'within a generation' in the event of a settlement. This was apparently kept a close secret from the Republican Army rank and file and it later led to accusations of deception and betrayal by some republicans. However, peace feelers had to be kept a closely-guarded secret because the revelation of them at that point had the potential to disorganise the movement when it was vulnerable and to reduce the momentum of the War at a time when that momentum was required to bring home a political settlement.

Bringing in Hume

The first part of the Peace initiative involved Adams and Fr. Reid. The second part involved Adams/Fr. Reid and Haughey. The third part involved Adams/Fr. Reid/ Haughey and Hume.

For a long time afterwards it was presumed, and the SDLP Leader was of the belief that his talks with Adams had begun the Peace Process rather than, as it really had, being begun by the Adams/Fr. Reid/Haughey axis. Hume had been 'protected' from this information for his own good at the time, lest his party colleagues and others in Dublin should learn of the tentative growth and ruin it all. It all remained hidden from the SDLP and from those outside of Haughey's close circle, to prevent it being assailed by the mainstream of 'Constitutional Nationalism' and destroyed, until Fr. Reid was instructed, by Haughey, to made tentative contacts with Hume, who was felt trustworthy enough to be let in on some of what was going on. After all, Hume had been taken into FitzGerald's confidence prior to Hillsborough and had remained tight-lipped about it to maintain the element of surprise against Unionistm.

In January 1985 Gerry Adams had surprised John Hume on a live radio show by issuing a challenge to the SDLP to meet Sinn Fein. A startled Hume responded to this by saying it was the leadership of the IRA which made all the important decisions and insisted he would only talk to them. On 1st February the IRA accepted Hume's request for talks, and Hume dismissed a further invitation to talks from Sinn Féin, labelling the party "mere surrogates" (IN 2.2.85). In response Taoiseach FitzGerald went on RTÉ Radio, reading a prepared statement in which he said that any meeting between Hume and the IRA should be "broken up" and warned that members of the Army Council, if identified, would be arrested. In contrast, Haughey expressed "full support" for Hume's "initiative".

Sean Donlon of the Department of Foreign Affairs, hearing that Hume believed "he could significantly damage them (the IRA. P.W.) in a confrontation", told the SDLP leader that he doubted "that he could at this stage discredit people like Adams and the provisional organisation in Belfast" (SI 3.1.16). Donlon was undoubtedly correct.

The meeting came to nothing when the SDLP refused to have it recorded and Hume's diversion with the IRA—undertaken instead of meeting Sinn Féin—just postponed the progress toward a peace settlement. It is possible that Hume's deep involvement at this point with the process that was to result in Hillsborough that year determined that he would take a different attitude in later years. When he saw the failure of the 1985 Treaty, and the potential of the Adams/Haughey process to produce a more all-embracing settlement, he grasped the Republican nettle. Hume's view in 1985—that IRA military capacity was in decline and Sinn Fein activists were mere "puppets" for those in the IRA who "called the shots" was also a judgement that he later discarded (Newsletter 30.12.15).

Hume finally met Adams in January 1988 when hostility toward Republicans in the aftermath of Enniskillen was at a very high level. When this was revealed, Haughey made a point of publicly backing the "integrity and judgement" of Hume in engaging in talks with Sinn Fein, against the SDLP Leader's critics, without saying anything about his own earlier initiative (IN 28.1.88). Hume then informed and instructed the SDLP to hold a series of talks with Sinn Fein at Clonard monastery in March 1988.

This was the first entry of the SDLP into the process and there was much reluctance and hostility among the rank and file about having to do so, as Currie reveals in his autobiography (p.364). The talks centred on the issues of the meaning of self-determination; the rationale for the armed struggle; the viability of the constitutional approach; the character of Britain's involvement in Ireland and the attitude to Unionism. At Clonard the SDLP put forward the argument that the Hillsborough Treaty had showed Britain to be neutral in Ireland and it was wishing to disengage—therefore violence was futile. Sinn Fein, in response, told the 'Constitutional' Nationalists of the SDLP some home truths about the failure of their approach to raise the position of Catholics in the Six Counties:

> "It should be noted that armed struggle is forced upon the IRA. Neither the IRA or Sinn Fein wants this war but the ineffectualness of all other forms of struggle, the conditions of repression that we have experienced, and British attitudes, have made armed struggle inevitable. The deaths and

injuries caused by the war are all tragedies which have been forced upon the people by the British presence. Your party's bargaining leverage, plus the continuous need for Britain to apply time and energy through the mechanism of its various political initiatives, are proof enough that the armed struggle has been beneficial to the political aspirations of the nationalist community" (Sinn Fein, *'Towards A Strategy for Peace'*).

There was much hostility toward what Hume was doing within the SDLP. A British official, reporting on a meeting between Mallon, McGrady and Brian Mawhinney, a Junior Minister, noted that "the Minister was impressed with the lack of enthusiasm by which they put forward the argument (for talks with Adams. P.W.) and what appeared to be their embarrassment/discomforture" (IN 31.12.15). By this time the British strategy of demonising Sinn Fein by association with violence/terrorism had amplified the latent hostility of the constitutionalists, making Hume's initiative a very difficult one.

The Sinn Fein/SDLP talks broke up without agreement. Currie wrote in his autobiography: "It was with a great sense of relief... that the Sinn Fein talks came to an end in September... My experience of the Sinn Fein talks convinced me more than ever of the necessity of finding a way of opening talks with the unionists" (p. 370).

What is apparent from a reading of newspapers and periodicals from this period is that the primary objective of many within the SDLP, particularly the high-profile figures outside of Hume's circle, was to use Hillsborough as a lever against Unionists to establish a return to devolution, with the 1985 Treaty acting as a kind of fall-back device pinning the Unionists into some form of power-sharing with the SDLP. This is very apparent from an interview with Currie, published in *Fortnight* magazine, June 1987, after the Loughgall Ambush and just before the Westminster Election which the SDLP hoped would strengthen its position. The *Fortnight* reporter wrote:

> "Austin Currie is optimistic. He has a vision of the post-election period in which things work themselves out and fall into convenient slots—with the Anglo-Irish Agreement playing a pivotal role... If the electoral geography of Fermanagh-South Tyrone denies him a Westminster seat he nevertheless is 'fairly certain' there is a safe seat for him in any new PR assembly... The election, hopes Currie, will 'isolate the two P's of Paisleyism and Provisionalism and create a greater coming together of the moderate elements in both traditions and communities'... He is not impressed by the intensification of the IRA campaign... There can only be a political solution and politically the IRA is dead, Sinn Fein is dead, if only they had the wit to stiffen...
>
> "Rumblings of discontent amidst the disarray of unionism are encouraging noises to Currie's ear... 'My pretty confident prediction in the aftermath of

the election the devolutionist argument will win'. Moderate devolutionist unionists, having come to terms with the fact that the Anglo-Irish Agreement is not going away, will sit down at the negotiating table. And… the SDLP will join them there, ready to talk about devolution… Indeed the presence of the Agreement—contrary to what certain people in the unionist and even Alliance ranks have been saying—is a spur to the SDLP to agree to devolution rather than a hindrance… The existence of the Anglo-Irish Agreement and the guarantee that gives to nationalists should encourage us to go into a power-sharing operation, rather than the reverse—simply because, if any arrangement we entered into were to fail, for any reason, then the position would revert to the Anglo-Irish situation…"

Currie admitted that, although he was "a Labour supporter and, of course, the SDLP is a social democratic party… in terms of Northern Ireland, and the nationalist position in Ireland generally, the Labour Party has been a disappointment". He therefore hoped for a comprehensive victory for Mrs. Thatcher and the Conservatives in the 1987 British Election:

"I'm sorry to have to say it but—From the point of view of nationalist Ireland a continuation of Maggie Thatcher in power, for a limited period of time, would be to our advantage… I believe that, while we have a strong Conservative government, that is a reason for optimism for the immediate future."

However, although Mrs Thatcher achieved another crushing victory over Labour in 1987, Currie's hopes for a devolutionist settlement and alliance with moderate Unionism was about to be shot down by Hume's wider strategic vision. And, of course, the Provos, who were far from "dead" after the Loughgall reverse, refused "*to stiffen*" and went on to form the stable centre with the other P—Paisleyism—a couple of decades later.

This account is not meant to denigrate Hume's role in the Peace. John Hume was absolutely indispensable to it. However, the standard account of Hume's role is wrong. Hume's crucial contribution to the Peace was in scuppering what the British and Dublin had intended for the SDLP at Hillsborough and in throwing his weight behind the other process that was developing through Adams, Fr. Reid and Haughey. That made all the difference to what subsequently was to occur. The moment where Hume accomplished this was in the mysterious goings on at Duisburg.

The Duisburg Division

One of the chief British objectives in agreeing to the Hillsborough Treaty was to lure the SDLP into a devolved government with unionists that would replace Direct Rule. The British saw Hume as the main obstacle to such an internal settlement and six months before the Hillsborough Treaty was unveiled, they sounded out the SDLP leader in a meeting at which he was assured about the concessions Britain was prepared to make. The object was stated "to test his reactions to our approach and, in particular, to gauge whether a limited agreement of the kind we have in mind will offer enough to the SDLP to allow them to consider seriously internal political development" (CENT 1/13/38, 17.6.85).

The moment for Hume and the SDLP to fulfil their part of the bargain arrived three years later, after the Unionists had been made, at last, pliable. However, whilst other SDLP leaders had been hooked (like a "*3 pound trout*"?), Hume refused to take the bait. As one senior negotiator on the British side of the Hillsborough Treaty remarked later: "the one thing none of us expected was that John Hume would shortly be talking to Gerry Adams" ('*John Hume, Irish Peacemaker*', kindle ed., chapter by Arthur Aughey).

The British had invested considerable political resources, including the unprecedented Hillsborough concession itself, to bolster Hume and Dublin against Sinn Fein and now Hume had betrayed that faith. This set everything on a path that Britain never intended and which the SDLP never expected.

The differences between Hume and his party colleagues emerged in striking form at the hush-hush talks held at Duisburg, a meeting that suffered a mysterious failure.

The October 1988 talks in West Germany were an attempt to break the Ice Age caused by Hillsborough. Present were the UUP, DUP, SDLP, and Alliance. Fr. Alex Reid was present to transmit the Sinn Fein view. The Duisburg Talks took place after two years of an absence of formal dialogue between the Unionist parties and the SDLP. The Unionist parties required a suspension of the Anglo-Irish Agreement, including the closure of the Maryfield Secretariat, to engage in formal talks on re-establishing devolution in the province. They had made an election pledge not to engage in talks while the Agreement was in place and they wanted sufficient time to elapse before the next meeting of the Anglo-Irish Inter-Governmental Conference in order to hold formal inter-party negotiations. So they requested a postponement by the two Governments of the next meeting of the Secretariat to justify taking part in talks while the Agreement was operating.

The SDLP, represented by Currie, felt the party should accommodate the desire of Unionists to hold formal dialogue, believing there to be a softening of Unionist resistance to Agreement and a potential for devolution. There was support from the other main personalities for this position, as well as from Fine Gael and Labour. However, Hume disagreed and communicated his displeasure to Currie, after a leak had suggested the SDLP delegation had agreed to such a postponement. Hume sent Currie a policy document he had drawn up himself saying that there would be "serious political consequences" if Hillsborough was suspended and he ordered Currie to stop pursuing the matter further (Belfast Newsletter 6.2.89). The objective was "to achieve an agreement that will transcend in importance any previous agreement ever made and... address all the relationships that can contribute to the realisation of peace and stability."

Currie noted in his autobiography:

> "I was very disappointed by this document. The whole purpose of Duisburg, as far as I was concerned, was... to enable the Unionists to get off their hook of not talking while the Anglo-Irish Agreement remained in existence. Devolution was part of the Anglo-Irish Agreement, supported by the two governments, and... a central plank of SDLP policy... The SDLP response to the Unionists, which was effectively John Hume's response, did not cover the exigencies of the political situation. I began to fear another agenda was at work... What I did not recognize at the time, because I was not party to everything that was happening, was that the end of Duisburg was a watershed and that devolution had been moved down the list of SDLP priorities" (pp. 361-2).

Currie, McGrady, Hendron and Mallon had wanted to see a devolved Power-Sharing Government established within 'Northern Ireland' on the basis of Article 4 of the Hillsborough Treaty. A working party had been set up with this objective in mind (IT 12.9.87). But it seems that Hume let the devolutionists go through the motions before calculating, after his talks with Adams, that an all-Ireland settlement which included Sinn Fein should be held out for, rather than surrendering the position hard-won at Hillsborough.

Hume must have seen that the Treaty of 1985 had failed in its objectives and would, at best, only lead back to the situation of Sunningdale in 1974. That was good enough for many in the SDLP, but not for Hume any more, especially since he became aware of the peace initiative that involved Haughey and the Irish Government. Hume decided to bank the main gains attained at Hillsborough, with its all Ireland component and the Dublin's role in 'Northern Ireland'. He then focussed his efforts on the all-Ireland settlement which included Dublin and Sinn Fein. The devolutionists were shoved aside. In 1988 Currie had fronted for the 'socialist' SDLP at Duisburg. Less than a year later he left 'Northern Ireland' and was standing for Fine Gael, the most bourgeois of Southern parties, in opposition to the SDLP sister-party in the South, Irish Labour.

Hume's adaptation to a pan-Nationalism with Sinn Fein, to achieve a wider settlement beyond devolution, had won out. And this was indeed a watershed in political affairs, as Currie noted. If it had just been the SDLP, without Hume, there would have been no Peace Process and no Good Friday

Agreement. This was a product of the Republican Leadership around Adams, with Haughey's facilitation, plus the strategic vision of John Hume.

After the death of Mrs. Thatcher in April 2013, many Dublin commentators took the view that the Hillsborough Treaty had helped to begin the Peace Process that led to the Good Friday Agreement. For example, Stephen Collins in *The Irish Times* of 8th April 2013 claimed Thatcher was "a pivotal figure in creating the conditions for the Belfast Agreement", and that the 1985 Agreement was a "stepping stone" to the 1998 Agreement. Presumably this was because the Iron Lady had "faced down the Unionists".

The policy of Mrs. Thatcher was never aimed at accomplishing something like the Agreement of 1998, by the including of Sinn Fein in a political settlement. It was meant to defeat the IRA and not to make peace with it. The purpose of the 1985 Treaty was part of this strategy, intended to isolate Republicans politically and produce an overall defeat of the IRA. Mrs. Thatcher's policy of 1985 failed and Hume came to recognise its failure in a *de facto* manner, although never saying as much. Adams and Hume therefore determined to carve out a different future in line with Hume's wider strategic vision. And then, after the Iron Lady had been put out to grass by the Tories in an internal coup during November 1990, Britain became open to peacemaking with Republicans, leading to Good Friday 1998.

Talks about Talks

The new British Secretary of State, Peter Brooke, who took over in July 1989, had had no involvement with the Hillsborough Treaty or its promotion. He was therefore ideal to move things on after the Hillsborough Ice Age. A series of negotiations involving the British and Irish Governments, as well as representatives from four of Northern Ireland's political parties (UUP, DUP, SDLP and Alliance), took place from April 1991 until November 1992. The Anglo-Irish InterGovernmental Conference was suspended on 26th April 1991 for 10 weeks, to enable the talks to proceed. But the objective was now not devolution but a much broader settlement.

The Unionists were comprehensively outmanoeuvred by Nationalism in these "*talks about talks*". All the Unionists got was the short suspension of the hated Treaty in which they had been hung out to dry. The talks were organised around three strands, with both Unionist parties conceding that strand two—the relationship between Dublin and London—was entirely legitimate and was an essential part of the solution to the conflict.

The *Irish News* editorial of 24th June 1991 noted:

> "There has been very little political activity over this past 16 years, but what there has been has resulted in the Anglo Irish agreement, and the

recognition by the British government that the Irish dimension has a real and legitimate part to play in the affairs of this part of the island. And by their presence at the Brooke talks (for however long they last out) Unionists have conceded that fact too. That is no mean achievement for constitutional politics."

The *Irish News* was being triumphalist as a result of a series of climb-downs by Unionists from their position after the 1985 Treaty. Apart from the fig-leaf of not engaging in talks while Anglo-Irish Conference meetings were taking place, Unionists accepted the agenda laid down by the John Hume in its entirety. They committed themselves to three strands of talks: within 'Northern Ireland', between the NI parties and the Irish Government, and between the British and Irish Governments.

These talks were not separate entities; they were all of a piece; there was to be "*no agreement without overall agreement*" (as Hume insisted), including the agreement of the Irish Government. In other words, Unionists had accepted the principle that the Irish Government had a right to a say in the North, the principle embodied in the Hillsborough Treaty and Articles 2 and 3 of the Irish Constitution, which they had previously rejected and gone into turmoil about. When the talks began, the reason given by Unionists for entering into them was to get rid of Dublin interference in 'Northern Ireland' affairs. However, in entering into these talks, they accepted the principle that Dublin had the right to interfere. As a result Nationalist politicians were exultant that the Hillsborough Treaty had achieved its largely unspoken aim of breaking the Unionist will six years on and '*lancing the Unionist boil*' in John Hume's phrase.

By their acceptance of the Three Strands of the Brooke talks, defined as the process for a solution by John Hume and through their surrender of a position as part of the UK delegation, the Unionists conceded a major point of Hume's argument. Hume's analysis of the problem and his process of solving it were accepted by the Unionists as fact and his work of years was proved not to have been in vain. Having entered into the talks with a view to ending the Hillsborough Treaty and with it the Republic's say in 'Northern Ireland' affairs, the Unionists ended up accepting that Dublin had a right to dictate the form of the talks and had a veto over the actual outcome. The only logical explanation for this behaviour was that the Unionist parties seemed to have believed that Dublin was going to voluntarily surrender, through Unionist negotiating skill, the foothold in 'Northern Ireland' that they had been granted in the 1985 Treaty, without gaining something more substantial.

The name of the game being played by Lord Carrington and the British Foreign Office, which was eager for a settlement, was to lure Unionists into a form of negotiations which accepted Dublin's role in the affairs of the North. And that is what was effectively done. And so a moral victory was achieved in the Brooke talks by 'constitutional' Nationalism that gave further momentum to the political initiative begun by the Provos. And the leaders of Ulster Unionism were shown to be rather inept in the art of politics—a fact that was demonstrated to the British Government.

As the academic Harvey Cox noted, what was particularly concerning for Unionists

"... was the clear evidence that the British Government valued its relationship with Dublin, and specifically the Agreement's legacy of the Inter-Governmental Conference, more highly than the sensibilities of their own citizens of the British tradition in Ireland. This might have offered proof, if proof were needed, that the Anglo-Irish Agreement was coming into its own as a permanent feature of the management of Northern Ireland." (*From Hillsborough to Downing Street*' in '*The Northern Ireland Question in British Politics*', p. 189-90)

Hume had noted in a BBC Radio Ulster interview after the Hillsborough Treaty on '*Inside Politics*': "This Agreement is not a solution. This Agreement is only an opportunity" (25.4.86). The Hillsborough Treaty was, for Hume, a means to an end in a wider scheme of things of his. The SDLP presumed that meant an unlocking of the devolution door to the advantage of the party and Power-Sharing. But Hume changed course and the Hillsborough Treaty was a means to a much greater end he had in mind, involving a complete political settlement involving Republicans.

Hume Changes Course

During the talks on Strand One—the internal aspects—Hume advanced a position that was clearly unacceptable to both the British Government and Unionists. He demanded direct Irish and European involvement in the internal government of 'Northern Ireland'. The SDLP proposed a system of government by Six Commissioners and an elected assembly to question and make further proposals. Three Commissioners would appoint a Cabinet to run the various 'Northern Ireland' Executive Departments.

Hume probably adopted this strategy to show Unionists how bad it could get for them—with the intention of facilitating the bringing of the Republican movement into the negotiating process and the acceptance of their involvement in a final settlement. On 28th September 1992 in a BBC *Radio Ulster* interview Hume described the SDLP's proposal, already outlined at the political talks, for the governance of 'Northern Ireland'. In the course of doing this Hume declared that 'Northern Ireland' was "not a natural entity and therefore you cannot have a normal democracy". This was Hume being unusually unambiguous to set the goalposts. He was declaring that he could not accept 'an internal solution', involving SDLP power-sharing with Unionists and was holding out for something broader.

The majority of the SDLP would have preferred strengthening the role of the Maryfield Secretariat and the scope of the Hillsborough Treaty. Tom Kelly, SDLP member and former Election Agent for Joe Hendron, told Gerard Murray:

> "Hume having won the battle to get the Secretariat up and running... I don't think he won the battle in getting it teeth. That is the route they should have gone down. Unionists learned to live with the Secretariat; Mallon and McGrady's view would have been the route to go was to strengthen Anglo-Irish relations and everything else would have fallen into place. That was the big stumbling block for Sunningdale... that they didn't get a Secretariat like that established. Now that they had it established they should have tried to get it pushed out in the public role and after a while it would wear people down. It is already there ten years' (*'John Hume and the SDLP'*, p.191)

The SDLP thought it best to grind the Unionists down through the Hillsborough Treaty but Hume, by 1992, concluded that it had served its purpose and there was little further mileage to be had from it or with what was emerging as an alternative. Hume seems to have had little interest in the Brooke/Mayhew Talks for this reason, because without Sinn Féin they were worthless. He privately believed the framework for the talks over the Brooke/Mayhew period was designed to exclude the Republican part of the Nationalist continuum and this element was essential to achieve a more enduring settlement.

In 1992 the SDLP achieved its best ever electoral result, at the British General Election, taking 24% of the total vote and Joe Hendron captured West Belfast from Gerry Adams. In rural areas the gap between the SDLP and Sinn Fein vote also widened. It must have appeared to the SDLP that all was going nicely to plan. The Unionists were where the SDLP wanted them and the Sinn Fein threat was being seen off. However, Hume's horizons were wider than the mundane electoral contest between the two wings of Northern Nationalism and temporary party advantage in that contest. He saw and knew of the wider picture and opted for the bigger prize for his community, one for which he had entered politics originally.

By 1990 the Republican military surge in Tyrone had been contained; Sinn Fein's electoral advance in the North had been halted and turned back, and the party had made little impression politically in the South. At this point Hume detached himself from the SDLP and joined the Republican Peace Initiative that had originated with Adams and Fr. Reid and which had been facilitated by Haughey. An effective Nationalist continuum was developing. Hume's political risk for peace and the initiative undertaken by Adams came together at the start of the 1990s and began to complement each other, pushing things in the direction of Good Friday 1998. But many in the SDLP were bewildered at Hume's behaviour.

In essence what separated Adams and Hume from others within the ranks is that they had, through the political experience of two decades, developed an understanding of the continuum that existed between Constitutional and non-Constitutional Nationalism. This included an awareness of the limitations of both. They appreciated that a combination was essential for the progress of their community and were prepared to ditch the dogmatic positions held by others. That was the secret of what happened.

The Brooke Speech

In October 1989 British Secretary of State Peter Brooke gave an interview to mark a hundred days in Office, in which he stated that the IRA could not be defeated militarily and made a guarded offer of talks with Sinn Fein in the event of a Republican Ceasefire. In such a context he suggested the British Government would be "imaginative". A year later, in October 1990, British Intelligence, authorised by Prime Minister Thatcher, made contact with Martin McGuinness and begun a dialogue to tease out positions on both sides. Brooke made a speech on November 9th in which he stated that "The British Government has no selfish strategic or economic interest in Northern Ireland: our role is to help, enable, encourage" (IN 10.11.90). This statement followed the script of the Fr. Reid/Adams Peace Note of May 1987 and seems to have been asked for by Hume as an explicit British declaration, to back up the argument the SDLP had advanced to Adams about British intentions in Ireland.

In 2015 Martin Mansergh commented that

> "The missing adjective between 'strategic' and 'economic' was 'political', and the British in the Downing Street Declaration declined to renounce any 'selfish political interest' in Northern Ireland" (Irish Catholic 27.8.15).

It is of course correct that Britain does indeed have a continuing political interest in 'Northern Ireland'. But it is actually in Ireland that the political interest lies, rather than specifically in 'Northern Ireland'. 'Northern Ireland' was created to be a political lever to be applied on the part of the island that was slipping away from Britain. That is why Britain imposed a pseudo-state on the Six Counties, rather than just Partition. It had to be suggested that Partition was only 'temporary', to give the South hope that it would someday regain the Fourth Green Field. To achieve this, it had to be on its best behaviour. Any movement in the independence direction would reduce the probability of 'unity'. And so the North could obstruct the independence of the rest of the island, whilst developing British hegemony on the South.

That was the dilemma which De Valera faced. Although he never declared himself a Partitionist, Dev chose Independence before Unity within the dilemma that faced him. The Brooke formula was very clever. Britain's selfish strategic interest in 'Northern Ireland' had diminished by 1990, with the ending of the Cold War, but its political interest in retaining at least a degree of hegemony over Ireland remained.

Claims that the Republican Army Council was considering a ceasefire were published in early 1991 in the *Irish Press* by Tim Pat Coogan, who had played a role in the Adams/Fr. Reid/Haughey diplomacy. In an interview soon afterwards with Mary Holland, broadcast by Channel 4, Adams said that the IRA "would not be found wanting" in the event of a British offer of negotiations. Soon after that the IRA called a temporary ceasefire over the Christmas period.

Thirty years after the Catholic Insurrection, the British State reached a decisive point with regard to the Republican War. The war of attrition conducted against the Republican Army through Ulsterisation, Criminalisation and Normalisation had contained but failed to defeat the IRA. The policy options open to Whitehall were summed up neatly by David McKittrick in the British *Independent on Sunday* in 1991 in an article headed, *'Internment: the big gamble for both sides'*:

"Security chiefs have reached the sombre conclusion that a defeat of the IRA is not on the horizon while current security policies are maintained... it is clear that the urgings of senior RUC and army officers have made internment a realistic option after a long period when it was considered out of the question... It came as something of a shock to hear the authoritative military assessment that internment may represent the only prospect of defeating the IRA before the end of this century... The assessment is that the IRA has very substantial stockpiles of weaponry, enough recruits to maintain its campaign for the foreseeable future, and a highly-experienced command structure. Its leadership has moved away from the 'Armalite and Ballot Box' strategy and is instead placing its faith in straight militarism as the way to sap the British will. The approach of paying less attention to political constraints means the organisation has felt free to use tactics which previously would have been regarded as unacceptable, such as bombing the military wing of a Belfast hospital and the 'human bomb' technique... It is from this cheerless perspective that military and police minds have increasingly turned to the idea of internment... in some senior circles internment is being presented, not only as a desperate attempt to deal with a dire situation, but also as something close to a panacea... Internment... is still the highest of high-risk strategies. It remains a gamble; it might work, but if something went wrong, it could turn the clocks back 10 years" (17.11.91).

This assessment is accurate except in its view that Republicans had abandoned politics for War. What was actually happening was that the War was being stepped up in parallel to the developing Peace initiative that was taking place behind the scenes. This was necessary to achieve a strong bargaining position and deter Britain from believing that military victory was possible in the transition from War to politics that made the Republican movement vulnerable to disorganisation.

Unionist politicians demanded both Internment and a continuation of the situation which was beyond the resources of law to cope with, in which the State thought it expedient to maintain the pretence of the *'rule of law'*. However, the British Government rejected calls for Internment, realising that interning Republicans would do away with the facade of them being presented to the world as a criminal conspiracy and disturb the pretence of the 'rule of law'. If Republicans were locked up without trial, it would be an effective concession of Prisoner of War Status and there was no desire to revisit that policy again. The Criminalisation fig-leaf would be blown and the Government would be forced to challenge the Republican political case or to concede it. As so much of British Government policy rested on Criminalisation, the re-introduction of Internment was never on the cards.

The plan now mooted was for 'selective internment', a refined version of the policy of 20 years earlier, aimed at capturing the IRA command structure —which British Intelligence believed it had identified—and disorganising its units. Loyalists would be interned immediately too, to demonstrate even-handedness. There is little doubt that there was significant support in the security apparatus for such a policy and a more aggressive approach to the IRA. And yet Britain baulked at the challenge presented to it. It understood that Internment would be a last desperate measure for which the IRA would have had made contingencies. It had failed before and it had had the effect of escalating the conflict. If it failed again, what next? The Government was faced with the stark choice of locking up the Republican command or doing business with it to find an acceptable settlement to the conflict.

The British Government's miserable political response to the upsurge in the Republican campaign was to remove the traditional *'right of silence'* in court and to ban Sinn Fein from the media. After a while this involved the ludicrous situation of actors speaking the words of Sinn Fein politicians. Perhaps nothing expressed the political bankruptcy of the British Government in relation to 'Northern Ireland' more than this policy. (To emphasise the ridiculous nature of this policy: Sinn Fein representatives were allowed to speak on the media at election time, due to the Representation of the People

Act.) The British Government, through these piecemeal political initiatives and tit-for-tat atrocities against Republicans made little impression on the "*mind of the enemy command*" which was already proceeding toward a political settlement whilst maintaining the War effort. In 1990 an IRA leader described the Republican military campaign as "armed propaganda". He said that the Republican Army was "prosecuting a political struggle through military means—there are armed and unarmed political actions" (The Independent, 12.3.94).

Robert Ramsey, who had surveyed Republicanism for many years from the standpoint of an official within the Stormont and Direct Rule administrations, has made this accurate estimation of things, that admitted the Republican struggle to be essentially political in essence:

> "On the wider political front, it was not obvious how far the IRA's armed struggle could now lead. They had never had any serious ambitions to win militarily, or to change basic unionist attitudes. Their aim had been to bring pressure to bear, from within Northern Ireland, the Republic, the United States and world opinion, on the British government, to move in the direction of leaving Northern Ireland in the medium to longer term" ('*Ringside Seats*', p.287).

Manoeuvring for Position

In the twilight of the War both Britain and the Republican Army pursued parallel policies of war and peace. The Republican Army was not convinced of Britain's peaceful intentions because of the stalling by new Conservative Prime Minister John Major, and it decided to ratchet up the pressure to see if the British State was really serious about making peace. In February 1991 the Provos signalled to Major that they were determined to counter the British Government's 'not in my backyard' policy by mortar bombing its backyard in Downing Street during a Cabinet meeting. In April 1992 a bomb at the Baltic Exchange in the City of London bomb caused £800 million worth of damage —substantially more than the total costs of damage resulting from all 10,000 previous IRA bombings in the North. Just a year later the IRA detonated a huge truck bomb at Bishopsgate, which caused a further billion pounds worth of damage. The insurance payments that resulted were so large that Lloyd's of London almost went bankrupt and there was a short-term crisis in the London insurance market. The Bishopsgate bomb was also hugely expensive for the British Government itself, forcing it into a position of becoming "re-insurers of last resort" for the finance houses of the City.

The effect on British policy of bombing England has sometimes been exaggerated. Britain has, after all, been a militaristic state for at least three centuries and is not very impressionable in that way. Peace has never been an objective of the British State, if its history since 1688 is anything to go by, and it has fought more wars than any other country in the world, doing so with relish. Its culture is saturated with militarism and nostalgia for wartime and would not be complete without remembering the War Years, which is not difficult as there has hardly been a time when war was not a recent memory. Britain also has prided itself on its substantial powers of endurance and thrives on a *'spirit of the Blitz'* mentality and putting up a *'business as usual'* front to hardships associated with war. And it is very unlikely that the Provisional IRA was going to succeed in breaking the British will when the Luftwaffe failed.

However, a number of bombings had a significant political effect, including the one that killed Airey Neave, the one that almost killed Margaret Thatcher, and those that targeted the City of London between 1992 and 1993.

Forces on the British side also employed bombs to political effect in Dublin, particularly in 1974. The Republican Army identified where Britain was vulnerable and open to influence—where its capacity for making money by moving money about the world was threatened, in the City. Under Thatcher, British industry had been devastated and the British economy became heavily reliant on the City. What the City said went with the British Executive and if you could influence the City you could influence the British Government.

These bombs were much more effective than the thousands that went off in the North of Ireland because they concentrated the enemy mind on the issue to a much greater extent than anything before. Such actions also enjoyed much greater tolerance amongst the community and they also emphasised the Republican power of endurance—which is the thing which most impressed Britain about the Republican Army. Thus these actions began to make Westminster responsive to peace overtures at this particular moment, after 28 years of failing to defeat the Republicans.

The continuation of contact by the British after these attacks, through the secret channels, indicated to the Republican Army that Whitehall not only was serious about dialogue to end the War but that the attacks themselves had brought home the message that the IRA was militarily undefeatable. The back-channel kept the Republicans informed of the details of the inter-party talks that were going on, the scepticism of the British with regard to them, and their view that only an 'imposed solution' involving Republicans was believed workable.

In March 1993 the British Government representative told his Republican contact that the British position, represented by the Secretary of State, Sir Patrick Mayhew, was changing:

> "Mayhew has shed marginalisation, defeating the IRA etc. That's gone...
> Mayhew is now determined. He wants Sinn Fein to play a part, not because

he likes Sinn Fein, but because it cannot work without them. Any settlement not involving all of the people north and south won't work. A north/south settlement that won't frighten Unionists. The final solution is union. It is going to happen anyway... Unionists will have to change. This island will be as one."

This statement is part of the correspondence published by Sinn Fein after the British attempted to doctor the published version of communications between themselves and Republicans, to save face and cover their tracks after they had been found to be *"talking to terrorists"* in late 1993, after long-standing denials. The statement is, of course, constructed in the usual language of British diplomacy, enabling it to be interpreted in differing ways, as circumstances dictate. However, Republicans decided to put it to the test.

Hume/Adams

Five years after Adams/Fr. Reid and Adams/Fr. Reid/Haughey came Hume/Adams. In 1992 Sinn Fein published *'Towards a Lasting Peace in Ireland'*, in which the armed struggle was described as "an option of last resort", and Sinn Fein said it was looking for "an effective unarmed constitutional strategy". At Bodenstown in June 1992 Jim Gibney said that:

"we know and accept... that the British government's departure must be preceded by a sustained period of peace and will arise out of negotiations involving the different shades of Irish nationalism and unionism" (Ed Moloney, *'A Secret History of the IRA'*, p. 400)

Talks between Adams and Hume, that had taken place in 1988 but which had gone nowhere, recommenced in April 1993. This second series of talks went on until September 1993 and joint statements were issued by the two leaders. They are usually termed the *'Hume/Adams'* talks to signify the primacy of the SDLP Leader, despite the originator being Adams. However, Conor Cruise O'Brien called them the *'Adams/Hume'* talks. O'Brien saw Adams as the "predominant partner" and explained this by suggesting that it was Hume who had come round to Adams' definition of self-determination from his position in the mid-1960s (*'Memoir'*, pp. 421-4). Perhaps we should credit O'Brien for that insight, although it was meant malevolently, to damage Hume.

Be that as it may, Adams was also the *'predominant partner'* because he carried the more substantial force behind him, despite the electoral balance of power in favour of the SDLP at that moment. (The phrase *'predominant partner'* was used in the early Home Rule debates when English Unionists asserted that, because England was the main basis on which the UK existed, it had the right to determine whether anyone else could leave the State. i.e. there was not a unilateral right to secede.)

Adams/Hume or Hume/Adams was an agreement between 'Constitutional' and unConstitutional Nationalism that the ending of the War should not depend on a British military withdrawal; that the consent of a majority in the North was required for political unification of the island; and that the War should be called off if the British Government undertook to become *'persuaders'* of the Unionist community, to persuade it that in the course of a generation it should adapt to making a future for itself in an all-Ireland State.

Usually the process is presented as Sinn Fein coming round to Hume's way of thinking. That is, of course, more accurate than the idea that Sinn Fein was coming around to the SDLP way of thinking. But it is still not accurate. In effect, Hume was moving away from the strategy of *"lancing the Unionist boil"* which had begun at Hillsborough a decade earlier and which, by then, had served its purpose, in order to become a partner with Adams and Sinn Fein in their Peace initiative. This development was not a matter of Adams coming around to the viewpoint of Hume or being 'brought in from the cold' by the SDLP Leader. Adams had privately and publicly outlined this scheme of development, which became known as the *Peace Process,* before there had been any 'Adams/Hume' meetings.

Hume was careful to exclude the rest of his party from the process he entered into with Sinn Fein. He allayed any suspicion they might have had in relation to what he was doing by assuring them that he was taking the task upon himself to limit the damage to the SDLP of the inevitable fall-out, should the whole thing came to grief. But there was certainly more to it than that. Hume was able to improvise effectively and enter uncharted waters without the dead-weight of his party pulling him back. Once begun there developed the kind of symbiotic relationship between Hume and Sinn Fein, characteristic of the old Nationalist continuum, Hume needed the Republicans to see his project through and the Republican peacemakers needed Hume to help bring the War to a close.

The Hume/Adams process led to some elements in the South turning on Hume with a vengeance, for implicating himself with Republicans and "orchestrating the nationalist consensus" in the North that was preventing a Unionist military settlement of the conflict. Hume in exasperation about these hurlers on the ditch told a journalist who questioned the advisability of contaminating himself with Sinn Fein that he "didn't give two balls of roasted snow what anyone advises me. I will continue these meetings" (IN 1.9.93).

Typical of the *Sunday Independent*'s approach was its issue of 1st October 1993. An article by Conor Cruise O'Brien argued that the Hume-Adams talks "cannot possibly lead to lasting peace, only to further disaster". Beside the article there was a grotesque cartoon of Hume, which appeared to show one blood-stained hand (presumably from shaking hands with the Sinn Fein Leader). The cartoonist later claimed that she had not meant the hand to be blood-stained but a mysterious piece of "bad print quality" had intervened to darken it (ST 11.10.15).

The SDLP was forced to make an approach to Aengus Fanning, the Editor of the Dublin-based *Sunday Independent,* and then to its owner, to try to curb the propaganda appearing in the newspaper, week on week through various columnists, which they felt was setting up their leader for assassination by loyalists. Brian Lenihan, the Chairman of the Oireachtas Foreign Affairs Committee, said that the attacks from Dublin had been based on "hatred and personal viciousness", rather than "reasoned argument. He accused O'Brien of having become "a terrorist intellectual who increasingly employs rhetorical devices, labels and slogans that are… undemocratic and hate-filled (*Irish Political Review,* November 1993).

Hume's frustration with all of this was revealed at the SDLP Ard Fheis in November 1993 when he accused the British of choosing,

> "… the easiest option when it came to Northern Ireland. Their only policy was maintenance of the Unionist veto which was central to the mess that Northern Ireland is in. The unionist mindset—the classic Afrikaner mindset—is that the only way of life is to hold all power in their hands and exclude everyone else" (IT 29.11.93).

A joint statement issued a couple of weeks after Hume/Adams said:

> "We accept that the Irish people as a whole have a right to national self-determination. This is a view shared by a majority of the people of this island though not by all its people. The exercise of self-determination is a matter for agreement between the people of Ireland. It is the search for that agreement and the means of achieving it on which we will be concentrating" (IN 24.4.93).

This represented a clear statement that a very different attitude to Unionism was being advocated by both Adams and Hume.

Loyalist/British Reaction

What was new about the hysterical propaganda produced by the O'Brien coterie about "*pan-nationalism*" was that it eroded the distinction which had previously been made between the two forms of Nationalism. There was nothing new in the idea that the two forms had much in common but the idea that, because of the common element, the difference between them did not count at all, was novel. The general impression given was that all Northern Catholics were to blame for the trouble up North. There is no way in knowing if that withdrawal of distinction influenced Loyalist militants—who were more likely readers of *The Sunday World* than the *Sunday Independent*—but the O'Brien rhetoric was an element which fed into the general social atmosphere in the North, fitting in well with Loyalist perceptions. Loyalists were also not discerning enough to notice the change that had been stated in the Hume/Adams position of April 1993.

London had placed a major responsibility for defending 'Ulster' in the hands of Unionists through its *Ulsterisation* policy of the mid-1970s. However, at the same time, the British Government maintained control over these forces, refusing to let them "*deal with the IRA*" in the way they thought fit. In this context the killing of local members of the security forces by the IRA, which the Unionists were not permitted to get to grips with, had the effect of driving many in the Protestant community to distraction. This was the motivating force behind the leaking of information to the loyalist paramilitaries and the active participation of some members of the security forces in death squads. The Stevens Inquiry found that the most senior British Army Intelligence Officer had taken Johnny Adair, a Shankill Loyalist paramilitary leader, to dinner and oversaw the leaking of information to him. (Henry McDonald revealed in the *Guardian* of 27th April 2003 that Adair's fingerprints had been found on at least a dozen Military Intelligence dossiers on Republicans).

Whitehall's Ulsterisation policy made it a virtual certainty that the leaking of information by the 'security forces' about people they suspected of being Republican, or dangerous in some other way, would take place to Protestant paramilitaries. This was to lead to the assassination of a substantial number of Catholics—Republican, or more usually, otherwise. The 'security forces' which were almost wholly Protestant and were put in the front line against the IRA by the British Government through Ulsterisation had to have access to Intelligence, such as photographic montages, and it is not surprising they made use of it.

The only effective way of combating the problem of collusion was to put the British Army back in charge of security, disband the UDR, and remove the RUC from an 'anti-terrorist' role. However, the British Government proved unwilling to do any of these things, particularly when the loyalty of the RUC was so vital to it after the imposition of the Anglo-Irish Agreement on the Protestant community.

The Ulsterisation policy, therefore, created an issue for the British in relation to the direction of operations against the Republican War. By placing the responsibility on the Ulster Protestants for their own defence, it had the effect of producing an upsurge in Loyalist activity in conjunction with the locally-recruited militias. The solution to this problem seems to have been for the British security services to undertake a greater penetration within Loyalist groups and to place a guiding hand on them, to 'refine' their activities. This was another consequence of the Hillsborough Treaty. It became necessary for Britain to redirect Loyalist anger, and the new breed of *les enragés,* away from anti-State activity toward something more useful for Britain.

Agents like ex-soldier Brian Nelson were well-placed to influence their activities. Supplied with armaments from the apartheid South African regime, and lavished with security force information on Republican suspects in the form of the photo-montages the Loyalist groups began to target Republicans and their families to a much greater degree—whilst at the same time not abandoning the everyday assassination of Catholic civilians. Nelson's notes, published by a Sunday newspaper in 2015, reveal that he worked closely with British Military Intelligence—which not only encouraged the UDA to target prominent Republicans but also put into operation a bombing campaign against economic targets in the Republic, to pressurise it into extraditing Republicans, which its judiciary was resisting. This plan was scuppered when the IRA assassinated the UDA leader in charge of the operation in late 1987.

The Loyalist tactic of random assassination of Catholics with the object of stimulating the Catholic community to turn on the IRA was in line with the standard practice of British colonial warfare. In conflicts like Malaya and Kenya these tactics were used and some of the practitioners of counter-insurgency techniques were employed in 'Northern Ireland', working closely with Loyalists, imparting their knowledge and skills to them. The Loyalists viewed their campaign as an extension of State activity, doing the work the official forces could not be seen to be getting their hands dirty with, and securing a degree of State protection as a result. Their motto expressed this succinctly: *"Their only crime was Loyalty"*.

In the last decade of the war, with Britain taking control of the Loyalist paramilitary groups, particularly through its Force Reconnaissance Unit, and its multitude of agents, attempts were made to refine Loyalist targeting. The work of the FRU included collecting, assessing and refining Intelligence data held by Loyalists, so it could be handed back to them, making their killing more effective from the State's point of view. The information that found its way into their hands came from all sections of the security forces, as the FRU acted as a conduit between British and RUC Intelligence organisations and the Loyalists through its many agents.

The managing of these groups also involved limiting their activities. For example, much time was spent frustrating their attempts to develop a large bombing or heavy-weapon calibre capability. The British also acted to prevent them from assassinating potential 'compromisers' within the enemy who might be useful for British strategy in time. The Loyalist groups became a useful adjunct to the British war effort against Republicans, which in the final stage of the War, often directed itself against the Sinn Fein electoral rise. (There is much information on this in a book *'A Very British Jihad: Collusion, Conspiracy and Cover-up in Northern Ireland'* written by the English journalist Paul Larkin. Larkin, was a producer on the BBC's *Spotlight* current affairs programme, for which he made a number of programmes on this aspect.)

The period between 1988 and 1994 seems to have represented a last attempt by elements within the British State to divert Republicanism into a sectarian civil war with the Loyalists who were targeting the Republican community with assistance from State forces. There were calls from the Republican heartlands for the Provos to meet lead with lead, but these were resisted by the Republican leadership. Resistance to engage in this kind of warfare subsequently led to charges of betrayal of the Republican base from some, who wanted their families and supporters protected through a reprisal policy and a general arming of the community. But, despite the Loyalist provocations, the Republican Army remained resolute and determined on its direction.

The year of 1991 saw the greatest number of people killed in the North since the mid-1970s. It was said at the time that this was due to the 'political vacuum'. But the political vacuum had lasted for 15 years with a much lower killing rate, a rate which was in steady decline until the 1985 Treaty. The increased killing rate was intimately related to the collapse in the Unionist political leadership, which put fresh vitality into 'Constitutional Nationalism' and gave Loyalist militants a motivation to counteract Nationalist victories in politics.

A number of other things caused the upsurge of Loyalist terrorism. The old Loyalist leadership had been imprisoned after the Stephen's Inquiry into Collusion and it had been replaced by a vigorous younger element, more eager to flex their muscles. The Loyalist impression that a 'pan-nationalist front' was developing against them and something sinister was going on behind their backs between Hume and Adams (and the London and Dublin Governments) resulted in a great upsurge in assassination activity, particularly in Belfast. One well-known Shankill loyalist boasted in *The Guardian* of his exploits, courtesy of an article by Maggie O'Kane.

The Shankill Bombing was the IRA's response to the wave of killing of Catholics by the UDA and UVF. The Provos chose to target the Loyalist Prisoners' Office above a fish shop on the Shankill Road, after observing that the UDA leadership met there at a regular time, and deal a spectacular blow to the directors of the death-squads. However, the operation, which was improvised at the last minute, went disastrously wrong. The fuse of the bomb proved to be too short, blowing up the bombers and killing nine civilians in the explosion. The loyalist leadership was curiously absent at the time.

The killing of large numbers of Protestants on the Shankill Road brought a predictable response against Catholics from the UDA and UVF over the following days and nearly derailed the Peace Process.

There has never been an equivalence between Loyalist terrorism and Republicanism, either in military or political character. The Republican Army formed itself from the most able, the most purposeful, and the most political, elements of the Catholic community in the aftermath of August 1969 and not just from the most fearless. They were the vanguard of their community and the most vigorous elements within it in both politics and War. The Loyalists, by contrast, were drawn from the backward mass of Protestant society, whose political function over the generations was to be a battering ram, set in motion by respectable people who then denied all knowledge of them when blood began to be spilt. And, increasingly during the 1980s, after Thatcher had devastated the heavy industry that was the bastion of Protestant working-class employment, Loyalism took on a negative character.

The Downing Street Declaration

The British Government and Sinn Fein exchanged 16 written and four oral messages in the Spring of 1994 and Prime Minister Major decided he would make open contact with Republicans. However, he was dissuaded by his Cabinet, which believed that the withdrawal of Unionist support, along with that of some backbenchers, would be fatal to his Government. Instead, therefore, Major turned to seeking an Accord with Dublin in an attempt to over-ride the Hume/Adams talks and deflect any fall-out upon the secret talks with Republicans being revealed.

In November 1993 *The Observer* broke the story that the British Government had been secretly negotiating with the IRA for the previous three years. This revelation encouraged Whitehall to act, to prevent further speculation and instability, by bringing things out into the open. The result was the *Downing Street Declaration* of 15th December. The kernel of the Downing Street Declaration was that Britain was a "disinterested party" as far as Ireland was concerned: It was suggested that Britain had no preference as between the Union or a United Ireland or anything in between; the Irish could have whatever political arrangements they could agree amongst themselves. Until agreement was arrived at, 'Northern Ireland' would remain in its semi-detached relationship to Britain, as long as there was a majority in the Six Counties to retain it. Republicans demanded clarification of this

Declaration in the light of the Hume/Adams proposal. However, the Declaration was pretty clear. So what Sinn Fein was interested in when it demanded clarification was what lay behind the Declaration in the mind of the British Government. In particular, it wished to know whether the British Government was prepared to work towards the creation of a United Ireland.

In the Declaration there was a broad hint that the British Government saw the future of the Six Counties in an all-Ireland context and there was evidence for this, in the shape of the increasing role the Irish Government had been given in the affairs of 'Northern Ireland' to demonstrate that this was the thrust of British policy over the previous decade. The overall impression given was that it was "a statement of withdrawal in spirit from Northern Ireland by the British government" and "a shedding of the British population of Ulster". The indication made by the Declaration was that there was only one direction in which the Six Counties could go and, whilst Unionists "would not be thrown out of the British house against their will, theirs was the guest room..." (John Wilson Foster and Feargal Cochrane, Fortnight, March 1994, pp.35-6 and pp.16-19).

The main difference between the Declaration and the Adams/Hume principles was the lack of an overt commitment from the British Government to become *'persuaders for Irish unity'*. If the British Government were to declare itself willing to undertake that role, and this process was to be aimed to be completed *'within a generation'*, the Provisionals campaign would be over.

The *Irish Press* of 22nd January 1994 had an account by Emily O'Reilly giving an explanation of the relationship between the Adams/Hume document and the Declaration. The story she told was that the first version of the Declaration, tabled by the Irish Government in June 1993, was in effect the Adams/Hume document, which Adams said he was happy with. Crucially, the two elements of the document that were subsequently rejected by the British Government were that the British would become *'persuaders'* of the Unionist community to agree a political settlement with the nationalist community on the island as a whole and that the process would be completed within in the time frame of 'a generation'. And that is why Republicans sought 'clarification' from the British Government.

It was understandable that Sinn Fein insisted on these provisos before accepting the Declaration as a basis for calling off the War. This was because up to that stage the Republican Army had provided the main momentum for Anti-Partitionism. If the military campaign was ended, something else would have to provide momentum in its place. Also, Hume had been facilitated in applying political pressure on the British Government by Adams' substantial political innovation that created the unprecedented Republican offer. Without Britain applying alternative pressure on the Unionists, the question had to be asked whether progress in the direction of a United Ireland could be maintained or would politics just freeze in a Partitionist mould, as things had done under the Anglo-Irish Agreement?

The IRA's immediate response to the confidence trickery that the Major Government was engaging in was to take the British approach to these matters and apply the carrot and stick. After launching a mortar attack on Heathrow Airport in London, it called a post-Easter Ceasefire for 72 hours. The problem that Republicans faced was that the Major Government was driven by short-term party political considerations, which meant that it did not dare offend its remaining unionist elements in the Conservative Parliamentary Party at the same time as alienating the Ulster Unionists, who supported the narrow Tory majority at Westminster. Also, the Labour Opposition had dropped its formal commitment to Irish unity by consent, in order to present a united front with the Tory Government on the Downing Street Declaration.

Gone were the days when Britain could pursue long-term projects in the world—particularly one that might undo the damage Westminster did in 1920. The British political system entered a phase long ago of living from hand to mouth, in which damage limitation and fire-fighting were the order of the day, rather than purposeful political action that might pay dividends in the long-term. Its only consideration, it seems, was to neutralise the Republican Army in one way or another, rather than taking remedial action in respect of the underlying problem of the 'Northern Ireland' it had created, when an excellent opportunity presented itself. And the Major Government would not have been dissatisfied to have the Provos reject the Downing Street Declaration out of hand, of course.

Differences within the SDLP

The Downing Street Declaration led to differences within the SDLP regarding the Peace Process. Hume's position was that the British Government should hold face-to-face negotiations with Sinn Fein and issue 'clarification' of the Declaration for Republicans. He was very careful not to attempt to 'clarify' the Declaration himself and make things uncomfortable for Republicans with the result that they might reject the Declaration completely.

Seamus Mallon, to the delight of British Secretary of State Sir Patrick Mayhew, badgered Sinn Fein to call off the War on the grounds that the Declaration encompassed the Adams/Hume principles fully. In the House of Commons on 21st January Mallon said:

> "On the issue of self-determination, there is not a whisker between what is in the joint declaration and what is in the (Hume/Adams) document... if

the IRA believed that the core element of self-determination, but is continuing to kill people because of that core element, that is spurious and cynical because there is no difference between what the IRA agreed in any other document and what was agreed in the joint declaration" (IN 22.1.94).

Mallon was playing party politics, to secure an advantage for the SDLP, in a delicate situation that Hume knew demanded a higher, more subtle approach, in the interests of the process as a whole. Mayhew praised Mallon for his "devastating examination of the claim of the IRA and Sinn Fein to justify the perpetration of violence in the circumstances applying now, after the joint declaration by the two governments" (IN 22.1.94).

Mallon's position was incomprehensible. It was clearly the case ever since 1973 that the unification of Ireland could be formally achieved if a majority in the North voted for it. And that was probably the case in substance long before then. It needed no high-level negotiations in 1993 to establish that Irish unity might be achieved with the agreement of both parts of Ireland and Adams had conceded as much some time before. It was also very unlikely that Adams agreed unconditionally that unity should depend on gaining the consent of enough Unionists to constitute the majority of the Northern electorate and then thought better of it demanding that the British Government should become *'persuaders for Irish unity'*.

In the Summer of 1994 there was great discontent with Hume's conduct of relations with the Republican Leadership. Mallon made public a part of the Hume/Adams Agreement, even though it had been negotiated on the condition that neither side would make it public without the consent of the other. Mallon attempted to expose a part of the Agreement, presumably to show that it was identical to the Downing Street Declaration and to put pressure on the Provos to declare an immediate ceasefire, despite the fact that this would undoubtedly provoke a split.

It became clear at this time that a number of the SDLP rank and file members had never liked the Hume/Adams talks in the first place, on the grounds that 'Constitutional Nationalists' would only lose out from them: they largely supported the British Government's position on the Declaration. A senior NIO official, Chris McCabe, made an official Note of a meeting with Eddie McGrady on 18th May 1994 that revealed: "Mr. Eddie McGrady is not a happy man. He disagrees fundamentally with the way John Hume is acting, which he thinks is elevating Sinn Fein/PIRA to a position of respectability they do not deserve (more than once he described them as the 'scum of the earth')..." (IN 12.4.03). McGrady publicly referred to the joint-venture his leader was engaged in as *"the Provo Peace Process"*. And Seamus Mallon kept saying that Hume had to disengage with Adams unless the IRA campaign ended immediately.

Conor Cruise O'Brien gave his backing to ousting Hume. He wrote in the British *Independent* under the banner, *'It's Time for Mr. Hume to Go'*:

"... many SDLP members have become increasingly restive about Hume/Adams... Mr. Mallon is at the head of those in the SDLP who have had enough of Mr. Hume as their leader, if he seeks to continue that partnership with Mr. Adams. For my part, I hope that Mr. Hume will step down, and that he will be replaced by Mr. Mallon. A Mallon-Adams partnership is simply not on the cards. The change would be a most healthy development. For more than a decade now, John Hume has been in the pocket of Sinn Fein/IRA—the pocket labelled 'peace'. His utterances, from out of that receptacle, have had a deeply damaging effect on the positions of the Dublin and London governments; especially Dublin. They have also blocked all possibility of serious talks between nationalists and unionists... So roll on the change" (31.3.94).

But Hume and Sinn Fein were drawing closer together. When Hume achieved 29 per cent of the European poll in 1994, nearly toppling Paisley from the top spot, *An Phoblacht* congratulated him for his "excellent performance". Disappointment was expressed privately that he had not topped the poll. During the election campaign Sinn Fein desisted from criticising Hume whilst support for their leader was restrained (Suzanne Breen, *Fortnight* July/August 1994).

There were two wings to the SDLP—John Hume and the rest of the party. Hume was becoming increasingly out of joint with the party he led, which displayed some of the antagonism Fitt had developed toward the Provos. These elements wanted a peace, it seems, but one without the Provos—which was impossible. Hume pulled them along behind his strategic vision but they seemed to have felt that they could outmanoeuvre the Republicans in the transition between War and Peace, securing an electoral advantage in the process. All the while, the Catholic community, particularly the working class, rewarded Hume for his efforts, and demonstrated clearly their views on the matter.

CHAPTER 13

Retreat from the Battlefield

Wars are difficult things to stop. The greatest and most experienced warfighting nation, England, found them hard to call a halt to, even in the days when its wars were aristocratic affairs that were largely uninfected with morality. Jonathan Swift helped stop a war with a famous pamphlet, *'The Conduct of the Allies, and of the late Ministry, in beginning and carrying on the present war'* (1711). The Tories, who had come to power and inherited a Balance of Power War against France, found it difficult to stop fighting it to an emphatic conclusion. The public had been worked up by the previous Government and was in the mood for a crushing of the French. It took Swift's pamphlet to point out the benefits of ending the War at an advantage, to take the momentum out of the war mood. In the settlement, England availed of the Treaty of Utrecht and secured a slaving monopoly for its Empire to go from strength to strength.

From 1994 the Republican Army began its retreat from the battlefield. This is the most dangerous manoeuvre in military affairs. There is a great danger that retreats can be turned into routs and can result in defeat.

Britain, the most military state in the world, which has fought more wars than any other, is supremely experienced in such matters. It knows about conducting retreats and regrouping to fight another day. A book about its bungled Second World War on Germany was called *'Dunkirk—Retreat to Victory'*. It lost its war on Germany in 1940 but managed to still end up on the winning side in 1945 after the USSR and US defeated Germany and Japan.

This side of things must have been known to the Republican High Command—that Britain, being supremely experienced in these things, would also be very good at frustrating retreats and scattering the forces of those attempting them. Cromwell after all had introduced this practice into English military affairs during the Civil War. So it was a big challenge for the Republican Army to remove its forces, intact and in an orderly fashion, from the battlefield in order to pursue the final phase of the struggle through politics.

IRA 1994 Ceasefire

In early Summer 1994 Republican leaders drew up a paper known as TUAS. TUAS, it has been suggested, stood for *Totally UnArmed Strategy*. It explained the main strategic objectives of the Republican movement as "the construction of an Irish nationalist consensus with international support as the basis of the dynamic contained in the Irish Peace initiative". It suggested that the Peace initiative—

> "should include the strongest possible political consensus between the Dublin government, Sinn Fein and the SDLP; A common position on practical measures moving us towards our goal; A common nationalist negotiation position; An international dimension in aid of the consensus (mainly from the U.S.)."

It also noted a combination of circumstances that gave the Republican Army the best opportunity for securing a political settlement:

> "Hume is the only SDLP person on the horizon strong enough to face the challenge. Dublin's coalition is the strongest government in 25 years or more. Reynolds has no historical baggage to hinder him... There is potentially a very powerful Irish-American lobby not in hock to any particular party in Ireland or Britain. Clinton is perhaps the first US President in decades to be substantially influenced by such a lobby."

The document of over 1000 words concluded:

> "It is the first time in 25 years that all major Irish nationalist parties are rowing in roughly the same direction. These combined circumstances are unlikely to occur again in the foreseeable future. The leadership has now decided that there is enough agreement to proceed with the TUAS option."

The TUAS document formed the basis on which the Republican Army Council decided to call a Ceasefire. Only senior members of the movement were shown the TUAS document and the rank and file were told that the ceasefire was conditional—if the British did not respond in a satisfactory manner to the initiative, it was back to War.

Some have suggested that TUAS actually stood for *the Tactical Use of Armed Force*. However, that was hardly an innovation in Republican strategy needing a new policy paper. The tactical use of armed force was a long-standing characteristic of the Republican campaign and the only sense in which TUAS could have any meaning in relation to it would be in expressing the point that armed force was merely a Republican tactic rather than a principle.

Having first settled some local accounts, on August 31st 1994 the IRA declared a complete cessation of military operations. Mitchell McLaughlin of Sinn Fein said that the Provos had learnt lessons from the 1975 Truce that made them much more politically-savvy in 1994:

> "It could be argued that the IRA was at the height of its powers in the mid-1970s, and much more active than it was when it eventually declared a Ceasefire in 1994. But that is a mistaken analysis both from a military, and

more important, from a political point of view. In 1974 the IRA was in military decline. It retained a vigorous capacity, but had lost the military ascendancy to the British. In late 1974 British Army commanders believed that they were close to defeating the IRA—more so than they ever were subsequently. So, while the 1975 truce was called from what the British saw as a position of disadvantage by an IRA in fast decline, by 1992 there were no such illusions as to the substance of what was being dealt with."

Politically, Republicanism had not yet proven its powers of lasting endurance in the middle of the 1970s. Endurance in war is the quality that Britain respects most, since endurance is what it itself is all about. Britain always played the long game in war due to its geopolitical aspect—its island position and the strength of its Navy—and it presumed that the Irish, like the stylish Continentals, were good for a short fight before inevitable failure.

The IRA had put up an intense effort over three or four years in the early 1970s. But every year it had claimed *'Blian an Bhua'* (Victory Year), as if one more last push was all that was needed, and by the same token, that the fighting would last just one more year. A year is a mere blink of an eye in British warfare, so the proclamations of *'Victory Year'*, year after year, suggested to the British that the IRA was reaching the end of its tether.

It wasn't unreasonable for the British Government to suppose in the mid-1970s that a short war was all that the IRA had in it. After all they were Irish and so they would have their frenzy of excitement and then burn themselves out while Britannia would still be there, playing the long game. And, when the Irish had exhausted themselves, things would settle down again. In 1994 the IRA could call a Ceasefire with more well-placed confidence in a favourable political outcome than in 1975. It had taken everything the British State could throw at it and was still standing. And its battle-hardened political expression was confident enough to believe that it could see a political process through to fruition over an extended period of time.

But the Republican Army was not naïve enough to place all its faith in the unarmed process. Its volunteers were assured that there would be a return to armed struggle if the peace strategy proved to be a blind alley. Renewed training was instituted, Intelligence-gathering and targeting were continued and Nationalist areas were policed, both against anti-social elements and those who might want to carry on the War independently. And, as a last insurance card, preparations were made for the mounting of attacks in England, in case the British Government had any ideas of using the Ceasefire against the Republican Army, as it had done in 1975. These measures were all necessities of the situation but afterwards convinced die-hard Republicans who were not in favour of calling off the War that the leadership had been playing a double-game with the rank and file for a number of years.

The Republican ceasefire was not the end of the problem of 'Northern Ireland', as many in Dublin imagined, because the Provos were never the problem of 'Northern Ireland'. What it did was to shift the problem from the British context to the Irish context and that is probably irreversible.

Unionism seeks Victory

Almost immediately after the IRA Ceasefire both the British and the Unionists declared that the Republican Ceasefire could not be treated as effective until the IRA handed in its arms to the British Government. There was also a demand that the IRA used the word *'permanent'* in relation to its ceasefire. It became clear that John Major's Government in London was trying to ward off the day when it would have to begin playing its part in the Peace Process.

The 1992 British General Election produced a slim Conservative majority of 21 and a situation in which Ulster Unionists constituted a vital reserve of lobby fodder for the Government. In July 1993 the nine Unionist MPs helped secure the Maastricht Treaty for Prime Minister Major when reliance on his own Euro-sceptic backbenchers was doubtful. This was part of an *'understanding'* in which Major put a brake on the political process that could have led to a settlement. Having pursued a peace-making initiative in clandestine fashion, the Major Government began to dread the implications of the open Peace Process because of its small majority, which left little room for manoeuvre, and which could shrink drastically at any moment if a Tory died or was caught with his trousers down while ejaculating 'Victorian Values'. And it needed desperately to hang on for the better part of two years, to stand a chance of winning the next election, after Major had won it an unexpected extension of power in 1990.

The British Government itself, therefore, was the weak link in the chain. It had to stay friendly with the Unionists to preserve its existence. However, at the same time it needed to stay friendly with Dublin and appear to be abiding by an unspecified but assumed understanding enshrined in its *Downing Street Declaration*. So the IRA decision to call the Ceasefire placed the British Government in a great dilemma.

The Unionist Party gave the impression that it had little or no regard for the Ceasefire and seemed to view it as something worse than the state of war that had preceded it. The Leader of the Unionists, James Molyneaux, said it was the most "*destabilising event to happen to Northern Ireland in 70 years*" (Sunday Business Post, 30.4.06). This was an echo of Faulkner's view over 30 years earlier that a Catholic reform movement would be much more dangerous to Unionism than the standard Nationalist approaches— 'Constitutional' or the straightforward unConstitutional.

The Unionists seemed uncomfortable in unfrozen politics and what they wanted was an unconditional surrender of an undefeated army. *Unconditional Surrender* meant that the IRA should place itself unreservedly at the disposal of the British Government. Of course, if Adams and McGuinness had accepted such terms, and declared that all arms should be handed over to the RUC and the Republican command structure dissolved, it is certain that the Republican movement would have assumed that they were British agents, disengaged from the entire process and resumed the War immediately—which it was more than capable of doing.

That might or might not have satisfied the Ulster Unionist leadership, since it still hankered after total military victory and a humiliation of Republicans. The present writer clearly remembers the *Belfast Telegraph* column of Eric Waugh expressing the view that many he knew in the security services, including those that had directed the ambush at Loughgall, wished to use helicopter gunships and an Israeli-style approach along the Border to finish off the Provisionals, believing that the British had them on the run. Waugh lamented that this course had not been taken up and a kind of Chamberlainite appeasement of *'peace in our time'* had been shamefully resorted to.

Of course, the 'military victory' approach died with many of its advocates in a mysterious helicopter crash off the Mull of Kintyre just before the Ceasefire. That event, even though it is not included in the *'Lost Lives'* volume, commemorating the deaths that occurred during the 'Troubles', was certainly of fundamental military importance and a great stroke of luck for the Peace. A great quantity of British military expertise, information and contacts were lost with the 24 senior Intelligence Officers who died. The British were fond of describing IRA bombers killed by premature explosions as having scored "own goals", but this was the biggest "*own goal*" of the War. The senior leadership of RUC Special Branch was decimated in the crash, British Army Intelligence was severely damaged, and MI5 lost almost all of its senior personnel in Ulster. The British capacity to engineer a breakdown of the Ceasefire and exploit the aftermath by provoking a military rout of the Republican Army was lessened thereby. (The Jack Holland book, *'Phoenix, Policing the Shadows'*, has much information on this. See also Patrick Fitzgerald, *Fortnight*, July/August 1994.)

I can only think of one case of the unconditional surrender of an undefeated army. This happened in the Autumn of 1918, with the surrender of the undefeated German Army—which was achieved by a political stratagem of war. A political revolution was provoked in Germany by an Allied confidence trick, utilising the US President. The Allies declared that, if Germany got rid of the Kaiser and established a Republic, *'peace with honour'* could be negotiated and a new settlement of Europe would be worked out at the Peace Conference in which all would participate as equals. At least, that is what President Wilson said and his British allies did not publicly contradict him—although they had no intention of delivering on its promises. The leadership of German Social Democracy was naive and innocent and believed the Allied peace propaganda that was directed at them. This resulted in a botched political revolution in the midst of a War which the Allies did not expect to win by battle before 1920. The subsequent political bungling brought about a great demoralisation in the German army which then fell apart without having been actually defeated. The Allies then treated Germany as a conquered country which had no rights, forgetting the promises they had made—or allowed President Wilson to make as if he was speaking for all. The new Republican government in Germany was compelled by the Royal Navy, which was inflicting a Starvation Blockade upon the German people (which was maintained until July 1919, eight months after the actual Armistice) to accept *'war guilt'* on behalf of the German nation and to agree to a destructive scale of reparations. A consequence of all this, and the chaos it brought about in Germany, was Hitler and the Nazis.

For a semblance of an Irish precedent, there was the Winter of 1797-8, when many of the United Irishmen in Wexford responded to an appeal by the Catholic clergy that they should hand in their arms under a Government offer of amnesty. Those who did so were viewed by the Government as self-confessed rebels and were dealt with accordingly. And that double-dealing was in great part responsible for the ferocity of the mass rebellion in Wexford just a few months later.

An example on the other side was during the Treaty War of 1922-23. The defeated IRA refused the offer of unconditional surrender from the Free State. It called a Ceasefire, dumped its arms, kept its command structure intact, and largely evolved into the *'slightly constitutional'* party, Fianna Fail. And it was through the efforts of that party that a functional constitutional order was given to the Free State, enabling it to become something more in time. If in 1923 the so-called *'irregulars'* had confessed their *'irregularity'*, had repented of their sins, had expressed remorse for all the trouble they had caused, and had crawled humbly into the Southern Parliament with their tails between their legs, the Free State would in all probability have remained a loyal part of the British Commonwealth.

History therefore shows that the character of the retreat from the battlefield is all-important, and this was well understood by the Republican Command.

Major Problems

The conduct of the Major Government in the year and a half following the *Downing Street Declaration* and in the year after the IRA Ceasefire confirmed that the London Government had been bounced into the *Declaration* by Hume and Adams and that the *Declaration* merely served the purpose of the moment for Britain. It also seemed to be the case that Whitehall would have been happy to see Hume cut down to size by a failure of the IRA Ceasefire.

Insofar as the Major Government had a strategy, it lay in the hope that the Ceasefire would lead to the Republican movement falling apart, so that the problem of what to do next would simply disappear. In many ways this British disorientation provided great encouragement for the IRA, not only to call the Ceasefire in the first place, but to persist in its unarmed strategy in the face of a perceived political bankruptcy within the mind of the enemy command.

The Major Government probably hoped that the great hopes surrounding the *Declaration* would develop such an expectation of peace on the part of the ordinary citizens of the North that the IRA would find itself stranded, unable to develop its unarmed strategy due to discontent within Republican ranks, but also incapable of going back to War due to the public backlash it would suffer if it chose to do so. In such circumstances, the IRA would either break up into incoherent chaos due to internal dissent, or would lose its structure and ability to resume the War through inactivity.

As was noted earlier, there is a deeply-rooted British conviction about the Irish that the Irish are a volatile and hot-headed people who lack the power of endurance—which the English have in great abundance. From the British perspective, the Irish were merely a *'mob trying to realise themselves as a nation'* (to use Pearse's phrase). They indulged in periodic rebellions, but like their game of hurling, their span of activity in each engagement was very sharp and short. The British State, which is all about endurance, as reflected in its game of cricket, therefore always wins in the end, in one way or another. And it was always reasonably content to lose early battles if it won the war.

However, the Northern Catholics had developed something of the English capacity for endurance, after being subjected to a form of British administration for generations—and some of the qualities of the people who surrounded them in that corner of Ireland rubbed off on them. And that made them into a different sort of force to be reckoned with than was expected both in 1970 and 1994.

Fr. Faul, who knew the Provos very well and who, whilst being a solid Nationalist himself, spent much effort attempting to prevent young folk joining them, commented around the time of the Hunger Strikes that there was something different about the new Republicans—something almost British-like about their power of endurance, their capacity to be flexible and to play the long game. He noticed this about Bobby Sands, in particular, who was a good poet and who apparently had a liking for the poet of Empire, Kipling. And since then, of course, it has become well-known that they had someone in their high command with a love of that quintessentially English strategically long game of cricket (Martin McGuinness)!

Adams said in a *Radio Ulster* interview on 3rd September 1995:

> "In my view the British government has not yet committed to the peace strategy. And the British government in my view is committed to a strategy of trying to win through the peace process a victory which it had failed to achieve during the years of conflict."

Adams formed this view as the British Government was beginning to insist on prior IRA decommissioning, to make the IRA ceasefire *'meaningful'*, before political progress—after earlier encouraging a very different understanding among Republicans.

Clinton and Major

The interference of the United States Government in 'Northern Ireland' was an important factor in convincing the Republican Army of the wisdom of a Ceasefire. This is an area in which the 'Hume factor', along with Irish American influence, came in very handy in 1994. Haughey had realised the importance of opening this Front against the British. Back in 1977, Hume and Dublin had procured a statement from President Carter offering US intervention to help solve the 'Northern Ireland' problem. This created an important precedent that Britain did not like and sought to avert. Haughey had attempted to remove Dublin's Anglophile Ambassador in Washington, Sean Donlon, from his post during his 1979-81 term of Office. However, Haughey's efforts were blocked by Fine Gaeler Garret FitzGerald, who used the Irish American Establishment to bolster Donlon's position. It was only after Donlon saw that Haughey was about to return as Taoiseach in 1987 that he decided to leave for a job in industry. (He re-entered the political scene in 1995, when Taoiseach John Bruton, appointed him Chief of Staff and Special Adviser with particular regard to Northern Affairs. This is when the IRA Ceasefire was ended with regard to operations in England.)

In January 1994 the British Government exerted its influence to prevent Adams from gaining entry to the US, but "was filled with astonishment and annoyance" when President Clinton granted him a visa, overriding the Anglophile State Department and British diplomatic lobbying. Major told Taoiseach Reynolds, who was lobbying for the visa with Clinton, that he would "oppose it with all I had". At the time the British Ambassador told *CNN* that the President was granting a visa to "Sinn Fein's Dr. Goebbels", and the *Daily Telegraph* spoke of "the worst rift since Suez" in the "special relationship" between Britain and its Anglo-Saxon cousin (Conor O'Cleary, *'The Greening of the White House'*, p. 89 and pp.117-9).

Although Bill Clinton had been a Cecil Rhodes scholar at Oxford, he considered himself an Irish-American. His Presidential campaign of 1992 had been bankrolled by prominent Irish-American businessmen and he had heavily courted the community in the US. Sinn Fein was fortunate as regards Clinton. He was a President almost wholly focussed on domestic politics and had little strategic interest in foreign affairs. (It was Clinton who began to expand NATO into Eastern Europe, to garner support from expatriate communities in the US, without care for the long-term consequences.) The Anglophiles in Washington were unable to persuade him not to support the Irish lobby against British interests.

During the Presidential campaign the British Tories made the mistake of interfering in US politics on the side of the Bush campaign. They misjudged the American electorate, whom they thought would re-elect the victorious war President who had pulverised its former ally, Iraq, to lay down a marker in the post-Cold War world.

The part of this interference that Clinton never forgot was the checking of his passport details by British officials, to provide the US Republican campaign with information that might tar him as a Soviet sympathiser in his youth. Clinton was outraged by this and blamed the British Prime Minister for authorising it. Clinton took no time to get even with Major, appointing Jean Kennedy Smith of the Kennedy clan as Ambassador in Dublin and Mayor Flynn of Boston to the Vatican. Lord Hailsham, Thatcher's Lord Chancellor, had made his displeasure about Irish American interference known to the *Irish Times*, as well as the fact that the spirit of Anti-Catholicism had not died, when he is reported to have exclaimed: "Those Roman Catholic bastards! How dare they interfere" (*'The Greening of the White House'*, p. 39). But British displeasure at US interference was not confined to the Right—the *Guardian* also expressed its outrage and said that America should stop doing this sort of thing (18.3.95).

British vulnerability to US interference had come about due to its failure to prosecute two World Wars to a finish. It had had to be rescued by America for its failures to destroy Germany with its original allies, and this left it open to Irish-American consent in return tor US aid. The Irish lobby then made certain America took full commercial advantage of its bargaining position with relation to Britain. And so, through the British mismanagement of its world domination, the US was brought into predominance over Britain, with the Irish lobby emerging in the process as one of the major influences in American affairs.

President Clinton wanted to send a US Peace Envoy to Ireland and was only dissuaded by the Taoiseach Albert Reynolds, who felt he could use the favour in preventing this US interference with Major in talks over the Downing Street Declaration. The US President then lifted the ban on Sinn Fein fundraising in the States. St. Patrick's Day, a major event in American life, became a lever of the Irish Americans that could not be ignored by the President and it began to be used to good effect.

Clinton's visit to Belfast in November 1995 preserved the Peace Process by pressurising Major into giving a wider remit to an International Commission with regard to arms decommissioning. Up until then, the British side was making a partial IRA surrender of arms a condition of starting Talks. After Clinton's visit, it was decided that preliminary talks would start whilst a Decommissioning Commission sat, and there would be great pressure all round to accept the recommendations of the Commission as regards demilitarisation to enable substantive talks to take place.

The change Clinton's visit brought about in the position of the British government can be seen in two Communiqués issued either side of his visit. In September 1995 a statement saw the International Decommissioning Commission's role as being the attainment of full and verifiable decommissioning on 'illegally held arms by paramilitary organisations' (IT 30.9.95). However, a new communication on 28th November, after Clinton had made his mark, did not refer to paramilitary arms at all but to 'the desire to see all arms removed from Irish politics' (IT 30.11.95).

The result of this change was a dose of reality in the recognition by the British that the IRA was not militarily defeated and could not be treated as if it were. Presumably what helped the US administration to make resolving the 'Northern Ireland' question one of its priorities and its willingness to pressurise the British Government into seeing things in a different way was the persuasion of John Hume and some powerful Irish American entrepreneurs who had supported Clinton in his 1992 Presidential campaign.

Major Miscalculation

Immediately after Clinton's visit the British Prime Minister came to Ballymena and made a very strange statement about the Republican movement—strange in view of British policy over the previous 20 years. He said:

> "They're trying to maintain the fiction that I think most people in Northern Ireland will find laughable: that Sinn Fein and the IRA are wholly separate organisations. We know that not to be true. The people of Northern Ireland know that not to be true" (IT 22.12.95).

Major's statement was strange because it had been British Government policy to make a qualitative distinction between Sinn Fein and the IRA, with the object of bringing on Sinn Fein as a political force which would complicate the 'Northern Ireland' situation and open up the possibility of developments which, as things then stood, were right out of the question. In the early 1970s there was certainly nothing much to choose between Sinn Fein and the IRA but the British Government chose to find a difference between the two in 1975 and to work at developing it forever after, in order to open up the possibilities of negotiations with Republicans.

What began to happen in the early 1990s was the development of a new Republicanism which displayed a dimension of originality and flexibility that was not present in the movement from the 1920s to the late 1960s. The ideological medium in that period was a Southern doctrinaire Second Dáil Republicanism that had no truck with compromise.

This Anti-Treaty Republicanism had maintained itself in existence, preserving its purity, despite becoming increasingly unrealistic once De Valera had begun to erode the Treaty and establish the Southern State as something independent in the world, during Britain's Second World War on Germany. After that, there was little or no basis in political conditions in the 26 Counties for Anti-Treaty Republicanism. Only the National antagonism over the North kept the Republican movement alive and gave it a second innings.

The Republican Army was a new creation after August 1969 out of the ashes of Bombay Street etc. It was not created by Republican doctrine, but by fresh experience. In its dynamic mass, it was the specific creation of 'Northern Ireland'. The British Government obviously saw in the new Republican Army something different with which it could ultimately do business, even if it went to the wrong door first. This new Republicanism took up the suggestion, first put to it 20 years earlier, that there was Sinn Fein and there was the IRA, seeing that great potential lay in that distinction— a potential that began to be realised in the 1990s. But Prime Minister Major seemed to forget all about this or cared to forget it as *'the bastards'* in his own party began to get to him.

The Mitchell Report

The appointment of Senator George Mitchell, a leading Clinton supporter, as Chairman of the Decommissioning body showed the depth of US involvement in the Peace Process. By Britain's past standards of rejecting international interference in its affairs, having the arms decommissioning body chaired by an outsider was an innovative departure. Whitehall agreed to authorise the Mitchell Commission only because it did not dare to spoil

President Clinton's visit by refusing to do so. However, once Clinton was gone, Major found that he had to please the Unionists in Westminster so that they did not commit against him in the lobbies of Westminster. So he treated the Mitchell Principles upon their publication as things of no consequence.

With his majority in Parliament approaching nil, Major's main priority during 1996 was to hold onto Office for another year to maximise his chances of re-election. There is, after all, no higher motive in British politics. Major's plan to maintain himself in power seems to have been to humour the US President while he was in the province, play for time when he had gone, and prevaricate on the Peace Process which Clinton had reinvigorated through his visit.

The sidelining of the *Mitchell Report* was an example of the lowest form of political expediency by the British Prime Minister. The Report was anything but a one-sided document favouring Sinn Fein and, if the Westminster Government had supported it, very great leverage could have been applied to Sinn Fein to make compromises which it did not relish making in a hurry. But the Report was instead brushed aside at the hour of its publication because it was known that any other course of action would have jeopardised the support of Unionist MPs for Major's crumbling Government.

But what was probably more damaging was the half-baked response of the Dublin Government to Major's dismissal of the *Mitchell Report*. A sharp diplomatic response, that maintained Republican confidence in the relationship it had forged with the previous administration in Dublin that had created the necessary momentum in the process, would probably have held things together. But the Dublin Government was at that time no longer that of Albert Reynolds and Fianna Fail, but was headed by John Bruton, an enthusiastic Redmondite, in a Fine Gael/Democratic Left/Labour Coalition.

Mansergh had informed Bruton of the position of Republicans with regard to the Peace when Fianna Fail had handed over to the Coalition. A written Note of Bruton's records a summary of what Mansergh told him:

> "Too quick a move on arms could break the Sinn Fein leadership... They don't contest the process of decommissioning. There was little real disagreement on the shape of a political settlement. Adams agreed that a united Ireland was impossible without unionist support. Fifty per cent plus one was not enough" (Kevin Rafter, *'Martin Mansergh'*, p.233).

All Bruton had to do was to maintain this position to sustain the Peace Initiative. However, the new Taoiseach instead attempted to impose his own version of what the Peace Process should have been on what actually constituted it.

John Bruton had become Taoiseach unexpectedly when Albert Reynolds' Labour partners had pulled the plug on the Coalition. As Taoiseach Bruton all of a sudden had to start playing a part in support of Republicans which was he was ideologically ill-disposed to play—being an admirer of John Redmond and believing 1916 and the independence struggle to have been a mistake. He had to carry forward the Peace Process which, in so far as it involved the Irish State, had originated with, of all people, the hateful Haughey and which then had been brought to spectacular success by Haughey's successor, Reynolds. It really went against the grain of Bruton's character and his view of the North with which he had identified himself as Leader of the Fine Gael Opposition to do this.

Brian Feeney has noted that—

> "Bruton... remains the only Taoiseach in history ever to be criticised in an editorial of the... nationalist Irish News for his mishandling of the peace process. Within a week of his taking office, he stated that 'substantive progress' on decommissioning was required by the IRA, thereby adopting the British position" (*'Sinn Fein, A hundred turbulent years'*, p.412).

The political circumstances he had inherited dictated that he had, of course, at least to go through the motions of supporting the Peace initiative and he did well enough to carry the process forward for about a year. But on the one critical day he failed badly to provide leadership. This was the day of the Mitchell Report, when it was treated as a thing of no consequence by Major. And that was the moment that effectively led to the ending of the IRA Ceasefire. (However operations were not resumed within Northern Ireland.)

The Dublin Government that assisted Major to escape the Peace Process was not only handicapped by being led by Bruton but also by containing as a significant element members of *Democratic Left*—formerly the Worker's Party, formerly Sinn Fein the Worker's Party, formerly Official Sinn Fein, formerly Sinn Fein. Bruton had the anti-Republican, law and order, Treatyite/ Blueshirt view of things which corresponded closely with an Anglophile view of the world that disabled him at the vital hour whilst WP leader De Rossa's ideological view of the world was coloured by the feud of the Official IRA with the upstart Provos. This combination prevented Dublin doing the necessary when Major had fobbed off the Mitchell Report and it unravelled the front assembled to pursue the Peace.

End of Ceasefire

That was the moment that effectively led to the ending of the IRA Ceasefire and the resumption of the War against the British Government on the territory of Great Britain (the Provos were careful to signify this by a restriction of military activity in the Six Counties to virtually nothing). Having informed the Sinn Fein leadership that the War was about to be renewed, the

Sinn Fein leadership informed the US Government, through its diplomats, that this was the case. This emphasised to the Americans—the predominant element in the new disposition—their importance and the nature of the resumption of the War. London and Dublin found themselves relegated to secondary status by Sinn Fein and having to find out afterwards what their bungling had resulted in.

The IRA called off its Ceasefire on 9th February 1996 in spectacular fashion because the British Government had failed to comply with the understandings which had led to the Ceasefire. The two Governments in London and Dublin condemned the ending of the Ceasefire in terms that were not consistent with their positions over the preceding two years. If there had never been a semblance of justification for Republican military activity, it was hard to see how such a thing as the Peace Process was justifiable in the first place. States do not engage in peace processes with criminals, so the mere fact that the Peace Process was entered into with the IRA represented a formal recognition that the Republican struggle was not an campaign of criminality. Coming to an accommodation with Republicans carried the implication that there was justification for the Republican military campaign in the first place.

The Republican leadership had acknowledged a number of years earlier that a simple military victory was an impossibility. After many years of stalemate, the political initiative launched by Hume and Adams had obliged the Irish and British Governments to launch initiatives of their own and to produce their highly ambiguous *Downing Street Declaration*. Nine months of intensive discussions between the two Governments and the Republican leaders followed and had produced the Republican Ceasefire. There could be no reasonable doubt that the Ceasefire was called on the strength of certain understandings established within those discussions. The only conclusion that could be reached was that the British Government did not comply with those understandings and therefore the British element of the Ceasefire ended with a spectacular explosion in Canary Wharf.

Brian Feeney gives a description of how Bruton bungled the Peace in his book, '*Sinn Fein, A Hundred Turbulent Years*':

> "What was particularly frustrating for Sinn Fein was that, after the 1993 Downing Street Declaration, Irish officials had rapidly taken the process on to the next phase, which was the plan to devise institutions to give expression to the self-determination described in the Declaration. By the summer of 1994 a blueprint for such institutions had been sketched out by Irish and British officials. It was shown to Sinn Fein to help them move the IRA to a ceasefire. Sinn Fein's leaders were quite encouraged by the plans, which contained all Ireland bodies with executive powers. Yet when the completed plans were published in early 1995 by John Bruton and John Major as the

Frameworks Documents, Sinn Fein had still not met any British minister and was no closer to talks than it had been when the IRA had declared a ceasefire five months earlier.

"The thinking behind the Frameworks Documents was absolutely fundamental to removing the basis for a Republican military campaign, and that thinking was one of the reasons why all party talks on the documents were so important to Sinn Fein... The idea of the Frameworks Documents was that the all-party agreement on new Northern Ireland and all Ireland institutions would be put to the Irish people in referendums north and south. Those referendums would be a new expression of the self-determination of the Irish people... The whole process—Declaration, Frameworks Documents, referendums—that had been devised by Irish officials was being held up at a crucial stage by the absence of any negotiations. The British government was blocking it by refusing to talk to Sinn Fein at ministerial level about anything but decommissioning of IRA weapons. There the matter stood throughout 1995. Tensions rose within the Republican movement... As the first anniversary of the IRA ceasefire approached, very serious strains built up within the IRA. Adams desperately needed action from the British on the main front; a date for talks. But by the end of the summer John Bruton seemed, on the contrary, as if he was going to agree with the British government to establish a body to supervise decommissioning before talks, another delaying tactic. Sinn Fein sent out frantic signals that this would be the last straw... After more rumblings in the IRA, Adams and Hume together asked to meet Bruton. He refused. The basis for the ceasefire in TUAS therefore no longer obtained. It is now known that from this time, October 1995, Adams had lost the support of the Army Council. Work had begun in South Armagh on converting a vehicle to transport a huge bomb to London" (pp.412-5).

Hume's difficulty

John Hume was put in a difficult position within the SDLP by the collapse of the Peace Process. When the IRA ended their Ceasefire in Britain, Hume came out vigorously against Sinn Fein. In an article entitled *'Why voters must turn away from Sinn Fein'*, he said Republicans "got it wrong over the last quarter of a century, the SDLP are the people who got it right" (IN 10.2.1997).

Frustrated at the collapse of the IRA Ceasefire, Hume panicked. He began to move toward the position of Hendron and Mallon. But, with Orange conduct at Drumcree radicalising the Nationalist population across the province, the position held by Hendron and Mallon began to become a losing hand.

It was becoming apparent that Hume's difficulty was that Sinn Fein had taken over much of what used to be his position and it was advancing this position as effectively as the master, if not more so. That may be one explanation of why Hume seemed to retreat from the position he had taken up during the Hume/Adams talks towards the scepticism and hostility of Mallon and Hendron.

He came under severe pressure from the other three SDLP MPs and it looked as though Mallon would make a bid to replace him. The Dublin media certainly championed the pretenders to Hume's throne. Everything had hinged on the attainment of the IRA Ceasefire. His great performance in the European elections, and then the IRA's Ceasefire caused Hume's stock to soar and his leadership was put beyond challenge. However, there remained two SDLPs—John Hume and the rest. And this was very apparent to the Nationalist electorate.

The SDLP as a body would have been much more representatively and appropriately led by Hendron or Mallon at this juncture. But the standing of Hume through his efforts in the Peace Process and the functionality and effectiveness of his political position made this an impossibility.

Hume's collaboration with Sinn Fein to bring about the Peace Process was not an SDLP/Sinn Fein collaboration. It was a John Hume/Sinn Fein collaboration. Hume acted against the instincts and bias of his own party structure in that business, but in the knowledge that, at grassroots level, there were, for the most part, no hard distinctions between the SDLP and Sinn Fein. When Hume embarked on Sinn Fein's political initiative with Adams, and it began to gather a political momentum, it became clear that this was a 'solo run' by Hume, dragging the rest of the SDLP behind him. And it was inevitable that the choice Hume made, putting the interests of community above party, was not popular in all sections of his party. There were plenty of murmurings and expressions of *angst*. It was said that, when Hume was confronted by his colleagues, concerned that the negotiations with Adams were damaging the SDLP, he replied: "If it's a choice between the party and peace, do you think I give a fuck for the party?" (F. O'Connor, *'Breaking the Bonds: Making Peace in Northern Ireland'*, p.25).

It was not surprising that much of Hume's position started slipping away from him to Sinn Fein, once Republicans started taking up his position. Sinn Fein gave it a much sharper expression and provided a greater number of people who could advocate it effectively, without divided minds about it.

In a series of three elections from May 1996 until May 1997, the Northern Catholics delivered their verdict on the Peace Process and the two Nationalist parties. In the elections to the Belfast Forum, on an abstentionist policy, Sinn Fein took 15% of the vote. A year later, in the British General Election of May 1997 the party took 16%. And in the Local Government Elections in the same month this increased to 17%. In 1993 the ratio of SDLP votes to Sinn Fein votes had been 75 to 25. In 1997 it was down to just 55 to 45 in favour of the SDLP.

Catholic voters not only wanted to encourage Sinn Fein to pursue its Peace Initiative; they were also showing that they did not hold the IRA responsible for the partial breakdown of the Ceasefire, despite the SDLP's best efforts to tar it with this. They were in the process of making a decisive change, backing the Republicans to secure the best deal possible for the community, and were starting to abandon the SDLP.

High Noon at Drumcree

In July 1997 Northern Ireland came closer to what is called 'civil war' than at any time since August 1969. The Nationalist community across the north was outraged by the confidence trick at Drumcree (near Portadown) perpetrated by the new Labour Government and its Secretary of State, Marjorie Mowlam. The protesting Catholic residents were led to believe that the Orange March would be prevented but were then taken unawares by a British Army operation in the early hours of the morning that sealed them into their homes to enable the Orangemen to march. This set the scene for a battle royal to take place later at the Ormeau Bridge in Belfast. Here, the Catholic community deployed in force days before the event to prevent a repeat of the events in Portadown and to stymie a military curfew similar to that imposed a year earlier, to ensure the Ballynafeigh Orangemen got down the road.

If the Orangemen had been reinforced from other areas, there would have been the prospect of a confrontation which would have surely been the end of the Peace Process and much more besides. However, this time the Orangemen backed down and everyone lived to fight another day. It was also one of the two occasions when the INLA had a significant effect on political events in the province. The INLA's intervention on the Ormeau Bridge in 1997 concentrated minds on what wider mayhem could follow in the absence of a political solution. The Drumcree and Ormeau Bridge events were a game changer. (The other was in the assassination of Airey Neave and the Tory policy of Integration.)

In 1997, in response to the *'pan-nationalist front'* in politics, a *pan-unionist front* had been organised in support of Orangemen against Catholic residents, in order to push the Orange march down the Garvaghy Road. While succeeding on the Garvaghy Road, that success was not repeated at Ormeau. It was the defeat inflicted here that really signalled to the Catholic community that things were changing in the North.

The situation in 1997 had been transformed since 1994, as Unionist power had been blunted. Two years earlier, in 1995, after a compromise had been reached whereby the 800 strong Orange were allowed to march along

Garvaghy Road on condition that they did so silently, without accompanying bands, Ian Paisley, leader of the DUP, and David Trimble, who was to win the leadership of the Ulster Unionist Party within weeks of this event, had held hands in the air in a triumphalist gesture while doing what resembled "*a victory jig*" with the Orange marchers down the road. Trimble later claimed that he only took Paisley's hand to prevent the DUP leader from getting all the media praise, but large graffiti went up across the Province saying '*Well done, David*' at his success at making the Croppies lie down again.

Unionists had threatened to withdraw from the Peace Process if the Orangemen were not allowed down the Garvaghy Road and exercise their supremacy on the "*traditional routes*".

During the standoffs in 1995, 1996, 1997 and 1998 thousands of Orange and their supporters, including well-known loyalist celebrity paramilitaries, gathered at Drumcree and put the Garvaghy Road under siege for several days. Numerous roads were blocked across the province and illegal checkpoints set up which the RUC made little effort to interfere with. Many Catholic families were burnt out of their houses and a number were killed by Unionist militants. The concentrated power of the Protestant community was applied to achieve the annual objective of getting Orange feet on the Garvaghy Road. This went on until the massacre of the Quinn family in Ballymoney in 1998, after which mainstream Unionism began to disassociate itself from what they had helped call forth, although lower key protests continued.

The annual events at Drumcree between 1995 and 1998 were very important in mobilising the Catholic community and this signified an altering in the balance of power between the Protestant and Catholic communities that had been proceeding in other areas of life. This complemented what was happening in the Peace Process. Gerry Adams later told an RTE journalist:

> "Ask any activist in the north, 'did Drumcree happen by accident?', and he will tell you, 'no'. Three years of work on the lower Ormeau Road, Portadown and parts of Fermanagh and Newry, Armagh and in Bellaghy and up in Derry. Three years of work went into creating that situation and fair play to those people who put the work in. They are the type of scene changers that we have to focus on and develop and exploit" (Irish Independent 14.7.02).

The really significant thing about the Drumcree stand-offs was how they helped to radicalise the Catholic community. The intransigence, bigotry and blustering of all shades of Unionism in the marching season between 1995 and 1998 diminished Catholic willingness to tolerate the *status quo* in the province and Sinn Fein was the ultimate beneficiary of this. Catholics in parts of the province which had seen little of the warfare of the previous 25 years, and which had accepted Orange marchers as part and parcel of life in Ulster, began to counter parades that had previously been unchallenged. Sinn Fein activism in residents' groups was rewarded by the election of more Sinn Fein Councillors.

The fact that the British Government finally applied the power of State, after the Catholic community had shown its determination to counter the Orange, had important implications for Catholic confidence in the future and the willingness of Catholics to swing behind Sinn Fein. In 1997 the Orangemen of Portadown walked down the Garvaghy Road for the last time and subsequently Orange parades in contentious areas dwindled.

Ceasefire Resumed

The resumption of the IRA's campaign brought about a refined and politically-selective military activity, waged almost exclusively in Britain. Although the Ceasefire had formally ended it continued to exist in *de facto* form in 'Northern Ireland', despite every opportunity to relaunch it over the period when the Drumcree stand-offs were at their height.

Aside from the bombing of the British Army Headquarters in Lisburn (which was a kind of symbolic operation to prove they hadn't gone away), the renewed Provo campaign in the province was almost non-existent. The Republican Army did not want any military stimulus to upset the prospects for peace in the Six Counties, so they did not respond to Unionist provocation at Drumcree, keeping a tight discipline over the rank and file. The fact that there was no High Noon at Drumcree was due to Republican commitment to the Peace Process.

Ed Moloney has argued that the renewed military campaign had signified "military weakness" in the IRA. But this view overlooks the politics of the situation. The Republican command had the objective of a return to the negotiating table chiefly on the mind, so operations were controlled and limited, with experienced volunteers not risked after years of contribution to the struggle.

The renewed military campaign was tightly controlled and politically focussed so as not to wreck the pan-nationalist consensus, which was under strain, or squander the political gains made, particularly in the US. Some controlled and carefully targetted military operations were aimed at keeping Whitehall on its toes and at the same time placate more hard-line Republicans, with Sinn Fein continuing to point up the political alternative available to the British Government if it chose to take it. The more vigorous elements of the Republican Army were occupied in the execution of a number of drug dealers and the breaking of their networks during 1995-6.

The British understood the situation too and lethal force was held back. Both sides did not wish to endanger the prospects of resurrecting the process of negotiations, so what transpired was a kind of military sparring before the main event in the political ring.

An extraordinary Republican Army Convention took place in October 1996. Around 60 delegates attended, about one-tenth of the Republican Army's Volunteers. The Leadership saw off a motion that would have prevented a return to the conference table. Another motion sought to limit the Army Council's power to call or prolong ceasefires by binding it to strict conditions of Army Executive review. This motion would have delivered a present to the British if they wished to provoke splits in the movement, and it would have weakened those within the British State who were favourable to peace since they could no longer depend on any commitments made when negotiating with the Army Council. The leadership managed to water this amendment down and to prevent the meeting from changing the Constitution of 1986, which had given the Army Council complete control of the IRA's arsenal. This was vital if Decommissioning was ever to take place.

The Republican Army Executive elected an Army Council that was in favour of the peace strategy and managed to beat off the challenge of those sceptical of further negotiations, although there was a strong element on the Executive of this mind.

The Republican leadership realised that the Major Government, with its slim and declining majority, was a beaten docket, incapable of doing the necessary to advance toward Peace. However, the new British Labour Government under Tony Blair, with its landslide victory in 1997, took a different attitude and, instead of requiring Republicans to use the word *'permanent'* in relation to their Ceasefire, it exhibited an apparent eagerness to make it actually permanent. Blair's Chief of Staff from 1995 to 2007, Jonathan Powell, later revealed the thinking of the new Government as it came to power:

> "Our analysis was that John Major had run into trouble because he had let it drag out too long... he had let it go on and on and on, and the republicans had begun to believe that he was not serious about it at all, that he was just trying to string them along, which is why they went and did Canary Wharf... John Major... tried to get the ceasefire declared as permanent; to get PIRA to say it was permanent. When he could not get this, he then moved onto decommissioning as a surrogate to show that it was permanent... I think the mistake John Major made was that he allowed the issue of decommissioning to become a complete hurdle they had to cross, when there was no way republicans were going to cross it. They would not have gone on the ceasefire if they knew that this was going to be required of them right up front in the process. Decommissioning is something that happens right at the end of the

process, not at the beginning. I think the trouble was that Major made it a precondition. He said that we could not come into talks until this had happened. At first he said complete decommissioning, and then backed down from that and said token decommissioning... It was a terrible mistake to allow decommissioning to become this blockage and it should never have been put up front as a precondition." (Graham Spencer, *'The British and Peace in Northern Ireland'*, p.303 and pp.327-8)

As luck had it, just when things improved in London, they improved in Dublin with Bruton's exit from power. On 24th July 1997 the new Taoiseach, Bertie Ahern, made a significant speech which outlined the results of the private dialogue that had begun between Fianna Fail and Republicans. Ahern made a commitment to a re-opening of negotiations with the British:

"... not just of the Anglo-Irish Agreement but of the 1920-1 settlement... and a new approach to constitutional doctrines on both sides. The Government of Ireland Act of 1920 and subsequent constitutional development failed to resolve the conflict of political allegiances within Ireland. A deep settlement, incorporating positive elements that have been identified, would address and overcome previous failures going back to 1920, to achieve the basis of a just and durable settlement " (IT 25.7.97).

Republicans entered talks at Stormont on 10th September 1997. Blair's Chief of Staff noted the openness of the Sinn Fein leaders from the outset, something apparent when they went to Downing Street around Christmas 1997:

"When we met for the first time in Downing Street in the Cabinet Room, Martin McGuinness wanted to break the ice and said, 'So this was where all the damage was done?' I thought he was referring to when the PIRA bombed Downing Street in 1991 where they nearly wiped out the War Cabinet who were meeting to discuss the Iraq War. But McGuinness was referring to where the treaty was signed by Michael Collins and Lloyd George...

"I think they had made the decision in the late 1980s that they wanted peace, and they knew approximately the terms they would have to settle on in the end and that would include the Union going on. If they had said that to the movement in the 1980s they would have been rejected, so they had to lead the movement crab-like to a peace process... Adams was very explicit at the first meeting that we had in Downing Street when he took Tony and me to a part of the room where the pillars separated people off and said he could deliver the PIRA, but that it would be better to do it with the whole movement rather than just reaching agreement with some of them. He argued that it was important to win the movement over, and we accepted that... The peace process was about getting to a fundamental fairness that they felt had been denied... they did not just want to have their grievances heard, but to change things and get a practical approach for going forward" (*'The British and Peace in Northern Ireland'*, pp. 305-6).

Powell understood that, whilst Sinn Fein wanted to negotiate a settlement that fell short of their objective, that it had not abandoned that objective but simply had determined to achieve it through politics: "I think this is very important to understand, that what republicans were really demanding was change and the ability to bring about change without the unionists being able to veto it. The issue was the unionists always being able to block change…" (p.321).

It soon became apparent that the Ulster Unionists were reluctant participants in any talks that would end their position of dominance. David Trimble, the new Unionist Leader, who had replaced Molyneaux, delayed his party's return to the talks until 17th September when they were accompanied into Castle Building by leaders of the loyalist parties in a scene reminiscent of the film *'Gunfight at the O.K. Corral'*.

Once inside the Talks, the Unionists sought the immediate exclusion of Sinn Fein by the two Governments. The Unionists were intent on characterising what they called *'Sinn Fein/IRA'* as one indistinguishable organisation, which, of course, they were not. This was a fiction maintained so that Sinn Fein could be isolated from the process, even if it did have the electoral mandate to be there. The Ulster Unionist submission to the Talks was headed *'Notice of Indictment'* and, having indicted the Republicans, Ken Maginnis and Trimble immediately left with the rest of the Pan-Unionist front. In his remarks to the media, the new Unionist leader indicated that his party would pursue a strategy of negotiating with all the participants—except Sinn Fein, saying "there is no need for us to engage with Sinn Fein at all".

Mallon Takes Control of the SDLP

In August 1997 there was speculation that Hume might stand to succeed Mary Robinson as President of the Republic. This would have removed one of the main architects of the Peace Process and it would have been very damaging to it. Firstly, Hume's stature was required at the Talks as a counterweight to Unionism, since there was no other 'constitutional nationalist' of such credibility. If any other member of the SDLP delegation apart from Hume had led the party, Sinn Fein would have been in a very isolated position and the whole process could have fragmented and collapsed.

By this time Hume appeared to be beleaguered within the SDLP. He was getting his way most of the time by overawing the party with his substantial will and his even more substantial stature but, if he was taken out of the frame the Mallonites with their devolutionist perspective, might well have ruined everything. There could be little doubt that Hume's departure would not only have compromised the Peace Process but would eventually have damaged the SDLP as against Sinn Fein. An SDLP Councillor in Armagh told the *Irish News*, "I do feel very, very strong about it. I do feel very, very strong. I am very concerned that the whole thing will fall around him if he goes. The party will fall" (IN 22.8.97).

Hume was being pushed forward as a possible President by Fine Gael and the *Irish Times*. Two things were significant about this alliance. Firstly, they seemed to want Hume out of the way so that a more devolutionist and anti-Sinn Fein SDLP would emerge. The *Irish News* Editor, Tom Collins, came out for the removal of Hume from the Peace Process in support of the Mallonites. The paper's Editorial of 19th August 1997 suggested that Hume was past his 'sell by' date and "would undoubtedly be keen to avoid the mistakes made by the likes of James Molyneaux and Ian Paisley, who damaged the credibility of their parties by clinging to power at an advanced stage".

How misconceived this view was was later illustrated by the fact that Paisley provided the immensely important act of leading the DUP into government with Sinn Fein over a decade after this was written. The remarks show that there was no appreciation whatsoever of the fact that Hume had helped to establish the context of politics in Ireland at this point. Collins's underlying message was that the Mallon wing of the party, which seemed to have the ascendancy at the *Irish News*, simply could not wait for Hume to go.

The objective of establishing a real antagonism between the SDLP and Sinn Fein was counter-productive to the overall interests of Nationalism. It could only result in the splitting apart of the Nationalist movement, with the detached part having to form an alliance with the liberal wing of Unionism. And what bargaining power would it have in such a situation, depending on Unionists to offer a favourable deal?

Catholics in 'Northern Ireland' are largely ambivalent about the SDLP and Sinn Fein. There is a continuum of attitude within the SDLP, ranging from violent antipathy to Sinn Fein at one end, to virtual Sinn Fein supporters at the other. Many upwardly mobile Catholics found outright support for Sinn Fein to be an impediment to their careers. But quite a lot of people, regardless of party affiliation, wanted Sinn Fein to do well in elections so that the democratic argument of Nationalism in the peace talks would be unanswerable.

A good example of the Northern Catholic attitude toward Sinn Fein and the SDLP was that of the successful Presidential candidate Mary McAleese. McAleese described herself as "an SDLP supporter" in an interview with the *Irish News* on 21st October 1997 after it was reported in the *Irish Times* on the previous day that Brid Rogers, an SDLP Councillor, had suggested McAleese was "pushing the Sinn Fein agenda" (along with Fr. Alex Reid). However, a leaked Minute from the Republic's Department of Foreign Affairs (dated 26th May) published in the *Irish News* described McAleese's attitude more frankly:

> "She was very pleased with Sinn Fein's performance in the general election and confident that they will perform even better in the local elections... Ms McAleese feels a lot of the 'new' Sinn Fein support has come from the young middle-aged and upwardly mobile nationalists rather than first-time voters, and that they see Sinn Fein as far more likely to deliver on the political front than the SDLP. She attributed the SDLP's failure to pick up either of the mid-Ulster or West Tyrone seats in part to their poor PR. The same tired old faces continued to front the SDLP while Sinn Fein publicise a range of candidates who all look young and fresh by comparison. She has not had much contact with Adams since the election although she returned from London last Monday evening on the same flight as Adams and McGuinness. Both of them were in great form and thoroughly enjoyed their visit to Westminster! ... She is confident that... Sinn Fein will agree to go into the talks only if they received guarantees on the timing of their entry into and on the duration of the talks and on 'decommissioning'. After the specified duration of the talks has passed and, in the strong likelihood that the talks will not produce an agreed outcome, the 'torch' will go back to the two governments, who will propose a solution as set out in the Framework Document" (IN 20.10.97).

Sinn Fein and the SDLP had been mutually complementary expressions of the will of the Northern Catholics. That is how they had been treated by the electorate, though others tried to impose a hard and fast difference of a fundamental kind between them. The combination of 'constitutional' and unConstitutional politics was nothing new in Irish National politics. 'Constitutional' only really meant pacifist. It did not mean a commitment to development as part of the British state, which is what constitutional really means. 'Constitutional' Nationalism did not denote a Nationalism seeking to find a place within the British Constitution. It meant nationalism which did not seek to use force itself to achieve its aim of leaving the British state and it was quite prepared to benefit from the efforts of those who did.

There was little difference in policy terms between the SDLP and Sinn Fein after Sinn Fein adopted a policy of Nationalist development by peaceful methods that was similar to Hume's—and that is why the SDLP begun to go into decline. But there had been for some time an element within the SDLP, held largely in check by Hume, that shared something of Fitt's attitude and hankered after a constitutional position in the proper meaning of the term.

Mallon evidently decided to do business with the reluctant Unionist participants in the Talks and attempted to establish a relationship with them that went beyond the one that was desired by Hume. The objective seems to have been to strike out independently of the broader Nationalist movement, to establish an embryonic devolutionary arrangement with Trimble. Deaglan de Breadun, the *Irish Times'* Northern Editor, recalled that the SDLP had felt marginalised since the time of Haughey Governments in Dublin:

> "The SDLP had worked closely with different Irish governments for many years and benefited from the political support and backup of Dublin and its bureaucracy. There was a close relationship between the... Department of Foreign Affairs... and the SDLP, indeed the mandarins were believed to have an input into SDLP speeches at times. Lately, however, the party seemed to be feeling squeezed, neglected and, to some extent, taken for granted... During the week beginning 8 December, the SDLP secured a deal with the Ulster Unionists on the list of key issues... the SDLP looked for support to the administration in the South, but this was not forthcoming... In the circumstances, SDLP sources felt Dublin should have put the heat on the republicans. Instead, Dublin sat on its hands. The rationale for Dublin's behaviour was that the situation inside the republican camp was still too delicate for such robust handling... 'Sinn Fein could only sign up to certain things as part of—and in the context of—an overall package' according to Dublin sources...
>
> "The time might come when Dublin turned its back on Sinn Fein, but to do so at this time would have placed the whole process in jeopardy... As a result the SDLP had found itself on its own on the nationalist side. Indeed, UUP sources claimed that when push came to shove, only Seamus Mallon was prepared to stand by their earlier deal. There was angry SDLP reaction to this and outright rejection of persistent suggestions in some quarters that Hume had been less enthusiastic about the initiative... It would also have caused serious problems among republicans on the ground if the final list included an assembly but left out, say, equality and demilitarisation. That was why Dublin was refusing openly to take sides... My report led Mallon to condemn breaches of confidentiality in the talks... In an apparent rebuke to Dublin, Mallon added: 'those who have chosen to distort or misrepresent a serious attempt to reach agreement have damaged the trust which is needed if these talks are to succeed. We hope that damage can be repaired when we return on January 12th'...
>
> "The latest attempt to advance the process ended in failure on the night of 16 December amid recriminations between the Ulster Unionists and the SDLP... SDLP sources said that the Ulster Unionists had 'got it in the neck' from all the other parties because of 'gratuitous leaking' about an 'alleged agreement' on the key issues between themselves and the SDLP. For their part, sources in the UUP insisted that the agreement had been made with the main nationalist party but that Mallon was the only SDLP representative prepared to stand by the deal." (See IT 18.12.97, IT 19.12.97 and *'The Far Side of Revenge'*, pp.86-90).

What seemed to be happening was that, in his eagerness to establish devolution and an internal governing arrangement with Trimble and the UUP, Mallon was breaking with the pan-Nationalist front that Hume, with Adams, had painstakingly established over the previous years. But, at the same time, the UUP and Trimble were reluctant participants in the process of establishing a settlement. So the breaking with Sinn Fein, Dublin (and Hume) was premature, even to those who wished to follow Mallon in striking out independently and establishing an independent 'constitutional' force in Northern politics.

Trimble was well aware of the devolutionary tendency within the SDLP and his objective was to form an alliance with it in order to break up the pan-nationalist front and isolate Sinn Fein. In an interview with Radio Ulster's *Inside Politics* on 20th September 1997 he made this strategy is clear:

> "There is far too much emphasis on Sinn Fein in this. Sinn Fein are marginal to the process, bear that in mind... It is not necessary for Sinn Fein to agree to anything, nor does Sinn Fein have a veto, unlike Unionists, because assent by our party is essential to any proposition and in fact in terms of the operation of the talks we have a veto. Sinn Fein does not. So Sinn Fein's participation is not essential... Are they [the SDLP and Irish government] going to shield Sinn Fein; are they going to help them continue with their alliance with them; or are they prepared to join with us in trying to build a better Northern Ireland for everybody here?... Now I could understand why in the past the SDLP were reluctant to do so, because John Hume wanted to see Sinn Fein involved in the process and you can understand the political and electoral considerations that may have led him to put that as a priority. Now that has been achieved he... has a very important strategic decision to take which will be more influential, more important in terms of the progress of the talks than the entry of Sinn Fein."

Trimble's view must have impressed Mallon since it was taken up by him. And this was an early indication that the SDLP under Mallon was going to attempt to hitch its political destiny to Trimble and Ulster Unionism within a devolutionary framework and live or die by the success of it. It seems to have been determined to move beyond Hume and to test the party's mettle, along with its political pretensions to be an independent force, apart from the Nationalist continuum.

CHAPTER 14

The Long Good Friday

The 1998 Agreement came about because the Republican Army had succeeded in waging War on Britain for over 28 years without being defeated. The Agreement and its new Constitution was the price Britain paid to end the War. Nothing like it would have been contemplated by Whitehall but for the Republican ability to sustain the War, and the willingness of the community to keep supporting it through thick and thin.

David Trimble, the new UUP Leader, attempted to minimise the importance of the Republican presence in the Talks that led to Good Friday, telling BBC Radio that "Sinn Fein are only bit players. They're a small group, a minority of a minority" (IT 14.10.97). He seemed to want to wish them away as unwelcome guests at a dinner he did wish to attend himself. But Trimble was evidently influenced against his will to sup with the Devil and then conclude a pact with him. Following this, the minority status of the Catholic community began to alter as a result of the Unionist signing of the Agreement and the Republican minority status within the former minority was transformed into a majority one. Those were the political effects of the long Good Friday.

Republicans and the 1998 settlement

The IRA and Sinn Fein were, of course, indispensable to the settlement of 1998 and both London and Dublin knew it. That was the major difference between 1973 and 1998. All the attempted settlements between 1973 and 1998 had been negotiated without Republicans, were aimed at undermining Republicanism, and they had all failed. But, while there was willingness in varying degrees to admit Sinn Fein to the table in 1998, the objective of the main players in 1998 was to marginalise the Republicans in the settlement. Deaglan de Breadun of the *'Irish Times'* let that slip when he wrote in 1997: "The time might come when Dublin turned its back on Sinn Fein, but to do so at this time would have placed the whole process in jeopardy". Sinn Fein's proposal at the Talks of an all-Ireland state with one parliament and 15 Regional Councils was ignored by the other participants, who had their set *'Three Strand'* agenda, ready to be imposed on the Unionists.

Sinn Fein complained that the *'Propositions on Heads of Agreement'* paper represented an Irish Government breaking of ranks, setting up institutions that would not be a basis for a lasting peace settlement (IT

22.1.98). That was very true. But the surprise was that it was Sinn Fein which, more than any other party, contributed most to their eventual functionality.

It was thought at the time that Good Friday was a settlement on SDLP terms and this view was re-inforced by the Mallon phrase that it was *"Sunningdale for slow learners"*. It was also the case that Hume took a back seat in the negotiations in favour of Mallon, Sean Farren, Denis Haughey, and Mark Durkan. However, years later, after the SDLP found itself reduced to a minor party in its political utopia, Mallon conceded that the settlement was pre-decided: it only appeared to have been got through SDLP negotiation:

> "In the two years of talks prior to the Good Friday Agreement there was little negotiation done by them (Sinn Fein, P.W.). Why? Because they'd already done their negotiations with America, with the Irish government, the British government. They had already got assurances as to the things they wanted and demanded. In other words they were telling the sovereign governments that they were writing the script" (IT 12.12.15).

A few days before the Agreement was finalised, Sinn Fein settled with the British Government on the prisoner issue. Sinn Fein had sought advice from the African National Congress, and had been warned to make sure the deal was clear, so there would be no mistake that a war had ended and an agreement had been made. And Nelson Mandela advised Adams not to give up weapons until the institutions were functioning.

William Beattie Smith of the United States Institute of Peace in Washington DC made the following estimation of the 1998 settlement:

> "The IRA's mission was to create an independent all-Ireland socialist republic… The IRA campaign did not attain its ultimate objectives. Northern Ireland remains in the United Kingdom… Nevertheless the IRA did achieve clear and substantial gains. The British terminated the majority-controlled administration that had run Northern Ireland since its creation in 1920, undertook to work for a united Ireland if a majority of the electorate supported it, introduced new power-sharing arrangements designed to guarantee minority participation in a new devolved administration, promoted new all-Ireland institutions that were presented as a step towards unification, and gave the Irish government substantial influence over British policy discussions. These were considerable achievements for a force of under two thousand fighters confronting one of the world's most experienced and best-equipped armies.
>
> "Why did the British yield so much? Did they appease violence or respond pragmatically to the changing elements of an intractable problem with no perfect solution?" (*'The British State and the Northern Ireland Crisis, 1969-73'*, p.2)

The Republican War was finally brought to a close by an arrangement that was fully in keeping with the self-defence Insurrection that began everything in August 1969. August 1969 was thus the *Alpha* and the *Omega*, the beginning and the end.

What originally caused the Insurrection that began the War was the structural fault-line of having an Ulster Unionist sub-government outside the democracy of the State, and what ended the War was the State finding it necessary to structurally negate the majority-rule in the sub-government, and to create a sharing-out of the government apparatus in proportional measure. Of course, the region still remained outside the democracy of the State. But that has been Britain's one fundamental and constant requirement of it since 1920. And that, one presumes, is how it will remain until it is completely detached towards Dublin.

Irredentism or Misgovernment?

There was a Constitutional dispute during the negotiations over the 1998 Agreement about where British sovereignty to the Six Counties actually lay. The Nationalists required the deletion of Section 75 of the *1920 Government of Ireland Act*, which claimed sovereignty over Northern Ireland and reserved ultimate authority to Westminster. They saw this as expressing the British territorial claim to the Six Counties, despite the consent clause inserted into the Hillsborough Treaty. This demand had been included in the Adams/Fr. Reid Peace Note of May 1987.

The demand seems to have been made by Sinn Fein to cover its consent to the Agreement. The thinking was that under it Britain could block a future majority within the Six Counties voting itself into an all-Ireland state. Removing it was probably regarded as furthering the objective of eroding Britishness in Ulster. When the deal was done, Taoiseach Ahern claimed that "The British Government... are effectively out of the equation" (Ian Ward, *'The English Constitution; Myths and Realities'*, p152). Subsequent events have shown this claim to have been either a false claim, used to lure Sinn Fein into the Agreement or naïve wishful thinking. Westminster sovereignty was not removed and it would also have been self-defeating to do so, since it would have thoroughly Ulsterised the problem of the divided society.

Trimble and the UUP argued that the British claim of sovereignty over Northern Ireland rested on the *Act of Union* and actually went back to the Norman conquest of 1177. The Unionist Leader even attempted to rewrite Article 3 of the Republic's Constitution for the Twenty-Six County State — although his offer was not taken up by Dublin.

The Unionist view that it was the Act of Union of 1801 that protected the Union says much about the character of modern Ulster Unionism. The Act of Union had quite obviously been breached, not only by the 1920 Government of Ireland Act, but also by the Anglo-Irish Treaty of 1921. To a lawyer like Trimble legalities seemed to override political realities. The Union may have existed as a legal entity but in practicality the detachment of the Six Counties from the UK State and its party politics made 'Northern Ireland' only formally part of the Union and in character, a place apart.

The intention of the Southern Government was to obtain the concession of the repeal of the remaining sections of the 1920 Act, in return for the amendments to Articles 2 and 3 of the Republic's Constitution. The British agreed to this, whilst taking steps to reserve powers essential to sovereignty elsewhere. The symbolic legitimation for a Republican invasion of the North contained in Articles 2 and 3 was removed, but the Good Friday Agreement legitimised the Republican War within the North by the settlement Britain conceded, in *de facto* form at least. A referendum was held in the 26 Counties in 1998, in which overwhelming approval was given to amendments of the Articles, dropping the claim.

It is often said that Articles 2 and 3 gave legitimacy to the IRA. That might have been the case until 1969, when IRA activity largely came from the State whose Constitution contained the Articles. But, after 1969, when the IRA became an indigenous development within the Six Counties, Articles 2 and 3 were really of no consequence in relation to the Provisionals. As Danny Morrison told a Dublin magazine in 1988:

> "The IRA doesn't claim to be representing the people in the Twenty Six Counties. Nor does Sinn Fein. The IRA claims to represent the IRA and the oppressed nationalists who support it. The IRA don't plant bombs in the name of the people of the Twenty Six Counties—the IRA plant bombs to bring about a political resolution to the problem of the North" (*Hot Press*, 25.8.88).

Articles 2 & 3 of the Twenty Six County Constitution are sometimes described as being 'irredentist', in that they claimed a right of sovereignty over an area that lay outside the borders of the Irish State. The claim of sovereignty had stood in the way of any real Southern approach for *rapprochement* with the North. In fact, no credible effort of that kind had ever been made by Government or Opposition in the South. Dublin Governments had routinely condemned the use of force to further the Constitutional claim, whilst retaining the 'irredentist' Articles. However they made little attempt to understand the Ulster Protestant community so that they might engage with it culturally in an historic compromise.

However, the War itself was not 'irredentist' because it was an internal uprising of the Northern Catholics against the conditions of life they suffered from within the Six Counties. It was not the influence of the 'irredentist' claim on the Northern Catholic community that prevented them from participating in the democratic politics of the British State, in which they were required to live. The Northern Catholics did not participate in the democratic politics of the State in which they lived because those politics were closed against them by Westminster.

Back in 1955 Michael Sheehy noted that:

> "It is natural that the Catholic minority take their cue from... the official Southern attitude to Partition. They are thereby encouraged to take the view, prompted by their own aggrieved feelings, that the Northern government lacks a foundation in justice and should be overthrown. The nationalist minority then constitutes a threat to the stability of the Northern government, and leaves that government no choice but to treat it as a subversive element... Southern statesmanship is primarily responsible for the hopeless position in which the Northern nationalists now find themselves... This incitement to intransigence has contributed to place the Northern nationalists in a dilemma; for they are neither prepared to accept the Northern government nor are they capable of destroying it" ('Divided we Stand', p.67).

In 1955 Sheehy was an almost lone voice in the wilderness but today his book is included in a select list of *"The books that define Ireland"* (Irish Independent 13.4.2014). Sheehy was both right and wrong: useful in 1955 and less useful today. In 1955 he was pointing to the Catholic predicament brought about partly by being let down by a Southern Nationalist Establishment that was bankrupt in relation to understanding the Northern Protestants through its *One Nation* dogma. However, the Insurrection that began in August 1969 was not brought about by Southern provocation but by the raw experience of life in the Northern statelet. The conditions that brought about the War in the North was not the 'irredentist' clauses of the Southern Constitution, but the governing arrangements made by the British State for its Six County region since 1920. Those governing arrangements were sectarian in a *de facto* way and that was important because all citizens were therefore under necessity to adapt themselves to that fact and behave accordingly.

The term *'Irredentism'* began to be used critically by some members of the Southern Establishment (most notably Conor Cruise O'Brien) during the 1970s, but they made no attempt to delete the 'irredentist' Articles of the Constitution when it actually mattered, at the height of the crisis over the Council of Ireland in 1974. The Articles were retained by Dublin Governments of all shades until the leadership of the Provisional IRA consented to their deletion in 1998. That was despite the fact that they denounced the

Provos during most of the conflict, particularly since it became apparent they could not deal a knock-out blow.

When Articles 2 and 3 were amended in 1998, it made little difference in relations between North and South, aside from providing Trimble with an argument in the Protestant community for accepting the Good Friday Agreement. However, the then small DUP argued that the Republic's amendments to their Constitution were too inconsequential to be called a concession of any real value to Unionism.

It was in Nationalist Ireland that the change had the greatest effect. From 1922 until 1998 the official Dublin position was that British Government in the Six Counties was illegitimate, usurping Irish rights of sovereignty over its island. There were Dublin Governments that wanted to acknowledge the North as a legitimately-governed part of the UK but they dared not say it, or interfere with the Articles that denied such a thing.

The repeal of *de jure* sovereignty over the Six Counties was only done with the permission of the Republican Army in 1998. That is evidenced clearly by the fact that no such thing was ever attempted before, despite the fact that it would have been very politic to do so at important moments. The fact that the Northern Republicans had to give consent to this fundamental change in the 26 County State was a measure of the change in relations between the Northern Catholics and Dublin Governments, brought about by the sustaining of the Republican War. And it was an indication of something that was to come—the rise of Sinn Fein as a serious political force in the Southern body politic.

The force that grew up because of the internal events of 1969, from the conditions of life within the perverse political entity of 'Northern Ireland', and which won a settlement on behalf of its community that rectified the most humiliating parts of these conditions of life, demonstrated that the conflict had nothing to do with irredentism and everything to do with misgovernment.

As for Article 75 of the Government of Ireland Act; it was transferred into the 1998 British Act of Parliament passing into Law the Agreement. It is in Clause 5.6 reaffirming the power of Westminster to make laws for 'Northern Ireland'. The British Constitution is, of course, something that can never be nailed down. It is largely what the Westminster Government at the time says it is. This is born out by Westminster overriding Stormont in 2015 over Welfare Reform. Here the financial power of Westminster was used to force the devolved Government to accept Conservative policy in an area over which it had been given authority under the 1998 Agreement.

Neither State, therefore, surrendered its Constitutional claim to 'Northern Ireland' in 1998, although Dublin's modification expressed more of a retreat from its original position than Britain's.

The Good Friday Agreement

The Good Friday Agreement was signed on 10th April 1998. It provided for the establishment of subordinate government in 'Northern Ireland' on the basis of a division of power between the Unionist and Nationalist communities. It formally acknowledged that that the two communities did not form part of a single body politic within the Six Counties. There were two national communities, which elected their own representatives and parties. Power was to be shared out on a community basis, and there would no longer be a government reflecting the majority of the electorate. It thus recognised that the 'Northern Ireland' part of the UK was not a suitable place for democracy on the Westminster model.

Mark Langhammer, an independent Labour councillor in Newtownabbey, summed up the political meaning of the Good Friday Agreement and the governmental institutions it established to a fringe meeting at the British Labour Party Conference in Blackpool on 28th September 1998. His speech, made before the institutions had even begun even to function, has stood the test of time and is worth reproducing as an analysis of them:

> "From the British government point of view and from an Irish government point of view, the Agreement has been and is a roaring success. It is not self-evident that it has been a success from a socialist point of view. Taking the British viewpoint first, it's been my view for a long time that Britain has operated an arm's length policy, a policy to insulate Britain from Northern Ireland politics: a form of bipartisanship. Certainly British policy, pretty well since 1914, has been to insulate Britain from the effects of politics in Ireland. And, from that point of view, Northern Ireland through this Agreement has well and truly sealed off from Britain. It has been a great success for the British political establishment.
>
> "The Irish government point of view is similar. It is not so long-standing, but now the Irish political establishment operates a similar arm's length policy. It probably dates from the Ulster Workers Council strike of 1974, and the Dublin and Monaghan bombings that year: Irish policy has been to keep Northern Ireland bottled up, sealed off, and distanced from Irish politics. And, in that respect, the Agreement is a marvellous success for Ireland...
>
> "The main part of the Good Friday agreement is really related to the new Northern Assembly, the new Stormont... for want of a better word, I would call it a Confessional Assembly. The Confessional Assembly has been set up as an unashamedly sectarian institution. It is set up with an intricate system of institutionalised sectarianism. When you enter the Assembly, after election, you register as 'Unionist', as 'Nationalist', or as 'Other'. Effectively what you register as is Protestant, Catholic or Other. When it comes to an important vote in the Assembly... the voting system that is used is one called Parallel Consent. There are two separate and quite detailed formulas for assessing

Parallel Consent, but to the layperson, it means that for any vote to go through the Assembly, you need the majority of the voters registered as Protestant, and the majority of the voters registered as Catholic, but—crucially—you need no majority, or no members, of those registered as 'Other' ...

"One result of this Parallel Consent is that the electorate, which doesn't like voting for losers, and therefore which will not want to waste its vote on an 'Other', will vote for whichever affiliation, Protestant or Catholic... Thus, the manner in which registration works, and the manner in which Parallel Consent works, is a major disincentive to anyone trying to develop cross-community, left of centre politics. It's just not possible...

"The other interesting thing about the Agreement is the manner in which it is perceived in both the Protestant and Catholic community. In the Protestant community it is very definitely perceived as a line in the sand: this is the end of everything; thus far and no further... this is the final solution. That's the way it is seen by Protestants, undoubtedly.

"On the Catholic side, there is a different perception... It's seen as an evolutionary thing. It's seen as a process that might evolve into something else. It might get a bit of dynamic. The North/South bodies might move onto something else. There is a tremendous faith in the present Republican leadership. Most of the folk in the Republican movement—and there are divisions, obviously, in the Republican movement, but most of the folk in the Republican movement would have a very high degree of respect for their current leadership. They probably feel themselves to be better led by them than they have ever been in their history. The attitude really is to test it, to see where it goes, it's an evolutionary thing: quite different altogether from the way in which the thing is looked at in the Protestant community" (*Irish Political Review*, October 1998).

'Northern Ireland' was set up in 1920-1 in a way that the only possible politics within it would be conflict between Nationalism and Unionism. The 1998 Agreement effectively formulated that reality by institutionalising it into a Constitutional structure similar to apartheid (separate development). The big difference between what formerly existed in 'Northern Ireland' and what existed in South Africa lies in the altering of the dominating/dominated statuses of the two communities. In 1998 power was formally equalised between them.

The Purpose of the Agreement

The central strategic purpose of the Agreement was to enable the Dublin and London Governments to distance themselves from Six County affairs on the pretext that a democratic settlement had been made there between the different factions. Underlying the Agreement was an assumption that the Six Counties did not belong within the United Kingdom and the implication was that they would eventually be reunited with the rest of the country.

The Agreement restored Six County devolved government in the only way it could have been restored after 28 years of warfare—with an all-Ireland dimension signposting the direction in which a settlement would eventually be arrived at. That is what made it attractive to Republicans, apart from the measure of power it gave to nationalists within the Six Counties and the opportunity to engage positively with Unionists in order to convince them of good Republican intentions. It was not that the institutions gave any real power to Ministers beyond local matters, but it provided Republicans with a power base in which they were given legitimacy by the State and through which they could demonstrate a growing popular support in the North without fear of future political initiatives aimed at undermining them.

But although the Agreement seemed to represent a transitional arrangement towards some form of Irish political unity, it had no real mechanisms within it to facilitate such a transition. (There was a provision for a Border Poll to be conducted, but no mechanism for setting it in motion.) The omission was presumably to placate Unionists. Therefore, the transition would have to take place outside the institutions if it was going to take place at all. This was mainly because the structures established by the Agreement would have the function of maximising communal conflict. More important, in the short term the whole arrangement lacked an internal dynamic that would maintain momentum in the process. So its functioning depended on continual pressure from exterior agency.

As Mark Langhammer noted, a new form of Confessional apartheid was being established on a formal basis. Representatives in the new Assembly were required to identify themselves in confessional form through *'designation'*, voting would take place confessionally, and the formation of the devolved sub-government known as the Northern Ireland Executive would also be a confessional construct. What counted was not majorities in the Assembly as a whole, but majorities within each of the confessional blocs of which it was composed. There would, in effect, be two confessional assemblies to match the two confessional voting blocs, and decisions would be taken by agreements between them.

Elections to the Assembly were to be political contests only within each of the two communities which were explicitly recognised as the institutional and permanent separate but component parts that made up 'Northern Ireland' politics. By giving formal structural expression to the social reality of 'Northern Ireland' the 1998 Agreement thereby entrenched and enhanced the communal reality of it. That is not a criticism of, since it only formalised what was meant to be in 1920.

An Equalisation of Power

The Republican War on the British State led the State to exert pressure on the Unionists to submit to a rearrangement of the internal mode of government in the North. The Unionists under Trimble submitted—or formally/partially did so. Paisley and his DUP resisted this equalisation of power by remaining outside the Agreement.

This is what made the 1998 Agreement different from previous attempts to reform structures within Northern Ireland—the balance of power was changed between the two communities. Power was now equalised between the communal blocs instead of the former one-sided structure of Confessional dominance which existed under the Stormont system. This equalisation of power was a radical change, given the fact that 'Northern Ireland' was set up as an arena for communal conflict and Unionism had chosen communal conflict as its eternal battleground. It therefore represented an adjustment in formal political relations which greatly improved the position of the Catholic community whilst worsening that of the Protestant community. And, because of that, it was bound to have an invigorating effect on Nationalism as it had a disorientating effect on Unionism.

The 1998 Agreement took account of the fact that 'Northern Ireland' was only a pretend-democracy, in which actual democratic politics played no part: the essential governing politics for 'Northern Ireland' being always externally-based, at Westminster. The Agreement made detailed arrangements for a subordinate administration in which ministries were shared out in proportion to the voting strength of parties, and were to be operated independently of each other.

This made the 1998 arrangement fundamentally different from the 1973 agreement for semi-voluntary power-sharing. The 1998 Constitution represents a mandatory division of power between the parties within two independent blocs rather than a sharing of power within a coalition cabinet, managed by the British Secretary of State. The First/Deputy First Ministry is shared between the two largest parties, with co-equal powers within a single Office. However these Ministers have no say in the allocation of Ministries, which are chosen by the elected parties on the basis of size. The Ministers are not subordinate to a Cabinet. They answer to their parties, which can replace them at will and which determine their policies.

Ministries are granted as of right, according to strength in the Assembly, and allocated under the d'Hondt formula, which ensures the largest parties get the most Ministries. Ministers are chosen by party leaders from MLAs (Members of the Local Assembly). The parties can change their Ministers without reference to the Cabinet or to the Assembly. No doctrine of Cabinet collective responsibility is possible within such a system. The Government is not responsible to the Parliament/Assembly, which cannot bring it down by No Confidence motions

In the negotiations over Strand One the Unionists had been against the idea of a 'cabinet' at all and had only conceded it to the SDLP when the SDLP agreed to the Unionist scheme for the North/South bodies in Strand Two. The Unionists were against these altogether but knew Nationalists would not accept the Agreement without them. So Reg Empey proposed a scheme which involved authority flowing from the Assembly to the cross-border bodies, rather than from the proposed North/South Council. The Unionists wanted to avoid a situation where the North/South bodies were a power unto themselves with areas of authority delegated by London and Dublin and defined by the Agreement.

While this form of government was wholly undemocratic, it was the only kind of progress that could reasonably be expected within the closed structure of the 'Northern Ireland' entity. What it did was provide a fairly level playing field for the process of communal conflict, which is the only possible content of politics in 'Northern Ireland', as a place apart from the two states. The main advantage of the arrangement in this respect is to transfer that conflict, which had previously been played out in violent form, to the political arena—without, of course, doing anything to overcome its root in any fundamental way. But, most of all, the Agreement of 1998 represented a Constitutional revolution in the structure of the British state, placing the way the Province was governed largely beyond the play of politics at Westminster, in a suspended medium.

Sinn Fein did not sign the Agreement and was non-committal on the day of its signing, Good Friday. But it quickly called a special Ard Fheis, turned party policy on its head, and embraced the deal fully as its achievement—as indeed it was, in substance.

Manufacturing Consent

The Unionist case that no Agreement should have been made with the Republican Army and that the War should have gone on until it was defeated is understandable but not realistic. The War had been in stalemate for years and it was publicly recognised by authorities connected to the British State, both military and political, that a decisive British victory was no more in prospect than a clear Republican victory. The deal was a tacit acknowledgement that the War could not be ended by a defeat of the Republican Army. It could only be ended with an arrangement which facilitated the transfer of the unstoppable Republican activity from the military to the constitutional sphere.

The British Government understood that the War was fed on the Republican side by the unique political structure it had imposed on the Six Counties and, since it was determined that the North should not be incorporated into the political life of the UK State, it saw that some kind of deal must be made with the Provos sooner or later—and that meant including an all-Ireland dimension. Such an agreement would, by implication, legitimise the Republican campaign and confirm the assertion of Republicanism that it was a necessary and legitimate component of the situation— although this could never be admitted openly by the British. This point was underlined by the release of the Prisoners of War and the dropping of the insistence that they were criminals.

On Good Friday 1998 the Republican movement made a historic compromise which involved the abandonment of much of its previous position. But it was clear that Sinn Fein could bring the bulk of its support along in supporting this new departure. SDLP voters were a given because the Agreement corresponded most closely to that party's policy and to Hume's vision. The problem lay in manufacturing consent for it within the Unionist community, in order to create the majority that was necessary for its actual functioning as a Confessional system.

Arthur Aughey had this to say about the Unionist position in 1998 in the context of the 1985 Hillsborough Treaty:

> "The signing of the Anglo-Irish Agreement in 1985 had been a tremendous shock to the Unionist community… the lesson of the Anglo-Irish Agreement… appeared to be that Unionists could not afford to be on the outside of a process which would determine their future. The fear of exclusion was… deeply imprinted on Unionist minds. Unionists might be pessimistic about the trend of events and feel that the bias of political forces were still ranged against them. But it was better to be in than to be out. That was the judgement of the UUP" (*The 1998 Agreement: Unionist responses'* in Michael Cox *et al*, *'A Farewell to Arms?'* p.65).

The Unionist dilemma in 1998 was just as Hume intended it to be in 1985 but now, with Sinn Fein as allies, Hume had achieved much more.

While devolved government was restored by the Agreement, the majority status of the Unionist community was negated politically in the process. It was a shock to the Unionist community that Trimble had compromised their majority status by signing up to the Agreement and had ushered in a new balance of power within 'Northern Ireland' as a result. That balance of power inclined towards the Catholic side over the subsequent period, but it might have been different if Trimble had decided to gain the benefits that would have come by operating the new development with a positive purpose and a good will. If he had done so Paisley and the DUP might have been a mere footnote in history.

Before the referendum on the Good Friday Agreement, senior Unionists, who were half-hearted in their support for it, neglected the referendum campaign. In their absence some of their colleagues, including Peter King and Peter Weir, actually drifted off to the 'No' camp, after they had thought about what they had done. The UUP found that it could not get its members to campaign for a 'Yes' vote, so small was the enthusiasm for the Agreement. Opinion polls began to show a great reduction in support for the Agreement amongst the Unionist community and Blair had to fly in to rescue the situation, for fear the referendum should destroy everything he had taken time to piece together.

There is little doubt that the Protestant community was hustled into supporting the Agreement. This was done by means of a written plan for controlling political opinion in 'Northern Ireland'. This was devised by Tom Kelly, the former Chief Political Correspondent of BBC NI, who had become Director of Communications in London. It involved using an extensive propaganda campaign in favour of the Agreement and assumed the most intimate kind of relationship to exist between Government and the broadcasting media in 'Northern Ireland' (which of course it did).

Kelly's plan gave advice on the presentation of the Government's message and emphasised the need to give the impression that the deal was not being imposed but was actually giving the public 'a choice'. It gave advice on how opinion polling was to be manipulated to show majorities for the upcoming agreement: "it will be important to ensure that not all of the results of opinion-polling, etc., will be in the public domain". It also suggested how personalities and a wide range of organisations were to be used to reinforce the message "without it being seen to be government-inspired". It advised that: "While any overt manipulation could only be counter-productive, a carefully co-ordinated timetable of statements from these people will be helpful in giving our message credibility with those they represent". Kelly's plan also advised the Government about how resistance to the GFA was to be overcome.

Its most revealing phrase is: "advertising on its own will not convince the public to vote in favour of the referendum" — which seems to give the lie to the idea that the public was engaging in a free choice. It revealed how far the British Government was from viewing the referendum in its generally accepted sense, as a question referred to the people for decision. Instead this referendum was seen as a process in producing a predetermined outcome — in much the same way as a sausage machine produces a sausage.

What Kelly envisaged was an intensive manipulation of public emotion, which distracted attention from the actual matter that would be put to referendum. The voters were bombarded from all sides to vote in favour of the Agreement, without being given a chance to think about what they would actually be voting on. Copies of the Agreement were posted to all householders with no attempt to facilitate discussion. And the scheme worked.

The Agreement was approved by a substantial majority of all those who voted, and in the end by a bare majority of Protestant voters. Elections to a devolved Assembly were held quickly on the heels of the referendum. The UUP gained 28 seats but the openly anti-Agreement DUP and Bob McCartney's UKUP (United Kingdom Unionist Party) got 25 between them, leaving Trimble with a slender majority. The SDLP got the majority of seats in the Nationalist election, with 24 to Sinn Fein's 18. The Assembly met in shadow form in July 1998 and, under the dual voting system, elected David Trimble First Minister and Seamus Mallon Deputy First Minister. The understanding was that Ministers would be appointed to an Executive in a matter of weeks, and by September 1998 at the latest.

Blair's Letter

However, as soon as Trimble had been elected First Minister, with the support of Sinn Fein, he made it clear that he would not agree to the formation of the Executive according to the d'Hondt system until the Republican Army had decommissioned its arms. In other words, he refused to do what he agreed to do by signing the Good Friday Agreement.

The relevant terms of the Agreement were that, when a devolved Executive including Sinn Fein Ministers was set up, and the Ministers of this Executive began to operate cross-border bodies, Sinn Fein Ministers would use their influence with a view to securing arms decommissioning from the Republican Army within two years.

The practical assumption was that this would leave about a year and three quarters of functioning devolution and cross-border administration in which to gradually achieve decommissioning in a situation where confidence was established by the working of the new system.

Trimble was encouraged and supported in his obstructionist stance by Prime Minister Blair who, having signed the Good Friday Agreement, also gave the Ulster Unionist Leader a letter which effectively contradicted what was said in the GFA. This gave Trimble a written assurance that Sinn Fein would not be admitted to an Executive without prior Republican decommissioning of arms. In the letter Blair referred to Trimble's problem with

Strand 1, Paragraph 25, of the Agreement that required exclusions from Office to be the result of a cross-community vote. This meant that SF Ministers could not be ousted from Government without the consent of the SDLP:

> "This letter is to let you know that if, during the course of the first 6 months of the Shadow Assembly or the Assembly itself, these provisions have been shown to be ineffective, we will support changes to enable them to be made effective in preventing such people from holding office. Furthermore, I confirm that in our view the effect of the decommissioning section of the Agreement, with decommissioning schemes coming into effect in June, is that the process of decommissioning should begin straight away."

The letter carefully did not say that decommissioning was a requirement of the Agreement but encouraged Trimble in his stance that it was and to believe that Blair would support him in this with action.

Trimble insisted at a press conference on 16th April, a week after the Agreement was signed, that parties he linked with paramilitary groups would have to decommission before holding Office in the Executive, declaring there would be a "major crisis" if they didn't. And, a day later, in an article in the *Belfast Telegraph*, he spoke of toughening of measures to exclude these groups if the existing provisions did not prove adequate (BT 17.4.98).

The personal letter contradicting what was actually signed up to by all and sundry in the Good Friday Agreement meant that Blair spent a year trying to find a way of making good his undertaking to David Trimble without placing himself in clear breach of the Agreement itself. But the wording of the Agreement was so clear that this proved to be impossible. And, since the Agreement was given the public status of a kind of international treaty, sanctioned not only by prime ministers and parliaments but also by referendums, the British Government was eventually obliged to require Trimble either to deliver on his undertaking under the Agreement or to renege on it.

On the morning of the Agreement Referendum, Blair made the following statement in an article published both in the *Irish News* and the Belfast *Newsletter* that went far beyond the terms of the Agreement:

> "Representatives of parties intimately linked to paramilitary groups can only be in a future Northern Ireland government if it is clear that there will be no more violence and the threat of violence has gone. That doesn't just mean decommissioning but all bombings, killings, beatings, and an end to targeting, recruiting and all the structures of terrorism. I have set out the tests for this. They will be enshrined in law and these tests will be applied more and more rigorously as time goes on. There can be no fudge between democracy and terror. The people of Northern Ireland will not stand for this. As prime minister of this country nor will I."

This wholly unrealistic set of standards, which was in effect a wrecker's charter with regard to the Agreement, convinced Trimble that he had signed a completely different deal to the one he actually signed and would have greatly encouraged him in obstructing the workings of the actual Agreement he actually did sign, along with his Prime Minister.

As David Morrison subsequently wrote:

> "Anybody reading that before going out to vote could be forgiven for thinking that they were voting on an Agreement which required the IRA, not just to decommission arms, but also to disband, before Sinn Fein would be allowed into a Northern Ireland government, and that the Government was going to legislate to ensure this. There is, of course, no such pre-condition in the Agreement" (*Irish Political Review*, July 2003).

'Pro-Agreement' Unionism?

After the Hillsborough Treaty of 1985, ten years before he became UUP leader, David Trimble had written a pro-Ulster Independence pamphlet called *'What Choice for Ulster?'* In it he called for "an orderly transfer of power to an Ulster government" because:

> "We have been turned into an internal colony. Worse still, the diktat has changed the status of Ulster by formally associating a foreign country in the government of Ulster; a foreign country, moreover, which still maintains a formal claim to Ulster... the Union as we know it has ended. It died first in the mind of the establishment some time ago and the diktat is merely the outward and visible symbol of its determination to bury it"

The Leader of Ulster Unionism was an unlikely signatory of the Good Friday Agreement, given these thoughts about the Hillsborough Treaty of 1985. It has to be presumed that, against his better judgement, Trimble was cajoled and bullied into signing the Agreement by Blair and it was then sold as something Trimble could accept. The *Irish Times* (07.06.98) claimed at the time that the British Prime Minister threatened to hold an all-UK referendum on the future of the North—that would have supposedly led to dire prospects for Unionists, if Trimble did not sign up to the Agreement. That, of course, would have been a very high-risk gamble on Blair's part but he seems to have called Trimble's bluff and induced him to sign up to something he was not at all in favour of.

Because Trimble signed the Agreement while disagreeing with it, the result was that a kind of parallel leadership of the Unionist Party ensued, led by Jeffrey Donaldson, whose conscience had made him head for the car park when the UUP had signed up. Donaldson and his supporters in the

UUP wanted assurances on the future of the RUC and IRA decommissioning before a Sinn Fein entry into Government and the release of any prisoners. The Orange Order backed Donaldson in refusing to support the Agreement.

Trimble claimed that the only difference between his position and that of Donaldson was on the effectiveness of mechanisms that were to be used to exclude Sinn Fein if decommissioning did not take place. Trimble relied on Tony Blair's letter, whilst Donaldson wanted an effective rewriting of the Agreement before he would support it. The result was that everything that Trimble did and said after Donaldson walked out on Good Friday was thereafter determined by Donaldson's principled opposition to the Agreement and resulted in a hardening of opposition to the Agreement within the Ulster Unionist Party itself and the Protestant community as a whole.

It would be true to say that Trimble's heart was never in the Agreement. He seems to have seen some things in it for Unionism but mainly on the lines of being able to taunt Republicans about abandoning its earlier position. But, if the Unionist Leader had followed his heart, he would have joined Paisley and McCartney in opposing the Agreement, and a version of Joint Authority between the two Governments would surely have followed, which Unionism was deeply opposed to. Trimble, therefore, followed his head in signing up to the Agreement but he could never quite put his sentiments aside—what his heart of hearts told him—and focus single-mindedly on the new situation he had placed himself within. This led him to fight a half-hearted campaign in favour of the Agreement he had signed and then continue to try and re-write it ever after, as Donaldson wished. He joined some Tories in a futile attempts to amend it in the Westminster Parliament—futile since it was an agreement with another Government and therefore Parliament could not alter a single letter.

The Omagh Catastrophe

Two events had important ramifications for the Peace Process: The Real IRA bomb at Omagh of August 1998, and the Loyalist killing of the Quinn children in Ballymoney. The deaths of the Quinn children disabled Protestant support for the Drumcree Orangemen, in the light of incessant political and media pressure holding the Orangemen at Drumcree directly responsible for the separate event at Ballymoney. After that, Orange protests at Drumcree were never the same again and an important destabilising element was removed from the scene.

The Real IRA, was a potentially destabilising element, composed of a group of senior and experienced Provos who had had enough of the unarmed strategy and decided to return during late 1997 to tried and trusted methods.

It quickly revealed itself to be a force to be reckoned with, mounting devastating bomb attacks it made on a number of town centres. The sheer scale and success of these attacks put in doubt the Republican peace strategy. But then a similar attack on Omagh resulted in the deaths of 29 people—Catholics and Protestants as well as visitors to the province amongst them.

The Omagh Bombing was a deliberate attack on a non-military target. The Omagh killings, on the other hand, were accidental in the sense of being unintentional. The other town centres had been blown apart by the Real IRA without killing anybody and that was presumably the intention in Omagh. However, in the bombing of towns, there is a high risk of killing substantial numbers of people, who in view of those carrying out the bombing are not legitimate targets.

Knowledge and truth about what happened were things not sought in the commentary on the Omagh bombing. The media acted instinctively as a propaganda organ of State, in creating an atmosphere around the bombing of unquestionable evil that defied any thought about why it had resulted in so many deaths. The objective was to finish off physical force Republicanism at this opportune moment by not letting any facts get in the way of a higher moral and political purpose. The relatives of those killed in Omagh were understandably unsatisfied with this approach, particularly after it subsequently emerged that security force agents had had prominent roles in the bombing operation.

Some of this was given the light of day in the report of Nuala O'Loan, the Policing Ombudsman. After she had given the relatives a briefing on what she had discovered about the Omagh Bombing, one of the relatives, Laurence Rushe, told the *Sunday Business Post*:

> "The work of British dirty tricks and the security services underworld makes me sick… It is obvious to everyone that the so-called Real IRA are infiltrated with informers and cowards. The Real IRA is controlled by the state and the state knows more about the Omagh bombing than they are telling us." (9.12.01).

Following this the *Irish News* carried a Real IRA statement admitting that "MI5 had handled two agent provocateurs whose identity was known" to them and "who were instrumental in the planning and implementation of the bombing" (14.12.01).

O'Loan's effort at uncovering the truth about Omagh was given little support by the Secretary of State and she ran into a great storm of hostility from Unionists. However, despite the obstructions placed in her way by the police and other agencies of the State, O'Loan did not go the same way as Stalker, Stevens *et al* because the Omagh relatives had been given such a prominent media profile that it would have been impossible to have buried the Omagh Report as other State investigations had been buried in the past.

The State then did an unprecedented thing in relation to Omagh. In breach of the normal practice of criminal law, established over a thousand years, the British Government instigated the families of the Omagh victims to take the law into their own hands by means of a civil action, treating murder as a mere civil offence, and to seek a money settlement against the people whom they held to be responsible, whose names (minus its agents, presumably) had been provided to them by the State.

This raises the question of why the State did not itself prosecute: it had changed the criminal law to make prosecution easier than it had been before. The State gave every impression that it was uncharacteristically paralysed by the fear of failure in relation to Omagh prosecutions. The only explanation for this seems to be that it was not fear of failure that paralysed the arm of the State in this respect, but fear of prosecution itself, or what might emerge in any prosecution taken against those that it chose to put on trial.

It must have been calculated by the Government, knowing it had agents in the Real IRA, at the heart of things in relation to the bombing, the Defence might have made a credible case in court that the State itself was partially responsible for the high casualties at Omagh. That, of course, would have been disastrous. So it was decided to overturn the normal rule of law, that the Crown acts for society and the victims must make do with whatever satisfaction that that gives them. In the instance of Omagh, the victims were encouraged to act in place of the State, at the instigation of the State, and with the support of the finance and propaganda operation of the State, in order to achieve 'justice' in financial form, in an unprecedented civil case that would not expose the hidden behaviour of the State to the wider public.

To this day there remain many unanswered questions about the Omagh Bombing and why it resulted in such a high death toll. Information subsequently came to light in the civil inquiry, and through agents, which showed: that the car used for the Bombing was stolen by a Garda agent; that an FBI agent video-taped the town for Intelligence purposes before the bombing; that the bomb was apparently made by a British agent; that the car had a tracking device planted in it pin-pointing it through a live satellite receiver; that those driving the car to the target were being tracked by GCHQ in Cheltenham via their mobile phones; that pedestrians were moved away from safety towards the car bomb, without any police supervision of them in the area; that the car was the only vehicle illegally and suspiciously parked in the street; and that Intelligence material was deliberately held back from the police investigation.

In September 2013 the NI Secretary, Theresa Villiers, refused to authorise a fresh Inquiry demanded by the relatives, to consider new evidence that had emerged. The revealing of information held by the State has been resisted to the extent that the only conclusion possible is that the State played a prominent role itself in the catastrophe.

The Omagh catastrophe served its purpose in a political way by bringing about a great popular reaction against the physical force men—without the awkward questions that, in the past, might have persisted when such political consensus did not exist. It affected even those Republican die-hards who were opposed to the Agreement but who now refused to support a resumption of the armed campaign. Armed Republicanism was dealt a deadly blow from which it has not recovered.

Gerry Adams said after the bomb on September 1st: "the violence we have seen must be for all of us a thing of the past, over, done with and gone" (IN 02.08.98). This statement prompted Trimble to agree to meet Adams for the first time.

John Hume opts out

Hume sprang a major surprise when he unilaterally nominated Mallon for the post of Deputy First Minister in the Assembly after GFA was signed. That raised the question of whether the devolved arrangements established by the Agreement could work without him at the helm of the SDLP. A crucial element in the delicate balance of the Peace Process was that Sinn Fein be given the political power according to its mandate and that the Agreement was implemented with some dynamism. The retirement of Hume, who had facilitated the transmission of Republican energy from the military to the Constitutional sphere, put this plan in doubt by putting those who had opposed it at the head of the SDLP.

Hume refused to take a seat in the Assembly on the stated reason of ill-health. He was certainly strained by the efforts of Trimble to destroy his great project of a quarter of a century and was suffering health problems. But he kept up his roles as an MP in Westminster and an MEP in Strasbourg.

The reason he decided to step down from the greatly important role of nurturing his creation into maturity at Stormont, and maintaining the delicate and important relationship with Republicans that he had developed, therefore remains a mystery. It may be that he was sidelined by the devolutionists who wished to show him how it should be done. Or perhaps he just came to the conclusion that he had got them what they had always wanted and his critics within the party could operate their heart's desire without hassling him again in his ill health.

Mallon, who now effectively led the party, represented the Constitutional tendency within the SDLP which refused to acknowledge that it was IRA unconstitutionality that had largely brought about the realisation of Hume's scheme and the Constitutional change from which the 'Constitutional Nationalists' had benefited. Hume took a less moralistic view of the matter and showed political courage in coaxing Sinn Fein into the constitutional sphere.

Hume's withdrawal at that point was damaging because only the sketchiest guidelines had been set out for the future governing structures in the Agreement. The party which he led also seems to have had little idea of how to operate the GFA without the architect present in the building to direct them.

Mallon suffered a blow to his authority very early on when he went to the Garvaghy Road and suggested to the residents that, having got the Orange march banned, they had made their point and should then agree to let it go through. The residents held the position that the point at issue was the Orangemen's refusal to directly negotiate about access to the area with the people living there, and they sent Mallon packing empty-handed. Hume would probably have never made that visit, but the result may have been different if he had, rather than the new Leader—despite the fact that the dispute centred itself near Mallon's home ground.

Mallon's Offer to Trimble

By this time, nine months had elapsed from the signing of the Agreement, and there was no sign of its implementation. The time frame for the establishment of the institutions under the Agreement was October 1998. However Trimble announced at the UUP Conference, just before the designated date, that he would not allow Sinn Fein to become part of new institutions before IRA decommissioning had taken place.

On 18th January 1999 Trimble said in an Assembly debate: "I have heard people sitting elsewhere in this assembly make the statement that for entry into the executive there is no precondition and in a technical sense, a very narrow technical sense, they may be right" (IN 19.01.99).

This was an admission by Trimble that the Agreement, in its clear and actual words as distinct from its so-called '*spirit*', did not make IRA decommissioning a precondition of Sinn Fein having its seats in an Executive. Signatories of the Agreement placed themselves under obligation to use their best endeavours to secure paramilitary decommissioning within two years if the parties held seats on an Executive. The Executive was to function for two years before decommissioning became an issue. That is what Trimble put his name to, and that is what was enacted as a constitutional document by the two referendums. But Trimble continued to delay the setting up of an Executive.

In exasperation Seamus Mallon made an offer to the UUP Leader on the opening night of the SDLP Conference at Newry on 13th November 1998. This was that, if Trimble agreed to the Executive structures being put in place, the SDLP would vote for the exclusion of Sinn Fein, if IRA decommissioning did not happen within the time-scale of the Agreement i.e. before May 2000. That was possible at the time within the rules set by the Agreement, because the SDLP was still electorally dominant in the Catholic community and could have delivered the consensus element needed to exclude Sinn Fein from government on the ground that it was in breach of the Agreement. Sinn Fein did not have a blocking vote at the time.

This part of Mallon's speech appeared in the press under the heading *'Solemn Guarantees from the SDLP'*. Mallon said that the SDLP would "remove from office those who have so blatantly dishonoured their obligations". No comment was made on Mallon's offer by Hume, and the text of the speech was issued from Mallon's Office, not from SDLP headquarters — arousing speculation that divisions continued between the SDLP and its former leader (*'The Far Side of Revenge'*, p.195).

Mallon believed that London and Dublin "should have been tougher and demanded decommissioning" and that the IRA should have been "pressurised" into it (IT 12.12.15). He was prepared to help Trimble and force Blair's hand. If Trimble had taken up Mallon's offer, the outcome would have been what was in effect a Unionist/'Constitutional Nationalist' coalition directed against Sinn Fein. The isolation of Sinn Fein, which was the declared object of the Dublin and London Governments, and of Unionist leaders over the decades, would have been accomplished. But Mallon's offer to Trimble was ignored by the Unionist Leader.

The only rational object of Unionist Party policy within its chosen 'Northern Ireland' Constitutional framework was to cause a substantial breach between the SDLP and Sinn Fein and, on that basis, bring about a coalition with the SDLP. So why did Trimble not take up Mallon's offer and put it to the test? The only logical answer to this is that, in order to do so, Trimble would have had to agree to implement the Agreement in its other aspects, to satisfy the SDLP.

The rejection of Mallon's proposal demonstrated that Unionist objections to operating the Agreement, despite the UUP endorsing it, went far beyond the Decommissioning issue. A Unionist leader who supported the Agreement, but who had tactical difficulty with the Decommissioning issue, would have seized upon Mallon's offer as a life-line.

Sinn Fein maintained that Trimble was making use of the Decommissioning issue in a way not warranted by the Agreement, in order to ward off the Agreement itself. Trimble's rejection of Mallon's offer to support him on the decommissioning issue, even though Mallon was offering to exclude Sinn Fein from the Government, was conclusive proof of the Sinn Fein argument to those who were most concerned, and they responded appropriately.

Mallon must be given credit for being 'constitutional' by conviction and for being willing to engage in a basic confrontation with Sinn Fein in alliance with the Unionist Party—something which Gerry Fitt was never able to bring himself to do when he led the party. But Mallon's willingness to act independently at the moment of truth was not put to the test because of Trimble's rejection of the offer and, as a consequence, the SDLP was undermined by the conduct of Trimble and of the Unionist Party.

That Unionist objections to operating the Agreement, which the party had endorsed, went far beyond the decommissioning issue, were demonstrated in November 1998, when the Unionist Party obstructed the setting up of the Cross-Border institutions in negotiations between themselves, Premier Tony Blair, Dublin and the SDLP. This obstruction of the implementation of the Agreement by the UUP was conducted purely against the 'constitutionalist' Nationalists. And it had very negative effects for the SDLP.

Surrender Demands

In February 1999 Trimble suggested that, if Republicans did not decommission, "then we will have to find some way of going forward without them" (IN 06.02.99). Having rejected the SDLP offer, this meant getting the two Governments to move against Sinn Fein. This UUP obstructionism prompted Taoiseach Ahern to speak out against Trimble, saying that the formation of an Executive would be impossible without Sinn Fein. But Ahern then made the mistake of departing from the terms of the Agreement when he stated that the IRA had to hand over weapons "because Mr Trimble has made it abundantly clear that he will not set up the executive until this issue is resolved" (IN 16.02.99).

Ahern coming down on the Unionist side in the Decommissioning argument had an unsettling effect within the Republican leadership, which relied on him to uphold the Agreement. The *Sunday Times*, a long-standing conduit for Establishment attempts to undermine Republicans, ran the headline across the top of its first page: *'No power-sharing before arms handover, Ahern tells Sinn Fein'*. Featuring an interview with the Taoiseach, the paper stated; "Bertie Ahern has said that Sinn Fein should be barred from the new Northern Ireland government unless the IRA starts to decommission its weapons'..." (14.2.99).

A campaign developed in which the London and Dublin Governments, and much of the British and Irish media, sought to put pressure on Republicans to decommission even though it was not a condition of the Agreement. In response to this, Adams made it clear to Ahern and Trimble that a Republican surrender was not on the cards and he could not deliver a *'decommissioning event'* for Unionists, stating: "I cannot deliver from the IRA what the British government could not achieve in the last 30 years" (IN 19.02.99).

Blair and Ahern put together the *Hillsborough Declaration*, which attempted to set out how things might move forward from the impasse. The statement declared that devolution should take place, followed by a running of the d'Hondt process to select Ministers for the Executive and then, within a month, a collective *'Act of Reconciliation'*, involving the IRA putting their arms beyond use, could take place in a way that the Decommissioning Commission could verify. This *Hillsborough Declaration* initially pleased Trimble, particularly in the way that it sought to amend the Agreement. However, the bulk of the UUP, following Jeffrey Donaldson, still demanded a firm timetable for IRA decommissioning.

Sinn Fein rejected this scheme outright, as an alteration to the Agreement. The party emphasised that it and the IRA were two quite separate organisations and that Sinn Fein had an electoral mandate quite apart from the IRA. It only had a responsibility to encourage the Republican Army to decommission under the Agreement, as did other parties to the Agreement, and it could not to be held responsible for IRA actions. The two Governments had to recognise the validity of the Republican argument and Blair then set a deadline of the 10th March, then 30th March, for devolution, in an attempt to put pressure on Trimble. However, the *"absolute deadline"* of the 30th March, as Blair called it, came and went. Things were no better under a revised deadline of 30th June

Trimble "jumps first"

For a full year the Unionist Party ensured that the process set out in the Agreement did not start. It then gave an ultimatum that, unless the terms of the Agreement were changed, by making prior Republican Decommissioning a condition of Sinn Fein participation in the Executive, the Agreement would never start.

Blair and Ahern produced their *'Way Forward'* document. This suggested the Executive should start functioning, and this should be followed by a Republican indication that it would decommission. Trimble rejected this document, but Blair explained to him that the document meant something quite different. The idea was to get an Executive up and running and then apply pressure on Republicans to quickly decommission soon afterwards. If the IRA did not decommission, the whole thing could be suspended again, using the *Northern Ireland Constitution Act*, Act, which was being rushed through the British Parliament to provide the UK Government with powers of suspension over the Agreement, with the blame falling on the Republican movement. It was also suggested to Trimble that, when Republicans were excluded, every other party could then move forward without Sinn Fein (IN 06.07.99).

In some ways this was Seamus Mallon's offer to Trimble of November 1998, appropriated by Blair. This new Law, pushed through Parliament to introduce the power of suspension, was a breach of the Agreement, introducing an element into the situation that Sinn Fein had not signed up to. It was up to Dublin, as the guaranteeing signatory of the Agreement, to object to these new rules. Ahern, realising the implications of this British manoeuvre, changed his position, changed his position back to supporting the terms of the Agreement and warned against the consequences of excluding Republicans from the settlement.

It was July 1999, 15 months after the Agreement and there was still no sign of its implementation. By this time, Mallon had hung on month after month hoping, where there were little grounds for hope, that Trimble would agree to an Executive, while Trimble showed that his primary object was to waste time in the hope that the Provos would go back to War or else disintegrate. When Mallon finally resigned his Office as Deputy First Minister in July 1999, it was not the SDLP itself that forced the issue.

The two Governments decided to put Trimble on the spot on July 15th by going ahead with the running of d'Hondt. On July 16th Trimble announced to the Ulster Unionist Council that he would be boycotting the Assembly while d'Hondt was run. A DUP *'exclusion motion'* had been tabled against Sinn Fein, and Trimble was keen to avoid being seen to exercise the logic of his position by supporting it, or abstaining from it and giving the DUP ammunition against him for his hypocrisy. So he stayed away with his entire Assembly team.

Sinn Fein and the SDLP attended the Assembly and nominated their Ministers. In the absence of the UUP and the DUP, an all-Nationalist Executive was on the cards. Seeing that, the Speaker, Lord Alderdice of the Alliance Party, decided to put an end to business.

With Trimble having reduced proceedings to a farce by boycotting the Assembly, Mallon's hand was forced and that is how he came to resign as Deputy First Minister before an Executive was even established for him to become Deputy First Minister of.

Deaglan de Breadun said that Trimble's policy had the greatest effect on 'Constitutional Nationalism':

> "The biggest loser was the SDLP. This, after all, had been John Hume's scheme planned for at least a quarter of a century. Out of many bitter and disappointing days of the SDLP leader, 15 July, 1999, must have been among the worst. The strain on the man was visible... it was a bitter day too for Seamus Mallon" (p.272).

The result within the Nationalist bloc of Trimble's efforts to *"bleed the process dry"* was a great undermining of the SDLP, Trimble's natural partners in an Executive.

Trimble was eventually cajoled into 'jumping first' in December 1999—to agree to the triggering of an Executive a year and a half after it should have been up and running. Trimble probably intended to be a First Minister without a Government for the two year period set in the Agreement for the Executive to function before Decommissioning was required. That expired in May 2000. The idea was then to claim that Sinn Fein was in breach of the Agreement because the IRA had not surrendered arms. Preferably it would then disband and express remorse for having ever existed! However, Trimble failed to see out the two years because something was done at the end of November 1999 which obliged the Unionist Leader to allow the Executive to be formed.

After Trimble's boycott of the Assembly, it was decided that some US muscle was required to move him along. The two Governments commissioned a review into the workings—or non-workings—of the Agreement in which Senator George Mitchell acted as facilitator. During this review the IRA, in an attempt to break the log-jam, announced that it would appoint a representative to the Decommissioning Commission of General de Chastelain. Senator Mitchell then stated that devolution should now take place and left Ireland.

The *Mitchell Review* was about digging David Trimble out of the unnecessary hole he had dug himself into, by getting the IRA to throw him a lifeline. But it remained to be seen if the lifeline was enough for his party, or if the *'No Guns/No Government'* hole was too deep for him to get out of. In response, Trimble finally agreed to the establishment of an Executive—which was then elected under the d'Hondt system, with parties choosing Ministerial portfolios in turn in November 1999. The UUP and the SDLP took three positions each and the DUP and SF two each. Trimble became First Minister and Mallon Deputy First Minister. However, further convolutions meant that the first meeting of that Executive was not held for another two years, in November 2001—two and a half years after the signing of the GFA.

At the same time as starting to operate the GFA, Trimble deposited a post-dated letter of resignation with Joshua Cunningham, who had the trust of the straightforwardly anti-Agreement Unionists in the Ulster Unionist Council, setting an arbitrary deadline for the start of IRA decommissioning of February 2000. This was to convince his party of his intention to bring everything down if Decommissioning was not immediately forthcoming.. This really was a straightforward surrender demand for the IRA to start handing in its arms within a month, prior to any Executive having been in actual existence. The Agreement had envisaged two years of Executive operation before such an event so Trimble must have known that his demand would not be met by the IRA and his move actually did not involve any 'jumping', but rather a quick and momentary dipping of the toe before a retreat back to his redoubt.

The Agreement Suspended

The manoeuvrings within the UUP had all the character of a 'sham fight', in which the Ulster Unionist Council became the arena for a theatrical sparring match of shadow boxing between Trimble and Donaldson. The dispute had all the characteristics of a 'double act'. Trimble had accepted the Agreement on Good Friday to prevent something worse befalling Unionism. His *persona* was that he wanted to work the Agreement, but was being prevented from doing so because of Unionist opposition led by Donaldson.

His 'predicament' led some nationalists to effectively propose setting the Agreement aside, in order to make concessions to help Trimble in his shadow-boxing with Donaldson.

At one point Donaldson explained on television that Trimble had to threaten to collapse the Agreement institutions by resigning, because Sinn Fein had not met its commitments under the Agreement. He spoke as if he were a disillusioned supporter of the Agreement, rather than opposing it because it failed to make prior disarming of the IRA a condition of Sinn Fein participation in the Executive (see *Irish Political Review*, March 2000).

At the end of each meeting of the Ulster Unionist Council there was the same result—give or take a couple of percentage points—57 to 43, 55 to 45, 54 to 46, etc. always in favour of Trimble, as the 860-odd members of the UUC held the whole process to ransom—with Blair's connivance.

The overall effect of Trimble's obstructionist strategy was to make Decommissioning more difficult for the Republican leadership to achieve. And the crucial thing for the UUP was that, the longer Decommissioning took and the closer it got to an election, the less time Trimble would have to show the Unionist electorate any benefits of the Agreement. Therefore, even if Trimble was sincere in wanting to make the Agreement work, by delaying Republican reciprocity he was making it imperative for his own electoral interests to actually prevent it. The arbitrary deadline for the start of IRA decommissioning of February 2000, set by Trimble in his post-dated letter of resignation to Joshua Cunningham, led to the predictable outcome of the IRA refusing to move on Decommissioning.

The ploy was naturally seen by the IRA as a Unionist ultimatum, conceding to which would be humiliating. It therefore achieved the intended result. Although the Decommissioning Commission under General de Chastelain stated that it was certain Decommissioning would occur, the new Secretary of State, Peter Mandelson, called the IRA's position *"totally unacceptable"* and threatened to put the institutions *"on hold"* if some decommissioning were not immediately forthcoming.

On 11th February 2000, with the Ulster Unionist Council scheduled to meet again and Trimble likely to fulfil his promise to resign, Mandelson suspended the Assembly and the long overdue establishment of the Executive. The view at the highest level of the Northern Ireland Office was that, if Trimble resigned, he would encounter great difficulty getting re-elected under Assembly rules because of UUP discontent. It was calculated that the Executive could be re-assembled after a short suspension and review, and Trimble could continue in position.

This British suspension, after only eight weeks of the Executive being elected, pulled the rug from the Republican leadership which was arguing for the Peace strategy. In an interview with Radio Ulster's *'Inside Politics'* on 29th January, Adams had warned that, if the institutions were suspended by the British Government, the IRA would probably withdraw from talks with General de Chastelain.

Just before Mandelson announced the suspension, the Decommissioning body reported an IRA statement committing Republicans to future Decommissioning. But Mandelson decided that, because weapons de-commissioning was unlikely to have happened by the 22nd May deadline *"set out in the Good Friday Agreement"*, he would suspend the institutions. The fact that the Agreement had envisaged the institutions in operation for nearly two years before decommissioning was to take place was taken as of no consequence by the British Secretary of State. As a result, on 15th February, the IRA announced that it would no longer co-operate with the Independent Commission on Decommissioning because of the suspension of the Assembly.

Peace or Pacification?

Trimble had not been satisfied with the IRA commitment to decommission and insisted that decommissioning was to be on his terms alone. He stated that any further plans to re-enter government would have to have the prior consent of the 860-strong UUC.

On the morning of the first Decommissioning Report from General de Chastelain, a triumphant John Taylor said of Sinn Fein, on BBC Radio Ulster, "We put them on trial for two months and they failed to come up with the goods".

There was no doubt that the Republican leadership and bulk of the movement was committed to an exclusively political struggle —if it could be shown to be workable. Republicans had committed themselves to achieving Decommissioning as part of a process of complete demilitarisation. Decommissioning, in any form, was a very difficult bridge to cross for the Republican Army. It could only begin to take place when the Process was seen to be well established.

The problem with Trimble's behaviour was that the process was hardly off the starting blocks when it was put under continual threat from within the Unionist Party. The setting up of the Executive and cross-Border bodies had missed their deadlines by over a year, due to Unionist prevarication, and yet the Provos were expected to dance to the Unionist tune, after they had been *"put on trial for two months"*.

It was said that the retention of arms by the Republican movement was a threat of force by one party to the democratic process. But, of course, 'Northern Ireland' itself was a product of the threat of force by the Unionist Party, and it was the Republicans who were most earnest about removing it from politics.

Trimble's obstruction of the Peace Process was designed to concertina the time available to the Republican leadership to develop a case for Decommissioning down to the bare minimum. Trimble had squeezed what should, under the Good Friday Agreement, have been two years of political development and demilitarisation down to "two months". And he had been allowed to do this by Blair, despite the impending consequences of his actions. His only logical motive could be the desire to the desire to bar Sinn Fein from the Executive, or force an IRA split. Trimble knew that any Republican leader would not have a case for putting arms beyond use at an IRA Convention at that point in time. He knew that a Convention would not be called unless the IRA Leadership could count on taking the bulk of the movement with them. He prevented the conditions developing in which a case for Decommissioning could be made. And he hoped the world would fall in on Sinn Fein as a consequence.

When the IRA agreed to appoint representatives to the Decommissioning Body, it threw Trimble a lifeline into the hole which he had dug for himself. Instead of taking that lifeline, he instead tried to pull Republicans into the hole, whilst simultaneously escaping up the line!

Trimble and the Republican Position

Trimble's strategy in the aftermath of the Agreement seems to have been to attempt to transfer the general sense of defeat within Unionism to Republicanism. He tried to do this by using the die-hard element within Republicanism, that did experience a parallel sense of defeat, to spread defeatism amongst the Republican rank and file.

The present writer wrote a series of articles for the *Irish Political Review* to explain the change within Irish Republicanism that had taken place over the preceding years. There was much scepticism amongst Unionists at this time about that change and the belief was that the new development in Republicanism was merely a tactic to outwit them. That could be described as the mainstream Unionist view that was held by much of the Protestant community.

The period in which the articles appeared was marked by a trial of strength between Trimble and Sinn Fein. Sinn Fein did nothing to initiate this trial of strength but had to accept it when Trimble made the challenge, to preserve the Peace Process.

Trimble seemed to hold two views about the Provos simultaneously. He held one view that they were trying to outwit the Unionism and that the Ceasefire was really just a tactic. But he was also influenced by some people, including Republican die-hards and people like Eoghan Harris, who were telling him that Unionism had won a great victory over Republicanism and his object should be to turn it into a rout. Harris told Trimble that Sinn Fein was very interested in being part of a functioning Executive and Trimble should "*call their bluff*". Trimble made Harris his adviser.

Harris had been the chief theorist of the Official Republicans while they were waging their war in a medium of ideological fantasy. He was the Marxist-Leninist leader of Sinn Fein the Workers Party when it came close to superseding the Communist Party in Ireland in Moscow's favour. Then, after the collapse of the Soviet system, he became a Liberal authoritarian, under the tutelage of Conor Cruise O'Brien, and a Neo-Conservative in deference to US power and the 'New American Century'. He even sought to help to reorder Iraq through his working for a potential puppet ruler, Ahmed Chalabi, before the puppet was discovered to be a con-artist and dropped by his US sponsors.

Harris popularised his views every week in the *Sunday Independent* in provocative rhetoric against traditional Ireland. He summed up his basic position on independent Ireland, which he has propagandised every week for around two or three decades in his column, in the following description:

> "... squalid murder in an unnecessary War of Independence, which led inexorably to civil wars, and to a prolonged cult of the gun that equally inexorably produced the Provos—and will produce more of the same as long as the cult is not challenged" (15.9.13).

Harris introduced himself to Trimble in 1995 and became adviser to the Unionist Leader, writing his Oslo speech accepting the Nobel Peace Prize for the Agreement (which Trimble had done his best to prevent!). According to Dean Godson, the UUP Leader's biographer (*'Himself Alone'*), Trimble liked using Harris to shock the UUP membership.

Harris addressed the UUP Assembly group in Glasgow and the Party Conference in Enniskillen in late 1999 and told them to take the historic opportunity of going into government with Republicans in order to *"secure the Union"*. This was at the point of Trimble's *"jumping"*.

I do not have transcripts of what Harris said to the Unionist Party but the article below, written at much the same time, probably gives a flavour of the things he presented to the UUP. Harris, writing in the *Sunday Times* the week before the suspension of the Agreement by Mandelson, said under the title, *'Face It: The IRA Has No Future'*:

> "...David Trimble's dialectical strategy of going into government with Sinn Fein has been a stunning success. I say dialectical because he took an intelligent each-way bet. He went in sincerely, and if Sinn Fein were sincere too, then all would be well. If they were not—and they were not—then Sinn Fein would suffer. Saying yes has worked. For the first time in 30 years, the unionists are the good guys. Not just the British and Irish governments, not just British and Irish public opinion, but the heavy newspapers such as The New York Times and The Washington Post are all singing from the same sheet and bearing down grimly on Gerry Adams and Sinn Fein... Whatever formula Sinn Fein comes up with, then the UUP should not accept delivery but pass the parcel swiftly to the people best able to open it—Mandelson, Blair and Ahern... Why should the Irish Republic be forced to run the risk of civil war for the sake of a couple of hundred thugs? Bertie Ahern, like Cosgrave, de Valera, Lemass and Lynch before him, must soon answer... He must tell the IRA that it has no future, as an idea or as an institution, that it must disarm or be disarmed. In short the kissing has to stop" (6.2.00).

The 'dialectic' strategy presented by Harris was more easily explained as an each-way bet. If Republicans disarmed and tamely joined the Executive, only good could come of it for Trimble in "*securing the Union*". Alternatively, if Republicans baulked at the logic of their initiative, and refused to hand over their arms, they would be vilified generally and go into a political oblivion.

The Unionist delegates were not convinced by this simplistic university Marxism. They did not see the Provos through the fantasy prism of Official Republicanism. They had a much more fundamental basis of antagonism to them, and it was not just with the Provos, but with the community that produced them. And they were not about to take Harris's advice to rely on Blair and Ahern for their future.

After Mandelson had suspended the institutions, Harris penned another piece, '*Let Sinn Fein Lassoo Its Cowboys*' for the *Sunday Independent*:

> "…Adams needs to… deal with the problem he brought into being. Why should the Irish people be chained to the treadmill of Northern Ireland by 137 cowboys in south Armagh or wherever?… In short, when is Adams going to stop being a girl's blouse [sic], purge the cowboys and let Sinn Fein get on with politics? The myth is that the worst thing you can have is a split. Not so. Michael Collins had to split the IRA in 1922 to set up the Irish Free State. Goulding had to split the IRA twice, in 1970 and in 1974, to allow the Workers Party to make political advances. Provisional Sinn Fein only made political progress after it had dumped the Continuity and Real IRA factions.…" (13.2.00).

Adams, of course, did not bring "*the problem*" into being. The problem came into being long before the Sinn Fein President came along. Decades earlier, Harris had supported the efforts of the southern IRA to destroy the Northern entity through invasion, so he must have once seen it as "*the problem*" then. But, when the entity produced something internally and of itself, Harris condemned the thing it produced and called that "*the problem*" instead!

Adams had not even brought the Provos into being—another product of the problem. By all accounts, he had been inclined to remain a 'Stickie' and a comrade of Harris. He had wanted the Abstention issue shelved for the time being in the wake of August 1969, and the movement to give priority to dealing with the situation in the North. He wanted the movement to remain united. But then Goulding and the Dublin leadership disciplined him for questioning their policies and excluded him from the Abstention votes. So in frustration he joined the emerging Provos.

As to Michael Collins: Harris does not mention that it was the Free State Leader who made war on the North to preserve Republican unity in the South as the British boxed him in on the Treaty he had signed up to, and which he was hesitating to implement.

Collins had *"to split the IRA in 1922 to set up the Irish Free State"*. But he made his moves on the insistence of Churchill, surely. Collins actually relied on his charisma and his secret network, the Irish Republican Brotherhood, to impose his will on the Army. But the bulk of the Republican movement had outgrown the conspiratorial structure, which had been necessary to its survival before 1916 and which had given cohesion to those defending the Government formed after the 1918 Election, and Collins (unlike Adams) did not dare to call an Army Convention to support him. So he was reduced to scheming and trying to break up the Army which had fought the British to the negotiating table, by individual approaches to various elements within it, while he built up a regular/paid Army with British support.

But whatever policy Collins had in mind at the outset, he became increasingly incapable of implementing it, as he became ever more dependent on British support: and eventually Whitehall gave him orders to make war on the Republican Army—or else the British Army proper, which had not left the country eight months after the signing of the 'Treaty', would do the job for him.

That was the scenario which Adams and the Republican leadership insisted would not be repeated in the North. They bound the movement into the deal they had made by means of extensive discussion at every stage before moving forward and thus carried the movement with them united. Some detached themselves from the new departure, but there was no rupture as in 1922. And that, presumably, is why Harris would have much preferred the Collins disaster to the Adams success.

The Crusade and the Cruiser

As has been noted, Trimble was encouraged in his obstruction of the Agreement by an assortment of people with a long-standing anti-Republican orientation, whose main desire was to see the Provisionals humiliated. This assortment was blinded by their hatred of the Provisionals (and by extension of the community that supported them), and they encouraged Trimble into positions that threatened the continuance of the Republican Ceasefire. They were only interested in breaking up the Republican movement without a care for the long term position of Northern Catholics.

The attacks from Dublin motivated Deaglan de Breadun to write a piece in the *Irish Times* early in the new century, in which he suggested that *"a crusade against Republicanism"* was being launched:

> "The prospect of casting the Provisionals into exterior darkness and setting up a coalition of the Ulster Unionists and the SDLP has been the dream of

many unionists and some nationalists for a long time. But even some unionists who would like to see such an outcome dismiss it as unrealistic: Sinn Féin is too strong at this stage. A tempting possibility for elements in the Establishment would be to demonise Sinn Féin to such an extent that it was demolished in the next Westminster election...." (IT 5.2.00).

One of the chief agitators for the aforementioned '*crusade*' was Conor Cruise O'Brien who wrote in the *Sunday Independent*, the chief organ of the crusaders:

"The stand the British government is now taking over decommissioning, and the threat to suspend the Good Friday institutions unless decommissioning is made good, constitute the first major act of resistance to the IRA threat to be offered by any British government for many years now. I welcome this act of resistance, and hope the resistance will be maintained. But it cannot be denied that there are serious risks involved. As Neville Chamberlain found, just over 60 years ago, when you stop appeasing an aggressive power, the threat by reason of which you offered the appeasement is likely to be activated. I believe that, if the British government continues on its present course, the IRA leadership will feel as affronted as Hitler did when Neville Chamberlain offered his guarantee to Poland. The blackmail had stopped working, and the threats which underlay the blackmail had to be made good. If the present notice of intent to suspend the Good Friday institutions becomes operative—as now seems likely—the Sinn Féin-IRA leadership will experience a peculiarly keen humiliation... The ministers held their offices courtesy of the British government, which, according to Sinn Fein's basic philosophy has no right to be in Ireland at all, and consequently no right to appoint ministers. Conversely—and more to the point—no people claiming to be republicans had any right to accept appointments in Ireland which the British government had conferred and had the power to suspend or terminate. By exercising its power to suspend, the British government exposed Sinn Féin-IRA to the ridicule of more consequential republicans, like the Real IRA. In these circumstances it seems certain that the IRA, in the wake of the suspension of the Good Friday institutions, will consider carefully the option of renewing the armed struggle... The two governments should be aware of the threat, take it very seriously, and make constructive use of the breathing space. For the British government this should mean stalling on the implementation of the Patten Report, and seeking to rebuild the morale of the RUC. It should also mean alerting the military to the existence of a serious and urgent threat to the peace" (6.2.00).

O'Brien had developed a passionate hatred of Republicanism, which he passed on to others in his social and professional milieu. He could not bear to think that any good could ever come of what Republicans did and determined that this should not happen, even if the IRA was sincere in its good intentions as peacemakers. His hatred led him to take up the cause of Ulster Unionism.

The cause of O'Brien's hatred of the Northern Republicans is unclear and it was not always there. In the early 1970s he had the *'colon'* view of the Ulster Protestant—a term used at the time to describe the French in Algeria whose will needed breaking by De Gaulle in order to make an Algerian settlement possible. A few years later, when O'Brien was a senior Cabinet Minister in the Coalition at the time of Sunningdale, he was part of the Government that attempted to force the Council of Ireland on the reluctant Unionists, even after they had been outraged by the plea of Dublin concerning Articles 2 and 3 in the Boland case, with catastrophic results for the power-sharing Executive.

This traumatic experience seemed to prompt a revulsion against everything Nationalist in O'Brien, and he started chastising everyone and everything implicated in traditional National culture, without regard for consequences. O'Brien had developed a totalitarian disdain for the course that Irish history had taken. Haughey warned him not to base his politics on the premise that Irish history had been a mistake. But O'Brien persisted in his ideological thrust to the periphery of things in the 26 Counties. He became a Unionist. And, in becoming a Unionist, his influence reinforced the most reactionary and rejectionist aspect of Unionism which was oblivious to the predicament of the Catholics of the North and which, in turn, ensured that community's commitment to Anti-Partitionist politics.

It was very clear what O'Brien was saying. The British Government, in suspending the Agreement, was humiliating the Republican leadership which had invested its credibility in an unarmed approach. The acceptance of participation in the Stormont institutions, to engage with Protestant Ulster, left Sinn Fein vulnerable to those who had the power to cut the Republicans down to size whenever they thought fit. This would surely result in discontent and strong pressure from those within Republicanism who suspected they had been tricked, which would force the Provos back to war. And then the British would be well prepared to smash them!

O'Brien, lost in his Churchillian mythology, may have forgotten that the British guarantee to Poland, far from saving the Poles, led to a World War, the loss of a very substantial number of Poles, and fifty years of Soviet occupation of Eastern Europe. But O'Brien viewed the Republican Ceasefire in a tactical manner: the general thrust of his utterings was that the British and Irish Governments and Unionist Party should use the good faith of the Republican leadership as a point of weakness to produce a final solution to the problem of the Northern Catholics—who were by implication seen as the main problem, rather than the perverse construct of 'Northern Ireland' that actually generated the conflict.

Trimble's 'sophisticated analysis'

Prof. Henry Patterson, one of Trimble's advisers, has an interesting passage in his book, *'Ireland Since 1939, The Persistence of Conflict'*, reporting the thoughts of the Unionist leader around the time of the 1994 IRA ceasefire:

> "Even though the cease-fire may be merely a tactic, the fact that they have had to change their tactics is an admission that the previous tactic (armed struggle) has failed. Although there are elements in the republican movement that desire a return to violence, they will be returning to a tactic that was not working… So, in that sense the republican movement is being defeated slowly. It is a slow process but that is what is happening. From our point of view, what we have to ensure is that while their campaign is winding up it does not cause any political or constitutional change which is contrary to the people of Northern Ireland. And we also want to do everything possible to ensure the Union is strengthened" (p.332).

Prof. Patterson comments:

> "This was a sophisticated analysis, too sophisticated for many unionists, who still preferred the Paisley-McCartney vision of a republican movement with almost demonic powers that was moulding Anglo-Irish policies to its will through the continuing threat of force."

What Trimble was describing to Patterson was surely a winning hand. The IRA campaign was in decline and it was going over to an unarmed political strategy of what was termed 'constitutional nationalism' because it could achieve no more through unconstitutional methods. All that Unionists needed to do was to oversee this process and make sure, quietly and calmly, that the Republicans obtained nothing injurious to Unionism in the transference of their War into politics. Perhaps the Union could even be strengthened by the process! And, best of all, in September 1995 Trimble had become the Leader of Unionism to bring his *"sophisticated analysis"* to bear on the situation at the ideal moment. In view of this *"sophisticated analysis"* in the mind of the undisputed Leader of Unionism, really all that needed doing was to do as Napoleon famously advised and *"never interfere with the enemy when he is destroying himself"*!

Convincing the rest of Unionism—which was incapable of such a "sophisticated analysis"—of the situation, of the positive benefits of the Agreement that had been signed up to, should, therefore, have been the obvious strategy for Trimble. However, it is perhaps significant that the Trimble *"sophisticated analysis"* comes from a Spanish publication which Patterson took the trouble to translate himself. This seems to suggest that Trimble did not publicise this view to Unionism after 1994. And, having made his "*sophisticated analysis*", Trimble made nonsense of it by attempting to seriously interfere with the enemy by destroying them himself: In other words he reverted to his Ulsterish instincts in attempting to achieve a Protestant victory over the Fenians in the old struggle of communal attrition. So why did he do this?

Trimble's 'Exotic Advisers'

In his quest for the Holy Grail of "*sophisticated analysis*" ,Trimble assembled a raft of exotic advisors. Many of them were former Official Republicans including Harris, Prof. Bew and his colleague, Henry Patterson. (There was also Ruth Dudley Edwards, the revisionist historian who revised into a unionist, and her friend, Sean O'Callaghan, a former Provo who turned informer and anti-Provo and tried to put some politics into the Unionist Party.)

Trimble seems to have been attracted by these ex-Official Republicans because of their special 'inside' knowledge of Republicanism and their offers of help in destroying it. The ex-Official Republicans were motivated, so far as the North was concerned, by a profound resentment of the Provisional movement and its successful War. They botched their own '*Lost Revolution*', and evolved from a National Liberation Front into an Ulster Unionism preservation society.

Official Republicanism had been something substantial in the early 1970s, But the sheer contradictions of its messed-up mind had splintered its base. Many went over to the Provos or the IRSP and others gave up in disillusionment after their "*Revolution*" turned sour. But many of the splinters took their intellects into the Liberal professions to make a living as thorns in the side of those who had hi-jacked the 'Revolution'. So, long after the guns had rusted, the Officials were still conducting their feud with the Provos, this time in the political sphere, as if it were still the 1970s when they had been competing as rivals in waging war. They were, therefore, most inappropriate allies of Trimble because they had one intention alone—that of humiliating the Provos to gain the satisfaction of saying: "*I told you so*" to them.

Trimble should have realised that an attempted humiliation of Republicans was the worse possible strategy to take. But the fundamental Ulsterish instinct in him, that desired to see a Protestant triumph in the province, drove him to leap into bed with the bearers of the forbidden fruit at the expense of his "*sophisticated analysis*". But what Trimble never understood was that the Good Friday Agreement put Ulster Unionism in the position of having to do what was required of it in the British interest. The Agreement was already an accomplished fact, established by a Prime Minister who was winning elections with landslide majorities, who felt the '*hand of history*' on him and was on a mission that was all the more irresistible because it was personal. And Trimble was being advised that he could see all of this off!

If, instead of listening to this misguided advice, Trimble had taken on board the view that the Good Friday Agreement had resulted in an end to the Republican campaign without the realisation of its Anti-Partitionist objective, and championed the deal as a means of proceeding towards peace and stability against the more fundamentalist positions of the DUP and Bob McCartney, he stood a chance of preserving himself, his party and the Agreement. But what he proceeded to do was embrace the worst of all worlds. He decided to take it that the Republicans had been defeated, had no capability of resuming the War, and needed to be forced into a humiliation in order to satisfy his Unionist opponents. That policy, by equating IRA decommissioning with Republican surrender, meant that decommissioning could not and would not take place.

The articles the present writer wrote at that time suggested that Trimble had miscalculated and was playing a very dangerous game for all concerned. Danny Morrison, the author of the *'Armalite and ballot box'* phrase summed up Republican thinking very neatly in November 1999 on the BBC Radio Ulster programme, *'Talkback'*. He said that Republicans realised that, after 28 years of war, while the British Government had been unable to defeat the IRA, the armed struggle was no longer advancing the objectives of the movement. The British Government and Unionism were united in their opposition, and the military campaign was simply cementing their opposition. The Peace Strategy was launched with the calculation that Unionism in particular would not be able to cope with an honourable settlement of the conflict without itself fragmenting.

It was apparent by this time that Sinn Fein was making a serious attempt to engage with Unionism. When the Republicans first embarked on warfare nearly 30 years earlier, they had shared the widely-held Nationalist view that the Protestants in the North of Ireland were suffering from some kind of *'false consciousness'*, and only needed to be given some strong medicine and their bluff to be called by the British to knock the stuffing out of them. I recall, however, that that view was held most strongly and ideologically by the Official Republicans of the early 1970s and by their IRSP offshoot. But it was the Provos who actually put it to a thorough test, proved it to be basically unsound, and then began the very different approach of unsettling Unionism by means of an interim Six County settlement.

The Peace initiative and the working of the Agreement represented a serious Republican initiative to engage with the reality of what constituted 'Northern Ireland'. This followed on from the implicit acceptance of Unionism as a second Irish nation with which a working relationship had to be established. The old ideas of Unionism as a *'colon element'*, or as a British *'fifth column'* began to disappear.

Republicanism had undergone a cultural revolution and was responding to Unionist petulance about the new political developments with considerable maturity. Time after time, the Republican constituency stretched itself to reassure Unionists that it remained committed to a majority decision within the Six Counties with regard to a future United Ireland. The fact that they could not explicitly say this had everything to do with a desire not to fracture its political base before some confidence had been built up through Unionists engaging in this new departure with Republicans. If Unionists persisted in their former ways, no such confidence could be established and it would be very difficult to convince the sceptical Republican base that the new departure was worthwhile.

At this time, the Sinn Fein leadership would have found it impossible to sell a deal involving substantial IRA decommissioning in their local areas, let alone the Republican heartlands outside Belfast and Derry. Even with the Executive set up and some progress made, it wasn't going to be easy. No matter what criticisms can be made about Republicanism, on a fundamental point it was right. If Britain was not prepared to disengage from Ireland and let progress take place in an all-Ireland context, then the Government had to take political responsibility for the area it claimed jurisdiction over until it was prepared to leave.

While Trimble was trying to politically defeat Republicans, he should really have been trying to establish a functional relationship in government with the SDLP to make life difficult for Sinn Fein. But the fact that he was intent on attempting to deliver a Republican rout, rather than accommodating the SDLP, had disastrous repercussions for both his party and for the SDLP, from which they both have never recovered.

Trimble and Athol Street

Trimble's 1994 "*sophisticated analysis*" bore a resemblance to some things Athol Street had been saying about the decline in the IRA's military campaign—*some* being the operative word. Athol Street had been trying to get the Unionist community to see some political sense and to stop its wilder elements killing Catholics at random. This was only a minor part of what was said by Athol Street. The main thing was that the Provos were well able to keep fighting because Six County political conditions created by the 1921 system generated the conflict to which the IRA gave expression—a conflict that only could only be ended by ending the detached status and entering the political life of a state, either the state administering it, or the one to the South of it.

The sophisticated Unionists made debating points out of some things in the Athol St. analysis but the main Athol St. view was completely rejected by them.

Athol St. was, however, given as "one unexpected source of inspiration" to David Trimble in the mammoth biography of him, *'Himself Alone, David Trimble and the Ordeal of Unionism'*:

"These were the publications the British and Irish Communist Organisation (first known as the Irish Communist Organisation). Many then considered B&ICO a self-consciously Stalinist (but non-sectarian) faction. A substantial number of its leading lights believed that the British multinational state was invested with certain progressive possibilities... Adapting Stalin's theory of nationality to the Irish context, B&ICO had come to conclude that Irish republicans had fundamentally misanalysed the situation. Far from Northern Protestants being a minority within the Irish nation, they were a distinct nation of their own, no less entitled to the Catholics to political self-determination; any attempt to coerce them would not merely be foredoomed to failure, but would also lead to a bloodbath by virtue of dividing the working class. This became known as the two nations theory (at the same time, B&ICO also believed in civil rights for Catholics—and that the British state was the best vehicle for achieving these complimentary ends). He was particularly influenced by three of their pamphlets; The Economics of Partition, The Birth of Ulster Unionism and the Home Rule Crisis 1912-14. In time, Trimble also became a fan of Workers Weekly, the newsletter of an allied organisation the Workers Association for a Democratic Settlement of the National Conflict in Ireland—a compliment which that Journal did not always reciprocate through the late 1970s and 1980s. It found him too devolutionist and Ulster Nationalist for their more integrationist tastes... After Trimble became leader, the links with the left endured. Thus Paul Bew, Professor of Irish Politics at Queen's and Henry Patterson, Professor of Politics at the University of Ulster—both of them formerly of the Workers Association—became two of his strongest supporters in academe. And John Lloyd, the staunchly Trimbleista former editor of the New Statesman who later worked for the Financial Times, had been in B&ICO itself for a time" (pp.29-30).

The main advice which the B&ICO gave to Unionism is not mentioned at all by Godson: that it should dissolve itself into British party politics, and recognise that Northern Ireland was not a possible framework for a stable settlement. Neither does Godson mention the B&ICO conclusion that Unionist rejection of British party politics had the effect of turning the direction of events towards the Irish framework.

Trimble throughout his political career was committed to Unionist victory in the Six County area of communal attrition, and restoring the 'Ulster' idyll of 1921-1968. He had been an active member of William Craig's Vanguard movement, which the B&ICO had described as fascist. He had the politics of the Unionist family. He had opposed the extension of the British Labour Party to the Six County region of the State, and the Campaign for Labour

Representation is not mention by Godson. Neither is the Campaign for Equal Citizenship, which gained some support within a traumatised Unionism following the shock of Margaret Thatcher's Hillsborough Agreement with Dublin.

The most that Ulster Unionism would take from Athol St. was a garbled version of the 'two nations theory'.

The Two Nations view had its origin behind the barricades, on the Catholic side, in August 1969, in the defence of Catholic working class districts against an assault by Protestant police and populace. What became the Provos had the same origin.

Appeal across the barricades to a common national sentiment was put to the test. What it proved was that there was a basic conflict of national sentiment.

B&ICO, which was both Catholic and Republican in origin, decided to deal with the internal Six County conflict openly as a conflict based on national difference, which could not be resolved on the ground of that difference in the artificial Northern Ireland construct.

It tried to explain Protestant Ulster to nationalist Ireland so that it would understand that Ulster Unionism was not a superficial piece of Tory political manipulation, or of outmoded religious bigotry, that could be blown away. The common view of Fine Gael, the Irish Labour Party and Fianna Fail in that period was that Ulster Unionism would crumble if it was given a severe shock. B&ICO tried to persuade them that it was the expression of a stubborn historic community with a will of its own, and that the view that it was *"loyal to the half-crown rather than the Crown"* was not well-founded. It also tried to persuade them that Britain remained a militarist state, that war was its natural element, and that the financial cost of the North to it was slight in terms of the UK Budget, and that for these reasons the Border could not be carried by assault.

In explaining Protestant Ulster to nationalist Ireland, the B&ICO found that it was explaining it to the Ulster Protestants too. Ulster Unionism had been living in a mindless routine for half a century during which it had been detached from British political life and all it had to do at home was count Protestant heads at every election. It never had a political problem to deal with until August 1969, so that after 1969 it was unable to think politically. It had nothing that could be called an intelligentsia in its middle class. The middle class was bewildered when the crisis came. All it could do was remember some echoes from 1912-14 and imitate them. But in 1912 it had a leadership structure for dealing with a crisis, and the community was organised from top to bottom under Carson. In 1969 it was in disarray.

And all the active parts of the middle class could do was encourage elements of the working class into wild actions.

Doing the thinking that should have been done by the Protestant middle class was never the B&ICO intention, but it found that some Unionist elements were trying to catch onto its publications and take something from them for their own purposes. But they usually distorted what they took when they tried to assimilate it.

William Craig's Vanguard manifesto was a pamphlet called *'Ulster A Nation'*. The last thing that could be logically inferred from B&ICO publications was that Ulster was a nation. If it was not an integral part of the Irish nation, still less was it a nation itself. It was, when Craig published his pamphlet, a region with a sharp national division of about 60-40.

Trimble possibly did try to borrow from the B&ICO, but he could not borrow usefully because the basic B&ICO analysis was completely unacceptable to him. Perhaps he did want to be British, but he could not set about it by letting go of Ulsterism. And, in the end, he did become British by following in the footsteps of Fitt the Brit and entering the House of Lords.

He took as his advisers in 1998, Official Republicans, chief among them being Eoghan Harris, who had vehemently rejected the B&ICO analysis right at the start.

The Neo-Conservative connection

Dean Godson's biography of David Trimble contained acknowledgements to Richard Perle (Assistant Defence Secretary in President Reagan's administration, adviser to President George W. Bush), David Frum (speech writer for President George W. Bush), Ahmed Chalabi (groomed as leader of 'democratic Iraq' by the US administration and Eoghan Harris), and Devon Gaffney Cross (who served under Perle on Bush's Policy Board). Godson, the chief leader writer for *The Telegraph*, Associate Editor of *The Spectator* and Research Director of the right-wing *Policy Exchange* think-tank, was a very well connected US Neo-Conservative/British Tory opponent of the Irish Peace Process.

The Telegraph group had important connections to British Intelligence and received leaked information for dissemination. Godson also had a significant family background in US Intelligence, and a penchant for 'political warfare' against those the West saw as a threat: first Russia and then the new enemy, political Islam.

Godson had been a Research Fellow in the late 1980s at the Institute for European Defence and Strategic Studies and had an outlook which saw any

British accommodation with Irish Republicans as dangerous Chamberlainite appeasement, along with other contemporary examples in the world. He preferred the aggressive Israeli approach to the Palestinians to British peace-making with the Irish.

In October 2004 Godson wrote an article for the *'Jerusalem Center for Public Affairs'* entitled *'Lessons from Northern Ireland for the Arab-Israeli Conflict'*, in which he condemned British appeasement. Below is a flavour of the world-view that Trimble came into contact with and which, presumably, was another influence on him:

> "While there are obvious limitations in any analogy between the situation in Northern Ireland and the Israeli-Palestinian dispute, many in the British government and military believe there is such an analogy. As a consequence of the Troubles of the last 30 years, Northern Ireland has become the defining national security experience for that generation of people who now have stewardship for British policy.
>
> "Many British officials see a strong resemblance between the Israelis and the Unionists, both of whom have to be pulled down a peg or two. Both are now perceived as 'Afrikaaners', or 'settler' groups who have driven out indigenous peoples.
>
> "According to the 'consent principle', which has governed British policy throughout the Troubles, Northern Ireland's position as part of the United Kingdom is recognized as long as the majority of its population wishes to uphold the existing constitutional settlement. In the Israeli context, the consent principle is known as the Jewish state's 'right to exist'. Beyond that, though, almost everything else is up for grabs...
>
> "Blair certainly expresses himself more cautiously on these matters when it comes to the Israeli-Palestinian dispute (though not necessarily his wife!); and his perspective on how to handle the Unionists is not always the same as the Northern Ireland Office, the department of state responsible for running Ulster on a day-to-day basis. Blair effectively says, 'I'll be tough on terrorism. But I will also be equally tough on the causes of terrorism.' The implicit cause of terrorism is a state run on Unionist majoritarian lines in Northern Ireland. And he certainly views many of Israel's current policies as the root cause of terrorism there. This is where Blair's pragmatism vis-a-vis both the Northern Ireland Office and vis-a-vis the more traditional Arabist approaches within the British Foreign Office come into play. The Blairites know that neither Northern Ireland nor Israel can be wished away in this generation. Whether Northern Ireland should have been created originally or whether Israel should have been created originally is not really the point; the fact is that neither entity can be destroyed in the here and now. Indeed, if the name of the game is to persuade both Unionists and Israelis to abandon their hardline redoubts, then the first phase of the end game of a peace process, at least, requires a charm offensive...
>
> "Blair is seen as being very tough on American-related terrorism, but

specifically excluding terrorists who had killed a very substantial number of British citizens. Indeed, the UK government was perhaps the only government in the world that did not use the events of September 11th as an excuse to engage in a crackdown on its own insurrectionists. Now why was this? There is a profound belief, which existed in official British circles prior to 1997 but which skyrocketed since then, that tough measures against terrorism in Northern Ireland and against Palestinian terrorism are massively counter-productive, and that they are especially counter-productive once the British have selected partners for peace from within the relevant insurgent movements. In the case of Northern Ireland, the partner for peace that they have selected is the current generation of the Sinn Fein leadership, personified by Gerry Adams…

"A key theme in this mindset is that there can be no purely military defeat of insurgents. If this is true, then one has to make a massive number of political concessions. Some of the more robust elements within the British system believe that the Royal Ulster Constabulary… was stopping between 7 and 8, and in some cases even 9 out of 10 IRA operations during the latter years of the Troubles. Indeed, year by year we learn just how riddled the IRA was with British informers. But notwithstanding that achievement, the British government decided to give disproportionate political concessions to ensure that the IRA never had 'an excuse' to go back to armed struggle. In other words, they believe that the IRA, like the Palestinians, has a great number of very good excuses to go back 'to war'. That process, of depriving the insurgents of 'excuses', inevitably comes at the expense of Unionists and the Israelis.

"But what is the definition of victory in Northern Ireland? The British do not define 'victory' as the military defeat of the IRA. Firstly, they do not believe it was possible, but even if it was possible, they do not believe in such a defeat as a matter of principle. Victory, as far as they see it in Northern Ireland, is to persuade Sinn Fein/IRA to accept the use of democratic methods. In other words, they have a methodological definition of victory, but have no particular end point of a settlement in mind…

"Indeed, one unique aspect of policy in Northern Ireland is that the British state is well-nigh unique in advertising, quite openly, that it does not really mind if it is dismembered—subject, of course, to the consent principle. All it wants is that the IRA and the Republican movement—in the main—abandon full-scale violence, and then all other roads are open. To ensure that abandonment of violence, the British will maintain the pace of concessions, at least for as long as the Unionists are prepared to tolerate them. And because the British have been working on the Unionist community for so long, they reckon that they have a very good chance of maintaining that grip on events" (No. 523, 1.10.04).

It is important to note that Godson spent five years working closely with Trimble to construct his biography, between 1999-2003. Godson's book is in one way a critique of Trimble, but sympathetic to his predicament as a victim of a diabolical appeasement. Godson's view certainly must have chimed with that of Trimble, particularly with regard to Blair, and would undoubtedly have encouraged him to resist the Good Friday Agreement as some kind of Munich.

With powerful US Neo-Conservatives and elements within British Intelligence behind him, Trimble would have been encouraged to hold out against the mistaken Blairite appeasement of evil. After all, these important people around Godson, in the US and the UK, had seen off Russia, leaving the field open to American preponderance. And, in the new century, after launching their Global *"War on Terror"*, these personages were in the process of remaking the world—and they were on the Unionist leader's side!

There was, therefore, every reason for Trimble to hold out against Blair and resist implementing his Agreement, since the Prime Minister would ultimately have to dance to the American tune, particularly after the events of 9/11 in 2001.

CHAPTER 15

Whither Republicanism?

Whither Republicanism? That became an important question with the British suspension of the 1998 Agreement. Would Sinn Fein be able to see through the transition between War and politics that it had embarked upon, or would it fragment in the face of the obstacles placed in front of it? There were many hoping it would—and they weren't all in the British or Unionist camps.

The Sinn Fein objective of replacing War with politics was put in doubt after Mandelson's unilateral decision to suspend the Agreement. Conor Cruise O'Brien accurately described Mandelson's demonstration that International Treaties could be ripped up upon the whim of the *"predominant party"* as a calculated humiliation of the Republican leadership. O'Brien's assertion that the IRA was being goaded back to War could not be dismissed out of hand, especially with the appearance in the press of *'leaked'* security assessments of the Republican Army's supposed inability to re-launch a credible military campaign.

This was a crucial point in the Peace Process. When the Peace went into crisis through the suspension of the institutions by the British Secretary of State, the Leader of Ulster Unionism went into collaboration with Republican die-hards. The die-hards, having concluded that the Republican War had ended in a Republican defeat, determined to do their best to undermine the Sinn Fein leadership and their political strategy. This unlikely alliance had lasting repercussions for subsequent politics and deserves some attention at this point.

The *Republican Defeat* View

After the Good Friday Agreement, Anthony McIntyre, a former Provisional, wrote an article for the Liberal part of the British press, called *"We, the IRA, have failed"*. He said that the view the War had ended in a draw was false:

> "To claim... that the IRA did not win but had not lost either is demonstrably wrong. The political objective of the Provisional IRA was to secure a British declaration to withdraw. It failed. The objective of the British state was to force the Provisional IRA to accept—and to respond with a new strategic logic to—the position that it would not leave Ireland until a majority in the north consented to such a move. It succeeded" (The Guardian, 22.5.98).

This was the All-or-Nothing, Republican defeat, view, advanced by the die-hard opponents of Sinn Fein's embrace of the Good Friday settlement. The most significant of the opponents of Sinn Fein was Brendan Hughes, a very able IRA Commander who had led the first Hunger Strike. In an interview with McIntyre on his website, *The Blanket*, Hughes said:

> "From a nationalist perspective alone what we have now we could have had at any time in the last 25 years... In 1969 we had a naive enthusiasm about what we wanted. Now in 1999 we have no enthusiasm. And it is not because people are war weary—they are politics weary. The same old lies regurgitated week in week out. With the war politics had some semblance. Now it has none. The political process has created a class of professional liars and unfortunately it contains many republicans."

Hughes seemed to have come to the opinion that the conflict in which he played a very active and effective part was not worth a single life—at least not since 1974. McIntyre concurred with this view: "To bring the North to this point was not worth one drop of blood, republican or any other. The SDLP gained more in 1974 and its leadership... killed nobody."

It was true that the SDLP leadership killed nobody. But it was less true to say that they got what they got in 1974 without an awful lot of people being killed—in fact, the bulk of those who died in the War in the two previous years. It was an unfortunate fact of life in 'Northern Ireland' that most things were got through the killing of people, by one side or another.

The other implication of this position was not drawn out—that, if the War was still ongoing for the purpose of making a Republican Socialist revolution, it would be worth expending all the lives, and many more. And that is the implication that was carefully ignored by the British Press that took a liking to what Hughes and McIntyre were saying and began to popularise it. Both Hughes and McIntyre supported the continuance of the War when it was actually being waged in 1992-3 in the face of attempts to wind it down.

It is nonsense for the opponents of Sinn Fein to say that the deal of 1998 was available to it in 1974, and the struggle since then had been a waste of effort and of unnecessary lives, or alternatively, that the Sunningdale Agreement was a better deal for Nationalists than the Good Friday Agreement. For a start, the 1974 deal was never offered to Republicans. They were excluded at the outset by the Constitutional Pledge, and it was presented to the SDLP as an attempt to undermine the Republican effort. The Unionist Party had it as its official policy not to enter government with anyone who sought to end the Union. Faulkner took a chance with the SDLP and it ended in tears. If Sinn Fein had been amenable to a deal with Faulkner, is it likely to have worked, when it didn't work with the SDLP?

Moreover the 1974 deal was for weighted majority rule—which gave far less power to the minority than did the GFA, which made each Minister supreme in his own field, within the bounds of law and financial constraints.

The real historical question is: why didn't the SDLP achieve a settlement with Faulkner? Why did it not pursue an evolutionary line of development in a relationship with willing Unionists? Why did it welcome Faulkner's 1971 offer of development through Parliamentary Committees, only to pull out of Stormont immediately afterwards? The answer to these questions must lie in the fact that it lacked the substance needed for an independent course of action and the ability to transfer the momentum of the Insurrection into structural advancement for the community—something that the Provos provided and were able to accomplish two decades later.

It is also handily forgotten that the 1974 settlement with the SDLP in government was not acceptable to the very people—Trimble and Empey—who signed up in 1998 to a deal with the un-decommissioned Provos as Ministers. Something about inter-community power relations had to have changed during the intervening period for this to happen, which very much suggests that the intervening period had an effect on politics in a way that what happened before 1974 did not.

So the contention that the War was unnecessary for the achievement of what *was* actually achieved by the War is a debating point, pitched at a very remote level of abstraction from the historical course of the actual events themselves.

Leaving aside the fact that the settlements of 1974 and 1998 were very different settlements indeed, an important consideration is ignored here. A political settlement is not the end of history. It is the start of a new political process. The development of a political process in a favourable direction is dependent on the development of durable political substance in a political movement that has capable and flexible leadership.

The Republican political substance was, and was seen to be, far more substantial in 1994 than it was in 1974. Republicans had grown in understanding and determination in the course of the 'Long March' to 1998. And that is very important because the durability of political forces, as has been noted, is what impresses Britain most.

Over the centuries Britain developed a peculiar form of warfare that, in comparison with the military behaviour of other states, seems to be slow and inefficient—almost bungling. That is before everything finally comes together for it, of course. This approach had a lot to do with it being an island and having had a Navy as its senior service for war-making. It could do something that Continental nations could not do—retire behind its island defences and wait, even when it initially bungled things, as it did in 1914-

17, when it was saved by the US, and in 1939-41, when it was saved by the USSR. As a consequence, British wars tended to be long and attritional. And they were made immensely painful for opponents, who they ground down in prolonged agony. Britain found this form of attritional warfare to be more beneficial to its interests than the short, stylish and relatively humane form of warfare that is devastating and quick. Its slow grinding wars disrupted the world over an extended period, producing unexpected opportunities to extend British influence in multiple spheres.

Whilst the Provos fought their Long War through necessity, the British fought their long wars through choice. However, Britain was always going to respect the opponent who stayed the distance in its long wars above the adversary who could only put up a short resistance and go down in a blaze of glory. The former were rare and worthy of recognition whereas the latter, for Britain, were ten-a-penny in its history books.

Furthermore, the more dogmatic 1974 Republican leadership was unlikely to conclude, or be able to sell, a functional settlement to the Northern base. They were from the old Southern incorruptible Republican rump, and they had the added disadvantage of being not strictly from the people who were doing the fighting. McGuinness and Adams and the new generation of Republicans were of Six County origin and knew what the War was actually about.

Surrender and Re-grant?

The criticism made by the Republican die-hards—which Ulster Unionists then took up in order to use as jibes against Sinn Fein—was that, as a result of the Good Friday Agreement, it had ended up *"administering British rule"* in the Six Counties, *"in a Partitionist assembly"*.

What was the *"British"* status of 'Northern Ireland' after 1998? Sinn Fein knew all too well that 'Northern Ireland' was a place apart and was only *de jure* under the 'British government'. By administering something that Britain set apart from itself, it was not conniving at a strengthening of the British presence but playing a part in loosening it. It was facilitating the further distancing of Britain, after forcing the British engagement to equalise the status of its community with the community that regarded itself as British.

It was neither a Republican nor a British war aim that the War would result in Sinn Fein being in the government of the Six Counties. But war is the sort of catastrophic activity that results in such unpredictable events. The British way of dealing with *"armed rebellion"* is to resist it, testing the quality of what it represents, and then to compromise with it, if it deserves compromising with. That has been demonstrated many times.

One of the most popular phrases used against Sinn Fein by its die-hard opponents was that it had agreed to a form of "*Surrender and Re-grant*", like the Earl of Tyrone, Hugh O'Neill, at the turn of the 17th Century. This phrase was used by Bernadette McAliskey-Devlin, Tommy McKearney and McIntyre. But it was not the Treaty O'Neill signed with the Crown in 1603 at Mellifont that did for the Ulster Earls and let in the Plantation, but what happened afterwards. O'Neill having survived the War was routed in the peace.

Hugh O'Neill may have made a formal submission to the Crown after he failed to win in the Nine Years War, but he was treated with great respect at the English Court and secured a good settlement at Mellifont that left him in charge of his territory and with rights over his lordship largely intact. The Treaty he made caused great annoyance, both in England and amongst the Crown's representatives in Ulster, where it was felt to have been far too generous to be allowed to a defeated rebel. But the Crown obviously felt that O'Neill was still a substantial force that needed to be taken account of in any settlement. The Treaty of 1603 was not an end to history. The English in Ireland took it that there was unfinished business and began undermining O'Neill in the peace, with Sir Arthur Chichester and Sir John Davies attempting to *shire* Ulster, dispossess the Irish of their land, maintain garrisons at O'Neill's expense, and work up trouble against the Gaelic Chiefs through their subjects. The English peace took a familiar course:

> "Government officials were constantly around watching for any information which might be used against him. His friends were arrested and questioned and were offered bribes to incriminate him, and attempts were made to assassinate him" (Micheline Kerney Walsh, '*Hugh O'Neill and the Flight of the Earls*', p.15).

Hugh O'Neill said of the English: "They themselves . . . teach us this manner of feigned friendship and of destruction by peace" (Micheline Kerney Walsh, '*Destruction by Peace: Hugh O Neill After Kinsale*', p. 350)/

Kerney Walsh found a letter from O'Neill to the Spanish Council of State, written whilst in exile in Rome (23.5.1615), asking for the King's help against England:

> "We beg His Majesty to be moved to help us, remembering what the Engslish have done many times despite their peace treaties… The English… using the name of peace as a deception, teach us this manner of feigned friendship and of destruction by peace" (p. 350)

Despite a peace treaty between England and Spain in 1604 that agreed neither side would support the other's rebellious subjects, O'Neill and Red Hugh O'Donnell attempted to manoeuvre against England with Spain, anticipating a breach and renewal of war. In 1606 the Treaty nearly collapsed. The Gaels were willing to break the Treaty and renew the war with England if Spain provided the necessary support. Then, an English event, the Gunpowder Plot, had an impact on the situation. When O'Neill was invited to London to answer in a dispute over land ownership, he was warned by friends of his on the English Privy Council that evidence would be presented against him that would result in his arrest on charges of treason. Whether this was a ruse to secure the Earl of Tyrone's departure or not, O'Neill decided to take no chances and he left with Red Hugh O'Donnell in what is known as *"the Flight of the Earls"* to obtain foreign help.

The Preface to Micheline Kerney Walsh's book, *'Destruction by Peace'*, was written by Cardinal O'Fiaich. The Cardinal did not like to hear of Tyrone's departure described as a *flight*. He knew O'Neill to be a proud Ulsterman who would not flee but was engaging in a tactical retreat so that he could take on the Crown in the future in another round with England. Cardinal O'Fiaich noted that, after the reverse at Kinsale, O'Neill brought his troops back to Tyrone, "defeated but still strong and full of fight". Although his allies began to seek peace terms with the Crown, and there was a massive price placed on his head, none of his community would betray him. They determined to remain a cohesive force in their retreat from the battlefield.

The Cardinal also admired the Earl of Tyrone for his complexity:

> "His Pale upbringing, his education in England, his marriage entanglements, his combination of attachment to traditional ways and preparedness to experiment in the organisation of Ulster, his durability as a 'survivor' in an era when so many of his contempories met death on the battlefield, by political assassination or by execution, his military prowess in defeating, defying or evading some of the greatest English commanders of the Elizabethan age, all of these things gave him a complexity which has never been adequately explored" (p. xii).

The Republican die-hard view of O'Neill is, like its view of Sinn Fein, simplistic. O'Neill was a complex 'national' manifestation, being a protégé of the English Court and an ally of the Crown in earlier Irish conflict. He was educated by one of the great aristocratic families at a time when England was generating its own national State. If O'Neill learnt 'nationalism' anywhere, it was among the English, rather than within the fragmented Gaelic system. And he proved very capable of exploiting internal contradictions within the English Tudor State, as he did regarding the Earl of Essex (or arranged for Elizabeth to do, in punishment for calling off the war in Ireland).

There are certain similarities between O'Neill and the Provos in their intimate understanding of the State they were up against: a perception that had something to do with their origin and development, that they used to their advantage. However, whilst both conducted effective retreats from the battlefield, where O'Neill was unable to overcome internal Irish rivalry that the English State utilised against him, the Provos remained coherent and capable against it.

The Cardinal, being a keen student of history, must himself have seen the parallels between O'Neill and the modern force O'Fiaich himself was, helping to move towards a functional settlement. And, having a good knowledge of O'Neill's experience and the fate he suffered, he knew the difficulties faced in dealing with those who made a speciality of destroying in peace.

The Cardinal had played an important role in assisting the Provos to retreat from the Hunger Strike in 1981. That was a dangerous moment for the Republicans, at which they required protection from the Nationalist mainstream to prevent a disorganisation in the ranks. That protection would not have been forthcoming from 'Constitutional Nationalism'. But it was provided by Cardinal O'Fiaich, Fr. Faul and Fr. Murray—who emphasised the Nationalist continuum between the spiritual and political causes. And they did this for the good of their community, which could not afford a rout occurring in the wake of the Hunger Strike, after all it had endured for a decade. The Cardinal then provided the moral authority for the beginnings of the Peace Process, something which he would have been strongly associated with, if he had not died of a heart attack in 1990.

What is interesting here is that the die-hards opposed to Sinn Fein relied on a view of O'Neill formed from hostile English sources. And, within this English world-view, they made a parallel with Sinn Fein. But the Cardinal knew his history better than the die-hards. He could, using the continental sources used by Kerney Walsh, place Tyrone in a wider world-view. The Cardinal had a historical appreciation of the two situations, which was lacking in the die-hards with their foreign/academic ideologies. And he knew that Tyrone had not surrendered and been put to flight but had been destroyed in the peace.

The Trouble with Treaties

Anyone aware of Irish/British history should know that too much can be read into the formalities of Treaties. Didn't De Valera once say that *"the history of Ireland is a history of broken treaties"*? There was the Treaty of Limerick less than a century after Mellifont—*Cuilidh ar Luimneach agus ar felne Sasanach*—which rendered Ireland helpless for 200 years as it was under a regime of very effective oppression. Two centuries later it was never a British aim to put Michael Collins and Sinn Fein in power through the Articles Of Agreement 'Treaty'. The majority at Westminster that agreed to that 'Treaty' could not even countenance the thought of Redmond as Prime

Minister under a system of meagre Home Rule governance in 1914. But, when the assertion of Irish democratic will in 1918 was backed up with a resolution not seen before and not anticipated at the time, England had to alter its Imperial aims in Ireland, sign an Agreement, and pursue its aims in relation to the Irish independence movement differently.

It was not the signing of the 'Treaty'. and the administering of Crown authority by Collins, that had the desired effect upon the Irish Independence movement from the British standpoint. It was the subsequent disorganisation of the Republican Army of the Irish democracy, by the way Collins implemented the 'Treaty', that helped impress the British agenda on Ireland and let Britain recover some lost ground. And it was not the Partition of the country that produced a continuation of Imperial hegemony in Ireland, but the establishment of a semi-detached pseudo-state in the North that acted as a lever on the whole island for the future. A simple Partition would have exerted little influence in the South.

In the 1990s it would not have been Britain's intention to see Sinn Fein in government, calling the shots in the Peace Process, and emerging as an increasing political power on the island. It would have been the intention to disable and disorganise it by preventing it completing an orderly retreat from the battlefield to the political sphere. Destruction by Peace would have been welcome after destruction by War had failed.

What Britain understands in these matters is that treaties simply put conflict onto another plane, where new varieties of power are employed in different ways. There are, after all, more ways than one to skin a cat. So the continuing political substance and durability behind the parties who conclude agreements is very important in such matters.

War Aims

The basis of the McIntyre/Hughes criticism of the Provos is that Republicans were defeated in their stated primary War aim, that of forcing a British withdrawal. It is suggested that Sinn Fein refused to admit that it had retreated and conned the rank and file into believing that they were still Republicans. And therefore all the *"deaths were needless deaths"* — those occurring after 1973-4 anyway. One thing that can be said immediately about this argument is that Britain did not get where it was in the world by taking such a naïve view of politics and war. England has not gone into its many wars with definite, formal demands. Formal demands have the effect of limiting aims. The actual but unstated aim is always to get the greatest possible advantage from the war, seizing opportunities as they arise.

If there is a standard British aim in war at all, it is to disorganise and weaken the enemy of the moment to such an extent that England gains a position of advantage from which it can proceed to greater things. As a result British wars have tended to be both very numerous (with countless enemies) and *continuous*—that is continuing in political form long after military engagements have ceased. War is politics by other means and politics is war by other means.

In making its wars, England made plans for many eventualities and engaged in conflict on some excuse or another when advantage was sensed. It then decided what could and could not be gained in the fluctuating course of war and formulated demands on this basis. At some times, war aims were expanded in the course of conflict and, at others, they were contracted. It all depended on the strength and skill of the opposition as to what could be won or not won, or on what necessity there was to satisfy the allies who were necessary for a successful conclusion. Victory has often been proclaimed by Britain, despite the non-achievement of objectives—aims which hardly seem to matter after the event.

The Republican War was a declared war carried through to a Ceasefire and a Peace settlement. It is argued that the primary War Aim was not achieved in the Peace settlement. That is often the case with wars whose character as legitimate wars is never disputed.

The declared British war aim in 1939 was to uphold the integrity and independence of Poland. Although 50 million people were killed in that war, a peace settlement was made in 1945 without Polish independence—with Britain's new enemy, Stalin, occupying the country instead of Hitler. The ally became the enemy. And the territorial integrity of 1939 Poland has never been restored. War is, therefore, a complicated business when it comes to deciding what is victory and what is defeat, and the outcome never rests on the static articles of Treaties but more on the position attained for a subsequent push forward. And Britain understands this better than anyone.

One of the British objectives in the 1998 Agreement was to soak up Republican energies in the mundane affairs of provincial life through the 'Northern Ireland' Assembly. That showed some signs of success between 1998 and 2000. And it has not been abandoned as a long-term objective. It is an example of how Britain moves on and starts again after signing Treaties and there is never an end to it.

It did not stop acting in this way after the signing of the Agreement and the granting of a new Constitution to the Six Counties. It continues to exert its charms and pressures, probing for weaknesses to exploit. If Sinn Fein were to generate sufficient power in Ireland, Britain would accept that position and treat with it in the context of a United Ireland. After all, if republicans overcame Unionist resistance, all the better for the prospects of a stable and honourable settlement which might bring Ireland back into a closer orbit with London! It can hardly act otherwise than to attempt to mould such a close neighbour.

One thing is certain: Britain will always be working on it and would rule nothing out. Look at what it has achieved in relation in the 26 Counties from a very unpromising position in 1969-70.

As for the republican dissidents, they might consider the dictum of Basil Liddell Hart, the famous British military theorist, who pointed out that "Victory in the true sense... surely implies that one is better off after the war than if one had not made war" (*'The British Way in Warfare'*, p.41).

Following the Long War, the Republican Movement achieved an immensely more powerful position, compared to 1969, before War was embarked upon, when it was a small rump. And, as for the people they fought for and who comprised its activists, the Northern Catholics, well that is a 'no brainer'. It has been argued that the working-class did not benefit as much from the Peace as the middle class, but that would have been the case even if the Provos had achieved military victory and it ignores the transformation wrought in the slums of the major towns and cities. There is simply no comparison between the morale and the conditions of life of working class people before and after the War.

Can the same be said of the State that squandered its Empire in trying twice to cut Germany down to size? Or can it be said of the Ulster Unionist Party—which lost the Union in 1920 and its parliament in 1972, and was detached further from Britain after 1985 and 1998?

Both the Ulster Unionist Party and Sinn Fein were founded in 1905. What a change there has been in the balance of power on the island of Ireland since then. In 2014 a Leader of the Unionist Party—a Party which had been provided with a 'state' to govern in perpetuity by Westminster—was concerned that Sinn Fein might give up on Stormont in pursuit of its "all-Ireland agenda" (BT 15.12.14). Could such a thing be ever imagined in 1921? These things need to be put in historical perspective and not seen through the British narrative.

Politicians and Spooks

Writing after Mandelson's suspension of the Agreement, McIntyre made the following comments about the situation: "Small wonder that the British diplomat Sir David Goodall said of the Good Friday Agreement that 'it is working almost exactly to plan'. Who else knew the plot?" (Fourthwrite, Spring 2000).

From the start those who opposed calling off the War have been uttering dark hints of treachery and collusion between the Republican Leadership and the British State. The fact is that it had been an objective—at least since 1972—of some elements within the British State to 'politicise' the Provos as a way of ending the conflict. It had been the objective of other security force elements to destroy the Republican movement and claim outright victory. The British State is not a monolith: it is multi-facetted and devises many possible policies to achieve its broad objectives.

England has supped with much greater devils than the Irish Republican Army. After the Bolshevik Revolution, alone among the Western Powers, it maintained a backchannel with Trotsky. R.H. Bruce Lockhart published an account of such dealings in his *'Memoirs of a British Agent'*. The British intention at the time was to strengthen the Soviet Government so that it could break the Treaty of Brest-Litovsk it had signed with Germany and renew the War. Lenin dealt with the British agents in a pragmatic fashion, seeing what he might obtain from them until breaking off relations. In modern times the British Prime Minister and Queen supped with the leader of the world's largest Communist Party to further the perceived interests of the British State. Martin McGuinness is welcome on the same basis.

The vigour of the British State results from the great variety of things, often contradicting each other, that go on within it. The key is to be prepared for every eventuality—even for what amounts to defeat—if it can gain a rewarding position!

It would be safe to say that the preferred option of the British State was to destroy the Republicans as a political force and cobble together a settlement with some compliant Catholics who would pose no problems for anyone. The second option would have been to reduce the Provos to political insignificance. The third best option would be to politicise them and remove the military threat (mainly to stop bombs going off in Britain) so that they could be dealt with in politics—an art which the British State is immensely skilled at. A final option was to concede and withdraw from Ireland (though not necessarily bring about Irish unity). There were occasions in which some people probably toyed with the fourth option but these were momentary and discounted quickly.

It should be said that withdrawal would not have necessarily resulted in a Republican victory—much killing, and re-partition were just as likely. It would not be surprising or sinister for a part of British Intelligence to have been the promoters of the third best option—that of facilitating the Republican movement's political development.

Over the years it became a common refrain in the British democracy that there could be "*no talking to terrorists*", to the "*men of violence*". That became the public position of the parties of State that was rarely challenged. Furthermore, politicians, who after all are merely temporary creatures of party in Britain, would not have had the staying power to '*talk to the terrorists*'. Whitelaw was the most substantial political talent that was applied to the sorting of 'Northern Ireland' and he was moved on before his work was complete. 'Northern Ireland' only appeared on the political agenda momentarily when there were great upsurges of trouble there or when the trouble visited the 'British mainland'.

That was the case in the mid-1970s when British politicians made the last concerted effort to tackle the problem. But, with the decline of the Republican military capacity and the containment of the War, 'Northern Ireland' went off the British political agenda. British politics are about parties winning votes in elections to gain the power to govern and 'Northern Ireland' was detached from the party politics of the State on purpose to prevent it interfering in this contest between parties of State.

With the Republican Army contained, and 'Ulster' ring-fenced, it was business as usual for the British State, and Ulster was way down its political agenda—until the next bomb in London or large dose of killing. So the British democracy would have been the last place that such a long-term and delicate project as negotiating with the people who mattered would be undertaken: it was much more likely to be found elsewhere within the more permanent and stable architecture of the British State.

The Intelligence services have much more freedom of action than democratic politicians in the British system. For one thing, they are largely beyond democratic control and the short-termist hysteria of democracy. They predate the British democracy by many centuries—from the time of the Cecils during the Tudor period. They represent continuity in the State and are there for both the long-haul and the long-term interest.

It is one of their characteristics that they often contain innovative mavericks who have a tendency to 'go native' and start apparently acting more in the interests of those they are supposedly countering than those they are working for—until the time comes when the natives have to be shafted (Lawrence of Arabia being an example). Their purpose is to 'think outside the box' and 'think the unthinkable' because the politicians might one day come to them for a solution.

It could be said that during the 1980s elements in the Republican Leadership started to think on similar lines to elements in the British State and began working toward a bisection of purpose from different directions. They had differing objectives in mind, but they met within the understanding that a political solution was necessary because a military one was not on. While continuing overt and covert warfare in the late 1980s-90s, crucial elements on both sides were convinced of the direction things were heading in.

Peter Taylor demonstrated in his television series, *'Brits'*, that from 1974 onwards the running of British State policy in 'Northern Ireland' was effectively ceded by the Government to its security services. The democracy largely washed its hands of the mess it had made of things after the huge effort put into pacifying the province with the Power-Sharing solution failed in 1974. After that there were minor initiatives, which had little hope of success. The Brighton Bomb jolted the Thatcher Government into action in the shape of the Hillsborough Treaty, but it too foundered.

That helps to explain why politicians would abandon power and responsibility to the *'securocrats'* in important affairs of State. But, when one considers that the British political parties have no electoral interest in 'Northern Ireland', and have detached it from their body politic for a century, it becomes apparent why they despaired of making a settlement themselves and handed responsibility over to those who had more experience in non-domestic and colonial environments.

The key figure in political dialogue between British Intelligence and Republicans was Michael Oatley of MI6. Oatley was instrumental in the talks leading up to, and during, the 1975 IRA Truce. Later, when the Government policy of criminalising Republican prisoners ran into crisis in the H-Blocks in 1980, he came up with a functional settlement of the first Hunger-Strike, which should have averted the second one. And he re-emerged to see through the process which put an end to the War in the early 1990s.

Interestingly, on the Taylor programme, he ridiculed Trimble's demand for an IRA arms handover as *"meaningless"* and *"politically counter-productive"*. Where would the British State be without people like Oatley?

The sneer is that the British had successfully moulded a compromising Irish Republican leadership. It would be more accurate to say that compromise suited both sides in the military stalemate situation. The compromisers talked to each other. Only in the long term will it emerge which side will achieve its objectives. So far the Provos have not put a foot wrong.

It was not the Provos who miscalculated in relation to the British intention of continuing the war at the political level after they had concluded an Agreement. As we shall later see, that miscalculation was made by the die-hards in connection with the naïve venture involving the Boston College Tapes.

Secret History?

That brings us to Ed Moloney and his *Secret History*. Much of the political analysis of the Provos has been coloured by Ed Moloney's 2002 book, *'The Secret History of the IRA'*. Moloney is an English journalist who as a young man took part in the People's Democracy radical activism in 'Northern Ireland' in 1968-69 and who went on to make a successful career in international journalism. *'The Secret History of the IRA'* is based on interviews the journalist conducted with Brendan Hughes and others—interviews which remained secret at the time.

The die-hards greeted Moloney's book with great enthusiasm, as confirming their view of things with 'evidence'. It went much further than previous accounts of the IRA, suggesting the Provos *'lost'* the War in 1994 and asserting that the leadership of the movement conned the grassroots into the Ceasefire and "*surrender*", having operated a secret agenda for Peace over many years. Never far from the surface are hints that the Sinn Fein leadership were either the willing or unwilling tools of the British Intelligence services and might even be British agents who conspired with person, or persons, unknown to eliminate their Republican opponents in one way or another in furtherance of their own despicable agenda.

While there is much of interest in Moloney's book, its main thrust is that Adams sabotaged the striking power of the IRA and manoeuvred it towards negotiations and compromise, using an apparatus he had constructed behind the IRA official structure. He manipulated the Republican movement into surrender and a betrayal of principles, according to Moloney. So Adams is the 'Stalin' of the piece. From almost page one he is presented as a devious political manipulator, learning from the mistakes of Cathal Goulding, and perfecting the art of political manipulation and elimination. Almost singlehandedly, he deals ruthlessly with competitors for power, first by allying with them, then isolating them and finally destroying them, along with the Revolution, Socialist and Republican. And the only thing missing is a Trotsky!

In his tale of the Great Betrayal, Moloney completely loses sight of political reality. His account is of one Provo disaster after another, of one military catastrophe after another, of one political setback after another, until the greatest defeat of all—the surrender dressed up as a victory in 1998.

He neglects the fact that the Republican offensive, even at its height, when very respectable people—including senior members of the SDLP and the Dublin Establishment—were utilising it to play Machiavellian power-politics, could not have achieved outright victory. Unionist resistance, not the British State, was the crucial factor in halting the offensive, and this was clear by the Winter of 1972-3—when the IRA ceased to conquer. But from 1976-7 onwards, when Republicans began to realise this themselves, the IRA did a remarkable job in sustaining itself in order that the effects of the military campaign could be translated into political dividends for its community.

Of course, the policy of the British State—keeping the province at arm's length, and continuing to treat it as a semi-detached pressure cooker of communal attrition—not to mention the political ineptitude of Unionism, provided the hope that often sustained the deed. But the Republican Army took everything that the British State could throw at it (and the British have immense experience in this department) and continued to possess the capability of maintaining a forceful campaign, even in the twilight years of its War.

It is a long time since the Provos declared that they were going to drive the British out of Ireland. And in those times many in Dublin and the SDLP would have pocketed such a victory with relish. But in the last decade of the conflict it was pretty clear that the War was continued, not to achieve military victory, but to bring about the best possible transitory settlement that would lead to an ultimate realisation of political objectives.

At the time the Insurrection began, Nationalism was in long-term decline in the South and the Republican Army could expect decreasing assistance from that quarter, unless it made continual advances. The Republicans found they had to remain in the field until the British were prepared to make a deal with them, so that the maximum political advantage could be secured for their community for the sacrifice that had been made in lives.

The political advantage gained was clear to the community who lived through the Stormont system and could remember the relative political, economic, and social positions of the two communities before 1972. The Provos also knew that the British would not address the situation in 'Northern Ireland' unless forced to. That was the political reality of the perpetual arm's length promotion of communal politics that the British State pursued in the Six Counties since 1921. It was this attitude that the Provos sought to break.

The Sinn Fein strategy became one of maximising its political power in the North, and using this political base to advance Republican objectives in the rest of the island. The political power of Sinn Fein, which proved remarkably resilient despite British and Irish attempts to undermine it, expanded considerably in the aftermath of the 1998 Agreement, as a consequence of the political success it had achieved in advancing the Nationalist interest within the North—something which Northern Catholics astutely credited Republicans with, despite all the attempts to promote the view that the SDLP was right all along and had won the political settlement.

In the South the retreat from national culture and the atrophy of National life created an opening for the expansion of Sinn Fein and an increase in Republican influence which could hardly have been predicted in the Haughey era.

The Republicans settled on the alternative route to a United Ireland— minimising the communal grind in the North and diminishing the antagonism between North and South that was produced by 'Constitutional Nationalist' initiatives like the Hillsborough Treaty. The Republican objective became to assuage and/or wear down Unionist resistance to a United Ireland over the next couple of decades in an atmosphere of general political co-operation. In one sense this was a tall order because the communal grind of politics is always likely to keep antagonisms simmering on one issue or another. But Sinn Fein were confident that its ability at politics would work to undermine its political opponents whilst its power base continued to exert a wider influence, even into parts of the Protestant community.

The majority of Republicans saw the Peace Process as being, not the ending of the War, but the closing of one and the opening up of another Front in the struggle. And, most important, the community which had supported the Provos in their War, far from abandoning them when they called a halt to it, began to increasingly register support for Sinn Fein. Over three decades, the Republican movement had stayed in the field because of its ability to improvise and open new Fronts on which to fight. When the War began to run out of steam in the late 1970s, the prison campaign was opened, leading to the Hunger Strike, the rejuvenation of recruitment and the electoral rise of Sinn Fein. The growth of Sinn Fein and the establishment of a significant electoral mandate were a useful adjunct to a less vigorous military campaign in the early eighties. Military activity was refined to suit the electoral development and the Long War strategy was theorised.

By the early 1990s, Republicans realised that Sinn Fein could not in the near future overtake the SDLP as the majority Nationalist party, and the attempt to extend Republican military hegemony from South Armagh into East Tyrone had not succeeded. It was decided that a new Front needed to be opened up as the long War was taking too long.

The IRA was a hierarchical military organisation through necessity. But outside it lay a substance it had to relate to and take account of—the community which produced and sustained it. Although the Republican Army could exist apart from the majority will of its community, it depended on that community because it was ultimately its creation and was its instrument to bring improvement. Elements within the IRA desiring to act against the community's interest on behalf of a disconnected Republicanism could not do so without becoming isolated. That has been made very evident by events since 1998.

The 'Revolutionaries' and the Nationalist Continuum

After the 1998 GFA the die-hards and their left-wing supporters made Sinn Fein their principal enemy. Hatred toward Adams and Sinn Fein became the main feature of die-hard political orientation, in much the way as the Trotskyite Fourth International's main preoccupation became the undermining of Moscow. And, just as the left-wing opponents of the Soviet State began to absorb the world-view of the opponents of Communism, and added to its arsenal, the Republican die-hards similarly helped swell the ranks of the opponents of Sinn Fein. Many of the Trotskyites and other leftists moved on to ultra-Liberalism or *"neo-conservativism"* and many die-hards are gravitating in that direction too.

At the root of disappointment about the Republican Army concluding its War before the attainment of its full objective, lay a spirit of restlessness similar to that in Trotskyism. It was also the *"Revolutionary"* looking at the Partisan.

The German philosopher Carl Schmitt once made the useful distinction between *Partisans* and *Revolutionaries*. In his *'Theory of the Partisan'* he noted that, whilst the Revolutionary and Partisan share certain similarities, like engaging in irregular warfare and being civilians who take up arms, rather than being professional soldiers, one important thing divides them. Partisans tend to have a telluric character (*Das tellurisch*) that connects them to the earth. The Partisan has objectives that are limited and territorially-based, such as toppling a regime or ending the foreign occupation of a particular area. The Revolutionary activist, on the other hand, has no telluric character, and has universalist objectives which do not limit the field of action.

Schmitt saw the Revolutionary activist as beginning with Lenin and the Bolsheviks.

The events of August 1969 coincided with the importation of ideas from the International Marxist Student Revolution of the period. In some ways the ephemeral Student Revolution in Northern Ireland—in the shape of People's Democracy—helped to spark events, but what was more important, it saturated the atmosphere in which the Catholic Insurrection occured. The ideas of the Revolution permeated the older Irish Republican ideology and put a revolutionary gloss upon the substance. During this time the old certainties of Catholic Nationalist Ireland became more fluid and new ideas, seen previously as alien ideologies, became fashionable.

The nature of the British State in 'Northern Ireland' meant that the revolutionary atmosphere generated a volatile situation that resulted in the overthrow of Stormont. But, when the revolution had overthrown Stormont, what it found was a constant confronting it—the British State. Revolutionary ideas persisted, but it should have been quickly understood that there had been no revolution in substance. What had happened was just a peeling away of a façade.

The new Republican Army were always Partisans, rather than Revolutionaries, because it was grounded in reality. Even Traditionalists sometimes expressed revolutionary ideas, as a defence against jibes from the Revolutionaries about being "*right wing*" and "*fascist*". And naturally Republicans wanted to achieve social change. They refused, however, to be diverted from simple anti-Partitionism into theoretical Marxism that messed with the head.

However, it is understandable that some flavour of revolution should have permeated the ranks in the revolutionary situation surrounding the fall of Stormont and, when many in the ranks were confined indefinitely by the State, they educated themselves in the international literature of the period. The H Block library of a thousand or more books on Marx, Marxism, Lenin, Trotsky, Mao, Castro, Fanon etc. reinforced the revolutionary self-image. The State, it seems, facilitated this. Britain, which sheltered Marx, knows a thing or two about utilising revolutionary ideas in its own interest.

During the early 1980s Gerry Adams was keen to distance the Republican Army from the ultra-Leftist 'revolutionaries' the British Left wanted to connect it with. He was eager, instead, to connect the Republican movement with very conservative Nationalists instead. Fionnuala O'Connor commented about this in her book '*In Search of a State, Catholics in Northern Ireland*':

> "No 'lumpen-nationalists' for Gerry Adams: instead he uses the words 'nationalism' and 'republicanism' interchangeably, keen to outline a unity among Northern Catholics which others believe no longer exists."

And she quotes Adams as saying:

> "There is... group Catholic thinking... there's a tendency within this state for some aspects of life to remind you where you come from... The Unionists have shown no great effort to accommodate, the British are not prepared to push the issue forward, and that brings people back to this group Catholic thinking... If the emergence of Sinn Fein means a slight radicalising of the non-unionist section of the community, so much the better'..." (p.87).

Northern Nationalism is said to be 'Constitutional' or 'Revolutionary'. However, neither term is accurate. 'Constitutional Nationalism' is far from being Constitutional, that is, accepting the British Constitution or the Constitutional position of 'Northern Ireland' within the UK. And 'Revolutionary' Nationalism is far from revolutionary, as should be very clear by now. It espouses social improvement within the parameters of the society in which it functions, rather than a root and branch overthrow of existing structures.

Irish Republicanism in its actual manifestation was never very 'Revolutionary'. In the 1960s some began to connect it to French revolutionary politics through the United Irishmen. But there was little continuity between the 1790s and the Republicanism of the 1950s, beyond the ideals of breaking the connection with Britain (which was confined to only a section of United

Irishmen), and replacing the name of Protestant, Catholic and dissenter with *Irishman*. And many of the United Irishmen became Constitutionalists when they were admitted to the Constitution.

In 1919-21 Sinn Fein attempted to replace the British authority over the Kingdom of Ireland with a native one. The Irish democracy assembled to replace the Dublin Castle administration and constructed a legal system designed to maintain ordinary bourgeois order and quell any disorder that might arise in the transition. One of the publications it issued was called *'The Constructive Work Of Dail Eireann'* which described how it suppressed anything that hinted of social conflict. That reflected the fact that Ireland was not as stratified a society as England.

There was very little alteration of anything else and, if Britain had accepted the democratic verdict in 1918, there would have been a peaceful and smooth transition of ownership of the Kingdom that became a Republic in the absence of a monarchy.

If anything, the revolutionary element in the situation was Britain, which subverted its unitary policy with regard to Ireland, and constructed something without political precedent: the Six Counties.

One of the most noticeable things about Northern Nationalism after Partition was the sheer lack of *'Revolutionary'* sentiment directed against the *'Constitutionalists'*. I have no idea when the term *'Constitutional'* came into currency to describe parliamentary Nationalism but the Northern IRA was remarkably restrained in issuing condemnations of their Nationalist brethren.

What actually existed in the North was a continuum of two wings of Nationalism rather than two distinct political movements. Revolutionary Ideology was a luxury that Northern Nationalists could not afford in the face of the forces arrayed against them. The men who favoured physical force periodically used electoral politics, and the electoral wing of Nationalism never ruled out physical force, if it had any hope of success. And there were many like Cahir Healy, the most representative Northern Nationalist of the Stormont period, who transferred between the two easily, bringing the bulk of his community with him.

The Officials contained more *"revolutionaries"* than the Provisionals but the British Communist ideology which the leadership had imported was a rigid Stages theory of economic determinism. However, the Provos were also able to gather in people seeing themselves as being Revolutionary, or who became Revolutionaries after contemplation in gaol. And such people would tend to feel disgruntled with an *'Unfinished Revolution'* and see the unfinished nature of the struggle as evidence of a defeat—rather than an incomplete victory, which is how the Partisan tends to see it. Such activists are nearly always inspired by Lenin in one form or another.

That is not to say that the Partisans lacked a social agenda—as would have been the case with mainstream Republicans of an earlier generation. Gerry Adams certainly has a social vision which is well encapsulated by the *1916 Proclamation*.

The disgruntled revolutionaries of the Officials went on to supply the first wave of anti-Republican journalists for the British State. They became 'Irish' correspondents for the *Sunday Times* etc., supplying a native service not otherwise available. Then the die-hards become incorporated into the process which Britain accomplishes so well.

Politics and Ideology

Britain has always believed in the primacy of Power Politics over ideology. For centuries England was an anti-Catholic state, largely held together internally by anti-Catholicism. It persecuted Catholicism in Ireland with its Penal Laws but it still made alliances with Catholic Powers in furtherance of power politics. Ideology, therefore, was always the servant of Power: that is the secret of England's success. Its ideology is tempered with pragmatism.

The Republican Leadership has acted likewise, placing Power Politics to the fore, whilst retaining its Ideological lodestar: and that seems to be what most bothers the die-hards. Ideology has a tendency to disorientate practical politics. It represents a rigorous system of ideas which has the effect of disconnecting its adherents from political realities. It is a substitute for an understanding of the society and its historical development.

Now it must be said that there is little of traditional Republican ideology in the position of Anthony McIntyre, a leading diehard. He is a Northerner and has nothing of the Living Dáil Republicanism of Ruairi O Bradaigh. He largely defines Republicanism on its rejection of the 'consent principle' with regard to Ulster Protestants. That is what, for McIntyre, sets the IRA and Sinn Fein apart from the SDLP.

Of course, the rejection of the 'consent principle' was not confined to Republicans. Up until quite recently, it was a characteristic of the entire Nationalist movement, both North and South of the Border, stretching from Fianna Fail to Fine Gael and Labour to the Nationalist Party and Sinn Fein. This rejectionism was eventually dropped, as the events of the decades after August 1969 brought nationalism up against the reality of the situation.

But there is another ideological influence on McIntyre, one he shares with Professors Bew and Patterson, and that is Marxism. Academic Marxism has tended to see ideology as a bourgeois/ruling class phenomenon, something that creates *'false consciousness'* in the proletariat. Those who become Republican Socialists find a neat complementarity in this idea of 'false consciousness' as it helps to explain Protestant Unionist opposition to a United Ireland: which is explained as *'deluded'* and being under some Orange-bourgeois spell. Long ago, however, the Professors went on to reject such crudity and retreated into an Althusserian discourse—before re-emerging as reconstructed (or is that unreconstructed?) Liberal Unionists.

The Provos learnt from Britain the mastery of the art of Power Politics: in which Ideology is taken to be subservient to Power. That is what has marked them out from the old Republicanism and from the academic snipers. This can be seen in the ability of Sinn Fein to function effectively within the transition between War and politics. If Sinn Fein had found itself floundering and fragmenting in the new situation which it had carved out for itself, and then resorted to ideology to know what to do next, it would have been clear that it had failed in the art of Power Politics. And that is just what Britain tested it for in the in the nine years between the signing of the Agreement in 1998 and it becoming functional in 2007.

Sinn Fein had found itself in unchartered waters. It had attained a position but it needed to know what to do with it. It might have fallen between two stools and done neither one thing nor the other. It could easily have run out of perspective in the new situation—if it had not got the relationship between Ideology and Power Politics right. If the die-hard's general position had been that of the Republican Movement, it is most probable that is just what would have happened.

McIntyre, having ruled out a return to the military campaign, put as an alternative to the Sinn Fein strategy a kind of Republican version of the old Nationalist Party—boycotting Stormont to maintain its dogmatic purity and Anti-Partitionist credentials. But the history of the Catholics of 'Northern Ireland' as detailed in the first volume of this series demonstrates that this would surely have just resulted in an impetus to participate as a minority in devolutionist politics and government again—repeating all over again the cycle that began in 1920-1.

The Missing Subject

It is an unpalatable, but important, fact for the Republican die-hards that it was not Republican ideals that generated the Catholic Insurgency that became the Republican War. The War was actually generated by the perverse system of government imposed on the North in 1920, which necessarily preserved and intensified sectarian animosities and finally produced the interregnum of August 1969. This misgovernment was a thing quite distinct from Partition, although it gave the appearance of being part and parcel of the Partitionist settlement because the two things were born at the same time.

What should be more palatable is the fact that 'Northern Ireland' continued, after the Good Friday Agreement, to be an unstable and aggravating political entity no matter how it was reconstructed. The nature of the situation would, therefore, prevent Sinn Fein stabilising and legitimising it, even if that were the Sinn Fein intention—which it obviously is not. The Sinn Fein intention seems to be the management of the communal conflict generated by 'Northern Ireland' in a way that will lead to Irish unity at some future date. That communal conflict is something that agitates 'Northern Ireland' to no great purpose, aside from the purpose intended by Whitehall back in 1920. But it requires management to prevent it being manipulated for other purposes.

The die-hard opponents of the Sinn Fein accommodation developed the view that the British Direct Rule structures helped defeat the Republican Army by buying off the Catholic community. The gist of the argument is that the British subvention that constituted about 7% of the North's finances in 1970 increased to about 33% by the mid-1980s (Bob Rowthorn & Naomi Wayne, *'Northern Ireland: The Political Economy of Conflict'*, p. 98). Concurrent with this was a great expansion of the public sector. In 1960, 22% of the economically active population of the Six Counties worked for Stormont, but by 1992 the British State employed nearly 40% of the workforce.

It is suggested that these interventions of the British State were a form of *"counter-insurgency Keynesianism"*, producing an upwardly-mobile Catholic middle class, dependent on the British State for its position. This contrasts with the old, much smaller, Catholic middle-class of the Stormont period, that aside from teachers was mainly a petty-bourgeois phenomenon of publicans and book-makers. Better quality housing, more employment in the public sector, as well as community development posts and funding, have also bought off a section of the working-class, according to this argument.

It is undoubtedly the case that Direct Rule and the expansion of the British State economy in the North have improved the economic position of Catholics, removing their dependence on the Unionist Establishment and their own petty-bourgeoisie prior to the August 1969 explosion. However, this *"counter-insurgency Keynesianism"* view only brings the discovery that the Republican War was ultimately self-defeating. This is because Direct Rule was both a Republican War Aim prior to its achievement, and a Republican achievement when Stormont was brought down. It is certain that, without the Republican War, Britain would never have contemplated Direct Rule, which was a defeat for its 1920 settlement. So the Republican War brought about Direct Rule which, by holding at bay a return to rule by the Unionist sub-government that Britain desired, greatly improved the social and economic position of the Six County Catholics, which then eroded Catholic participation in the War—or, at least, participation in a war that could be taken to a level to force a British withdrawal.

The primary Republican War Aim, the destruction of 'Northern Ireland', always offered the ultimate solution to the Catholic predicament in the Six Counties—and still does. That is the preferred option. But it was, and is, not available and a transitional stage which has buried all chance of a restoration of Unionist sub-government forever constituted an acceptable stepping-stone for the community. That was the Secondary War aim and it was widely understood within its community as such—except by the 'Revolutionaries'. And Sinn Fein—as the Republican Army before it—is a product of the Northern Catholic predicament and historical experience, not a disconnected Revolutionary ideology.

Sinn Fein seems to have learnt the art of compromise, so important to statecraft, as described by John Morley in 1875:

> "In politics we have an art. Success in politics, as in every other art, obviously before all else implies both knowledge of the material with which we have to deal, and also such concession as is necessary to the qualities of the material. Above all, in politics we have an art in which development depends upon small modifications... To hurry on after logical perfection is to show oneself ignorant of the material of that social structure with which the politician has to deal. To disdain anything short of an organic change in thought or institution is infatuation...
>
> "That fatal French saying about small reforms being the worst enemies of great reforms, is, in the sense in which it is commonly used, a formula of social breakdown.
>
> "On the other hand, let us not forget that there is a sense in which this very saying is profoundly true. A small and temporary improvement may really be the worst enemy of a great and permanent improvement, unless the first is made on the lines and in the direction of the second... the small reform, if it be not made with reference to some large progressive principle and with a view to further extension of its scope, makes it all the more difficult to return to the right line and direction when improvement is again demanded... Compromise may mean... either the acceptance of the instalment as final... or... a mistaken reversal of direction, which augments the distance that has ultimately to be traversed. In either of these senses, the small reform may become the enemy of the great. But a right conception of political method, based on a rightly interpreted experience of the conditions on which societies unite progress with order, leads the wise... to accept the small change, lest a worse thing befall him, and the wise innovator to seize the chance of a small improvement, while incessantly working in the direction of great ones.
>
> "The important thing is that throughout the process neither of them should lose sight of his ultimate ideal; nor fail to look at the detail from the point of view of the whole; nor allow the near particular to bulk so unduly large as to obscure the general and distant" (On Compromise, pp.187-190).

This was the secret of British Statecraft and the question was how successfully could Sinn Fein apply it against 'Northern Ireland'.

The Anti-Sinn Fein Symbiosis

Trimble and the *crème de la crème* of Unionism came to be influenced by the ex-Provisionals who saw what Sinn Fein was doing as a sell-out of Republicanism. This republican opposition to the Sinn Fein Leadership first appeared in intellectual form in a magazine published by the Irish Republican Writers Group (IRWG) called *'Fourthwrite'*, along with an Internet site called *'The Blanket'*, in the efforts of former Republican prisoners Anthony McIntyre, Tommy McKearney, Tommy Gorman and Brendan Hughes.

In their opposition to Sinn Fein, the die-hards apparently decided to make contact with Trimble Unionism to pursue a common objective against the Adams Leadership. That interpretation of things most probably would be denied as their primary motivation and the argument advanced that the construction of a new republican opposition was the main aim. In 2000 the first issue of the Irish Republican Writers Group magazine, *Fourthwrite*, carried a lead article under the headline, *'Parliamentary Plot May be Unravelling'*:

> "...For a period Sinn Fein could cloud its outright parliamentarianism behind the whiff of sulphur but now the radical balloon may be about to be pricked. Outmanoeuvred by Trimble's UUP on the 'Guns or Adams must go' issue, the Sinn Fein leadership's life support machine—The Executive—is now suspended. Denied administrative power, Sinn Fein's position in the North may soon become like that of Plaid Cymru prior to the formation of the Welsh Assembly... One unnoticed casualty in all of this has been the intellectual authority of the Sinn Fein leadership... Sinn Fein's grand strategy is now in doubt and the leadership's judgement open to question. Thinking republicans must inevitably fill this intellectual vacuum or Irish republicanism shall wither and fade away" (Issue No. 1, Spring 2000).

But if no "*thinking*" republican alternative was developed to Sinn Fein, all that would be left would be sniping and providing ammunition to Unionism and elements in the British State which were determined to turn the Republican retreat into a rout. It is interesting, however, to be reminded by *Fourthwrite* that the "*Adams must go*" project had its origins in the early collaboration between the Trimblites and the ex-Provos. It remained an ongoing demand, taking in a much greater spectrum of interested parties across the island of Ireland. But it failed to make him *go away, you know*.

The link between the die-hards and Unionism was presumably forged in

McIntyre's relationship with Prof. Bew, Trimble's adviser. This culminated in the Boston College Tapes Project, in which republicans (and loyalists) could make recorded statements about the war, on the assurance that these would remain confidential until after they died. This provided the opportunity for Dissidents to make allegations about Gerry Adams. In the event, police in Northern Ireland gained access to the Tapes, the upshot being that Gerry Adams was arrested just before the May 2014 General Election for questioning, and held for four days in Antrim Police Barracks.

After being released, Adams made a point of drawing attention to Prof. Bew's role in the Boston College Tapes project, on which he worked with McIntyre. In response to this, Prof. Bew defended his relationship with McIntyre in a *Sunday Independent* article revealing that he had first come across the IRA man when "he opened a dialogue from prison with me on the subject of my recent book and a Thomas Davis lecture given on RTE." Lord Bew continued;

> "Strangely, McIntyre became my own personal peace process with the provisional republican movement, which he left only in 1998. McIntyre got a first class degree at the Open University in prison and then a PhD when he got out. He had also published in academically respectable places. It is not obvious to me that there are many people with that background and experience together with academic credibility" (11.5.14).

In the same article Prof. Bew also related the value McIntyre had for Trimble:

> "In the mid-Nineties young republicans of my acquaintance all appeared to believe, on the basis of the testimony of Joe Cahill, that the ceasefire had been called because the British had given the 10-year signal for withdrawal. McIntyre never believed that and it is obviously true today that he was right. But the fact that he was prepared to write and say it openly paradoxically strengthened the ability of unionists to make the necessary compromises embodied in the Agreement."

McIntyre projected the idea that Sinn Fein willingness to work within the 1998 Constitution amounted to defeat. Bew and Trimble attempted to impress this assessment of republican defeat on the Unionist Party, supported by Eoghan Harris and Sean O'Callaghan. (But fellow Unionist Jeffrey Donaldson was not convinced by this ideological simplicity. He continued to contest Trimble's view and had at least half the Unionist Party with him. He later joined Dr. Ian Paisley's DUP—which rejected the GFA, describing it as a Republican/Catholic victory.)

The IRWG were ex-prisoners but they welcomed Unionist input into their own anti-Sinn Fein output, despite having no tolerance for the principle of Protestant consent for a United Ireland. Two of Trimble's advisers, Stephen

King and Henry Patterson, engaged with the disgruntled republicans—even though they had a more fundamentalist hostility to Unionism than did Sinn Fein—for their own communal reasons, wanting to damage Sinn Fein.

Patterson contributed an article to the first issue of *Fourthwrite* (Spring 2000), entitled *'Towards 1916'*, which dismissed Gerry Adams claim that "there may be a united Ireland by the year 2016". He gave the Sinn Fein Leader faint praise:

> "... while a critic of the republican tradition I would be the first to recognise the truly historic achievement of Gerry Adams who has done more than any other republican leader apart from Eamon de Valera to reconcile subtly all but the most intransigent idealists to a settlement which contains nothing that can realistically be seen as even 'transitional' to a united Ireland."

Another one of Trimble's advisers, Steven King, was given space to write in an article, *'Not a Proud Record'*:

> "The Republican project as prosecuted by the Provisionals lies in ruins. There is now no attempt to distinguish between Catholic, nationalist and republican. Far from being even a source of embarrassment, it is a determined policy of the Adams faction. There is no conversion strategy aimed at Protestants and dissenters, only a questionable conviction that Catholic birth rates will break the connection with Britain, such is the poverty of ideas. Behaving as Catholic sectarians, the modern-day woodkerne, would be excusable, in a sense, if it was any more successful... Neither truly republican nor truly Defenderist, the Provos have had two successes. They have succeeded in grabbing a slice of the Stormont action—and on the evidence so far—used it for good Catholic purpose. More disturbingly, they have produced a new class of the permanently enraged demanding Catholic power. When this new breed's great expectations are disappointed and Ulster remains stubbornly apart, the seeds of more mindless violence will germinate."

Fourthwrite described itself as *"inclusive"*, meaning that it included jibes from those who were irked by the thought of the dispossessed re-forming as a continuum to maximise their power and equalise things for their community. And, at the same time, the Trimble Unionists felt free to cherry-pick from the shibboleths of the ideological republican die-hards in order to goad Sinn Fein—although Sinn Fein remained unresponsive.

The German mycologist Heinrich de Bary defined symbiosis as *"the living together of unlike organisms"*. And that seemed to be the relationship between the disgruntled republicans and the Trimble Unionists. Symbiotic relationships are close, and often long-term, interactions between two or more different biological species. They tend to be of two types. Some symbiotic relationships are 'obligate', meaning that both symbionts depend entirely on each other for survival. Others are 'facultative', meaning that one symbiont does not necessarily have to live with the other organism. Unionist symbiosis with disgruntled republicans was definitely of the latter type—Unionism could easily persist without the ideological republicans, but the Trimble Unionists certainly fed on the ideas of the other organism.

The main thrust of the IPRG was anger at the Sinn Fein leadership for stealthily running down the military campaign, negotiating a settlement with the enemy, and calling off the War before the full achievement of Republican objectives. The understanding was that accepting a settlement with continued Partition and legitimising Stormont spelled the defeat of the Republican Army. This then metamorphosed into the view that the War had not been worth the effort, with much disillusionment at the melting away of the Army after the settlement.

It was not only Unionism that became receptive to these arguments of the ex-Provisionals. They were also taken up with relish by a number of 'Northern Ireland' journalists who went on to publicise them in the mainstream press. Why they were disgruntled at the equalising of power between the two communities without Republican victory is never explained by them. Perhaps it is in the nature of dissatisfied student revolutionism. But 'left' British papers, like *The Guardian* and *The Independent,* promoted this Provo-defeat view of the former Provos and their professional adherents, and regularly gave over their columns to them. The 'left' of the English Press knows how to act in the overall interests of the British State with regard to 'Northern Ireland' in these matters.

Was Britain fighting itself?

Anthony McIntyre, who heads the intellectual opposition to Sinn Fein, had defended the Long War within the Republican Movement when there had been some suggestions of a Ceasefire around 1991. He described the *Downing Street Declaration* as a settlement of the conflict on Unionist terms (Fortnight, February 1994). He was against the 1994 Ceasefire and in September 1995 urged the movement to go *'back to war'*, at an internal Sinn Fein Conference in Dublin, according to a copy of his speech left in the Linen Hall Library, Belfast. By 1996, McIntyre had gone into full opposition to Sinn Fein, seeing what it was preparing itself to accept as "*Sunningdale Mark II*".

As Lord Bew noted in the *Sunday Independent*, McIntyre completed a PhD thesis at Queen's University upon his release from prison. It is called *'Modern Irish republicanism: the product of British state strategies'*, and was approved by Adrian Guelke; the *Guardian* (3.9.94) states it was supervised by Prof. Bew.

It is important to examine the main arguments of the thesis, to understand the intellectual basis of opposition to the Sinn Fein project and why it ultimately failed in its objective. McIntyre gave the gist of the argument of his thesis in *'The Blanket'* (23.8.04):

> "Those seeking an insight into the origins and development of the Provisional IRA campaign need look no further than 1969 and subsequent state policy. British indifference created the organisation; British repression sustained it. Its volunteers did not carry some genetic code dating back to 1916 predisposing them towards physical force. How otherwise can it be explained that the settlement of Good Friday 1998, so readily embraced and celebrated by those volunteers, does not vaguely resemble the objectives of Easter Sunday 1916?"

Early in his thesis McIntyre says:

> "The implicit contention in this thesis is that the dynamics of Provisional Irish republicanism are to be primarily found in the post-1969 relationship between large elements of the nationalist working class and the British state" (p.7).

From this we can presumably take it that the fortunes of the Provos were largely determined by what the British State chose to do and the effects its policy had on working-class Catholics. That sounds very like saying that the British State both created and destroyed the Provos—or perhaps that it was fighting itself all along! However, McIntyre makes the valid point that the Provos represented a distinct break with the old Anti-Treaty Republicanism:

> "The material representation of the ideology of traditional republicanism, the Republican Movement, was a vehicle swept aside in the popular upsurge generated in the wake of August 1969. A new body filled the vacuum—the Provisionals" (p.342).

Something entirely new was created in West Belfast after August 1969 that only *appeared* to be the old Republicanism and McIntyre makes the observation that: "The Northern nationalist tradition impacted more on the development of Provisional republicanism than did the physical force influence of 1916" (p.66). This means that the Provos were much more in spirit and character a product of the experiences of Northern Catholic within the Six Counties than of traditional Republicanism.

McIntyre says in his thesis that the Provos were about "improvisation rather than tradition" (p.7); and: "A methodological tracing out of the detail of Provisional republicanism shall demonstrate that there is no reason to see traditional Republican ideology as a determinant of primary significance" (p.37). He argues that the character of the Provos, shaped by the practical experience of life of Northern Catholics in the Six Counties, rather than Anti-Treaty ideology, was also its weakness making it liable to compromise before its formal objectives were achieved:

"Provisional republicanism would always be vulnerable to outcomes that did not specifically address the question of the British presence nor the indefinite continuation of partition. In other words there always existed the structural potential for an outcome that would constitute the outworking of structural processes of grievances regardless of how the latter might be ideologically defined" (p.67).

And so, since the driving-force of the Provo campaign was the grievances held by Northern Catholics, it began to falter when the British began to address these same grievances:

"Provisionalism was republicanism in a mass form. In order to sustain that form it had to be fed with material needs rather than vaporous ideology. Provisional republicanism went into serious decline as a result of those material needs being addressed from late 1972 to 1974" (p.347).

In one chapter of his thesis McIntyre addresses previous writing on the Irish Republicanism of the period. He compare the present writer's thesis, *'Irish Republicanism and Socialism'* with Prof. Henry Patterson's book, *'The Politics of Illusion'*:

"Pat Walsh at least does not make the mistake of Patterson in ignoring the politics of the era being researched. However, his account is much too conspiratorial and ascribes to the Provisionals much greater strategic foresight and capability than is merited" (p.60).

Later on he clarifies this point in relation to the Provos: "That they had a design is not in dispute here. The evidence suggests that such a design simply did not matter" (p.101).

This point seems to suggest, as the title of the thesis does, that fundamentally the Provos resulted from British actions in 'Northern Ireland' between August 1969 and 1973: the Provos grew, largely due to the military response of the British Government in events like the Falls Road Curfew, Internment and Bloody Sunday. And the Provos declined as Britain took a new 'political' approach and took the wind out of their sails—finally, presumably, finishing them off in 1998, bringing about *'The Death of Irish Republicanism'* (the title of a collection of McIntyre's writings published in book form). McIntyre suggests that the Provos were "thrown up at a *particular* juncture *primarily* by conditions *within* the northern state, rather than because of the mere existence *per se* of that state, and because the republican tradition was more of an 'enabling surface' factor than a dynamic or primary structural determinant" (p. 67).

But, if McIntyre saw the Provo development in this way, then surely he should not have been surprised that the new Republican Army called a halt to its campaign before achieving its Republican objective. But McIntyre seems to have wanted them to act like Anti-Treatyite Republicanism whilst conceding that they were nothing of the sort.

There is a strong parallel between McIntyre and Trotsky here. Trotsky predicted the inevitable failure of the Revolution when it was isolated and failed to be internationalised. But when the Revolution failed in the way he had predicted Trotsky instead described it as 'The Revolution Betrayed'. It seems that McIntyre has the same problem with Adams as Trotsky had with Lenin (and then Stalin) after Brest-Litovsk. McIntyre explains what he sees as the inevitable degeneration of Irish Republicanism from the understanding that it was a mere product of British State strategy and then describes it as a Great Betrayal from within!

To justify the title, McIntyre really would have to examine the mode of existence of the British State in general, and its relation to the anomalous 'Northern Ireland' part of it in particular. But he does not do that. Whilst his title suggests that the Republican Army British strategy created the Provos, he says little about Britain except that it tried a military solution which helped generate and develop the Provos and then instituted a political and economic strategy which contained and ultimately defeated them. In other words, Dr. Frankenstein, having created his monster then destroyed it. But McIntyre concentrates almost exclusively on the character of the monster and says very little about the intentions and motivations of its creator.

Lord Bew and Prof. Patterson certainly take a similar view to McIntyre, if from a different perspective. For them Whitehall is innocent, as regards the Six Counties, and 'Northern Ireland' is a state within the state, a state within which political activity could be effectively conducted. Perhaps it is to avoid confronting this view that McIntyre steers clear of analysing events before 1969 or examining the political context in which the events from August of that year took place. What emerges, therefore, is Hamlet without the Prince—an analysis that views the Provos as central to the 'Northern Ireland' conflict whilst seeing them as primarily a manifestation of short-term British policy.

The Republican Army, of course, is not the central issue in the 'Northern Ireland' problem. It was merely a temporary product of it—although a most important and significant product—one that actually changed 'Northern Ireland' like no other element within it ever succeeded in doing.

The general point of the thesis leads to this conclusion but the author cannot seem to accept it. Perhaps the personal element comes into play here: losing the central point of one's life is bound to be traumatic when so much of it has been invested in a struggle that turns out to have been about something other than what the sacrifice was imagined to have been about.

It is in this light that the 'Boston Tapes' saga (to which I will return)—a project bringing together Prof. Bew, Anthony McIntyre, Brendan Hughes and Ed Moloney—should be seen.

CHAPTER 16

Winning the Peace

It is worth setting out a chronology of the fate of the institutions agreed upon on Good Friday 1998 to show how First Minister Trimble and British NI Secretaries obstructed the development of functional government:

10 April 1998	Good Friday Agreement signed
25 June 1998	Elections to Assembly
1 July 1998	First and Deputy First Ministers elected, but no Ministers
14 September 1998	Assembly convenes
29 November 1999	Ministers appointed under D'Hondt system
2 December 1999	Devolved government institutions established
11 February 2000	Mandelson suspends Institutions
30 May 2000	Mandelson restores Institutions
1 July 2001	Trimble resigns as FM
18 October 2001	Other UUP Ministers resign
10 August 2001	Reid suspends Institutions
11 August 2001	Reid restores Institutions
22 September 2001	Reid suspends Institutions
23 September 2001	Reid restores Institutions
5 November 2001	Trimble re-enters Institutions
14 October 2002	Reid suspends Institutions
26 November 2006	New election: DUP overtakes UUP
13 October 2006	St. Andrews Agreement
8 May 2007	Devolved Institutions restored

In total the institutions agreed upon on Good Friday 1998 were functional, on a stop-start basis, for a total of only 18 months in the nine years following the signing of the Agreement, which had envisaged a decommissioning of arms taking place over a two-year period of functional government.

Between the first suspension of the Good Friday institutions in May 2000 by NI Secretary of State Mandelson and the fourth suspension in October 2002 by his successor, John Reid, Republicans were harried by elements within the British State and a range of political interests. This was, in military terms, an attempt to turn the orderly retreat from the battlefield of the Republican forces into a rout. History shows that Britain realises that wars do not end with peace treaties. Wars are often won and lost in the process of making peace.

Trimble, the Unionist Leader, wanted to impose a political defeat on Republicans and was intent on developing the Republican Ceasefire into something resembling an unconditional surrender. It was presumably calculated that, with the end of the 28 Year War, Republican solidarity and morale would begin to weaken, and that the Republican Leadership, exposed by the leap in a new direction, could be caught between the devil and the deep blue sea. From such an exposed position, it was imagined they could be negated as a political force, pulled between ever-increasing demands made upon them that would be unacceptable to the Republican rank and file but which would be desired by the Catholic community, weary of War.

The Agreement and Decommissioning

The main issue that was made the occasion for the collapse of the new-born institutions was Decommissioning. The relevant part of the Agreement about how this should work said:

> "All participants accordingly reaffirm their commitment to the total disarmament of all paramilitary organisations. They also confirm their intention to continue to work constructively and in good faith with the independent commission and to use any influence they may have to achieve the decommissioning of all paramilitary arms within two years following endorsement in referendums."

That is what the parties to the Agreement signed up to in 1998. But the only participant who abided by this provision was Sinn Fein. It might be argued that, while Sinn Fein abided by the letter of the Agreement, everyone else abided by the spirit of it. But there was no description of the spirit of the Agreement in existence. And it would be a strange state of affairs if the spirit of something ran so contrary to the letter. The letter required **all** participants to use *"any influence they may have to achieve"* the objective, whereas the *"spirit"* required it of only one of the participants, while the other participants put up conditions and obstacles which made attaining that objective impossible.

Much of the blame for the impasse that followed lay with Sinn Fein's 'constitutional nationalist' allies in the making of the Agreement. Dublin and the SDLP endorsed Trimble's demands, helping to paralyse the Agreement by wasting effort in trying to help Trimble out of the hole he had dug himself into. In doing so, they created a climate whereby the political agenda in the post-Agreement period was set by the Trimble/Donaldson double-act and the Ulster Unionist Council. The focus was on the decommissioning of Republican arms, to the exclusion of other stabilising factors.

The general impression created was that the Peace Process was entirely to do with something which had not even been part of the Agreement, but which Sinn Fein had the total moral responsibility for achieving. Taoiseach Ahern and the SDLP played fast and loose with words and undermined the relationship which Haughey/Reynolds and Hume had meticulously built up with Republicans. The importance of that relationship could not be overestimated. It was both the engine of the Peace Process and the device which made Nationalist advance possible in the North without the necessity of war.

The SDLP's Paradise Lost

More than a decade before the 1998 Agreement, during the aftermath of the 1985 Treaty, Fionnuala O'Connor wrote an article she called, *'Nationalism: Faith in John'*, published by *Fortnight* magazine (November 1987). In it she noted:

> "Mr. Hume may not encourage discussion on where the Agreement is taking the party, but it will probably be some considerable time before unease supplants the still almost mystical belief that 'John knows what he is doing'— even if nobody else does."

Although the 1998 Agreement was more in accordance with SDLP policy than Sinn Fein's, it was very much more Hume's independent achievement than the achievement of the SDLP. Without Hume the SDLP was a lacklustre affair of dogmatic and futile constitutionalism, limited by Northern Ireland horizons. Hume had largely done his own thing and the party had been content for him to do it. Some whinged, but they didn't have the nerve to act against him. If it had been up to the party, there would have been no Peace Process at all, because it wished to reduce Republicanism to insignificance before making a deal with Unionists—and the Republican Army could not be reduced to insignificance. It was Hume, acting freely on his own understanding of possibilities, who engaged in the negotiations with Adams and set the Peace in motion.

After the Agreement was signed and the elections were held, and the difficult business of implementation came on the agenda, Hume went to the backbenches and handed the effective leadership over to Mallon. (Hume remained formally as Leader of the Party.) Mallon was suddenly required to do something he was ill-fitted, both by temperament and experience, to do. He could not consolidate in politics the advance made by the Republican Insurrection because he saw it as something that was antithetical to what the SDLP was about. And so, under his leadership as Deputy First Minister, support within the community began to slip away from the SDLP.

Towards the end of April 2000 a proposal was floated by Hume and supported by Martin McGuinness that the Executive should be established in accordance with the terms of the Agreement, but with the addition of an undertaking by Sinn Fein that it would withdraw voluntarily from the Executive, leaving it in being, if the IRA ever acted in breach of the Ceasefire. This was well beyond anything required by the Agreement. However, Mallon did not follow up the proposal and Hume was otherwise engaged and did not ensure that he did.

The Agreement created a new situation in 'Northern Ireland' which could have evolved in various directions. One of those directions was a partnership between the SDLP and the Ulster Unionist Party which would have increasingly marginalised Sinn Fein. For that to happen, the UUP would have had to embrace the Agreement and work it with enthusiasm—particularly the parts of interest to Nationalists. But that would have involved statesmanship. The last chance for that to have happened was probably Mallon's offer to the Unionists in June 1999 to collapse the Executive himself if there was no decommissioning within a year—if the Unionists would agree to start working the institutions of the Agreement.

By fighting a tough rearguard action against the Agreement, from within the pro-Agreement camp, the Unionist Party began to undermine the SDLP. Sinn Fein was the great beneficiary of this process. Instead of being challenged by Unionist support of the Agreement, it was able to stand as the main defenders of the deal in the face of Unionist intransigence and SDLP wavering. Sinn Fein showed how embracing an Agreement, despite its shortcomings, could pay political dividends.

It was the SDLP which should have reaped political benefits from the Agreement. The world created by Hume was designed to be a Paradise for his party but it was soon lost as the SDLP looked increasingly aimless and incapable in politics in its Garden of Eden, after attaining its heart's desire. For years the SDLP functioned politically as the recipient of British concessions to Nationalism—concessions which had been hard won by the Republicans' War. The Party won little through its own efforts, aside from Hume's lobbying in the US. It was drip-fed a series of measures, designed merely to keep it top-dog in the Catholic community. But now Sinn Fein was in a position to cut out the middle-man in this process and was receiving the fruits of its own labour. Unable to rise to the test of making the Agreement work, the SDLP proved within a couple of years of the Agreement being signed to be the biggest loser in the political manoeuvring that followed the ending of the War. And it was the slowest learner of the fact that post-War politics were to be conducted in an entirely different way.

Mallon, eager to get on with operating the Agreement in long-desired alliance with the Unionist Party, was given the run-around and undermined by Trimble's in-out hokey-cokey tactics. Twenty odd years later Mallon told the *Irish Catholic* that "1921 was a contrivance. Sunningdale was a contrivance. The Good Friday Agreement is a contrivance... These are all contrivances because the North of Ireland itself is a contrivance" (1.10.15). And yet Mallon was too straightforwardly 'Constitutionalist' to be able to counter Trimble's tactics to his own advantage. Consequently, the Unionist Leader's playing fast and loose with the institutions began the process that took the SDLP down—along with himself and his party.

This outcome gives some clue about what would have happened if there had been no Republican participation in the Agreement and shows why Hume had insisted on the Republicans being on board for the making of a potentially functional settlement within the "*contrivance*" of 'Northern Ireland'.

The British drew their own conclusions from these events. Sir John Chilcot, Permanent Secretary at the NIO, revealed to Graham Spencer:

"... there was a dawning realisation, which I think I had as early as anyone, that John Hume was ready to sacrifice the SDLP and the nationalist interest because the ultimate deal had to be the bigger one... I could not put a note to it, but it became apparent as the UUP declined in power and influence over the unionist majority, and as Hume and Mallon started to lose control and split and factionalise" (*The British and Peace in Northern Ireland*, p.87)

After 28 years of bolstering the SDLP the British began to see that its bulwark against Republicanism was disintegrating.

Republicans Call the Shots

In February 2000 the devolved institutions were suspended after two months of operation. In May the two Governments made a *Joint Declaration* stating that, subject to a positive response to their statement, the British Government would bring forward the necessary Order to enable the institutions to be restored, begin the demilitarisation of the province, and undertake reform of the police. The IRA replied to this Declaration saying it would "completely and verifiably put IRA arms beyond use" and to do this it would resume contact with the Decommissioning Commission, which it had ended contact with after Trimble's failure to maintain the promised institutions of government (IN 07.05.00).

The IRA offer involved a decommissioning on its own terms. The Republican Army would seal their arms bunkers after inspection and allow further inspections afterwards to verify that they continued to be sealed. The international inspectors who would oversee this process were the former Prime Minister of Finland and the former General Secretary of the African National Congress. There was to be no "decommissioning event" that Unionists could present as an IRA surrender. In June 2000 the arms inspectors inspected the arms dumps and observed that the weapons and explosives "were safely and adequately stored" (IN 26.06.00).

Chris Thornton, writing from a moderate Unionist perspective in the *Belfast Telegraph* on 8th May, 2000, under the headline, *'It's Win-Win for Adams'*, recognised the political significance of the course of events:

> "Peter Mandelson is said, privately, to rank Sinn Fein among the best negotiators he has ever seen. The sudden thump of a new deal over the weekend helped show why. After weeks of gloom and playing dangerously close to taking the blame for a collapse of the peace process, the republican movement has remarkably reversed its fortunes. The latest twist in the process has put Sinn Fein in a win-win situation. The Ulster Unionist Party, while not in exactly the opposite position, is nevertheless painted into a corner. For Sinn Fein either way the deal now falls is a victory of sorts. If an executive is returned to Stormont, it is on the terms they have always argued should be there; with the decommissioning question put off for a long period—in this case a year—while the baby government beds down. But if Stormont doesn't return, it will be because the unionists said no. And in whatever form the process picks up after the dust settles, unionists will be on the back foot. Some in the UUP may well be scratching their heads at this latest turn of events. When Stormont was suspended in February they had seized the moral ground and portrayed the failure to decommission as the only obstacle to progress. Now the onus is upon them again to say yea or nay. And the delegates of the Ulster Unionist Council, who will be asked to decide the issue inside the next two weeks, will be wondering what suspension has advanced."

Thornton's analysis said more about Unionism than it did about Republicanism. For Republicans, the process was a genuine and serious initiative to make politics a viable alternative to war. For the Unionist Party the Agreement was increasingly a thing to be escaped from, without taking the blame for its collapse, back to the more comforting realm of conflict— an Anti-Agreement position from within the Agreement ranks. Trimble had been encouraged by Eoghan Harris to believe that he was the one with the *"Win-Win"* position but he had apparently squandered a winning hand. Harris had *"called it"* (to use one of his favourite phrases) wrong again.

The IRA offer on weapons was a sensible and reasonable one. It was the only move that could have been made which gave the two Governments leverage on Trimble whilst not involving a surrender of weapons and consequent criminalisation of the Republican struggle. It maintained the pro-Agreement forces intact, chief of these being the Republican movement itself. And that was the essential prerequisite for any political development at the level of politics. Mandelson acknowledged this in the House of Commons on the 8th May 2000. When answering a question from Trimble about imposing time limits on Republicans, he said that he had been down the road of deadlines before, and he wasn't going down that road again. As Thornton noted the political skills of Republicans had impressed in Whitehall.

Adams said at the Easter 2000 Commemorations that Republicans were not being given full credit for the movement Sinn Fein had made away from the traditional Republican position. Brian Feeney, who was producing a history of Sinn Fein at that time, wrote in his column in the *Irish News*:

> "Republicans speechifying at the weekend were especially conscious of tension within the republican movement because the current political path has turned into a cul de sac and the aims of 1916 are no closer... The IRA Easter... statement accurately portrays republican disarray. It's a textual and intellectual mess. It begins as normal... then the message disintegrates into sections reflecting the different factions in the group that wrote it... while the IRA asserts the British presence is the root of all evil, SF speakers are urging the British proconsul, Peter Mandelson, to implement the Good Friday agreement which guarantees the north will remain British as long as the majority wishes. While the IRA says partition is a cause of all our woes SF demands in the same message the immediate re-establishment of an assembly at Stormont to run partition... It reveals a movement at odds with itself trying to keep on board militarists who have not come to terms with their changed role since 1997 and who cling to an analysis of the problem which has been superseded by the votes of the Irish people in 1998" (26.4.00).

But this was how Republicanism was kept together during a difficult political transition. This *"intellectual mess"* in *"disarray"* and *"at odds with itself"* was holding together and getting the better of the Peace.

A New Orbit

From the Catholic-Nationalist perspective, what Sinn Fein was trying to do seemed a contradiction. But the Republican leadership was moving out of the usual orbit of Catholic-Nationalism into the realms of something else that involved a serious attempt to engage with the Unionist community. Martin McGuinness, giving his view of "the way forward in peace" in *The Sunday Observer* (4.6.00) made the clearest possible statement of Republican political intent:

"As an Irish republican, I will continue to work towards the day when we have an Irish Republic free from interference, from the political influence, of a British government... I know that unionists do not share in my vision of a united Ireland and that they will work just as diligently to prevent such an eventuality. But I have to say that, although I accept their right to do so, I also believe that many of them accept that, as we build a society of equals, all of the reasons of privilege and position—most of them, particularly for the working class unionist, a misconception—that sustained the desire by the unionist population to maintain the union with Britain will become irrelevant. It is for precisely this reason that the rejectionist unionists are fighting so hard to prevent all of the changes envisioned in the Good Friday Agreement. My greatest hope is that, through peaceful and democratic means, and by building on the Good Friday Agreement, we can convince unionists that a united Ireland is the best option for us all."

Previous attempts in this direction had all ended in failure, with former Republicans becoming virtual Unionists, and in the process becoming detached from their Republican base. But the Sinn Fein project was nothing like the Stickie slope. A battle-hardened and self-confident Republican leadership was bringing along its movement and its community towards its objective. And, like the All-for-Ireland League at the turn of the twentieth century, it no longer defined its community as being only the one in which it originated.

For 28 years Republicans fought the British Government, with which Protestant Ulster was aligned despite its exclusion from British politics. Because of this engagement, it got to understand the Protestants in a way that no Catholic force had done before. The Provos did not have the same 'one nation' illusions (or pretended illusions) that the Officials and Southern Nationalists had about the Ulster Protestants, illusions which were put to the test by what happened between 1970 and 1974 and were found to be inadequate. Now Republicans were in the process of engaging with the local Protestant basis of the British State in a different way, to resolve the problem of 'Northern Ireland'.

There were many who were genuinely taken aback by the IRA initiative. But there shouldn't have been any surprise. The IRA had concluded a long time earlier that the War was unwinnable, and, being an unwinnable war, it was a futile one. It takes humanity to end a futile war. (The War had become futile when it could not be advanced to the achievement of its full aims, but the problem lay in how to stop it.) Republican humanity brought the War to a close because of an unwillingness to see people die in vain—and not alone their own. And it probably would have ended earlier if an earlier British Government had agreed to do business.

On the British side, strategic rather than humanitarian considerations predominated in bringing about a negotiated solution to the impasse. The

English are at ease with war and there is only a handful of countries they have not fought against at some point or other. At the time of the British engagement in 'Northern Ireland', there was no other military theatre in which its armed forces could gain practical experience. However, there was little other benefit to Downing Street in its Northern Ireland War, which diminished rather than enhanced its reputation around the world and the winning of which could not advance its world interests. The Blair Government which made the peace in Ireland went on to deploy its military forces in other situations in which power politics were a direct consideration such as Iraq and Afghanistan. By contrast, an end to their War in Northern Ireland allowed Irish Republicans free to go home and settle down to civilian life.

A Worrying Development!

Eoghan Harris became a worried man in the midst of the peace negotiations. He wrote in the *Sunday Times* of the 7th May 2000:

> "This time we have to be tough because Sinn Fein's abuse of the peace process is causing a decline of democracy in the Republic. Make no mistake about it, Irish democracy is in danger. The danger arises from the fact that, for the first time in our history, we are letting northern nationalists set our agenda. Since northern nationalists, like northern Protestants, have been damaged by history, I do not think they are the right people to regulate the public culture of the Republic."

Here was Harris blurting out what the Southern State had since 1922 maintained in relation to Northern Catholics—a determination to keep their influence out. Part of the reason Sinn Fein was becoming relevant again in the Republic was because people like Harris had begun to bring about a great confusion of its history. Northern Catholics had never been open to revisionism because they have indeed been "*damaged by history*". Hard experience of historical reality had given them a healthy immunity to media and academic falsification and an excellent understanding of political reality. It could not be otherwise, due to the success of the revisionist destruction of political understanding in the South and its failure to penetrate the substance of the Catholic community in the North.

As for "*Irish democracy*", it only existed because of Sinn Fein. The history of Sinn Fein is the history of Irish democracy.

Over subsequent decades the Southern Establishment was to use every dirty trick to combat the transfer of the momentum of the Northern War and Peace Process into Southern political life, which constituted the second stage of Gerry Adams' vision. And, as the advance of Sinn Fein in the South seemed unstoppable, the effort was then directed to replacing Gerry Adams with a Southern leader limited by a 26 County horizon, with the object of reducing Sinn Fein in the South to a 26 County party.

Sinn Fein embarked on the radical departure of engaging with the Northern Protestant in a new process of understanding. It did so in a more substantial way than anything the Southern State had ever done in relation to Ulster Unionism.

Consequent on the belief that *"northern nationalists were setting our agenda"*, Harris and others attempted to make the Southern Protestants, who had been effectively integrated into all political shades by the Republic's parties of State, feel themselves to be a persecuted minority. This was done by manipulating history: attempting to redefine the War of Independence as a squalid sectarian land grab. The object was to introduce in the South the ethnicist politics of the Six Counties. The desire was to undermine the new Republicanism as it began to accomplish that which Harris' Official variety had botched in its *'Lost Revolution'*. But the revisionists failed to discredit those whose sacrifices founded the state and failed to prevent a revival in fortunes for Sinn Fein in the Republic.

The North Turned Upside Down

The IRA Decommissioning initiative of May 2000 forced Trimble to change his tactics and to work for a tactical resurrection of the Executive. He secured a temporary triumph over Jeffrey Donaldson at another UUC meeting. There was a 1% swing to Trimble and away from Donaldson in the UUC—or was it 2%? Trimble called the IRA initiative "an unprecedented offer", but announced that the UUP would quit a new Executive if the IRA "failed to honour its pledges" on disarmament. He then attempted to warn Donaldson's supporters that, if Unionists rejected the Agreement, it would be replaced by an even greener mode of government, and that the party would be in the wilderness for years with Sinn Fein becoming the largest party in 'Northern Ireland' (IN 18.05.00).

But, by that time, Donaldson's influence within the party had become irresistible. The point of the role-playing of a fundamental antagonism between Trimble and Donaldson was that the Unionist Party would be enabled to subvert the Agreement more effectively by making the rejectionists the focal concern of the process. Trimble could not have subverted the Agreement so effectively if somebody performing Donaldson's function had not enabled him to give the appearance of being under the practical necessity of doing what he did at each juncture, leaving it up to certain others to deceive themselves into believing that he would really have liked to implement the Agreement if he had been given a free rein to do what he wished.

It was eventually put to Trimble on '*Inside Politics*' on BBC's Radio Ulster on 4th November 2000 that he was scheming for a suspension of the Executive all along. Trimble replied:

"I didn't set that out as an objective. I think you have to look at what I said in context. The object is to put pressure on republicans and nationalists. This might result in a crisis, but is not actually my objective. My objective is to achieve progress" (*Irish Political Review*, December 2000).

Trimble's colleague, John Taylor, was not so coy however, when he explained that the objective of the Ulster Unionist Party was to achieve a suspension of the Executive with a view to negotiating a new Agreement.

The conduct and behaviour of Sinn Fein with regard to Stormont turned out to be entirely different to that predicted. Republicans became the element most dedicated to the effective political functioning of the Stormont institutions, and the Unionists, of both varieties, most involved in its dysfunction. The world had been turned upside down.

After Mandelson had suspended the institutions set up by the Good Friday Agreement, it was Sinn Fein which undoubtedly felt most hurt. Taylor said he was delighted with the return of Direct Rule. Conor Cruise O'Brien said at the time that Republicans would be acutely embarrassed by the overt demonstration that the British Secretary of State was boss and Sinn Fein Ministers were only in Office at his behest. And he predicted that War would resume. But the Sinn Fein hurt was of a different kind. It was a genuine sense of loss at the demise of political institutions that were seen as essential to the Republican project.

If Republicans had been insincere about their intentions, they would have walked away after Mandelson had suspended the Agreement institutions. And they would have been perfectly justified in doing so. But it was Sinn Fein which put in the effort necessary to secure the IRA initiative that brought about the re-establishment of the institutions. Unionists, on the other hand, sought concession after concession, endangering a return to government.

The IRA offer on arms put momentum back into the Peace Process. And it also had another dimension. It forced the British State to admit failure in its efforts to criminalise Republicans, and by implication it recognised the armed struggle to have been a legitimate response to the political conditions of the past—conditions that Britain had itself established. The two components of the Republican military campaign, its volunteers and its arms, were being treated by the British Government as justifiable expressions of abnormal circumstance. The prisoners were being released, and the State was assisting the IRA, through chosen third parties, to maintain and supervise its arsenal while the causes of the conflict were being addressed politically so that weapons, were no longer necessary.

Steak Knife Unionism

The date of 28th October 2000 was set for a fresh meeting of the Ulster Unionist Council to encourage Trimble to withdraw from the Executive.

With Republicans keen to move the Process on and work the institutions whilst proceeding towards decommissioning, Trimble joined the Dissidents. That is not to say that he joined the Donaldson opposition to himself, but that he took up the arguments of the Republican Dissidents against his own Unionist dissidents, arguing in favour of his continued participation in government with Sinn Fein.

Trimble's speech to his party conference was a series of taunts and jibes at Sinn Fein for having abandoned the armed struggle; for administering British rule in a Partitionist Stormont. One would think that, if a Unionist leader really believed he had secured the defeat of Republicanism, he would have let it have its fig-leaf and not try to goad and provoke it back to war. But Trimble seems to have believed that the Republican Army was fatally compromised and would be only capable of a half-hearted effort, and a war at half-cock would be good for Unionism in its difficulties.

Here is the nub of his speech to the Unionist unfaithful at the Waterfront Hall on 14th October 2000:

> "Unionism is on the inside now. Some think being inside is outweighed by having Martin McGuinness as a Minister. Let's be honest—Martin McGuinness has had influence over Government policy since he met Willie Whitelaw in 1972. That influence was hidden. Now it is in the open where he is accountable for his actions. The man who tried to destroy partition is helping to administer Northern Ireland within the United Kingdom, on behalf of Her Majesty and on the basis of British law. This is a real seismic shift... We are in a new situation. The Provos' armed struggle is over. After the thousands of needless deaths, the armed struggle failed. There is no united Ireland, but the guns are now being used as bargaining chips for more concessions. Until the Government stands up to this blackmail it will rightly be accused of a craven approach. But we have forced Republicanism to face up to the reality of Northern Ireland's place within the United Kingdom. All they have left is rhetoric about the inevitability of Irish unity. And it is rhetoric. The consent principle in the agreement drove a steak knife through that. The rhetoric only disguises their ideological defeat."

Why did David Trimble use the phrase "*steak knife*" in his speech? The allusion was to revelations a month earlier about a high-level informer in the IRA, code-named 'Stakeknife' or 'Steak-knife'.

"Steak knife" was supposed to be the code name of a highly placed informer in the ranks of the Ballymurphy IRA, a supporter of the Peace Process. The story was that in 1987 the UFF planned to kill this important British source, so one of the British Special Forces got their double agent in the UFF, Brian Nelson, to sow a false trail and convince the UFF that another man, Francisco Notorantonio, a former internee, was the IRA leader in the Ballymurphy. Notorantonio was killed by the UFF and the British source was protected. Or so the story that was 'leaked' went. The story first surfaced at the end of 1999.

Then there was an extraordinary series of events whereby a paper was banned from running the story that had already appeared. And the paper was banned from even saying that the story had been banned. Then the ban of talking about the ban was lifted, and then the ban itself was lifted. This unprecedented charade of heavy-handedness all created the impression that there must have been a lot of substance in the leak, as the State wanted it covered up so badly.

In Ballymurphy, the story that British Intelligence had set up the murder of a local did not cause any great surprise. How could it? The main concern centred on who was this *"steak knife"* and, if he existed and had not fled, surely he was still there in the Republican movement? Tension began to rise as speculation grew about the tout. Rumours were rife about his identity, and senior Republicans in the area fell under suspicion. Even Adams was mentioned as the possible *"steak knife"*. All this coincided with the dissident Republican characterisation of the Provo leadership as a moulded product of British manipulation. Ah ha! British agents all along!

The missing piece of the jigsaw was the fact that the alleged leader of the Real IRA in Ballymurphy at the time was Joe O'Connor. He was killed in mid-October 2000 and just happened to be a member of the Notorantonio family: grandson to the man who had been killed by the UFF in 1987. (The British were, of course, well aware of the individual's position in the Real IRA, and were not slow to publicise their knowledge of this after his killing.)

What conclusion could the Dissident draw from all this, but that the same Provo traitors who were up in Stormont were British agents all along who had set up the grandfather for assassination? After O'Connor's death, his mother said just that. Whether the killing was sanctioned by the Provos, or it was done by individual Republicans who had a difference of opinion with him over something, is impossible to say. One thing could be said with certainty, however—it took place in the charged atmosphere of the *"steak knife"* intrigue referenced at the Unionist Party Conference.

Trimble's advisor, Steven King, writing about the killing in Ballymurphy, in an article entitled: "*The Pain Is Shifting On To Republicans. Isn't it Time for UUC Delegates to Put up Their Feet and Enjoy the Spectacle?*" wrote in the *Belfast Telegraph* (24.10.00): "Isn't the real lesson of O'Connor's murder not that the Provos are only semi-house-trained but that the logic of the Agreement is sinking in, even in deepest Ballymurphy?"

He quoted from Marion Price's oration at the Real IRA man's graveside: "the Provos... are now reduced to an armed militia of the British State", and commented:

> "As Ulster Unionists embark on an unarmed feud this week, they could do worse than bear in mind Ms. Price's words. Unionists have suffered great pain over the last couple of years... Now the pain is shifting on to republicans, is it time to pull the plug on a partitionist settlement and Stormont rule? Isn't it time, instead, for UUC delegates to put up their feet and enjoy the spectacle?"

What was the Trimble leadership of Ulster Unionism reduced to when it had to rely on the death of a dissident anti-Agreement Republican, whose arguments it had adopted, to carry forward its policy within its own party?

At the end of his speech, Trimble declared:

> "It has been said that war is a continuation of politics by other means. In Northern Ireland today that is reversed. Politics are the continuation of the so-called war by other means. We cannot run away from the political struggle."

Trimble was not saying that this was the thinking of the Provos. The statement was made in the context of what he felt the Unionist Party must do to safeguard the Union. From the start, Trimble's main interest in the 'Peace Process' was not a positive one. His political manoeuvrings around the Agreement were all geared towards continuing the War in the political sphere and attempting to deliver a fatal blow to the Republican leadership which signed the deal. It was strange to hear this admitted from the horse's mouth but it elicited no comment from the media at the time. But that is really all that could be taken from Trimble when he chose to equate politics with war in the context of military intrigue.

Whatever the explanation of Trimble's reference to *"steak knife"*, it cannot be denied that he approved of security force intrigue. And, since that was very much the sort of activity that was conducted in the *"so-called war"* and supposedly brought the Provos to the conference table—and McGuinness's influence into the open—it cannot be denied that it was the type of thing Trimble approved of in the *"political struggle"*, which was, after all, *"a continuation of the so-called war by other means"*.

What could have been better for Trimble at this point, with his party difficulties, than if a Republican feud could be manufactured (as had happened in the past)? Obviously, Republican shooting Republican would give Unionists great pleasure and Unionism leverage with the British Government in obstructing and watering down the imminent and much-feared Patton Report on Policing that was going to pose great difficulty for Trimble's hard-line

Unionism in his constituency. It would also have had the benefit of making things very difficult for the Republican leadership. If the Republican Army found itself attacked, and its arms dumps threatened by those who wanted to start a new war, how could it respond without losing out politically and militarily? Having seen the difficulties within Loyalism, it must have surely crossed the minds of those given to intrigue that a Republican bust-up would have done very nicely at such an opportune moment.

The Battle of Ideas

Here is another part of Trimble's Waterfront Hall speech:

"…we got what unionists have always wanted. At Sunningdale when the anti-union vote was in the low 20's, Articles 2 and 3 were not changed, there was a Council of Ireland, not answerable to the Northern Ireland Assembly. This party was right to reject Sunningdale. In 1998, when the combined anti-unionist vote was over 40%, Articles 2 and 3 have changed decisively. The North-South Ministerial Council is answerable to the Assembly. The cross-border cooperation takes up just 0.1% of our budget. Unionists have a veto. This party was right to run with the agreement."

But no matter how many times Trimble said *"we got what unionists always wanted"*, he never believed it himself—or if he did, he always communicated in his political actions that he didn't believe a word of it. It was widely believed or understood that Trimble had signed the Agreement under duress, because he was persuaded that the consequences of him not signing it would have been much worse for Unionism. And Mandelson had made it clear to him only a couple of weeks previously that this continued to be the case. It was hard for Trimble to be taken seriously as an advocate of the Good Friday Agreement when he was the most reluctant signatory of it and would have given more than anyone to have gotten out of it there and then. It was harder still therefore to make the case that the Agreement had destroyed Republicanism when Trimble acted as if it would have been preferable if it had never happened.

Trimble felt he had to justify putting McGuinness in government, having thirty years earlier rejected Fitt and Devlin as "Republicans". And he tried to do this by saying that Unionism got a better deal in 1998 when Nationalism was stronger, than in 1973 when it was weaker. Now anyone with any memory knew that the Catholic vote was smaller in 1973 because sizeable numbers of Catholics followed the Republican call to boycott the elections. So that argument was nonsense. But, if the position of Nationalism was much stronger in 1998 than it was in 1973, surely that had something to do with the Unionist rejection of the 1973 deal? It was certainly not just purely a product of demographics.

Trimble had read the heart-searching of disgruntled former Provos, who saw the difference between Sunningdale and The Good Friday Agreement as not being worth the killing and dying done to supposedly achieve the latter. But Unionism had a much greater responsibility for *"the thousands of needless deaths"* than Republicans had if that argument was accepted, since it was Unionists, not Republicans, who actually brought down Sunningdale. But the die-hards neglected that part of the story.

Trimble was expecting people to believe that he was trying to destroy Republicanism by luring it into government. If that was so, he was the first Unionist leader who was concerned with the defeat of ideological Republicanism at all. Unionism had never been very concerned about it in the past. The Unionist statelet was always able to deal with the small ideological Republican rump which periodically ventured across the Border over the years. In fact, Unionism had an active interest in preserving ideological Republicanism. Its existence, whilst offering no serious threat to the Six Counties, gave the Unionists leverage with the British Government for the upkeep of strong security and provided the handy justification for more vigorous policing of the Catholic community.

Trimble's Unionist view of Republicanism was by this stage bolstered by the arguments of the die-hards. With a slight difference of emphasis, Trimble's speech could have been turned into something from the disgruntled Republicans of *Fourthwrite*. And there was little doubt that Trimble's 'smart' advisors from academia and 'thinking' Unionism were encouraging him to gather up ammunition from the Republican die-hards to use against those responsible for calling off the War.

In September 2000 Prof. Bew told a campaign rally in support of David Burnside's failed candidature in South Antrim that:

> "It is not enough to say that the agreement is a partitionist settlement and unionists should go home contented. Many ordinary unionists are not buying this agreement so those in favour of the agreement must take a more active approach. There has to be a battle of ideas across a wide front. The only grand unionist narrative of what has happened must not be the DUP one of betrayal."

Trimble's Waterfront speech was an expression of this *"battle of ideas across a wide front"* against *"the DUP narrative of betrayal"*. But the sum total of this battle appeared to be Trimble's firing of dissident Republican ammunition to justify his policy to the Unionist Party. If Trimble had been successful with this form of politics, he would undoubtedly have brought about a rejuvenation of armed Republicanism and he would then have been able to tell everyone 'I told you so'. But neither the Unionist faithful nor the wider Protestant community believed him.

On 25th October the IRA released a statement saying it would allow some of its arms dumps to be re-inspected and on the following day it was announced that a second inspection by international observers of the IRA's arms dumps had taken place.

On 28th October Trimble won the backing of the UUC, beating off a challenge from Donaldson by 445 votes to 374. At the 24th meeting of the UUC to discuss the Agreement Trimble announced that he was going to *'sanction'* Sinn Fein through the Office of First Minister: he would prevent them from participating in the North-South Ministerial Council. He did this despite getting assurances from Taoiseach Ahern that the IRA was about to re-engage with de Chastelaine. On 5th December the IRA stated that it had not broken contact with the decommissioning body—but that decommissioning "cannot and will not happen on terms dictated by the British government or the unionists" (IN 6.12.00).

Sinn Fein brought a legal challenge to Trimble's *'sanction'*. In January 2001 the High Court ruled that Trimble's ban on Sinn Fein Ministers attending North-South ministerial council was illegal. But Trimble announced an appeal to the decision and kept the ban in place.

Patton and Policing

An Independent Commission on Policing was established under the chairmanship of Chris Patten as part of the 1998 Agreement. The imminence of the Patton Report on the reform of the police was a big problem for Trimble because of his reluctance to positively embrace the Agreement. Both Sinn Fein and the SDLP demanded fundamental change to policing as part of the Agreement. They saw the RUC as part of the Unionist government apparatus of the old Stormont system and noted that it had remained fundamentally unchanged under Direct Rule. Sinn Fein wanted the RUC disbanded while the SDLP policy was for reform.

Trimble treated the SDLP position on policing as an attempt to "*out-Sinn Fein, Sinn Fein*". But the SDLP position always was that it would not encourage Catholics to join the police force unless there was a substantial reform of it.

When the Patten Report was published in 1999 the SDLP welcomed the changes it suggested to policing and the establishment of a new police service. Sinn Fein, which preferred disbandment, took Patten, if implemented in full, to be the "*minimum threshold from which to achieve acceptable policing*". In May 2000 the British Government introduced the Police Bill but significantly watered down the Patten Commission's recommendations. Legislation to reform the RUC was passed into law at Westminster.

The question of what the new police force would be called remained undecided as the Secretary of State, Peter Mandelson, retained the power to decide that at a later date. On 5th December 2000, in response to the passing of the Police Bill, the IRA issued a statement saying that the British Government had failed to keep to its side of the bargain by failing to implement in full the Patten Report on policing reform.

In August 2001 the British Government published revised plans to reform the police. The new plan included significant changes to the Policing Board and some powers of investigation of police activities. In August the Catholic Church officially backed the revised policing plan of the British Government. The Bishops pronounced that they still had some reservations but there was now "*real hope for a new beginning in policing*". The SDLP then endorsed the policing plan and announced that it would nominate members to join the new Policing Boards. These were established, despite Sinn Fein's refusal to endorse the reforms or to nominate members to the bodies, in view of the fact that only 11 of Patten's original recommendations had remained undiluted.

Here is a die-hard Republican view of Sinn Fein and the Patten proposals, expressed by Anthony McIntyre in an article entitled, '*Getting Ready to Jump Again*':

> "How do we get a measure of Patten from a republican perspective? One way is to contrast objectives sought to gains achieved. The Ulster Unionist Party aimed to preserve the RUC. This is accomplished. The SDLP sought to reform the RUC. It succeeded. Sinn Fein wanted the RUC disbanded. It failed... Republicans considering the clawing back on Patten would do well to regard such as peripheral to the real issue which is the extent to which the acceptance of Patten underlies Sinn Fein's commitment to an internal solution dressed up by what Henry Patterson once referred to as 'necessary nonsenses' to keep republicans happy" (The Blanket).

Republicans were faced with a problem over the British watering down of Patten to help Trimble. Republicans had argued that the discredited RUC should be totally disbanded. Of course, in an ideal world it should have been. And, if it weren't for the existence of rejectionist Unionism, it undoubtedly would have been. But Republicans were now taking into account the existence of Unionism and engaging with it. Political reality meant that the RUC wouldn't be disbanded, but would be incorporated into the new police service in some way or other. The Republican leadership consequently began to move to the more practical position of defending the Patten proposals from dilution, and getting the most accountable and acceptable police service possible, so that Catholics could be encouraged to join. In October 2002 Adams said he could "conceive of a world in which it would be appropriate for Sinn Fein to join the Policing Board" (IN 27.10.02).

The situation was that Sinn Fein was trying to establish a normal and functional police service which could only have a stabilising effect on politics, while Unionists were attempting to retain the old Protestant force and its Unionist symbols—which could only have an antagonising effect on the Catholic community and a destabilising influence. What was happening was that Republicans were engaging in politics by taking into account the substance of the Protestant community, whilst Unionism continued to flounder by acting as if the Catholic community simply did not exist and would hopefully go away or return to the former passivity of the Stormont era—now that Stormont was occupied again.

The policing issue brought another attempt by the SDLP to isolate Sinn Fein and put it under pressure to toe the 'democratic' line and pose problems for its base. But, even on this policy difference, where it looked as though the SDLP had secured a significant victory over Sinn Fein, it turned out that its endorsement of policing was premature and the course of events actually enhanced the credibility of Sinn Fein as the party which had the better political grasp of the situation in which the Catholic community found itself.

The SDLP's political difficulties were compounded by its implication in a Policing Board with little actual power over policing, but which took the blame for the shortcomings of the RUC/PSNI. Its membership of the Board prevented it from launching any agitation for effective police action in combating the street violence with which Unionism tried to undermine the political institutions of the Agreement. The SDLP probably hoped that Sinn Fein's refusal to nominate representatives onto the Police Authority would be its undoing, exposing Sinn Fein to the charge of not being serious about transforming 'Northern Ireland'.

However, Sinn Fein's contention that the Police Authority was a bogus institution, short on authority, was borne out by subsequent events. The political policing that was a continuing feature of 'law and order' in the province, the obstruction of the Ombudsman's reports on the Omagh bombing, police collusion with loyalist instruments and general anti-Sinn Fein activity all clearly demonstrated to the Catholic community that policing had a long way to travel before it could be described as representative and "normal".

Trimble Resigns

On 8th May 2001 Trimble told the UUP that he would resign as First Minister on 1st July if there was no progress from the IRA on Decommissioning. He called this the *'nuclear option'*. As a result of this manoeuvre, Trimble emerged from the Ulster Unionist Council's annual meeting in June as the unopposed Leader: party opponents chose not to challenge him ahead of his scheduled resignation. Trimble duly resigned, nominating Reg Empey as his caretaker, and triggered a six-week period in which he hoped to force the IRA's hand on the surrender of arms.

The *New Statesman* of 2nd July 2001 carried an account of an interview with Trimble by John Lloyd, its former Editor and a staunch supporter of Trimble. It was published on the day after the Unionist Leader put the Agreement into what might have been a terminal crisis and it revealed his thoughts just before he made his fateful decision. The interview reveals that Trimble's motivation in provoking the new crisis was a restoration of the status quo before the Agreement of 1998:

> "It is clear... that he... sees the future shape of the politics of the province as being up to him: to produce a stronger bond between the mainland and that part of the UK... It is not a direction that Sinn Fein can be expected to endorse; it carries, itself, the risk of renewed terror. But it is the route Trimble now maps, and on which he now seems likely to begin to march."

Lloyd also noted:

> "one of Trimble's closest advisers told me that he feared civil war... in this bleak landscape, however, Trimble walks with a conviction of a politician who sees himself as a large player in British as well as Northern Irish politics..."

Trimble "seems almost serene" about it all, according to Lloyd.

A few weeks later, on July 20th, Trimble appeared on Radio 4's *Any Questions*. He dismissed the idea that the breakdown of devolved government might lead to a return to war. He said that the IRA had only embarked on the Peace Process because it was on the verge of being defeated by the British Army, and it was therefore in no condition to resume its War. By combining the two positions revealed to the *New Statesman* and Radio 4, the core of fundamentalist Ulster Unionist aspiration was revealed; a return to warfare in such a way that the British would 'take off the gloves', smash Republicanism and put the Fenians back in their place. Trimble had used the phrase *'bringing them to heel'* a few months earlier. It was only through this *'bringing to heel'* that the spiritual needs of Unionism could be satisfied, it appeared.

Ulster Unionism, a spiritual rather than a political entity, could be manoeuvred by a superior authority (Britain) into a semblance of realistic political activity if it was forced to choose the lesser of two evils. But it could not be manoeuvred into engaging with a will in the implementation of an Agreement which it had felt itself compelled to accept. So Trimble evidently felt he could, like the proverbial horse, be led to the water by his master but refuse to drink of it, if he saw it as dirty. And his master would then have to think again and set off on a different course of action instead.

In the interview with Lloyd the Unionist leader refused to criticise Tony Blair "personally"—but he made the following criticism all the same:

> "The great mistake of the first period was the release of the prisoners for no gain. Their release should have been linked to decommissioning… Releasing prisoners who had committed serious crimes… was a judicial abomination; but if you are going to do it for reasons of political gain, then at least make sure you get the gain!"

This was the Major position of preconditions on Republicans that was brought to an end at Canary Wharf. If it had been maintained, there would have been an end to the Peace Process and no Agreement. So Trimble's position amounted to a statement that the Agreement was plain wrong and that he should never have been forced to sign it, or later on, operate it temporarily, when sufficient pressure was brought to bear by the superior authority.

The Arms Issue Again

In May 2001 the Independent International arms inspectors said that they had carried out a third inspection of IRA arms dumps and that the weapons had remained out of use. At that point the IRA had held four meetings with the arms decommissioning body. It had honoured every commitment it had made, although the British Government continued to renege on its commitments on both policing and demilitarisation. In early August, General de Chastelain said the IRA put forward a plan to put its weapons "*beyond use*" and made the statement that his Commission believed the IRA's proposals "*initiates a process that will put IRA arms completely and verifiably beyond use*". The IRA then released a statement confirming the details of what the Decommissioning Body had stated and revealed that it had had eight meetings with General de Chastelain in the preceding five months to discuss its arms.

Despite these developments the latest NI Secretary of State, John Reid, suspended the devolved institutions for 24 hours from the 11th August 2001. This occurred because the British Government had given the parties in NI a week to respond to their August 1st proposals. The IRA had responded, with the deal concluded with the International Arms decommissioning body. Trimble, however, stated that he could not return to his post as First Minister until he was satisfied with the way the Republican Army disposed of its arms. He required an immediate formal surrender of weaponry rather than the process which had been agreed between the Republican Army and General de Chastelain, so he refused to play ball.

Reid decided on a "*temporary suspension*" of the institutions, returning the clocks to zero and so giving another six weeks for Trimble to be sated.

This device was required because, if six weeks had elapsed without a First Minister, or without a Deputy First Minister, the 1998 Act required the Secretary of State to call an election. Reid's decision was to avoid the final whistle and conclusion of the game for Trimble. It was like a referee adding on extra time in a game for time-wasting by one of the sides. However, in this case the captain of the losing team was being rewarded, by a dramatic extension of time, for taking the ball away home and refusing to play until he got the result he desired.

This was a calculated move by the British Secretary of State to subvert an Agreement enshrined in British Law. It was essentially taken to protect Trimble against the democracy. In any normal democratic system, if one party to a coalition walked away from government, as the UUP had, then the usual consequence of such a decision would have been fresh elections and a new mandate with a more realistic political landscape emerging. But that was the last thing Blair and Reid wanted and they effectively subverted the democratic imperative and prolonged the agony of all concerned.

The IRA responded to this trickery by releasing a statement withdrawing its offer to put in place mechanisms to put arms beyond use, describing Reid's actions as† *"totally unacceptable"*.

During the six week extension Hume signalled he had had enough and resigned as formal leader of the SDLP. Mallon then announced he was also stepping down as deputy—or acting—leader and would not stand for the leadership. A couple of days later the Republican Army announced its intention of "intensifying its engagement" with the International Arms body, in order to "accelerate toward a comprehensive resolution" if others also played their part—meaning Trimble. However, with no response from the UUP leader, Reid decided to suspend the institutions again on 21st September to protect Trimble, but giving notice this would be the last "technical suspension" he would be given.

In October Trimble tabled a motion in the Assembly to exclude Sinn Fein from the Executive. But this failed after the SDLP refused to support it. Trimble then announced that he was withdrawing his Ministers from the Executive and that they would eventually resign.

The Ulster Unionists' three Ministers in the Executive then resigned, putting a seven day deadline on the IRA to initiate decommissioning. On 22nd October 2001 Adams announced that he and McGuinness had urged the IRA to make a *"groundbreaking move"* to save the Peace Process. On the next day the IRA announced that it had begun a process of putting arms beyond use in line with an agreement with the Independent International Decommissioning Commission. Hours later the IICD confirmed it had witnessed the disposal of arms and described the act as *"significant"*. Trimble then renominated UUP Ministers to the Executive, thereby preventing its collapse. The Secretary of State also announced the scaling down of military forces and installations in South Armagh.

In November 2001 the IRA made a significant act of putting weapons beyond use. Trimble claimed it as his *"El Alamein"* (a skirmish in the desert during Britain's Second World War on Germany that is pretended to have been a turning point in the conflict—when in fact it was the substantial Soviet victories at Stalingrad and Kursk which actually broke the German Armies).

Within an hour of Adams' announcement that he had made a proposal to the IRA about putting arms beyond use in order to save the political process, Alan MacFarland, UUP Assembly member for North Down, appeared on Radio Éireann to say that arms were never the issue. Everybody knew, he said, that arms could be procured at a moment's notice and their destruction was therefore of minimal consequence. The issue was now the existence of the IRA as an organisation, a command structure, with or without arms.

MacFarland's contention and his demand bore out the Sinn Fein view that arms were never the issue and indicated that the Ulster Unionist Party was prepared to move to the next ditch to impede the operation of the Agreement again.

Opponents of Sinn Fein ridiculed the suggestion that the IRA had not acted under compulsion, claiming that it only ever acted under compulsion and the compulsion in this instance had come from the arrest of the Columbia Three and the events of 11th September 2001 in the US. However, Peter King, the US Republican Congressman, denied that Columbia or September 11th had anything to do with it. He was not aware that any particular pressure had been brought to bear on Irish Republicans by the American Republican Party. He said that, long before the arrest of the Columbia Three, the IRA had done what he understood it had intended to do and would have done earlier but for Trimble's breaches of the Agreement. However, as Jonathan Powell noted, the events of September 11th had a hardening effect on Trimble, who wanted the British to push "them much harder after 9/11 because they had no choice, that they had to sign up for a peace agreement, and we should have just forced the issue and given an ultimatum" (*The British and Peace in Northern Ireland,* p.312).

If Trimble had read Leo Abse's fascinating biography of Blair (written before he was Prime Minister), he would have realised that the Prime Minister's character had been formed around "an idealised mutuality and an avoidance of acknowledgement of strife, a wish which reflected his essential mode of thought: all differences of views should be minimised" (Leo Abse, *The Man Behind the Smile,* p.60).

Blair was all about the creation of "false consensus" which would portray all those outside it as mentally suspect due to their inability to conform to it. And of course, Blair was the definer of the consensus. Blair's authoritarian political character, which Abse called "the politics of perversion", which was more suited to the perverse pseudo-state of 'Northern Ireland' than to the real State he led, posed problems for both Unionists and Republicans. But Sinn Fein was better at dealing with Blair than Unionism, because Unionists had a strong moral imperative and found it difficult to accept a greater moral force making it toe the line. Republicanism was used to that in dealing with Britain from an independent standpoint and so was better at handling Blair's peculiar character.

Saving Dave I

Trimble was still seen by the British Government as indispensable to the Agreement and, in the years which followed, the NIO proceeded to make a series of extraordinary efforts to 'save' him from his Unionist opponents, some of them within his party. Trimble's power to obstruct the implementation of the Agreement largely depended on the threat of him being 'finished' and the thought he projected: "*Après moi le deluge*".

David Morrison (*Irish Political Review,* December 2001 and January 2002) detailed the extraordinary measures, including the passing of an Act of Parliament, which were taken from 1998 onwards to *save* David Trimble from having to face a leadership contest in the UUP or an Assembly Election before it was due in 2003. These measures were taken because anti-Agreement Unionism was getting stronger.

It would be tedious to follow the intricacies of the stop-go years between the signing of the GFA and its starting to function on a stable basis. The following, however, are just some of the examples of the constitutional contortions engaged in by the British Government to try to keep the Agreement afloat in these years.

One of Trimble's obstructive tactics was to threaten to resign as First Minister. If six weeks elapsed without a First Minister or a Deputy First Minister, the *Northern Ireland Act 1998* required the Secretary of State to call an election—which it was generally thought would produce an unequivocal anti-Agreement Unionist bloc and make the re-election of Trimble and Mallon, or another acceptable alternative, absolutely impossible. At all costs David Trimble had to be protected, first from his Assembly Members and, if that failed, from the electorate.

Mallon resigned as Deputy First Minister in July 1999 but, when the Assembly met again after the Mitchell Review, the pretence had to be made that he hadn't resigned after all. It was on the basis of this piece of trickery devised by Peter Mandelson that devolved government, and the other institutions prescribed in the Agreement, were established in early December 1999.

When Trimble threatened to resign in February 2000, an Act of Parliament was passed to enable the mandate of 1st July 1998 to be extended indefinitely. And when Trimble did resign on 1st July 2001, getting him and the new proposed Deputy First Minister, Mark Durkan, elected required more political trickery. This time, in November 2001, the temporary transfer of Alliance and Women's Coalition Members from the 'Other' bloc to the Unionist bloc, had to be arranged, for the sole purpose of the electing of the First Minister and Deputy First Minister. These two parties had to briefly give up their non-sectarian designation in the Assembly and designate themselves as 'Unionist' because there was insufficient Unionist support for re-appointing Trimble as First Minister.

Peter Robinson of the DUP took two legal actions seeking a judicial review of the Secretary of State's failure to call an election before May 2003 and the other seeking to challenge the election of the First Minister and Deputy First Minister in November 2001, arguing that it should have been declared illegal on the grounds that it took place outside the six weeks time limit specified by the 1998 Act. Both actions failed in the High Court in December of 2001. Trimble was, therefore, successfully protected from the electorate until May 2003.

Trimble certainly needed protecting from the electorate. In the British General Election of June 2001 there were two dramatic movements of political support. Within the Protestant community there was a great swing away from Trimble's UUP to Paisley's DUP, although the Ulster Unionists remained the major Unionist party. The UUP started the election with 9 seats at Westminster and finished it with 6, losing 3 seats to the DUP and 2 to Sinn Fein (they had regained 1 from the DUP and 1 from Bob McCartney). The DUP increased their seats from 3 to 5 and would have won more if the Alliance hadn't withdrawn its candidates in some constituencies to save Trimble.

The preservation of Trimble meant that he could continue making difficulties for the Republicans. If Unionists had embraced the Agreement, a process would have started of the IRA withering away.

In the early days of the Agreement the Loyalist parties were willing to give a lead in building working-class acceptance of the deal within the Loyalist communities. However, that position was steadily complicated and subverted by Trimble's chipping away at the Agreement, with the ground being taken by militant rejectionists.

Things began to get very difficult for Loyalists who remained in support of the deal. As a consequence of this poisonous atmosphere, by the Summer of 2001, attacks on Catholics reached a level not seen for three years. This meant that the Republican Army had to maintain itself in constant readiness to defend the community against possible Loyalist attacks, or to be able to resume the War if the Peace Process and Good Friday Agreement collapsed. This was a situation which had negative political implications for all. What was an army that had to continue to maintain itself in readiness to do? And this was probably one of the reasons for the Colombia Three affair.

Sinn Fein overtake the SDLP

In the Nationalist part of the June 2001 Election, Sinn Fein started with 2 seats and increased to 4, over-taking the SDLP which had just 3. The Sinn Fein vote went up substantially and it now became the leading party in the Nationalist bloc. The SDLP—the fast learners, according to Mallon—had had the framework for 'Constitutional Nationalist' action laid on for them by the Good Friday Agreement. But the 'constitutionalists' began to wither in Paradise, undermined by the attempt to work the new Constitution.

Protest had been the routine of the SDLP and its political forte. And, because the opportunity for 'constitutional' Nationalist action was not brought about by its own efforts, but was a product of the unconstitutional action of the Republican Army, it was unable to avail of the opportunity it received. It began to be displaced in the sphere of 'Constitutional' action by the unconstitutional or 'slightly constitutional' force which had created the opportunity and the new Constitution. And really there was nothing paradoxical in that.

When the SDLP was set up there was no Constitutional wing to the Republican movement. When Sinn Fein made its transition to using the electoral system, the Catholic community had a choice of two 'Constitutional' parties, one a bit less 'Constitutional' than the other. During the period when this new form of politics was developing there was a definite role for the SDLP. It was to that party that the British Government gave concessions for the Catholic community, in order to undercut Republican electoral support. That phase began to come to an end as Sinn Fein began to outstrip the SDLP, which then struggled to find a reason for its existence to present to Catholic voters beyond a kind of distaste for those who had got their hands dirty in the struggle.

The SDLP found it could not outdo Sinn Fein in appeal to working class voters and there was not sufficient electoral power in the rural community to keep it as the dominant party. And soon Sinn Fein began to supplant it there as well due to the radicalisation of the rural Catholic community which came about as a result of Drumcree and other Orange marching stand-offs.

Neither party was able to cross the community divide. The SDLP often claimed to be a socialist party representative of both Protestants and Catholics and as such it joined the Socialist International. However, the SDLP was unable to broaden its appeal to include Protestant workers and actively discouraged the British or Irish Labour Parties from doing so.

In July 2002 the new SDLP Leader Mark Durkan, who had replaced Mallon a year earlier, came up with the idea of a *'new nationalism'*, which was to make the SDLP more meaningful. He announced it at a symposium in New Ross, Co Wexford. This was a Nationalism with cross community appeal. But very problematic to this vision was the fact that the SDLP had been the architects of the Good Friday Agreement, which institutionalised the communal division into a permanent feature of electoral politics. The GFA minimised the possibility of cross community politics and provided an arena for communal conflict at the political level, to compensate for the reducing of it at the physical force level. There has, predictably, being little heard of this 'new nationalism' (until Colm Eastwood, elected leader in November 2015, promised it again in 2016).

Saving Dave II

The second phase of 'Saving Dave' involved an offensive by some parts of the security services to discredit Sinn Fein's commitment to the Peace Process. It involved an Intelligence war on Republicans waged by the Intelligence services and culminated in three main events: The Colombian Three affair, the Castlereagh 'Break-in' and the Stormont 'espionage'. These events occurred because the British State continued its operations both against the IRA and Sinn Fein in a kind of 'Cold War' mode, forcing Republicans to counter these manoeuvres to demonstrate continued operational capacity.

The Colombian Three were Irish Republicans who in 2001 went to assist a liberation movement in Columbia with advice and training. They were arrested and threatened with lengthy jail terms. The episode was taken to be a breach of the GFA. However, it is difficult to see how such an activity by members of the IRA, while they were waiting around to be disbanded in Ireland, had anything to do with the Agreement. Apparently it was perfectly alright for the British Army to leave Ireland and engage in conflicts such as Afghanistan and Iraq, or for individual former soldiers to become mercenaries across the world for the most brutal regimes, without being in breach of the Agreement. The IRA, like the British Government, had a long-standing foreign policy but now it was taken to come within the terms of the Agreement, unlike British foreign policy.

A Not Guilty verdict for training FARC rebels was returned in Bogota on the Columbia Three. But that decision was overturned on Appeal. Conor Cruise O'Brien was certain that this was a political decision taken in the wake of the 9/11 attacks in New York:

"the Columbian Courts, while nominally independent of the Columbian Government, are actually tightly controlled by that Government... the Columbian Government is totally dependent on the Government of the United States for its financial and military backing" (Irish Independent, 18.12.01, *'Sentences Reflect Clear Sign of Bush's Order to Get Tough')*.

Whatever the quality of Columbian justice, using such an incident to bring down the institutions of government in 'Northern Ireland' was entirely spurious.

Next, on the 18th March 2002 the police revealed that there had been a 'break in' at the Special Branch offices of Castlereagh Police Station in Belfast. The 'break in', at one of the most secure police stations in the world, shocked security analysts, who immediately speculated about it being an inside job and another incident in the long line of incidents related to the Stevens Inquiry into Collusion, during which the security services caused vital documents to disappear. It was generally assumed, even outside the Catholic community, that the robbery was a security operation designed to remove documents which would be embarrassing if they fell into the hands of those who were investigating police conduct with regard to the Omagh Bombing and examining the allegations of collusion with Loyalist paramilitaries.

There had already been two publicised occasions in which documents required by investigators were found to have been destroyed by accidental fires in high security installations. The robbery was carried out by a group of men without masks, who seemed to know all the security requirements needed to walk right into the heart of the building ,and immediately find what they were looking for. The cameras which were supposed to keep a permanent watch had been switched off.

Separate investigations were launched by the police and the NIO. On 24th March, PSNI Chief Constable Sir Ronnie Flanagan said he would be "most surprised" if paramilitaries or civilians were responsible for the break-in at the Special Branch's office at Castlereagh. Despite this statement, a week later, hundreds of his police officers were involved in the raiding of Republican homes. The police swoops directed against Republicans were obviously meant to convey the impression that Republicans were responsible for the break-in at Castlereagh.

A leak by Sir John Chilcot, the MI6 man brought in by the Secretary of State to investigate the incident, was then taken as establishing as fact that the IRA had done it.

Although many senior Republicans were arrested for the Castlereagh 'break in', only one person, a cook working in the establishment, who was living in America when the charge was brought, was ever indicted. However, the charges were then dropped on the pretext that evidence of his guilt would damage security if presented in Court.

That would have spoken volumes about the nature of the State's interest in the 'break in', if the media had shown any interest. Some fourteen years later, an *Irish News* editorial noted that, when the incident was sent to the Ombudsman, a decade after the event:

> "… within a short time different theories began to emerge including the suggestion that the raid was actually an in-side job, possibly involving rogue Special Branch officers and IRA officers."

And it was disclosed,

> "that a former Special Branch officer whose details were stolen has come forward to claim the police allowed the break-in to take place. This astonishing allegation now forms the basis of an official investigation" by the Police Ombudsman (7.11.15).

However, a year later, according to the same paper, it was claimed that the IRA did in fact do the Castlereagh job. Which shows that a reliance on security sources is a very dangerous game for security correspondents and their editors to play.

The 2016 revelations by Alison Morris suggest that the IRA pulled off the Castlereagh job on St. Patrick's Day 2001, deciphered the encrypted codes on the documents obtained, and thus found agents working for the State within Republican ranks, both military and political. On this version, one of the agents turned out to be the IRA commander who planned the Shankill bomb of 1993, who was said to have provided the State with advance warning of the attack, which it did nothing to avert. Another of the agent codenames broken by Republicans was allegedly that of Special Adviser, Denis Donaldson (Irish News 25.1.16).

'The *Irish News*, however, has not as yet produced the documents it has claimed to have seen, which were stolen from Castlereagh, and therefore their authenticity remains in doubt. At present, it can only be concluded that the British Intelligence services seem to have been engaged in a continuing war on Republicans in which the latter may have taken retaliatory action to demonstrate continued defence capability.

The third event in the security offensive against Republicans, one in which Donaldson featured prominently, has been called *'Stormontgate'*. The Sinn Fein offices at Stormont were raided by Sir Hugh Orde, the new Chief Constable of the new Police Service, with the approval of the Secretary of State, for the purpose of providing a big media event to undermine Sinn Fein. This event, in October 2002, was political policing at its most vulgar.

Following other raids in private houses the police charged a Sinn Fein official with being in possession of political information (which he took to be so dangerous that he kept it in a rucksack!). The Police spin on this was that political information could be of use to 'terrorists'. Sinn Fein stood accused of trying to find out what its political opponents were intending, which seems to be what all responsible political parties aim to do in a normal democracy. It was doubly ironic that the sort of information gathered was the kind of thing that was routinely leaked to the media in Great Britain, a process which had been turned into a normal process of government by the New Labour Government and its spin doctors. But in 'Northern Ireland' it was used to suspend the institutions of government.

At the same time the British Government was overseeing communications by Sinn Fein and other parties in Northern Ireland in every way it could—for example, through the use of spies, by planting listening devices in the cars of elected MLAs, and expanding the role of the security services that specialised in such activities in the province. Whitehall had failed to reconstruct the 'Northern Ireland' security apparatus long after its reform had been pledged at the inception of the Agreement. Security force/Loyalist collusion continued unabated after the IRA had called a halt to war and resulted in the deaths of a number of prominent non-Republicans who sought to expose it, including the solicitor, Rosemary Nelson in March 1999, and the journalist Martin O'Hagan in September 2000, as well as a number of individuals who were involved in investigations, who met mysterious deaths along the way.

What was politically afoot was an attempt to stage-manage the withdrawal of the Unionist Party from the devolved government in such a way that Sinn Fein could be blamed for it. To achieve this, the British Government had one of its main agents within the Republican movement, Denis Donaldson, arrested and charged with espionage. It did not, of course, come to light until later that Donaldson was working for British Intelligence: that is, he was helping to bring down the institutions of government in 'Northern Ire—land',when he was supposed to be working *for* the Republican movement.

In the Castlereagh expose of 2016, Alison Morris alleges that the "Stormontgate" arrest of Donaldson was also orchestrated by the Intelligence services to protect their agent after Republicans had broken the codes from the documents they procured at Castlereagh.

The State case against its agent predictably collapsed in December 2005 and Donaldson made a dramatic public confession of being a British agent for a long number of years. What was interesting was the fact that Donaldson was allegedly a political rather than military spy for the State. He provided information from within the high levels of Sinn Fein during the negotiations about the Good Friday Agreement.

Donaldson was later killed by a person or persons unknown after a *Sunday World* 'Exclusive', which pin-pointed his location in Donegal.

If the Allison Morris story is to be believed, the IRA, after identifying the State agents by breaking the codes in the Castlereagh files, decided to allow them to 'retire' quietly into private life, or to leave the country if they felt endangered from former comrades. That was proof positive that the War was over.

Donaldson was living among Republicans in Donegal, with little sign of molestation: he was only targeted when his presence was made known to the world. In an interview Donaldson told the journalist who had tracked him down that the Stormont espionage event was staged and that he was sacrificed by the British so that Republicans would take the blame for the suspension of the institutions.

Both the Castlereagh 'break-in' and the political espionage which Republicans were supposedly engaged in had ended a whole year before the British Government decided to take down the institutions at Stormont after 'Stormontgate'. Seeing that Donaldson was working for the British Government all along, and his activities were known about by the Secretary of State for a whole year before he decided to act, the timing must have had some political significance. It, presumably, had to do with internal Unionist affairs—helping the UUP hold onto its slender electoral lead over the DUP to *'save Dave'* Trimble from the wolves of the electorate.

Bringing the House Down

In early October 2002 the UUP committed itself to collapsing the structures established under the Agreement unless Whitehall did what it wanted by some other means. An election was looming. It was taken to be a virtual certainty that the parties favoured by Whitehall, the UUP and SDLP, would lose their majority status to the DUP and Sinn Fein.

Majority status within the communal blocs was all-important in what went on at Stormont, due to the confessional apartheid system that the British Government had established under the Agreement. It would have been an entirely different ball game which Whitehall was unprepared to play at that stage to have dealt with Sinn Fein and the DUP. So, when Unionist leader and First Minister Trimble threatened to bring the house down, as a way of rescuing his position against the DUP, Secretary of State Reid, identified the interests of the State with Trimble's interest and acted on his behalf, keeping Sinn Fein and the DUP away from the levers of power for the time being.

Whitehall came to Trimble's aid by both ordering a police raid on the Sinn Fein offices at Stormont, with television cameras in attendance, and launching an espionage propaganda campaign against Sinn Fein while suspending the Power-Sharing institutions.

This kind of activity formed part of a long-established pattern. Republicans were arrested at critical points in the Peace Process and allegations were put into circulation by the Chief Constable. Unionists were appeased by the exclusion of Sinn Fein. And then, a few months later, when the incident had served its purpose, those who had been arrested were released without charge and without publicity.

All the allegations (The Columbia Three, the Castlereagh 'break-in', and the Stormont 'espionage') which led to collapses of the Executive and of Power-Sharing arrangements were presented as established facts by the British State media (as were Saddam Hussein's weapons of mass destruction in Iraq, at the time) despite the fact that they were unproven.

It was not important that they ever were proved—just that they provide political cover for the British Government to do the thing they wanted— 'saving Dave'. All three planks justifying the British Government's actions in October 2002 turned out to be not what they seemed. All three were quickly and quietly forgotten, without any official acknowledgement of the truth. They could be quietly forgotten about because the stories released to the media were not actually believed by those who used them to political effect and the media in 'Northern Ireland', being strictly controlled, showed little interest after the event.

It was somehow expected that this pattern would result in the Catholic community deserting Sinn Fein in droves as it recoiled from such dishonourable and disreputable behaviour. And it was hoped that Republicans failure to do and say certain things, which the Agreement never required them to do or say in the first place, would put them beyond the Pale with the media and in consequence with the electorate, which in Britain seems to be gullible in that way. Instead, the strategy had precisely the opposite effect on the Catholic community and ended up in severely damaging the SDLP.

The great hope of the SDLP was that Sinn Fein had misjudged the situation when it refused to sit on the Police Authority of the supposedly new police force. But the events of early 2002 showed that it was the SDLP that had misjudged the situation. The party found itself implicated in the Policing Board with little actual power over policing. It found itself taking the blame for the continued political use of the police as a battering ram against Republicans when the British wanted to prop up Trimble.

Ever since 1998 the British State has conducted war by other means against Republicans. Hot War has become Cold War. Britain could not rest easy, with the result that the Republican ceasefire developed into a political victory which the securocrats continue to try to undermine.

The Republican scheme, on the other hand, was for a gradual withering away of the Republican Army over a couple of years in the context of the operation of Power-Sharing and North-South institutions, reform of the governing apparatus of the Six Counties and of the police, along with British demilitarisation.

Saving Dave III

During its holding operation, British pressure was ratcheted up on Republicans in various ways. Having failed to shatter, split or humiliate the Republican movement by means of incessant piecemeal demands that went beyond the scope, spirit or letter of the Agreement, the British then attempted to demoralise it with revelations of Intelligence penetration at the highest level. Stories began to appear about the IRA having been riddled with informers and British spies, including the infamous 'Steak knife'. This kind of thing became so transparent and vulgar that even the commentator Denis Bradley, and the SDLP, had to call for the British to call off their Intelligence war on the Nationalist community (IN 14.05.03).

The British Government had established the institutions for their own purpose and supported them while they fulfilled that purpose. But when the parties that it did not want in power began to flourish within those structures they were promptly pulled down to prevent an election formalising the shifting balance of power within the two communal blocs.

Prof. Patterson, adviser to Trimble, appeared on Radio Éireann on Good Friday 2003 to defend the British decision to suspend institutions. He said he saw "no democratic imperative to hold elections", even though the law required them. Elections, he said, "would reward the bigots and extremists": by which he meant the DUP and Sinn Fein. So, because Trimble would lose an election, elections and the democratic process were to be abolished!

Prof. Patterson also claimed that the SDLP did not want an election but could not say so publicly. He said this was because it was apparent in the Catholic community that "essentially the war is over" and that "so long as Sinn Fein is committed to peace" the demise of the SDLP was inevitable. This evaded the question of why Trimble sought to bring down the institutions if the War was over and Republicans were committed to peace. What Patterson said was more than likely what Trimble believed, but it was still not enough to satisfy Unionism desire for spiritual satisfaction. What was required was an act from Republicans that could be presented as *surrender,* so that Trimble could gain ground against the DUP. And, since that act had not been forthcoming, the institutions had to come down and the election cancelled. Such is democracy— the democratic process had to be killed in order to save it!

In November 2003 an election finally took place to an Assembly that no longer existed. In the Nationalist election, Sinn Fein changed places with the SDLP; and in the Unionist election the DUP changed places with the UUP. The campaign to *save Trimble* had gone on, even during the suspension of the institutions. Having put off the impending election, time was bought for a third instalment of *'Save Dave'*. But it was to be the final instalment.

Ultimately, Trimble was expendable and the Republican leadership was not. The British realised what was at stake. As Sir John Chilcot in a revealing interview related:

> "I have never forgotten that moment when Adams, talking about decommissioning with his head in his hands, said something like 'That is a really tricky political problem' because that was a sharing moment. That was not about getting enmeshed by us, but a sign that we all had to find a way through... It was more difficult for them than us actually. I think it was politically difficult for us, but for them it was a matter of real principle because they were facing possible insurgent civil war, while we were facing a terrorist threat that we could 'sit on' for as long as it took... while they saw that as an existential threat for us it was not. It was more something to cope and deal with and take a bit of pain and spend a bit of blood and treasure on" (T*he British and Peace in Northern Ireland,* p90).

In the *Joint Declaration* of April 2003 Blair modified the 1998 Agreement, with the consent of Taoiseach Ahern, to make Sinn Fein membership of the Executive conditional on the decommissioning of IRA arms and its disbandment. By doing this the two Governments broke the Agreement, which set out an automatic right of Ministerial position on d'Hondt lines.

They conceded to Jeffrey Donaldson's position: on the basis of which he had refused to sign the Agreement and on which he harried Trimble at the UUC meetings. But, having made that concession, they found Donaldson was not moving into the *'pro-Agreement'* camp but was taking himself and two of the UUP's remaining heavyweights at Westminster, Martin Smyth and David Burnside, out of Trimble's Parliamentary Party altogether. Donaldson then proceeded to take the Disciplinary Committee of the UUP to court for withdrawing his party membership and won. Role playing died hard in the Unionist Party.

Trimble was left at Westminster with just two comparative lightweights to accompany him—Roy Beggs and Lady Sylvia Hermon—and facing an Assembly election, fourteen months after Reid had shut down the institutions in order to save him. The Ulster Unionist leader, despite having split his party and been defeated by Paisley, was satisfied that he had frustrated Sinn Fein and nullified the possibility of the Agreement functioning. He told Malachi O'Doherty in early 2004:

"'What are the DUP going to do? Paisley's language indicates that he is still mentally thinking of himself as being in opposition, but if the DUP continues to think of itself an opposition there isn't going to be an assembly. Will the DUP get a nationalist partner that has a majority of nationalist seats?' He can't see it. 'There is only one available'... He anticipates a long period of political deadlock... Trimble has accepted that Sinn Fein is his likely partner if he ever restores the fortunes of his own party and sees the end of the suspension of the Agreement. 'It's not a problem. There are a lot of good people in the SDLP and I am sorry that the SDLP have got themselves where they are. I think that mistakes were made at an early stage after the Agreement and it is not Mark Durkan's fault they are where they are. It was the previous leadership that made the mistake of positioning itself so close to Sinn Fein. If they can rebuild themselves and come back I will be very happy about that'... He wants the government to squeeze the IRA while he gets on with making use of the interim to restoring the party.... So he's ready for a fight" (Fortnight, February 2004).

But there was to be no come back for Trimble and the Unionist Party. And there was no revival for the SDLP.

Whither the SDLP?

Provisional Sinn Fein and the SDLP had their origins in the same place and in the same year—the year when the Unionists went over from policing to militarily attacking the Northern Catholics in response to rather modest demands that any functional state could have conceded. The SDLP and Sinn Fein were both products of the Northern pseudo-state (as Henry Harrison called it), of fifty years of the political policing of that 'state', and of the Catholic predicament in 1969-70 in relation to the Unionist policing which had become military assault.

But Sinn Fein and the SDLP represented different responses to that predicament. The basic difference was that one was pacifist and one was not. SDLP leader John Hume came to understand the origins of the two responses, minimised the conflict between them and always realised that they were working for a common objective, born from a common experience.

There was no real division over 'the Constitution' because 'Constitutional Nationalism' was really a misnomer. 'Constitutional Nationalism' was no more constitutional than was Republicanism. Its aims lay outside the Constitution: in a separation of 'Northern Ireland' from the British Constitution. The Good Friday Agreement was not a Constitutional settlement, and it certainly did not make 'Northern Ireland' into a democracy. In essence it formalised the Limbo position of the Six Counties as a transitional arrangement between one constitution and another ('Limbo' is a kind of detachment from Heaven and Hell but exit in only one direction is possible from 'Limbo'). It met the requirements set out by Gerry Adams twenty years before as conditions for the operation of a peaceful policy by the Republican movement. But Peace in this matter meant the absence of military activity only—and not an end to Republican politics and objectives.

The conflict of communities went on after the War as it did before the War was ever declared. And it would undoubtedly go on as a process of communal attrition even if Sinn Fein dissolved itself and handed the leadership of Nationalism back to the SDLP.

The SDLP was, in fact, in some ways affected by the IRA Ceasefire more than Sinn Fein. Its new leaders after Hume began to take the conflict with Sinn Fein in earnest with no one to put them right. They portrayed Sinn Fein as doctrinaire sell-outs, knowing full well that they were nothing of the sort. But, at the same time, the party depended on republicans to obtain the settlement they desired but which they had not the political power to obtain by themselves.

The new SDLP, freed of Hume, had got used to thinking and believing its own propaganda that political advance had been achieved through its own political talents and did not realise that its own punching power had gone when the Provos called a halt to the armed struggle.

The Good Friday Agreement was made by and for the SDLP to flourish in. In the Summer of 1998 the party looked forward towards a bright future as the major Catholic party as the Agreement was implemented. The DUP had wanted no part in it. The UUP Leader signed under duress and then sought to undermine the deal from within. And Sinn Fein was lectured about being a 'slow learner' for not having grasped a political settlement earlier. Only the SDLP was truly happy with the GFA: how could it have been unhappy with a project shaped to its own design?

But the day of the SDLP was a short one. Others had been learning all along in the real field of political education—people who knew that the realisation of a programme was not the end of history but just another chapter along the way. And, worse still, Hume had been one of their main educators. In their triumph, the SDLP was exposed as mere bantamweights in politics. The real power behind the partnership stepped forward to claim the belt for its efforts.

So where did it all go wrong as the working of the Agreement caused electoral support to slip away from the SDLP to Sinn Fein? And how did the SDLP change places with Sinn Fein, not only electorally, but also in terms of political disposition? Obviously, the SDLP was greatly undermined by the behaviour of Trimble after the signing of the Agreement but there was also something suicidal in its very political understanding of its own achievement that disabled the party.

It went wrong because the SDLP, the architect of the Agreement, did not really understand its construction. It did not understand that 'Northern Ireland' is one of the least suitable places in the world for the operation of devolved government. It is the area for a profound social antagonism between two communities whose allegiance is given to different States. It is not itself a state and is therefore incapable of being a democratic state. It has no capacity for evolving away from that. Its internal arrangements facilitate communal antagonism and provide an arena for conflict which naturally tends towards the emergence of the most able forces in each community, which attain primacy at the expense of the rest. So the SDLP became also-rans in the system it helped construct—or re-construct. 'Northern Ireland' did not become a democracy in 1998 and there was not an end to history in which a new politics was going to develop, despite all the good intentions.

The *Guardian* of 29th November 2003 had this comment:

> "it is difficult to disagree with the sombre observation of Professor Paul Bew that the Good Friday agreement has not generated the dialectic of compromise that its authors hoped, but instead has generated a dialectic of antagonism that has not yet run its course".

When one sees the word "dialectic", it suggests an ex-Marxist is speaking. Bew's *"dialectic of antagonism"* was inherent in the 'Northern Ireland state' from the beginning. The Agreement of 1998 gave formal structural expression to the inherent antagonism of 'Northern Ireland', and could not have produced a *"dialectic of compromise"*.

The SDLP went off chasing the *"dialectic of compromise"* and the *'centre-ground'* in their Promised Land. But the new structures established in 1998 removed the very notion of a *'centre-ground'* from the political agenda. Those who presented themselves as occupying the *'centre-ground'*—the Alliance Party and the Women's Coalition in 1998-2003—were shunted to the margins as the "Other" becoming make-weights or melting away. Between the two organised communities on which the Agreement was based there were only the strays in a No-Man's Land between the lines—and that is not a place to be if continued existence is desired. When the strays wanted to be players they had to re-classify themselves as 'Unionist'.

And yet the SDLP, the architect of this tightly-structured communal system, refused to act according to its logic and went chasing the non-existent *'centre-ground'* by encouraging 'swing' voting between the communities as Sinn Fein gobbled up the Catholic vote. What the logic of the system required was that each community should maximise its representation in the Assembly, and form a voting alliance for that purpose. Sinn Fein, the most thoroughly pro-Agreement party, was willing to have a voting alliance with the SDLP. The SDLP refused on more than one occasion. Sinn Fein urged their voters to give their transfers to the SDLP, but the SDLP urged their voters to give their transfers to the Unionist Party (which did not reciprocate by giving votes to Fenians unless it was to keep out a Sinn Fein candidate). The strategy of the SDLP just made no political sense and it could only have the effect of losing Nationalist seats to the Unionists, with the result that the nationalist community would be entitled to fewer Ministers.

How Sinn Fein Won the Peace

One of the hardest things to accomplish in war is an organised retreat from the battlefield. Accomplishing an organised retreat often makes the difference between complete defeat on one hand and the ability to fight another day or to continue to be able to advance the strategic objectives of a campaign in a different form. If the German Army in 1918 had conducted an orderly withdrawal, and if Germany had not suffered a collapse behind the lines induced by the Royal Navy starvation blockade and the gullibility of the German Social Democrats in the face of Wilson's '14 Points', there would have been a real 'Armistice' and the Great War would have had very different consequences and the subsequent history of Europe would have been entirely different. The formal military position in late 1918 represented a stalemate. The Entente, despite possessing a great superiority in blood and treasure, had never set foot on German soil in four years of war. It was what happened after the 'end' of the fighting in the War on November 11th that really determined its result and outcome.

After the signing of the Agreement in 1998 there was still unfinished business. The Republican Army had still to retire in good order to maintain cohesion. If it managed to complete its withdrawal from the battlefield in an orderly and disciplined manner, it would enhance the overall position of Sinn Fein and the community it stood for. It could preserve itself intact for a new campaign of a very different type. Its major advantage was that the community that produced it understood that the most important thing was to preserve its military capacity—rather than going down in defeat. The memories of 1922 that persisted in the community ensured that this happened.

Sinn Fein agreed to operate this system from a position of initial disadvantage, but it made a great success of their role in consolidating the Agreement and the Catholic community, which is for the most part satisfied with the part that it has played, rewarded them with more votes.

British attempts to subvert the Republican Peace project foundered on the inability of the media and Establishment figures to utilise the series of Whitehall manufactured "*crises*" to break the will of the Northern Catholics. They had stuck by the Provos through thick and thin during the War, realising what the Provos were doing for them was the 'only game in town', and refused to be taken in by all the talk of *'frightfulness'* in their midst. They refused to take heed of SDLP condemnations, suspecting they went beyond electoral opportunism and reflected a deeper game. At election after election they returned to the ballot box to vote Sinn Fein and put it up to the British to ensure that community bargaining power was maintained.

Part of the reason why the Northern Catholics have been impermeable to British ideas was that during the War they were subject to so much black propaganda and untruths by the State and its compliant media. They developed a healthy disregard for what was told them. It was a situation reminiscent of how Redmondite war recruiting propaganda, relatively successful in the towns and cities, fell on deaf ears in the countryside of Munster which had witnessed so much lying about the Land War. It was presumed thereafter that anything coming from Britain and its native friends was bunkum.

It is an unpalatable fact to the Ulster Unionist or to 'right-thinking' people that the Republican War gave the mass of Northern Catholics a measure of self-respect that changed everything in the North. That is one of those truths that dare not speak its name, although it is well understood within both communities. The Republican Army that faded into history did not raise the respect and confidence of the Northern Catholic community by killing people, and least of all by killing Ulster Protestants. It was entirely through the continued ability of Republicans to frustrate and outmanoeuvre the British State and through the preparedness of ordinary young men and women within local communities to sacrifice their existences for the Republican cause that produced a great lifting of confidence generally and led to the Great Transformation. Terence McSwiney's view that *"It is not those who inflict the most, but those who suffer the most who will conquer"* comes to mind here.

The Northern Catholics had been condemned to live in a political strait-jacket by the 1920 settlement and the dysfunctional form of government that was imposed on the province. That was not a situation that could create any kind of self-respect in a community. Catholics had waited for half a century for deliverance from the South from this state of affairs and when the moment of truth came, in 1969-70 they had been badly let down. Then they produced something from themselves and of themselves that began to call the shots—and not only in relation to those who kept a heel upon them locally but also in relation to those in Dublin who had let them down in their hour of need, and in relation to the imperious British State to boot. When the British State threw its vast political experience and military resources at the Republican Army and it remained standing and its volunteers coming back for more, in each new generation, the Northern Catholics knew that they had produced something very special indeed. So they stuck by it, helping it to deliver for them. And all the considerable efforts of the British and Irish States proved incapable of separating the community from the remarkable military/political development it produced by its own efforts.

CHAPTER 17

The Functional Peace

The six months following the British pulling down of the institutions to save Trimble was one of very little activity. The big beast, Reid, was replaced as Secretary of State by the smaller specimen, Paul Murphy, to signal a holding operation on the part of the British State. Blair, having made a mess of the Agreement, then went off to wage war on Iraq with the US and proceeded to turn the country (and thereafter the region) into a glacis (killing field) after 'liberating' its discordant elements from social order.

Trimble, who ruined the Unionist Party, was put out to grass by Blair and he was joined by Prof. Bew in the Upper House of the British Parliament. They complained that they were undermined by Whitehall—which, they claimed, was so intent to do a deal with Republicans that they killed the Unionist Party to draw Sinn Fein into the system. But who else was there for Blair to deal with if he was to ever solve the Irish question after *'feeling the hand of history'* on his shoulder? Blair had invested so much time and effort on *'solving'* the 'Northern Ireland' problem that he was not going to see peace and the Agreement go down for Trimble and the UUP.

Had Trimble and Lord Bew forgotten the basic fact that the solution must relate to the problem? And it was Republicans that constituted the 'Northern Ireland' problem for the British and it was Sinn Fein who had the capability of constituting it into something that could be handled, at least for the time being. And the time being is what British politics is very much about in the democratic era.

Triumph of the "*Extremes*"

In the elections to the Assembly at the end of 2003 the DUP triumphed in the Unionist bloc and Sinn Fein triumphed in the Nationalist bloc. The DUP took 30 of the 108 seats, an increase of 10 over 1998. The UUP took 27 a fall of 1. Sinn Fein won 24 seats, an increase of 6 and the SDLP took 18, a loss of 6. The Sinn Fein percentage of votes had risen to nearly 24% against 17% for the SDLP, a complete reversal of fortunes from 1998. And Sinn Fein beat Trimble's party into 2nd place. And so, all the anti-Sinn Fein manoeuvrings of the two States in support of *saving Dave,* and his 'moderate' counterpart in the Green bloc, came to nought.

After the election, the elected representatives were due to meet at the Assembly but there was no prospect of their doing so. If Trimble's strategy had been to wear down the Agreement and finally see it off he had succeeded, like Lord Nelson, in the moment of his own demise. He had signed the Agreement in 1998 for fear of something worse and cooperated in implementing it by becoming its First Minister. But thereafter he had largely concentrated on preventing it from being implemented, in conjunction with his alter-ego Donaldson. The start of devolved government was delayed for a year and a half and then it was suspended for most of the next three and a half years. And so the Democratic Unionist Party rose to dominance within the Unionist community andDonaldson (plus future leader, Arlene Foster) jumped ship to join it.

A new deal between the DUP and Sinn Fein looked very unlikely at the start of 2004. The DUP, triumphant from the election, was giving every indication that it was irretrievably committed to removing the Agreement and establishing a different system of devolution after a *'renegotiation'* of the Agreement. It was demanding the banning of Sinn Fein from Office, regardless of its electoral support, and the establishment of Cabinet government responsible to the Assembly. Of course, its heart's desire was a restoration of the old Stormont system with itself taking the place of the Unionist Party. But that was hardly a possibility after 1998. However, it was becoming clear, even in 2004, that Paisley was intent on making a settlement in a way that Trimble never was.

The other cause for optimism was that for the first time in 80 years a functional all Ireland political party existed in the shape of Sinn Fein. The Catholic community in the North had protected Sinn Fein from every manoeuvre made against it and the party had responded to the challenge by increasing its representation. And it did so as a means of self-preservation as much as anything else.

High-powered talks were held between the British Government and the DUP and between the British Government and Sinn Fein at Leeds Castle in September 2004. The SDLP had a peripheral presence at Leeds Castle, denoting its fall from grace.

Northern Bank and the McCartney Killing

Two incidents temporarily derailed any chance of progress being made between Sinn Fein and the DUP. A large bank robbery took place in Belfast about a week after the DUP scuppered an attempt to manoeuvre it into coalition with Sinn Fein. The Chief Constable said he believed it to be the work of the IRA. Taoiseach Ahern said he 'knew' that the Provos were planning the bank robbery when they pretended to be negotiating a settlement with him. But, when the Taoiseach was challenged to have them arrested and charged with the crime, he desisted from his allegations.

The van in which the money was taken from the Bank was caught on CCTV, and was followed on a series of cameras until it disappeared somehow. A bank clerk was prosecuted, but, in the absence of evidence, the case failed. Only one identifiable bit of the stolen money was ever found. The fact that it was found in a Social Club of the RUC was immediately understood by all 'right-thinking' people to be proof positive that the RUC had not done the robbery but the Provos had.

A man from Cork, who was a property speculator, was later tried on a charge of receiving some of the stolen money, knowing it to be the proceeds of the Bank Robbery. But no evidence was presented that the man had received any of the money taken in the robbery, even though he was convicted of possession of it. Some Northern Bank notes were found amidst notes in his wheelie-bin. But there was no evidence that they had come from his house or directly into his hands from the robbery. However, this 'evidence' was taken to be good enough to surmise that they had come from the robbed bank at the other end of the country and to conclude from that that the Provos had robbed it.

The Northern Bank robbery was said to have been conducted like a military operation, but that is often the case with organised crime gangs. It could have been the work of dissident Republicans. Or it could have been organised by some arm of the British deep state in the Six Counties, intent on scuppering a deal that would put republicans into government.

It has become part of the received wisdom that the robbery was the work of the Provos, despite the lack of evidence, arrests or charges pressed. Jeffrey Donaldson has said he is perplexed as to why the IRA should conduct a high-profile robbery at such a sensitive time. But he too firmly believes it is the case.

In another incident blamed on the Provos, a Belfast man, Robert McCartney, was killed after a friend was involved in a bar-fight with some men, who were or had been, allegedly, Provos. Sinn Fein was held responsible for this act, as well as for the Northern Bank robbery, on the grounds that the IRA was said to be still in existence and operational because its former volunteers still socialised together and acted in a comradely manner during a fight.

The McCartney killing was a tragic incident in a pub brawl, but it was hyped into an international incident. McCartney's sisters received big media coverage for their campaign to get a criminal conviction against IRA men involved in the fracas. In the event they were set up for a painful disillusionment, finding there are limits to the effectiveness of these State-sponsored politically motivated campaigns.

Following these events the main feature of the 2005 UK election campaign was the deployment of the propaganda apparatus of two States—led by RTE and the BBC—in the attempt to use the death of Mr. McCartney to collapse the Republican vote. The pretence was made that Sinn Fein was the oppressor of the Northern Catholic community rather than its creation and representative, and it was hoped to implant this impression as a false memory in voters.

The purpose was to engineer an SDLP revival that would make a DUP/SDLP coalition possible in a future revived Assembly so that Sinn Fein could be isolated. The SDLP candidate in West Belfast, Alex Atwood, was quick to support the Chief Constable's statement about the Northern Bank robbery. But the SDLP vote nevertheless collapsed in the constituency.

The Southern Government sent two Cabinet Members North to canvass for the SDLP and to solicit Unionist votes for it in a couple of other constituencies, helping it to gain South Belfast on a split Unionist vote, and to hold Foyle (Derry), though with a reduced majority. It was said that some Unionists voted SDLP to prevent Sinn Fein becoming the largest party in the North—though in the event there was no danger of that with the UUP being reduced to 1 seat to the DUP's 9. The SDLP gained one seat but lost another, Newry & Armagh, by a landslide to Sinn Fein.

Around June 2005 Fr. Reid, of the Clonard Monastery, who had acted as conciliator and facilitator in the Republican peace initiative, was provoked into saying that the Dublin politicians were becoming the greatest danger to the Peace Process through their behaviour and he told them in effect to shut up.

The game of blaming Republicans had been going on at this point for 20 years, ever since Sinn Fein had entered electoral politics in earnest. It had been encouraged to enter electoral politics, only to find the propaganda apparatuses of two States deployed against it in the Peace Process and continually in the electoral arena. The propaganda enjoyed considerable success where it did not matter, across the media and in the better parts of Dublin and beyond, but it was a complete failure where it really counted. The only place where blaming the Republicans counted was in the Catholic community in the North but the Northern Catholics proved to be beyond the reach of the propagandists of the British and Irish Governments and of the Unionist Party. They maintained a healthy disrespect for anything that was churned out by the media to get them to desert Sinn Fein and they put their crosses on their ballot papers increasingly next to those who had made the settlement.

The Republican Army bows out

When Trimble was First Minister, Arms Decommissioning was detached from its conditional place in the Agreement and made into an unconditional demand in a manner that was intended to actually obstruct its achievement. This was clearly not because Unionists thought the Republicans would revert to military activity as an adjunct of political office in a guns *and* government strategy. It was because the basic spiritual need of Unionism had been affronted by the Agreement, and, once the State propaganda conditioning of Blair's Press Secretary, Tom Kelly, wore off, Unionist unwillingness to share power without a prior humiliation of the enemy re-asserted itself.

As Trimble gave way to Paisley, and the DUP Leader gave something of the appearance of reaching an agreement with Sinn Fein, Ahern supported him in making a decommissioning demand which Paisley had frankly declared to be for the purpose of humiliating Republicans—getting them to *'wear sack cloth and ashes'*. When the IRA rejected that demand, and refused to implement the Decommissioning measure which would have been part of the deal, Ahern turned on Sinn Fein in a reckless manner, and made wild accusations which he hoped would break the Republican will. Sinn Fein handled what Ahern and his Justice Minister, Michael McDowell, threw at them and actually emerged stronger as a consequence of it.

The Northern Catholics had by then asserted themselves in such independent substance that they no longer took orders from Dublin, as their community had done in the past. At this point the practical assumption on all sides was that the Republican Army had called off the War for good and had no intention of resuming it. Anybody who was seriously concerned that a general Peace should be the outcome, and who had any sense of reality at all, understood that the Republican Army must be accorded a fair degree of autonomy during the process of demobilisation (partly in order to curb other potential military developments that might emerge if the process was not handled responsibly). But some saw that as turning a blind eye to *'criminality'* and wanted the Republican Army to disarm, with instant law and order springing up in the North maintained by the official forces of the law. The idea that new and ideal social forces would instantly emerge to replace the imperfect products of reality is really one for the birds. That was shown in Yeltsin's Russia, in post-Saddam Iraq, and in Syria where, when Government authority was removed, the gap was filled by Islamic State and other groupings.

The demand that began to emerge at this point was that Sinn Fein should end its association with the Republican Army and condemn all forms of behaviour that might ensue in the transition to Peace and 'normality'—even though that was a totally unrealistic demand. However, the IRA went ahead and initiated the decommissioning process itself, in conjunction with General de Chastelain's Independent International Monitoring Commission—as distinct from the fake group headed by Lord Alderdice which impersonated the IIMC by giving itself a title with very similar initials.

This was another confidence trick played by the British Government during the Peace Process. The Independent International Commission on Decommissioning was a formal part of the Good Friday Agreement. It was chaired by General De Chastelain, former Canadian Chief of Defence Staff and Ambassador, and had its own investigative team, and was independent of the Government. It acted strictly in accordance with the remit given to it by the Agreement and the General refused to play politics for the British Government.

The British then set up a Committee to play politics for them and selected someone who would head it. The Governments called the new body the Independent Monitoring Commission. Its members were all British Government appointees and it had no investigative apparatus of its own. What it therefore knew was what the British Government and its security services told it and it issued reports to serve the political purpose of the moment, in competition with the real independent body.

The Republican Army made a statement of final decommissioning in September 2005. The decommissioning was supervised by de Chastelain's team, with two clergymen as observers and the arms were "*banjaxed*" in McGuinness' words. Having engaged in this disarmament, the new Republican Army passed into history. This unilateral disarmament angered the Democratic Unionist Party, which felt it had been swindled out of a moral triumph over evil that could be played out to the world. And the British Government's own monitoring body had no part in the process, which was carried out strictly within the terms of the Agreement.

The political situation at this point was that the DUP had won the Protestant Election and was refusing to form a devolved administration with Sinn Fein, which had won the Catholic Election. The stated reason for the DUP refusal was that the IRA had not engaged in final disarmament along the lines of the DUP demand that the destruction of arms should be filmed and the film made public.

In its Election Manifesto for the May 2005 British General Election the DUP stated that power-sharing with Sinn Fein under d'Hondt was out of the question. It therefore had to persuade the SDLP to form a coalition—in breach of the Agreement. The SDLP, however, was not prepared to enter a Power-Sharing Government without Sinn Fein. Earlier in the year, in February, Mark Durkan claimed on Radio 4's *Westminster Hour* that Blair had asked him to go into coalition with the DUP but he said he could never be sure if Blair would then secretly negotiate with Republicans, having banked his promise.

It was agreed with the Dublin Government that there should then be a six-month delay, to see if the Decommissioning held, before it was put to the DUP that its reason for refusing to form a government had been met. The IMC delivered a report at the end of January 2006, saying that the Provos had met their obligations. But it became evident that the DUP was still no more willing to take part in the formation of a government under the terms of the Agreement than it had been the year before.

In February 2006 Paisley was still not a believer in the potential of the political process being pursued by Sinn Fein. He told the DUP Conference that there were—

"a mighty host of forces intent on pushing down the throats of the Ulster people the blatant lie that the IRA has decommissioned all its weapons. That falsehood was so blatant even Lord Haw-Haw would have blushed to utter it" (Irish Independent, 6.2.06).

The Policing Obstacle

Having cleared the decommissioning obstacle—although not to the satisfaction of all—the next hurdle Sinn Fein had to clear was policing. At the time of the Ceasefire Sinn Fein had demanded the disbandment of the RUC. In 2000 the party reduced its demands to full implementation of the Patten Commission report on Policing. The Patton recommendations, however, suffered substantial dilution by the British Government. The SDLP was enticed on to the new District Policing Partnership Boards but Sinn Fein declined to take its seats, judging that Patton had largely not been implemented and only 11 of the original proposals had not suffered amendment. Although some of Sinn Fein's concerns were addressed in the Police Act of 2001 that set up the new Police Service Of Northern Ireland in place of the Royal Ulster Constabulary, Republicans judged that not enough had changed to justify supporting the police. They were proved correct in their estimation by the role of the police in facilitating the pulling down of the political institutions in 2002.

On 13th May 2006 the *Irish Times* front-page head-line read: *'Paisley Says Progress Hinges on SF Support for Police'*. Another headline on an inside article read: *'There is No Way Forward without Resolving Police Issue'*. Both articles were written by Frankie Millar, the former UUP member who had become a journalist and now inclined toward Paisley, and the message of the headlines was that devolved government could be up and running at Stormont if Sinn Fein joined the Policing Board. But the operative word was '*could*'. Paisley would not move without Sinn Fein toeing his line on policing—but neither might he move with it doing so. And he was also insisting that the PSNI had to be 'fully embraced' by Republicans as well as a whole series of other things.

Millar revealed that IRA Arms Decommissioning and Disbandment were not enough for Paisley:

> "You do all that, but that is not sufficient. We must be able to build upon something that is a democracy…' Paisley confirms this means provision for 'collective responsibility' in any executive, 'and especially the fact that you cannot forever be stuck, that you have to get agreement between two diverse agencies. There's bound to be a time when we have to go to a majority weighted vote. I am prepared to have a weighted majority. I'm prepared to go as far as any real democracy goes, but I'm not prepared to tie my country in with people who at the end of the day want to destroy it.' …On one specific, he has previously said he would not accept the concept of co-equal First and Deputy First Ministers…"

That was the DUP position in 2006. But it had eventually to abandon its objective of attempting to create a normal Executive with Cabinet Government and a 'democracy' of 'Northern Ireland.'

Policing was a thorny issue for the Republican Movement, which was always a conglomeration of people with different motivations. These were, however, united in their belief that the conditions of life under the Stormont period should never be permitted to return. And the conditions of life in the Stormont period for Catholics were little more than the experience of being policed by armed Protestants. Many would never accept any sort of policing, given the policing experiences of the past. But the logic of the new Republican strategy meant that the policing issue had to be dealt with so that one community would no longer be policed by the other and the conflict in armed form did not begin again.

Allowing that the entity called 'Northern Ireland' had to exist for the time being, the most obnoxious feature of it was the fact that the power of policing was farmed out to the Protestant community (with some disconnected Catholic involvement for practical reasons). This meant that the communal antagonism was conducted on grossly unequal terms. But the effect of the reform was to reduce the inequality as regards policing. Reform in policing was essential unless this extensive area of public life were to be surrendered completely to the other side. The Catholic community could not exist in perpetuity with a police force that was completely unaccountable to it. Such a situation would ultimately lead to friction and conflict.

In a transitional situation, the control of an indigenous police force, or a large section of it, was vital. There would always be significant opposition amongst Ulster Protestants to equality within the Six Counties and eventually to majority rule in an all-Ireland context. A Unionist-dominated police force could not be expected to keep order in such a situation.

The Republican Army had developed its own form of policing, through necessity, in the areas in which it had substantial support. This was performed by the Republican Civil Administration that had grown out of the 1975 Truce. The Civil Administration system, although functional and generally widely supported in areas like West Belfast, was not adequate to the situation after the Agreement of Good Friday. An attempt was made to develop a system of Community Restorative Justice to put in its place. It is not clear if this was a serious attempt to establish a parallel Republican system of policing in justice or something that could be used as a bargaining chip in Sinn Fein agreeing to work inside the policing and justice structures of the North. However, the scheme met with strong opposition from Michael McDowell (the anti-Republican Irish Minister for Justice/Tánaiste) and from Mitchell Reiss (the US policy advisor).

Eventually Sinn Fein obtained sufficient reforms in policing arrangements to enable it to bring most of its hinterland to acceptance of a still imperfect system as part of the price to get devolved government up and running in 'Northern Ireland'.

However, Sinn Fein acceptance of the PSNI prompted a minor split among Republicans. In 2008 a section left the organisation after refusing an order to collaborate with the new police. This group, which was disenchanted with Sinn Fein strategy—viewed as achieving equality for Catholics, rather than Irish unity—went on to form *1916 Societies*.

The belief also developed among Republicans who had formerly supported the Sinn Fein project that the Good Friday Agreement had no dynamic in it towards Irish unity. These issues were argued over most noticeably in East Tyrone.

Another set of opponents in Belfast formed the Republican Network for Unity.

These Republican groupings differed from the Dissidents of 32 County Sovereignty Committee, Oglaigh na Eireann and the Real IRA, in being supportive of the IRA Ceasefire as the most advisable policy at the time. But they would not bring themselves to give aid to the police against any Republicans who might choose to continue war.

Sinn Fein managed to cross the policing Rubicon intact, and its support in the community strengthened as a result. The transfer of policing to Stormont was the most sensitive measure involved in the 1998 Agreement.

Under the new system there was to be some kind of supra-communal or trans-communal system. Sinn Fein was reluctant to play a part in the Policing Boards until the RUC was remade. That was at the time a strong Unionist point against it. Then Sinn Fein began to participate and this too caused Unionist hostility.

Paisley's purpose

Paisley had agreed with Molyneaux, the Ulster Unionist leader at the time of the Republican Ceasefire of 1994 that this event was *"the worst thing that ever happened to us"*. In 1998 the DUP understood the Agreement as a Unionist defeat in its Referendum Manifesto:

> "The Agreement will lead to a united Ireland... The Government of Ireland Act which established the supreme authority of the United Kingdom Parliament over Northern Ireland is abolished immediately. In contrast the illegal claims in the Irish Republic's constitution are merely amended... The Agreement takes precedence over the Act of Union" (*It's Right to say 'NO' to the united Ireland Process*).

However, having opposed the Agreement that the Ceasefire produced and having threatened to smash it along with Sinn Fein, Paisley began to conceive a different strategy in relation to it and the Republicans. Paisley realised that the Agreement of 1998 made it impossible for the DUP (and Unionism in general) to have any say in the governing of the territory that had been set up for it to govern, without a willingness to share power with Sinn Fein. Paisley decided that sharing the cake with Republicans was preferable to no cake at all. But Paisley also had a purpose when he decided to operate the Agreement, and that was to implicate Sinn Fein in it, in conjunction with the strong Unionist presence that his party represented. And this made him amenable to devolving policing authority, and binding Sinn Fein into policing.

In doing this Paisley was branded a 'Lundy' by the 'moderates' of the Unionist Party. While the Unionist Party was the major Protestant party, the story was that it could not operate the Agreement wholeheartedly because it had to guard itself against the DUP. Then the DUP became the major party and, against expectations, undertook to operate the GFA with some goodwill. If the apologia of the Unionist Party had been in earnest, it would have welcomed this new departure by the DUP and helped to consolidate it. Instead of doing that, it reversed roles with the DUP and accused it of selling-out to Sinn Fein. That is to say, it adopted what was called the *'extremist'* position when held by the DUP, and set about attempting to destabilise the developing DUP/SF accommodation.

The political Commentator Alex Kane has said that it was Peter Robinson rather than Paisley who delivered the DUP over the line to make a deal with Sinn Fein in 2007. He has suggested that Robinson saw in the Summer of 1999 that the Good Friday Agreement was not going to be wrecked and that the DUP would have to win the battle with Trimble within Unionism and accept the deal for a share of power. Paisley's instincts were against a deal with Sinn Fein up to 2005 and it was Robinson who kept him in check to pursue the logic of the new strategy (IN 24.1.14).

The anti-Paisley campaign launched by the Unionist Party, appealing to the most primitive element of Ulster Protestant culture, operated on an element of the DUP which had gone along with the Paisley approach in the first instance. The Unionist 'moderates', being overtaken by the Unionist 'extremists', set about recovering ground by attacking the 'extremists' for selling out to Republicans. But in the official nomenclature the UUP remained 'moderate', even when attempting to destabilise the DUP/SF arrangement and the DUP remained 'extremist', even when making a deal with Sinn Fein.

The game was to destabilise the deal made between the 'extremists' who were acting moderately. And the SDLP attempted to join the game on the other side, but with even less success. Any attempt by the 'moderates' to outflank the 'extremes' on the oppositionist edge of politics inevitably led to a bolstering of the most extremes—the Loyalists and Republican Dissidents.

It was therefore a counter-productive activity for the 'moderates'—unless they wished to throw the situation back into its fundamentals in which the extremes returned to flourish. There are indications that this lesson is still lost on the 'moderates' in NI politics.

The DUP Accepts

The October 2006 St. Andrew's Agreement enabled the DUP insistence that they had renegotiated the 1998 Agreement to be squared with the Sinn Fein insistence that it could not be renegotiated. There was no referendum held, despite the Dublin Government suggesting it, and despite the fact that this would have legitimised St. Andrew's as superseding Good Friday.

The Agreement involved a number of changes to governmental procedures in the light of the previous experience of devolution.

The 2006 St Andrew's Agreement Act provided for a new Ministerial Code of Conduct and placed a duty upon Ministers and Junior Ministers to act in accordance with the provisions on Ministerial accountability of the Code. It also amended the 1998 Act to allow the Assembly to refer important Ministerial decisions to the full Executive. It did this by enabling 30 MLAs to initiate such a referral within seven days of a Ministerial decision or notification of decision. This was done at the insistence of the DUP which was concerned at *'unaccountable'* Sinn Fein ministerial *'fiefdoms'* in the lapsed institutions, when Martin McGuinness and Bairbre deBrun had used the independence of their Offices to take decisions that were unpalatable to Unionists, such as the abolition of the 11 plus exam.

St. Andrew's also amended the Pledge of Office to require Ministerial commitment to participate fully in the Executive, the North-South Ministerial Council (NSMC) and the British-Irish Council (BIC). This was included at the insistence of Sinn Fein which was determined to prevent the non-participation of Unionist Ministers in cross-border institutions. It also amended the provisions of the 1998 Act that dealt with the NSMC and BIC, providing for the Minister or Junior Minister responsible for an issue under consideration at a Council meeting to be entitled to attend. This was also a demand of Sinn Fein which was determined to prevent Unionist Ministers from excluding SF from participation in cross-Border institutions as Trimble had done earlier. Finally, it created new arrangements for the appointment of the First and Deputy First Ministers, who were to be nominated by the largest parties in each of the two largest designations within the Assembly. This was conceded to the DUP, so that it would not have to nominate a Sinn Fein DFM as part of a joint team to the OFMDFM.

A final amendment was a change to the Good Friday Agreement rules so that a Petition of Concern could now be raised within the Executive as well as in the Assembly. This provided the DUP with a potential block on Nationalist Executive actions if it could muster 3 Ministers with the First Minister. The effect of this reform did not become apparent until years later when it began to be put into use by Robinson, under pressure from his party, after Paisley's departure.

There was considerable disquiet over the St Andrew's deal within the DUP and it would not have been carried without Paisley's imprimatur and Robinson's drive. And, although the DUP agreed the St. Andrew's deal with Sinn Fein, the party still tried to avoid going into government with Republicans. The DUP programme for the election held under the St. Andrew's modification of the Good Friday Agreement included a promise to bring about the ousting of Sinn Fein, the largest Catholic party, by the British Government. It knew that instances of Republican 'misbehaviour' which it could bring forward would not bring about a cross-community vote to sanction Sinn Fein and relied on pressurising the Secretary of State to do what a cross-community vote would not do. The DUP objective was still 'voluntary' power-sharing with the SDLP as a stepping-stone to a revived majority-rule constitution in place of the 1998 Constitution. That was its essential programme in 2007 going into the Assembly Elections.

The Sinn Fein policy was to make the 'Northern Ireland' institutions work as a transitional stage to an abolition of the sub-government.

The DUP programme was frustrated by the election result in which Sinn Fein held its ground and actually strengthened its position as the dominant Nationalist bloc party. In 1998 the SDLP had got 22% of the vote and 24 seats in the Assembly whilst SF had 18% and 18 seats. By 2003 the SDLP achieved 17% and 18 seats to SF's 24% and 24 seats. By 2007 the turnabout was complete with the SDLP declining to 15% of the vote and 16 seats to SF's 36% and 28 seats.

Twisting the DUP arm

Seeing the failure of its latest propaganda offensive against Sinn Fein, the British Government instead turned the screws on Paisley. As a result the DUP entered government with Sinn Fein in May 2007.

There are three grounds for the DUP accepting the invitation to go into government with Sinn Fein.

Firstly, there was the threat of Plan B—*Joint Authority*, exercised by the two Governments, alluded to by Paisley himself when he told a BBC Radio show: "How could I have faced my people if I had allowed this country to have the union destroyed and a setting up of a joint government by the south of Ireland?" (David Gordon, *The Fall of the House of Paisley*, p.14).

Secondly, Westminster engaged in a direct form of economic and cultural blackmail against Unionist voters. This was through a big raft of legislation that Blair threatened to impose on Northern Ireland if no devolved administration was formed. The DUP opposed these measures, which could have severely damaged the party's future electoral prospects. The measures included Water Charges for every household, an Irish Language Act, an end to academic selection, and a streamlining of Local Government.

The logic here was that the DUP could claim credit for preventing these measures if it was prepared to resurrect the Good Friday Agreement devolutionary institutions. If the DUP left the power with Westminster to impose these changes, it would be blamed by the Protestant electorate for measures favourable to nationalists, detrimental to unionists, and imposing extra costs on every household.

A third motivation was that Paisley had come round to the view that the only way of obstructing the drift toward a United Ireland was to gradually implicate Sinn Fein in the government of 'Northern Ireland' and to attempt to narrow its horizons in the process.

The alternative was for Paisley to call Blair's bluff, as he had the year before, and to play for more concessions that would have really broken the Agreement. This would have pleased Robinson and others who seemed reluctant to enter government with Sinn Fein. In the event, Paisley must have judged that the prospects of successfully achieving a fundamental change in the Agreement were minimal. So perhaps Paisley used the threat of Plan B—the Irish Republic exercising governing powers along with Britain in a Joint Authority—to pull the stubborn elements in his party into line in accepting the deal with Sinn Fein.

But there were attempts made to subvert Paisley's accommodation with Sinn Finn and make the discontent within Paisley's rank and file effective. This resulted in some loss of electoral support. But, the defections from the DUP did not go to the 'moderates' of the UUP, who began to stir up fundamentalist passions against Paisley. It went into the birth of a third Unionist movement, the Traditional Unionist Voice, which split the Unionist vote in the 2009 European Election and enabled Sinn Fein to top the poll.

The DUP accepted the St. Andrew's Agreement as meeting some of its demands for an alteration in the Good Friday Agreement, but its position of primacy in the Unionist camp meant it did not feel obliged to implement it. If it rejected the St. Andrew's Agreement outright, the probability is that an alternative, a kind of Joint Authority by London and Dublin, would have been put into operation. It obviously did not want that. But neither did it really want to sit in government with Sinn Fein. So, whilst the DUP endorsed St.Andrew's, it insisted that there was a set of further conditions to be met before the St.Andrew's Agreement was fully implemented. As a result, the DUP dragged its heels on the issue of Transfer of Policing and Justice Powers to the Assembly, in the expectation that the Tories would win the next Westminster Election. (In the event, it did not get the result it hoped for.)

If Unionism had accepted the Agreement in the first instance when the SDLP was the leading Catholic party, there might have been a different outcome to the Good Friday Agreement initiative, with a more compliant spirit developing amongst Republicans. What Unionism did though was try to diminish Republican standing in the Catholic community, and thereby it maximised Republican dissent from the Agreement. By the time the DUP became the leading Unionist Party and the SDLP faded from the picture, the only prospect for devolution was through a sharing of power with Sinn Fein. Probably only Paisley had the stature within Unionism to implicate Unionists in working with Sinn Fein in a functional accommodation.

The Centre Can Hold?

The long search for a 'centre-ground' in 'Northern Ireland' was finally successful when the 'extremes' of the DUP and Sinn Fein came together in a devolved government. Paisley, for his part, overcame his fundamentalist urge to humiliate Sinn Fein and struck a deal with it instead. And Catholics began to free themselves from the mirage of 'Constitutional' Nationalism, taking a rational view of the predicament that Partition had put them in, and backing the party which had been the means of improving their position through warfare transformed into politics.

The campaign against Paisley was fed from two opposite sources—the extreme extremists in the Unionist movement and the moderate extremists in the Nationalist camp. The latter had made Paisley their bogeyman for 40 years and it was intolerable that he should be the Unionist who made a workable settlement. From the 1960s Paisley had been viewed as a *"Demagogue"* by Nationalist Ireland (The *Irish News* headline on his death in September 2014 was *'Death of a Demagogue'*). In 1970 Andrew Boyd published a famous and popular book called *'Holy War in Belfast'* that argued that much of the trouble in the North had been caused by Protestant demagogues like Roaring Hanna—whose statue at the bottom of the Antrim Road was destroyed by a mysterious explosion shortly afterwards.

Andrew Boyd was a major influence in *The Irish News* at the time and the newspaper greeted his book with headlining attention. The basis of it was the neat 'transformation thesis' that seemed to explain why the people of the United Irish had become rabid Unionists in the 1820s through a doctrinal dispute within Protestantism. It was nonsense, of course, for a number of reasons that space does not permit me going into. Suffice to say that many former United Irishmen, like Samuel Neilson, had become supporters of the Union before the dispute. And Boyd took no account of the much greater *'transformation'* that overtook Ulster Protestantism—the 1859 Revival.

Demagogues were much in evidence in turning the Protestants into Unionists in Boyd's account and Paisley was the latest, and greatest, of them. Similarly, the South needed a scapegoat for Protestant hostility to Southern advances, to avoid pinning the blame where it really was deserved. There was much sniping done by the Southern press at Paisley and the DUP. Paisley represented the bogey man on the Unionist side, corresponding to the Republican bogey on the Northern Nationalist side. And so the Demagogue Paisley was ideal for demonising, as Northern intransigence personified. But then the intransigent became the dealmaker.

Around 1970 a common Nationalist explanation of unionism was that its working classes were the dupes of aristocracy. Perhaps that was due to seeing the Londonderrys and Brookeboroughs at the head of the Unionist movement. But it has been a generation since the last two aristocratic Prime Ministers of 'Northern Ireland', O'Neill and Chichester-Clarke, were blown away by the developing conflict and Unionism democratised itself down to Paisley.

The reason why an aristocracy imposed itself at the head of Unionism had nothing to do with servility. It was due to the extensive links with governing circles in Britain this class once had, which proved indispensable to the resisting of Home Rule.

Once Britain began to detach itself from 'Ulster' in 1920 the aristocracy at the head of the Unionist Party lived on borrowed time. As long as it conducted affairs to the satisfaction of the unionist mass base it remained at the head of the movement. However, when its leverage over London appeared to have vanished in 1969-70 and nationalists began to run rings around Unionism, it was cast aside.

Paisley developed his DUP into the working class unionist party and then the unionist party. He democratised Unionist politics in the only way it could be democratised in the absence of the parties of State. Paisley was successful because he adjusted to the changed political circumstances that faced his community. The Westminster Government had interposed itself between Unionism and Nationalism, fighting the Republican Army with its own army, but making concessions to Dublin at the expense of Unionism, in order to defeat the IRA.

Paisley's DUP learnt to deal with the complex and shifting Westminster manoeuvring in a way that the official Unionists had been incapable of since the fall of Faulkner. Paisley destroyed any number of Westminster schemes to undermine his community in the short-term. He held the last ditch even if the ground around it was being occupied by the enemy. He did this through shadow-boxing rather than actually fighting, having the prudence to realise that fighting would be what John Hume wanted and would prove fatal. Having finally seen off the official Unionist Party he had nothing more to conquer within Unionism and needed to do something else. He had also seen off his original enemy, Rome, in Ireland—if not the Fenians who had followed it.

There is a strong sense in which Nationalist Ireland made Paisley the man he was. He was a sectarian rabble-rouser on the fringe of Protestant religious culture when he emerged as the handy demon of Dublin. And being the demon of Dublin turned him into the hero of Protestant Ulster since, if the Nationalists hated him that much, there had to be something substantial about him.

Paisley was interviewed by BBC journalist Andrew Marr in 2014. He claimed he had 'smashed Sinn Fein' by driving it into politics: "I did smash them because I took away their main plank. Their main plank was that they would not recognise the British government. Now they are in part of the British government" (IN March 10th).

Marr did not press the matter any further. As a British political correspondent with intimate access to the 'Westminster bubble', he knew very well that 'Northern Ireland' is purposely a place set apart from *'British government'*. But it is something he could not say or base a question on, since it was one of the fundamentals of good behaviour that journalists, if they value their careers, should not stray into thinking too deeply about. It is part of the great consensus that 'Northern Ireland' exists apart from the party conflict at Westminster that is Marr's bread and butter. 'Needs must' was the watchword at Westminster and the less said the better!

Paisley too knew that 'Northern Ireland' is a place set apart. About 25 years earlier he adopted the policy of bringing it into the British system and even proposed integration at one point. He was presumably talked out of it by some powerful figures behind the scenes, and retreated from a policy of 'integration' to the firmer ground of local Protestant/Catholic squabbling in an assembly, which was in his background and is also the main ground of 'Northern Ireland' politics.

Paisley upset all calculations—except those of Sinn Fein—by making a deal with Republicans. Blair said to McGuinness at a private meeting after the DUP victory in 2007: how are we going to get Trimble back now for a deal? McGuinness told Blair to forget Trimble because he was confident that the real deal was going to be done with Paisley and the DUP. Blair was sceptical (having put the best years of his life into 'saving Dave') but McGuinness was proved dead right.

A Prophecy?

Back in 1971, at the height of the War, Daithi O'Connell of Sinn Fein made the following observation about the Rev. Paisley after he had established the DUP:

> "He is... perhaps the most genuine representative of the unionist viewpoint of the north... On that basis we look to the people who are genuine representatives for meaningful dialogue... Paisley, like ourselves, is realistic... We have noted with interest the development of Paisley's social conscience... We know for a fact that in his constituency he gives equal treatment to Protestants and Roman Catholics alike... We realise that over the years Paisley has changed. Lately, we have heard much more of him as the politician rather than the Minister of religion" (Belfast Newsletter, 13.12.71).

O'Connell derided the Ulster Unionist *'fur-coat brigade'* as unrepresentative of Protestant Ulster and for being not as consequential as the DUP. The understanding seems to have been there from the early days that a deal with Paisley was possible to do, was likely to stick, and to prove the most likely of arrangements in ending the conflict. Paisley was earmarked from the beginning as a man whom Sinn Fein could do business with—and meaningful, practical business at that. And so it came to pass.

Paisley not only proved Blair's initial instincts wrong about the possibility of a deal with Sinn Fein he also upset the calculations of the DUP. Resentment within the DUP over the deal with Sinn Fein led to Paisley's retirement under pressure from his lieutenants. Paisley was accused of too much amiability in public with McGuinness—their affable relationship leading them to be called *'the chuckle brothers'* by the media.

Paisley had been very useful to the DUP in doing the dirty deed with Sinn Fein. Only he could have carried it off and given it sufficient legitimacy. But, once he had done it, he had outlived his usefulness and he was ditched by his party and his Church. The concern that a dynasty might emerge through Ian Junior, who was sidelined when a building development scandal was utilised to see him off with his father.

Many in the DUP probably thought they could revert to a simple hostility to Sinn Fein—but within the power-sharing structure laid on for them by Paisley, so that they might have it both ways. But they found that they couldn't. They found they had to play the game because Sinn Fein still had the power under the d'Hondt system to ensure that there was no other game to be played. Robinson could not take over from Paisley without the consent of Sinn Fein. Such was the logic of the ingenious system devised by the architects of the GFA. And any hopes that Gordon Brown, the son of the manse who succeeded Blair as British Premier, would be more sympathetic to Unionism were quickly dashed.

Sinn Fein eventually agreed that Robinson should take over as First Minister, and then effectively prevented him from establishing anything like Cabinet government. Robinson maintained the policy of Paisley and the party had to fall into line. Despite the St Andrew's reform/renegotiation of the 1998 Agreement, the various Ministries remained largely independent of each other within the Executive. The DUP conducted its Departments independently when Trimble was First Minister, but aimed to bring about Cabinet Government when it became the major party. It failed to do so. However, what it achieved was a strengthening of the veto points of the GFA system that would make it dysfunctional if the main partners in government began to fall out.

Bringing about change in an orderly way is difficult under the power-division system which operates and which was strengthened at St Andrew's. Legislation on contentious issues is all but impossible under the double-mandate safeguards requirement of the devolved system. There must be administrative autonomy for the various Ministers if there is to be any government at all. Without that there is paralysis, as was to be found out in time. Initially, however, DUP/Sinn Fein devolution began working so well that police powers were then devolved—the last piece in the jigsaw and a thing inconceivable under the UUP/SDLP-dominated Executive. And a touch of desperation engulfed the former centre—that now constituted the fringe parties. Something of a *de facto* coalition against the functioning Executive by the SDLP and the UUP emerged—despite the fact they were members of it themselves.

The Illusory Opposition

Having failed to flourish in the Paradise of its making, the SDLP flirted with unravelling its own creation with the absurd proposal for the construction of an Opposition at Stormont—in other words the creation of something that in large part began 'The Troubles' in the first place. In the Parliamentary system it is essential that an Opposition can be an alternative Government, but that runs counter to the essence of the GFA, which empowers all parties according to their elected representation

The Unionist Leader who succeeded Trimble, Sir Reg Empey, suggested what amounted to a kind of losers' Executive to circumvent the declining election results of the UUP and SDLP. He called for the scrapping of the d'Hondt system, which distributes Ministries according party strength in the Assembly. He said that "there was a role for a 'real opposition' like that seen in the US and other democracies" (IN 9.8.07).

It was increasingly argued in the 'moderate' media that the SDLP should join forces with the UUP and thus constitute an Opposition within Stormont through which a 'normal' political system might develop. In March 2013 Brid Rogers, the former SDLP Agricultural Minister, called on the SDLP to give up its one remaining Ministry in the Executive and take up the position of Opposition in the Stormont parliament (IN 9.3.13). Margaret Ritchie and Dolores Kelly repeated this call at the SDLP Conference in November 2013.

Patrick Murphy in an *Irish News* column entitled *'Stormont's d'Hondt set-up haunts SDLP'* put forward the fullest case for Opposition and undermined that case in the same breath in an interesting series of thoughts:

> "The theory supporting power sharing is that democratic elections can never remove a Unionist government in a state designed to have an inbuilt

Unionist majority... So power-sharing is seen as our best option. Here's a thought how worse off would we be if Stormont had been run by the Unionist majority for the past six years?... Why are there no non-sectarian parties to argue the case? Perhaps that has to do with the institutionalised communal bloc system that the SDLP insisted on in 1998? Perhaps it is to do with SDLP opposition to non-sectarian politics in the form of Labour organisation in the province? And perhaps it is to do with what 'Northern Ireland' was meant to be in 1920? The SDLP was the architect of the present power-sharing system. The party's weakness was its interpretation of the concept. Does power sharing mean sharing power voluntarily across the two communities or compulsorily across all elected parties? Initially it simply meant the inclusion of non-Unionists in government but the SDLP extended it to mean the inclusion of every major party. It advocated the d'Hondt system, a complex mathematical formula for awarding Cabinet seats for all elected parties. Is that power-sharing or an example of one for everybody in the audience? John Hume insisted on these provisions when there were some suggestions from his devolutionary colleagues that they did not need to be so robust. But it most probably boiled down to Hume's calculation that a Sinn Fein presence was very necessary in the Executive to act as a check on Unionist desire for majority rule. Or perhaps he just did not entirely trust his colleagues in being an effective bulwark against Unionism on their own?" (IN 8.3.13).

That last paragraph really gets at the crux of the matter and what separated Hume from the party he led. Hume realised, it seems, that the SDLP was fundamentally a protest movement and did not have the skill of political manoeuvre that could transform it from a party of protest into a government.

Murphy then suggested how voluntary coalition and opposition would work in practice: leading to a minority party (the SDLP) representing Nationalism in most voluntary coalitions because this would be Unionism's preferred option every time. Far from being a means of the SDLP becoming an Opposition, it would essentially be a way of the party getting back into government with the Unionists without Sinn Fein.

The SDLP and UUP criticised Sinn Fein and the DUP for operating an 'Executive within an Executive' and maintaining a hold on decision-making. The Good Friday Agreement had been constructed to produce weak government at Stormont by using the STV version of Proportional Representation for elections with six member constituents favouring the election of Independents and smaller parties. As in Germany after the Great War, this electoral system, which Britain would never touch itself, envisaged widespread dilution of power constraining the 'extremes' and empowering the 'moderates'.

However, the tendency has been for the two leading parties from the two communities that get the First Minister and Deputy First Minister Offices to dominate. This is partly because the leading party in each community has an inbuilt majority within its designation (Nationalist or Unionist), and can therefore dominate voting within its communal bloc. It is then in its interest to form a good relationship with the dominant party in the other bloc to get policy through.

What has tended to happen is that, because elections in 'Northern Ireland' are really contests within each community, the DUP and SF began to support each other to maintain a stable and business-like relationship, to counter those who had been unable to accomplish this when the Executive was first established (the UUP and the SDLP), and who were reduced to whingeing after losing their majorities in their respective communal blocs.

That working relationship between the DUP and SF, ironically, is what made the Agreement functional and seemingly is what constitutes a menace to those who wished it to be otherwise.

Jim Gibney of Sinn Fein in his *Irish News* column has noted:

> "The assembly cannot have a formal opposition; a formal opposition is based on a parliamentary system which rests on democratic institutions and democratic culture. The current parliamentary arrangements have been carefully structured. These are novel arrangements and are needed because the Six County state is not a democratic entity" (IN 25.10.07).

It might be said that a pre-requisite of a democracy is a Government and an Opposition. But 'Northern Ireland' is not a democracy and anything resembling democracy is what had to be got away from if a functional settlement was to be made at all.

The real reason why the SDLP could not constitute itself into an Opposition is what would happen then? The old Nationalist Party, of which the SDLP is in substance a continuation, agreed in 1966, under pressure from the Taoiseach, Sean Lemass, to accept the status of Loyal Opposition in the old Stormont. Lemass had not taken the trouble to analyse the 'Northern Ireland state' before exhorting the Nationalist Party to engage in the charade of Loyal Opposition in it, and the Nationalists did not have the character to refuse, even though they knew from long experience that Northern Ireland was not a state, that Stormont was not its democratic Parliament, and that Opposition was futile within the structures of the sub-government which had been farmed out to the all-class (and in a sense all-Party Party) alliance of the Protestant community. All that participation did was to bring out the futility of it and ripen conditions for the new departure of 1969.

When the SDLP was formed, and even before, the young Turks of Hume,

Currie, Fitt and Devlin announced that they would succeed and transform 'Northern Ireland' by going into Opposition just like the people who they said were failures and who they were replacing. All that was needed was youth and vigour. But youth and vigour were not enough to overcome the system that had been designed to make it all so inconsequential.

Liberal democracy, as it is presently constituted in the western world, cannot work in 'Northern Ireland' because it cannot reduce the political arena to the business of a political Establishment and foster an apolitical mass in the society. The atomised individual is curtailed by the persistence of the community—and there are two of those. In Western states these days Liberal democracy has made political projects unattractive and unpopular unless they appeal to economic interests and the promotion of the market. This seems to be what is meant by Progress. Within such a project the State is reduced to the role of night-watchman, managing the population. However, in 'Northern Ireland' the populace keep reasserting itself against the politicians, and there is no State to conduct the business of real politics to rectify the inconvenient activism of the masses.

Liberal democracy and parliamentary politics aim at the curbing of popular power. But this has proved impossible in 'Northern Ireland' because it is cut off from the democratic State in which it is held. What exists in 'Northern Ireland' is perhaps closer to what constitutes true democracy—but it is dysfunctional for all that.

Stormont politics are ultimately futile and have been shown to be. The Stormont system is a closed system where the only really worthwhile thing is a break-out. And Britain has determined that a break-out is only really possible in one direction—although a veto has been placed on such a direction for the present. But Sinn Fein has been breaking out, whilst conducting a holding operation on behalf of its community in the North. And this seems to be at the root of attempts to undermine the peace that was so painfully constructed in the two decades between 1987 and 2007.

In March 2016 a Private Members' Bill succeeded in making provision for a Her Majesty's Opposition to be established at Stormont if any party so chose. John McCallister's *Assembly and Executive Reform Bill* had proposed a complete restructuring of the Good Friday institutions to restore majority rule and collective cabinet responsibility on the Westminster model. It sought to abolish community designations and the Petitions of Concern safeguard. Sinn Fein and the SDLP blocked most of the proposed reforms but the SDLP, supported the clauses allowing for the establishment of an Official Opposition, while SF voted against. Thus the SDLP removed the Nationalist veto on this proposal (IN 2.3.16). In May 1916 the new SDLP Leader took his party out of the Executive, along with the UUP, to be an Opposition to John Hume's achievement.

CHAPTER 18

Restless in Peace

The settlement Britain made in 1998 did not work out as intended, despite giving 'Northern Ireland' the best government it ever had. The objective of the Agreement was to establish a harmless middle-ground Unionist Party/ SDLP coalition, along with a marginalised Sinn Fein and DUP. That would have succeeded, after 28 years of trouble, in putting 'Northern Ireland' back in the box that was closed in 1921 and marked with the words: "*Do not open under any circumstances*". The '*consociational*' principle, on which the new political structures were based, envisaged the establishment of a moderate political elite, which would nullify the '*extremes*' and the activist elements of society. The Executive Ministries were initially allotted considerable independent power and the Assembly was rendered weak by placing nearly all the parties within it in government.

After the failure to save Trimble from the electorate, something very unexpected happened. Sinn Fein and the DUP led by Paisley cobbled together a functional arrangement to work the Agreement. The '*extremes*' began to operate it with much greater success in terms of peace and stability than was ever managed by the 'moderate centre'—or imagined possible at all. And, when Paisley gave way to Peter Robinson, this functional arrangement continued for a time, with the communal conflict being blunted by the '*extremes*' in power, whereas the '*moderates*' had only sharpened it.

But things can never rest in 'Northern Ireland' and those who did not like the settlement such as it actually was—who were many and varied—could not help but set about undermining and unravelling it, despite knowing full well the consequences of doing so: '*Northern Ireland*' *RIP*—Restless in Peace.

Three important developments followed that deserve our attention. Firstly, there has been the spread of Sinn Fein across the Border and the reaction to that. Secondly, there has been the Boston Project and associated pursuit of the Sinn Fein leader, Gerry Adams. Thirdly, there has been the destabilisation of Unionism, brought about by the equalising effects of the Agreement. These three developments have run in parallel, feeding off one another and tending towards what could result in an unravelling of the Peace, so painstakingly put together over two decades.

The Spread of Sinn Fein

The achievement of the 1998 Agreement in the North had repercussions for the political prospects of Sinn Fein in the South. For most of its existence, since the rise of Fianna Fail, Sinn Fein had been an ideological rather than a political force in the 26 Counties. De Valera reduced it to little more than the *Wolfe Tone Annual* and Brian O'Higgins' marvellous Christmas cards. At times Sinn Fein had political effect but its main influence was as a kind of guardian of principle.

In the aftermath of August 1969 Fianna Fail wondered why the Northern Catholics had not developed a Fianna Fail of their own, rather than the miserable thing they had produced in the Nationalist Party. But, since the 1998 Agreement, after the Republicans had fought a long war and remained undefeated, many Southerners began to see Sinn Fein much as Fianna Fail had been seen in the 1920s.

The governing parties in the South (unintentionally) provided the space for this new Sinn Fein to step into. As a reaction to the War in the North, they had been increasingly denying their history, allowing it to be written by those who left the country for retraining at Oxford and Cambridge, people who came to see a different world than that derived from independent Irish experience. Within Ireland the aim seemed to be a rehabilitation of British rule and a denigration of the independence movement. The skewed academic history of the 'Trinity History Workshops' and others was allowed to go unchallenged, except by vigorous groups of amateur historians and community groups from the substance of the country.

The South began to bask in the prosperity that Haughey had created, while increasingly denigrating the maker of their place in the sun, and they got very *blasé* about such worthless commodities as 'history'. Politics was about facilitating property speculation and money-making.

The party had become the fourth largest party in 2002 but its representation in the Dail dropped from 5 TDs to 4 five years later.

After the party's poor performance in the Southern General election of 2007, Sinn Fein was widely ridiculed by commentators as Northern blow-ins, ignorant about the South. Its leaders were portrayed as economically incompetent. And then crash went the Tiger! The governing parties were confronted with a vibrant and subversive political force, flooding into the national political space they had evacuated, in a situation where the populace felt cheated by those elected on promises of prosperity. In the 2011 General Election, in which Fianna Fail suffered a dramatic collapse, Sinn Fein increased its representation to 14 seats, its highest total since 1923.

The Establishment parties dealt with this problem by abandoning what they had been saying about the North for a generation—that it produced trouble because of what it was: a Partitionist entity that oppressed its Nationalist minority. Now suddenly it was Sinn Fein, the rising force, which was responsible for all the ills of the North: it was the Republicans who were the source of the problem that had brought them into being! However, this about-turn just did not wash with the people, after all they had been hearing over the years. So Sinn Fein became a Going Concern in the South.

The primary stimulant disturbing the Northern settlement seems to be Sinn Fein's structure as an all-Ireland party. The organisational range of Sinn Fein poses a problem for both Dublin and London. The Dublin Establishment, right across the political spectrum, became concerned at the State ambitions of the blow-ins from the North. They represented something that Fianna Fail was in its past, a vigorous and 'slightly constitutional' party, that was not entirely manageable by the State apparatus constructed over the generations. Interestingly, it was the thing that Tánaiste Erskine Childers thought was needed in the North in the aftermath of August 1969, but, when it actually appeared in substance three decades later, Dublin went into panic mode.

The historic policy of Dublin since Partition, despite all its Anti-Partitionist rhetoric, was to seal off the North as a thing dangerous to its national independence and sovereignty. Perversely, since the Southern State began surrendering its independence of mind—largely because Britain succeeded in making it feel guilty over the Northern conflict—it has had to face a potential disruption to both its cosy set-up and to its developing relationship with Britain.

Sinn Fein blossoming as an all-Ireland party was also problematic for Britain. The original purpose of 'Northern Ireland' was to exert leverage over the bulk of the island and it performed this function spectacularly well, particularly in the half-century after 1970, as England extended its influence.

However, what would happen if the same party had power and influence on both sides of the Border and that party had proved itself able to deal with Britain by being impervious to British wiles? Where would the lever be then?

The secondary problem was the DUP. Sinn Fein's partner in government in the North was also a less malleable force than the Unionist Party. It was far more representative of the Protestant community and had an independence of spirit that the *"fur-coat brigade"* of Unionists never had. From O'Neill through to Trimble the Unionist Party always did what Britain required of it. Even Faulkner, the best Unionist politician by a long way, was persuaded to drop his demand for political integration when Whitehall had a word in his ear.

On the other hand, Paisley continuously frustrated British initiatives and Peter Robinson, through his adventurist actions in 1986, alarmed those implementing the Hillsborough Agreement, deterring its full application.

And, of course, the DUP then embarked on a functional arrangement with Sinn Fein, against all odds and expectations.

For the simple-minded in Dublin, Paisley and the DUP had never ceased to be the principal hate-figures in the *'Black Protestant North'*. Paisley remained a religious enthusiast when the South began to become confused about its Catholicism. So he was labelled a bigot in Dublin and by the Southern media—taking the attention off its own bigotry—although there is a strong historic strain of liberalism in Ulster Presbyterianism and Paisley was very representative of it (That idea will, of course, be appalling to the simple-minded.)

It was such considerations that seem to have prompted the extraordinary informal grand alliance which is determined to undermine the functional DUP/Sinn Fein cooperation which, from various political positions, is believed should never have happened.

British Roll-back of the Agreement

The famous British jurist, F.E. Smith (Lord Birkenhead), who introduced the 1920 Act into Parliament and prosecuted Roger Casement, once stated that the measure of success in war and "who wins is found in the answer to the question: who is punished? There is no other test" (*The Speeches of Lord Birkenhead*, p108). At the conclusion of the War the Republican POWs were released and Sinn Fein took their place in government.

The 28 Year War could not be won by the British Army. It goes against the grain for Britain not to win in war, or at least to give the appearance of having won. In 1998 it admitted in effect its inability to win and, by the settlement it agreed, *de facto* at least, that the War waged against it by the Republican Army was legitimate. But the only sense that can be made of its policies in the years which followed is that it continued hoping to free itself from the concessions it had had to make in order to end the War. The idea is to restore a modified version of the system it set up in 1921, an arrangement more to its liking. Its intention has been to recover the ground, all or in part, it had to concede in 1998.

The first manifestation of this was in the attempts to 'roll-back' the policing reforms. This has involved a subversion of the Patten changes, which were intended to introduce a new culture into the police. Under these reforms, large numbers of RUC personnel took golden handshakes, amounting to a half billion pounds in total. Then many of the same people were re-hired under civilian contracts—putting themselves outside the legal requirements of the new policing and the Ombudsman's authority, while also undermining the Patten provision for a temporary 50/50 recruitment policy to correct the Protestant predominance in the police force.

Further British measures against the settlement included the arrest of pivotal Republicans for alleged IRA activities not covered by the 1998 Agreement—because they occurred after it and were therefore beyond its scope. For instance, Padraig Wilson, an individual who was instrumental in carrying through the Republican transition from War, was charged with the offence of investigating the circumstances surrounding the killing of Robert McCartney—a thing which at the time it was widely demanded Republicans should do. Later he was charged with conducting a Republican internal investigation into the alleged rape of Mairia Cahill (the charge being later withdrawn). Then he was arrested again in connection with the killing of Kevin McGuigan (and released again). There was also the arrest of John Downey, an *"on the run"*, who had been given a *'Letter of Comfort'*—in effect an immunity from prosecution by the Blair Government. Gerry Adams was arrested and questioned for three days over the murder of Jean McConville. Ivor Bell was charged in connection with the same offence. When a republican was killed in 2015, the Power-Sharing institutions were brought near to collapse by PSNI assertions that mainstream republicans were to blame, an assertion never backed up by proof. Nor did charges follow—although there were widespread, well-publicised arrests. And in the South Thomas Murphy was arrested for financial irregularities, while Bankers walked away unmolested.

The strategy of embarrassing Sinn Fein with arrests of Republicans was presumably directed towards dividing and fragmenting the Republican base. Perhaps the most remarkable achievement of the Provos was to hold the Republican movement together, except for some fragments, as they negotiated the Agreement and carried it through. They said at the outset that their great concern was to prevent a repetition in the North of what happened in the South in 1922. And they have succeeded in this for now.

These arrests have been illustrative of the political policing that still remains on the British agenda, mainly concentrating on republican misdeeds in *"legacy issues"*, whilst ignoring those on the other side, like the Ballymurphy Massacre. And there is a straight refusal to reveal information sought by relatives over killings in the past that the State possesses but wishes to conceal.

The Boston College Tapes

With the War over for the best part of two decades, attempts continued to resurrect particular incidents in it, to undermine the Republican leadership which successfully brought it to a close. A wide range of political forces have participated in this, including Whitehall itself, the British Security Services, the Unionist Party, the SDLP, the British media (from the *Daily Telegraph* to the *Guardian*), the Nationalist media, Fine Gael, Fianna Fail, and Republican die-hards of various kinds—all sharing the intention of pinning something on Gerry Adams and his comrades that would shred the functional arrangement arrived at between Sinn Fein and the DUP. It seems that 'Northern Ireland' cannot but help undermining itself from within and without.

As we have seen, because the War ended without the ending of Partition, some of those who waged and supported the campaign turned against the leaders that ended it, regarding them as traitors. They set about subverting the Agreement by discrediting the leadership that made it. In this endeavour they found themselves being facilitated by parts of the British State, angered at having had to negotiate following the failure to win the War and inclined to engage in wrecking activity.

The Boston College project was conceived by Professor Paul Bew and operated with the assistance of Dissident Anthony McIntyre and journalist Ed Moloney. The idea was for former paramilitaries to confidentially record memoirs, with the tapes remaining confidential until after they died. Within this general remit, an essential element of the project was to provide republican opponents of the Good Friday Agreement with an opportunity to vent their spleen. The venture came into the public eye when the PSNI succeeded in over-turning the confidentiality provisions of the scheme. This caused the Project to explode in the faces of its originators, with a continuing fall-out.

The General Editors of the Boston project, Thomas E. Hachey and Robert K. O'Neill, in a Preface to Ed Moloney's book based on the tapes, *'Voices from The Grave'*, thank particularly "Paul Bew, politics professor and senior political adviser to a Northern Ireland first minister, together with two historians who remain anonymous" for assistance. They give the overall impression that the Republican War was sectarian in nature:

> "In an assessment of the information contained in the recorded interviews, Lord Bew strongly encouraged Boston College to document and archive the stories of paramilitaries who fought on both sides of that sectarian divide, known more popularly as the Troubles, because it was such a natural fit. Boston College has had a long interest in Ireland and offered a welcoming and neutral venue in which participants felt a sense of security and confidentiality that made it possible for them to be candid and forthcoming. What Bew perceived as the real value of the IRA/UVF accounts was in what they revealed about the motives and mind sets of participants in the conflict, a resource of inestimable value for future studies attempting better understanding of the phenomenology of societal violence..."

The British construction of the thing called 'Northern Ireland' is completely omitted from what the Editors call "*the phenomenology of violence"*: as if the War was suitable for sociological investigation as a kind of ethnic/religious conflict quite detached from the political problem produced by the existence and functioning of 'Northern Ireland'.

Republican die-hards, disgruntled by the realpolitik of Adams and Mc Guinness in terminating the War, agreed to tell their tales to a tape-recorder, with the tapes being held in Boston College until their death. That is important—not the death of people implicated by the tales on the tape, only the deaths of the tellers of the tales. The project was, therefore, very political and not historical—a fact confirmed by the publication of the aforementioned book, *'Voices from the Grave'*, with the war stories of republican Brendan Hughes and loyalist David Ervine, edited by Ed Moloney.

The interviews on the tapes were sponsored by what was called the 'Boston College Center for Irish Programs IRA/UVF Project'.

The Editors explained in a Preface to the book that:

> "The transcripts of interviews… are subject to prescriptive limitations governing access. Boston College is contractually compelled to sequestering the taped transcriptions unless otherwise given full release, in writing, by the interviewees, or until the demise of the latter…"

That meant, in effect, that the interviewees were encouraged to speak freely about what they had done in the War, and who they had done it with, and to whom, on a guarantee of impunity. The guarantee came from the assurance that the tapes would remain secret until they died, unless they chose to make their stories public. This arrangement meant that the interviewee might give 'evidence' against others, and also against himself or herself for plausibility, without being subject to prosecution. It meant too that they would not have to defend any allegations against cross-examination with regard to the implication of others or as to hearsay. The effect of this was that Brendan Hughes, who was unhappy at how the Republican leadership ended the War, was able to make accusations about Adams without challenge, allegations that have been used by the British authorities and their media to re-open the War on a political level, in an attempt to undermine Sinn Fein's move Southwards.

The British Government, through its police service in 'Northern Ireland', demanded the tapes and the American Courts upheld the demand under a treaty Moloney and McIntyre failed to notice. The tapes relevant to the case of Jean McConville were handed over to the PSNI in July 2013. Other tapes followed.

A dozen or so Republicans were arrested and questioned concerning the killing of Jean McConville, on the basis of 'evidence' provided by the Boston Project. These included Adams and other senior Republicans. Ivor Bell has been charged with aiding and abetting murder after recording an interview with McIntyre. His lawyer argued in court that the Boston Project had been "a complete sham" and had been operated "with no validation of any of the work carried out" (IN 23.12.14).

The whole business is at the very least symptomatic of a tremendously naïve understanding of how the British State has operated historically—surprising amongst Irish Republicans, but perhaps less so since they came under academic tutelage and became prone to naïve ideas about *"freedom of speech"* and the like. What is undeniable is that the tapes were seized upon by the British State in its efforts to wear away the movement that facilitated the rise of the Catholic community out of the predicament it found itself in from 1921 and to keep it hemmed in to its ghettoes.

An Unfinished War?

Ed Moloney, who had previously been of the opinion that the Provos had lost the War—and who had published the most substantial argument in favour of that view in *'The Secret History of the IRA'*—changed his mind when Britain overturned confidentiality clauses of the Boston project, in order to make use of the tapes in criminal cases. The War is not over, he suggested—as he became personally embroiled in a legal case to fight British demands for access to the tapes—and the British Government continues to pursue victory in it. The logic must therefore be, he concluded, that, if it continues to pursue victory, then it surely did not win.

In an article in the *Belfast Telegraph* of 4th August 2012, entitled, *'Peace Process Could Unravel Over Tapes Fight'* and sub-titled, *'Legal moves to seize taped IRA interviews from Boston College are nothing less than the Government tearing up the peace process'*, Moloney argued that the War had ended in *"a draw"*:

> "The IRA didn't achieve its goal of a united Ireland, but did get into government, while the British and unionists failed to inflict a military defeat on the IRA in the conventional sense; for example, combatants were let out of jail, not imprisoned, while the IRA's leaders were invested with a new respectability and political power. People may quibble about what 'victory' and 'defeat' in such circumstances really mean, but it is undeniable that our 'war' did not end in the way such things normally do… the arrangement which ended our conflict was agreed to in negotiations between the major forces involved in the conflict. It is no exaggeration to say that, without it, our 'war' may never have ended, but that agreement carried the obligation that the deal would and should be honoured. There was no doubt, however, that our 'war' did end and the evidence was unmistakable, because what had

happened during the 'war' stopped... In spite of reservations about true IRA intentions... there is little doubt that it has kept to its side of the 'peace' by ending its warlike activities. But can the same now be said of the British side of this equation? Recently, the Historical Enquiries Team (HET), in conjunction with the PSNI's criminal investigations branch, has delved into the past to frame criminal charges against people who were active as combatants when the 'war' that has now ended was still raging. The subpoenas served against the Belfast Project archive at Boston College, which I was involved in establishing, is a potential example of that type of activity, but it is not, by any means, the only one. How and why the political blessing was given for this to happen is a question that so far seems not to have been even asked much less answered, but prima facie it looks very much as if someone on the British side, at some level, has decided to resume the 'war' that was supposed to have ended, by agreement, in a draw, by trying to put people who fought against them in that 'war' into prison... You cannot unilaterally renew a war that ended in a draw, by agreement and with considerable compromise, without there being negative repercussions. A move like this amounts to a de facto abrogation of the peace deal by one side. It would be foolish to attempt to predict when, or what form, such a backlash might take, but our knowledge of Irish history tells us that there will be harmful ramifications at some point."

The War was not over and the Boston College Tapes became central to the campaign to 'get' Gerry Adams. This campaign came to a head in May 2014, during the election campaign for the European Parliament, with the arrest of the Sinn Fein leader and his detention for a number of days. Martin McGuinness made the allegation that the timing was politically-inspired. The arrest was most probably a probing of the situation, to see how things would pan out. But its effect was to destroy the Boston College Project—which was forced to decommission its tapes after the surrender to the police.

Lord Bew was forced to defend himself, after the political policing arrest of Adams by what the Professor in his Althusserian days would have called the Repressive State Apparatus. Bew came into focus for his pivotal role in the Boston College Tapes as the Ideological State Apparatus, which was fingering Adams for the Repressive State Apparatus to detain him for the killing of Jean McConville. The Sinn Fein leader made a point of drawing attention to the role of Lord Bew in all of this in an impressive post-arrest press conference.

Lord Bew penned an article for the *Sunday Independent*, clarifying his position in relation to Boston College, Moloney, McIntyre and the tapes. He said he regretted the decommissioning of the Boston tapes after their surrender to the Repressive State Apparatus:

> "It is clear... that... McIntyre believed that the Burns Library in Boston College would always be a safe place for these papers. For almost a decade

that belief was vindicated and the archive was quietly built up. The recent PSNI interest in the tapes came late in the day. Both Moloney and McIntyre were disturbed at the turn of events and fought a legal battle to prevent premature disclosure. McIntyre said on the BBC programme Spotlight last week that, in hindsight, it was a mistake to publish Brendan Hughes' tape following his death. At any rate, the police interest in the archive has ended up destroying the project" (11.5.14).

It is suggested here that the Boston College project and other oral histories were destroyed, first by Moloney's decision to publish '*Voices from the Grave*' for commercial or publicity purposes and then by the actions of the British State in wishing to utilise Moloney's and McIntyre's work to criminalise Adams.

Moloney defended the Boston Project in May 2014 as facilitating "a different account of events from the one peddled by the Sinn Fein leadership" and being "a liberating experience" for those critical of the latter. The important thing for Moloney was: "it is about who controls the narrative of the IRA's part in over 30 years of violence in the North" (IT 20.5.14).

On *Radio Ulster* (6.5.14) Jack Dunn of Boston College revealed that Moloney and McIntyre neglected to know about the MLAT Treaty between US and Britain—which Maloney as a journalist should have made his business to know about—even though it dated back to the time of the IRA Ceasefire.

Dunn added that Moloney and McIntyre did not make it their business to check the Contracts given to contributors that stated the protection of their testimonies was subject to existing US Law. In other words, misplaced faith was placed in British 'goodwill' after 1998 and in the strength of will of a US University to defend the project against the US judiciary!

Origins of the Pursuit of Adams

The Boston College Tapes played a fundamental part in what might be termed the pursuit of Gerry Adams. This long-standing campaign, aimed at undermining the authority and "credibility" of the Sinn Fein Leader, is essentially a political campaign, waged in humanitarian guise, to remove Adams from Southern politics and to undermine Sinn Fein's advance in the 26 Counties.

The hope is that, if Adams could be replaced as leader of Sinn Fein by a Southern-based person, the all-Ireland nature of the party could be gradually undermined and the party reduced to just another Free Statist radical grouping. In this way the most practical route to a united Ireland could be closed off.

Removing Gerry Adams from active politics would also take out the master strategist who transferred the energy of the Northern fight from the military to the political fields—first in the North and then in the South—

and who master-minded a rapid growth in Sinn Fein, bringing it to a position where it could challenge the two major Southern parties.

The publication of the second edition of Moloney's book *'A Secret History of the IRA'* in 2007, to coincide with the functional arrangement Sinn Fein was making with the DUP, began the attempt to undermine Adams—despite protestations to the contrary. A year later Moloney published *'Paisley, From Demagogue to Democrat?'* which attempted to shake the other pillar of the Peace.

A reading of the reviews of Moloney's book on the IRA that McIntyre published on his website, *The Blanket*, is enlightening about the origins of the political and media obsession with Adams. In an editorial on the collection of reviews McIntyre assembled in praise of Moloney's efforts, the former Republican volunteer stated:

> "Allegations of previous involvement in war crime, no matter how distant in time, will cause serious concern for any politician with the slightest awareness of the pitfalls of public perception, especially when situated in an ever growing discourse of human rights."

The objective of the 'Get Adams' campaign, that has been taken up by a wide variety of political interests in Ireland, is pretty much summed up in that sentence.

One of the first reviews assembled by McIntyre was one by Jim Cusack, the very anti-Sinn Fein Security Correspondent on the *Sunday Independent*. Cusack's article entitled: *'Exposing Adams' secrets to the light of day'* states the main allegations that have been levelled at the Sinn Fein Leader were for being "... the man in charge of the IRA in west Belfast when it kidnapped, murdered and secretly buried Jean McConville, and that he was also in charge of the IRA in Belfast on Bloody Friday". Cusack concedes that "A Secret History of the IRA, unfortunately, does not offer conclusive proof on either issue". But that does not prevent him from making the allegations.

The killing of Jean McConville was a tragic incident in a War, one of many tragic incidents. The community of which Jean McConville was part recognised her death as a shocking event in a war situation. Single incidents in war do not alter the character of conflicts and wars are not usually judged on the basis of them. There have been many mothers of large families killed in British and US military operations, operations which are supported by the same people who make a point of singling out the death of Jean McConville.

Cusack is followed in McIntyre's selection by Prof. Patterson, former Official Republican, adviser to Trimble, and Unionist academic. The article *'How Clever Was Adams?'* in which the answer is *too clever by half* is republished from *Fortnight* Magazine of October, 2007. Patterson also concedes that:

"Moloney provides no evidence... However he (Moloney) does emphasise the degree to which... botched or betrayed operations greatly assisted the progress of Adams' pursuit of his 'secret peace process' with the London and Dublin governments."

Also in McIntyre's selection of witnesses bearing testimony against Adams is Prof. Bew. McIntyre describes his former mentor thus: "Paul Bew is the Professor of Irish Politics at Queen's University, Belfast. This article first ran in the Daily Telegraph and is carried here with permission from the author". The title is: '*At Last We Know the Human Cost of Gerry Adams*':

"Today, Gerry Adams presents himself as a folksy, slightly pompous avuncular figure in Irish politics: a moralist who chides the politicians in Dublin for their embarrassingly corrupt ways... Mr Adams emerges from... A Secret History of the IRA... smelling like a rotten cabbage. If the author of the book—an award-winning Irish journalist—is to be believed, Mr Adams knew about the killing of Jean McConville, the widowed mother of 10 children who was murdered by the IRA in 1972... But even now, is there any hard proof against the Sinn Fein president? Mr. Moloney relies heavily on a range of interviews with republican activists, many of whom, it will be said, have an axe to grind against the leader who brilliantly manipulated them to the point where the IRA campaign ended without achieving its stated objective of British withdrawal from Ireland. All that could be said here with certainty is that Mr. Moloney presents the evidence by means of relentless accumulation of precise detail that may convince many readers. Some of the naive liberals who got on the Adams bandwagon in recent years will be shocked... Ulster Unionists will be less shocked. They have never believed anything other than that Mr. Adams is a bad man, and a bad man who compounds his badness by endless displays of slippery hypocrisy. David Trimble will, however, add that, while Mr. Moloney's book proves that Mr. Adams is a troublesome and dishonest adversary, there is little alternative to dealing with him as the leader of a formidable section of Northern nationalist opinion... Irish republicans, or rather those Irish republicans who sincerely believed in the project of the 'Republic', will be appalled. For such people, the moral price of this squalid war was only worth paying if the end result was the triumph of their particular political vision. Instead, they have witnessed a new ethnic bargain, one available in most essentials since the mid-1970s, which has revised Stormont, albeit along power-sharing and Irish dimension lines... Mr. Moloney's real achievement is to remind us of the human cost of the 'Troubles' and the policy of human sacrifice pursued for so long by Mr Adams and his colleagues at surprisingly little risk to their own lives..."

Again, the important factual sentences in this piece are: "*But even now, is there any hard proof against the Sinn Fein president? Mr. Moloney relies heavily on a range of interviews with republican activists, many of whom, it will be said, have an axe to grind against the leader."* Prof. Bew buries this fact beneath a pile of unsubstantiated accusations from Adams' political enemies with political axes to grind. And his intention seems to be to cultivate a great and one-sided moralism in the minds of Republican die-hards in order that they do down their former comrade in the interests of Ulster Unionism.

From all the accusations and abuse levelled at Adams we should conclude that he is an extraordinary man, apparently almost single-handedly waging a 28 Year War on the British, commanding IRA units across the city, 'disappearing' people who stood in his way, sending forth his comrades to lay waste to Belfast and its civilians and not being satisfied with his handiwork, single-mindedly deciding to call a halt to his War, deceiving his old comrades, having some of them killed by the Brits, whilst all along engaging in secret, shady dealings with Charlie Haughey and British Intelligence. And the only thing the powerful and well-resourced British Justice system could ever lay on him was escaping from their Internment. Mick Collins really had nothing on the man!

"Unlike Hume, Adams was a team-player, with the discipline that comes with having to consult your immediate colleagues about both strategy and tactics." That estimation comes from an unexpected source, Ruth Dudley Edwards, writing in the *Sunday Independent* (3.1.16). It is also very true.

There was a great "manipulator" about all this time, and his name was John Hume. Hume from the beginning worked behind the back of his party colleagues and of his leader, following his own agenda. He spied for Dublin as the SDLP was being established; he plotted with Taoiseach Lynch to destroy Stormont behind the back of his party leader; he was consulted with regard to the Hillsborough Treaty whilst keeping his colleagues in the dark; he consorted with Adams, acting independently of the party of which he was leader to bring about the settlement he had personally in mind. He frustrated his party colleagues in their devolutionary desires and facilitated an Agreement between the mortal political enemy, Sinn Fein, and the British, which had the effect of undermining his own party.

That is not a criticism of Hume. It is high praise. But it is amazing that such a blind spot exists in those who line up to condemn Adams for something that they have not chosen to say about Hume.

Sex as a Political Weapon

Sexual impropriety and how it is dealt with is the political weapon of today. A significant part of the pursuit of Adams involved allegations of sexual abuse made against Republicans. Sex abuse allegations have long been used by the British State during the conflict. There has been little concern for the victims of such abuse. What has been of concern to the security apparatus is how knowledge of sexual abuse could be employed to recruit informers—whether they were paedophiles, rapists or murderers—or be used to undermine the opposition to 'Northern Ireland'. The last thing that was desired was that victims should use the criminal justice system to get justice—since that would expose the perpetrators of such acts, who the Intelligence services would no longer have any leverage over.

A number of attempts were made during 2013-15 to implicate the Sinn Fein Leader personally and the Republican Movement generally, in cases of sex abuse. And this presented an opportunity for the State to arrest Republicans who had made honest attempts to get to the bottom of accusations of such crimes and to deal with them in the absence of a legitimate State legal apparatus.

By this time it had been demonstrated in the 26 Counties how sex abuse could seriously damage some of the main institutions of Nationalist Ireland, particularly the Catholic Church. All the main political parties of the Southern State, along with the Gardai, were in some way culpable for letting this abuse go unexposed and unpunished over generations. Only Sinn Fein, having never held power in Dublin, was completely innocent. But a model had been established and the cultivation of moral panic was seen to have the potential to achieve what normal political argument could not, in stemming the Sinn Fein tide in the South.

Many of these attempts to discredit Sinn Fein, and its leader in particular, followed on from TV documentaries. There was once a time when these documentaries exposed dark State activities to the benefit of democracy. However, the subsequent generation of 'investigative journalists' seems to have been 'turned', to give service to the State instead. A difference between a trial and a TV programme is that there are no Rules of Evidence on TV and only as much cross-examination as the producer desires there to be. The producer is judge, jury and executioner rolled into one. Assertions are treated as facts and there is less justice than in the celebrated Show Trials of the past. Impression and emotion replaces reality.

The major features of this process were: trial by media, directed not at the perpetrators of the alleged crimes but at those who had made attempts to deal with them; a complete ignoring of the ordinary standard of '*innocent until proved guilty*'; the smearing of the Republican movement with the paedophile demon, an obsession of '*post-modern*' society; moral judgements made against Republicans for their inadequacy in dealing with issues that the major institutions of the Irish State had spectacularly failed in dealing with themselves with every service of a modern state available to them in peaceful, stable conditions; and above all, to pin everything, ultimately on the prime target of their political campaign—the Leader of Sinn Fein, Gerry Adams.

In the most startling incident, despite the fact that Adams actually gave evidence against an alleged abuser—his own brother—in a trial at Belfast, he was effectively made the defendant by the media. The anti-Adams political/media alliance quickly concentrated their efforts on putting Adams on trial, rather than his brother and there was liberal use of the word *'Paedophile'* in newspaper headlines next to the words *'Adams'*, *'Sinn Fein'*, *'IRA'*. The same formula, pioneered by the salacious British tabloid press, was used subsequently during the Mairia Cahill allegations (e.g. *'Are IRA's rapists and paedophiles still here?'*, in relation to an alleged Republican practice of expelling alleged sex offenders to the South: IN 23.10.14).

The Republican die-hards, out to get Adams, devised a case against the Sinn Fein leader based on his cross-examination at his brother's first trial by the Defence barrister employed by his brother. It was suggested that Adams gave perjured evidence in support of his niece and against his brother, bearing out their contention that lying was second nature to him. By deception he took control of the Republican War effort, and by deception he entangled it in the Peace Process, from which it could not escape. And now, it was alleged, he had been shown under oath to be a liar.

However, if there was a plausible legal case that Adams had withheld information from the police in breach of law, or that he gave perjured evidence, then he would have been prosecuted. Powerful interests in North and South would have loved to bring him down and would have taken such an opportunity. But they obviously couldn't.

A wide range of political opponents thereafter attempted to make political capital out of this personal family tragedy, including senior figures in Fianna Fail and the Dublin media, as well as Unionists. This bizarre and incongruous grand alliance against Adams, fed by widely conflicting motives, could only be seen as farcical but for the fact of its actual existence and the common purpose of the participants.

Following the political pressure and newspaper campaigns, four official agencies in 'Northern Ireland' started investigating whether Adams had a case to answer about withholding information about his brother from the police. But apparently no findings emerged and, if things go true to form, there will presumably be little reporting that all the efforts that were trumpeted across the media to discredit the Sinn Fein Leader came to nothing in the end.

In late 2014 the Mairia Cahill case followed a similar pattern. She was from an influential Republican family, had been a member of Sinn Fein for a number of years, even after she had made serious sexual allegations against a Republican. She had decided, after leaving Sinn Fein and joining a dissident group, that she had failed to get the justice she wanted from Republicans, and turned to the British justice system. However, bizarrely, the State relegated to a secondary position her complaints—along with those of other women—against the alleged abuser, in order to charge republicans who had conducted investigations at the request of the victims with IRA membership (IN 2.11.14). When presented with social crime of this kind, it was customary for the RUC to give priority to its war on the IRA, as opposed to protecting individuals. The actions of the PSNI in this instance was a continuation of that policy. This threw the communities back on their own resources.

Catholics in the North were aware that the community in the North had little means to deal with social crime. After August 1969, it was forced into constructing a rudimentary alternative State apparatus behind the barricades because of the absence of a normal State. This apparatus existed prior to the formation of the Republican Army and was acting independently of it when the IRA emerged.

It was not the Republican Army that suspended the normal due process of law in 'Northern Ireland'. That had already been done by the State through the Special Powers Act (1922), The Detention of Terrorists Act (1972), The Emergency Powers Act (1973) etc.—not to mention illegal activities by the State's forces and the refusal of the State to hold its enforcers to account when they transgressed the law. It was within this framework of law, or its absence, that the Republican Army conducted its impromptu judicial functions and maintained a kind of order in communities which were No-Go areas for the police.

The Republican Army certainly acted the part of a State in certain areas of the North, acting as peace-maker in local disputes as well as war-maker on the State. It did not fight a War and let things run wild in its hinterland. It kept the peace within its area. What the State would not do, the Provos found it necessary to do for their community. They began to act as the State, less as usurpers of the State (which they would have liked to be able to do), but more in the absence of the State. And there is certainly a good deal of nostalgia in Catholic areas for the times when Republican policing kept the areas relatively crime-free.

Southern Discomfort

During the offensive against the Sinn Fein Leader and his party in the South, *The Irish Times* revealed the main interest the Dublin media had in these victims of abuse:

> "Much of the media focus has been on Gerry Adams and Sinn Féin. Just as it was last year in the case of Áine Tyrell, and just as it was in the case of

Jean McConville earlier this year. At stake is Adams's credibility. Last November questions were asked about when and what the Sinn Féin president knew after his brother Liam was sentenced to 16 years in prison for raping his daughter, Áine. In April and May this year more questions were raised about what the Sinn Féin president knew about the 1972 IRA murder of Jean McConville after he was questioned by the PSNI at Antrim station. Now questions are being asked about what Adams knew about the alleged rape and interrogation of Maíria Cahill. Questions are also being raised about how the republican movement dealt internally with IRA sexual abuse. As with the Catholic Church, it is asked, did the IRA "institution" come before the victims?" (Gerry Moriarty, *'Maíria Cahill: unanswered questions. Will other victims come forward? Will there be lasting damage to Adams? And who do we believe?* 25.10.14).

The principal thing driving the *'Get Adams'* campaign in the South was the fear of a Northern contamination of the cosy Partitionist Southern body politic. Adams went South to capture the Louth seat and the people put a Northerner in the Dail. But Adams as the leader of an all-Ireland party crossed the line which no Northern Catholic is supposed to cross—unless they have become harmless, and fully integrated cogs of the party system of the South, like Frank Aiken and Austin Currie.

Adams, in coming South, was confronting the 26 Counties with the fact that the issue of the Northern Catholics was not put to bed in 1925 or indeed 1998 and that there was still unfinished business in the North. Jack Lynch is praised by all shades in the South for having kept the North at bay but the presence of Adams and the rise of Sinn Fein in the Opinion Polls was a sharp reminder that Lynch failed.

The North was allowed to stew in its own juices but refused to continue there in perpetuity. And so the Southern political Establishment and its media pulled out all the stops to remove Adams from the scene before the centenary of 1916, which they would have liked to commemorate without much thought about embarrassing matters outstanding.

Even though the Southern Establishment has an inkling that it is playing with fire, and at moments of impending crisis fears the consequences of what it does by way of destabilising the North with its reckless attacks on republican leaders, a fear which makes it stop short of destroying what it helped to put in place, it does not seem to be able to stop itself pushing towards the brink.

There is a complete absence from the Irish National press of any publication sympathetic to the predicament of the Northern Catholic community. Such sympathy is seen by the social stratum that produces the media as sympathy with Sinn Fein.

The fact that Sinn Fein was produced out of the situation in which the

Northern Catholic community was placed, not by Partition as such, but by the political arrangements made by Britain as the means of enacting Partition and maintaining it, is denied. The implications of admitting it are too awful to contemplate for those in control of the media. This is an issue which goes beyond careerism and is connected to the basic orientation of the State. It is a remarkable fact that there is no mainstream media organisation which fully reflects the true national interests of the Irish state. There was one newspaper in the past which represented native Ireland, the *Irish Press*. It was brought down in 1995 and has not been replaced. Martin O Muilleoir, the Belfast publisher, attempted to establish a newspaper on an all-Ireland basis, but was blackguarded by the Southern Establishment, with the Progressive Democrat Minister for Justice, Michael McDowell, in the lead. It started publication in January 2005 and closed down in September 2006.

In the Irish media dispassionate description of British political conduct, whether in 'Northern Ireland' or in the world, is put down as *Anglophobia*, a product of the bad old world of backward, independent Ireland. A *phobia* is defined as a groundless, irrational fear or hatred of something. But, in Dublin a strictly accurate, rational and factual account of how Britain managed the Six Counties is decreed to be Anglophobic and not helpful. In short, the truth cannot be told in Dublin about the North because the truth might be of benefit to Sinn Fein. So the conflict 'up there' needs to be presented as a campaign of murder and mayhem against lawful activity.

That Britain is not responsible for the political condition of the 'Northern Ireland' region of its State is held as an article of faith, in defiance of all fact and reason. But, if that is the case, it rules out all understanding of the problem and all effective solution. The problem is presented as being *the Provos* — who didn't actually come into existence until 50 years after 'Northern Ireland' came into the world on the whim of Whitehall—and, in recent years at least, they have been much more part of the solution than the problem.

The fear in Dublin that Sinn Fein was gaining traction in the South produced a pulling together of the 'Civil War' parties against the threat of the Northern hordes. Some even came out for a realignment of the established party system as an emergency front against Sinn Fein, rather like the one against Fascism mooted in the 1930s. Micheál Martin, as Leader of Fianna Fail, made a number of highly-publicised attacks on Sinn Fein in company with elements who had regarded Fianna Fail in the same light not so long before. "*Martin claims SF and Provisional Movement sullied the name of Republicanism*" was the headline in *The Irish Times* (22.4.13) above the following:

> "Mr Martin asserted that if people wanted to know where the men and women of 1916 would have stood in later years, they would find out by looking at what they did: taking the route of constitutional republicanism."

But surely that— *"taking the route of constitutional republicanism"*—is actually what Adams is being damned for by Martin's die-hard allies in the *'Get Adams'* coalition: Which only goes to expose the bizarre alliance between unconstitutional die-hards and Constitutional Nationalism and reveals the multi-dimensional character of the campaign against Sinn Fein.

The Fianna Fail Leader launched a full-scale assault on Sinn Fein in April 2015 using RTE's *Late Late Show* and a double page interview in the *Sunday Business Post* to suggest that the Northerners were seeking to "undermine the very institutions of the state" (19.4.15). Martin then went on to devote half his speech at the Fianna Fail commemoration on Arbour Hill to lambasting Sinn Fein, saying the party was "unfit for participation in democratic republican government" (IT 20.4.15). Martin's attack won praise from Eoghan Harris in the *Sunday Independent* (26.4.15).

It is evident that Constitutional Fianna Fail finds it very difficult to deal with Constitutional Sinn Fein without disowning its own history. Astonishment at Martin's behaviour towards Sinn Fein even reached the *Irish Times*. Eugene McEldowney (admittedly a Northerner) wrote:

> "His attacks on Sinn Fein smack of opportunism and desperation. They also reveal a woeful ignorance of his own party's early history... His remarks show he is rattled by the advances Sinn Fein is making on the Fianna Fail base. And he is right to be worried. Whole swathes of voters have already gone over to Sinn Fein and more are expected. Martin is getting bad advice from someone..." (IT 31.10.15).

The peaceful transition from Treatyite to Anti-Treatyite government in the South in 1932 was accomplished peacefully because of the backing of a well-organised and highly-motivated IRA—which had not surrendered a decade earlier but had merely dumped arms. This provided Fianna Fail with military protection against the Treatyites, whose own official military expression had declined since the Treaty War and who were developing Fascist pretensions to prevent those it accused of being *"Communists"* obtaining power. The fact that no armed attempt was made to prevent the IRA/Fianna Fail 'Communists' from taking power must surely have been because of the military backing behind the Anti-Treatyites, which could come into play if the democratic process was not honoured—rather than any Blueshirt commitment to democracy. Does Martin really forget all of this?

The Fianna Fail leader might just ponder on something Kevin Boland said:

> "I think it is clear from our history that there must always be a Republican Party... and that, if Fianna Fail ceases to be the Republican Party, whether through the assertion of mere pragmatists or through its leaders succumbing to the lure of office, then there will be a vacuum which will have to be filled" (*Voice of the North*, 18.11.70).

The following week, speaking at the Royal College of Surgeons (Dublin), Adams replied to the Fianna Fail leader's attacks at Arbour Hill. The Sinn Fein leader told Martin:

> "Let there be no doubt about it, war is terrible. All war. War is desperate. And those of us who have lived through the recent conflict are the ones who have worked to ensure that the conflict is ended for good, and that we never— none of us, ever—go back there again. That's why Sinn Fein is and was pivotal to the peace process. So those of us... who have come from communities that were ravaged by conflict... don't need lectures from Micheal Martin or anyone else about conflict. We have been there. Let me say this: Republicans did not go to war: the war came to us... Micheal Martin needs to wake up and realise that the war is over..." (Deaglan de Breadun, *Power Play—The Rise of modern Sinn Fein*, pp. 18-19)

Another manifestation of the attempt to stem Sinn Fein has been a rather obvious attempt to create the impression that Sinn Fein's political prospects were hindered in the South by keeping their *"toxic"* Northern Leader, with the hope that the naïve come-lately Southern Shinners could be persuaded to give up Adams for another who would be more malleable by the 26 County State. This element of the *'Get Adams'* campaign involves the working up of an antagonism within Sinn Fein against their Leader to get him replaced by somebody from the South who can be 'house-trained'.

However, there is not the slightest suggestion that there is any part of the Republican movement, the voters of Louth or the Northern Catholic community generally, that views Adams as a liability—precisely the opposite is the case.

Adams was somewhat insulated from the on-going campaign to undermine him by the death of Nelson Mandela. In December 2013 the Sinn Fein Leader formed part of the Guard of Honour at the funeral of Mandela—the ultimate peacemaker. The ANC had fraternal links with Sinn Fein over decades and a military alliance with the IRA. Kader Asmal revealed in his memoirs, *'Politics in my Blood'*, how the IRA helped carry out a spectacular *coup de main* against one of the South African regime's most important strategic installations, an oil refinery at Sasolburg in 1980. This was the most significant military blow against the Apartheid regime and it was facilitated by Asmal, Adams and Michael O'Riordan, the General Secretary of the Communist Party of Ireland. It involved IRA training of MK cadres as well as reconnaissance of the target by Irish Republicans (See Manus O'Riordan, *Irish Political Review*, January 2014).

In 1990, on a visit to Dublin, Mandela shocked the Dublin and London Establishments, along with their respective medias, by continually insisting that Britain should be negotiating with Sinn Fein, without preconditions, to end the conflict in Ireland. In 1998, when a deal had been concluded, Cyril

Ramaphosa, who led the ANC in its war on the white supremacist Government of South Africa, assisted the Republican leadership in selling the peace agreement to its rank and file in the Republican heartlands.

Dublin in Denial

The scapegoating of Sinn Fein in the South for the conflict in the North has portrayed it as having wantonly began an illegitimate and unnecessary War against a normal system of government, despite the fact that, up until the Republican War had achieved the Agreement of 1998, the Republic's Constitution had asserted that, not only was the system of government in the North undemocratic, but that British sovereignty over it was illegitimate.

This denigration has come about through Dublin's increasing denial of Britain's fundamental responsibility for establishing and maintaining the thing—'Northern Ireland'—that caused the War in the first place—something which Dublin was certain about as that War got started in 1969-70. Dublin has revised its view of the fundamentals of the problem of the North in the course of the War. It issues only mild criticisms of Britain's lack of will to see that justice was done internally in the Six Counties but steers clear of acknowledging its central responsibility for the existence of 'Northern Ireland'. There is no consideration of Britain's motivation in setting up its undemocratic system of government for its own interests.

That has presented Dublin with a political predicament it does not wish to confront as it abandons its convictions and moves towards becoming normal, ordinary, liberal and progressive in the world—which means, of course, more British. And so it scapegoats Sinn Fein, a symptom of 'Northern Ireland', rather than its cause.

It is unsurprising that Sinn Fein gathered real momentum in a society that is in denial about the North after its efforts to encompass it went awry. Sinn Fein, a coherent, rational and purposeful force, was confronted by the hysterical reaction of time-servers who have made no attempt to understand what now confronted them.

Sinn Fein, in its Northern manifestation, has itself shown great willingness to learn about and adjust to the South, whilst the political class that went into hysteria preferred to know nothing about the North. Dublin even found itself wrong-footed by Sinn Fein in the Republican reconciliation with the British Monarchy. Under such circumstances the centenary of 1916 presented a great problem for Dublin.

Dublin's purpose in helping things towards the edge was partly to stop the momentum gathering in the South around the 1916 Centenary, which showed itself in the tremendous enthusiasm that manifested among the Dublin working-class during Sinn Fein's re-enactment of the O'Donovan Rossa funeral. At that point the *Irish Times* almost immediately began linking the shooting of Kevin McGuigan, an ex-Provo with a hot-head and a long-standing grudge against those who attempted to calm his hot temper, with the O'Donovan Rossa event (Stephen Collins, *'McGuigan killing raises questions for Rising tributes'* 22.8.15). The wind needed taking out of the Sinn Fein sails by the tried and trusted (though previously unsuccessful) method of linking it to sporadic violent events in the North. So, by late 2015, with Sinn Fein having established a substantial electoral presence in the South, the strategy was to deal with the party's rise by denying it voting transfers. Transfers are vital in PR systems and analysis of data showed this to be Sinn Fein's weakness (see Stephen Collins, IT 31.10.15).

The 2016 General Election became the anti-Sinn Fein election. Before the poll the chief objective of all the main parties was to prevent Sinn Fein being in government. The sentencing of Thomas Murphy, the South Armagh Republican, in the Special Criminal Court for minor tax arrears was arranged to occur on Election Day and featured in news broadcasts during the day. Sinn Fein had itself closed off the possibility of going into government through Motion 52 passed at the Derry Ard Fheis in March. This forbade the party from entering "a Fianna-Fail led or Fine Gael led government". The party won 23 seats and narrowly lost out by transfers in a number of close contests.

After the election the objective of both Fianna Fail and Fine Gael was to prevent Sinn Fein becoming the main opposition. Sinn Fein had succeeded, at least temporarily, in altering the basis of politics in the Southern State.

The threat of Sinn Fein also forced the political Establishment in Dublin to move beyond the low-key, mealy-mouthed *"shared history"* approach that it had planned for the 1916 Centenary to a more enthusiastic embracing of the event which produced the founding of the State, and that new approach was welcomed by the mass of the people.

It is possible that the relentless offensive waged by the Southern political Establishment will stem the Sinn Fein tide and keep the Northern Catholics boxed in to the confinement they were sentenced to in 1921. However, the mere existence of 'Northern Ireland' condemns the rest of the island to its political consequences for as long as it is maintained in separate existence. That, after all, was the original intention of it. And the mess the South has made in reconciling itself to the obvious political facts of life in the North is no insulation against it.

Unionist Discomfort

And so back to the "Black North". The Good Friday Agreement also came under attack due to the discomfort of Unionism in the face of its equalising process. This has had the effect of disabling the Paisley/Robinson accommodation with Sinn Fein that lies at the heart of Stormont's brief functionality.

The first stirrings of discontent came within the Unionist mass base, particularly in the Unionist capital, Belfast. Marginalised Loyalist unease at the Agreement was not just about what flag would fly over Belfast City Hall. It had another fundamental cause—a new Census result that was predicted to show a position of relative numerical equality between the two communities in 'Northern Ireland'. The population balance of two-thirds Protestants to one-third Catholic, established in 1921, had been sustained for 40 years without much movement. The majority fear of being out-bred by the minority was not increased by the Censuses of 1971 and 1981 which still put a Catholic majority way into the future. But the Census of 1991 had a significant psychological effect on the Protestant community as it suggested that a Catholic majority was only a generation away.

As the prospect of Northern Catholics achieving a small majority in the entity established in 1921 became more of a probability with every Census, more ingenious ways of disguising that fact had to be come up with by London. The raw facts of life of a sectarian headcount, in which there appears to be an irresistible momentum in one direction, intrudes into a situation that is usually tightly controlled by the media in the province. The new 'identity' questions in the 2011 Census were undoubtedly an attempt at sociological mystification on Whitehall's behalf. What Unionists were being told by the Census propaganda department was that, though Catholics had increased, the numbers describing themselves as 'Irish' had declined! A similar piece of subterfuge was engaged in by the Census makers during the 2001 Census when returns were 'cooked' by reallocating 'Others' overwhelmingly to the 'Protestant' category in a desperate attempt to save Trimble as First Minister against the Unionist electorate. But it was ultimately in vain, like all the other methods employed in the losing battle of *'saving Dave'*.

There were about twice as many Protestants as Catholics when 'Northern Ireland' was concocted. To prevent the numerical superiority from being eroded, it was necessary that the Protestant breeding rate should be kept up. But Catholic life, being based on a lesser attraction to material things, was more child-friendly and tended to produce a higher breeding-rate (even independently of political concerns). This was, of course, compensated for by a higher rate of emigration that affected Catholics disproportionately, due to the lack of work and housing provision. But that head-counting constituted the basis of 'Northern Ireland' politics for two generations. The

Catholic community was demographically curbed to prevent out-breeding but it was otherwise left to its own devices and given up as a lost cause to Unionism—until the point when it has become demographically threatening.

There is the growing probability that there will be either demographic equality or Catholics becoming the slight majority in 'Northern Ireland'. This suggests there will be an extended transitional period in which life within the Six Counties is shaped more to the liking of nationalists—if that isn't occurring already. The Unionists would be in the novel position of being a minority in their 'own wee Ulster', with the maintenance of their detachment from an all-Ireland state depending on their coming to terms with the Catholic community. It was the realisation of this predicament which caused the growing discomfort among Unionism which began to destabilise the political settlement.

Despite the Census manipulations to reassure Unionists that a Catholic majority would not mean an instant United Ireland, the partial removal of the Union flag over Belfast City Hall (bringing its flying into line with British practice) at that moment indicated that the Unionist citadel was no longer a Protestant city and would henceforth have to be shared. The reality of the demographic danger to Unionist supremacy in 'Northern Ireland' spoiled the carefully engineered Census mystification and could not disguise the fact that the results marked the formal end of the 'Protestant majority' position and made the 'majority' in the territory carved out for them in 1920-1 into just another minority.

Disputes over flags and marching are the routine of politics in 'Northern Ireland'. The conflict in the Six Counties is formally about the Border but in actuality it is never really about Partition, since Border Polls are rare. By the same token it is never really about *the Union*—most of which went in 1921, a little more in 1985 and even more in 1998. It is about the political limbo of 'Northern Ireland' in which communities adopted shibboleths with little practical political meaning beyond the eternal routine of conflict they were condemned to.

From 1921 *the Union* was reduced to the mere ceremonial symbols of the State—the Crown, the Queen, the Union Jack, etc—for Unionists. And one of the chief petty concerns has been the flying of flags around localities— or more accurately the flying of them in the face of Catholics—presumably to show who still holds the whip-hand (or doesn't, as the case may be). That is why the restriction on the flying of the Union flag above City Hall provoked such consternation.

Flag waving certainly became a prominent feature of Protestant communal identity after the community was cut off from the UK state in 1921 and asked to perform a new Imperial duty as a semi-detached outpost. There is some evidence that it greatly increased in the Terence O'Neill years when the Protestant masses became uneasy about concessions to Catholics. Flag waving is a sign of insecurity in the sense that it seems as if it has to be done to reassure Unionists that they are still 'British' and still top-dog in their backyard—in 'our wee Ulster' as it is sometimes put. It is proof that the Unionist community was vitally damaged by the arrangement of 1921 which cut it off, along with its Catholic neighbours, from the political life of the State.

In resisting the Equality Agenda of Sinn Fein within 'Northern Ireland', the mass base of Unionism helps to fragment the Protestant bloc and produces the further withdrawal from politics of its middle-class component, accentuating Unionism's yahoo and religious fundamentalist character. And that in turn leads to the production of increased discontent among the Unionist mass base that transmits itself into Unionist politics.

Robinson's Retreat

In the middle of the Flag Dispute, during May 2013, Jim Allister, the one-man opposition at Stormont, scored a rare political success for the Unionist ethnic bloc in the passing of a Private Member's Bill on Special Advisers (SPADS). This was an anti-Sinn Fein measure on the part of the Traditional Unionist Voice that managed to ensnare the SDLP. The Assembly voted to bar anyone with a *"serious"* (i.e. 5 year) conviction from being a special political adviser at Stormont. It was passed with the support of Unionist and Alliance MLAs. Sinn Féin and the Green Party voted against the Bill, while the SDLP abstained. If the SDLP had united with Sinn Fein to call for a *Petition Of Concern* to ensure that the measure enjoyed the support of both communities, the Act would not have passed.

The Act was called *'Anne's Law'* after Anne Travers, the campaigning sister of the woman who had been accidentally killed by the IRA in an attempt on the life of her father, a senior Catholic judge. It was this aspect— the Catholic victim—that enabled the SDLP to be ensnared and separated from the Nationalist bloc.

The issue of Special Advisors itself was minor but the small Unionist victory had repercussions. From the contributions of some of the DUP members in the Assembly, it was clear that they greatly enjoyed this sojourn into the past and the indulging of fundamentalist instincts, after being nudged into a more accommodationist position by Robinson in the aftermath of the Flags dispute. As a result of the letting loose of basic instincts, the DUP/Sinn Fein relationship, which depended much on Robinson, began to fracture. Under pressure from the Flag protesters, the Orange Order, the TUV, and Victims campaigners, Robinson decided to pull down the Long Kesh Peace and

Reconciliation Centre project (which was to be symbolically sited in the former Maze Internment Camp) he had unveiled only four months previously, to steady his party. Sinn Fein had agreed to a DUP majority on the Board of this project and it was a massive blow to the relationship built up between Sinn Fein and the DUP when Robinson unilaterally ditched agreed plans and it led to deterioration in the relationship between the two parties.

It was said that Republican "*insensitivity*" pushed Robinson into this change of course but the issues cited in Robinson's letter (written from his American holiday home), on which Unionists had found Sinn Fei*n* "*insensitive*", had all occurred before June 2013, at a time when he continued to support the Long Kesh Peace Project against its detractors. One of the issues cited was the Tyrone Volunteers march, which had taken place for many years without comment, and which took place in Castlederg (without incident) after Robinson had written his 13 page letter from America. In fact, as Liam Clarke revealed in a radio interview with a New York-based station, Robinson and other DUP members had told him that they pulled down the project because they feared that it would be used against them within Unionism in elections over a considerable period, as the project was being built.

Robinson became vulnerable after the small TUV victory in the Assembly, which caused rejectionist Unionists to scent an opportunity to undermine his relationship with McGuinness and thereby destroy the coalition with Sinn Fein. The nonsensical behaviour of Dublin down the years, which was aimed at undermining Adams and Sinn Fein by highlighting the fate of victims, also sent out a message to those wishing to break the functional arrangement. The Northern rejectionists thus found that they were part of mainstream politics across the island. Up until then Robinson had risen above this fundamentalist behaviour, by pursuing Paisley's broader strategy of implicating Sinn Fein in the government of 'Northern Ireland', hoping thereby to quell the Republican storm and halt its momentum.

Robinson gave an indication of the broader policy in a speech to Castlereagh Council. Here is the report from the *Belfast Telegraph*:

> "Insisting that the Union was stronger than ever, he cautioned unionists not to 'turn the clock back to a bygone era' and urged them to have more self confidence. 'Unionism has historically had a siege mentality', he said. 'When we were being besieged it was the right response. But when we are in a constitutionally safe and stable position it poses as a threat to our future development. Demographic changes and social change mean that we need to build bigger and broader coalitions and not to retreat into an ever-diminishing core.'
>
> "He said unionism should not be defined simply by the issues of 'flags and parades' but by what he described as the benefits of living in the UK.

'Unionism needs to think and act strategically... because if unionists are not seen to make Northern Ireland work within the Union then no one will. Unionism will only succeed if it is a broad coalition of interests. I accept that not every person who wishes to remain part of the United Kingdom will share my affection for the national flag or even my cultural heritage. My responsibility as leader of the largest unionist party is to seek to hold that broad coalition together for it is only the capacity to bring together those with differing views under a common banner that gives unionism its strength.'

"Mr Robinson... challenged the view that unionist culture was being eroded. 'Unionists are the purveyors of unionist culture. Nobody can take our culture away from us. It's within us... Outsiders might try—and from time to time succeed—in limiting our cultural expression in a specific place or manner but they have no power to stop us increasing our expression in other ways. Such a nationalist strategy doesn't make me feel culturally diminished. It just makes me angry. Angry that people cannot respect and tolerate diversity. But that anger should be channelled into overcoming such intolerance...' The First Minister said unionists and nationalists had to work together to secure progress.

"Mr Robinson said it was foolish to think that the collapse of the Assembly would not result in further conflict. 'Happily, it's only an academic argument but I have absolutely no doubt that if the Assembly were to fall it would leave a void which every malign force would seek to exploit and profit from', he said. 'Paramilitary organisations which are presently contained would be reinforced and bracing themselves for an opening to wage terror'..." (19.10.13).

There was much sense in Robinson's argument to Unionism. The former days were over where the 'minority' could be presided over as a second-class community. They were no longer a 'minority' because of demographics and soon they might be a majority. And, as a result of the Republican War, they were no longer second-class. So Unionism had to take account of them and even court them, or a section of them, to survive. Robinson was also aware of the antagonising effects of 'Protestant culture' on Catholics. Whilst many aspects of the British State are attractive to Northern Catholics, the Ulsterish variant of Britishness repels them.

It was not those who had the Union flag waved at them who took away the Union. The Northern Catholics led by Joe Devlin were enthusiastically Imperial. Devlin's Hibernians were helping to integrate Ireland into the developing British welfare state, and West Belfast was one of the great recruiting centres for Britain's Great War. It boasted of being more loyal to England's cause than the loyalists. But they don't make Northern Catholics like that any more. 'Northern Ireland' saw to that. The major political effect of 'Northern Ireland' has been to make its inhabitants less and less British as the years rolled by—something which Carson predicted and feared.

The symbolism of the flag dispute set off a chain of events that resulted in the bulk of the DUP and the Protestant middle-class—which had not retreated from politics altogether, was discontented with being hustled into the Agreement, and was never comfortable in the potential of the Paisley/Robinson strategy to blunt Republicanism—losing its faith in the strategy.

Moving towards the edge

The success of the Paisley/Robinson project depended on Unionism being amenable to Six County Catholics and making 'Northern Ireland' possible for them to live in contentedly. And that meant holding a tight control over all the instinctive reflexes of Ulsterish Unionism. That was proving a difficult project to see through, given the nature of 'Northern Ireland' and its communal blocs. By 2013 the Unionist mass base had been on the streets, Jim Allister was harassing the DUP, and its rank and file were growing in discontent.

With the Northern Ireland institutions under threat, talks were held under the Chairmanship of American Richard Haass. Unionist discomfort over issues like flags, parading, and coming to terms with the past was clear during the Haass Talks on these issues in late 2013, despite the 'hush-hush' nature of the negotiations. Surrendering ground on unrestricted flag-waving and parading through the territory of other communities is a painful, divisive and fragmenting experience for a Unionism whose remaining Britishness was almost entirely based on such things. It was caught in a contradiction between making the necessary compromises to establish the required equality under the 1998 Constitution to please the British and the US Governments on the one hand, and keeping its base happy by preserving some majority/dominant status, on the other. And all the time the secular Protestant middle-class was walking away from politics, or voting Alliance, at the unpleasantness of it all. For both Unionist Parties there was the realisation that any compromise with equality could be used opportunistically by the other and, if both compromised, Jim Allister, leader of the tiny Traditional Unionist Voice, would be the winner. And increasing Protestant fragmentation and withdrawal from politics could only benefit Sinn Fein electorally, turning it into the dominant party in 'Northern Ireland', the territory carved out for Unionism.

The failure of the Haass Talks demonstrated that the 'Northern Ireland' system was not capable of autonomous functioning beyond anything but the mundane. It is a system that requires active supervision from London and Dublin. And, when necessary, Washington intervention is needed to jump-start it when it stalls. That is because, within its delegated affairs, it operates as two separate communal blocs voting on matters in parallel—so it is incapable of resolving issues of fundamental difference internally.

The Good Friday institutions lack the dynamic of internal development. Any dynamic that has existed has centred on the tying up of loose ends, of completing unfinished business from the 1998 Agreement. And the local parties are incapable of following through on even this without the requisite muscle from London, Dublin and Washington. In a speech to the British-Irish Association Conference in September 2013 the Secretary of State for 'Northern Ireland' signalled that what was required from Haass was an *"internal solution"* and a blame-limiting process confined to the two communities.

Robinson and McGuinness called in Haass presumably in order to implicate the Ulster Unionists and DUP rank-and-file in a deal on the issues that were destabilising the functional settlement in 2013, but to no avail. The Nationalist bloc made compromises, feeling able to compromise because it had no opposition outside the negotiations to worry about. But the Unionist ultras and the volatile yahoo element of Unionism lay in wait for the Unionist bloc delegates and they did not dare to make the necessary compromises by signing up to the Haass Document No.7. The Nationalists salvaged a moral victory out of the wreckage by accepting Document No. 7 and pleasing Washington. But that was that.

There was another crisis in February 2014, when DUP First Minister Robinson threatened to bring the devolved system down if *Letters of Comfort* given many years earlier to republicans liable to prosecution were not withdrawn by the British Government. A Judicial Inquiry was conceded by the British Prime Minister. This concession was something entirely different to what the First Minister was demanding and much less consequential. However, Robinson accepted it, drawing back from the abyss.

The Westminster Government helped to accentuate the instability within Unionism. From 2011 the British began stripping the North of about £1.5 billion pounds of its annual Block Grant. Large cuts to public services pushed the administration to breaking point. Westminster also required Belfast to impose welfare cuts in line with Britain but found that, due to the Good Friday Agreement, this was now a devolved matter. This meant that Nationalist consent was necessary. Although the decision not to cut welfare benefits when they were being cut in Britain was made within the authority devolved to Stormont, Whitehall decided to override that authority. The Cameron Coalition, in line with its austerity policy, imposed a cut of £1 billion a year in the North, over four years, and demanded that welfare cuts be implemented largely on the same basis as in Britain.

When the Government of the State decided to impose cuts on its sub-government's welfare provision and Sinn Fein and the SDLP attempted a stand against the cuts, Whitehall replied with drastic fines on Stormont, starting at £87m for 2013-4, rising to £114m for 2014-5, out of its general Budget. NI does not have its own revenue streams as such: taxes are raised as an integral part of the UK (whilst being excluded from the politics of the State). As such, it can only distribute what is given to it by Whitehall, and its electorate can do nothing about it every five years, even if it is unhappy about such things, as it does not elect the governing parties.

Sinn Fein made two reasonable proposals for resolving the issue: either let the Assembly, freed of communal voting rules in this instance, decide it, or put it to a referendum. These proposals were rejected. The Government of the State replied that it was exploring "all options which were legally and constitutionally possible" to impose its will, including a suspension of the Assembly but a leaving in place the façade of an Executive on the Stormont hill. Another option was a short suspension and return to Direct Rule, to impose the new financial arrangements (BT 1.11.14)

Around this time the Tories were courting the DUP as possible electoral support at Westminster in the event of a tight 2015 election. The DUP broke ranks by accepting the cuts, to show their amenability.

Sinn Fein, as the only party which aspired to govern a state, and as the only cross-Border party in 'Northern Ireland', was vulnerable to political manoeuvres by its opponents in Dublin. It was attacked by Charles Flanagan, the Fine Gael Irish Foreign Minister, for having *"failed to take the tough budgetary decisions that have to be made in government"*. And, of course, if Sinn Fein had tamely accepted welfare cuts in the North, it would undoubtedly have been the subject of the opposite criticism—opposing austerity in the South whilst implementing it in the North. The SDLP was absolved from such criticism being only a local party of 'Northern Ireland' and having no pretensions for real politics or government. However, it was again placed in an awkward position by the British economic assault on the North.

In the event, Sinn Fein negotiated the Stormont House Agreement of December 2014 that ameliorated the welfare cuts in return for Britain making concessions on three key issues discussed by Haass. However, Sinn Fein made it clear that it was protecting both present and future claimants from the full impact of the 'reforms'. It appeared that Sinn Fein had managed to avert the fall of Stormont and agree to the social welfare cuts in a way that prevented political damage to itself. The Dublin Government publicly implicated itself in this deal and was thereby disabled from criticising Sinn Fein for accepting austerity, admitting that it was an external imposition from London, one which it supported. The rest of the Stormont House deal was a kind of 'keeping the show on the road' operation, with nothing of substance solved but everything put up for negotiation/conflict. The deal included: a Commission on Flags, Identity, Culture and Tradition; a transfer of the business of the Parades Commission to the Assembly; the establishment of an oral history archive; a Historical Investigations Unit to deal with legacy issues; an Independent Commission on Information Retrieval to help relatives of victims to gain information confidentially; the possibility of establishing an Official Opposition; and a reduction of the Stormont Ministries from 12 to 9.

Just before the 2015 General Election the DUP, which had been courted by the Tories (fearing they were not going to get a working majority) and seeking to establish distance from its Sinn Fein partners in government for electoral purposes, decided to use an accounting manoeuvre to welch on the deal. It restricted protection to existing claimants. Learning of the manoeuvre, Sinn Fein responded by opposing the Welfare Bill by tabling of a Petition of Concern—a legitimate mechanism of the Good Friday Agreement. Stalemate ensued again.

During the UK election campaign Unionists were reminded again that they were not fully British or part of the Union. 'Northern Ireland' parties were excluded from the TV Election debates, as inclusion of NI parties would have made them too unwieldly. Lord Hall, replying to a DUP complaint about the unfairness of this, when other regional parties in the UK were included in the debates, pointed to the fact that the parties of State do not compete for seats in the 'Northern Ireland' region. This is the fundamental test of membership of the Union and its politics. 'Northern Ireland' is a place, formally part of the UK, but actually apart from it. Cameron, embarrassed at this blurting out of the political facts of life when he was attempting to court the DUP as future lobby fodder, said he was in favour of including the party in the debates. However, he was only playing political games, as TV debates did not favour his position.

Stormont House Crash

In May 2015, Cameron, having secured a majority for the Tories at Westminster without requiring support from the DUP, moved to strip public services and welfare in the North of a further £25 Billion. This would have made the financial situation of the Executive at Stormont unsustainable. The DUP, having thought it would be indispensable to Cameron, found itself expendable. However, Unionism went along with the cuts, even though a substantial part of its own community was affected. Presumably the issue was judged a useful diversionary action to avoid a compromise with Sinn Fein on legacy issues, flags and parading.

Sinn Fein is the only party in 'Northern Ireland' which aspires to govern a state. Its constituency in both States demands that it opposes the Tory welfare cuts—which were actually opposed by many in the UK, including a substantial number of Conservatives. Stalemate set in. Then in August 2015, after the shooting of two former members of the Provos in Belfast, PSNI Chief Constable George Hamilton, after media provocation promoting political policing, claimed that the IRA still existed and had carried out one of the killings. This enabled the Unionist Party to attempt to out-flank the DUP. UUP Leader Mike Nesbitt withdrew his only Minister from the Executive, to distance the party from the DUP: the two parties that had drawn together in support of the Tory welfare reform cuts. In this way, the subordinate part of Unionism hoped to recapture lost ground to the dominant part in the 2016 Assembly Election.

The UUP leader described the Executive as a *"busted flush"* and stated he was going to form an opposition (BT 26.8.15). The UUP walked away, calling for the DUP to withdraw from the Executive: effectively a call to bring down the institutions.

Robinson, not wanting to do the UUP bidding, and also reluctant to end power-sharing, then *"stepped aside"* with four of his five Ministers, but failed in a motion to have the Assembly adjourned as the SDLP supported Sinn Fein in opposing the proposal.

Robinson then called on the British Government to suspend the institutions, but the proposal was rejected. The conflict within Unionism was all about who could push things closest to tipping point without actually taking everything over the cliff.

It was clear that Robinson, after a period of maintaining stability at Stormont, had been unsettled by a revival of the fundamentalist instinct within the DUP. On top of this, the recent semi-resurgence of the UUP under its new leader, had stirred up discontent amongst the DUP to a level that made Robinson's earlier project, outlined in his Castlereagh speech, of stabilising 'Northern Ireland' in the Unionist interest, untenable.

All in all there was little reason to doubt Sinn Fein's view that the crash of the Stormont House Agreement in late 2015 was *"a contrived crisis"*, brought about by the electoral rivalry between the two branches of Unionism. The *casus belli* of the crisis was flimsy in the extreme—the killing of two former Republican prisoners, not usually a concern of Unionism.

The impasse that developed threatened the continued existence of devolved government. All-party talks were convened and these led to a deal called *"Fresh Start"*, under which the devolved administration would be able to partially protect welfare recipients until the next British General Election.

Stormont temporarily ceded the devolved power of welfare to Westminster to enable the sovereign Government of the State to over-ride it and impose its policy on a UK-wide basis. If it hadn't done so, Westminster could have taken back the powers by suspending the Good Friday Agreement or restricting devolved powers—it is the sovereign power after all. But that would have endangered the Agreement.

Sinn Fein could have called Britain's bluff on the matter and provoked a major crisis. However, if it had, it would have made itself dependent on Dublin's will to defend the Agreement, as its Guarantor in 1998. It chose not to risk what it had gained on that and agreed to deal with Westminster. The SDLP took the opportunity to make some easy criticisms of Sinn Fein for bowing to the Westminster diktat by giving away powers devolved to the Assembly.

A Position of Stalemate

Sinn Fein submitted to that Westminster diktat in order to preserve the substance of the arrangement that had been achieved on the basis of the 1998 Agreement because that arrangement was advantageous to the position of its Northern constituency, the Six County Catholic community. Others were willing to collapse those arrangements because they did not find them advantageous.

The overall situation continued as one of stalemate, with the two communities in the North each having a veto on changes proposed by the other. But, within that overall stalemate, little changes are made which do not impinge on the Constitutional arrangement immediately but will probably do so in the long run.

Brian Feeney, a former active member of the SDLP who became an objective political commentator in the SDLP-oriented *Irish News*, recognised this and saw its significance. On 11th April 2012 he commented:

> "Sinn Fein has been unashamedly taking ownership of the North. Areas of life here which for generations unionists believed were exclusive to them and of which they had sole possession have now been invaded and taken over by republicans. It gives another meaning to a shared society. Unionists look on in bewilderment as Sinn Fein confidently assert control of what are called 'signature' projects that unionists expected might have caused embarrassment to republicans. Not a bit of it. They own the north as much as any unionist. 'An Ireland of equals' you see... Unionists stand open mouthed as Republicans appear to promote 'Norn Irn'. Of course, in the next breath republicans remind them it is all part of a larger project to make unionists feel safe in a future united Ireland... At the same time no unionist could fault McGuinness for the commitment with which he operates the institutions of the local administration here. In fact, he and his fellow republicans have taken complete possession of all aspects of that administration, haven't they? They're making *'Norn Irn'* work, aren't they? Unionists couldn't complain about that, could they? It has baffled some Sinn Fein supporters who write to this paper objecting that Sinn Fein has 'sold out'—

but these supporters fail to see... that by embracing fully all the north's institutions Sinn Fein is irrevocably changing the north into a place unionists no longer own or even recognise but can't object to."

Involvement in commemorating Somme events and engaging with the British Royal Family were outstanding instances of this approach. These were the sacred icons of the Unionist Family after it allowed itself to be shunted into Northern Ireland semi-detachment from Britain in 1921. They were what made it British and distinguished it from the Fenians / Papists / Rebels. But this was the case no longer. Fenians now appeared at Somme commemorations and were guests of the Royal Family—and remained Fenians still.

It disconcerted Unionists to find that the enemy shared their shibboleths— and all the more so because they sensed that the enemy did not really share them.

Sinn Fein did not celebrate the event of the Somme: it commemorated the dead of that event. Six County Catholics took part in the Great War, having been recruited in large numbers into the British Army by the Home Rule leader, Joe Devlin. They went over the top at the Somme because the Home Rule leadership had told them this was the way to get the Home Rule Bill implemented. They died—but Home Rule was not implemented. And the survivors came home to find that there would be no Home Rule; that they were to be excluded from the British political life of which they had seen themselves a part; and that they would be required to live under the local rule of the Orange Order. When they had gone off to the War, there had been no hint that this was in prospect.

The Somme was a real tragedy for the Home Rulers who died there, and it is right that it should be commemorated as a tragedy. In Imperial memory, however, it is a glorious event to be celebrated. The difference between the two has profound implications.

And the Queen? Well, she isn't really a monarch at all. Tom Paine, the pioneer of English Republicanism, recognised over two centuries ago that England was a republic using monarchy as a convenience, and for camouflage. Martin McGuinness met the Queen as the figurehead leader of the state against which he had made war and with which he had made peace. The actual peace negotiations had been conducted with the elected Government that gave the Monarch her orders.

And Gerry Adams shook hands as an equal with the future King at the place where the future King's uncle, Lord Mountbatten, had been killed in a Republican act of war.

It is a very long time since the British State made peace on terms like that with an enemy against whom it had fought a War.

The new post-Republican middle class of the 26 County Establishment were honoured by invitations to meet British Royalty. Sinn Fein met the Royals as a matter of practical political business.

This difference in state of mind is sensed by Unionists. They know very well that Sinn Fein did these things in a different spirit. But what could they do about it?

The Fenians moved in, onto their ground. And did it in a way that demystified it. At the same time, the mystique still works on those who are enraptured by it.

Sinn Fein, in the British sphere of its activity, has acquired the skill of doing politics in the British way, while remaining Irish Republican in outlook.

Republicanism Or Anti-Partitionism?

Is Republicanism the same thing as Anti-Partitionism? Does a detour, a manoeuvre, on the way to ending Partition, mean the end of Republicanism?

Anti-Provo Republican Dissidents think that it does: Republicanism is equated with simple Anti-Partitionism.

Martin McGuinness said in a radio interview at the Sinn Fein Ard Fheis of 2012:

"I recognise that there are one million people on this island who are British and let me state here and now that as a proud Irish Republican I not only recognise the unionist and British identity, I respect it. People who think that a new Ireland, a united Ireland can be built without unionist participation, involvement and leadership are deluded... The war is over and we are in the process of building a new Republic" (Irish Independent, 23.6.12).

This was, *de facto*, the 'two nations' view of the Northern situation as put by the Irish Communist Organisation (more conveniently known as 'Athol St.') in 1969.

The ICO, as an active element in Northern politics, had its origin, along with the Provos, behind the West Belfast barricades in August 1969. Republicanism was almost dead as a movement in 1969. As far as it was present, it called itself *"Republican Socialism"*. But Republican Socialism had no currency when the masses were impelled into action by the events of mid-August. Socialist appeals could not cross the barricades in a situation in which the sense of nationalist difference was uppermost.

The ICO therefore said that the fact of national difference must be acknowledged in order for there to be any practical possibility of cross-community rapprochement. It proposed this to the Dublin Establishment, which was very anti-Partitionist in its rhetoric at the time. Taoiseach Lynch issued a formal rejection of the proposal at the Fianna Fail Ard Fheis about a month later.

The Republican Socialist IRA of 1969 became the Officials, or Stickies, in 1970, and it condemned both the *"two-nationists"* and the new Republican body that began to organise itself on the evident realities of Northern life. It condemned the Provos as sectarian bourgeois nationalists in the pay of the Dublin Establishment. And it condemned the ICO as Imperialist. And then, in the course of about a decade, its members entered the Dublin Establishment, qualifying for entry by the vehemence of their condemnation of the Provos.

The Provos also condemned the *"two nationists"*—or some of them did. In 1972, when military action was at its most intense, the *Republican News* (April) derided the "two nationism" being published down in Athol St. *Liam Mac's page* denounced the ICO as a "true blue unionist organisation" (30.4.72). But there were also others who knew better, Ruairi O Bradaigh being one of them.

The *Workers Weekly* (Athol St: a precursor of the present *Irish Political Review*) replied to *Republican News* that—

"In August 1969 it contributed more to the defence of Catholic areas than some bodies with very great pretensions. As a consequence of its involvement in this it was led to do some serious thinking about the developments that led to August 1969, and about the general national question. It came to the conclusion that there was no validity in the 'one nation' dogma which it had taken from the Catholic bourgeoisie. There were no national ties between the Catholic and Protestant communities. They were two distinct historical communities. They could form a common state by agreement, but for either to assert national rights over the other was completely undemocratic... Furthermore, we have observed that for all practical purposes nobody believes in the 'one nation' theory. Everybody, be he Republican or Unionist, who makes practical political calculations reckons the Protestant and Catholic to be distinct and separate communities... The inevitable outcome of the national conflict will be a compromise between the two nations" (*Workers Weekly* 5.5.72).

The view of the Dublin Establishment of the early 1970s was that Ulster Unionism was a kind of illusion that would soon be blown away, or a delusion that would be rectified by a sharp shock. It saw the North as being run by a feudal aristocracy that was manipulating the masses by means of an obsolete form of religion that had somehow dragged on from the 17th century and would soon be overcome by modern fashion. Brendan Clifford was derided for mistaking this concoction, that would collapse, for a nation. He replied in a pamphlet, published about that time, that he was sure the Ulster Unionist morale would long outlast the morale of Dublin Establishment anti-Partitionism. That was borne out over subsequent decades.

Dublin Governments in the new millennium have even less understanding of basic facts of life in the North than they had in the 1960s and 1970s. The Provos grew in strength by coping with facts. And they have long coped with the fact that the difference running through the North is a *national* difference, and that it must be worked around.

Dissident Republican intellectual Anthony McIntyre expressed the opinion that anti-Partitionism is Republicanism, and that any admission of a national complication in the North abandons Republicanism:

> "Republicanism is dead in my view because it lacks the capacity to overcome the bedrock of partition—the refusal of the unionists to consent. Republicanism as we knew it had a coercive attitude to unionism. Republicanism sought to coerce the Brits out of Ireland and the unionists into a united Ireland. It failed absolutely and nobody yet has put forward a plausible strategy for making coercion work. And once republicanism abandons coercion and acquiesces in the consent principle it is no longer republicanism, but merely embracing the Brit/unionist/constitutional nationalist means of getting the Brits to leave and getting the unionists into a united Ireland... The unionist question is the central question and one that can't be wished away. The unbridgeable cleavage between the British state and republicanism was not on whether Ireland should or should not be united. It was on the terms it would be united. The Brits insisted on the partition/consent principle. Republicanism dissolved itself in order to acquiesce in the Brit position. Once the consent principle is accepted it is an acknowledgement that partition has a democratic basis and is therefore legitimate. That is something which is irreconcilable with the republicanism we knew... There are only two ways to unite the country: coercion of the North or consent. The republican position is one of coercion. The British state's position is one of consent. The coercive position does not have to be one of armed struggle. The Brits or the international community could arrive at a conclusion that the six counties are Irish territory and should therefore be returned... Republicanism can do everything... apart from signing up to the consent principle which legitimises partition. The entire philosophical basis of republicanism is that... no minority on the island has the right to rupture the national unity and that to recognise the consent/partition principle is to give them that right" (From the Pensive Quill, September 2014).

Academic history is doctrinaire and merges conveniently with doctrinaire notions of Republicanism. And it contrasts with Sinn Fein's understanding of social reality, of the *"bulks of actual things"*, as Pearse once put it, in relation to the substance of the Northern Protestants.

What was it that Wolfe Tone actually said? He did not say: *There are no Anglicans, Dissenters and Catholics, only Irishmen.* He said his aim was to bring it about that Anglicans, Dissenters and Catholics would all become citizens of an Irish nation. He wanted to make them into Irishmen

because the nation was what was becoming the general form of socio-political organisation.
That surely was what Martin McGuinness set out to do.
McIntyre said Republicanism was dead because the Republican War to knock down the British State in the Six Counties and set up an all-Ireland state failed in that object, and that what it succeeded in doing counted for nothing.
The War failed in one object and succeeded in another. It caused the British State to exert pressure on the Protestant community to submit to a re-arrangement of the internal mode of government in the North. That rearrangement gave the Catholic community a guaranteed position in public life which enabled the Republican cause to be pursued Constitutionally.

McIntyre said that Republicanism is Anti-Partitionism pure and simple, and that it was a matter of "*all or nothing*". If an interim settlement, that was much more more than nothing, was achievable as a result of the military action, it should not have been achieved or accepted. The Republicans who achieved it, and used it as ground for achieving Irish unity by other means, killed Republicanism.
The right thing for Republicans to have done was to admit defeat, plead guilty to having waged an unjust war, and walk away from the situation.
The revisionist historians depict Republicanism as an elitist ideology that despises the people. That was a caricature of the Republicanism of the past, but it seems to be true of the rejectionist Republicanism that sees no value in the interim settlement which greatly improved the political and social position of the Catholic community, and which that community had experienced as a victory that opened the way to further development.

At the time of the 1998 Agreement McIntyre wrote an article for the *Guardian* headlined "*We, the IRA, have failed*". What failed was the One Nationism on which the War was launched in 1970. But that denial of national diversity within the North was not an IRA position particularly. It was the general position of nationalist Ireland as a whole, from the President and the Taoiseach downwards—barring Athol St. (and some isolated individual voices, like Desmond Fennell). The Provisional leadership felt its way towards an interim settlement taking account of the fact of national difference within the North. McIntyre and his colleagues continued in denial of that fact.

"The republican position is one of coercion. The British state's position is one of consent... Republicanism can do everything... apart from signing up to the consent principle which legitimises partition. The entire philosophical basis of republicanism is that... no minority on the island has the right to rupture the national unity" (Pensive Quill, September 2014).

There was a war between the British State and the Provisional IRA on the issue of uniting Ireland by force. If the War had not been fought with the British State, it would have been fought with a military force of the Ulster Protestant community. That was the case on the island in 1919, and in the North in 1970.

Redmond denied that *Ulster Would Fight*, and he expected the British Army to bring it into line for him.

Sinn Fein in those times was not so certain that Ulster would not fight. It knew that the British Army would not force 'Ulster' into an all-Ireland political structure. And there were prominent members of Sinn Fein who did not see the coercing of 'Ulster' into the Republic as being Republican in spirit.

The Vice-President of Sinn Fein recognised in 1916 that:

> "The Unionists of Ulster have never transferred their love and allegiance to Ireland. They may be Irelanders, using Ireland as a geographical term, but they are not Irish in the national sense..." (Fr. Michael O'Flanagan as reported in *Freeman's Journal*, 20.6.1916).

The question now is whether the political force generated out of the segment of the Irish Nation which was trapped on the wrong side of the Border, and subjected to hostile government by the Unionist Irish nation for 50 years, can succeed where the one-nationist Anti-Partitionism of the 26 County State failed so completely.

The Constitution of the 26 County state denied the legitimacy of British sovereignty in the 6 County secession until 1998, and it never paid any attention to the anomalous form of government established by the British State in its Six County region. The North was undemocratically governed even by British standards, regardless of rhe question of legitimate sovereignty, but Dublin Governments never made that an issue with Britain.

The Southern sovereignty claim was repealed in 1998, with IRA approval, but no definite view of what Northern Ireland was then was ever published by the Southern State or its major political parties. The sovereignty claim was replaced by an "*aspiration*" to unity, but no political engagement with Ulster Unionism with a view to achieving that aspiration followed.

The first nationalist political force that ever came to a close political engagement with Ulster Unionism is Provisional Sinn Fein.

Consent?

As the position of the nationalist community in the north strengthens with Republicans in government under the 1998 Agreement, and the nationalist population increases proportionately, the consent principle with regard to unity will possibly become a live political issue. The expectation of this was a factor in the making of the 1998 settlement. Consent was not a pig in a poke.

The Unionists chose their ground. They chose, or agreed to, a kind of minimal Home Rule, connected with Britain but detached from British politics.

Unionism has not flourished under this form of Unionist Home Rule. The nationalist minority of a third in 1921 maintained itself for half a century, and it has done much better than maintain itself since Unionism threw itself into crisis by its conduct in 1969.

Sinn Fein has signed up to *consent*. So has the SDLP. (It is too often forgotten that the 'Constitutional nationalists' rejected the principle of consent for most of this period, calling it the "*Unionist veto*".)

Which consent is meant—Unionist consent or Northern Ireland consent?

The constitutional position under the Good Friday Agreement is that, once a first Border Poll is held, it will be repeated every seven years. That provision has kept the peace since 1998 and it is impossible to see it abrogated.

Some people are trying to move the goalpost from Northern Ireland consent to Unionist consent. They want to reassert the principle that was adopted in 1912 that there must be an agreement acceptable to Unionism. In the end that meant Ulster Unionism.

But Unionism chose Six Counties as its safe haven, and surely the ground on which consent must operate is the Six County voting population.

Will Unionism agree to that, if there is a danger of the consent vote going against it?

History is not yet at an end.

Bibliography

Bew, Paul	*Ireland, the Politics of Enmity, 1789-2006*, in *Ireland* volume of the *Oxford History of Modern Europe*
Bishop, Patrick & Bloomfield, Ken	*Stormont in Crisis. A Tragedy of Errors, The Government and Misgovernment of Northern Ireland*
Bleakley, David	*Faulkner*
Brady, Seamus	*Arms and the Men*
	Eye-witness report by Seamus Brady on events in Derry, NAI, 2000/6/658
British Government	*The Future of Northern Ireland*
	Northern Ireland Constitutional Proposals
Burton, Frank	*The Politics of Legitimacy*
Cahill, Joe	*The Provisional IRA*
Callaghan, James	*A House Divided*
Clifford, Angela	*August 1969: Ireland's Only Appeal to the United Nations — a cautionary tale of humiliation and moral collapse*
	The Arms Conspiracy Trial. Ireland 1970: the Prosecution of Charles Haughey, Capt. Kelly and Others
	The Arms Crisis
Clifford, Brendan	*Against Ulster Nationalism*
Currie, Austin	*All Hell Will Break Loose*
de Baroid, Ciaran	*Ballymurphy and the Irish War*
Devlin, Paddy	*Straight Left*
	The Fall of The Executive
Doherty, Paddy	*Paddy Bogside*
Downing Street Communiqué and Declaration	
Faulkner, Brian	*Memoirs of a Statesman*
Fisk, Robert	*The Point Of No Return: The Strike Which Broke The British In Ulster*
Harnden, Toby	*Bandit Country: The IRA and South Armagh*
Heath, Edward	*The Course of My Life*
Hughes, Brendan	*Voices from the Grave*
Irish Government	*Pamphlet on the current and historical situation in Northern Ireland and the need for reform*
Kelly, Capt. James	*The Thimble Riggers*
Kelly, Stephen	*Fianna Fáil, Partition and Northern Ireland, 1926-1971*
McAllister, Ian	*The Northern Ireland Social and Democratic Party*
MacDonald, Darach	*The Chosen Fews, Exploding Myths in South Armagh*
McKearney, Tommy	*The Provisional IRA, From Insurrection to Parliament*'
MacStiofain, Sean	*Memoirs of a Revolutionary*
Mallie, Eamonn	*The Provisional IRA*

Maudling, Reginald	*Memoirs*
Moloney, Ed	*Voices from the Grave*
Morgan, John	*The Dublin/Monaghan Bombings 1974, a military analysis*
Mumford, Andrew	*The Counter-Insurgency Myth: The British Experience of Irregular Warfare*
Murphy, Michael	*Gerry Fitt—A Political Chameleon*
Murray, Gerard & Tonge, Jonathan	*Sinn Fein and the SDLP*
O'Duffy, Brendan	*The Price of Containment*, in *The Northern Ireland Question in British Politics*
Ó Fearghail, Seán Óg	*Law (?) and Orders—The Story of the Belfast Curfew, 3-5 July 1970*
Patterson, Henry	*Ireland Since 1939*
	'Deeply anti-British'? The Irish State and Cross-border Security Cooperation 1970-1974
Phoenix, Eamonn	*Irish Times* 1.1.00
(Provisionals)	*Eire Nua*
Ramsey, Robert	*Ringside Seats*
Routledge, Paul	*John Hume*
SDLP	*Constitution*
	Towards a New Ireland
	Another Step Forward
Smith, Wm. Beattie	*The British State and the Northern Ireland Crisis 1969-73*
Staunton, Enda	*The Nationalists of Northern Ireland*
Sunday Insight	*Ulster*
Swan, Sean	*Official Irish Republicanism, 1962 to 1972*
Taylor, Peter	*Provos—the IRA and Sinn Fein*
	Brits: The War Against the IRA
Treacy, Matt	*The IRA 1956-69, Rethinking the Republic*
White, Barry	*John Hume; Statesman of the Troubles*
Workers' Association for the Democratic Settlement of the National Conflict In Northern reland	*War Mongering! The Irish Press and the Troubles in Northern Ireland*

CAB 128/46; CAB 128/48; CAB 130/560; CAB 134/3011;
CJ 3/98
DFA 305/14/360
FCO 33/575, PRO FCO 33/759
NA 2003/16/465
NAI, 99/1/76
NAI, TSCH 2000/6/657
NAI, TSCH 2000/6/658
NAI, TSCH 2000/6/659
NAI, DFA 2000/6/660
NAI, TSCH, 2000/6/662
NAI, DEA 2001/6/513
NAI, TSCH 2001/6/517
NAI, TSCH 2001/8/15
NAI, DFA 2001/43/1392
NAI, TSCH 2002/8/481

NAI, TSCH 2002/8/483
NAI, DFA 2002/19/500
NAI, TSCH 2002/8/484
NAI, TSCH 2002/8/78
NAI, DFA 2003/13/16
NAI, TSCH 2004/21/254
NAI, TSCH 2005/7/627
NAI, TSCH 2005/7/629
NAI, TSCH 2005/7/630
NAI, TSCH 2005/7/631
NAI, TSCH 2005/7/633
NAI, TSCH 2005/7/649
NAI, DFA2003/17/30
NAI, DFA 2003/17/269
NAI, DFA 2003/17/335

NIO, CJ3/18
PREM 15/476
PRO, CJ 3/18
PRO DEFE 25/273
PRO PREM 15/476

PRONI, CAB/9/J/37/2
PRONI D/3072/4/1/1

UCDA P104/8822, 14.3.67, Aiken papers

An Phoblacht, September 1971;
Belfast Newletter, 3.1.72
Belfast Telegraph, 26.5.75
Daily Telegraph (2.7.00), *Political Guidelines for the Pacification of the Province* by Oliver Wright
Free Citizen, no 10
Evening Standard, 20.10.69
Fortnight, 21.5.73
Guardian, Seamus Twomey, 24.7.72
Hansard, 29.10.70; 22.9.71; 3.6.74
Independent, 14.12.87
Irish News, 11.8.69, 29.8.69, 4.9.69, 11.9.69, 24.9.69, 18.10.69, 11.10.69, 11.11.69, 17.11.69, 24.11.69, 1.1.70, 5.1.70, 20.1.70, 22.1.70, 23.1.70, 24.1.70, 1.1.70, 5.1.70, 22.1.70, 7.2.70, 2.3.70, 6.6.70, 7.7.70, 18.8.70, 19.8.70, 22.8.70, 23.8.70, 15.10.70, 1.6.71, 22.6.71, 25.06.71, 12.7.71, 17.7.71; Paddy Devlin 2.8.71, 10.8.71; 22.8.71; 16.12.71; 3.1.72; 26.1.72; 1.2 72 ; 4.2.72; 7.2.72; 27.3.72; 6.6.72; 27.11.72; 21.3.73; 2.7.73; 14.7.73; 21.9.73; 11.11.73; 12.12.73. 31.1.74;
Irish Press, 10.8.71, 1.2.72; 2.2.72; 27.3.72; 24.7.72; 27.7.72;
Irish Times, Austin Currie 20.6.88; Desmond Fennell 19.8.69 and 15.9.69; 14.11.70; Internment 15.7.71, John Hume, 16.8.71, 6.11.71, 31.12.71; SDLP 2.8.72, 11.8.72; Paddy Devlin, 7.11.72; Ronan Fanning, 26.2.00; Cosgrave 14.6.74; Hume 17.6.74; British withdrawal 29.12.05; UDI 3.9.75;
News Letter, 27.7.71
Republican News, Truce 5.4.75
SDLP News, Austin Currie 5.10.72
Sunday Express, Heath/Internment 28.11.93
Sunday Independent, 5.10.69; Eoghan Harris, 17.12.06; British withdrawal 1.1.06; Ceasefire, 1.1.06
Sunday Times, Truce 18.6.78
The Times, UDI 10.9.74, 23.6.75;
This Week, Ruari O'Bradaigh, 14.8.70
United Irishman, Nov. 1969, May 1970, September 1970, June 1972
Voice of the North

Index

32 County Sovereignty Committee 518

Act of Union 398,410
Abse, Leo 493
Adair, Johnny 362
A House Divided 15,63
Adams, Gerry 82,202, 374,415,444,479,532
Adenauer, Konrad 336
Afrikaner 361
Against Ulster Nationalism 261
Ahern, Bertie 120,339, 390,418,419,426
Aiken, Frank 87,548
Albert St. 64
Alderdice, Lord 421,515
Algeria 252
All Hell Will Break Loose 158,175,299
Alliance Party 141,145, 216,260,421
Allister, Jim 556,559
Alternative Assembly 160, 167,175-7,184-5,215
Althusser 461,540
Amritsar 187
Amsterdam 260
ANC 397,475
An Phoblacht 171,266, 320,367,369
Anglo-Irish Agreement 308,346,367,390
Anglo-Irish 'Treaty' 5,7, 399,447,448
'Anne's Law' 556
Another Step Forward 249
Anti-Paritionism 566, 568-9
Anti-Treatyites 10,266
Apprentice Boys 13
Ardoyne 13,68,124,129
Arlow, Rev. Wm. 258
Armagh 21
'Armalite & Ballot Box' 296

Armistice 375
Arms and the Men 21
Arms Conspiracy Trial, The 86,116
Arms Trials 115,117-19, 123,126,128,138,140,146, 152,184,335
Armstrong, Sir Robert 301-2,306-7,329
Articles 2&3 399,401,410
Asmal, Kadar 551
Athol St. 435,566
Atkins, Humphrey 280, 290,294,306,334
Aughey, Arthur 407

B&ICO 261,435,436,437
'Bandit Country' 261
B Specials 20-24,27, 30,31,33-5,37,49,50-1,53,72,100,129,223
Balance of Power 370
Ballyclare 223
Ballymacarret 131
Ballymena 379
Ballymoney 387,412
Ballymurphy 110,112, 114,131,155,187,203,269
Ballymurphy and the Irish War 127
Ballynafeigh 386
Ballyvoy/Murlough Bay 251
Baltic Exchange 357
Barricades Bulletin 64
Barry, Peter 299,318,320
Battle of the Bogside 18
Battle of the Bogside 18-19,25-6
Ballygawley Bus Bombing 328
BBC 65
Beattie, - 159,167
Beggs, Roy 504
Belcoo 191
Belfast Forum 385

Belfast Newsletter 50, 349,526
Belfast Telegraph 32,91, 110,374,410,476,483,539
Bell, Ivor 264,536
Benn, Tony 30
Bennett, Huw 268
Bennett, Jack 28
Bermuda 14
Bessbrook 262
Better Govt. of Northern Ireland Act 1920 5
Bew, Prof. 99,104,110-12,114,257,269,283,432, 460,465,467,470,485, 510,537,540,543-4
Birmingham 256
Birth of Ulster Unionism, The 435
Bishop, Patrick 26
Bishopsgate 357
Black & Tan terror 6
Black, Sir Harold 15-16,176
Blair, Tony 389,409, 412,418,419
Blaney, Neil 19,24,104, 105,118,119,120,137,140
Blanket, The 442,464, 468,488,542
Bleakley, David 157, 230-1
Blian an Bhua (Victory Year) 372
Bloody Sunday 185,187-8,190-2,194,204,212
Bloomfield, Ken 31,167, 194,224,302,304,306
Boal, Desmond 284
Bodenstown 287,359
Bogside 12,16-18,21-2, 26,34,204,205
Boland, Kevin 19, 104-5,119,225-6,550
Bolsheviks 451
Bombay High Court 186

575

Bombay Street 24,34,65, 80,115
Bord Bainne 117
Boston 260
Boston College Centre for Irish Programs IRA/UVF Project 538
Boston Coll. Tapes 453, 465,470,532,536,540,541
Boundary Commission 10,333
Bowen, Muriel 289
Bow Group 214
Boyd, Andrew 524
Bradley, Denis 503
Brady, Seamus 18,19,21, 117,142,148
Brandywell 18
Breaking the Bonds: Making Peace in N. Ireland 385
Breen, Suzanne 367
Brest-Litovsk 451,470
Brighton Bomb 304,307, 339,453
British and Peace in N. Ireland, The 288,390
British Foreign Office 13
British Foreign Sec. 14
British-Irish Association Conference 560
British-Irish Council (BIC) 522
British Labour Party 56, 60,61,63-4,142,143, 145-6,148-51
British & Peace in N. Ireland, The 330,493,504
British State & the N. Crisis, The 194,215,397
British State in Northern Ireland, The 283
Brits: The War Against the IRA 186
British TUC 234
British Way in Warfare, The 450
Broadcasting Authority Amendment Act 285
Brooke, Peter 319,350-1
Brooke speech 354

Brookeborough, Lord 35
Brown, Gordon 527
Bruton, John 377,381
Bunbeg 44,251
Burke, Danny 108
Burton, Frank 123,210
Burnside, David 486,504
Bush, G.W. 378,437
Business Week 337
Butler St. 33
Byzantine 11

Cadwallader, Anne 269, 272
Cahill, Joe 465
Cahill, Mairia 536,546, 548
Calcutta 289
Callaghan, James 13,15- 16,30,34,37-8,49, 51- 4,56,61,63,65,66,68,80, 83-4,86,142,146-50
Calvert, Prof. Harry 212
Campaign for Equal Citizenship 436
Campaign for Labour Representation 435
Canary Wharf 383,389, 491
Cappagh 325
Caraher, Ben 143
Carrington, Lord 183,351
Carron, Owen 292-4
Carson 200,310
Carter, President 377
Carthill, Al 186
Carver, Michael 171,268
Casement, Roger 172, 535
Castle St. 64
Castlederg 557
Castlereagh break-in 497-502
Castro 458
Catastrophe 5
Catholic Bulletin 336
Catholic Predicament in N. Ireland, The 5
Ceasefire (1994) 370, 376,467,519

Celtic Tiger 301
Census 2011 554-5
Chalabi, Ahmed 425,437
Chalfont, Lord 80
Chamberlain, Neville 35, 429
Chichester, Sir Arthur 445
Chichester–Clarke 13, 29-31,33-4,38,45,49, 61,87,147,155-6,158
Chilcot, Sir John 288, 330,475,498,504
Childers, Erskine 73,91, 534
Chosen Fews, Exploding Myths in South Armagh, The 262,264
Christ, Jesus 27,265
Christian Democracy 334
Churchill 428
Citizen News 34
Citizen Press 32-5,37
Citizens Defence Ctte 32, 34-5,37,50,71,80,81,96, 112,117,119,123,125-6, 127,130,-1
Citizens Press 64
Clancy, Basil 175
Claudy 191
Clifford, Angela 79,86, 110,116,128
Clifford, Brendan 261
Clinton, Bill 371,377- 9,381
Clonard Monastery 24, 330,345
Clonard St. 65
Coagh 327
Coalisland 21
Cochrane, Feargal 3 66
Colley, George 86
Collins, Michael 10,79, 112,115,153,333,390, 427-8,447,544
Collins, Stephen 334, 350,553
Collins, Tom 392
'Colon view' 430
Columbia Three Affair 496-7,502

Commonwealth 375
Communist Party 177, 234,425
Community Relations Council 157
Conaty Tom 50
Conduct of the Allies 370
Confraternities 330
Connolly Association 82
Connolly, James 143,208
Constitution Bill 216
Constituent Assembly 238
Constitutional Convention 249,254,277
Constitutional Pledge, The 442
Constructive Work Of Dail Eireann 459
Convention Repeal Act 176
Conway, Card. 188,289
Conway Mill 319,320
Conway St. 34,65
Coogan, Tim Pat 191, 289,330,333,355
Cooney, Paddy 228,236
Cooper, Ivan 42,45,177, 252
Cooper, Frank 2 46,257
Cooper St. 34,139
Council of Ireland 184, 217,220,221,224,226-8,231,234-5,238,240
Counter-Insurgency Myth: The British Experience of Irregular Warfare 169,205
Cork Examiner 284
Cosgrave, Liam 217, 226,242
Course of my Life, The 193
Cox, Harvey 319,352
Cox, Michael 407
CRA 42,43,67,75,97
Craig, Bill 129,156,164, 193-4,200,217,219, 222,276,435,437
Craigavon, Lord 44
Creggan 205,206
Cremin, Mr. 190
Criminal Law Jurisdiction Act 285
Cromwell 307,370
Croppies 40
Croppies lie down 200
Cross, Devon Gaffney 437
Crossmaglen 261,262
Crumlin Road 334
Cunningham, Joshua 422-3
Cupar St. 65
Currie, Austin 24,45,51, 53,56-7,72,139,142-4,154,158,162-3,166-7,173,175,177-8,184, 233,280,299,346,348,548
Cusack, - 159,168
Cusack, Jim 542

De Baroid, Ciaran 127
de Bary, Heinrich 466
de Breadun, Deaglan 394,396,421,551
de Brun, Bairbre 522
de Chastelain, General 423-4,487,491,515
De Gaulle 239,430
d'Hondt process 419,421, 504,515,528
De Valera 101,115,120, 152,426,466

Dail Eireann 176
Dail Uladh 176
Daily Mirror 170
Daily Telegraph 38,378
Daly, Fr. 188
Daly, Cathal 302,330
Darlington Conference 206,222
Das tellurisch 457
Davies, Sir John 445
Death of Irish Republicanism, The 469
Decommissioning 389, 417,418,422-4, 475,492,514
Democratic Left 109, 136,382
Derry Citizens Defence Association 16-17

'Derry taig' 281
Destruction by Peace: Hugh O Neill After Kinsale 445-6
Detention of Terrorists Act, The (1972) 547
De Valera 335,355, 380,447
Devenney, Samuel 16
Devlin, Bernadette 52, 136
Devlin, Joe 7,88,101, 124,145,558,565
Devlin, Justin 215
Devlin, Paddy 24,44,81, 130,136,139-41,145-6, 152-4,158,172,173, 180,202,216,226, 232,235,253,485
Direct Rule 30,48,56, 83,146,156,162,181,191, 192-3,196,201,223, 277-8,281,312
Divided we Stand 400
Divis Flats 22,64
Doherty, Paddy 12,17-18,26,42,45,122
Dolly, Michael 1304
Donaldson, Denis 499-500
Donaldson, Jeffrey 411-12, 419,422,465,480,501,504
Donlon Sean 42,151, 164,230,232,247,345,377
Dorr, Noel 306,307
Dover St. 65
Downey, James 246
Downey, John 546
Downing St. Communiqué and Declaration 31,365, 367,373,375-6,383,467
Downing Street Years, The 308
Drogheda 280
Drumcree 384,386-7,412
Drumm, Jimmy 287
Drumm, Maire 160
Drumnakilly 327,328
Dublin/Belfast Secretariat 313

577

'Dublin Fund, The' 152-3
Dublin/Monaghan Bombings, The 242
Dublin Mountains 27
Duffy, Paddy 232
Duisberg Division 347, 348
Dundalk 80
Dungannon 21,228,281
Dungiven 13,160,167, 175-7,179,184,207,215
Dunkirk—Retreat to Victory 370
Dunloy 327
Dunn, Jack 541
Dunree 80
DUP 230
Durkan, Mark 397,495, 497,505,515

Eastwood, Colm 497
Economics of Partition, The 435
Edwards, Ruth Dudley 544
EEC 194
Eire Nua 92,100,176,284
Eksund, The 324
'El Alamein' 493
Election, 1918 428
Emergency Powers Act (1973) 285,547
Empey, Reg 406,443
The English Constitution; Myths & Realities, 398
Enniskillen 21,322, 328,342
Entente, The 507
Ervine, David 538
Essex factory 205
Evening Standard, London 107
Eye Witness in Northern Ireland 117

'Facing Reality' 282
Facts and Figures of the Belfast Pogrom 1920-22 328
Fairwell to Arms, A 407

Faith of Our Fathers 185
Fall of The Executive, 235,253
Fall of the House of Paisley, The 522
Falls Curfew 129
Falls Park 177,311
Falls,The 23,37,44,64-5,84,138
Fanning, Aengus 360
Fanning, Ronan 39
Fanon 458
FARC 497
Farren, Sean 290
Far Side of Revenge, The 394,417
Faul, Fr. 289,376
Faulkner, Brian 11,38, 57,155-60,163-7,169-70,172,175,178,181,187, 192-4,196,212,218-19, 222,224,233,276,373,534
Feakle 257,258
Feehan, Sean 336
Feeney, Brian 315,382, 477,564
Fenians 13,28,53,200
Fennell, Desmond 92, 569
Fianna Fail 56,70-1, 73-6,78,88,97,105-6,117, 119,142,150,152,190, 192,333,375,533
Fianna Fáil, Partition and N. Ireland 153
File on Four 315
Finchley 322
Fine Gael 150,260
Finland 475
Fisk, Robert 261
Fitt, Gerry 10,44,45,55-7,81,139- 42,145,152-4,160,164,168,173,176-7,180,185,207,209,223, 225,227,232,233,279, 281,296,485
Fitt, Gerry: Political Chameleon 279,281
FitzGerald, Garret 217, 225,295,300,307,315,

332,334,338,377
Fitzpatrick, Fr. Noel 185
Fitzgerald, Patrick 374
Flag Dispute 556
Flanagan, Charlie 561
Flanagan, Sir Ronnie 498
Flynn, Mayor 378
Force Reconnaissance Unit 363
Ford, Major General 186
Fourthwrite 450,464, 465,486
Fortnight 346,367,369, 374,467,473,505,542
Foster, Arlene 511
Foster, John Wilson 366
Fourth International 457
Frameworks Documents 384,393
Frankenstein, Dr. 470
Free Belfast 64
Free Citizen 52
Freeland, Sir Ian 130
Freeman's Journal 570
Free State 75,297,375
From Hillsborough to Downing Street 319
Future of N. Ireland (Green Paper) 214

Gadaffi, Col. 306,323
Gallagher Eamonn 42-4, 60,84,136-7,139,140,160, 164,178,180,183,195-6
Gardai Special Branch 264
Gardiner St. 17,99
Garron Tower Conference 175
Garvaghy Road 318,386-8,416
GCHQ 414
GEN 47 192,193
General Absolution 24
General China (Waruhiu Itote) 267
German Army 374,507
Germany 323
Gibbons, James 19,119
Gibney, Jim 359,530

Gibraltar 323,327,342
Gibson, Justice 328
Gilchrist, Sir Andrew 62,81,109,110,118
'Glenanne Gang' 269
God 103
Godson, Dean 435-6, 438-40
Goebbels, Dr. 377
Goodall, Sir David 306-7,450
Good Friday Agreement 35,223,349-50,354, 396,399,402,407-9, 411,422-3,440-2,450, 462,478,486,496, 505,554,560,571
Good Friday Agreement suspensions 471
Goodison Sir Alan 337, 339
Gordon, David 522
Gorman, Tommy 464
Goulding, Cathal 17-18, 27,106,107,427,454
Government of Ireland Act 1920 46,76,343, 398,401
Gowrie, Lord 306-7
GPO 134
Great War 6,301,508,529
Greaves, Desmond 17, 28,82
Green Briar 290
Greening of the White House, The 378
Gresham Hotel 106
Grosvenor St. 101,112
Guardian, The 186,302, 378,441,467,507
Guelke, Adrian 467
Guildford 256

Hachey, Thomas E. 537
Hailsham, Lord 378
Hall, Lord 562
Hamilton, George 563
Harris, Eoghan 103,425-8,432,465,476,479,550
Hartley, Tom 321

Haas, Rich 559,560
Hassan, Fr. 328
Hastings Street 22
Haughey, Charles 19,24, 87,105,110-11,115-20, 137,142,291,295,300,318, 332-3,335-6,340-1, 344,347,350,353,359, 430,473,533,544
Haughey, Denis 397
Haughey, Sean/Jock 107,333
Haw-Haw, Lord 516
Hawthornden Road 234
Hayes, Maurice 34,157, 187,221,276
H-Block 320
Healy, Cahir 144,459
Healey, Denis 30,151
Heath, Edward 66,171, 181,183,188,192-4,213
Heath Threat 218
Hendron, Joe 278,296, 385
Heenan, Cardinal 188
Herbert St. 33
Hermon, Sir John 326
Hermon, Lady Sylvia 504
Hibernia 117
Hibernians 7,89,101-3, 253,264,558
'Hidden Hand' 263
Highfield 114
Hillery, Dr. Patrick 13-14,29,76-7,79,80, 83,86-7,90,130,164, 173,195
Hillsborough Agreement 234,239,284,304,306, 311,314,315,319,321,326, 332,338,342,345,348, 353,363,398,407,411, 436,453,456,534
Hillsborough Declaration 419
Himself Alone, David Trimble & the Ordeal of Unionism 435
Historical Enquiries Team (HET) 540,562

Hitler 175,375,449
Hoggart, Simon 186
Holland, Jack 374
Holland, Mary 307,316, 334,355
Holy War in Belfast 524
Home, Sir Alec Douglas 192,195
Home Rule Crisis 6,58, 76,124
Home Rule Crisis 1912-14, The 435
Hooker St. 33
Housing Executive 157
Hot Press 331,399,410
Howe, Geoffrey 306
Howell, David 241
How Stormont Fell 159
Hugh O'Neill & the Flight of the Earls 445
Hughes, Brendan 101, 264,265,290,442,448, 453,464,470,538
Hume, John 10,42-8, 50,55,57,139,141-2, 144,149,159,160,162,165, 173,176-80,184-6, 188-90,195,202,209, 214,217,221,224,226,232, 236,247,250,283,305, 315,332,344,359,367, 385,415,530,544
'Humespeak' 282
Humiliation & Disgrace 28
Humpty-Dumpty 49,195
Hunger strikes 288,290, 295,305,311,329,376, 447,456
Hunt, Lord 49,50,51,53
Hurd, Douglas 302,313-4
Hussein, Saddam 502,514

India 112
Independent, The 467
INLA 265,280,306,386
In Search of a State, Catholics in N. Ireland 458
Inside Politics 352,395
Institute for European Defence & Strategic Studies 437

579

Internment 155,162-3, 167-9,171-2,191
International Decommissioning Commission 379,515
IRA 1956-6, Rethinking the Republic, The 107
IRA—From Insurrection to Parliament 272
Iraq 1 01,510
Ireland since 1939: the persistence of conflict 17,104,270,334,431
Ireland: the Politics of Enmity 99,104,111, 257,269
Ireland's Violent Frontier 273
Irish Catholic 354,475
Irish Communist, The 322
Irish Communist Organisation 566-7
Irish Constitution 230
Irish Dead, The 132
Irish Independence Party 289,295-6
Irish Independent 16,497
Irish Labour Party 136
Irish National Archives 14
Irish News 16,50,53-5, 64,71,79,83-4,89, 94,120,125,127,154, 178,185,207,216-8, 220,296,350,391,477
Irish Political Review 111,361,403,411,422, 425,481,494,551,567
Irish Press, The 191,246, 549
Irish Republican Army 17,30,49,57,58,63,66,68, 95,96,10 2,103-5,115, 122-6,169,172,-5,177, 179,185,187,199,207,215, 257,262,276,344,451,475
Irish Republican Writers Group (IRWG) 464-5,467
Irish Supreme Court 225

Irish Times 16,56,87,92, 95,141,159,170,179-2,246,257,316,329,378, 411,547
Irish Worker 209
Iron Lady 309,314
IRSP 260
Iveagh House 164

Jay, Peter 265
Jerusalem Center for Public Affairs 438
John Bull's Political Slum 104
John Hume and the SDLP 300,316,353
John Hume, Irish Peacemaker 151,164,247, 276,348
John Hume: Statesman of the Troubles 235
Johnston, Ray 106
Joint Declaration 475, 504
Judgement Day 24
Junior Orange Parade 15

Kaiser 374
Kane, Alex 310,520
Keenan, Sean 17,26,42,45
Kelly, Basil 176
Kelly, Captain James 79-80,107,117-23,125-6
Kelly, Dolores 528
Kelly, Henry 159
Kelly, John 119-20, 122-3, 125-6,128,140
Kelly, Stephen 153
Kelly, Tom 353,408,514
Kennedy, Hugh 117
Kennedy, Paddy 24,81, 140,142
Kenya 267,363
Keogh, Dermot 76,90,116
King, Sir Frank 269
King, Peter 493
King, Steven 110-12, 114,466,483
King, Tom 318,330
Kingsmill 263

Kinsealy 339
Kipling 377
Kitson, Frank 2 69
Kursk 493

Labour Party Conference 1998 402
Langhammer, Mark 402, 404
Larkin, Aidan 251,252
Larkin, Paul 364
Late Late Show 550
Law (?) and Orders—The Story of the Belfast Curfew,3-5 July 1970 130
Leeds Castle 511
Leeson St. 22,101
Legacy Of History, The 342
Lemass, Peggy 77,82
Lemass, Sean 5,73-77, 81,82,87,115,128,144, 152,182,335,426,530
Lenin 17,457,458-9,470
Lessons from Northern Ireland for the Arab-Israeli Conflict 438
Letters of Comfort 560
Libya 306
Liddle Hart, Basil 450
Lillis, Michael 314
Limbo 152,505
Linehan, Brian 19,361
Linen Hall Library 467
Lloyd George 390
Lloyd, John 435,490-91
Lockhart, R.H. Bruce 451
Logue, Hugh 237
London Underground 256
Long, Arthur 50
Long Bar 50
Long Kesh 125,267, 287,288
Long Kesh Calendar 185
Long Kesh Peace and Reconciliation Centre project 556-7
'Long March' 443
Long Road, The 321
Lost Dominion, The 186

'Lost lives' 374
Loughgall 327,347,374
Lourdes 330
Luftwaffe 358
'Lundy' 519
Lurgan 21
Luykx, Albert 119-20
Lynch, Jack 11,17,19-25,28-9,46,52,56,62-3,70-3,75-6,78-84, 86,87,902,105,107,109-11,115-16,118-23,125, 130,136-8,140-2,152, 160,165,172,173,181,184, 188,190-1,210,242, 312,332,426,544,566

Mc Laughlin, Mitchell 371
McAirt 100
McAleese, Mary 392-3
McAliskey, Bernadette 289,319,445
McAllister, Ian 55,145, 149,187,207
McAteer, Fr. 138
McAteer, Eddie 5,16,73, 81,94,138,152,182
McAteer Hugh 138
MacBride, Sean 284
McCabe, Chris 367,368
McCallister, John 530
McCann, Eamonn 52, 136
McCartney, Bob 303, 409,412,433,495,536
McConville, Jean 536, 538,542,543
McCorry, Kevin 185
MacDonald, Darach 262, 264
McDonald, Henry 362
McDonnell, Joe 294
McDowell, Michael 514, 518,549
McEldowney, Eugene 550
MacFarland, Alan 493
MacFarlane, Brendan 293
McGill, Mr. 173
MacGiolla, Tomás 25, 27,106,108

McGrady, Eddie 346, 367-8
McGrady, Eddie 278
McGuigan, Kevin 536, 553
McGuinness, Martin 202,297,374, 390,377,444,451,474
McGurk's Bar 180
McIlhone, Michael 126
McIntyre, Anthony 441-2,448,460,461,464-5, 467-70,488,537,539, 542,568-9
McKeague, John 15,445
McKearney, Tommy 267,272-3,286,324, 445,464
McKee 100
McKee, Billy 264
McKittrick, David 272, 355
McLarnan, Sammy 33
McMillen, Billy 26-7,50
MacStiofain, Sean 133, 171,202,253
MacSwiney, Terence 509
McWilliams, Sarah 333

Maastricht 373
Machiavelli 28,454
Maginnis, Ken 391
Maguire, Frank 290
Maguire, Noel 290
Major, John 357,367, 373,375,377-8,380, 389-90
Malaya 363
Mallie, Eamonn 27
Mallon, Kevin 52,96,144
Mallon, Seamus 212,230-2,281,346,369,385,393-4,409,416-7,421,473,492
Malt St. 101
Man behind the Smile, The 493
Mandela, Nelson 297,551
Mandelson, Peter 423, 426-7,441,450,471, 476-7,485,488

Mansergh, Martin 341, 354,381
Mao 17,458
Marr, Andrew 525-6
Martin, Micheál 549-50
Marx 17,458
Marxism 96-7,460
Maryfield Secretariat 326,353
Mason, Roy 223,264, 277,279,286,288
Mater Hospital 157
Maudling, Reginald 160, 170,172,177,178,180,183,195
Mau Mau 268
Mawhinney, Brian 346
Mayhew, Sir Patrick 338,358,367
Mellifont, Treaty of 445, 447
Memoir, A 289
Memoirs of a British Agent 451
Memoirs of a Revolutionary 134,171
Memoirs of a Statesman 160,165,181,202,219,234
Methodist 308
MI5 374,413
MI6 453,498
Miami Showband 263
Millar, Frankie 516
Milltown 132,342
Minority Verdict; Experiences of a Catholic Public Servant 34, 221,276
Mitchell, George 269, 380,421
Mitchell Principles 381
Mitchell Report 381-2,494
MLAT Treaty 541
Modern Irish republicanism: product of British state strategies 467
Moloney, Ed 101,268, 269,323,338,359,388,454, 470,537,539,541,543
Molyneux, James 310, 313,373,391,373

'Monaghan' 110
Monday Club 194
Morgan, John 242
Moriarty, Gerry 329,548
Morley, Sir John 463
Morris, Alison 499,500-1
Morrsion, Danny 293, 320,411,433
Morrison, David 494
Mossadeq 337
Mother Teresa 303
'Mountain Climber' 293, 294
Mountbatten 247,280, 565
Moyard 114
Mowlam, Marjorie 386
Mull of Kintyre 374
Mumford, Andrew 170, 205
Munich 440
Murlough Bay 172
Murphy, Prof. John A. 311
Murphy, Michael A. 56, 167,279,281
Murphy, Patrick 528,529
Murphy, Paul 510
Murphy, Thomas 'Slab' 536,553
Murray, Denis 313
Murray, Fr. Raymond 289,311,447
Murray, Gerard 353,144
Murray, Len 234,239

Nairac, Captain 263
Nally, Dermot 258,302,306
Napier, Oliver 234
Napoleon 431
National Archives 24
Nationalists of Northern Ireland, The 152,153
Nation's Honour, The 28
Neave, Airey 278,280, 306,308-9,358,386
Neilson, Samuel 524
Nelson, Brian 363
Nelson, Lord 511
Nelson, Rosemary 500
Nero 93

Nesbitt, Mike 563
New Barnsley 112-14,131
New Ireland Forum 298, 299-301,304,338
New Labour 500
New Lodge Road 140
Newe, G.B. 175
Newry 21
Newry march 188
News Letter 178,218
New Statesman 490
Newtownabbey 402
Newtownhamilton 262
New York Times 426
Nicholas Mansergh, A Biography 340
NICRA 21,28,43,172-3,185-6
NILP 61,142,148,151, 154,157,230
Nine Years War 445
Nixon 239
Nobel Peace Prize 426
No-Go Areas 213
North Began, The 25
North-South Ministerial Council (NSMC) 522
'Northern Ireland' 5,6,19, 23,29,31,38,40,44,48,58, 59,61,63-4,68,75-6, 95,109,114,143,145-9,155,166,183,220,222-3,238,239,241,245,259, 264,282,284,292,295,300, 310,311-12,316,333, 349,354,402-4,433, 449,453,461-2,470, 505,507,517,524,526, 529,531-2,534,537, 545,555,558,562
Northern Ireland Act 1998 494
Northern Ireland Assembly 216
Northern Ireland Constitution Act 420
Northern Ireland Constitutional Proposals (White Paper) 215
Northern Ireland Execu-

tive 222
Northern Ireland Problem, The 213
Northern Ireland: The Political Economy of Conflict 462
Northern Ireland, What is it? 316
Northern Resistance 176
Northern Star, The 103
Northview 316
The Northern Ireland Question in British Politics 165,352
The Northern Ireland Social and Democratic Labour Party 145,187,208
Notorantonio, Francisco 483

O'Bradaigh, Ruairi 104, 134,160,259,265,296, 425,460,567
O'Brien, Conor Cruise 110,225,243,284,359, 367,369,400,429,430, 441,481,497
Ó Broin, Gearóid 249,252
O'Callaghan, Sean 432,465
O'Caollai, Breasal 117
O'Cleary, Conor 378
O'Connell St. 24
O'Connell, Daithi 104, 202,253,258,265,296,526
O'Connell, Daniel 188
O'Connor, Fionnoula 385,458,473
O'Connor, Joe 483
O'Doherty, Malachy 504
O'Donnell, Hugh 445
O'Donnell, Peadar 101-2
O'Donovan Rossa 553
O'Dowd family 263
O'Duffy, Brendan 165
Ó Fearghail, Seán Óg 130
O'Fiaich, Cardinal 288-9, 330,341,446
O'Flanagan, Fr. Michael 89,570
O'Hagan, Martin 500

O'Hanlon, Paddy 24,53, 139,228,251
O'hAnrachain, Padraig 341
O'Higgins, Brian 532
O'Kane, Maggie 364
O'Loan, Nuala 413
O'Malley, Desmond 170
O'Malley, Padraig 296
O Muilleoir, Martin 54, 549
O'Neill, Captain 7,15,29, 33,40-1,49,77,82,94, 94,114,148,152-3, 158,162,201,534,556
O'Neill, Charles 132
O'Neill, Hugh 445-7
O'Neill, Robert K.- 537
O'Rawe, Richard 292-4,329
O'Reilly, Emily 366
O'Riordan, Manus 551
O'Riordan, Michael 551

Oatley, Michael 453
Observer, The 322
Offences against the State Act 285
Official Republicanism 28
Official Republicans 96-7, 99,103,105,107-8,114, 135,259,425,427,432,567
Oglaigh na Eireann 518
Omagh 21,228
Omagh Catastrophe 412-15,498
On Compromise 463
One Man, One Vote 60
Operation Boot 337
Operation Brogue 336-7
Operation Motorman 204,205-6,209-10,213
Orange Order 213,412,565
Orange Terror 7,412
Orde, Sir Hugh 499
Orme, Stan 240
Ormeau Road 387
Oslo speech 426
'Out! Out! Out!' 301,302, 304-5,314,401

Paddy Bogside 12,17, 26,122
Paine, Tom 565
Paisley, From Demagogue to Democrat? 542
Paisley, Ian 23,217,226, 313,408,465,505,522, 532,535
Pakistan 112
Pamphlet on the current and historical situation in Northern Ireland 182
'Pan-nationalism' 361
Parachute Regiment 280
Parallel Consent 403
Parliamentary Plot May be Unravelling 464
Parnell 208-9,303
Pat Finucane Centre 263
Patten, Chris 487,535
Patterson, Prof. Henry 17,75,76,79,90,104-5,116,270,272,283,334, 431,432,460,466,469-70,488,503,542
Peace-Keeping Force 20
Peace Process 332,337, 339,344,349,360,365,373,379, 382,384,387,391,441,448,456
Peace People 285
Peacocke, Anthony 30
Pearse, Patrick 376
Penal Laws 460
Pensive Quill, The 568
People's Democracy, 177,457
Percy St. 34
Perle, Richard 437
Peter Pan 25
Petition of Concern 522,556,562
Phoblacht, An 289
Phoenix, Policing the Shadows 374
Phoenix, Eamonn 16,294
Plaid Cymru 464
*Poba*l 206
Pocock,Tom 106
Pogrom, The August 44,

57,67-8,95-6
Poland 429,449
Police Ombudsman 499
Point Of No Return: The Strike Which Broke The British In Ulster 261
Police Commissioner 15
Policy Exchange think-tank 437
Political Guidelines for the Pacification of the Province 38
Politics in my Blood 551
Politics of illusion 270,469
Politics of Legitimacy: Struggles in a Belfast Community 124,210
Pompidou President 194
Pope, the 280
Poppy day 328
Portadown 388
Powell, Enoch 309
Powell, Jonathan 389, 391,493
Power Play—The Rise of modern Sinn Fein 551
Power-sharing 216, 226,228,235,245,352
Price, Marion 484
Prince, The 28
Prior Assembly 295
Proportional Representation 172
'Propositions on Heads of Agreement' 396
Protestant-Catholic Encounter (PACE) 175
Provisional IRA The 27,50
Provisional IRA, From Insurrection to Parliament 268,286
PSNI 516
Public Accounts Ctte of the Northern Distress Relief Fund 140
Public Record Office 38
Pym, Francis 241

Queens University 467

583

Quinn family killing 387, 412

Radio Éireann 316
Radio Free Belfast 34,65
Radio Ulster 377
RAF 132
Rafter, Kevin 340,381
Ramaphosa, Cyril 551-2
Ramsey, Robert 157,164, 166,187,192-4,246,357
Real IRA 518
Reavey family 263
Record of Constructive Change, A 157
Redemptorist Order 330
Redmond, John 88,382
Redmond, Sean 55
Rees, Merlyn 227,228, 230,240-1,245-6, 257-8,261,264,276-7,287
Reid, Fr. Alec 330,332, 337,339,340,341,344, 347,359,392,398
Reid, John 471,492,510
Reiss, Mitchel 518
Relief Fund 80
'Republican Action Force' 263
Republican Co-ops 176
Republican News 259, 266,289,567
'Republican Action Force' 263
Revolution Betrayed, The 470
Revolutionary Marxism 28
Reynolds, Albert 339, 343,377,379
Rhodes, Cecil 378
Rhodesia 35,38,264
Ringside Seats 157,193-4,246,357
Ritchie, Margaret 528
Robespierre 103
Robinson, Mary 391
Robinson, Peter 302,495, 556-7
Rodgers, Brid 392,528
Rome 9,445

Ronan, Sean 44
Rose, Richard 149
Rosemount 205
Rowthorn, Bob 462
Royal College of Surgeons (Dublin) 551
Royal Irish Academy 130
Royal Navy 375
RTE 16,188
Ruairi O'Bradaigh, *The Life and Politics of an Irish Revolutionary* 297,298
Rubicon 343
RUC 18,323
Rushe, Lawrence 413
Russia 112,440
Ryan, Mick 27

St. Andrew's Agreement 520,521-3,528
St. Comgall's School 100
St. Matthews 126,131

Sands, Bobby 290-3,329
Sandy Row 65
'Saving Dave' 494,495, 497,502-4,510
Sayers, Jack 32
Scenario for Peace, A 331
Schmidt, Helmut 336
Schmitt, Carl 457
Scots-Calvinists 58
Scullabogue 301
SAS 262,325-6,328
Secret History of the IRA, The 323,338,454,539
SDLP 10,42,55,117,138, 141-5,148-9,152- 5, 157-60,162-7,169, 172-7,179,180-1,184-5,187,201-4,206-7, 210,213-16,218,220, 223,232,237,245,247-8,255,277,282,295-96,394,434,455,505-6
Second Dail 267,296
Section 31 285
Shankill Bombing 364
Shankill Defence Assoc. 15

Shankill Road 15,23,65
Sheehy, Michael 400
Shorlands 22
Short Strand 129
Sinn Fein 88-9,96106, 109,149,24 2,304,319
Sinn Fein & the SDLP 144
Sinn Fein, A hundred turbulent years 382,383
Smith, F.E. (Lord Birkenhead) 535
Smith, Howard 210
Smith, Ian 35,38
Smith, Jean Kennedy 378
Smith, William Beattie 194,215,397
Smyth, Martin 504
Socialist Republicans 18
Somme, The 565
South Armagh 261,263-4
South Armagh Brigade 262
South, Sean 104
Special category 288
Special Powers Act 157,186,193,285,547
Spencer, Graham 330, 390,475
Spring, Dick 339
Springfield Road 22,64, 112
Springmartin 269
'Stake/steak knife' 482, 484,503
'Surrender and Re-grant' 445
Stalin 449,470
Stalingrad 493
Stalker Report 325,327, 413
Starvation Blockade 375
Staunton, Enda 152,153
Steele, Frank 201
Stevens enquiry 362
Stewart, Michael 13,30
Stormont 13-15,20,22, 24,29-32,35,37-8, 40,55-7,65
Stormont Green Paper 167
Stormont House Agreement 561

Stormont in Crisis 32,224
Strabane 21,228,327
Straight Left 153
Strasbourg 415
Studies in Conflict and Terrorism 268
Stormontgate 499
Sunday Observer 477
Suez 204,378
Sullivan, Jim 50,125
Sunday Business Post 258,373,413
Sunday Independent 45, 103,110,360-2,429
Sunday Insight 156
Sunday Press 276,312
Sunday Times 258,260, 294,418,460,479
Sunday World 362,501
Sunningdale 212,219-21,225,234-6,241, 246,249-50,275,312, 349,442
'Sunningdale for slow learners' 397
Supreme Being 103
'Supreme sacrifice' 7,155
'Surrender and Re-grant' 445
Swan, Sean 27
Swatragh 333
Swift, Jonathan 370
Sydenham 235

Taylor, John 44,424,481
Taylor, Peter 68,186,453
Television Trials 215
Terror in Northern Ireland 117
Tet Offensive 323-4
Thant, U. 189
Thatcher Foundation Papers 329
Thatcher, Margaret 278-9,284,290,318-9,327, 333
Theory of the Partisan 457
Thimbleriggers, The 80, 123
Thomas Davis Lecture 465

Thornton, Chris 476,477
Three Strand Agenda 396
Times, The 241,260
Tonge, Jonathan 144
Towards a lasting peace in Ireland 359
Towards a New Ireland 206-7,214,280
Towards a Strategy for Peace 331,346
Tragedy of Errors, The Government and Misgovernment of N. Ireland 195
Tralee 86-7
Travers, Anne 556
Treacy, Matt 107
Treaty War 101,375
Trimble, David 110,387, 391,395-6,401,407, 409,415-16,431,437, 443,472,482,484,489, 501,532
Trinity History Workshops 532
Trotsky 451,454,458,470
'Truceliers' 286
TUAS *(Totally UnArmed Strategy)* 370,371,384
Turf Lodge 37
TUV 555-6
Tuzo, General 170,186,268
Twomey, Seamus 98
'Two Nations' 89,92,436, 566-7
Tyrone Democrat, The 175
Tyrone IRA 325
Tyrell, Áine 547-8

UCD Law Society 72
UDA 199,365
UDF 173,365
UDI 38,194,247,248,259
UDR 51-3,173,272,318, 323
UKUP 409
Ukraine 112
Ulster A Nation 437
Ulster nationalism 259,

264,274
Ulster Unionist Council 219,224
Ulster Volunteer Force 16
Ulster Workers Council 228,230,234,236,238, 249,311
Ulster Workers Strike 230,232,233,236,242,2 53,260,402
Ulsterisation 262,270, 272-5,288,325-6,362
Ultach 7
United Irishman 25,28, 105-6,108,135
United Irishmen 99
United Nations 19-20, 87,189
United States Institute of Peace 397
Unity Flats 13,68
USSR 444
UTV 65
UUUC 156,234,275,476
UVF 33,132,230,310

Vanguard 194
Vatican 378
Very British Jihad, A; 364
Villiers, Teresa 414
Voice of the North, The 56,142,312,550
Voices from the grave 265,537,538,541
Waldheim, Kurt 189
Walsh, Micheline Kerney 445
Walsh, Pat 469
Ward, Ian 398
War Mongering! The Irish Press and the Troubles in Northern Ireland 191
War of Independence 426
Warrenpoint 280
Washington Post 426
Walsh, Kerney 447
Waterfront Hall 482,485
Waterville 282

Waugh, Eric 374
Way Forward 419
Wayne, Naomi 462
Weber, Max 19
Week, This 134
West, Harry 156
Westminster 13,25,31, 54,78,141,183
What Choice for Ulster? 411
White, Barry 235
White, Robert W. 297
Whitelaw, William 195, 197,201-3,213,215-6,
222,241,482
Whittaker, T.K. 73,75,82, 85-6,90,92,116, 300,335,342
Wilson Harold 13,34,35, 38,49,151,183-4,223, 2 30,234,240,246
Wilson, Paddy 278
Wilson, Padraig 536
Wilson, President 375,507
Winchester, Simon 98
Wolfe Tone 568
Wolfe Tone Annual 532
Women's Coalition 507
Won't stand (idly) by 20,22-3,26,70,86,116
Workers' Association 191,435
Workers Party 136,265
Workers Weekly 435,567
Wright, Oliver 37,38,41, 57-9,61-4,68,146

Year of Victory 202,286
Yelstin 13
Yorkshire Television 263

Available from Athol Books:

***Joe Devlin*: What Now?**, *His Confrontation of the British Parliament, After The 1918 Election.*Edited by *Brendan Clifford*
Orange Terror, *The Partition Of Ireland* (1943) by *"Ultach"*.
   A Reprint from *The Capuchin Annual*
The Grammar Of Anarchy: Force Or Law—Which? by *J.J. Horgan*. **Unionism, 1910-1914**. Introduction by *Brendan Clifford*
Roger Casement: *The Crime Against Europe*. With *The Crime* Against Ireland
Traitor-Patriots In The Great War: Casement & Masaryk by *Brendan Clifford*
Casement, Alsace-Lorraine And The Great Irredentist War by *Brendan Clifford*
Connolly And German Socialism by *Brendan Clifford*
Northern Ireland What Is It? Professor Mansergh Changes His Mind
   by *Brendan Clifford*
The O'Neill Years, Unionist Politics 1963-1969 by *David Gordon*.
   A detailed study of events within Ulster Unionism during Captain O'Neill's period as Prime Minister at Stormont
Belfast Politics (1794) by *Henry Joy* & *William Bruce*. First complete reprint.
   Introduction, *Brendan Clifford*. Includes *Thoughts On The British Constitution*
Ulster Presbyterianism, The Historical Perspective, 1610-1970 by *Peter Brooke*
The Economics Of Partition, A Historical Survey Of Ireland In Terms Of
   Political Economy by *B. Clifford*.
The Dublin/Monaghan Bombings, 1974, *a military analysis*,
   by *John Morgan, Lt. Col* (Retd.)
The Arms Conspiracy Trial. Ireland 1970: the Prosecution of Charles Haughey,
   Capt. Kelly and Others by *Angela Clifford*
Elizabeth Bowen: "Notes On Eire". Espionage Reports To Winston Churchill,
   1940-42; With an extended Review of Irish Neutrality in World War 2
   by *Jack Lane* and *Brendan Clifford*.
Dáil Éireann, *Irish Bulletin* Volumes 1,2 and 3. Reprint of official
   newspaper of Dáil Éireann with War Reports

https://www.atholbooks-sales.org